CW00742330

DUMBARTON OAKS
MEDIEVAL LIBRARY

Jan M. Ziolkowski, General Editor

HOLY MEN OF MOUNT ATHOS

DOML 40

Holy Men of Mount Athos

Edited and Translated by

RICHARD P. H. GREENFIELD

and

ALICE-MARY TALBOT

DUMBARTON OAKS
MEDIEVAL LIBRARY

HARVARD UNIVERSITY PRESS
CAMBRIDGE, MASSACHUSETTS
LONDON, ENGLAND
2016

Library of Congress Cataloging-in-Publication Data
Names: Greenfield, Richard P. H., editor, translator. | Talbot, Alice-Mary
Maffry, editor, translator.
Title: Holy men of Mount Athos / edited and translated by Richard P. H.
Greenfield, Alice-Mary Talbot.
Other titles: Dumbarton Oaks medieval library ; 40.
Description: Cambridge, Massachusetts : Harvard University Press,
2016. |
    Series: Dumbarton Oaks medieval library ; 40 | English translations on
rectos with Greek originals on versos. | Includes bibliographical
references and index.
Identifiers: LCCN 2015037313 | ISBN 9780674088764 (alk. paper)
Subjects: LCSH: Christian saints—Greece—Athos—Biography. |
Orthodox Eastern monasteries—Greece—Athos. | Byzantine Empire—
Church history.
Classification: LCC BX393 .H64 2016 | DDC 271/.81949565—dc23
LC record available at http://lccn.loc.gov/2015037313

Contents

CONTENTS

LIFE OF PHILOTHEOS OF ATHOS 613
Translated by Stamatina McGrath

Introduction

This volume presents selected *Lives* of holy men who lived on Mount Athos, the most famous Byzantine center of monasticism; it was often termed simply Hagion Oros, or the Holy Mountain. These vitae provide insights into both the history of monastic development on Athos between the ninth and fifteenth centuries and the varieties of monastic life practiced communally in large monasteries as well as individually in huts and caves. We have chosen six vitae of five different saints—Euthymios the Younger, Athanasios of Athos, Maximos the Hutburner, Niphon, and Philotheos of Athos—who were celebrated for their ascetic practices, the gifts of foresight and clairvoyance, and, in most cases, the ability to perform miracles. Euthymios and Athanasios were also famed as founders of monasteries. We offer two versions of the *Life of Maximos the Hutburner,* to demonstrate how hagiographic accounts of the same saint could vary, even when composed very close in time. It should be noted that, with the exception of Athanasios of Athos, the cult of these saints was essentially limited to the Holy Mountain, as can be seen by the manuscript tradition; almost all the surviving manuscripts of these *Lives* were copied on Athos.

Mount Athos is the northernmost promontory of the Chalkidike peninsula, which juts out into the northern Ae-

gean Sea like a hand with three fingers. The promontory is twenty-eight miles long, and quite narrow, with a width of three to six miles. It is connected to the mainland by a narrow isthmus just over a mile wide. Almost completely surrounded by the sea, it is the most isolated of all the Byzantine holy mountains, and the furthest from a major population center, being located about sixty miles east of Thessalonike.[1] The peninsula is dominated by the six thousand foot peak of Athos and its foothills, which break up the landscape into a series of deep gorges. In many places along the coast, the rocky cliffs plunge right into the sea, and there are few natural harbors. The craggy landscape, with little flat land, combined with the lack of good ports, is not inviting for human habitation, and as a consequence the Athonite promontory was only very lightly populated in classical antiquity, with perhaps five or six small towns. These settlements were abandoned by the third century of the Christian era.[2]

Athonite tradition traces the Christian character of the Holy Mountain back to the first century CE when the Virgin Mary, en route to Cyprus, was diverted by a storm to Athos and converted its local inhabitants. At the same time she supposedly prayed to her son to grant her the peninsula as her special place, and ever after it has been called the "garden of the Panagia."[3] Local legend places the origins of monasticism on the Holy Mountain in the early fourth century, attributing to Constantine I the foundation of the earliest Athonite monasteries.[4]

In reality, however, for six hundred years, between the third and eighth centuries, Athos seems to have been essentially uninhabited, frequented only by the occasional Greek

or Slav shepherd and his flocks.[5] This lengthy period of isolation from human activity permitted the Athonite forests to become dense and lush. The earliest documented hermits appear in the ninth century.[6] The tenth-century historian Genesios relates that in 843, on the occasion of the celebration of the restoration of icon veneration, the monks of Athos sent delegates to Constantinople to join in the festivities, so it seems quite possible that the occasional hermit had made his way to Athos before the year 800, without leaving any trace in the historical record. According to Athonite tradition, one of the first to settle on the Holy Mountain was a certain Peter, whose vita was written in the late tenth or early eleventh century by Nicholas, himself an Athonite monk.[7] We have not included his vita (*BHG* 1505) in this collection because it is a pastiche based on a variety of hagiographic sources, and Peter appears to have been a semilegendary figure.[8] Nonetheless, he is greatly hallowed in Athonite tradition, as one of the pioneers of eremitic life on the peninsula.

Life of Euthymios the Younger

We are on much firmer ground with Saint Euthymios the Younger, who became a hermit on Athos in the mid-ninth century. His vita (*BHG* 655) was written by his disciple Basil, who later became bishop of a town or city near Thessalonike. Basil received his tonsure from the hands of Euthymios, his spiritual father, and witnessed many of the events of the final quarter century of Euthymios's life, including a number of miracles and episodes illustrating his gift of clairvoyance. Basil's text contains a number of accurate chrono-

logical indications (although others are problematic),[9] and his description of the topography seems trustworthy, so we can have some confidence in his account of the holy man and Athos in its early days. He couches his vita in a relatively high level of style, quite different from the more vernacular texts about Maximos the Hutburner and Niphon written in the fourteenth and fifteenth centuries. He tends to use very long sentences and recherché vocabulary, makes classical allusions to Homer and Orpheus, and cites the works of Gregory of Nazianzos, Cyril of Alexandria, John of the Ladder, Theodore of Stoudios, and pseudo-Eustathios of Thessalonike.

Euthymios, whose traditional dates are 823/4–898, exemplifies the type of Byzantine monk who embraced a range of monastic experience during the course of his career and was frequently on the move: after a brief period of marriage, he took monastic vows at a cenobitic monastery on Mount Olympos in Bithynia, then moved to Athos where he lived as a hermit, spent some time on a pillar in Thessalonike as a stylite, founded a double monastery at Peristerai on Mount Chortiates not far from the same city, and at the end of his life moved to a solitary cave on an island. He was one of the pioneers on the Holy Mountain, where he had several extended periods of residence and tried to bring some organization and more formal liturgical services to the scattered hermits who were living there before the foundation of cenobitic monasteries. Among the noteworthy features of his vita is a vivid description of the three years he spent as a recluse in an Athonite cave, subsisting on foraged plants, his clothes reduced to ragged threads, at the mercy of the ele-

ments, his body ravaged by vermin. Also useful and important is Basil's detailed account of the foundation of the monastery of Saint Andrew at Peristerai, in which he was supported by generous donations from the local population. The church of the monastery still stands today.

Life of Athanasios of Athos, Version B

A half-century after the death of Euthymios, Athanasios of Athos (ca. 925/30–ca. 1001), a highly educated intellectual who abandoned a brilliant teaching career in Constantinople for the monastic life, arrived on the Holy Mountain. He first took the monastic habit on another holy mountain, Kyminas in Bithynia, at a *lavra,* a type of community where most of the monks lived as solitaries in individual cells *(kellia)* outside the monastic complex. About 957 he moved to Athos, where he spent some years as a solitary. In 962/3 Athanasios, who was initially very reluctant, was persuaded to establish the monastery of the Great Lavra at the tip of the peninsula, with the encouragement and support of the emperor Nikephoros II Phokas (963–969), whose spiritual father he was. The vita provides much information on the history of the early years of the Lavra, one of the first cenobitic monasteries on the Holy Mountain, nicely complementing the data found in Athanasios's own rule and *typikon* for the monastery.[10] Athanasios, who was intimately involved in the practical aspects of the construction and management of the monastery, would today be called a micromanager. He worked in the refectory, pulled heavy wagons like a draft animal, helped move huge logs, and nursed sick breth-

ren in the infirmary. He even sought to relieve the labor of his monks by inventing an ox-driven contraption to knead bread dough. Athanasios met his death circa 1001 when scaffolding collapsed while he was inspecting remodeling work on the main church (*katholikon*) of the monastery.

The Great Lavra continues to function to this day as one of the principal monasteries on the Holy Mountain, and Athanasios is venerated by Athonite monks as one of their most important holy men. His saintly character was revealed during his lifetime by his gift of clairvoyance and his performance of miracles. He stopped a plague of locusts, saved sailors in a shipwreck, made seawater drinkable, and healed numerous sick monks by the laying on of hands, by making the sign of the cross, or by striking them with his staff. Following his accidental death, his relics continued to effect miraculous cures, through the agency of oil from the lamp that burned above his tomb or the application of blood that had been collected from his corpse.

Two vitae of Athanasios survive: vita A (*BHG* 187) was composed in a high linguistic register by the monk Athanasios of the Panagiou monastery in Constantinople in the first quarter of the eleventh century; vita B (*BHG* 188) was written in a somewhat simpler style by an anonymous monk at the Lavra sometime between 1050 and 1150. We have chosen vita B for this volume, following the argument of Dirk Krausmüller that this version is closer than A to the original lost version of the vita of Athanasios, composed by Anthony, superior of Panagiou.[11] It is a good example of an upper mid-level style of Greek that combines a modest number of allusions to scripture with relatively frequent references to the

orations of Gregory of Nazianzos, and it would have been accessible to a general audience.

Lives of Maximos the Hutburner and Life of Niphon

Several centuries later, in the Palaiologan period, appeared the two versions of the *Life of Maximos the Hutburner* (1272/85–1367/80), one written by the hieromonk Niphon of Athos (1315–1411) (*BHG* 1236z) and the other by Theophanes of Vatopedi (*BHG* 1237), along with the anonymous *Life of Niphon* (*BHG* 1371).[12] Taken together, these closely related vitae provide a fascinating illustration of the genre of individualistic contemplative asceticism, which was evidently so admired in some circles in the Byzantine world of the fourteenth and fifteenth centuries and which has found resonance in modern Orthodox spirituality. They also give unique insight into the way in which the holiness of these men was recorded, interpreted, and communicated by those closely associated with them.

These two vitae of Maximos were both written by younger contemporaries of the saint and are thus probably to be dated in the last quarter of the fourteenth century. Although there is no evidence of Maximos's cult spreading beyond Athos in the Byzantine period, his importance in the context of the Holy Mountain is illustrated by the fact that two more versions of his *Life* were written by Athonite monks in the early years of the fifteenth century: Makarios Makres (ca. 1382/3–1431) and Ioannikios Kochylas (active ca. 1400).[13]

Niphon's *Life of Maximos* was, according to internal evidence, the first of the four accounts to be written,[14] although

he states at the outset that he never intended his work to be more than a rough account prepared from his personal recollections of the holy man and those of other witnesses with whom he was acquainted. The wording of Chapter 1.3 might in fact be taken to suggest he was writing notes specifically for his contemporary Theophanes, the author of the second *Life,* if the latter were to be identified with the "intelligent scholar from among the devout" who Niphon hopes will eventually produce a proper account. Niphon was evidently an ascetic associate of Maximos, even living with him for a time and inheriting his hut; it is also clear that he was present at a good number of the incidents he records. His memoir is idiosyncratic in content and largely unorganized—episodes appear to be grouped primarily according to their source, although he sometimes breaks this pattern by telling other stories of which he is reminded by the content. Appropriately, Niphon writes in an unpolished vernacular style and, interestingly, is almost entirely unconcerned with theological matters. He thus never once mentions Maximos's devotion to hesychast prayer, his visionary experiences, or his interview with Gregory of Sinai, elements which became central to Theophanes's telling of the *Life.* Niphon's Maximos is very much a down-to-earth person whose sanctity is rooted in his asceticism, his performance of extraordinary miracles of clairvoyance, and his sometimes dramatic transcendence of human nature.

By contrast with Niphon's work, Theophanes's *Life* is generally more polished and deliberately constructed. There are, for example, a number of quite elaborate and nicely turned segments in which the author demonstrates his superior education, stylistic skills, and grasp of theological is-

sues and language. These are appropriate to a man who, as the title of the *Life* indicates, was at one time superior of the Vatopedi monastery on Athos and a bishop in Thrace, although unfortunately nothing more is known of him.[15] A clearly apologetic strand is also visible here. Theophanes stresses, for example, the visionary legitimation of Maximos's abandonment of the communal norms of cenobitic monasticism at the Lavra. He also evidently feels the need to explain why no miracles were performed at Maximos's death and why his relics were never translated into the Lavra, as might perhaps have been expected for someone of the stature he claims for his hero. Elsewhere, however, Theophanes deliberately retains a vernacular, and hence convincingly authentic, Greek style for the miracles and the direct speech he records. Much is drawn directly, almost word for word, from Niphon's account, although he acknowledges his source only once (Chapter 31.1). Episodes are also sorted out quite neatly by type here, meaning that Theophanes sometimes splits up and often redistributes material derived from Niphon's more scattered recollections.

Set alongside each other, the two accounts thus provide a fascinating and revealing insight into the process of hagiographic composition and rewriting *(metaphrasis)*. On the one hand it is possible to see which of Niphon's stories were not included in Theophanes's *Life* and propose reasons for their omission. On the other, Theophanes's framing of Maximos as a holy fool and then as a hesychast visionary, ascetic, and teacher is so emphatically handled, yet so different from Niphon's perspective, that it must raise questions of authorial construction, or at least interpretation. In one or two places

each *Life* includes additional or variant factual information on Maximos, indicating a divergence of memory or tradition. Interestingly, Theophanes reveals that he himself was the eyewitness in the extraordinary story in which Maximos is seen to fly (Chapter 28 in both, see also the *Life* by Theophanes, Chapter 35.2), reversing the main flow of information from Niphon to Theophanes.

The third *Life* in this group is that of the hieromonk Niphon (*BHG* 1371), the author of the first *Life of Maximos.* The unidentified author[16] was evidently a near contemporary of his subject, since he "later" spoke directly to a monk who had been cured by Niphon (Chapter 13). Some doubts must be raised, however, about how close their relationship really was, for he appears confused on at least one key point of chronology: although Niphon himself states in his *Life of Maximos* (Chapter 3.3) that he inherited on Maximos's death the last and more permanent hut occupied by the holy man near the Lavra, the author of Niphon's *Life* states (Chapters 4.2–5.1) that Niphon inherited one of Maximos's earlier huts, subsequently moving, on Maximos's advice, to a cave. The author has organized his brief *Life* into two roughly equal sections. An account of the main points of Niphon's career and interaction with his associates is followed by a series of miracle tales, primarily involving Niphon's clairvoyance. Mirroring its content, the *Life* is written in a clear, straightforward style, with a number of vernacular elements once again lending authenticity, particularly to the direct speech.

The *Life of Niphon* contains one important nugget of historical information, in its report of an Ottoman attack on Athos, in 1372 or 1373, that was thwarted decisively by a Ve-

netian flotilla (Chapter 18).[17] The threat of Turkish piracy is a relatively persistent theme in this *Life,* more so than in those of Maximos, but otherwise the narrative is entirely focused on the holy man's relatively mundane interactions with the largely anonymous members of the extremely local and enclosed Athonite world that immediately surrounded him. What is striking here, and the same is true of the two versions of the *Life of Maximos,* is the general absence of reference to the many grim realities of the Byzantine world in the region of northeastern Greece in the fourteenth and early fifteenth centuries. The political, social, and economic mayhem prevalent across the region during most of this period thus finds almost no reflection in these accounts. Even the burning theological issues of the day, notably those surrounding "hesychasm" and the controversial theology of Gregory Palamas, seem somewhat remote. Although these issues are treated to some extent in Theophanes's more sophisticated account,[18] for both Niphon and his biographer "spiritual tranquility" *(hesychia)* seems to remain, primarily, a fairly straightforward requirement or goal of monastic asceticism. These *Lives* thus provide a healthy reminder to historians that high-level turmoil may leave relatively little mark on those in the lower levels of society who are not directly in its path.

According to Theophanes (who is the source of almost all biographical information on his early life), Maximos,[19] whose baptismal name was Manuel, was born to aristocratic parents in the town of Lampsakos on the Hellespont. Unfortunately, the *Lives* provide no evidence that allows specific dating for Maximos's birth, but references indicate this must have been sometime between 1272 and 1285.[20] Further-

more, Theophanes's account of Maximos's childhood not only is very brief but also contains a number of common hagiographic tropes. Maximos evidently acquired his initial monastic training in his late teens, first under an elder on the Thracian holy mountain of Ganos and then on Mount Papikion, some hundred miles to the west. He then moved on to Constantinople, where, Theophanes relates, he experienced an ecstatic vision of the Virgin, became known as a holy fool, and came to the attention of the imperial court and the patriarch, all the while living as a vagrant in the gateway of a church. Some time later he left the city, traveling to Thessalonike and then to Athos and the Lavra of Athanasios. There he began a regular course of training in obedience and humility as a cenobitic monk, eventually becoming a member of the choir and continuing to experience a high degree of spiritual inspiration while, somewhat unusually, maintaining his austere lifestyle by sleeping on the benches of the church narthex rather than in a cell.

At some point, however, there was clearly a break with the regime at the Lavra. Theophanes describes this in terms of conflict between Maximos's solitary, rather than communal, spiritual vocation, something in which he was encouraged and legitimized, the author argues, by visions of the Virgin. This culminated in an ascent to the peak of Athos itself, where he underwent a defining vision and ecstatic experience, which included being supplied with heavenly food. In Niphon's much vaguer account, the break comes when Maximos, who has gone directly to Athos from his earlier monastic training and has served as timekeeper at the Lavra, leaves the Holy Mountain for his visit to Constantinople, only returning some time later.

Both *Lives* agree, however, that this break was a turning point in Maximos's life. It was then that he gained both his sobriquet of the Hutburner (Kavsokalyves) and his early reputation as an extreme ascetic, for he began wandering about, living in isolation in a series of small grass huts, which he would burn whenever he was discovered. Even in the wilder parts of fourteenth-century Athos, this practice was unusual, and his eccentric behavior was evidently regarded with suspicion by his contemporaries, to a point where some apparently doubted his orthodoxy. His inability to fit in with the dominant cenobitic lifestyle of the larger Athonite communities and his seemingly exaggerated claims to inspiration clearly led to his being mocked by many of his contemporaries. The epithet "vagrant" was given to him, a term that not only described his behavior but also contained the implication that he was regarded as being in spiritual error and likely outright crazy. According to Theophanes, however (the episode is not mentioned by Niphon), a change in attitude occurred when Maximos was interviewed by the great hesychast teacher, Gregory of Sinai, perhaps in the early 1330s.[21] Gregory openly endorsed a very positive view of Maximos, as an inspired visionary filled with spiritual wisdom, and he helped persuade Maximos to settle down in one place.

In the last phases of his life, when he was living in a cave on the barren southern slopes of the Holy Mountain and then in a permanent hut closer to the Great Lavra, Maximos thus gained widespread respect, for his continuing physical asceticism and for being a spiritual advisor endowed with the grace of miraculous clairvoyance. He was also said to be able to heal the possessed and, more unusually, eyewit-

ness accounts are included in both vitae that tell of his being transfigured with light and fire, and, on one occasion, of his even flying. Fueled by reports of such evidence of divine blessing, Maximos's reputation spread beyond the confines of Athos; around 1350 he was visited by the two reigning emperors, John VI Kantakouzenos and John V Palaiologos, and, just over a decade later in 1363 or 1364, by the patriarch of Constantinople Kallistos I. Indeed, toward the end of his life, the impression is given that a visit to him had become something of an established feature on the itinerary of visitors to the Lavra.

Most commonly, however, Maximos, like Niphon, was visited by his fellow solitaries and cenobitic monks from the communities on the Holy Mountain. The vitae thus provide fascinating information about the day-to-day existence of these men and the network of interaction and support that evidently existed among them. A vivid glimpse is given of their mundane activities, of the ways in which they shared conversation and food, of their sufferings from physical deprivation, cold and health problems, of their petty failings and misdemeanors, of their aspirations and fears, and of the various remarkable events that stood out in their memories as having broken the pattern of their daily routines.

Theophanes reports that Maximos died at the age of ninety-five on January 13 in an unspecified year (Chapter 34.1). Based on the same internal evidence as that used for his birth, this places his passing sometime between 1367 and 1380.[22]

Nothing is known of Niphon beyond the information provided in his own *Life* and in the vitae of Maximos.[23] He was born in the village of Lukovë, situated on the coast of modern Albania. A careful process of deduction suggests

that this was probably in 1315.[24] At a young age he entered a nearby monastery, under the guidance of his uncle, and was evidently fast-tracked into the priesthood.[25] He was overcome, however, by the attractions of *hesychia* (spiritual tranquility) and went to the monastery of Geromerion, in the same general region, to pursue his training under the guidance of an elder. From there he traveled on foot to Athos, where he lived for three years with a hermit called Theognostos, before moving to the hermitage of Saint Basil for fourteen more. Following an epidemic, probably in the 1350s, he was persuaded to provide spiritual ministry to the hermitages associated with the Lavra before again seeking a solitary life of extreme asceticism at a number of isolated locations on the southern tip of Athos, including a cave facing the islet of Saint Christopher. At some point he ended up living alongside his "kindred spirit" Maximos the Hutburner and, when the latter died, inherited his cell near the Lavra.[26] His *Life* indicates that during these latter years, at least, he was assisted by several disciples who lived in close proximity and formed part of a network of other solitaries occupying the remoter slopes of the Holy Mountain. There is nothing in the immediate sources to support the assumption, made in some modern literature, that he is to be identified with the Niphon who was *protos* of Athos and who, after being accused of Bogomilism by Stefan Dušan in 1345, was defended by Gregory Palamas. Niphon died, aged ninety-six, in 1411.[27]

LIFE OF PHILOTHEOS

The latest of the Athonite monks to be included in this volume is Philotheos. His very short anonymous vita (*BHG* 1534) is written in an upper middle level of Greek and incor-

porates biblical allusions to both the Old and the New Testaments, references to homilies of John Chrysostom and Pseudo-Ephraim, and proverbial expressions. The introductory passage to the *Life* is lifted in its entirety from the tenth-century *Life of Saint Paul of Latros* with the exception of the saint's name and a play on words inspired by it. Internal evidence in the vita suggests that Philotheos was residing in the Macedonian town of Chrysopolis when the region came under Ottoman occupation in 1371.[28] He lived to the age of eighty-four, dying around 1450. As the author of the vita does not claim to have met the saint in person, but is rather writing to celebrate his commemoration day, the text of the *Life* probably dates to the second half of the fifteenth century.

The *Life* tells how Philotheos and his brother, the sons of refugees driven from their home in Asia Minor to Chrysopolis in Macedonia by the Ottoman occupation, were recruited by the Turkish child levy (*devşirme*) toward the end of the fourteenth century.[29] After escaping from the Turks, supposedly under the guidance of the Virgin Mary (who appeared to the boys in a vision in the guise of their real mother), Philotheos and his brother found refuge in a double monastery of the Virgin in Neapolis (probably Kavala). There they were eventually reunited with their mother, Eudokia, who by amazing coincidence had become a nun in the same double monastery. The perils of life in such a complex are revealed by the tale of a dissolute nun who attempted to seduce the youthful Philotheos. He resisted temptation, and the nun was expelled from the institution.

After his mother's death Philotheos moved to the cenobitic monastery of Dionysiou on Mount Athos, but in his fi-

nal years he adopted the eremitic life. During his years as a hermit he was renowned for his ascetic fervor, mortifying his flesh with fasting and vigils, and for his prophetic powers; he is also said to have suffered many temptations from the Devil. Like others in this volume, his life illustrates the way in which monks might espouse a variety of ascetic experiences during the course of their monastic careers. Before his death, Philotheos, imitating the practice of some early Desert Fathers, had instructed his disciples not to bury his body, but to leave it exposed to be eaten by wild beasts; and so they dragged his body some distance and abandoned it in the woods. Later on, a monk, out at night on a fishing trip, saw Philotheos's skull "shining like a star" above his bones, and took it back to his cell as a holy relic. A vision, however, warned him that he should return the skull to Philotheos's disciples, who kept the relic as an amulet. Despite the brevity of this vita, it is an important source of information on the child levy, as well as on double monasteries.

A Note on the Translations

All six vitae in this volume are presented here in English translation for the first time. The *Lives* of Euthymios the Younger, Maximos the Hutburner, Niphon of Athos, and Philotheos have never been translated into any other language.[30] A French version of vita B of Athanasios of Athos exists, but in an obscure and inaccessible journal.[31]

The two main translators carefully reviewed and revised each other's translations to such an extent that they can almost be considered joint translations, but Talbot took the lead in the vitae of Euthymios and Athanasios, while Green-

field was the primary translator for the vita of Maximos by Niphon and the vita of Niphon. The translation of Theophanes's vita of Maximos was truly a collaborative undertaking. Stamatina McGrath prepared the translation of the vita of Philotheos. With a volume of multiple vitae and three translators, it has been a challenge to achieve consistency in the vocabulary of monastic life, but we have done our best. We note in particular the difficulty of translating the frequent term *hesychia* (literally, "quietude"), a term describing the solitary contemplative life of hermits who withdrew to the wilderness. In the end we opted for "spiritual tranquility." We have rendered *theophoros,* a frequent epithet for these holy men, as "divinely inspired" rather than "Godbearing." We have chosen to translate *hegoumenos* as "superior," *hieromonachos* as "hieromonk," and *geron* as "elder." In the effort to make the translation more understandable, we have frequently added proper names, as, for example, where the Greek has only "that man" or "the elder" or "the monk."

All scriptural citations are italicized, and the references are indicated in square brackets in the Greek text; references to patristic authors are provided in the endnotes to the translation. We have used Sir Lancelot Brenton's Greek and English version of the Septuagint, the Nestle-Aland Greek text of the New Testament, and for the English translation the Revised Standard Version, occasionally modified.[32]

We here wish to acknowledge the role of two members of the Dumbarton Oaks Medieval Library editorial board in the review of this volume and their numerous excellent sug-

gestions for improvement of the translation: Alexander Alexakis reviewed the *Life of Euthymios,* and Claudia Rapp the vitae of Athanasios, Maximos, Niphon, and Philotheos. In addition, Alexakis collated the four surviving manuscripts of the *Life of Euthymios* and prepared a much improved version of the Greek text of that vita. We are grateful to both scholars for their invaluable assistance. We also note with gratitude Stamatina McGrath's contribution to this volume of the text and translation of the *Life of Philotheos,* as well as the section in the introduction on his vita.[33] Nathanael Aschenbrenner, a Tyler Fellow at Dumbarton Oaks, conscientiously assisted with the review of page proofs. Alice-Mary Talbot would like to thank the members of the Dumbarton Oaks Friday reading group, with whom she first began to translate the *Lives* of Euthymios and Athanasios many years ago. Finally, we should like to express our appreciation to Nadezhda Kavrus-Hoffmann and the library staff at the State Historical Museum for their assistance in our acquisition of a digital file of the Moscow manuscript of the *Life of Euthymios the Younger.*

Notes

1 It should thus be contrasted with Mount Latros near Miletos, Mount Galesion near Ephesos, (Bithynian) Mount Olympos near Prousa, and Mount Saint Auxentios near Constantinople.

2 Papachryssanthou, *Prôtaton,* 3.

3 V. della Dora, *Imagining Mount Athos: Visions of a Holy Place from Homer to World War II* (Charlottesville, Va., 2011), 24, 63. "Panagia" ("all-holy one") is a traditional name for the Virgin Mary.

4 Papachryssanthou, *Prôtaton,* 7.

5 Papachryssanthou, *Prôtaton,* 6.

6 Ibid., loc cit.

7 Ibid., 20.

8 The vita was edited by Kirsopp Lake in *The Early Days of Monasticism on Mount Athos* (Oxford, 1909), 18–39.

9 For a brief indication of the most problematic issues of chronology in this vita, see the notes to the translation; Richard Greenfield plans to publish a discussion of these at a future date.

10 On the rule and *typikon* of Athanasios, see *BMFD* 1:205–31, 245–70.

11 Krausmüller, "The Lost First *Life* of Athanasius the Athonite," 63–86.

12 For the context of these *Lives* in contemporary hagiography, see Angeliki Laiou-Thomadakis, "Saints and Society in the Late Byzantine Empire," in *Charanis Studies: Essays in Honor of Peter Charanis,* ed. Angeliki Laiou-Thomadakis (New Brunswick, N.J.,1980), 84–114.

13 The vita by Makarios Makres (*BHG* 1237f) was edited and translated into English by Sophia Kapetanaki in her doctoral dissertation, "An Annotated Critical Edition of Makarios Makres' Life of St Maximos Kausokalyves. . . . ," (PhD thesis, University of London, 2002, 146–81, 258–94). An earlier Greek edition was published by Asterios Argyriou in Μακαρίου τοῦ Μακρῆ Συγγράμματα (Thessalonike, 1996), 141–65. The vita by Kochylas (*BHG* 1237c) was edited by the monk Patapios Kausokalyvites, "Ιερομονάχου Ἰωαννικίου Κόχιλα, Βίος ὁσίου Μαξίμου τοῦ Καυσοκαλύβη [14ᵒˢ αἰ.]," Γρηγόριος ὁ Παλαμᾶς 819 (2007): 513–77. See also Kapetanaki, "Transmission of Byzantine Hagiographical Texts," 179–85.

14 Information provided in Chapter 21.1 of the vita may suggest a date in the early fifteenth century (1403 or 1408) for its composition. See the note to that chapter, below.

15 *PLP* 7616.

16 Conceivably, as Halkin argues ("Niphon," 6), this could be the same Jeremiah ὁ Πατητᾶς who wrote the canon in honor of both Niphon and Maximos.

17 On this and other Turkish attacks on Mount Athos in the fourteenth century, see Laiou-Thomadakis, "Saints and Society" (as in n. 12, above), 92–95.

18 For discussion, see Ware, "St. Maximos," 423–30.

19 *PLP* 16810.

20 Halkin, "Deux vies," 106 n. 2, suggests 1270 to 1285; Ware, "St. Maxi-

mos," 411, prefers 1270 to 1280. The mention of the silver *hyperpyron* coin in Niphon's *Life of Maximos* (Chapter 10.2) implies, however, that he must have still been alive in 1367 and, since he died aged ninety-five, cannot have been born before 1272 if his age is accurately recorded. The *PLP* prefers 1280, through a calculation based on dating his visit to Constantinople during the second patriarchate of Athanasios I, circa 1307.

21 The *PLP* dates this to 1331 or a little earlier. Ware, "St. Maximos," 418, is less precise, suggesting shortly before 1325 or in the 1330s.

22 The *PLP* suggests 1375. See further above, n. 20.

23 *PLP* 20687.

24 Halkin, "Niphon," 7–8.

25 On the issue of his uncanonical ordination, see Halkin, "Niphon," 8–9.

26 See above on the confusion between Niphon's own account and that of his hagiographer.

27 For the calculation of this date, see Halkin, "Niphon," 7–8.

28 The conquest of Thrace and Macedonia by the Ottoman Turks occurred between 1366 and 1371; see Machiel Kiel, "The Incorporation of the Balkans into the Ottoman Empire, 1353–1453," in *The Cambridge History of Turkey,* vol. 1, ed. Kate Fleet (Cambridge, 2006), 138–56.

29 Further on the institution of *devşirme,* see Basilike Papoulia, *Ursprung und Wesen der "Knabenlese" im Osmanischen Reich* (Munich, 1963).

30 Selected chapters of Theophanes's vita of Maximos and a few pages of the vita of Niphon were translated into Italian by Antonio Rigo, in *L'amore della quiete (ho tes hesychias eros), l'esicasmo bizantino tra il XIII e il XV secolo* (Magnano, 1993), 99–119, 121–24; these excerpts were also published in a Spanish translation, *Silencio y quietud. Misticos bizantinos entre los siglos XIII y XV* (Madrid, 2007), 97–114, 115–17.

31 Dumont, "Vie de saint Athanase l'Athonite."

32 Lancelot Brenton, *The Septuaginta with Apocrypha: Greek and English* (London, 1851); the Greek text and RSV English translation are conveniently combined in Eberhard Nestle, Kurt Aland, et al., *Greek-English New Testament* (Stuttgart, 1992).

33 She in turn would like to acknowledge her appreciation of the review of her contributions by Richard Greenfield, Claudia Rapp, and Alice-Mary Talbot.

LIFE OF EUTHYMIOS THE YOUNGER

Βίος τοῦ ὁσίου πατρὸς ἡμῶν Εὐθυμίου τοῦ ἐν Θεσσαλονίκη

Εὐλόγησον πάτερ.

I

Ὁ τῆς ἀνθρωπίνης οὐσίας γενεσιουργὸς καὶ συνοχεὺς Θεός, ὁ ἐπὶ διαμονῇ καὶ ἀφθαρσίᾳ τὸ ταύτης διαπλάσας φύραμα, κἂν παρατροπῇ καὶ παραβάσει τὸν θάνατον εἰσῳκίσατο, δυσὶ τούτοις ἐκ τῆς ἄνωθεν συγγενείας ἐρωτικῶς διακειμένους τοὺς ἅπαξ τὸ πρῶτον ἀπολωλεκότας ἀξίωμα προορώμενος, ἔν τε τῷ βίῳ τὴν διαμονὴν ἐπὶ μακρὸν ἀποκεκληρῶσθαι καὶ τὸ εὖ εἶναι μετὰ καὶ τοῦ εἶναι ἁρμοδίως συμπεριλελῆφθαι, ὡς ἂν αὐτοῖς ἀναλόγως τῷ θείῳ ἡ πρὸς τοὺς γονέας τιμὴ μεθοδεύοιτο, μιᾷ τινι θεσμοθεσίᾳ περιπλέξας ἀμφότερα καὶ ὥσπερ ῥᾴδια ταῦτα ἐκ δυσπορίστων ἀποφηνάμενος, ἐν τῇ πρὸς τοὺς γονέας τιμῇ τοῖς ποθοῦσιν ἑκάτερα συνωρίσατο· "Τίμα," γάρ φησι, "τὸν πατέρα καὶ τὴν μητέρα σου, ἵνα εὖ σοι γένηται καὶ ἔσῃ μακροχρόνιος ἐπὶ τῆς γῆς" [see Exodus 20:12].

2   Καὶ μὴν καὶ ἐκ τοῦ ἐναντίου, ὡς ἂν μὴ αὐθαιρέτου δόξῃ μόνον γνώμης τὸ ἐπίταγμα, πολλοῦ γε καὶ δεῖ,

Life of our blessed father Euthymios of Thessalonike
    Bless us, father.

Chapter 1

God, who is the creator and sustainer of human substance, originally formed its dough for permanence and incorruptibility, although, on account of its perversion and transgression He later introduced death. He foresaw, however, that those who had once and for all lost their initial standing were passionately attached to the following two things as a result of their kinship with heaven: to be allotted great length of life and to combine living well with plain existence. So that they might set about showing honor toward their parents in a way that would resemble their honor for the divine, God thus wove both these things, long life and living well, together in a single commandment, and declared, in the commandment to honor one's parents, that they were easy instead of difficult to achieve, bringing them together for those who desire both. For He said: "*Honor your father and mother, that it may be well with you, and that you may live long on the earth.*"

On the other hand, so that His injunction might not 2 seem to be only a matter of free choice but, far from it, a

ἐπαπειλημένης ἐντολῆς καὶ τὸ χρειῶδες ἀπαιτούσης τοῦ πράγματος· ἐπάγει γὰρ εὐθύς· "Ὁ κακολογῶν πατέρα ἤ μητέρα θανάτῳ τελευτάτω" [see Exodus 21:16]. Καὶ γὰρ οὔτε ζῆν εἰκὸς εὐπρεπέστατα οἷς τὸ εἶναι μετὰ τοῦ εὖ εἶναι ἡ πρὸς τοὺς τεκόντας τιμὴ οὐμενοῦν οὐ προεθησαύρισεν.

2

Ἐπεὶ οὖν οὕτω ταῦτα καὶ "πατρὸς μὲν εὐχὴ στηρίζει οἴκους τέκνων," ἤ φησι Σολομὼν ὁ σοφώτατος, "κατάρα δὲ μητρὸς ἐκριζοῖ θεμέλια" [Ecclesiasticus 3:9], φέρε πατρικῆς ἡμῖν ἐφεστηκυίας μνήμης καὶ τιμᾶσθαι παρ' ἡμῶν ἐποφειλῶς ἀξιούσης, αὐτοὶ τὴν ἰδίαν ὑπακοὴν ἐπιδειξώμεθα καὶ τὴν ἰσχύν, ὡς ἡ δύναμις, τῷ λόγῳ ἐπιτρέψωμεν, αὐτόθεν ἡμῖν τὴν πρὸς τὸ λέγειν χάριν ἐξ ἀκενώτων πηγῶν ἐπιχευούσης τῆς χάριτος.

2   Καὶ γὰρ ἄτοπον ἴσως καὶ γελοῖον δόξει τοῖς εὖ φρονοῦσι κρινόμενον τῷ διὰ τοῦ εὐαγγελίου ἡμᾶς ὠδινήσαντι [see 1 Corinthians 4:15], εὐχαῖς τε καὶ νουθεσίαις ἱεραῖς σπαργανώσαντι, γάλακτί τε ἀρετῶν παιδοτροφήσαντι καὶ ἄρτῳ ζωτικῷ θείας ἐπιγνώσεως θρέψαντι καὶ εἰς ἄνδρας τελεῖν, τό γε εἰς αὐτὸν ἦκον, τοῦ πληρώματος τοῦ Χριστοῦ [see Ephesians 4:13] παρασκευάσαντι, κἂν ἐξ ἀφροσύνης ἡμεῖς ἔτι ταῖς φρεσὶ νηπίοις ἀνοηταίνουσι σφᾶς αὐτοὺς παρενείρωμεν, μὴ τὴν ἑαυτῶν ἐν λόγοις ἐπιδείξασθαι

commandment that carries with it a threat and makes this a matter of necessity, He immediately added, "*He that reviles his father or mother, let him die.*" For it is not right for those to go on living very happily for whom honor toward their parents has in no way previously accumulated a store of simple existence together with living well.

Chapter 2

Since this is so, and "*The blessing of the father establishes the houses of the children, but the curse of the mother roots out foundations,*" in the words of the most wise Solomon, as the commemoration day of our father is upon us and demands to be deservedly honored by us, let me demonstrate the appropriate obedience and, to the extent of my ability, let me turn my strength to the narrative, as the grace flowing from inexhaustible springs spontaneously gives me the grace to speak.

In the judgment of sensible people, it would perhaps 2 seem inappropriate and even ridiculous not to demonstrate my strength in composition for my father Euthymios who *labored to give birth to me through the gospel,* who swaddled me with prayers and holy admonitions, who suckled me with the milk of virtues and nourished me with the living bread of divine knowledge, my father who also prepared me, at least as far as it depended on him, *to mature into a man of the company of Christ* (even if, out of foolishness, I am comparing myself with infants whose minds are devoid of intelligence).

δύναμιν, καὶ ταῦτα ἀκινδύνως ἡμῖν ἐχούσης τῆς ὑποθέσεως, εἴτε ἐξισουμένου τοῦ λόγου τῷ μεγέθει τῶν πράξεων ἢ καὶ ἀποδέοντος τῆς τῶν ἔργων μεγαλειότητος.

3 Εἰ μὲν γὰρ πᾶσαν αὐτοῦ τὴν ἀρετὴν ὁ λόγος εἰς θεωρίας καὶ ἀναβάσεως ὕψος ἐληλακὼς ἐπικαταλαβέσθαι καὶ ὡς μεταδοτική τις δύναμις τοῖς ἄλλοις διαπορθμεῦσαι δυνήσηται (ἄλλων μὲν ἴσως τοῦτο τῶν ὅσοι γεγυμνασμένοι τὴν ἕξιν καὶ τὰ αἰσθητήρια [see Hebrews 5:14], ἀλλ' οὐχὶ τῆς ἡμετέρας μεθημοσύνης), τῷ ἁγίῳ πάντως θήσει τὰ νικητήρια, καταπλήττων, οἶδ' ὅτι, τῇ τῶν ἔργων μεγαλειότητι τῶν ἀκουόντων τὴν σύνεσιν· εἰ δ' ἀπορήσει πως πρὸς τὴν ἰσότητα, ὃ πᾶσα παθεῖν ἀνάγκη τοῖς ἐκεῖνον ἐγκωμιάζουσιν, καὶ οὕτω τὸ περίδοξον τῷ ὑμνουμένῳ περιποιηθήσεται, τοσοῦτον ὑπεραναβάντι τὸ σῶμα τῆς ταπεινώσεως [Philippians 3:21] καὶ οὕτως ὑψηλῷ τῇ θεωρίᾳ καὶ πράξει χρηματίσαντι, ὡς μηδὲ λόγοις παριστᾶν ἡμᾶς δύνασθαι, ὅσα τοῖς ἔργοις αὐτὸς διηνυκὼς ἀναδέδεικτο. Καὶ ἐπεὶ ταῦτα προοιμιασάμενοι ἐποφειλόμενον ἡμῖν μᾶλλον τὸ ἐκ τῶν λόγων ἐφύμνιον, ἄλλως τε καὶ ἀκίνδυνον πανταχόθεν, ἀποδεδείχαμεν, τὸν ἐκείνου Θεὸν συνεργὸν ἤδη τῷ λόγῳ ἐπιβοησάμενοι, τῆς κατ' αὐτὸν ὑποθέσεως τὴν ἀπαρχὴν ἐντεῦθεν ποιησώμεθα.

And this is especially so since the endeavor I propose holds no danger for me, whether my narrative equals the magnitude of his deeds, or fails to match the greatness of his actions.

For if my narrative, having arrived at the height of contemplation and elevation, is indeed able to include all of Euthymios's virtue and communicate it to others like some freely available power (but perhaps this is a task for others who *are trained in their practice and their faculties,* and not for my inadequate self), it will surely bestow the prizes of victory on the holy Euthymios, astonishing, I know, the understanding of the audience with the magnitude of his deeds. But if, on the other hand, my narrative should somehow fail to match his achievements (which of necessity must always be the fate of his eulogists), even so it will still procure fame for the one who is being celebrated; for it is because he surpassed *the lowly body* to such an extent and was so lofty in contemplation and practice that I am unable to represent in words what he accomplished in deeds. And since in writing this prologue I have demonstrated that it indeed remains my obligation to produce an encomium of words, and besides it is totally without risk, after summoning Euthymios's God as a helper for my narrative, let me now make a beginning of this endeavor on his behalf.

3

Εὐθύμιος τοίνυν ὁ ἀοίδιμος ἡμῶν πατὴρ καὶ μακάριος, ὁ καὶ ἐν σαρκὶ ἄγγελος καὶ τῇ ἀποθέσει τοῦ σκήνους μετὰ τῶν ἄνω δυνάμεων περὶ Θεὸν χορεύων καὶ ἀγαλλόμενος, πατρίδα μὲν πρόσκαιρον καὶ ἐπίγειον τὴν τῶν Γαλατῶν χώραν ἐπεγράφετο, κἂν τῷ κάλλει τῶν ἀρετῶν καὶ τῷ ὕψει τῆς πρακτικῆς ἀναβάσεως τῇ ἄνω Σιὼν πολιτογραφηθείς, ταύτης οἰκήτωρ ἐνδίκως γνωρίζεται· Γαλατῶν ἐκείνων, οὓς ὁ θεῖος ἀπόστολος ὡς εὐήθεις καὶ ἀνοήτους [Galatians 3:1] ἐπιτωθάζων διὰ τὸ ἐπιρρεπὲς τῆς γνώμης καὶ εὐρίπιστον, τάχα ἂν ἐν τῷδε τῷ μάκαρι ὡς εὐσταθεῖς καὶ συνετοὺς ὑπεραγάσαιτο.

2 Κώμη δὲ αὐτῷ τιθηνὸς καὶ τροφὸς καὶ τῇ γεννήσει τὰ τῆς τιμῆς ἀντιλαμβάνουσα τροφεῖα Ὀψὼ προσηγόρευτο, ὑποτελὴς μὲν τῇ τῶν Γαλατῶν Ἀγκύρᾳ, εὔκρατος δὲ καὶ πίων καὶ πολυάνθρωπος, οὕτως δ᾽ ἂν εἰπεῖν τὴν αὐτήν, τῷ παρ᾽ ἡμῶν εὐφημουμένῳ θαρρήσαντας, καὶ ἁγίων ἔδος καὶ σῳζομένων μητρόπολιν καὶ διδάσκαλον ἀρετῆς καὶ ποδηγὸν εὐσεβείας καὶ πρὸς Θεὸν μετανάστευσιν (τῇ τῶν πρώτων μιμήσει, ὅσοι μὴ ῥᾳθυμίᾳ ἑαυτοῖς τὰς πρὸς ἀρετὴν ἀφορμὰς ἀποκείρουσιν), ἑπομένην δεικνῦσαν τῶν σῳζομένων τὴν εἴσοδον.

3 Γεννήτορες δὲ αὐτῷ εὐπάτριδες ἅμα καὶ δίκαιοι καὶ

Chapter 3

Euthymios then, my celebrated and blessed father, who was an angel in the flesh and, after setting aside his body, is now part of the choir surrounding God and rejoices together with the celestial powers, claimed the land of the Galatians as his temporary and earthly fatherland, even though, due to the beauty of his virtues and the extent of his elevation through his deeds, he was enrolled as a citizen of the celestial Sion, and is justly recognized as an inhabitant of that place. He came from the land of those Galatians whom the divine apostle Paul mocked as simple and *foolish* on account of the inconstancy and instability of their opinions, although surely, on the basis of this blessed individual, Paul would have greatly admired them as steadfast and intelligent.

The village that was his nursemaid and caregiver and that, 2 on account of his birth, received in terms of honor the wages of a wet nurse, was called Opso; it was subordinate to Ankyra of the Galatians, had a mild climate, and was both fertile and populous. I would say, moreover, drawing confidence from the subject of my praise (that is, Euthymios), that it was an abode of holy men, a metropolis of the saved, and a teacher of virtue; it was also a guide to piety and a migratory route toward God which, if followed (by imitation of those initial exemplars who did not idly cut off from themselves the occasions for virtue), pointed the way to the entrance of the saved.

Euthymios's parents were of good family and righteous 3

9

τοσοῦτον ἀλλήλους τῇ ἀρετῇ παραθήγοντες, ὅσον φιλο-
νεικεῖν ἑκάτερον, ὅστις τοῦ ἑτέρου τὸ πρωτεῖον τῆς ἀρετῆς
ἀπενέγκοιτο· καὶ γὰρ φθόνος μὲν αὐτοῖς ἀπῆν ἀναβάσεως,
ζῆλος δ' ἐνεκεντρίζετο καὶ ἔρις ἦν ἀγαθὴ καὶ φατρία περὶ
αὐτῶν ἐκράτει ψυχωφελὴς καὶ ἐπέραστος οὐ μόνον τοῖς
τὴν αὐτὴν κώμην οἰκοῦσιν, ἤδη δὲ καὶ τοῖς πόρρω τὴν
διαγωγὴν κεκληρωμένοις καὶ τὴν κατάσχεσιν.

4   Καὶ γὰρ ἐδόκει θαῦμα τοῖς ὁρῶσι καὶ τοῖς ἀκούουσιν,
ἀνθρώπους ὄντας βιωτικοὺς καὶ δημοσίοις τελέσμασιν
ὑποκύπτοντας καὶ στρατείᾳ τε καταλεγομένους καὶ τῇ
ταύτης βίᾳ ἐνδιδόναι μικρὸν τῆς ἀρετῆς ὥσπερ ὀφείλοντας, μηδ' ὁπωσοῦν ταύτης ἐκκλῖναι διανοουμένους τούτους ἐπικαταλαβέσθαι ἢ ἀπονεύοντας. Φαιδρὸν μὲν οὖν
εἰπεῖν, ὅτι καὶ μᾶλλον ταῖς φροντίσι περιαντλούμενοι καὶ
ταῖς ἀνίαις τοῦ βίου ἔσθ' ὅτε καταγχόμενοι, προτροπῇ
ἀλλήλους καὶ παραινέσει σχηματίζοντες, ἐπὶ Θεὸν ὀλοψύ-
χως τὴν ἑαυτῶν ῥοπὴν μετωχέτευον, ὃς δύναιτ' ἂν βουληθεὶς καὶ τὰ ῥάδια ποιῆσαι δυσπόριστα καὶ τοῖς ἀπόροις
αἰσίαν τὴν παροχὴν διαδαψιλεύσασθαι.

5   Καὶ μὴν τοῦ λυποῦντος τὴν παραψυχὴν ἐκεῖθεν ἀντι-
λαμβάνοντες *καὶ σιωπῶσα καὶ φθεγγομένη* τοῖς ἄλλοις
ὑπῆρχον *παραίνεσις, συμπαθεῖς, μέτριοι, εὐπειθεῖς, ἥμεροι,*
φιλόξενοι, φιλόπτωχοι, ἐκ τούτου δὲ καὶ φιλόθεοι, προσ-
ηνεῖς, κόσμιοι, σώφρονες, ἐπιεικεῖς *ἐν ἀνυποκρίτῳ ἀγάπῃ*
[2 Corinthians 6:6], *τοῖς πᾶσι τὰ πάντα γινόμενοι* [1 Corinthians 9:22].

6   Ποθεῖτ' οἶδ' ὅτι τῶν ἀρετῶν ἀκροασάμενοι καὶ αὐτὰ
μαθεῖν τὰ ὀνόματα. Ἐπιφάνιος ἦν ὁ πατήρ, ὁ θείας

and urged each other on in virtue to such an extent that each was competing to see which one could carry off the first prize of virtue from the other. For they did not envy each other's spiritual advancement, but zeal spurred them on, and their rivalry was a positive one, and a group formed around them that was spiritually beneficial and desirable not only for those who inhabited the same village, but also for those who had as their lot a life and property far away.

For it seemed wondrous to those who saw and heard 4 them that, although they were ordinary lay people and subject to public taxation and enrolled in the army and were seemingly obliged to surrender a little of their virtue to its violence, they neither considered any way of avoiding this or tried to dodge being involved <in military service>. It is amazing to say that rather, when they were completely overwhelmed by cares and sometimes suffocated by the troubles of life, molding each other through exhortation and encouragement, they wholeheartedly diverted their effort to God, who could, if He wanted, both render inaccessible that which is easy to procure and provide a happy solution to difficult problems.

Receiving consolation in their suffering from this source, 5 they were to the others *both a silent and vocal encouragement;* and they were compassionate, moderate, compliant, mild-mannered, hospitable, and charitable to the poor. As a result they were also lovers of the divine, gentle, decent, prudent, and fair *in genuine love, being all things to all men.*

I know that having heard about their virtues you want to 6 learn their names as well. Epiphaneios was the father, named

ἐπιφανείας ἐπώνυμος, ὁ φαεινὸς τῆς ἀρετῆς λύχνος καὶ εὐσεβέστατος, ὁ φάνας μὲν τότε δι' ἑαυτοῦ τοῖς ἐγγύς, φαίνων δὲ καὶ νῦν ἡμῖν τοῖς πόρρω που κατῳκισμένοις καὶ ἀπέχουσι τῇ τοῦ υἱοῦ λάμψει, ὃν ὡς πυρσὸν ἀνάψας τῇ οἰκουμένῃ ἐξαπέστειλεν. Ἄννα δὲ μήτηρ, ἡ χάρις μὲν προσαγορευομένη καὶ χάριτος Θεοῦ δοχεῖον καὶ τέμενος χρηματίσασα, χαρίτων δὲ καὶ ἡμᾶς ἐμπιπλῶσα θείων διὰ τῆς τοῦ παιδὸς χαριτώσεως.

4

Ἐκ δὴ τούτων ὁ ἱερὸς ἐκεῖνος ἐκβλαστήσας καὶ ἀληθῶς τοῦ Θεοῦ ἄνθρωπος, τί δεῖ λέγειν, ὅσης ἐξ αὐτῆς τῆς γεννήσεως χάριτος ἐπεπλήρωτο; Οἷος ἦν τοῖς ὁρῶσι καὶ πρὸ τῆς ἥβης κρινόμενος, προσηνής, κόσμιος, μειλίχιος, ἡδυεπής, εὔτακτος, εὐπειθής, γονεῦσιν ὑποτασσόμενος, τῶν παιδίων διϊστάμενος, τοῖς ναοῖς προσχωρῶν, τοῖς εὐσεβέσι τῶν συγγενῶν οἷα πατράσι προσκείμενος; Καὶ γὰρ ἐκράτει τῶν εἰκονομάχων ἡ βδελυρὰ τότε καὶ μισόχρι- στος αἵρεσις, ἀπὸ Λέοντος μὲν τοῦ θηριωνύμου καὶ δυσ- σεβοῦς λαβοῦσα τὴν ἔναρξιν, ὃς καὶ δίκην ἔτισε τῆς αὐτοῦ ἀξίαν παρενέξεως, ἐν τόπῳ ἁγίῳ, ᾧ αὐτὸς ἐξύβρισε, τὴν βέβηλον αὐτοῦ καὶ βάρβαρον τομῇ μαχαίρας ἀπορρήξας ψυχήν, καταλήγουσαν δὲ εἰς ἕβδομον ἔτος τῆς ἐπικρατείας, Μιχαὴλ τοῦ ἀπὸ ἐξκουβίτων παραχωρήσει Θεοῦ διὰ

after the divine epiphany, a shining and most pious lamp of virtue, one who shone then in himself upon his neighbors, and now shines upon us, who live far away and are distant, through the illumination provided by his son, whom he lit like a torch and sent to the inhabited world. His mother was Anna, who bore the name of grace and was a receptacle and precinct of God's grace, and fills us as well with divine graces through the grace shed by her child.

Chapter 4

Since that truly holy man of God sprang forth from such parents, why need I recount with how much grace he was filled from the time of his birth? Or how he was judged by those who saw him, even before he reached his maturity, as gentle, decent, gracious, well-spoken, well-behaved, compliant, obedient to his parents, avoiding children, attending church, and devoted to his pious relatives as if they were his parents? For at that time of Niketas's birth the abominable and Christ-hating heresy of the iconoclasts prevailed which began with Leo, that beastly named and impious man who, in a holy place which he had insulted, paid the just penalty for his rejection of icons, for there, with a blow from a sword, he ended his accursed and barbarous life, which terminated in the seventh year of his reign; and at that time Michael, the former *exkoubitor,* by God's will took

πλῆθος ἁμαρτιῶν ἡμῶν τῆς τῶν Ῥωμαίων βασιλείας τὰ σκῆπτρα τότε κατέχοντος, ὡς εἶναι ἔτος ἀπὸ κτίσεως κόσμου, ὅτε τῷ βίῳ ὁ μέγας ἡμῶν καθηγητὴς Εὐθύμιος ὑπὸ Θεοῦ ἐκεχάριστο, ἑξακισχιλιοστὸν τριακοσιοστὸν τριακοστὸν δεύτερον.

5

Εὐθυμίου τοιγαροῦν τοῦ ἁγίου πατρὸς ἕβδομον ἔτος ἐν ἀρετῶν ἐπιδόσει καὶ ἡλικίας αὐξήσει διανύοντος, ὁ μὲν πατὴρ πρὸς τὴν ἀγήρω καὶ μακραίωνα βιοτὴν μεταβιβάζεται, δύο θυγατέρων πατὴρ πρὸς τῷ ἀοιδίμῳ τούτῳ χρηματίσαι διαρκέσας, ὧν ἡ μὲν μία Μαρία, Ἐπιφανία δὲ παρωνύμως τοῦ πατρὸς ἡ ἑτέρα προσηγόρευτο. Ἡ μήτηρ δὲ τῇ τοῦ ἀνδρὸς ἀποβιώσει χηρείᾳ τε καὶ στρατείᾳ ἐξυπηρετεῖν οὐχ οἷά τε οὖσα, ἄλλως τε καὶ παιδὸς αὐτῇ ἑτέρου μὴ ὑπόντος ἄρρενος, ὃς καὶ τὸ πένθος τῆς χηρείας ἐπικουφίσει καὶ τῆς στρατείας τὴν λατρείαν ἀποπληρώσει, ἀνενδότως ταύτην κατατειρόντων ἑκατέρων καὶ μηδ' εἴ τι γένηται μεθήσειν ἀνανευόντων, τὰ τῆς χηρείας μὲν ἀρίστως διατιθεμένη καὶ ὡς γυναικὶ σωφρονεῖν μελετησάσῃ ἁρμόδιον, ἐπὶ τὴν τῆς στρατείας φροντίδα τὴν ῥοπὴν πᾶσαν μετατίθησι. Πάντοθεν οὖν περισκοπήσασα καὶ πολλαχῶς τοῖς λογισμοῖς διαφόρους ἐπινοίας ἀνατυπώσασα, ὡς οὐδεμίαν ἄλλην περιλειπομένην ἀντιλήψεως

possession of the scepter of the Roman empire on account of the multitude of our sins. So the year from the creation of the world, when our great leader Euthymios was brought to life by God, was 6332.

Chapter 5

When the holy father Euthymios was in his seventh year, increasing in virtue and stature, his father passed on to the eternal and long-lasting life, having survived long enough to be the father of two daughters in addition to this celebrated son, one of whom was called Maria, the other Epiphaneia after her father. His mother, as the result of the loss of her husband, was unable to provide in any other way for both widowhood and military service, because she had no other male child to relieve the sorrow of her widowhood and fulfill the obligation of military service, both of which weighed heavily upon her without cease and refused to let up no matter what happened. Dealing with her widowhood in an excellent manner and as appropriate for a woman who was concerned to act in a prudent fashion, she devoted all her effort to her concern for the obligation of military service. Looking all around and variously devising in her mind different ideas, once she understood that there was no other

ἐλπίδα ἑαυτῇ ἐπικατελάβετο, ἐπὶ τουτονὶ τὸν ἐν νέῳ τῷ σώματι φρόνημα τέλειον ἐπιδεικνύμενον παῖδα τὴν ἑαυτῆς σωτηρίαν ἀνατίθησι. Καὶ ὡς μὲν τέκνον μονογενὲς ἔχειν τοῦτον μεθ᾽ ἑαυτῆς φύσεως νόμοις ἠναγκάζετο καὶ τὰ σπλάγχνα ἐκινεῖτο καὶ μητρικῶς ἐπ᾽ αὐτῷ διεφλέγετο, μήπου τι τῶν ἀνιαρῶν ἐπισυμβαίη τούτῳ πρὸς ἀποδημίαν ἀπαίροντι, καταγχομένη δ᾽ οὖν ὅμως τῇ τῆς ἐκστρατείας ἐπιθέσει, ἀνάγραπτον αὐτὸν τοῖς στρατιωτικοῖς ἐκδίδωσι κώδιξι, Νικήταν τότε τὸ ἀπὸ γενέσεως ἀποκληρούμενον ὄνομα, οὐκ ἄνευ θείας ὀμφῆς ἢ θεοπρόπου τινὸς ἐπιπνοίας, ὡς οἶμαι, τούτου αὐτῷ ἐπιτεθέντος τοῦ ὀνόματος, ἀλλ᾽ ὡς νίκην εἰληφέναι κατ᾽ ἐχθρῶν, τῶν τε ὁρωμένων ὁμοίως καὶ τῶν ἀοράτων, φερωνύμως εἰς ὕστερον μέλλοντι.

2   Τελεῖ μέντοι κἀντεῦθεν ἐν τοῖς στρατιωτικοῖς καταλόγοις καὶ πάντα τῇ μητρὶ γίνεται, υἱός, ἀντιλήπτωρ, φροντιστής, προστάτης, τῶν ἀνιώντων ἐπικουφιστής, τῶν εὐθύμων περιποιητής, ἀντιχρηματίζει ταύτῃ κηδεμών, πατήρ, ὑπερασπιστής, τὸ μέγιστον, ἀνὴρ πάντων τῶν ἐν τῷ οἴκῳ τὴν φροντίδα καὶ τῶν ἐκτὸς τὴν ἐπιμέλειαν ἀναδεξάμενος. Ἐπικουφίζεται τούτοις τῶν ὀδυνῶν ἡ μήτηρ, παραψυχὴν εὐπορήσασα, καὶ τὴν διαμονὴν τῷ γένει καὶ τὴν αὔξησιν ἐπιμηχανᾶται τῷ πάντα αὐτῇ τὰ τίμια χρηματίζοντι καὶ γαμετῇ συνευνάσαι τοῦτον εὐστόχως στοχάζεται, ὡς ἂν καὶ τῶν φροντίδων αὐτῷ συγκοινωνήσῃ τὸ γύναιον καὶ τέκνου γονῇ προσθήκην οἴσει τῷ γένει ἐπιμειοῦσθαι κινδυνεύοντι. Καὶ δὴ ὁμότροπον τῷ παιδὶ τὴν σύγκοιτον ἐπιζητήσασα, εὑρίσκει τάχος συνετὴν οὖσαν

remaining hope of assistance for her, she entrusted her salvation to this child who had manifested mature judgment in a youthful body. She was compelled by the laws of nature to keep him with her as her only son, and she was moved in her heart and burned with maternal affection for him, lest anything grievous happen to him if he moved away. Constrained, however, by the obligation of military service, she handed him over to be enrolled in the military registers, at that time bearing his birth name of Niketas; in my opinion, this name was not given to him without a divine oracle or some prophetic inspiration, but he received it as one who would later achieve victory over his enemies, visible and invisible alike, as appropriate for one bearing this name.

Indeed, enrolled from then on in the military ranks, Euthymios was everything to his mother, a son, helper, caretaker, protector, reliever from distress, procurer of happiness; he served her as guardian, father, defender, and, what was most significant, as a man who assumed the care of all household affairs and responsibility for external matters as well. His mother was relieved of her sorrows at these burdens, enjoying consolation, and began to plan for the continuation of the family line and its increase through the son who was her complete pride and joy. She shrewdly endeavored to betroth him to a bride, so that his wife might share in his responsibilities and through the birth of a child add to a family that was at risk of being diminished. Thus seeking a partner who was of similar temperament to her son, she quickly found a woman who was intelligent and attractive,

τὴν αὐτὴν καὶ εὐθέατον, πολύολβόν τε καὶ τοκέων εὐπα-
τριδῶν ἀπόγονον, τῇ ἐπωνυμίᾳ καὶ μόνῃ τὸ κεχαρισμένον
δηλοῦσαν τῆς ἕξεως· Εὐφροσύνην γὰρ αὐτὴν οἱ τεκόντες
προσηγορεύκασιν, ἱκανὴν οὖσαν εὐφρᾶναι ἔφεσιν ἀνδρὸς
συνετοῦ καὶ θέλξαι πόθον συνεύνου πρὸς αὐτὴν ἐπινεύ-
οντος.

6

Ταύτῃ τοι καὶ πατὴρ θυγατρὸς μιᾶς τῇ συζύγῳ συνευ-
νασθεὶς ὁ τῆς σωφροσύνης πυρσὸς ἀποδείκνυται, μητρι-
κῆς βουλῆς καὶ οὐχ ἡδονῆς ἀποκύημα εὐπορήσας τὸ ἔγγο-
νον· Ἀναστασὼ δὲ αὐτὴν διὰ τὴν τῆς τοῦ γένους ἐκπτώσεως
ἐλπιζομένην προσαγορεύσας ἀνάστασιν καὶ δόξας ἱκανῶς
ἔχειν τὴν παῖδα τὴν ὑπὲρ ἑαυτοῦ λύπην τῇ τε συνεύνῳ καὶ
αὐτῇ τῇ μητρὶ ἐπιλύεσθαι, εἰ τῷ Θεῷ διὰ τοῦ μονήρους
προσχήματος αὐτὸς ἑαυτὸν ἀφιερώσας δωρήσοιτο, ἤδη
καὶ τῆς ἀδελφῆς Μαρίας τῷ οἴκῳ δι᾽ ἐπιγαμβρίας εἰσοι-
σαμένης αὐτῆς σύνευνον, καιρὸν ἐπιζητήσας τοῖς βου-
λευθεῖσιν ἁρμόδιον καὶ τούτου περιτυχών, ὡς πολλάκις
ἐπηύχετο, τὴν τοῦ τιμίου σταυροῦ ἑορτὴν ἐπιτελέσας, ἐν
ᾗ ὑψοῦσθαι ἐτησίως τοῖς εὐσεβέσι νενομοθέτηται ἐν τῇ
τεσσαρεσκαιδεκάτῃ τοῦ Σεπτεμβρίου μηνός, ἑστιαθεὶς
μεγαλοψύχως καὶ τῇ τοῦ προσώπου φαιδρότητι πολὺ τὸ
χάριεν ὡς οὐδέποτε ἄλλοτε τοῖς ἰδίοις ἐπιδειξάμενος, τῇ

wealthy and the child of wellborn parents, one who revealed through her name alone the gracefulness of her character; for her parents had named her Euphrosyne, a woman capable of pleasing the wishes of an intelligent man and charming the desire of a husband who was <positively> inclined toward her.

Chapter 6

After sleeping with his wife, Euthymios, the torch of prudence, became the father of one daughter, producing the child as the offspring of his mother's wish, not of his own pleasure. He named her Anastaso on account of the hoped for resurrection of a family in decline. In the belief that this child would suffice to assuage his wife's and mother's sorrow over him, if he were to dedicate and give himself to God by adopting the monastic habit, and since his sister Maria had already introduced her husband into the house by marriage, he sought an appropriate moment to carry out his wishes. He found it, as he had often prayed, after celebrating the feast day of the venerable cross, on which day, the 14th of September, it is customary for it to be raised on high every year for the pious. After a bounteous feast, he revealed his great joy to his family as never before through the radiance of his face. The next day, setting the feast day of his

ἐπαύριον ἑαυτῷ δεξιὰν ἀπαρχὴν τὴν τοῦ μάρτυρος Νικήτα ὡς συνωνύμου μνήμην ὑποστησάμενος καὶ τὴν τοῦ ἐκ νεκρῶν ἀναστάντος Χριστοῦ δύναμιν (ἥν γὰρ κυριακὴ τῶν ἡμερῶν, καθ᾿ ἣν ἔθιμον τὴν τοῦ ζωοδότου ἐκ νεκάδων ἀνάστασιν Χριστιανοῖς ἄγειν νενόμισται), τῷ οἰκείῳ ἵππῳ ἀπώλειαν ἐπιφημισάμενος, ὃς ἦν ἐν τῷ χλοηφόρῳ πεδίῳ προσδεθεὶς ὡς νομευθησόμενος, καὶ πρὸς τὴν τούτου ἔρευναν ἑαυτὸν σχηματισάμενος, ἀντὶ τῆς τοῦ ἵππου εὑρέσεως πάρεργον ἑαυτῷ τὴν τῆς οὐρανίου βασιλείας εἰσαγωγὴν ὁ ἄριστος ἐπραγματεύσατο, οὐδὲν ἧττον ἢ ὁ υἱὸς Κὶς ἀντὶ τῶν ὄνων τοῦ πατρὸς τὴν τῆς βασιλείας ἀρχὴν ἀντευράμενος. Ἔτος ἦν τοῦτο τῆς μὲν ἀπὸ γεννήσεως τοῦ ἁγίου ἀγωγῆς ὀκτωκαιδέκατον, ἀπὸ δὲ κτίσεως κόσμου ἑξακισχιλιοστὸν τριακοσιοστὸν πεντηκοστόν, τῆς σωτηρίου δὲ πρὸς ἡμᾶς οἰκονομίας ὀκτακοσιοστὸν πεντηκοστόν.

7

Χ ώραν τοίνυν ἐκ χώρας ἀμείψας καὶ πόλιν ἐκ πόλεως οἷά τις ἀεροβάμων παραδραμών, τὰς τοῦ Ὀλύμπου ἐπικαταλαμβάνει ἀκρωρείας· πολλοῖς δὲ ἐν αὐταῖς περιτυχὼν ἁγιωτάτοις πατράσιν (οὐμενοῦν εἴποι τις ἡλίκοις τε καὶ ὅσοις), Ἰωαννικίῳ τῷ θεοφόρῳ πατρὶ ὡς προφητείᾳ καὶ τοῖς ἄλλοις καλοῖς ὑπεραστράπτοντι τελευταῖος ὑπαντιάζεται. Καὶ δὴ συνάξεως οὔσης καὶ πολλῶν πατέρων ὡς

namesake the martyr Niketas as an auspicious one for new beginnings and also relying on the power of Christ who arose from the dead (for it was a Sunday, on which day it is customary for Christians to celebrate the resurrection of the giver of life from the dead), Euthymios alleged as a pretext the loss of his horse, which had been tethered in the grassy meadow to graze, and pretended to go out to look for it. But instead of finding the horse, which was a secondary matter to finding for himself an entrance into the kingdom of heaven, the excellent man accomplished nothing less than Saul, the son of Kis, who found the beginning of his rule over his kingdom instead of his father's lost asses. It was the eighteenth year since the holy one's birth, in the year 6350 from the creation of the world, and the 850th year of the incarnation of the Savior among us.

Chapter 7

Moving then from place to place and passing from city to city, as if walking through the air, Euthymios arrived at the ridges of Olympos; and after encountering many extremely holy fathers there (one could not describe how numerous and how great they were), he ended up meeting the divinely inspired father Ioannikios who outshone them all with the gift of prophecy and other blessings. And so, when there was an assembly and many fathers had come to visit

πρὸς ἀρχιπάτορα τοῦτον εὐχῆς χάριν καὶ ὠφελείας ἐλη-
λυθότων, καὶ ὁ νέηλυς οὗτος φοιτητὴς μέσος τῶν ἄλλων
τῷ ἁγίῳ ἐμφανισθησόμενος παραγίνεται.

2   Τοῦ δὲ θεοφόρου πατρὸς θεόθεν τὰ κατ' αὐτὸν ἐκ-
διδαχθέντος καὶ προγινώσκοντος ἤδη τήν τε διάπυρον
αὐτοῦ πρὸς τὸ μονάσαι σπουδὴν καὶ τὴν εἰς ὕστερον αὐτῷ
ἐπανθεῖν μέλλουσαν τοῦ Πνεύματος ἔλλαμψιν, ὅπως τε μοναχῷ γενομένῳ μοναχῶν ἀγέλαι εἰς ὀσμὴν μύρου [Jeremiah
25:10] τῆς αὐτοῦ πολιτείας ἀκολουθήσωσιν, οἷά τινι πανθῆρι
τῇ τῶν τρόπων ποικιλίᾳ ἐφεπόμεναι, βουλομένῳ δὲ καὶ τοῖς
ἄλλοις ἐκ μικρῶν τεκμηρίων τὴν κεκρυμμένην αὐτοῦ καὶ
τέως λανθάνουσαν ἀρετὴν ποιῆσαι κατάδηλον, καὶ διὰ
τοῦτο σχηματικῶς τοὺς συνελθόντας πρὸς αὐτὸν ἀποπει-
ρωμένῳ, τίς ποτ' ἄρα εἴη ὁ ἐν μέσῳ αὐτῶν ἐν σχήματι
λαϊκῷ τολμηρῶς συναυλιζόμενος, αὐτοὶ μὴ γινώσκειν
τοῦτον κραταιῶς ἀπεφήναντο.

3   Ὁ δὲ τὸ δόκιμον τοῦ ἀσκητοῦ καὶ πρὸ τῆς ἀσκήσεως
παραστῆσαι βουλόμενος καὶ τὴν μέχρι θανάτου ὑπακοὴν
καὶ ταπείνωσιν, "Ἀνδροφόνος," φησίν, "ἐστὶ καὶ κάκιστος
ὁ βλεπόμενος, ἀλλὰ συσχεθήτω καὶ σιδήροις πεδηθεὶς τῶν
πρακτέων ἐξειπάτω τὸ βέβηλον." Πυθομένων δ' αὐτῷ τῶν
πατέρων εἰ ἄρα φονεύς ἐστιν, ὡς ὁ μέγας Ἰωαννίκιος προ-
ηγόρευσε, κατέθετο ἑαυτόν, ἐν οἷς οὐκ ᾔδει, φονέα, ταπει-
νωθεὶς καὶ κωφωθεὶς καὶ σιγήσας ἐξ ἀγαθῶν [Psalm 38(39):2]
καὶ μᾶλλον ἑαυτὸν τιμωρίαν ὀφλεῖν τῆς μιαιφονίας διαβε-
βαιούμενος.

4   Χειροπέδαις οὖν σιδηραῖς ἐντεῦθεν τοὺς πόδας δε-
σμεῖσθαι ἀπαγόμενος, ὡς ἁγιασμοῦ μετοχήν, μετάνοιαν

Ioannikios, as if to a patriarch, for the sake of a blessing and spiritual benefit, this newly arrived disciple appeared in the midst of the others to be presented to the holy man.

The divinely inspired father Ioannikios had been in- 2 structed about him by God and already foresaw his ardent zeal for monastic life and the illumination of the Spirit that would later blossom in him, and how, once he became a monk, flocks of monks would follow *the fragrance of the perfume* of his way of life, as if *following a leopard* on account of the *versatility* of its ways. Since, however, Ioannikios wanted to reveal Euthymios's concealed and still unknown virtue to the others as well, <but only gradually> by means of small indications, for this reason he tried to find out by gesturing to those who came to him who it was who thus dared to join their assembly in lay garb; they responded forcefully that they did not know him.

So Ioannikios, wishing to present Euthymios's mettle as 3 an ascetic even before he embarked upon ascetic practice, as well as his humility and obedience unto death, said, "The man you see is a most wicked murderer; let him be seized and, after he has been bound in iron fetters, let him confess his abominable deeds." When the fathers asked him if he was indeed a murderer, as the great Ioannikios had declared, he admitted that he was a murderer, although he actually knew nothing about it, *humbling himself and remaining dumb and keeping silence from good words,* and instead asserting that he should pay the penalty for murder.

Thus, after being led off to have his feet bound in iron 4 fetters, as though this were participation in a sacrament,

βαλὼν καὶ εὐχὴν αἰτησάμενος, ἐν ταῖς χερσὶ τὰ δεσμὰ ὑπε-
δέξατο, καὶ ταῦτα περιχαρῶς ἀσπασάμενος τοῖς ἰδίοις ποσὶ
περιθέσθαι ἐσχημάτισατο. Τῶν δὲ πατέρων θαυμασάντων
τοῦ νέου τὸ πρόθυμον καὶ ὅτι τὰ τῆς καταδίκης δεσμὰ ὡς
ἀφέσεως περιεβάλλετο σύμβολα, καὶ τῷ μεγάλῳ προσ-
αναγγειλάντων τὸ δραματούργημα, αὐτὸς τὸ κεκρυμμένον
αὐτοῖς ἀνακαλύπτει τοῦ πράγματος καί· "Ἄφετε," ἔφη,
"τὸν ἀνεύθυνον κατάδικον, ἄφετε· οὗτος γὰρ μέλλει τῶν
μοναχῶν ἐπικοσμεῖν τὸ πολίτευμα· δοκιμῆς γὰρ χάριν τὸν
φόνον ἐπιφημισάντων ἡμῶν, ἔγνωτε πάντως ὅπως αὐτὸς
τὸ ἐπίμωμον οὐκ ἀνένευσεν. Εἰ οὖν νέος καὶ κοσμικὸς καὶ
τῆς ἡμετέρας πολιτείας ἔτι ἀπείραστος τηλικούτῳ ἐγκλή-
ματι δι᾽ ὑπακοῆς ἑαυτὸν ὑπεύθυνον καθυπέθετο, ποῖον
εἶδος ἀρετῆς μονάσας οὐ κατορθώσειεν;"

8

Θαυμασθεὶς οὖν ἐπὶ τούτῳ παρὰ πᾶσιν καὶ πλεῖστα
ἐπαινεθείς, ἀφιλόδοξος ὢν καὶ μισόδοξος, ὡς ἐπὶ ἀρετῇ
διαβοηθεὶς ἤδη καὶ πρὸ τῆς ἀποκάρσεως, ἐκεῖθεν ἀποδρὰς
ἑτέρῳ πατρὶ προσοικίζεται, πόρρω μὲν τοῦ μεγάλου Ἰωαννικίου ἀπέχοντι, Ἰωάννῃ αὐτῷ προσαγορευομένῳ καὶ ἐπὶ
ἀρετῇ ὑπὸ πάντων ἐξακουομένῳ. Προσληφθεὶς δὲ μεγαλοψύχως ὑπ᾽ αὐτοῦ, ὥσπερ θείας τινὸς προνοίας προοδο-
ποιούσης αὐτῷ τὴν κατοίκησιν, καὶ τὰ τοῦ μονήρους βίου

Euthymios prostrated himself and requested their blessing, and took the fetters in his hands; joyously kissing them he indicated that they should be put on his feet. The fathers marveled at the young man's eagerness and that he would put on the bonds of a convicted criminal as though they were symbols of release. When they reported to the great man how events had unfolded, Ioannikios revealed to them the hidden truth of the matter, and said, "Release the condemned man who is innocent, release him; for he is going to be an adornment to the community of monks. For I made the allegation of murder to test him, and you are fully aware how he did not deny his blame. If then a young layman, who still has no experience of our way of life, admitted his culpability for such a great crime out of obedience, what kind of virtue may he not attain once he has become a monk?"

Chapter 8

Euthymios was thus admired for this by everyone and was greatly praised, but being someone who was not vainglorious and who even despised glory, since he was being celebrated for his virtue even before his tonsure, he left that place and went to reside with another father, who lived far away from the great Ioannikios. This man was called John and was celebrated by all for his virtue. After being welcomed wholeheartedly by him, as if some divine providence was preparing the way for him to dwell there, he was in-

κατηχηθεὶς καὶ μαθητευθεὶς ἀγωνίσματα, τηρεῖν τε πάντα
Θεῷ καὶ τῷ καθηγητῇ ἀνθομολογησάμενος, κείρεται ὑπ᾽
αὐτοῦ καὶ τῇ εὐλογίᾳ καὶ ἐπιθέσει τῶν χειρῶν εἰς τὸ τῶν
μοναχῶν μεταμφιέννυται πρόσχημα καὶ τὴν Εὐθύμιος
προσηγορίαν τῆς Νικήτα ἀντικομίζεται, δηλοῦν (οἶμαι) τῷ
καθηγητῇ βουλομένου τοῦ ὀνόματος τὴν ἐξ ἀθυμίας τῆς
τῶν εἰκονομάχων αἱρέσεως εἰς εὐθυμίαν ἄρτι τότε τῆς τοῦ
Χριστοῦ ἐκκλησίας μεταποίησιν, πρῶτον ἔτος Θεοδώρας
καὶ Μιχαὴλ αὐτοκρατορικῶς ἀγόντων, ὅτε διὰ γυναικὸς
ἀσθενοῦς καὶ παιδὸς ἀτελῆ κεκτημένου τὴν ἡλικίωσιν εἰς
αἰσχύνην τῶν ἀφρονευσαμένων πρεσβυτῶν Θεὸς τῇ ἐκκλησίᾳ τὴν ἐν εἰκόσιν ἁγίαις ἀνατύπωσιν καὶ σχετικὴν
διαμόρφωσιν ἀνανεοῦσθαι ἐχαρίσατο.

9

Παραμείνας οὖν ἐπὶ χρόνον ἱκανὸν τῷ ἀρίστῳ καθηγητῇ ὁ νουνεχὴς καὶ εὐφυέστατος μαθητής, κραταιῶς τε
διδαχθεὶς τὰ τῆς ἡσυχίας καὶ ἀσκήσεως παλαίσματα ἐν
πρωτοδευτέρῳ τινὶ τάξει, τῷ τῶν Πισσαδινῶν λεγομένῳ
κοινοβίῳ, ὡς πλέον τι δυναμένῳ τῇ τῶν διακονιῶν ἀφθονίᾳ
καὶ τῶν ἤδη προβεβηκότων ἁμίλλῃ τοὺς εἰσαγωγικοὺς
ὠφελεῖν, ὑπὸ τοῦ καθηγουμένου ἐξαποστέλλεται.

2   Νικόλαος δ᾽ ἦν ὁ ταύτης τῆς μονῆς τὸ τηνικαῦτα προϊστάμενος, ὃς οἷά τισιν ἀγγέλοις τοῖς μοναχοῖς τάξεις καὶ

structed in the monastic life, being tutored in its struggles, and promising God and his mentor to observe all its requirements; he was then tonsured by John and, with the blessing and laying on of hands, changed his garb to the monastic habit and received the name of Euthymios instead of Niketas. In my opinion, this name was intended by his mentor to indicate the transition from the despondency of the iconoclast heresy to the good cheer at that time of the Church of Christ. For it was the first year that Theodora and Michael held imperial power, when, through the agency of a weak woman and a child of immature age, and to the shame of the churchmen who had lost their senses, God granted that the depiction of holy icons and relative representation be restored in the Church.

Chapter 9

After the intelligent and most talented disciple had thus remained for a long time with his excellent mentor, being instructed forcefully in the struggles of spiritual tranquility and ascesis in a sort of first and second stage, he was sent by his mentor to the cenobitic monastery named for the Pissadinoi, since it would have a greater capacity to assist beginners on account of the abundance of service positions and the possibility of competition with those who were more advanced.

The superior of this monastery at that time was Nicholas 2 who, in assigning ranks and responsibilities to the monks as

ἐξουσίας ὑποστησάμενος, ἀναλόγως ἑκάστῳ τὴν δυνατὴν καὶ ἁρμόζουσαν διακονίαν ἐνεχείριζεν, βαθμοῖς τισι καὶ ἀναβάσεσιν ἀπὸ τῶν ἐσχάτων ἄχρι τῶν ὑψηλοτέρων τοὺς ἀσκητὰς ἀποπειρώμενος, ἐν οἷς τοῖς διὰ πάντων εὐδοκιμήσασι μείζονα τὴν τιμὴν καὶ τὸ σέβας τῆς εὐκληρίας ἀπένεμεν, ἧττον δὲ τοῖς ἀμελείᾳ ἔν τινι διαμαρτήσασι καὶ τούτων ἔτι, ὅσοι ῥᾳθυμίᾳ τοῦ παντὸς κατημέλησαν, οὓς καὶ πολλάκις τῷ κέντρῳ τοῦ ὄνου καὶ τῇ μάστιγι τοῦ ἵππου [Proverbs 26:3] ὡς βοσκηματώδεις καὶ ἀνοήτους ἐπηνώρθου καὶ μετεσκεύαζεν.

10

Κ̅αὶ θαυμάσειεν ἄν τις εἰκότως, ἐνταῦθα τοῦ λόγου γενόμενος, τὸ τοῦ ἡμετέρου πατρὸς ἐφ᾽ ἅπασι περιδέξιον διὰ πάντων δοκιμασθέντος καὶ ἐν πᾶσιν εὐδοκιμήσαντος· ἅμα γὰρ τῷ τῇ μονῇ προσδεχθῆναι παρὰ τοῦ μεγάλου ἐκείνου Νικολάου, τῷ τῶν ἀχθοφόρων ζῴων τῆς μονῆς προστατοῦντι ὑπηρετήσων παραδίδοται. Προθύμως δὲ τοῦτο καταδεξάμενος καὶ εὐψύχως τῇ διακονίᾳ προσκαρτερήσας, ἐκεῖθεν τῷ μαγείρῳ διακονεῖν ἀποστέλλεται. Ὡς δὲ κἂν τούτῳ δόκιμος ἐκρίθη καὶ ἀξιέπαινος, τῷ κελλαρίτῃ πάλιν ὡς ἤδη προγεγυμνασμένος καταπιστεύεται, κἀκεῖ-θεν αὖθις ὡς ἀριστεὺς τῷ τῶν ζευγηλατῶν ἀριθμῷ συγ-καταμίγνυται, ἔνθα, ὡς αὐτὸς ἡμῖν ὁ μακαρίτης ἀτρεκῶς

if to angels, entrusted to each an appropriate position in accordance with his capabilities, testing the ascetics with levels and degrees of progress from the lowest to the highest. He assigned greater honor and respect for doing well to those who succeeded in everything, less to those who made mistakes in certain matters through their negligence, and even less to those who disregarded everything out of indolence. These latter he often corrected as brutish and foolish men and sought to improve them with a *goad for the ass and a whip for the horse.*

Chapter 10

Anyone who has reached this point in the narrative would rightly marvel at our father's skill in all things, being tested in everything and succeeding in everything. For after he was welcomed to the monastery by that great Nicholas, he was assigned as an assistant to the monk in charge of the monastery's pack animals. After he eagerly accepted this assignment and persevered cheerfully in his work, he was then sent to work for the cook. And when he was deemed experienced and praiseworthy in this as well, he was next entrusted to the cellarer as someone who was already trained, and then he was added to the ranks of ox-team drivers as an excellent fellow, and then, as the blessed one himself used to

διηγόρευε, καὶ τὴν τῶν γραμμάτων γνῶσιν ὑπὸ τῶν συν-
εργατῶν ἐκπαιδεύεται, μέχρι τότε τῇ ἐπιφορᾷ τῶν κοσμικῶν φροντίδων καὶ τῇ τῶν διακονιῶν ἀνενδότῳ ἐπιθέσει
ἀγνώς τις τούτων καὶ ἀδαήμων ἀποδεικνύμενος.

2   Καί μοι, ἐνταῦθα τῆς διηγήσεως γενομένου καὶ πολλὰς
ἀρετῶν ἰδέας ἐν βραχεῖ παραδραμόντος τοῦ συγγράμμα-
τος, ἐπικρινάτω εὐγνώμων ἀκροατὴς παρ᾽ ἑαυτῷ ἐνθυμού-
μενος, ὁποίου ἀγῶνος καὶ βίας ὑπῆρξε φύσεως <τὸ> του-
τωνὶ τῶν ἀοιδίμων ἀρετῶν ἑτέρῳ τινὶ κατορθωθῆναι κἂν
τὸ βραχύτατον, καὶ μάλιστα οἷς χαύνωσιν ὁ λογισμὸς
ὑποστὰς τῇ παρὰ μικρὸν παρανεύσει τοῦ παντὸς ὑπέμεινε
τὸ ναυάγιον· τῷ τε γὰρ ταῖς ἡδοναῖς ἀπομάχεσθαι, καὶ
ταῦτα ἐν νέῳ τῷ σώματι καὶ τῇ προλήψει τυραννουμένῳ,
γονέων τε πόθῳ καὶ συζύγου φίλτρῳ, ναὶ μὴν καὶ συγγενῶν συνουσίᾳ καὶ φίλων ἑταιρίᾳ καὶ τἆλλα, ὧν μόγις ἂν
ἀπαθῶς ποιήσαιτό τις κἂν τὴν ἀνάμνησιν, μηδόλως δὲ
τούτοις ἀποχαυνωθῆναι ἢ περιτραπῆναι τοῦ δέοντος ὀλίγοις ὑπῆρξε πάνυ τῶν τε νῦν καὶ τῶν πώποτε (ὀλίγοι γὰρ
ἐκλεκτοί, κἂν πολλοὶ οἱ καλούμενοι [Matthew 22:14]), μεθ᾽
ὧν καὶ ὁ ἱερὸς οὗτος ἀνὴρ καὶ τῆς ἄνω Ἰερουσαλὴμ
ἐπάξιον εἰληχὼς τὸ πολίτευμα.

3   Οὔμενοῦν οὐδενὶ τῶν προειρημένων ἁλούς, καίτοι
πολλάκις ὑπ᾽ αὐτῶν πολιορκούμενος, ἀπερίτρεπτος ἦν
οὐδὲν ἧττον ἢ κυμάτων προσβολαῖς πέτρα στερρὰ καὶ
ἀτίνακτος· καὶ γὰρ τοῖς τοιοῖσδε λογισμοῖς, εἴ που αὐτῷ
κραταιῶς ἐπετίθεντο, τὸ κυριακὸν αὐτὸς ἐπῇδεν ἀναλεγόμενος λόγιον· "Ὁ φιλῶν πατέρα ἢ μητέρα ὑπὲρ ἐμὲ οὐκ
ἔστι μου ἄξιος" [Matthew 10:37]. Οὐ μόνον δ᾽ ἐκ τοῦ

tell me with certainty, he was tutored in the knowledge of letters by his fellow workers, since up to that point he was unfamiliar with and ignorant of these on account of the constant pressure of worldly concerns and the continuous assignment of duties.

Since I am at this point in my narrative and my work has briefly touched upon the many forms of his virtues, let a gracious listener judge Euthymios's success for himself, bearing in mind what a great struggle and force of human nature it takes for someone else to succeed in even the least of these celebrated virtues, especially for those in whom the mind, having submitted to a slight slackening in their determination, has experienced a total shipwreck. For to fight off the pleasures, especially in a youthful body under the sway of its natural predisposition, love for one's parents and affection for a wife, as well as association with relatives and the companionship of friends, and so on, which one may scarcely recollect without emotion, and not to slacken off at all in these virtues or be diverted from the right course, is something that has befallen few men, either now or in the past *(for many are called, but few are chosen)*. But among those few was this holy man who had been allotted a mode of life worthy of the heavenly Jerusalem.

Taken captive by none of the previously mentioned temptations, even though he was often besieged by them, he was as immovable as a strong and unshakeable rock buffeted by waves. For if he was strongly assailed by such thoughts, he would call to mind and chant the words of the Lord, "*He who loves father or mother more than me is not worthy of me.*" And he used to strengthen his resolve not only by

ἀπηγορευμένου, πολλοῦ γε καὶ ἐκ τοῦ εὐθυμοτέρου τὸ νο-
ερὸν ὑπερρώννυεν, "Πᾶς ὅστις ἀφῆκε πατέρα ἢ μητέρα,"
διαγορεύων, "ἢ ἀδελφοὺς ἢ γυναῖκα ἢ τέκνα ἕνεκεν ἐμοῦ,
ἑκατονταπλασίονα λήψεται καὶ ζωὴν αἰώνιον κληρονομήσει"
[see Matthew 19:29].

II

Ἀμέλει ταύτῃ τῇ παραινέσει πάντων τῶν ἐν βίῳ περιφρονήσας καὶ αὐτοῦ κατεφρόνει τοῦ σώματος, πρὸς τὸ
πολύολβον ἀφορῶν τῆς ὑποσχέσεως καὶ τὸ πολύδοξον
ἐπιποθῶν τοῦ ἀντιδόματος. Ἐντεῦθεν ἑαυτὸν ἐταπείνου
καὶ ὡς εὐχερῆ κατεδέχετο τὰ ἐπίπονα· ἐντεῦθεν ἐν ἀγάπῃ
ἀνυποκρίτῳ [2 Corinthians 6:6] τοῖς ἀδελφοῖς διακονῶν,
ἀγογγύστως ἐξετέλει τὸ προσταττόμενον, οὐ μόνον οὐκ
ἀνανεύων οἷς πολλάκις ὡς ἀρχάριος ἐκελεύετο, ἀλλὰ καὶ
χάριν ἔχειν διωμολόγει τοῖς τὰ βαρέα τούτῳ τῶν ἐντολῶν
ἐπιτρέπουσιν· ᾔδει γὰρ ὁ γεννάδας οὗτος, ὡς οὐδὲν ἄμισθον παρὰ Θεῷ, οὐδὲ τὸ βραχύτατον, τῶν δὲ μεγάλων
κόπων αἱ ἀντιδόσεις πολυπλασίονες.

2   Ἐντεῦθεν καὶ ὑβριζόμενος πολλάκις ἐκαρτέρει, λοιδο-
ρούμενος εὐλόγει, βλασφημούμενος παρεκάλει, τυπτόμε-
νος οὐκ ἠπείλει, ἀλλὰ καὶ ἑαυτὸν ἐμπαρεῖχε τῷ παίοντι,
παρορώμενος εὐφήμει, ἄξιον ἑαυτὸν λογιζόμενος τοῦ
πάσχειν κακῶς διὰ τὸ ἐκεῖθεν ἐν ἀγαθοῖς ἀνταπόδομα.

remembering what was forbidden, but even more by recalling the rather encouraging verse, "*Everyone who has left father or mother or brothers or wife or children for my sake will receive a hundredfold and inherit eternal life.*"

Chapter II

Disregarding all material things as a result of this exhortation, he also despised his own body, anticipating this promised wealth and yearning for its glorious reward. Therefore he humbled himself and accepted laborious tasks as though they were easy ones; therefore he kept on serving his brethren, doing what he was told to do without complaint *in genuine love.* Not only did he not refuse those who frequently gave him orders as a beginner, but he even professed his gratitude to those who laid the burden of these commands upon him. For this noble man knew that nothing goes unrewarded by God, not even the smallest act, and that the rewards for great labors are manifold.

Thus even though he was often abused he would persevere, when reviled he would give a blessing, when slandered he would respond gently, when struck he would not utter threats but would hand himself over to the one who was delivering the blow, when overlooked he would keep silent, considering it worth suffering miserably on account of the blessings that would result from doing so. Due to his

Ἐντεῦθεν αὐτῷ διὰ τῆς ἀτιμοτέρας ἀγωγῆς καὶ χριστο-
μιμήτου ταπεινώσεως τὸ παθῶν ὑψηλοτέρῳ γενέσθαι
ἀξίως προσεγένετο, ἐξορίσαι τε ἀκηδίαν καὶ γαστρὸς
μανίας κρατῆσαι, γλῶσσάν τε χαλιναγωγῆσαι [see James
1:26] καὶ ἀκοὴν ἀποκαθᾶραι, χεῖρας ἁγνίσαι, ὥστε ὁσίως ἐν
προσευχαῖς αἴρεσθαι χωρὶς ὀργῆς καὶ διαλογισμῶν [see 1
Timothy 2:8], καὶ πόδας ἑτοιμάσαι, ὥστε τρέχειν ἀνεμποδίστως εἰς τὸν οἶκον Κυρίου [Matthew 12:4; Psalm
133(134):1] καὶ εἰς τὰς αὐλὰς τοῦ Θεοῦ ἡμῶν [see Psalm
133(134):1]· ἔτι δὲ ἦθος ταπεινόν, ψαλμῳδίας συντονία,
στάσις πάννυχος, προσευχὴ ἐκτενής, δακρύων ὀχετοί, τὸν
προγενόμενον ἢ καὶ ἐπιγινόμενον ῥύπον τῇ ψυχῇ ἀποκαθᾶραι δυνάμενοι, πρὸς δὲ τούτοις μελέτη θείων λόγων,
κλίσις γονάτων, νηστεία σύντονος, ἀμετεωρισία λογισμῶν,
νοὸς κάθαρσις καὶ ἀνάβασις καὶ τὸ ἄνωθεν λάμπεσθαι καὶ
φρυκτωρεῖσθαι θεοφανείας ἀξιούμενον.

12

Ταῦτα ἡμῖν Εὐθυμίου τὰ ἐν τῇ ὑποταγῇ κατορθώματα
καὶ (ὡς φέρε εἰπεῖν) προγυμνάσματα. Ἐν τούτοις τὸν ἀθλη-
τικὸν τῆς ὑποταγῆς τελέσας ἀγῶνα καὶ πρὸς τὸ βραβεῖον
οὐδὲν παραλείψας τῆς ἄνω κλήσεως [Philippians 3:14], ἐξ
ὧν στεφανοῖ Χριστὸς τοὺς αὐτῷ δουλεύοντας τῇ τοῦ
πνεύματος ζέσει καὶ τῇ περὶ τὴν ἄσκησιν ἀπληστίᾳ, ἐφ᾽

ignominious way of life and his humility in imitation of Christ he deservedly transcended the passions, drove out despondency, and controlled the mad cravings of the belly; he *bridled his tongue* and cleansed his hearing, purified his hands so as *to raise them in prayer in holy fashion without anger and quarreling,* and prepared his feet to run without obstacle *into the house of the Lord* and *into the courts of our God.* His other attributes included a humble character, constancy in psalmody, all-night standing vigils, prolonged prayer, torrents of tears, which were able to wash away any filth which accumulated or accrued in his soul, and, in addition, study of the divine scriptures, genuflection, intense fasting, concentration of thought, purification of the mind and spiritual ascent, and being considered worthy of heavenly illumination and of becoming a beacon of theophany.

Chapter 12

These were Euthymios's accomplishments in obedience and, as it were, his preliminary training. After completing the athletic contest of obedience with these accomplishments and having neglected none of the things that lead toward *the prize of the upward call,* on account of which Christ crowns those who serve Him with fervor of spirit and an insatiable appetite for asceticism, he gave himself over to

ἑτέραν παλαίστραν τῆς τῶν μονοτρόπων ἀγωγῆς ἑαυτὸν ἐπιδίδωσι, τὸν Κάρμηλον Ἠλιοῦ καὶ Ἰωάννου τὴν ἔρημον, τῶν ὀνομαστῶν καὶ μεγάλων, ἀπομιμούμενος. Ποιεῖ δὲ τοῦτο οὐ τὴν ὑποταγὴν ἀλεείνων ἢ τοὺς πόνους ἀπαγορεύων τῆς ἐπιπλήξεως (δι' αἰδοῦς γὰρ ἤδη τῷ περιόντι τῆς ἀρετῆς καὶ αὐτῷ τῷ καθηγουμένῳ ἐσεβάζετο καὶ πᾶσιν ἦν ἐφετὸς ὁρώμενός τε καὶ ἐξακουόμενος), ἀλλὰ Νικολάου τοῦ τῆς μονῆς προηγήτορος μετὰ καὶ τῶν ἐν τέλει ἀδελφῶν ταύτης ὑποχωρήσαντος.

2   Γέγονε δὲ καὶ τοῦτο ἐκ περιτροπῆς ἐναντίας τοῦ τῶν ζιζανίων σπορέως [see Matthew 13:25–27] τῇ τοῦ Θεοῦ ἐκκλησίᾳ τότε ἀπογεννήσαντος σκάνδαλα· τῆς τῶν εἰκονομάχων γὰρ αἱρέσεως ἤδη καταλυθείσης καὶ Μεθοδίου τοῦ ἁγίου μετὰ τὴν ἐπὶ πέντε ἐνιαυτοὺς τῆς ἐκκλησίας κυβέρνησιν πρὸς Κύριον ἐκδημήσαντος, Ἰγνάτιος ὁ ἱερὸς τῷ ἀποστολικῷ τῆς Κωνσταντινουπολιτῶν ἐκκλησίας θρόνῳ ἀναβιβάζεται. Ἐπὶ δέκα δὲ ἐνιαυτοὺς ταύτης ἰθύνας τοὺς οἴακας καὶ δεινῶς ὑπὸ τῶν τότε δυναστευόντων τῇ βασιλείᾳ σκευαζόμενος καὶ εἰς τοὔμφανὲς καθ' ἑκάστην ἀνενδότως καταθλιβόμενος, ἀπαγορεύσας ἔτι τοῖς ἀνίατα νοσοῦσι καὶ ἀμεταμέλητα δυσμενεῖν μελετήσασιν ἀνονήτως ἀπομάχεσθαι, τοῦ θρόνου καὶ τῆς ἐκκλησίας ὑποχωρεῖ, τὸ μὲν ἑκών, τὸ δὲ βιαζόμενος, καὶ τῇ ἑαυτοῦ μονῇ προσκαρτερῶν βιβλίον παραιτήσεως τῇ ἐκκλησίᾳ ἐπιδίδωσι, κρεῖττον εἶναι ἡγούμενος καθ' ἡσυχίαν ἑαυτῷ καὶ Θεῷ προσλαλεῖν ἢ τῇ τῶν κρατούντων ἀνωμαλίᾳ βλάβης αἴτιος ἑαυτῷ καὶ τοῖς ὑπὸ χεῖρα ἀποκαθίστασθαι.

3   Φήμης οὖν διαδοθείσης, ὡς ἄρα ὁ ἀρχιερεὺς καὶ μὴ

another wrestling arena, that of the solitary mode of life, in imitation of the Carmel of Elijah and the desert of John the Baptist, those celebrated and great figures. And he did this not to avoid obedience or escape painful criticism (for on account of his encompassing virtue he was already revered and respected by the superior, and all the monks desired to both see and listen to him), but at the time when Nicholas, the head of the monastery, left it, along with the brethren who held official positions.

This occurred as a result of a contrary development 2 brought about by *the sower of tares* who at that time was producing scandals in the Church of God. For when the heresy of the iconoclasts had already been destroyed and the holy Methodios had departed to the Lord after guiding the Church for five years, the holy Ignatios ascended the apostolic throne of the Church of the Constantinopolitans. And after guiding its rudder for ten years and being terribly treated and constantly and openly put under pressure on a daily basis by the men who at that time held power in the empire, he gave up fighting a pointless battle against men who were incurably ill and who unrepentantly plotted enmity, and stepped down from both the patriarchal throne and Church, from the first voluntarily, from the second under compulsion. Remaining in his own monastery, he handed the Church a letter of abdication, in the belief that it was better to converse in spiritual tranquility with himself and God rather than to become the cause of harm to himself and his flock as a result of the rulers' wickedness.

Thus when the report spread that the patriarch had been 3

βουλόμενος τῆς ἐκκλησίας ἀπελήλαται, πολλῶν τε διὰ τοῦτο τῆς τοῦ νέου πατριάρχου κοινωνίας ἀποκλινάντων, καὶ ὁ ὁσιώτατος οὗτος Νικόλαος, ὡς ἀκοινώνητος μείνειεν, τῆς μονῆς ὑπεξίσταται, καὶ ταῦτα ὀρθοδόξου ὄντος καὶ πάσαις ταῖς ἀρεταῖς ἀπαστράπτοντος τοῦ νέου πατριάρχου. Φώτιος γὰρ ἦν ὁ μακάριος, ὁ φωτὸς ἀκτῖσι φερωνύμως τοῦ ὀνόματος πλήθει διδασκαλιῶν καταλάμψας τὰ πέρατα, ὁ ἐξ αὐτῶν σπαργάνων ἀφιερωθεὶς τῷ Χριστῷ, ὡς ὑπὲρ τῆς αὐτοῦ εἰκόνος δημεύσει καὶ ἐξορίᾳ, τούτοις δὴ τοῖς ἀθλητικοῖς ἐκ προοιμίων ἀγῶσι, συγκοινωνήσας τῷ γεννήτορι, οὗ καὶ ἡ ζωὴ θαυμαστὴ καὶ τὸ τέλος ἐπέραστον, ὑπὸ Θεοῦ τοῖς θαύμασι μαρτυρούμενον.

13

Εἰ δέ τις τοῖς ἐπιγενομένοις τότε σκανδάλοις ἀνθρωπίνοις οὖσι τὸν λογισμὸν παραβλάπτεται, ἐκεῖνο καθ' ἑαυτὸν ἐνθυμείσθω ἐκ τῆς τῶν πραγμάτων ἀκολουθίας ἀναλεγόμενος, ὅτι ὥσπερ τῶν μεγάλων πραγμάτων τὰς ἀφορμὰς πόρρωθεν ἔθος τῇ θείᾳ χάριτι προκαταβάλλεσθαι, οὕτως καὶ ὁ τοῦ γένους φθορεύς, ὁ ἀποστάτης δράκων, ὁ σκολιόβουλος καὶ κακότεχνος, πόρρωθεν ἀντιτεχνάζεται τοῖς ἐγκρίτοις πράγμασιν ἀντεπιπλέκειν τὸ ἐπίμωμον, ὡς ἂν δυοῖν τοῖν ἐναντίοιν ἕν γέ τι πάντως αὐτῷ διανυσθῇ τὸ σπουδαζόμενον, ἢ μὴ γενέσθαι τὸ ὑπὸ τῆς

driven from the Church against his will, many people turned away from communion with the new patriarch for this reason. And this most blessed Nicholas withdrew from the monastery of the Pissadinoi, so as to avoid communion with the Church, even though the new patriarch was orthodox and shone brightly with all the virtues. For that was the blessed Photios, the man who, in accordance with his name, illuminated the ends of the world with rays of light through an abundance of teaching; he who from infancy was dedicated to Christ, since he shared his father's loss of his property and exile, and indeed from the very beginning shared in his athletic contests for the sake of His icon, a man whose life was wondrous and his death desirable, as attested by God through his miracles.

Chapter 13

And if anyone's thoughts suffer spiritual injury due to the all too human scandals which occurred then, let him call the following to mind as he recollects the sequence of events. Just as the causes of great matters are usually laid down from afar by divine grace, thus too the corruptor of the race, the apostate dragon, the one of crooked purpose and evil devices, contrives from a distance to interweave something blameworthy into divinely approved matters, so that, by the confusion of the two opposites, he may accomplish a single goal: either the operation of grace does not take place or, if

χάριτος ἐνεργούμενον, ἢ γενόμενον (ὡς ἅπαξ τὸ ἐν τῇ γνώμῃ τοῦ Θεοῦ κριθὲν ἀνασκευασθῆναι ἀδύνατον), ὡς ἐπίμωμον τοῦτο τῆς χρειώδους ὠφελείας, ἐφ' ὅσον πέφυκεν, ἀποδέειν παρασκευάσειεν.

2 Ὁ δὴ καὶ τότε ἐν τῷ μεγάλῳ ἀρχιερεῖ καὶ Θεῷ προεγνωσμένῳ καὶ πρὸ τῆς πλάσεως ἐπεμηχανήσατό τε καὶ ἐπετήδευσεν, τῇ πρὸς τὸν πρὸ αὐτοῦ ἀρχιερέα τὸ δοκεῖν παρενέξει τῶν πολλῶν τὰς ἀκοὰς παραχράνας, καὶ ἀποκλείσας αὐτοῖς τῆς ἐκ τῶν διδασκαλιῶν ὠφελείας τὴν πρὸς τὸ σῴζεσθαι εἴσοδον. Ἀλλ' ᾐσχύνθη τῆς δυσβουλίας ὁ ἀλιτήριος, τῆς τοῦ Θεοῦ εἰρήνης τοῖς ἀρχιερεῦσι τὴν ἀγάπην πρυτανευσάσης καὶ μίαν ἐκκλησίαν, τὴν τέως δοκοῦσαν διαιρεῖσθαι, ἀποτελεσάσης καὶ τῷ λύχνῳ φαίνειν τὸ ἐπιπροσθοῦν ἀποσκευασάσης καὶ ἀϊδίως ἅμα καὶ διαπρυσίως χρυσαυγίζειν χαρισαμένης.

14

Καὶ ταῦτα μὲν ὕστερον. Τότε δ' οὖν ὅμως ἐκ τῆς δοκούσης καινοτομίας τῷ Νικολάῳ φυγεῖν δόξαντι, καὶ μέντοι καὶ ἀποδράσαντι, ὁ μέγας ἡμῶν καθηγητὴς Εὐθύμιος τῆς τοῦ καθηγητοῦ προστασίας τὴν μονὴν θεασάμενος ἔρημον, φιλήσυχος ὢν καὶ φιλέρημος, τὸν καιρὸν ἑαυτῷ εἰς εὔλογον ἀφορμὴν ἐπιλογισάμενος, τὰς τοῦ Ἄθω κορυφὰς ἐπικαταλαβέσθαι διὰ σπουδῆς τίθεται, πάλαι αὐτῷ

it does (since what God's purpose once decides cannot be reversed), he may arrange, as much as he can, for it to be so lacking in necessary benefit as to be something blameworthy.

This then is what the Devil devised and contrived for the great patriarch Photios who was foreknown to God even before the creation, defiling the ears of many by his apparent disagreement with his predecessor as patriarch, Ignatios, and closing off to them the entrance to salvation as a result of the benefit of his teachings. But the wretched one desisted in shame from his wicked plan, for the peace of God caused love to prevail between the patriarchs and again reunited the Church which had recently seemed on the point of schism, and removed the shadow from the light of the lamp and granted that it shine eternally and brilliantly like gold.

Chapter 14

These things happened later. But at that time, when Nicholas decided to flee from the seeming radical innovation, and did indeed run away, our great teacher Euthymios, seeing the monastery bereft of the protection of its teacher, reasoned, inasmuch as he was a lover of spiritual tranquility and the wilderness, that this was an opportune moment for him; so he became determined to attain the summits of Athos, about which he had long heard and for which he

προφημισθείσας καὶ ἐν ἐφέσει κειμένας τῆς ἡσυχίας τῷ ἔρωτι. Καὶ δὴ ἀτελὴς ὢν τοῦ τῶν μοναχῶν ἁγίου προσχήματος διὰ τὸ ἐξ ἀφάτου ταπεινώσεως τὴν τούτου δόσιν ἀναβάλλεσθαι, ἐδυσφόρει καὶ ἐποτνιᾶτο καὶ ἤσχαλλεν, καὶ μάλιστα Ἰωάννου τοῦ ἱεροῦ ποιμένος αὐτοῦ πρὸς Κύριον ἐκδημήσαντος καὶ Νικολάου πάλιν τῆς μονῆς ἀναχωρήσαντος.

2   Ἀποροῦντι δ᾽ αὐτῷ περὶ τούτου, θεία τις ἐπίπνοια τὸν λογισμὸν ἐπιρρώσασα πείθει Θεοδώρῳ τῷ ἀσκητῇ προσελθεῖν καὶ παρ᾽ αὐτοῦ τὴν τελείωσιν τοῦ ἁγίου σχήματος ἐπιδέξασθαι· ὁ δὲ ἦν καὶ αὐτὸς ἐν ταῖς τοῦ Ὀλύμπου ἀκρωρείαις οἷα πυρσὸς ταῖς τῶν ἀρετῶν διαυγείαις φωτίζων τοὺς προσανέχοντας. Τούτῳ τοίνυν προσελθὼν καὶ τὸν σκοπὸν ἐξαγορεύσας τῆς ἐν τῷ Ἄθῳ μεταναστεύσεως, ἐπαινεθεὶς δὲ τῆς εὐβουλίας καὶ ἀποδεχθεὶς τοῦ ἐγχειρήματος, τοῦ ἁγίου καὶ σωτηρίου καταξιοῦται ὑπ᾽ αὐτοῦ σχήματος, καὶ τελειωθεὶς τῇ τῶν ἱερῶν ἀμφίων περιβολῇ ὁ ἐν ἀρεταῖς ὑπάρχων ὁλόκληρος, τῇ ὀγδόῃ ἡμέρᾳ, εὐχῆς αὐτῷ γενομένης τῆς ἀπολύσεως, μετὰ Θεοστηρίκτου τοῦ θεομάκαρος τῆς πρὸς τὸν Ἄθω πορείας ἀπάρχεται, πέντε καὶ δέκα ἤδη τῷ Ὀλύμπῳ προασκήσας ἐνιαυτοὺς καὶ Θεῷ μόνῳ καὶ τοῖς αὐτοῦ συνασκηταῖς μέχρι τότε καὶ γινωσκόμενος καὶ συνεξακουόμενος, τῇ μητρὶ δὲ καὶ ταῖς ἀδελφαῖς καὶ τῇ πολυωδύνῳ συνεύνῳ οὐδ᾽ ὄναρ ἐπιγινωσκόμενος ἢ κἂν διὰ φήμης ἀληθοῦς ἐξακουτιζόμενος.

yearned on account of his love of spiritual tranquility. And because he did not yet wear the holy habit of monks, as he had deferred donning it on account of his ineffable humility, he was upset and cried out in grief and distress, especially since John, his holy shepherd, had departed to the Lord and moreover Nicholas had left the monastery.

While he was in a dilemma about this, some divine inspiration strengthened his resolve and persuaded him to approach the ascetic Theodore, and to receive from him the consecration of the holy habit. This man was like a beacon on the heights of Olympos, illuminating his disciples with the radiance of virtues. Euthymios thus approached this man and explained his goal of moving to Athos; after being praised for his good initiative, his endeavor was approved, and he was deemed worthy by Theodore of the holy and salvific habit. On the eighth day after Euthymios, who was entirely devoted to virtue, had been consecrated by the donning of holy robes, he received a prayer of dismissal and set off on the journey to Athos together with Theosteriktos, the one blessed by God. Euthymios had already spent fifteen years as an ascetic on Olympos and, up to that time, he was known to and heard by God alone and his fellow ascetics. His mother and sisters and longsuffering wife, however, had no knowledge of his whereabouts, not even from a dream, nor had they received any reliable news of him either.

15

Τῇ Νικομηδέων οὖν μητροπόλει ἐληλυθώς, ὡς ἐκεῖθεν τὴν πορείαν ποιούμενος καὶ ὡς περὶ ἀλλοτρίων τῶν ἰδίων πυθόμενος καὶ μαθὼν ὡς ἄρα ζῶεν ἀμφότεροι, ἡ ζωὴ δὲ αὐτοῖς θανάτου χαλεπωτέρα διὰ τὸ μὴ γινώσκειν τὰ αὐτῷ συναντήσαντα, εἴτε ζῶν ἐστιν ἢ καὶ τεθνήκει μὴ γινώσκοντες, καὶ ἔτι τούτου ἀνιαρώτερον, εἴτε μοναστὴς εἴτε λαϊκός ἐστι, καθάπαξ οὗ κεχρημάτικεν μηδόλως ἐπιστάμενοι, οὔτε λαϊκοὶ μένειν διακαρτεροῦσι καὶ αὖθις μονάσαι δι' ἐκεῖνον δεδοίκασιν.

2   Ἐπεὶ δὲ τούτων ἤκουσεν ὁ μέγας ἐκεῖνος τῆς συμπαθείας βυθός, μικρὸν τῶν βλεφάρων ἀποστάξας δάκρυον καὶ οἷον εἰκὸς τὸν φιλομήτορα καὶ φιλάδελφον καὶ φιλότεκνον, ὡς ἐν ἑτέρου τάξει περὶ ἑαυτοῦ τὸν λόγον ποιούμενος, σταυρὸν ἱερὸν τῷ προσδιαλεγομένῳ δεδωκὼς καὶ τοῦτον αὐταῖς ὡς γνωρίμοις ἀποκομίσαι δι' ἐντολῆς καθορκώσας, ὡς καὶ αὐτὸς ἐν παραθέσει δῆθεν παρ' ἐκείνου εἰληφώς, τοιαῦτα εἰπεῖν τῇ μητρὶ καὶ ταῖς ἀδελφαῖς καὶ τῇ συνεύνῳ παρεκελεύσατο· "Ὁ ἀδελφὸς ὑμῶν Νικήτας, νυνὶ δὲ χάριτι Θεοῦ Εὐθύμιος μοναχός, ταῦτα δι' ἐμοῦ ἀντιδηλοῖ τῇ ὑμῶν ἀδελφότητι· 'μηδεὶς κοπτέσθω ἢ ὀδυρέσθω περὶ ἐμοῦ ὡς κακόν τι πεπονθότος ἀβούλητον· ἐγὼ γὰρ Θεοῦ χάριτι ζῶ καὶ πολιτεύομαι. Ἐπεὶ δ' ἔγνων, ὡς ἄρα παράγει τὸ σχῆμα τοῦ κόσμου τούτου [1 Corinthians 7:31] καὶ ὁ οὐρανὸς καὶ ἡ γῆ παρελεύσεται [Matthew 24:35], ἤκουσα δὲ καὶ τοῦ ἀποστόλου λέγοντος ὅτι καὶ "Οἱ ἔχοντες

Chapter 15

When he reached the metropolis of Nikomedeia, as he was continuing his journey from there, he made inquiries about his family, as if about strangers. He learned that they were all still alive, but that life was more grievous for them than death, because they did not know what had happened to him, whether he was alive or had died without their knowledge. Even more distressing than this was the fact that, since they had no way of knowing for sure what calling he had followed, whether he was a monk or a layman, they could not bear to remain lay people, but were afraid to take monastic vows for this reason.

When Euthymios, that great sea of compassion, heard this, he allowed a small tear to drop from his eyelids and, as was appropriate for one who loved his mother and sisters and daughter, speaking of himself as if he were another person, he gave a holy cross to his interlocutor and bound him by sworn oath to take it to them as though to acquaintances, saying that he had supposedly received it from Euthymios as a token of blessing. He asked him to say the following to his mother and sisters and wife: "Your brother Niketas, now by the grace of God the monk Euthymios, declares this through me to you, his womenfolk: 'let none of you beat her breast or mourn for me as if I have accidentally suffered some evil fate; for by the grace of God I am alive and leading my life. But when I realized that *the form of this world is passing away* and that *heaven and earth will pass away,* I also heard the apostle saying, "*Let those who have wives live as if they had*

2

45

γυναῖκας ἵνα ὦσιν ὡς μὴ ἔχοντες καὶ οἱ ἀγοράζοντες ὡς μὴ κατέχοντες [1 Corinthians 7:29–30] καὶ οἱ πωλοῦντες ὡς μὴ ἐξουσιάζοντες," ἄλλως τε καὶ τῶν εὐαγγελικῶν ἠκροασάμην φωνῶν, ὅτι πᾶς ὅστις ἀφῆκε πατέρα ἢ μητέρα ἢ γυναῖκα ἢ τέκνα ἕνεκεν ἐμοῦ ἑκατονταπλασίονα λήψεται καὶ ζωὴν αἰώνιον κληρονομήσει [Matthew 19:29].

3   Τούτου χάριν καὶ αὐτὸς οὐ μισῶν ὑμᾶς (μὴ γένοιτο), ἀλλὰ ποθῶν τῆς ἀλήκτου καὶ ἀϊδίου ζωῆς ἐπιτεύξασθαι, τῷ ταῦτα ὑποσχομένῳ Θεῷ ἐμαυτὸν ἀφιέρωσα, δυνατῷ ὄντι καὶ ὑμᾶς παραμυθήσασθαι ἐν ἐμοὶ κἀμοὶ τοῦ πόθου περατῶσαι τὸ ἐπιχείρημα. Εἰ οὖν βούλεσθε καὶ αὐταὶ τὸν αὐτὸν ἐμοὶ ἀναλαβέσθαι καὶ ζηλῶσαι σκοπόν, ὁ Θεὸς μὲν ὑμῖν βουλομέναις ἐπ᾽ ἀρωγὴν ἑτοιμότατος, ὁ προλαμβάνων ἀεὶ ἐξ ἀπείρου ἀγαθότητος τὰς προθέσεις τῶν προφθάνειν αὐτὸν ἀεὶ ἐπιχειρούντων· τύπος δὲ ὑμῖν καὶ ἐγὼ τῆς καλῆς ταύτης ἀποταγῆς οὐ σμικρότατος, ὡς οἴκοθεν ὑμῖν τῆς ὁδοῦ προαρξάμενος. Εἰ δ᾽ οὖν, ἀλλ᾽ ἔγωγε ἐμαυτῷ τὸ τῆς γραφῆς ἐπειπάμενος, "Σώζων σῷζε τὴν σεαυτοῦ ψυχήν" [Genesis 19:17], τῆς ἀρίστης βιοτῆς καὶ τῆς ἐνθέου πολιτείας, ὡς ἡ δύναμις, ἀντιποιήσομαι.'"

16

Ταῦτα τῷ ἀνθρώπῳ εἰπὼν καὶ τὸν τίμιον αὐτῷ ἐπιδοὺς εἰς τὸ ἀποκομίσαι σταυρόν, αὐτὸς μὲν σὺν τῷ Θεοστηρίκτῳ τῆς ἀγαθῆς ὁδοιπορίας εἴχετο καὶ πρὸς τὸν Ἄθω

none . . . and let those who buy live as though they had no posses-sions, and let those who sell live as though they have no power to do so," and I also heard the gospel verses, that *everyone who has left his father or mother or wife or children for my sake will receive a hundredfold and inherit eternal life.*

'For this reason, not out of hatred for you (God forbid!), 3 but in my yearning to attain the unending and eternal life, I dedicated myself to God who has promised this, He who can console you on my account and achieve for me the realization of my desire. If then you also wish to undertake and strive for the same goal as me, God is most ready to assist you in your wish, He who out of His boundless goodness always anticipates the purposes of those who always endeavor to reach Him. And I may be an important example for you of this good renunciation, inasmuch as I began my journey from your household. In any case, having declared to myself the words of the scripture, "*Save thine own life by all means,*" I will continue to seek the best way of life and divinely inspired conduct as I can.'"

Chapter 16

After saying these words to the man and handing over his venerable cross to him for delivery, Euthymios set off with Theosteriktos on his good journey and, after a laborious trip

47

μετὰ πολλοὺς τοὺς ἐκ τῆς βαδίσεως κόπους κατῳκίζετο· ὁ δὲ τὸν σταυρὸν ἀποκομίσαι τῇ μητρὶ καὶ ταῖς ἀδελφαῖς καὶ τὰς ἐντολὰς δεξάμενος ἄνθρωπος τῇ Ὀψῷ κώμῃ παραγενόμενος καὶ πάντα προσαναγγείλας ὅσα αὐτῷ διεντέταλτο, θάμβους μὲν κατ' ἀρχὰς τοῦ ὁσίου τὴν μητέρα ἔπλησεν, ὀδυρμῶν τε τὴν σύνευνον καὶ βοῆς τὰς ἀδελφὰς καὶ συγχύσεως.

2 Ἐπεὶ δὲ μικρὸν τῆς κατηφείας ἀνανήψασαι, ἀλλήλαις προτροπὴ καὶ παραίνεσις πρὸς μεγαλοψυχίαν ἐγεγένηντο, "Τί," φησιν, ἔλεγον πρὸς ἑαυτάς, "τὸν ἐν χαρᾷ ἀϊδίῳ ὑπάρχοντα ὡς ἀπολωλότα καὶ νεκρὸν μετὰ δακρύων ἀποδυρόμεθα; Δέον παυσαμένας ἡμᾶς τῶν ἀτάκτων κωκυτῶν, ἐπιπροσθούντων τῷ νῷ καὶ σκότωσιν τοῖς λογισμοῖς ἀπογεννᾶν πεφυκότων, τὰ περὶ τῆς οἰκείας σωτηρίας βουλεύσασθαι, καὶ εἰ μὲν ἀγαθὴν ὁδὸν ὁ ἀδελφὸς ἡμῶν προπορεύεται, καὶ ἡμᾶς τούτῳ συνέψεσθαι, παραζηλούσας τὸ ὁμότιμον· εἰ δὲ πονηρὰν καὶ ἀποτρόπαιον, τὴν ἀπάγουσαν ταύτης ἐπιποθῆσαι καὶ ἀντιμηχανήσασθαι· καὶ μὴν ἀγαθὴ ἡ τοῦ συγγενοῦς ἐπιτήδευσις. Οὐκοῦν καὶ ἡμεῖς τῷ αὐτῷ κανόνι στοιχήσωμεν, ἵνα καὶ τοῦ στεφάνου καὶ τῆς ἴσης ἀναρρήσεως ἐπιτευξώμεθα."

3 Ταῦτα εἰποῦσαι καὶ τῇ ἀγαθῇ βουλῇ τὴν ἀρίστην πρόθεσιν προσεπιπλέξασαι, Θεῷ ἑαυτὰς διὰ τοῦ μονήρους καὶ ἀγγελικοῦ προσχήματος ἀφιερώκασιν, Ἀναστασῷ τῇ τοῦ ὁσίου θυγατρὶ καὶ μόνῃ πρὸς διαμονὴν τοῦ γένους τὴν παιδοποιΐαν καὶ τὸν γάμον ἐπιτρέψασαι, ἥτις τῷ δοθέντι συνευνασθεῖσα συζύγῳ τριῶν θυγατέρων καὶ ἑνὸς υἱοῦ μήτηρ ἐγκαίρως ἀναδέδεικται.

by foot, settled on Athos. Meanwhile the man who had received the cross and message to deliver to Euthymios's mother and sisters arrived at the village of Opso. He recounted everything as he had been instructed, and at first filled the blessed man's mother with amazement, his wife with laments, and his sisters with cries and confusion.

But when they had recovered a little from their despondency, they encouraged and exhorted each other to adopt a positive attitude, and said to themselves, "Why do we tearfully lament as lost and dead someone who is living in perpetual joy? We should cease this unseemly wailing, which overshadows our minds and naturally produces darkness in our thoughts, and we should instead make plans for our own salvation. If our brother has preceded us on the right path, we should follow him, striving for equal honor; but if his path is wicked and ill-omened, we should desire one that leads in the other direction and strive against the wicked one. But our kinsman's pursuit is indeed a good one. Therefore let us also submit to the same rule, so that we too may attain the crown and equal acclamation." 2

After saying these words and combining their excellent purpose with goodwill, they consecrated themselves to God by adopting the monastic and angelic habit, entrusting to Anastaso, the blessed man's daughter, sole responsibility for bearing children and marriage in order to perpetuate the family line; and she, being joined in marriage to the husband given to her, in due time became the mother of three daughters and one son. 3

17

Ἀλλ᾽ ἀπίωμεν ἤδη τῷ λόγῳ καὶ τὴν ἐν τῷ Ἄθῳ τοῦ ἁγίου διατριβὴν ἀνατάξασθαι, ὑψηλήν τε οὖσαν καὶ ἀνωτέραν ἀνθρωπίνης διαγωγῆς καὶ βιώσεως, ὅμως ἀληθινὴν καί, ὡς Θεὸς ἰσχὺν τοῖς ἀγαπῶσι χαρίζεται, ὑπερτέρως τῶν πολλῶν καὶ διανυσθεῖσαν καὶ χρηματίζουσαν· ἄρτι γὰρ αὐτοῦ τῷ Ἄθῳ κατοικήσαντος καὶ ὥσπερ ἐξ ἐφέσεως παλαιᾶς καὶ μεμεριμνημένης τῆς ἀσκήσεως ἀπολαύσαντος, μικρά τις ἐδόκει ἐπίνοια ἡ πρὸς κακουχίαν αὐτῷ τοῦ σώματος ἐφευρισκομένη ἐγκράτεια.

2   Καὶ δὴ τοῦ Θεοστηρίκτου πάλιν τῷ Ὀλύμπῳ ὑπαναχωρήσαντος, Ἰωσήφ τινα μοναχὸν ἑταιρισάμενος, ὅστις ἐκ πολλοῦ προϋπῆρχε τῷ Ἄθῳ, μετ᾽ αὐτοῦ πρὸ τῆς ἀσκητικῆς αὐτοῦ παλαίστρας ἀποδύεται καὶ ὡς προγύμνασμα δῆθεν τῷ καλῷ Ἰωσὴφ τοιαύτην ὁ καρτερὸς ἀδάμας τῆς ἀσκήσεως τὴν ἀρχὴν ὑπεστήσατο, "Δεῦρο," λέγων, "ἀδελφέ, ἐπειδὴ τὸ πρῶτον ἡμῶν τῆς εὐγενείας ἀξίωμα τὴν ἐντολὴν τοῦ Θεοῦ παραβάντες οἱ ἄνθρωποι ἀπωλέσαμεν καὶ κτηνώδεις ἐντεῦθεν ἀντικατέστημεν ('Ἄνθρωπος γὰρ ἐν τιμῇ ὢν οὐ συνῆκε,' φησὶ Δαβὶδ ὁ θεόπνευστος, 'παρασυνεβλήθη τοῖς κτήνεσι τοῖς ἀνοήτοις καὶ ὡμοιώθη αὐτοῖς' [Psalm 48(49):12, 20]), καὶ ἡμεῖς ὡς κτηνώδεις ἑαυτοὺς ἐπιλογισώμεθα, καὶ ἐπὶ τεσσαράκοντα ἡμέρας ὡς τὰ βοσκηματώδη τῶν ζῴων εἰς τὴν γῆν συγκύπτοντες χόρτον ὡς βόες ψωμιούμεθα [see Daniel 4:29], ἴσως τὸ λογικὸν ἡμῶν ἐντεῦθεν ἀνακαθαίροντες, τὸ κατ᾽ εἰκόνα καὶ καθ᾽ ὁμοίωσιν

Chapter 17

But let me return to my narrative and describe the holy man's sojourn on Athos, which was lofty and superior to human conduct and lifestyle, but at the same time genuine and, since God grants strength to those who love Him, accomplished and carried out in a manner surpassing that of most monks. For soon after he took up residence on Athos and engaged in the ascetic lifestyle as something he had long desired and thought about, the abstinence he devised for the mortification of his body began to seem insignificant.

So when Theosteriktos went back to Olympos again, Euthymios took as a companion a monk named Joseph, who had lived for a long time on Athos, and together with him he stripped for the wrestling arena of asceticism. The mighty man of steel proposed to the good Joseph the following initial ascetic practice as a warm-up exercise, saying, "Come, my brother, inasmuch as we are human, we have transgressed God's commandment and lost the initial standing of our original noble state and thereby have become like beasts (for the divinely inspired David said, 'For *man being in honor understands not; he is compared to the senseless cattle and is like them*'). So let us think of ourselves as beasts and, crawling on the ground for forty days like grazing animals, *we will feed on grass like cattle,* perhaps thereby purifying our mind, and

2

[see Genesis 1:26], ὡς ἐπέοικε, πάλιν τοῦ κτίσαντος ἀπο-
ληψόμεθα."

3   Τοῦ δὲ Ἰωσὴφ ἐν τούτοις προθύμως ὑποκύψαντος καὶ
τὸ τεσσαρακονθήμερον στάδιον καλῶς σὺν τῷ προελο-
μένῳ κοινωνῷ διανύσαντος, ἐβάφη μὲν αὐτοῖς τὸ σῶμα τῷ
κρύει ταλαιπωρούμενον καὶ τοσοῦτον ὥστε τοῦ πρώτου
ἀγῶνος τὰ σύμβολα μέχρι τῆς ἐσχάτης ἀναπνοῆς τοῖς
ἀσκηταῖς διασῴζεσθαι.

18

Ἐπεὶ δὲ τὰ πρῶτα καλῶς εἶχεν αὐτοῖς καὶ εἰς συναίσθησιν ἤδη τῆς ἐκ τῆς καθάρσεως αὐτοῖς ἐγγινομένης ἐλλάμψεως προσειθίζοντο, ὡς ἐν κλίμακι τῇ ἀρετῇ ἀνυψούμενοι,
ἐφ᾽ ἑτέραν βαθμίδα τὴν ἑαυτῶν ἀναβιβάζουσιν ἄσκησιν
καί· "Δεῦρο πάλιν," εἶπεν ὁ ἄριστος προαγωγεὺς τῷ συν-
οπαδῷ τῶν ἀγώνων καὶ μιμητῇ, "ὦ καλὲ καὶ ἀγαθὲ Ἰωσήφ,
τὸ ἐπὶ κρύους ταλαιπωρεῖν αἰθρίως ἀφέμενοι, ἐν σπηλαίῳ
ἑαυτοὺς πᾶσιν ἀγνώστῳ κατακλείσωμεν καὶ νόμον ἑαυτοῖς ὡς ὑπὸ Θεοῦ νομοθετούμενοι τάξωμεν, μὴ πρότερον
ἀποστῆναι τοῦ τόπου ἕως τριῶν ἐνιαυτῶν παρέλθῃ διάστη-
μα· καὶ εἰ μὲν ἔνδον τῶν τριῶν τούτων ἐνιαυτῶν τύχοι τινὰ
ἐξ ἡμῶν μετατεθῆναι πρὸς Κύριον, μακάριος τοῦ τέλους
οὗτος ὡς μελέτην θανάτου τοῦ τέλους βίου προενστησά-
μενος καὶ προφθάσας ἤδη τὴν ταφὴν διὰ τῆς ἐνταῦθα

recovering again the quality of being *in the image and the likeness* of the Creator, as we ought."

Joseph readily bowed down under this yoke and accomplished in fine fashion the forty-day course together with his previously chosen companion; but their bodies were so tormented by exposure to the cold that the ascetics preserved until their last breath the marks of their first ascetic competition. 3

Chapter 18

When their first ascetic feat went well for them and they were already accustomed to a sensation of enlightenment as a result of their purification, ascending in virtue as if on a ladder, they raised the level of their asceticism to another rung. The excellent guide said to his companion and imitator of his labors, "Come now, my fine and good Joseph, let us leave off suffering outdoors in the cold and confine ourselves in a cave that no one knows about. Let us formulate a rule for ourselves as if we are regulated by God, that we will not leave the place until three years have elapsed. And if it should occur that during this three year period one of us should depart to the Lord, he will be blessed in this end as one who has instituted meditation on death even before the end of this life and anticipated his burial through

καθείρξεως, εἰ δὲ βιοῦν Θεῷ ἐπικριθῶμεν καὶ πολιτεύεσθαι, ἀλλ' οὖν γε τὰ πάθη καὶ τὰς τῆς σαρκὸς ὀρέξεις, ὡς
δυνατόν, θανατώσομεν καὶ τὴν καλὴν ἀλλοίωσιν Κυρίῳ
ἀλλοιωθησόμεθα."

2   Τοῦ δὲ τιμιωτάτου Ἰωσὴφ μηδ' ἐν τούτῳ ἀνανεύσαντος
(ἦν γὰρ οὐ κρυπτός τις καὶ ὕφαλος, κἂν ἀπ' Ἀρμενίων τὸ
γένος κατήγετο, ἀλλ' ἀπόνηρος ἅμα καὶ ἁπλοῦς τὸν
τρόπον καὶ ἄδολος, οἷον τὸν πνευματικὸν ὁ λόγος αἰνίτ-
τεται), τῷ θεόθεν αὐτοῖς ἐρευνήσασι προδεδειγμένῳ σπηλαίῳ ἑαυτοὺς προθύμως ἐγκατοικίζουσιν αὐτόθεν καὶ τὰ
τῆς τροφῆς ἀναγκαῖα ἐγγύθεν ἐρανιζόμενοι· τὰ δὲ ἦν
βάλανοι καὶ κάστανα καὶ οἱ τῶν κουμάρων καρποί, μόλις
ἂν καὶ μετὰ βίας τὸ ἀποζῆν χαριζόμενα.

19

Τὰ μὲν οὖν τῆς διαίτης αὐτοῖς ἐν τούτοις ἦν. Τὰ δ'
ἐντεῦθεν τί μοι κατ' εἶδος ἀναγράφεσθαι, τὰς ὁλονύκτους
στάσεις, τῆς προσευχῆς τὸ ἀνένδοτον, τὸ ἐν νηστείαις
εὔτονον (ὥστε μικροῦ καὶ ἀσάρκους αὐτοὺς καλεῖν καὶ
ἀναίμονας ἢ ὅσον τοὺς χαμεύνας ἐκείνους καὶ τοὺς γυμνό-
ποδας οἱ μῦθοι θαυμάζουσι), τῆς σιωπῆς τὸ ἐπίπονον (ὃ καὶ
θαυμάσαι ἄξιον, μὴ συλλαλούντων ἀλλήλοις τῶν ἀσκητῶν
πλὴν τῶν τῆς προσευχῆς ῥημάτων καί τινων ψυχωφελῶν
διηγημάτων, ἐπειδὴ καὶ τοῦτο αὐτοῖς προεθέσπιστο), τὴν

his confinement here. But if we should be chosen by God to survive and live out our lives, let us then mortify our passions and the desires of our flesh as much as possible, and *we will undergo the good change* in the Lord."

The most honorable Joseph did not refuse this proposal 2 (for he was not devious and crafty, even though he was of Armenian descent, but was without malice and simple in manner and guileless, like the spiritual man the scriptural passage hints at). At once, then, they eagerly installed themselves in the cave revealed by God to them in their quest, and gathered the necessary foods from nearby; these were acorns and chestnuts and the fruits of the strawberry tree, which provided barely enough to survive on with difficulty.

Chapter 19

Such then was their diet. As for the rest of their regimen, their all-night standing vigils, their unceasing prayer, their strenuous fasts (so that one could call these men all but fleshless and bloodless or the likes of those barefoot people who sleep on the ground whom mythic tales admire), their burdensome silence (which is worthy of admiration, since the ascetics did not converse with each other except for words of prayer and certain tales beneficial to the soul, since they had previously agreed upon this), their unceasing

τῶν γονάτων ἀδιάλειπτον εἰς προσευχὴν σύγκαμψιν, τὴν ἐν γυμνῷ τῷ σώματι ἐπὶ τοῦ ἐδάφους κατάκλισιν, τὴν ἄνευ πυρὸς διαγωγήν, τὴν ὅλης τῆς σαρκὸς νέκρωσιν καὶ (ὡς φέρε εἰπεῖν) παρόρασιν καὶ ἐγκατάλειψιν καὶ εἰς ἔχθραν ἀποκατάστασιν; δηλώσει δὲ προϊὼν ὁ λόγος.

2 Τρίχινος ἦν αὐτοῖς ἡ ἐσθής, ἐρρικνωμένη δὲ καὶ αὐτὴ καὶ εἰς δεύτερον μὴ λήγουσα περιβόλαιον. Ἐπεὶ δὲ αὐτοῖς ὁ καιρὸς ἐπετείνετο τῆς ἀσκήσεως καὶ εἰς ἐνιαυτὸν ἤδη ἐπιτροχάζων ἐτελεύτα τὴν κύκλευσιν, παντελῶς αὐτοῖς τῶν ῥακίων διαλυθέντων, οἱ μὲν ἀθληταὶ γυμνοὶ προσεκαρτέρουν τῷ σκάμματι (οὕτω γὰρ ἐγὼ καλεῖν τὸ ἄντρον ἐκεῖνο ἐκβιάζομαι, οἶμαι δ᾽ ὅτι καὶ τῶν ἀκουσάντων ἕκαστος), φθειρῶν δ᾽ ἑσμὸς εἰς αὐτοὺς ἐπλεόναζε τῷ τοῦ σώματος ῥύπῳ, καὶ τῇ ἐκ τῶν σεσηπότων ῥακίων σαπρίᾳ ὡς ἐν ἰχώρων ὕλῃ ζωογονούμενοι σκώληκες ἐπὶ τοσοῦτον, ὥστε μυρμήκων δίκην στιβαζομένους ἀπὸ τοῦ ἑνὸς μεταχωρεῖν πρὸς τὸν ἕτερον, ἀνιᾶν δὲ τούτους, ὡς τὸ εἰκός, καὶ τῆς ἀτροφίας καὶ ἀπαραμυθήτου διαίτης πολυπλασίονα ποιεῖσθαι τὴν βάσανον.

3 Ταῦτα τίς ἀποδέειν ἀθλητικῆς διορίσοιτο; Τίς δ᾽ οὐκ ἂν ἐκπλαγεὶς ὡς ξενακούστων αἴνεσιν προσοίσοι τῷ τὴν τοσαύτην ὑπομονὴν τοῖν ἀνδροῖν χαρισαμένῳ Θεῷ; Πλὴν ὅτι ὁ μὲν φθεὶρ ἐπὶ τοσοῦτον αὐξηθείς, θείᾳ νεύσει μετὰ τὴν χρονίαν τῶν ἀνδρῶν ὑπομονὴν ἐπιτιμηθεὶς αἰφνιδίως τοῦ τόπου ἀπηλλάσσετο, ὁ δὲ σύννομος Ἰωσὴφ καὶ ὁμόσκηνος πρὸς τὸ σκληρὸν τῆς διαίτης ἀπαγορεύσας μετὰ τὴν τοῦ χρόνου περαίωσιν τοῦ σπηλαίου ὑπεξέρχεται.

kneeling in prayer, their sleeping naked on the ground, their life without fire, their mortification and (so to speak) neglect and abandonment of their entire flesh and development of enmity toward it, how can I decribe it in detail? My narrative will make all this clear as it proceeds.

Their clothing was of hair, and this was tattered and was 2 not completed by a second garment. And when the period of their ascetic endeavor dragged on and passed through the complete cycle of a year, and their garments completely disintegrated, the athletes persevered naked in their trials in the ring (for I feel compelled to refer to that cave in this way, and I think that each of my listeners would too). Moreover a swarm of lice multiplied upon them due to the filth of their bodies, and worms were generated in their decaying and rotten garments as if in pus, to such an extent that, swarming about like ants, they migrated from one man to the other, and caused them distress, as is natural, and greatly increased their torments from lack of food and a regimen that provided no solace.

Who would say that these trials were inferior to athletic 3 feats? Who would not offer astonished praise, as though for unparalleled feats, to God who granted the two men such perseverance? However the lice increased so much that, with divine consent, they were punished and suddenly disappeared from the place after the men's lengthy perseverance. But Joseph, Euthymios's partner, who shared his abode, renounced the harsh regimen after the passage of a year and left the cave.

20

Εὐθύμιος δ' ὁ ἱερὸς λειποταξίου δοῦναι δίκην διευλαβούμενος, ἑαυτοῦ μᾶλλον τὴν τοῦ ἑτέρου ἀπόδρασιν ἡγησάμενος, πλέον ἑαυτὸν τοῖς γεννικοῖς ἀγῶσιν ἐκδίδωσι, μόνος τῷ κατὰ μόνας τὰς καρδίας ἡμῶν πλάσαντι καὶ συνιέντι εἰς πάντα τὰ ἔργα ἡμῶν [see Psalm 32(33):15] τὴν πάλην ἐπιδεικνύμενος. Οὐ μὴν ἀνεπίφθονος ἐντεῦθεν τοῖς δαίμοσιν οὐδὲ μὴν ἀπείραστος τῷ ὕψει τῆς ἀναβάσεως εἰς τέλος κεχρημάτικεν, ἀλλ' ὥσπερ ἀπομανέντων αὐτῶν σφοδροτέρας ἄγαν τῆς προσβολῆς πειρατεύεται.

2 Ἄθρει δ' οὖν ἐντεῦθεν παραδόξου βίου γενναῖα καὶ τὰ παλαίσματα· ὡς γὰρ μονωθέντα τοῦτον ὁ ψυχοφθόρος δυσμενὴς ἐπικατελάβετο, πᾶσαν κατ' αὐτοῦ κακίαν (τὸ δὴ λεγόμενον) κεκινηκώς, πάσαις μηχανῶν ἰδέαις τοῦ σπηλαίου ἀποσπᾶν ἐπιτηδεύει τὸν ἅγιον, λύπην αὐτῷ τὸ δοκεῖν καὶ ἀκηδίαν ἐκ τῆς τοῦ ἀδελφοῦ ὑποσπείρων ἀναχωρήσεως, ἔπειτα δειλίαν τῆς μονίας καὶ ὕπνου βάρος πρὸς ἔκλυσιν. Ἐπεὶ δὲ τούτων κρείττω τὸν ἀσκητὴν ἐστοχάσατο, οἴησιν αὐτῷ τοῖς λογισμοῖς καὶ κενοδοξίαν ὑποσπείρειν ἀντιτεχνάζεται καὶ τὴν ἐκ τοῦ εἶναι δοκεῖν ὑπερηφανίαν ὁ κακομήχανος. Ὡς δ' ἀμφοτέρωθεν ἀπεκρούσθη, ταπεινώσει καὶ τῇ πρὸς Θεὸν ἐλπίδι τοῦ ἀσκητοῦ ἑαυτὸν περιφράττοντος, ἀπορήσας τῆς διὰ λογισμῶν ἀοράτου πάλης, οὐκέτι ἀφανῶς, ἀλλ' ὡς τῷ μεγάλῳ ποτὲ Ἀντωνίῳ φανερῶς πολεμεῖν ἄρχεται.

Chapter 20

The holy Euthymios was afraid that he might be accused of desertion, since he considered the flight of the other man as his own, and so delivered himself even more to valiant trials, in solitude revealing his struggle to *the One who alone fashioned our hearts and who understood all our works.* He did not, however, escape envy from demons as a result but, on account of the extent of his ascent toward God, he continued to be tempted until the end, and was tormented by even more vehement attacks from them, as if they were enraged.

Consider, then, how noble were the struggles of his remarkable way of life. For the soul-destroying enemy, that is, the Devil, attacked him in his isolation, and exerting every wickedness against him (as the saying goes), used every device to tear the holy one away from the cave, sowing in him the feeling of sorrow and despondency on account of his brother's departure, and then fear of solitude and deep sleep to weaken him. But when he realized that the ascetic Euthymios was stronger than these temptations, the wicked plotter schemed instead to sow in his thoughts conceit and vainglory, along with pride from the notion that he was someone important. But when he was repelled on both counts, since the ascetic protected himself with humility and hope in God, then the Devil, frustrated in his unseen battle through the man's thoughts, began to battle him no longer invisibly but openly, just as he once fought against the great Antony.

21

Καὶ δὴ ἐν μιᾷ τῶν ἡμερῶν βαρβάρων σχῆμα ἀναλαβόμενος, ἐν σταθηρᾷ μεσημβρίᾳ τῷ ἁγίῳ προσευχομένῳ ἐπιτίθεται καὶ τοῦ ἄντρου τοῦτον ἀποχωρεῖν παρακελεύεται. Τοῦ δὲ ἑτοίμως ἔχειν, εἴπερ Ἄραβες εἶεν, τεθνάναι εἰπόντος ἢ τοῦ σπηλαίου ἐξελθεῖν καὶ τῆς προθέσεώς τι διαψεύσασθαι, αὐτοὶ ὡς δῆθεν ἀνήκοον σχοινίῳ ἐξ ἑκατέρων τῶν ποδῶν δεσμήσαντες ἕλκειν ἔξω καὶ μὴ βουλόμενον ἐπετήδευον. Ὡς δὲ μέχρι τοῦ κρημνοῦ ἀβουλήτως τοῦτον κατέσυρον, θείας αὐτοὺς αἴφνης δειματωσάσης χάριτος, μέγα ἑαυτοῖς "οὐαὶ" ἀνακράξαντες τοῦ ἀριστέως ἀπαλλάσσονται.

2 Μικρὸν οὔπω καὶ σχῆμα ἀναλαβόμενος δράκοντος ὁ καὶ τῇ προμήτορι δρακοντίοις συρίσμασι τὸν ἰὸν κερασάμενος, φοβεῖν ἐδόκει καὶ μεθιστᾶν τοῦ σπηλαίου τὸν δίκαιον. Ὡς δὲ καὶ ταύτης τῆς μηχανῆς ἀπεκρούσθη, τοῦ μάκαρος εἰπόντος αὐτῷ ὅτι "Εἰ μὲν θηρίον εἶ, τὸ βλεπόμενον, τῇ δεδομένῃ σοι ἐξουσίᾳ ὑπὸ τοῦ Θεοῦ κατ᾽ ἐμοῦ χρῶ· εἰ δὲ φάσμα ὑπάρχεις δαιμόνιον, τῶν ἡμετέρων προθύρων ἀπόστηθι," ἐπὶ ἑτέραν συμβολὴν ὥσπερ ἐξ ἥττης ἑαυτὸν ἀνακαλούμενος ὁ Πολέμιος μεταμφιέννυται, καὶ σκορπίων ἐξαίφνης ἀναπλήσας τὸ σπήλαιον οὔθ᾽ ἡσυχάζειν ἀδεῶς οὔτε μὴν εἰς προσευχὴν ἀβιάστως τῷ ἁγίῳ συνεχώρει διανίστασθαι, πάντοθεν αὐτὸν περιερπόντων τῶν φασματωδῶν ἐκείνων σκορπίων καὶ πλήττειν καιρίως δοκούντων ὡς καὶ ὀδυνῶν ποιεῖν δριμεῖαν τῶν πληττομένων συναίσθησιν.

Chapter 21

Thus one day the Devil took the guise of barbarians and set upon the holy one at high noon as he was praying and called on him to leave his cave. When Euthymios responded that, if they were Arabs, he would rather die than leave the cave and be false to his vow, they tied up both his feet with a rope on account of his refusal, and endeavored to drag him outside against his will. After they had dragged him unwillingly as far as the cliff, a sudden divine grace frightened them, and crying out loudly, "Oh no!," they left the valiant champion alone.

Shortly thereafter the same one who with serpentine 2 hissings concocted a venomous poison for our foremother Eve assumed the form of a serpent, and tried to frighten the righteous Euthymios and force him to leave the cave. But he was rebuffed from this ploy as well, when the blessed one said to him, "If you are a wild beast, as it appears, use your God-given power against me; but if you are a demonic apparition, get away from the entrance to my cave." The Enemy, as if recovering from defeat, then disguised himself for another hostile encounter, and suddenly filled the cave with scorpions, and did not permit the holy man to engage in quiet contemplation nor to arise for prayer with impunity, but those phantom scorpions crawled all over him and seemed to sting him severely so as to cause a fierce sensation of pain from the stings.

3   Ἐπεὶ δὲ καὶ τούτων Θεοῦ χάριτι κατηγωνίσατο, οὔτε τοῦ σπηλαίου ἐξελθὼν καὶ ἀποχαυνωθεὶς τῆς προθέσεως, κἀκείνους σοβήσας σταυρῷ καὶ τῇ εὐχῇ ὅπλῳ χρησάμενος, αὐτὸς μὲν ἀπείραστος ἔτι τῷ ἄντρῳ διεφυλάττετο, οἱ ἐχθροὶ δὲ τούτου ὡς ἡττηθέντες ἀπῴχοντο καὶ ὁ τῆς ἀσκήσεως τόνος θερμότερος διηνύετο.

22

Οὕτως οὖν τῶν τριῶν αὐτῷ περαιωθέντων ἐνιαυτῶν καὶ τῆς εὐχῆς αἴσιον εἰληφυίας τὸ συμπέρασμα, καὶ αὐτὸς τοῦ σπηλαίου ὑπεξέρχεται ὥσπερ ἐξ ἀδύτων ἱερῶν ἢ οὐρανίων ἀψίδων, τοῖς ἀσκηταῖς προσδοκώμενος, ἤδη πλείοσι γεναμένοις ἐκ τῆς πρὸς αὐτὸν μιμήσεως καὶ διὰ φήμης ἔχουσι τὰ περὶ αὐτοῦ, τοῦ Ἰωσὴφ τοῦτον ἀνακηρύττοντος καὶ μὴ βλεπόμενον. Ἐγχρονίσας δὲ τούτοις καὶ πλέον τῆς ἀοράτου φήμης τῇ βλεπομένῃ ἀρετῇ οἰκοδομήσας τοὺς αὐτῷ προσανέχοντας, ἐκεῖθεν πρὸς τὰς τοῦ Ὀλύμπου κορυφὰς διαβιβάζεται, ἐντολῆς αὐτῷ ἀποκομισθείσης διὰ Θεοστηρίκτου τοῦ ἀσκητοῦ παρὰ Θεοδώρου τοῦ σεβασμίου, ὅστις αὐτῷ καὶ τὸ ἅγιον σχῆμα ἐδωρήσατο, ὥστε αὐτὸν ἀνελθόντα ἀντιμίσθωμα τῆς τοῦ ἀγγελικοῦ σχήματος δόσεως ἀναλαβέσθαι τοῦτον καὶ μετ' αὐτοῦ ἄγειν τῷ Ἄθῳ προσοικισθησόμενον· ὃν καὶ εὐπροθύμως ἀναλαβών, πάλιν τῷ Ἄθῳ μετ' αὐτοῦ ὁ καλὸς ὑπήκοος ἐπανέρχεται.

But when, by the grace of God, he prevailed over the ₃ scorpions, not by leaving the cave and weakening in his avowed purpose, but by driving them away, using the sign of the cross and prayer as his weapon, he was then able to remain in the cave without temptation, while his enemies departed from him in defeat and the intensity of his asceticism became even more fervent.

Chapter 22

After he had thus completed the three year period and had received an auspicious conclusion to his vow, he went out from the cave as if from a holy sanctuary or the vaults of heaven; he was awaited by the ascetics who had already become numerous from imitation of his example and had heard reports of him, since Joseph had heralded his ascetic prowess even when he was unseen in the cave. After spending time with them and edifying those who devoted themselves to him with his visible virtue even more than he had by his reputation when he was unseen, Euthymios took himself off from there to the peaks of Mount Olympos. For the ascetic Theosteriktos had brought him instructions from the venerable Theodore, who had given him his holy habit, that he should come and, in compensation for conferring the angelic habit on him, he should take Theodore and travel with him to take up residence on Athos. So eagerly taking him along, the good disciple Euthymios returned with him again to Athos.

2 Ἐπεὶ δὲ τῷ μὲν Θεοδώρῳ πονήρως εἶχε τὸ σῶμα προσνεκρωθὲν τῇ ἀσκήσει καὶ γήρᾳ καὶ νόσῳ ἀπομαχόμενον,
ἐδεῖτο δὲ μικρᾶς εἰς παρηγορίαν ἀναπαύσεως, ταύτης δ᾽
ἐχρημάτιζεν ἡ ἐν τῷ Ὄρει κατοίκησις ἔρημος διὰ τὸ συν-
οικήσεως λαῶν βιωτικῶν πόρρω καθίστασθαι, τόπον ἐπιζητήσας τῷ καθηγουμένῳ ὁ ἄριστος φοιτητὴς καὶ διά-
κονος, τήν τε ἡσυχίαν τῷ γέροντι καὶ τὴν ἐπιμέλειαν τῷ
σώματι κατὰ ταὐτὸν ἐμπαρέχειν δυνάμενον, ἐν αὐτῷ κατ-
οικίζει τοῦτον, κελλίον αὐτῷ πρὸς κατοικίαν πηξάμενος.
Μακρόσινα τῷ τόπῳ ὄνομα, ἥτις πλησίον τῶν χωρίων
ὑπάρχουσα ῥᾳδίαν ἐδίδου τῷ ἐξατονήσαντι πρεσβύτῃ τὴν
τῶν τροφῶν ἐπιμέλειαν. Ὑπηρέτει δὲ καὶ αὐτὸς τῷ καθηγητῇ, ἐξ ὧν ἐκεῖνος ἐγλίχετο τιθηνίζεσθαι, ὡς ἂν αὐτῷ
μηδὲν λειπομένῳ, ᾧ διατραφήσεται, προθυμότερον ὑπάρ-
ξει τῷ διακονοῦντι καλῶς ἐπεύχεσθαι τὰ βελτίονα.

3 Πλὴν ὅτι κἂν τούτῳ Θεόδωρος ἀπηγορευκὼς δυσφο-
ρωτάτῃ νόσῳ στραγγουρίᾳ καὶ τῇ νεφρίτιδι παντελῶς
κατατείρεσθαι, τῇ ἐκ τῶν βαλανείων παρηγορίᾳ χρησόμε-
νος, τῇ Θεσσαλονικέων φιλοχρίστῳ καὶ φιλομονάχῳ
πόλει μετοικίζεται, ἔνθα καὶ τελειοῦται καλῶς ἐν Κυρίῳ
ἀναπαυσάμενος· καὶ κηδευθεὶς αἰσίως ἐν τῷ τοῦ μάρτυρος
Σώζοντος δόμῳ ἱερῶς ἐναποτίθεται, μόγις ποτὲ τὸ βριθὺ
τῆς σαρκὸς ἀποσκευασάμενος περιβόλαιον, ὑφ᾽ οὗ καὶ ὀδυ-
νώμενος ἀποστολικῶς τοῦτο ἐκδύσασθαι [see Colossians
2:11] ὑπεστέναξεν καὶ τοῦ σὺν Χριστῷ εἶναι ἀκωλύτως ἐπι-
τετύχηκεν. Καὶ ταῦτα μὲν ὁ Θεόδωρος.

Since, however, Theodore's body was suffering as a result 2 of mortification through asceticism and his battles with old age and disease, he needed some small concessions to comfort, but an abode on the Mountain was bereft of these because it lay far from any community of lay people. So the excellent disciple and servant looked for a place for his superior which could provide both tranquility for the old man and comfort for his body in the same location; he settled him there, after building a hut for him to live in. The name of the place was Makrosina, which was near the villages and permitted easy provision of food for the enfeebled old man. And Euthymios himself ministered to his mentor, providing those things with which Theodore longed to be nourished, so that he, lacking nothing in the way of food, would be even more eager to pray for the best outcome for Euthymios who was serving him so well.

However, Theodore grew weary even in this place on account of his being thoroughly weakened by the most unbearable illness of strangury and nephritis, and, in order to 3 have access to the comfort of a bathhouse, moved to the Christ-loving and monk-loving city of the Thessalonicans. There he died deservedly taking his repose in the Lord. And following appropriate funeral services he was buried in a holy manner in the church of the martyr Sozon, having removed at last the heavy cloak of the *flesh* by which he was pained and which he wished in anguish *to strip off,* in the words of the apostle; and he achieved his goal of being with Christ without hindrance. And that is the story of Theodore.

23

Εὐθύμιος δὲ ὁ ἱερὸς πλέον ἐν τῷ Ὄρει ἐπιτείνας τὴν ἄσκησιν καὶ μηδ' ὁπωσοῦν τῇ πόλει πλησιάσαι βουλόμενος, ἐπεὶ τὴν τοῦ καθηγητοῦ ἠνωτίσθη ἐκδημίαν πρὸς Κύριον, ἀπροαιρέτῳ βίᾳ καταγχόμενος τῇ Θεσσαλονίκῃ ἐπιφοιτᾷ καὶ αὐτός, ὡς ἂν ταῖς τούτου πρεσβείαις φρουροῖτο καὶ μετὰ θάνατον, ταύτας ἀντιλαμβάνων τῆς εἰς τὸ σῶμα τιμῆς καὶ τῆς τοῦ τύμβου προσκυνήσεως, ὡς δὴ νόμος ἐστὶ καὶ μετὰ πότμον γονεῦσι τὸ σέβας νέμειν τοὺς ἐκγόνους.

2 Πρώτως οὖν τῇ πόλει εἰσελαύνειν μέλλων, ἄγνωστος ὢν τὸ δοκεῖν καὶ πρὸς ἀγνοοῦντας τὴν εἴσοδον ποιούμενος, ἠρυθρία μὲν καὶ δι' αἰδοῦς εἶχε τὴν τοῦ ὄχλου συνάντησιν ὡς ἐν ἕξει τῆς μονίας ἤδη γενόμενος, ὅμως ἐπηύχετο τῷ Θεῷ μὴ ἄμισθον αὐτῷ τὴν πορείαν ποιήσασθαι μηδὲ τῆς προθέσεως πόρρω, ἀλλ' ἐνδίκως μισθῷ περατῶσαι τὴν ἔφεσιν. Καὶ δὴ ὡς ἐκεῖνος μὲν ταῦτα προσηύχετο καὶ ἅμα διηπόρει, ὅτῳ καταλύσειεν δώματι τῇ πόλει ἐπιξενούμενος, ἀθρόον διαδοθείσης τῆς περὶ αὐτοῦ γνώσεως (ἦν γὰρ διὰ φήμης ἐναρέτου ἐν αὐτῇ προσεξακουόμενος), παμπληθεὶ πάντες τῷ νέῳ Θεσβίτῃ προϋπήντουν καὶ γνησίως αὐτὸν κατησπάζοντο, ἁγιασμὸν ἑαυτοῖς ὁ καθ' εἷς δοκοῦντες πορίζεσθαι, ὅστις τοῦ χρωτὸς ἐκείνου καὶ τῶν ἁγίων ποδῶν ἐπιλαβέσθαι δυνήσεται, ἔτι δὲ καὶ φιλήματι ἁγίῳ μετοχετεύειν ἀλλήλοις τὴν εὐλογίαν ἐνόμιζον.

Chapter 23

As for the holy Euthymios, he had intensified his asceticism on the Mountain and had no desire at all to draw near to the city, but when he heard about the departure of his mentor to the Lord, he was caught in the vise of involuntary compulsion and he too departed for Thessalonike, so that he might be protected by Theodore's intercessions even after his death. And in exchange for these he concerned himself with honoring his corpse and venerating his tomb, as it is customary for children to honor their parents even after their passing.

Thus, when he was about to enter the city, thinking that he would be unknown and making his entrance among people unfamiliar with him, Euthymios at first blushed with shame and was embarrassed to encounter crowds of people, since he had been so long in isolation. He prayed to God, however, that his journey should not go unrewarded nor fail to achieve its purpose, but that he should attain his objective with a just reward. And as he made this prayer and at the same time wondered in which house in the city he might find lodging, information about him suddenly spread (for he was exceedingly well known there on account of his virtuous reputation). Everyone went out to meet the new Thesbite and embraced him heartily, each believing that whoever could touch his skin and holy feet would achieve sanctification for himself, and they also believed that they would bring a blessing on themselves through his holy kiss.

3   Ὡς δ᾽ ὁ μὲν λαὸς πολὺς ἦν συγκεχυμένος περὶ αὐτόν,
ἐκεῖνος δὲ ὡς ἀήθης βαρέως τὴν ὄχλησιν ἔφερεν, ἑαυτῷ
μὲν τὴν ἡσυχίαν, τῷ λαῷ δὲ τὸ ἐκ πίστεως περιποιούμενος
ὠφέλιμον, τὸν Θεοδώρου τοῦ ὁσίου τάφον κατασπασάμε-
νος, καὶ ὥσπερ εὐλογίας τῆς παρ᾽ αὐτοῦ ἐπαισθόμενος,
μικρὸν τῆς πόλεως ἐξελθών, ἐν στύλῳ ἑαυτὸν ὡς ὁ μέγας
Συμεὼν ἀναβιβάζει μετάρσιον, ὡς ἂν καὶ Θεῷ πλησι-
εστέρως ὑψωθεὶς ὀπτάνοιτο καὶ τοῖς φοιτῶσιν ἐκεῖθεν τὰς
νουθεσίας προσάγοιτο.

24

Χρονίσας οὖν ἐπὶ μικρὸν ἐν τῷ κίονι καὶ πολλοὺς μὲν
πρὸς ἀρετῶν χειραγωγήσας ἰδέας, πλείστους δὲ καὶ
μονάσαι τῇ διδασκαλίᾳ πεποιηκώς, ἔστιν οὓς καὶ νόσων
χρονίων ἀπαλλάξας ψυχῆς ὁμοῦ τε καὶ σώματος, ἀπαγορεύσας κἂν τούτῳ τὴν ἐκ τοῦ ὄχλου παρέδρευσιν, τῷ ἀρχιερεῖ τὰ τοῦ πράγματος ἀνακοινωσάμενος, τοῦ κίονος κατ-
ελθών, τῷ Ἄθῳ πάλιν ἑαυτὸν χαρίζεται. Θεόδωρος δ᾽ ἦν
ὄνομα τῷ ἀρχιερεῖ, ὃς ἀσκητὴς ἦν καὶ αὐτὸς καὶ ἀσκητῶν
ὁ περιώνυμος, ὑφ᾽ οὗ καὶ διακόνου χειροτονίαν ὁ δίκαιος
προτραπεὶς κατεδέξατο, οὐ φιλοδοξίᾳ κρατούμενος (ἣν
γὰρ αὐτῷ τύφος ἅπας καὶ ἔπαρσις δραπετεύσαντες), ἀλλὰ
διὰ τὴν ἐπ᾽ ἐρημίας ἀκατάγνωστον, εἴπου δεήσειεν, τῆς
θείας κοινωνίας μετάληψιν.

But as the mass of people was thronging around him in 3
confusion, he found it hard to bear the pressure of the crowd
since he was not used to it. So, in order to procure tranquility for himself and the benefit of faith for the mass of people, Euthymios kissed the tomb of the blessed Theodore
and, as if perceiving his blessing, went a little way out of the
city and climbed up high on a column like the great Symeon,
so that he might be seen as being elevated closer to God and
might provide advice from there to those who visited him.

Chapter 24

He remained on the column for a short time, guiding
many people toward the idea of the virtues, as well as causing very many people to adopt the monastic life as a result of
his teaching, and relieving some people of chronic illness of
both soul and body. But here too he grew weary of the
crowd's devotion, and, after making the archbishop aware of
the situation, he descended from the column and gave himself over once more to Athos. The name of the archbishop
was Theodore, an ascetic, indeed renowned among ascetics,
at whose urging the righteous man received ordination as a
deacon, not because he was overcome by vainglory (for all
vanity and arrogance escaped him), but so that he could partake of a canonically sanctified holy communion in the
wilderness, if it should be necessary.

2   Ὀλίγους οὖν καὶ τούτῳ διατρίψας χρόνους διὰ τὴν
ἤδη τῶν μοναχῶν ἐν τῷ Ὄρει τῇ πρὸς αὐτὸν μιμήσει
κατοίκησιν καὶ ὡς ἐν ἄστει σὺν ἀλλήλοις διατριβὴν καὶ
παρενόχλησιν καὶ μάλιστα πρὸς αὐτόν, ᾧ πάντες ἐφοίτων
ὡς πρὸς ταξίαρχον καὶ ἀκρέμονα, νῦν δ' αὖθις καὶ ἱερέα,
πρεσβύτην καὶ λευΐτην καὶ ἱερέων τὸν κύδιστον, Ἰωάννῃ
τῷ Κολοβῷ καὶ Συμεὼν συμβούλοις ἀποχρησάμενος,
ἀνδράσιν ἁγίοις καὶ τῆς ἄνω Σιὼν ἐπάξιον καὶ τὸ πολίτευμα
κεκτημένοις καὶ τὸ φρόνημα, τῇ τῶν Νέων ἐπιλεγομένῃ
νήσῳ ὡς ἀνθρώπων ἐρήμῳ τελούσῃ σὺν αὐτοῖς διαπορθμεύεται, ἐν ᾗ τῆς ἡσυχίας ἀπολαύσας ὡς ὁμοτρόποις περιτυχὼν καὶ ἰσορροποῦσι πρὸς τὴν ἄσκησιν μικρὸν ἔδοξεν
ὡς ἐν λιμένι ἐγκαθορμίζεσθαι.

3   Ἀλλ' οὐκ ἤνεγκεν ὁ φθόνος, μᾶλλον δ' ὁ τοῦ φθόνου
γενέτης, ὁμόγνωμον οὕτως κατ' αὐτοῦ τριῶν ἀριστέων
ἄσκησιν ἀνεμποδίστως ἐξανύεσθαι· πειρᾷ δὲ τούτους καὶ
ἀντιστρατεύει κατ' αὐτῶν ὁ παγκάκιστος, καὶ Σαρακηνοὺς
τῷ τόπῳ πλησιάσαι παρορμήσας, Θεοῦ συγχωρήσαντος,
ἐκδότους τοὺς ἀριστέας ποιεῖται τοῖς Ἄραψι. Δεδοίκατε,
οἶδ' ὅτι ἐναγώνιοι τῷ λόγῳ γενάμενοι, μήπου τι τοῖς
πατράσι τῶν ἀπηγορευμένων καὶ ἀνιαρῶν συνήντησεν,
ἀλλὰ θαρσεῖτε τῷ Κυρίῳ θαρρήσαντες· τοῖς αὐτοῦ γὰρ ἡ
νίκη καὶ μετὰ μείζονος τῆς ἐκπλήξεως. Ἄρτι γὰρ τῶν
Ἀράβων τοὺς ἁγίους τὸ δοκεῖν αἰχμαλωτισάντων καὶ ταῖς
οἰκείαις ναυσὶ ὡς ἑαλωκότας ἐμβιβασάντων, θεία τις
ἐπαρωγὴ τοῖς ἀσκηταῖς ἐπιλάμψασα τοὺς ὡς εὐτελεῖς

Euthymios thus spent a few years there, but then, taking 2
along as advisors John Kolobos and Symeon, holy men who
possessed a way of life and mindset worthy of the heavenly
Sion, he moved with them to the island called Neoi, because
it was empty of people. He did this on account of the settlement of monks on the Mountain in imitation of his example
and because of the way in which they spent time with each
other, as in a city, and became a distraction to each other
and especially to him, since he was someone whom everyone visited like some commander and eminent person, for
he was also now a priest, an elder and deacon and the no-
blest of priests. He enjoyed the spiritual tranquility on this
island, since he had found like-minded men with equal inclination toward asceticism, and he thus decided to remain anchored for a while as if in a harbor.

But envy, or rather the Devil, the progenitor of envy, 3
could not bear the three champions accomplishing their
unified ascetic regimen against him unimpeded. And so the
most wicked one made trial of them and launched a campaign against them, and after inciting Saracens to approach
the place, with God's permission, he betrayed the champions to the Arabs. Now I know that, since you are intensely
engaged with this narrative, you are fearful that something
untoward or grievous happened to the fathers, but pluck up
your courage, and have confidence in the Lord. For victory
belongs to His people and is a cause for great astonishment.
For after the Arabs seemingly took the holy men prisoner
and embarked them upon their own ships as captives, some
divine succor shone upon the ascetics, and caused those

συλληφθέντας ὡς θεοφόρους καὶ ὑψηλοὺς ἀπολυθῆναι πεποίηκε, πῶς καὶ τίνα τρόπον, λέξων ἔρχομαι.

25

Τριῶν ὄντων τῶν μακαρίων τούτων καὶ ἀοιδίμων ἀνδρῶν, δύο δὲ τῶν νηῶν, αἷστισι διαμερισθῆναι τούτους ὑπὸ τῶν ζωγρησάντων ἦν ἐπάναγκες, τοὺς μὲν ἁγίους οἱ κατέχοντες ἐν μιᾷ νηὶ ἐνεβίβασαν, ἐσθήματα δὲ ἐρρικνωμένα καὶ αὐτὰ τρίχινα, ἐργαλεῖα δὲ καὶ βιβλιδάρια, ἐν οἷς ὁ πᾶς αὐτοῖς βίος, ὅσα εὑρόντες ἀπεσύλησαν, τῇ ἑτέρᾳ φέρειν παραδεδώκασιν. Καὶ σκοπεῖτε ἐνταῦθα τοῦ πράγματος τὸ παράδοξον! Ἀνέμου αὐτοῖς ἐπιτηδείου συγκυρήσαντος, τὸν ἱστὸν ἄραντες ἐπανάγεσθαι τῆς νήσου ἐπεχείρουν ἀγαλλιώμενοι. Ὡς δὲ μικρὸν ταύτης ὅσον μίλιον ἓν εὐθυδρόμησαν, ἡ μὲν μία ἀκωλύτως τὴν θαλαττίαν ἐδόκει διαπλέειν κέλευθον, ἡ ἑτέρα δὲ ταύτης ἀορασίᾳ κρατουμένη τοῦ πνεύματος αὐτὴν αἰσίως ἐπιπνέοντος τῆς πορείας ἀνεχαιτίζετο· ἡ δὲ ἦν ἡ τοὺς ἁγίους λαχοῦσα ἀποφέρεσθαι.

2   Ὡς δὲ τοῖς Ἄραψι τοῦτο πάντη ἐδόκει παράδοξον, εἷς τῶν συμπλεόντων τοῦ πράγματος στοχασάμενος τὸ ἐξαίσιον, "Τί," φησίν, "ἐννεοὶ καὶ ἔξω ἑαυτῶν ἐοικόσιν ἐξομοιούμενοι ἵστασθε; Ταῦθ' ἡμῖν ἐπισυμβέβηκεν ἀνθ' ὧν τοὺς τοῦ Θεοῦ δούλους οὐδὲν ἡμᾶς ἀδικοῦντας βλάπτειν αὐτοὶ

who were regarded as insignificant creatures when they were captured to be regarded as divinely inspired and important individuals when they were released. And I shall narrate how and in what way this came to pass.

Chapter 25

There were three of these blessed and celebrated men, but two ships, between which they had to be divided by their captors, so those who held them embarked the holy men on one ship and, after robbing them of all the tattered haircloth garments, tools, and books that they found, which constituted their entire livelihood, they handed these over to be transported in the other ship. And see here the incredible occurrence! After a fair wind arose, the Arabs joyfully raised the mast and endeavored to sail away from the island. But when they had proceeded a short distance from it, about one mile, one ship seemed to sail along its watery course unimpeded, while the other, invisibly held fast, was checked in its course, even though a favorable wind was blowing. And this was the one that happened to be carrying the holy men.

Since this seemed very strange to the Arabs, one of the 2 sailors, attempting to explain the extraordinary nature of the episode, said, "Why are you standing there dumbfounded like people who are out of their minds? This has happened to us because we intended to harm servants of

διενοήθημεν. Ἀλλ᾽ εἴπερ σῳζομένους ἡμᾶς τὰ οἴκοι ἐπι-
καταλήψεσθαι βούλεσθε, πρεσβείαν αὐτοῖς ὑπὲρ τῆς εἰς
αὐτοὺς παροινίας ἀντεισοίσωμεν καὶ θᾶττον ἡμῖν τὸ τοῦ
πλοὸς ἐπακολουθήσει ἀκώλυτον· ἕως δ᾽ αὐτοὺς ταῖς ναυ-
σὶν ἐπιφερώμεθα, †δέος μέχρις ἐνθυμούμενον† καὶ τοῦ
πρόσω ἐπισχεθησόμεθα καὶ τάχα καὶ τῷ τῆς θαλάσσης
βυθῷ ὑπορροφηθείημεν, τῷ θείῳ δυσμενεῖν ἐπιχειροῦντες
βουλήματι."

3   Ὡς δὲ ταῦτα εἰπόντος τοῦ συμφυλέτου ἐπηκροάσαντο
καὶ δίκαια λέγειν ἕκαστος τῶν ἀκουσάντων ἐπευφήμησαν,
πρηνεῖς ἑαυτοὺς τοῖς ἁγίοις ἐπικλίναντες συγγνώμην λαβεῖν τῶν εἰς αὐτοὺς τετολμημένων ἱκέτευον. Τῶν δὲ ἁγίων
τῇ ἐξ ἔθους συμπαθείᾳ συγγνωμονησάντων τοῖς Ἄραψιν,
εὐθὺς ἡ ναῦς ποντοποροῦσα ἀνεμποδίστως ἐδείκνυτο. Τῇ
νήσῳ οὖν πάλιν ὑποστρέψαντες, τοῖς ἰδίοις κελλίοις τούτους ἀποκαθιστᾶν ἐπετήδευον. Τῶν δὲ ἀσκητῶν τὰ ἀφαι-
ρεθέντα ἐξ αὐτῶν ἐργαλεῖα καὶ βιβλία καὶ τρίχινα περι-
βόλαια ἐπιζητεῖν ἐπιχειρησάντων, ὡς ἄνευ τῆς τούτων
χρείας μὴ δυναμένων ἐπιβῆναι τῷ τόπῳ, οἱ βάρβαροι (ὅπερ
ἦν καὶ πανάληθες) μὴ ἔχειν ταῦτα διεξώμνυντο, ὡς τῆς
ἑτέρας νηὸς ταῦτα ἀποκληρωσαμένης ἀποφέρεσθαι. Ἐπεὶ
δὲ οἱ ἀσκηταί, ὡς τὸ πᾶν τῆς ἑαυτῶν σωτηρίας Θεῷ προ-
αναθέμενοι, τοιαύταις φωναῖς τοῖς Ἄραψιν ἀπεχρήσαντο,
ὡς "Εἴ γε ἄρα τῷ Θεῷ βουλητὸν ἡμᾶς τὰ ἑαυτῶν ἀπολήψε-
σθαι, πάντως τὸ ἀρεστὸν αὐτῷ εἰς ἡμᾶς διαπερανθήσεται,"
οὔπω τοῦ λόγου εἰς εὐχαριστίαν καταντήσαντος (φαιδρὸν
ἀκοῦσαι), ἰδοὺ καὶ ἡ ναῦς ὀπισθόρμητος, πνεύματος αὐτὴν
ἐναντίου ἀντεπιπνεύσαντος, τῇ νήσῳ ἐγκαθορμίζεται.

God who had done us no wrong. But if you want us to get home safely, we should ask them to forgive our abusive behavior toward them, and we'll soon have smooth sailing. But as long as we're transporting them on the ships, we will be prevented from moving forward and perhaps may be swallowed in the depths of the sea, if we try to oppose the divine will."

When they heard their fellow tribesman saying these words, each of the listeners praised him for speaking rightly, and they prostrated themselves before the holy men and prayed to receive forgiveness for their rash deeds against them. And as soon as the holy men with their customary compassion pardoned the Arabs, the ship was immediately seen to proceed on its voyage without any obstacle. Thus when the Arabs returned to the island once more, they set about restoring the monks to their own cells. But when the ascetics tried to ask for the tools and books and hair cloth garments that had been taken from them, since without them they could not live in that place, the barbarians swore that they did not have them (which was completely true), since the other ship had been assigned to transport them. And when the ascetics, placing in God all hope of their salvation, used the following words to the Arabs, namely, "If God wishes us to recover our possessions, surely that which pleases Him will be accomplished for us," their prayer had not yet reached the words, "thanks <be to God>," when (this is good to hear), lo and behold, the other ship came back, as a contrary wind had blown it in the opposite direction, and it anchored at the island.

4   Θαυμασάντων δὲ τῶν Ἀράβων τὸ ἐξαίσιον τοῦ πράγματος καὶ τῶν ἀσκητῶν βεβαιωθέντων τὴν παρὰ Θεοῦ τοῖς εἰς αὐτὸν πεποιθόσι ταχίστην ἐπικούρησιν, τὰ οἰκεῖα ἀναλαβόμενοι ἀπ᾽ ἀλλήλων διεχωρίζοντο. Καὶ δὴ τῶν Ἀράβων εἷς ἀφρονευσάμενος καὶ ὥσπερ διὰ τὴν ὑποστροφὴν τῆς νηὸς χολᾶν αὐτοῖς ἐπιμαινόμενος, τὸν Κολοβὸν Ἰωάννην μαστίζειν ἐπεχείρει λαβόμενος. Τῶν δὲ λοιπῶν Ἀράβων τοῦτον ἀναχαιτισάντων καὶ μόλις τῆς ὁρμῆς ἀποπαυσάντων, ὁ μέγας αὐτοῖς ὑπολαβὼν Εὐθύμιος ἀπεκρίνατο· "Εἰ μὲν ἀνυβρίστως ἡμᾶς λαβόντες, ὦ Ἄραβες, ἀνυβρίστως πάλιν τοῖς ἰδίοις κελλίοις ἀπέδοσθε, τάχα ἂν καὶ ὑμεῖς ἐν εἰρήνῃ τοῖς ἑαυτῶν οἴκοις ἀπεκομίσθητε· ἐπεὶ δὲ Θεὸν διὰ τοῦ ἀδελφοῦ παρωργίσατε, μικρὸν οὔπω καὶ μαθήσεσθε οἷον κακὸν ἀφροσύνη καὶ πρὸς Θεὸν ἐναντίωσις." Ταῦτ᾽ εἰπὼν ὁ μέγας ἅμα τοῖς σὺν αὐτῷ τῶν δυσμενῶν ἀπηλλάττετο.

5   Ἐκείνων δὲ τῆς νήσου ἀποπλευσάντων, ἡ τοῦ πατρὸς πρόρρησις ἔργῳ αὐτοὺς ἐπικατελάβετο· διήρων γὰρ αὐτοῖς συναντησάντων Γραικῶν, ἡ τὸν ὑβριστὴν ἐπιφερομένη ναῦς ἑάλω, καὶ ἡ πεποιθότως τοὺς ἁγίους ἐξαποστείλασα παρ᾽ ἐλπίδας διεσώσατο. Ταῦτα ὁ τῶν θαυμασίων Θεὸς καὶ δοξάζων τοὺς δοξάζοντας αὐτὸν [see 1 Kings 2:30] καὶ παραδιδοὺς εἰς ἡμέραν ἀπωλείας [Jeremiah 18:17] τοὺς ἀσεβεῖς τε καὶ ἄφρονας. Ἀλλ᾽ οἱ μὲν πατέρες οὕτως παραδόξως τῆς ἁλώσεως ἀπολύονται καὶ δοξάζεται Θεὸς καὶ μοναχοὶ ἐπευφραίνονται, αἰσχύνεται δὲ μόνος ὁ τὴν βασκανίαν αὐτοῖς ἐπικινήσας Διάβολος ὡς ἀνομήσας διακενῆς.

So, while the Arabs marveled at the extraordinary nature 4
of the episode, and the ascetics were assured of the swift
succor granted by God to those who have faith in Him, the
monks took up their possessions and the two groups went
their separate ways. One of the Arabs, however, went crazy
and, as though raging against the monks due to the ship's
return, tried to grab hold of John Kolobos and flog him. The
other Arabs restrained him and with difficulty checked his
assault, but the great Euthymios said to them in response:
"If you Arabs had seized us without abuse and without abuse
had returned us again to our own cells, perhaps you would
have returned to your own homes in peace; but since you
have angered God through <your attack on> the brother,
you will soon learn how bad frenzied madness and opposi-
tion to God can be." After the great man said these words,
he and his companions parted from their enemies.

When the Arabs sailed away from the island, the father's 5
prediction indeed came true; for they encountered Greek
biremes, and the ship carrying the abusive Arab was seized,
while the ship which trustingly let the holy men go was unexpectedly saved. This was the work of the God of marvels
and the One *who glorifies those who glorify Him* and delivers
unto the *day of destruction* the impious and foolish. The fathers were thus unexpectedly delivered from captivity and
God was glorified and monks were joyful, and only the Devil
who stirred up jealousy against them was disgraced for having committed a transgression to no purpose.

26

Ἐπεὶ δ᾽ ἐντολή ἐστι καὶ παραίνεσις φεύγειν τοὺς τῶν πτωμάτων τόπους καὶ μὴ ἐκπειράζειν Κύριον τὸν Θεὸν [Deuteronomy 6:16] ἐν οἷς δυνατῶς ἔχει τοῦ ῥύεσθαι, ὡς ἂν μὴ καὶ αὖθις ἁλόντες ἐπίβουλοι ἑαυτῶν τοῖς εὐσεβέσι κριθήσονται, τὴν νῆσον καταλιπόντες τῷ Ἄθῳ μετοικίζονται. Ἐπεὶ δὲ κἀνταῦθα βαρβάρων ἔφοδος ἐπλησίαζε καὶ ἤδη τινὲς τῶν ἀδελφῶν προεαλώκεσαν, ἐδεδοίκεσαν δὲ τὸ ἴσον καὶ οἱ ἔτι τῷ τόπῳ παραμένοντες, χωρία ἄσυλα ἑαυτοῖς ὁ καθ᾽ εἷς ἐπικαταλαβόμενοι, ἕκαστος αὐτῶν ἐν τῷ ἀρεσθέντι τόπῳ τοὺς οἰκείους μαθητὰς ἀναβιβάζουσι.

2   Καὶ Ἰωάννης μὲν ὁ μακάριος τοῖς Σιδηροκαυσίοις λεγομένοις προσοικίζεται, Συμεὼν δ᾽ ὁ θαυμάσιος τῇ Ἑλλάδι διαπορθμεύεται, Εὐθύμιος δ᾽ ὁ ἱερὸς καὶ ἡμέτερος ἐν τοῖς Βραστάμου λεγομένοις τόποις τοὺς ἑαυτοῦ μετατίθησι, μεθ᾽ ὧν καὶ Ἰωσὴφ ἐκεῖνον τὸν ἴδιον συναγωνιστήν, οὗ πολλάκις ἐμνήσθημεν, ὃς καὶ τελειοῦται τῷ τόπῳ, πρεσβύτης ἤδη γενόμενος καὶ μέχρι γήρως ἐνθέως τὸν καλὸν τῆς ἀσκήσεως ἀγῶνα τετελεκὼς [2 Timothy 4:7] καὶ διαγωνισάμενος καὶ τὸ στέφος ὑπὸ δικαίῳ ἀθλοθέτῃ Θεῷ ἀποκομισάμενος, οὗ καὶ ἡμεῖς ἐν τῷ σπηλαίῳ, ἐν ᾧ κοιμηθεὶς κατάκειται, τὸ τίμιον καὶ πολύαθλον σῶμα τεθεάμεθα καὶ ταῖς οἰκείαις χερσὶ ψηλαφήσαντες τῆς ἀφθορίας ὑπερτεθαυμάκαμεν οὐ μόνον δέ, ἀλλὰ καὶ μύρον ὁ Θεὸς ἡμῶν ἐκ τῶν κροτάφων τοῦ ἁγίου εὐῶδες ἔτι παρόντων ἐκεῖσε κενωθῆναι παρεσκεύασεν, ὥστε ἀπὸ τῆς ἱερᾶς αὐτοῦ

Chapter 26

Since there is a commandment and exhortation for people *to avoid dangerous places* and *not tempt the Lord God* even in places where He is able to save them, lest, by being captured again, they be judged by the pious to have brought it on themselves, the fathers left the island and moved back to Athos. And when the barbarian raids drew near here as well, and some of the brethren had already been taken captive, those who were still there feared the same fate; so each of them sought out a safe refuge for himself, and each of them moved his disciples up to the place he had chosen.

Thus the blessed John Kolobos settled in the so-called Siderokausia, and the wondrous Symeon moved to Hellas, and our holy Euthymios transferred his disciples to the place called Brastamon. Among his disciples was his fellow contestant Joseph, whom we have often mentioned, who died in that place; he was already elderly and, *having accomplished the good fight* of asceticism in a godly fashion until old age, had finished the contest and had received the garland from God, the righteous prize-giver. I myself saw his honorable and longsuffering body in the cave in which he died and was laid to rest, and I touched it with my own hands; and not only did I marvel exceedingly at its lack of corruption, but my God also caused fragrant, perfumed oil to exude from the holy man's temples while I was present there, so that it streamed from his holy head down to his

κεφαλῆς ἄχρι τῶν ἁγνοτάτων ποδῶν ποταμηδὸν κατα-
φέρεσθαι· τούτου τοῦ μύρου ἑαυτοὺς καταχρίσαντες, ἐπὶ
τρισὶν ἡμέραις (εὐλογητὸς Κύριος!) ὡς ἄρτι πνεόμενοι
ἡμῖν αὐτοῖς καὶ τοῖς πλησιάζουσι τὴν ἀσύγκριτον ἐκείνην
εὐοσμίαν διεσωσάμεθα. Καὶ ἄπιστον ἐνταῦθα, εἰ καὶ
παράδοξον, τῶν εἰρημένων οὐδέν· ἐξ ἔθους γὰρ Θεῷ τῶν
δι᾽ αὐτὸν ἀγωνιζομένων τοὺς ἱδρῶτας εἰς μύρον μετα-
σκευάζειν τελευτήσασιν, ὡς πολλάκις καὶ πολλαχόθεν ἐβε-
βαιώθημεν, τὰ μὲν γραφῇ, τὰ δὲ αὐτοῖς πιστωθέντες τοῖς
ὄμμασιν.

27

Καὶ ταῦτα μὲν περὶ Ἰωσὴφ τοῦ τρισμάκαρος. Τὰ δὲ τῶν
ἄλλων ἀδελφῶν καλῶς ὁ καθηγητὴς προνοούμενος,
κελλία αὐτοῖς ἑκάστῳ πηξάμενος, αὐτὸς πόρρωθεν βαθυτάτῳ χειμάρρῳ τὴν ἡσυχίαν μετήρχετο, πάντας τοὺς πρὸς
αὐτὸν φοιτῶντας ἐν τοῖς τῶν ἀδελφῶν κελλίοις ὑπο-
δεχόμενος, ἐν οἷς μετὰ τῶν ἄλλων καὶ Ὀνούφριον τὸν
περιώνυμον ἀσκητὴν ὑποδεξάμενος ἐν ἰδιάζοντι κελλίῳ
μονώτατον οἰκεῖν παρεσκεύασεν, ἀγγελικῶς βιοῦντα καὶ
ὡς ἀσώματον μετὰ τοῦ σκήνους πολιτευόμενον. Εἶπες ἂν
ὁ τὸν ἱερὸν ἐκεῖνον χῶρον ἐπικαταλαβόμενος ἀγγέλους
ὁρᾶν σαρκωθέντας ἢ βροτοὺς εἰς ἀγγέλους ἀϋλωθέντας,
οὕτως ἦν αὐτοῖς οὐράνιον καὶ ἐνάρετον τὸ πολίτευμα καὶ

most pure feet. And after anointing ourselves with this oil, for three days (blessed be the Lord!) I and those near me retained that incomparable fragrance, as if redolent with it. And there is nothing unbelievable in what I have said, even if it is amazing. For it is customary for God to transform into perfumed oil the sweat of those who have labored on His behalf when they die, as I have often been assured from many sources, receiving confirmation both from written texts and from my own eyes.

Chapter 27

And that is the story of the thrice-blessed Joseph. Our leader took forethought for the well-being of the other brethren, erecting cells for each of them, but himself practiced spiritual tranquility some distance away in a deep ravine, while receiving all his visitors in the cells of the brethren. Among others he received the celebrated ascetic Onouphrios and made arrangements for him to dwell all alone in a private cell, living like an angel and conducting his life within the body as if he were incorporeal. You might say that a visitor to that holy place would have seen angels endowed with flesh or mortals dematerialized into angels, so celestial and virtuous was their conduct and to such an

οὕτως τὴν τῶν ἀσάρκων διαγωγὴν οἱ σάρκινοι ἐπετήδευον. Οἱ μὲν οὖν ἐν τούτοις ἦσαν.

2   Εὐθύμιος δ᾽ ὁ πανάγιος ποτὲ μὲν τοῖς ἀδελφοῖς συν-
ανεστρέφετο, χειραγωγῶν αὐτοὺς καὶ ὥσπερ ἐπισκεπτόμενος καὶ τῶν οἰκείων χαρισμάτων ἐμφορῶν, ποτὲ δ᾽ ἐν
βαθυτάτῳ χειμάρρῳ ἰδίαζεν, πλειστάκις δὲ φιλησυχίας
ἐκνικώμενος ἔρωτι καὶ τῷ Ἄθῳ μολὼν κατὰ μόνας ἐπ᾽
ἐλπίδι κατῳκίζετο, Θεὸν ἀντιβολῶν καὶ μόνος μόνῳ προσ-
ομιλεῖν ἐφιέμενος.

3   Ἔνθα διὰ τῆς πράξεως τὸ ὀπτικὸν ἀποκαθάραντι καὶ
τῷ ὕψει τῆς θεωρίας τὸ γεῶδες βάρος ἀποσκευάσαντι καὶ
Θεὸν ὁρᾶν ἠξιωμένῳ, ὡς τῇ καρδίᾳ καθαρεύοντι, θεία τις
ἀποκάλυψις θεοπρεπῶς ἐναυγάζεται, "Ἄπελθε," λέγουσα,
"Εὐθύμιε, ἐν τῇ Θεσσαλονικέων μητροπόλει καὶ ἐν τοῖς
ἀνατολικωτέροις τοῦ ἄστεως ὄρεσι κορυφὴν ἐπιζητήσας
πηγὴν ὕδατος ἔχουσαν (Περιστεραῖς ὄνομα τῷ τόπῳ), ἐκεῖ
εὑρήσεις τοῦ πρωτοκλήτου τῶν ἀποστόλων Ἀνδρέου τὸ
τέμενος (πάλαι μὲν φιλοκάλως οἰκοδομηθέν, νυνὶ δὲ ἐρει-
πωθὲν καὶ εἰς μάνδραν προβάτων ὑπηρετοῦν τοῖς κατ-
έχουσι), καὶ τοῦτο ἀνακαθάρας ψυχῶν ἀπέργασαι φρον-
τιστήριον· ἐγὼ δέ σοι προπορεύσομαι καὶ τῆς ὁδοῦ
καθηγητὴς καὶ ἀντιλήπτωρ τοῦ πράγματος· οὐ καλὸν γὰρ
ἔτι μόνον ἐν ταῖς ἐρήμοις αὐλίζεσθαι καὶ δαίμοσιν ἀπομάχεσθαι, οἳ σοῦ τῆς ἀρετῆς ἡττηθέντες πρὸ πολλοῦ ἐδραπέτευ-
σαν."

extent did men of flesh practice the regimen of those without flesh.

So they lived like this. As for the all-holy Euthymios, he 2 sometimes associated with the brethren, guiding them and visiting them and filling them with his own graces, and on other occasions he spent time on his own in that very deep ravine; but most of the time, overcome by his passion for spiritual tranquility, he would go to Athos and dwell there by himself in hope, supplicating God and desiring to converse with Him on an individual basis.

After he had purified his vision there through his actions 3 and stripped off the earthly burden through his lofty contemplation and had been deemed worthy to see God, inasmuch as he was pure in heart, a heavenly revelation shone divinely upon him, saying, "Euthymios, go away to the metropolis of the Thessalonicans, and in the mountains to the east of the city look for a peak that has a spring of water (the name of the place is Peristerai). There you will find the sanctuary of Andrew, who was called first among the apostles (it was well built long ago, but is ruined now and serves its owners as a sheepfold); clean it up and make it into a monastery for souls. And I will go before you and be your guide on the way and your assistant in this matter. For it is not good for you to continue to dwell alone in the wilderness and to try to contend with demons, who fled long ago after being defeated by your virtue."

28

Ἐπεὶ δὲ τούτων ἤκουσεν ὁ θεοπειθὴς ἐκεῖνος καὶ ἐπέραστος, τὰ τοῦ Ἄθωνος λιπὼν ἀκρωτήρια τοῖς τῶν ἀδελφῶν κελλίοις πάλιν τὸ τάχος ἐφίσταται καὶ δύο μετ' αὐτοῦ συνοδοιπορεῖν ἐξ αὐτῶν διακελευσάμενος (ὧν ὁ μὲν εἷς Ἰγνάτιος, Ἐφραὶμ δὲ ὁ ἕτερος προσηγορεύοντο), τὴν Θεσσαλονικέων καταλαμβάνει μεγαλόπολιν. Ὑπεδέχετο δ' εὐθὺς ὑπὸ τῶν ταύτης οἰκητόρων ὥσπερ ἐξ οὐρανίων ἀδύτων ἐπιδημήσας ἄγγελος. Πυθόμενος δ' ἐμμελῶς καὶ μετὰ προσοχῆς τοὺς γινώσκοντας, ποῖος ὁ Περιστεραῖς λεγόμενος τόπος καὶ ὑπὸ τίνων τὴν δεσποτείαν ἀποκεκλήρωται, καὶ μαθὼν ὁποῖός τε εἴη καὶ τίνων δεσποτῶν ἀναγράφεται, προπομποῖς τε καὶ ὁδηγοῖς τοῖς εἰδόσι τὸν τόπον ἀποχρησάμενος τῷ ὄρει ἀναβιβάζεται, καὶ τῇ πηγῇ πλησιάσας εὐθὺς ἐπέγνω τὰ τῆς ἀποκαλύψεως σύμβολα.

2 Καὶ ὡς τὴν μάνδραν οὖσαν ἐν τῷ ναῷ ἐπικατελάβετο, "Ὤμοι," ἔφη στενάξας, "ὅτι καὶ παρὰ Χριστιανοῖς ἐξουθενεῖται τὰ τίμια." Τῶν δὲ σὺν αὐτῷ ἀνεληλυθότων μὴ συνιέντων τὸ λεγόμενον καὶ διὰ τοῦτο πυθομένων τὸν ἅγιον, "Ναός," ἔφη, "ὁ τόπος οὗτος ἱερὸς Θεῷ ἐχρημάτιζεν, ἐπ' ὀνόματι Ἀνδρέου τοῦ πρωτοκλήτου καὶ θεοκήρυκος ἀνεγερθεὶς τοῖς θεόφροσι, καὶ νῦν ἰδού, ὡς ὁρᾶτε, ἐρειπωθεὶς κατημέληται, τόπος ἀτιμίας τὸ θεῖον τελοῦν οἰκητήριον."

3 Ταῦτ' εἰπὼν καὶ διακηρυκευσάμενος, ὡς τοὺς ἀκροατὰς θαμβουμένους καὶ διαπιστοῦντας τῷ ῥήματι ἐπικατελάβετο, ὀρυκτῆρας λαβόντας ἀποπειρᾶν τοῦ ἔργου

Chapter 28

When that beloved man who was obedient to God heard these words, he left the heights of Athos and quickly went back to the brothers' cells; telling two of them to accompany him on his journey (one of them was named Ignatios, the other Ephraim), he arrived at the great city of the Thessalonicans. And he was immediately received by its inhabitants like an angel coming from a celestial sanctuary. He made diligent and careful inquiries of knowledgeable people about which place was called Peristerai and to whom it belonged, and, after learning which place it was and to which owners it was registered, using people who were familiar with the place as escorts and guides, he ascended the mountain; and when he drew near the spring, he recognized immediately the signs of his revelation.

When Euthymios came upon the sheepfold that was in 2 the church, he said with a groan, "How sad it is that places of honor are reduced to nothing even by Christians!" When those who had gone up with him did not understand his words and thus questioned the holy one, he replied, "This holy place used to be a church of God, erected by godly-minded people in the name of Andrew the first-called herald of God, but now look, as you see, it is in ruins and neglected, and a house of God has become a place of dishonor."

After he had said this and made this declaration, since he 3 realized that his listeners were astonished and did not believe his words, he told them to take spades and start work.

παρεκελεύετο. Τῶν δὲ μετ᾽ ἐπιμελείας ὑπειξάντων τῷ ἐπιτάγματι, μᾶλλον δὲ μετ᾽ εὐνοίας ἀπομιμησαμένων τὸν γέροντα (αὐτὸς γὰρ πρῶτος τοῦ ἔργου καὶ τῆς καθάρσεως ἤρξατο), μικρὸν ἀμφοτέρων διορυξάντων, εὐθὺς ἡ τοῦ ἁγίου θυσιαστηρίου κόγχη καὶ ἡ τοῦ ναοῦ θέσις αὐτοῖς ἐπεφανέρωτο.

29

Θαυμάσαντες οὖν ἐν τούτῳ τὴν τοῦ ἁγίου εὔστοχον πρόρρησιν καὶ πεισθέντες οἷς ἐπικατελάβοντο, ὡς ἄρα θεῖον εἴη βούλημα ἁγίων ἀνδρῶν κατοικητήριον καὶ θεῖον χρηματίσαι τὸν τόπον ἀνάκτορον, τὰ τῆς οἰκοδομῆς ἄμφω ὁ καθ᾽ εἷς ἀναλόγως τῆς προαιρέσεως ἐπιμεριμνήσαντες, οἰκείοις ἀναλώμασι τῇ τοῦ ἁγίου πρεσβύτου σπουδῇ τὸν ἱερὸν τῷ ἀποστόλῳ σηκὸν ἀνεδείμαντο, ἐχόμενα τούτου τῷ τε ἁγίῳ Προδρόμῳ καὶ Εὐθυμίῳ τῷ πάνυ τεμένη οἰκοδομήσαντες.

2   Διήνυσται δ᾽ οὖν αὐτοῖς οὐκ ἄνευ πόνων τὸ ἐπιχείρημα, δαιμόνων τῷ ἔργῳ ἐπιφθονησάντων διὰ τὸ ψυχῶν ὁρᾶν ἀνεγειρόμενον φροντιστήριον ἐπὶ τοσοῦτον, ὥστε μὴ κρυπτῶς μόνον ἀνέχεσθαι ἐπιβουλεύειν, ἀλλὰ καὶ φανερῶς ἀναβοᾶν καὶ λίθοις πειρᾶσθαι ἀποσοβεῖν τοὺς ὑπηρετεῖν λαχόντας τῇ ἀνεγέρσει τοῦ θείου τεμένους. Ποτὲ οὖν περὶ μέσην ἡμέραν τῆς οἰκοδομῆς τὰ ξύλα

They diligently complied with his command, or rather they followed the elder's example with goodwill (for he was the first to begin the work and the clearing away), and, after they had all dug for a little while, the apse of the holy sanctuary and the site of the church were directly revealed to them.

Chapter 29

The men marveled at the holy man's accurate prediction with regard to this building and, persuaded by what they had encountered that it was divine will for the place to be the abode of holy men and a divine palace, each one volunteered in his own way in the construction. Thus, through the zeal of the holy elder, they built a holy church for the apostle with their own funds, and nearby they constructed precincts for the holy Forerunner, John the Baptist, and for Euthymios the Great.

But they did not accomplish the undertaking without difficulty, since the demons were so jealous of their work, because they saw under construction a monastery for souls, that they could not bear to plot only in secret, but also called out openly and tried to scare away with stones those assigned to work on the construction of the divine sanctuary. Once, around midday, by twisting about the building's

περιστρέψαντες ἀπὸ τοῦ ὕψους τὸν τεχνίτην κατεαγῆναι παρεσκεύασαν. Τοῦ δὲ καὶ μετὰ τὴν πτῶσιν ἀβλαβοῦς διαμείναντος, τῷ γενομένῳ σημείῳ αὐτός τε καὶ οἱ ὑπηρετοῦντες πλέον ἀνερρώσθησαν, τὴν ἄπρακτον μηχανὴν τῶν δαιμόνων εἰς σωτηρίας ἀφορμὴν ἑαυτοῖς περιποιησάμενοι.

3   Νὺξ ἦν καὶ νυκτὸς τὸ μεσαίτατον (καὶ σκόπει μοι ἐνταῦθα τὴν τῶν δαιμόνων ἀναίδειαν!). Τῆς οἰκοδομῆς ἤδη συμπληροῦσθαι ἐγγιζούσης καὶ τῶν ὑπηρετῶν εἰς ὕπνον τραπέντων ἐκ τῆς ἄγαν κοπώσεως (ἄλλως τε καὶ τῆς ὥρας αὐτοῖς εἰς τοῦτο μόνον λυσιτελούσης), ἐπισείσαντες ἐκεῖνοι τὸ λαιὸν κλίτος τοῦ οἰκοδομήματος ὅλον αὐτὸ ἕως ἐδάφους εἰς τὴν γῆν κατέαξαν, βουλόμενοι κἀντεῦθεν τοὺς τὴν οἰκοδομὴν ἐπισπεύδοντας ἐνδοῦναι ταύτης, τῇ τοῦ ἔργου κατεάξει τὸν τόνον ἀποχαυνώσαντας. Ὡς δὲ τῇ τοῦ λαοῦ σπουδῇ καὶ ταῖς παραινέσεσι τοῦ ἁγίου πρεσβύτου τὸ πτωθὲν πάλιν αὐτοῖς σπουδαίως καὶ φιλοκάλως ἀνεγήγερτο, ἀποκαμόντες οἱ δαίμονες εὐσεβῶν βουλῇ καὶ προαιρέσει ἀπομάχεσθαι, ἐπὶ τὸν τῆς οἰκοδομῆς ἔξαρχον καὶ τοῦ ἔργου προασπιστήν, τὸν μέγαν ἡμῶν καθηγητήν, τὴν ἑαυτῶν ῥοπὴν μεταφέρουσι καὶ φανερῶς αὐτῷ δυσμενεῖν ἐπιχειροῦσιν οἱ τάλανες, τῆς προτέρας ἥττης ὥσπερ ἐπιλαθόμενοι.

4   Καὶ πρῶτον μὲν ἀπειλαῖς αὐτὸν ἀποσοβεῖν ἐπιτηδεύουσι καὶ τοῦ τόπου ἀπαλλάσσειν καὶ μὴ βουλόμενον διϊσχυρίζοντο. Ὡς δὲ γέλωτος ἀξίας τὰς ἀπειλὰς αὐτῶν ὁ ἱερὸς πρεσβύτης ἀπέφηνεν, ἐπ᾽ αὐτὸν καὶ δὴ νύκτωρ ἐφίστανται καὶ ὁδοστατεῖν ἐπεχείρουν τὸν ἅγιον. Ὁ δὲ τῇ

wooden scaffolding they contrived to crush the master builder in a fall from on high. But when he remained unharmed even after his fall, he and his workmen were encouraged even more by the miracle which occurred subsequently, as they transformed the ineffective trick of the demons into a means for their own salvation.

It was nighttime, indeed the middle of the night (and see here the shamelessness of the demons!). The construction was already nearing completion and the workmen had fallen asleep as a result of their hard work (especially as the time of day was only of use to them for this purpose), when the demons shook the left side of the structure right down to its foundation and smashed it to the ground. Their intention was that those who were zealously undertaking the construction should give it up, slackening their effort on account of the building's collapse. But when, as a result of the eagerness of the people and the exhortations of the holy elder, the collapsed portion of the structure was quickly and soundly rebuilt by them, the demons wearied of battling the will and purpose of the faithful, and instead turned their attention to the instigator and defender of the work, my great mentor, and the wretched creatures began to be manifestly hostile to him, as if forgetting their former defeat. 3

First they tried to scare him with threats and boasted that they would drive him away from the place even against his will. But when the holy elder showed that their threats were deserving of ridicule, they attacked him at night as well and tried to waylay the holy one. But he scared them off 4

σημειώσει τοῦ σταυροῦ τούτους φοβῶν καὶ ἀποτρεπόμενος καίειν ἐπεχείρει τούτους ταῖς ἁπτούσαις δᾳσίν, ἃς ἐν χειρὶ κατέχων ἐφεύρητο.

5 Ἐπεὶ δὲ καὶ πάλιν αὐτῷ παμπληθῶς τὸν κῆπον ἀρδεύοντι κραταιοτέρως ἐπέθεντο, τότε πλέον ἀναθαρρήσας τῷ πνεύματι, "Τί," φησι, πρὸς αὐτοὺς ἔλεγεν, "ἀδρανεῖς ὄντες καὶ ἄτονοι τοῦ Χριστοῦ ὑμᾶς ἐκνευρώσαντος τῶν αὐτοῦ λατρῶν ἀποπειρᾶσθε, ὦ δείλαιοι, ἐπιχειροῦντες ἀνατρέπειν ἔργον, ὃ Θεὸς περαιώσειν ἐπηγγείλατο; Εἰ οὖν δέδοται ὑμῖν ἐξουσία ὑπὸ τοῦ ὑμᾶς ἐκδειματώσαντος, ἰδοὺ αὐτὸς ἐγὼ μέσος ὑμῶν, ὡς ὁρᾶτε, μονώτατος· τῇ δεδομένῃ ὑμῖν ἐξουσίᾳ κατ' ἐμοῦ ἀποχρήσασθε. Εἰ δὲ οὐδεμία ἰσχὺς ὑμῖν παρεσχέθη πρὸς ἄμυναν, παύσασθε τοῦ λοιποῦ ἐκπειράζειν τοὺς ὑμῶν μὴ ἀγνοοῦντας τὰ νοήματα· ἐγὼ γὰρ μέχρι θανάτου τῶν ἐνταῦθα οὐκ ἀφίσταμαι."

6 Ταῦτα τοῦ ἁγίου πρεσβύτου τοῖς δαίμοσιν ἐπιτιμήσαντος, μεγάλα ἐκεῖνοι ἀναβοήσαντες, ὥστε καὶ τοῖς πόρρω τὸν ἐκ τῆς φωνῆς ἦχον ἐξακουσθῆναι, τοῦ τόπου καὶ τῶν ἐν αὐτῷ οἰκητόρων ὡς τὸ νικᾶν ἤδη ἀπαγορεύσαντες Θεοῦ χάριτι ἀποδιδράσκουσιν, καὶ οὕτως ἀκωλύτως ὅ τε ναὸς ἀποπληροῦται καὶ ἡ μονὴ ταῖς τοῦ ἁγίου πρεσβείαις ἀνίσταται. Ἔτος ἦν τοῦτο ἀπὸ μὲν κτίσεως κόσμου ‚ςτοθ', τῆς θείας σαρκώσεως ‚ωοθ', τῆς δὲ αὐτοκρατορίας Βασιλείου καὶ Κωνσταντίνου τῶν αὐγούστων ἔτος τέταρτον, ἰνδικτιῶνος ε'.

with the sign of the cross, and as he turned them away he tried to burn them with lit torches which he was holding in his hand.

They attacked him again in multitudes even more vigor- 5 ously while he was watering his garden, but this time he said to them, gaining greater courage in his spirit, "You are weak and feeble because Christ has unnerved you, so why do you attack His worshippers, you cowards, by attempting to demolish a building whose completion God has commanded? If you have been given power by the One who terrorized you, that is, Christ, look, here I am in your midst, as you see, completely alone; use the power given to you against me. But if you have been provided with no strength to defend yourselves, stop making trial of those who are not unaware of your intentions. For I will not leave here until I die."

After the holy elder issued this rebuke to the demons, 6 they cried out so loudly that the sound of their voices could be heard even by those far away, and through the grace of God they fled from the site and its inhabitants as if then despairing of winning the victory. Thus the church was completed without any further impediment and, through the intercessions of the holy one, the monastery was established. And this was the 6379th year from the creation of the world, the 879th from the divine Incarnation, the fourth year of the reign of Basil and Constantine the *augoustoi,* fifth indiction.

30

Ἄξιον δ' ἐνταῦθα τὴν ἐπισύστασιν τῆς μονῆς διηγησαμένους ἡμᾶς καὶ τὴν διὰ προσευχῆς τοῦ ἁγίου τῶν δαιμόνων ἀπέλασιν, μηδὲ τὸν σωματικὸν κόπον παραδραμεῖν ἀνιστόρητον, ὡς ἂν ἡμῖν ἀμφότερα ἀπομίμημα τοῖς τὰ ἐκείνου θαυμάζουσιν τὰ αὐτοῦ τῶν ἔργων κατορθώματα πέλωσι. Καὶ γὰρ τῷ ἁγίῳ τούτῳ πατρὶ αἱ μὲν νύκτες ἄϋπνοι ἐν προσευχαῖς διεπεραίνοντο, <...>, ὥστε τριῶν ἐργατῶν ἢ καὶ τεσσάρων τὴν λατρείαν ἀποπληροῦν μονώτατον. Ἐκίνει δὲ λίθους καὶ μόνος ἐπετίθει τῷ οἰκοδομήματι ἤδη ὑψωθέντι, οὓς μόγις ἂν δύο καὶ τρεῖς τῶν γενναιοτάτων ἀνδρῶν τοῦ ἐδάφους ἀποκουφίσειαν. Ὕδωρ δὲ κομίζειν τοῖς ἀδελφοῖς καὶ τὴν διακονίαν τοῦ μαγειρείου ἐπιτελεῖν οὐκ ἀπηξίου ὁ τῷ τρόπῳ πανευγενέστατος. Ἀλλ' εἴπου καὶ προελήφθη ὑπό τινος διὰ τὸ ἐν ἄλλοις εἶναι ἐνάσχολος, ζημίαν ἡγεῖτο τὴν ὑστέρησιν καὶ ἐν ἑτέροις τοῦτο ἀναπληροῦν ἐπετήδευεν, ἔσχατον ἑαυτὸν πάντων τῇ ταπεινώσει ἡγούμενος καὶ αὐτῷ μᾶλλον ἁρμόδιον τὸ διακονεῖν ἢ τοῖς ἄλλοις ἐπιλογιζόμενος.

2 Ταῦτα μὲν ὁ σοφὸς ἡμῶν Βεσελεήλ, ὁ τὴν σκηνὴν Κυρίῳ πήξας καὶ τῇ ἀρχιτεκτονίᾳ τῆς πίστεως λαὸν αὐτῷ περιούσιον ζηλωτὴν καλῶν ἔργων [see Titus 2:14] ἐν αὐτῇ ὑποστησάμενος, ὁ νέος Μωσῆς ὁ ἐξ Αἰγύπτου, τῆς κοσμικῆς συγχύσεως, ὡς ἐν ἐπαγγελίας γῇ μεταβιβάσας τοὺς ὅσοι τὴν φαραώνιον καὶ δαιμονιώδη τοῦ μαμωνᾶ διαγωγὴν ἀπετάξαντο, καὶ κληροδοτήσας αὐτοῖς τὴν οὐρα-

Chapter 30

It is worthwhile at this point, as I am describing the establishment of the monastery and the expulsion of the demons through the holy man's prayer, not to leave untold his physical labor, so that all this may be a model for imitation by us who marvel at the accomplishments of his deeds. For this holy father spent his nights sleepless in prayer, <and his days in work>, so that by himself he carried out the work of three or even four laborers. He used to move stones and place them singlehandedly on the building when it was already raised to a height, stones which two or even three of the strongest men could scarcely lift off the ground. And he who was most noble in character did not consider himself unworthy of carrying water to the brethren and serving in the kitchen. But if ever some other brother should perform a task in his stead, because he was engaged in other matters, Euthymios considered his own shortcoming a fault and strove to make up for it in other ways, believing, in his humility, that he was least of all and reckoning that it was more appropriate for him to render service than the others.

Our skilled Beseleel did these things, *pitching a tent* for the Lord and through the architecture of faith establishing in it a *special people who are zealous for good deeds.* He was also the new Moses who transferred from Egypt, that is, from the confusion of this world, as if to the Promised Land, those who had renounced the pharaonic and demonic life of mammon, and bequeathed to them the celestial possession

νίαν κατάσχεσιν, ὡς ἐντεῦθεν Αἴγυπτον μέν, τὴν σκυθρωπὴν ἁμαρτίαν, πενθεῖν τῶν ἰδίων πρωτοτόκων τὸν ὄλεθρον, ἡμᾶς δ᾿ ἑορτάζειν Κυρίῳ ᾠδὴν τὴν ἐξόδιον, ὑπὲρ οὗ ἵππον καὶ ἀναβάτην ἔρριψεν εἰς θάλασσαν [Exodus 15:1], ἤγουν τὴν ἀλόγιστον ὁρμὴν τῆς ἁμαρτίας, ἢ ὥσπερ ἵππῳ θηλυμανεῖ [Jeremiah 5:8] ἡ ἐμπαθὴς ἐπιθυμία ἐπιβεβηκέναι νομίζεται.

3 Ἐντεῦθεν σύστημα μοναχῶν πολυάριθμον καὶ ὁ ζῆλος ἀλλήλους ὑπερνικᾶν ἐκκαλούμενος· ἐντεῦθεν ἔρημος πολευομένη καὶ ἡ ἀοίκητος ἐν τοῖς τέκνοις πολύοικος· ἐντεῦθεν ἡλικία πᾶσα καὶ ἅπαν ἀξίωμα τὴν ἰδίαν διαγωγὴν ἀπαρνούμενον καὶ Θεῷ ἑαυτοὺς ἀφιεροῦν ἐπειγόμενον ὑπὸ μεσίτῃ τῷ αὐτοῦ ἀξίῳ θεράποντι· ἐντεῦθεν ἄνδρες μὲν γυναῖκας, τέκνα δὲ γονεῖς, ἀδελφοὶ δὲ τοὺς ὁμοίους καὶ φίλοι φίλους ὡς ἀλλοτρίους ἀποδιδράσκοντες, οἷς τὰ ἀντίθετα φρονεῖν ἡ πρὸς τὸν βίον ἄλογος προσπάθεια προεθέσπισεν.

4 Ἐντεῦθεν ἀρετῆς πυρσὸς ἀναφλεγόμενος καὶ κακίας τὸ σκότος ἀπομειούμενον· ἐντεῦθεν σωφροσύνη τιμωμένη καὶ ἀκολασία βδελυττομένη, ταπείνωσις ἐμπορευομένη καὶ ὑπερηφανία ἐπικοπτομένη, ὑπακοὴ δαψιλευομένη καὶ παρακοὴ μακρὰν ἐξακοντιζομένη· ἐντεῦθεν πολυσπερέων ἀγέλαι μερόπων εἰς μίαν γνώμης ταυτότητα συμβιβαζόμεναι, καὶ τῆς πολυσχιδοῦς ἀπάτης τὸ ἄστατον ὡς ἄπιστον διαχλευαζόμενον· ἐντεῦθεν τὸ τελευταῖον καὶ πρῶτον τῆς τῶν συντρεχόντων σπουδῆς ἐπιτήδευμα, Θεὸς ὑμνούμενός τε καὶ δοξαζόμενος νυκτερινοῖς ὕμνοις καὶ μεθημερινοῖς

<of the Promised Land>, so that thereby Egypt, *the gloomy sin,* might mourn the loss of its own firstborn, while we should sing the *song* of exodus in celebration to the Lord, because, for the sake of this new Moses, *He has thrown horse and rider into the sea,* that is, the irrational impulse of sin, through which passionate desire is believed to mount like *a horse in heat.*

Therefore a numerous assemblage of monks was called forth <to the promised land of Peristerai>, as was the zeal to compete with each other; there the uninhabited wilderness was turned into a place of many habitations for Euthymios's spiritual children. Therefore people of every age and every rank renounced their way of life and strove to dedicate themselves to God through the mediation of His worthy servant. Therefore husbands abandoned wives, children left parents, brothers left their siblings, and friends left behind friends as though they were strangers, people for whom their irrational attachment to secular life foreordained that they should take a different view from them. 3

Therefore the torch of virtue was kindled and the darkness of evil was diminished. Therefore moderation was honored and licentiousness abominated, humility prevailed and arrogance was checked, obedience was in abundance and disobedience hurled far away. Therefore flocks of *men from all over the earth* were reconciled into one identity of purpose and the instability of multifarious deceit was mocked as faithless. Therefore the first and last zealous effort of those who assembled was the praise and glorification of 4

μελῳδήμασιν οὐδὲν ἧττον ἢ ἐν οὐρανοῖς ὑπὸ ἀγγέλων
δοξολογούμενος.

5 "Ὡς καλοί σου οἱ οἶκοι, Ἰακώβ, αἱ σκηναί σου, Ἰσραήλ,"
εἶπεν ἄν τις τῶν ἐνθουσιαστῶν τἀνταῦθα ἐπικαταλαβόμενος, "ὡσεὶ νάπαι σκιάζουσαι καὶ ὡς παράδεισοι ἐπὶ ποταμὸν
καὶ ὡς αἱ σκηναὶ ἃς ἔπηξε Κύριος καὶ οὐκ ἄνθρωπος
[Numbers 24:5–6]. Ἀνέτειλε γάρ σοι ἄστρον ἐξ Ἰακὼβ
Χριστὸς ὁ Κύριος, καὶ ἀνέστησέ σοι ἄνθρωπον ἐξ Ἰσραὴλ
[Numbers 24:17], νοῦν ὁρᾶν Θεὸν ἐξισχύοντα, τὸν μέγαν
Εὐθύμιον, ὅστις θραύσει μέν σοι τοὺς ἀρχηγοὺς Μωάβ
[Numbers 24:17], τοὺς ἀντιθέτους καὶ σκοτεινομόρφους
δαίμονας, καὶ προνομεύσει τοὺς υἱοὺς Σήθ, τῆς εὐλογημένης
γενεᾶς τὰ σῳζόμενα ἔγγονα, καὶ ἔσται Ἐδὼμ κληρονομία
αὐτοῦ [Numbers 24:18], τουτέστιν ἡ ἐν Ἐδὲμ τρυφή, ἣν δι᾽
ἀκρασίας ἀπολέσαντες διὰ νηστείας πάλιν καὶ μετανοίας
ῥᾳδίως εὑρίσκομεν."

31

Λέγεται μὲν ἡ σκηνὴ τοῦ μαρτυρίου [Exodus 31:7] ὑπὸ
Μωσέως πεπῆχθαι, καθὼς αὐτῷ Θεὸς διετάξατο καὶ Βε-
σελεὴλ ὁ σοφώτατος τετελείωκεν, ἀλλ᾽ ἡ μὲν ἐπιστασία
τοῦ ἔργου τῷ Μωσεῖ ἐγκεχείριστο, ἡ δὲ προσένεξις τῆς
ὕλης τῷ λαῷ ἐπετέτραπτο, ὧν οἱ μὲν χρυσόν, οἱ δὲ ἄργυρον,
πλεῖστοι δὲ χαλκόν, καὶ σίδηρον ἕτεροι, εἰς τὴν τοῦ ἔργου

God in nocturnal hymns and diurnal melodies, no less than He is glorified in heaven by angels.

"*How goodly are thy habitations, Jacob, and thy tents, Israel,*" ₅ would say one of the inspired people who arrived there, "*as shady groves and as gardens beside a river, and like the tents which the Lord has pitched,* not man. For Christ the Lord *has made a star to rise out of Jacob* for you, *and has made a man to spring up out of Israel* for you, a mind which is able to see God, the great Euthymios, who *will crush* for you *the princes of Moab,* the hostile and dark-shaped demons, and *will ravage the sons of Seth,* the offspring of the blessed generation who still persist, and *Edom shall be his inheritance,* that is, the delight in Eden, which we lost through our intemperance and find easily again through fasting and repentance."

Chapter 31

The *tabernacle of witness* is said to have been pitched by Moses, just as God ordered him, and the most skilled Beseleel completed it, but the supervision of the work was entrusted to Moses, and the provision of the materials was left to the people; some of them brought *gold,* others *silver,* most brought *bronze,* and others iron for the completion of the

ἐκπλήρωσιν προσεκόμιζον, ὡς δὲ κἂν τοῖς ἐπίπλοις οἱ μὲν χρυσὸν νενησμένον, οἱ δὲ βύσσον ἢ κόκκινον, ἄλλοι δέρρεα ἠρυθροδανωμένα καὶ μέχρι τριχῶν αἰγείων [see Exodus 25:3–5] ἐποιοῦντο τὴν προσένεξιν, ἀναλόγως (οἶμαι) τῆς ἑαυτοῦ σπουδῆς ἢ περιουσίας τὴν προσφορὰν ποιούμενος ἕκαστος.

2 Σκόπει δ᾽ οὖν κἀνταῦθα, εἰ μὴ καὶ τῷ νέῳ ἡμῶν Μωσεῖ τὰ ὅμοια συνδεδράμηκεν· οἱ μὲν γὰρ αὐτῷ τῶν εὐσεβῶν εἰς τὴν τῆς μονῆς ἐπισύστασιν χρυσὸν παρεῖχον φερόμενοι, οἱ δὲ ἄργυρον, ἕτεροι χαλκὸν καὶ σίδηρον εἰς λειτουργικῶν σκευῶν ἀποπλήρωσιν. Ὡς δὲ κἂν ταῖς διατροφαῖς οἱ μὲν σῖτον καὶ ὄσπρια, ἄλλοι δὲ οἶνον καὶ ἕτεροι ἐκαρποφόρουν ἔλαιον, οἱ δὲ ζῷα εἰς θοίνην τοῖς ἐργάταις διάφορα, οἱ πλείους δ᾽ αὐτῶν μετὰ τὴν τοῦ ἔργου περαίωσιν καὶ ἔπιπλα σηρικὰ καὶ σκεύη ἱερὰ προσεκόμισαν. Καὶ οἱ μὲν γῆν ἀφιέρουν τῆς ἑαυτῶν ἀποτεμόμενοι, οἱ δὲ ἀγροὺς καὶ ἀμπελῶνας, βοσκημάτων τε ἀγέλας καὶ τὰ λοιπά, οἷς οἱ τὴν μονὴν οἰκοῦντες διατραφήσονται καὶ τὸ ἄλυπον καὶ ἀπερίσπαστον ἕξουσιν, ὡς ἂν καὶ Θεῷ ἀφροντίστως λατρεύωσι καὶ τοῖς προσκομίσασιν ἐπεύχωνται τὰ βελτίονα.

work, just as for the fabrics some brought spun *gold,* others *linen* or *purple,* others *red-dyed* skins and even *goats' hair,* each making his offering in proportion (I believe) to his zeal or his wealth.

So therefore consider what happened there at Peristerai, 2 and see if similar donations were not assembled for our new Moses. For some of the pious people brought him gold for the endowment of the monastery, others silver, yet others bronze and iron to manufacture liturgical vessels. Likewise for their nourishment some brought wheat and legumes, others wine and yet others oil, and some brought different animals as food for the workmen. After the completion of the work the people brought silk textiles and holy vessels, and some offered land, separating it off from their own property, and others fields and vineyards, and herds of cattle and so on, by which the inhabitants of the monastery would be nourished and be freed from worry or distraction, so that they might worship God without other concerns and pray for a better future for those who brought the offerings.

32

Ἀλλὰ ταῦτα μὲν κατὰ διαφόρους αἰτίας καὶ χρόνους ἀφιερούμενα εἰς πλάτος ἐπιδοῦναι τὴν μονὴν διαπετάσασαν τὰ σχοινίσματα αὐτῆς πεποιήκασιν· ὁ δὲ τιμιώτατος πρεσβύτης ὡς πλείστους ἀποταξαμένους καὶ ἀποταττομένους ἐν τῇ κατ᾽ αὐτὸν μονῇ ἑώρα τοὺς πάντας νεοπαγεῖς καὶ ἀγυμνάστους πρὸς τὴν ἄσκησιν, ᾔδει δὲ σαφῶς καὶ τοῦ Ἐχθροῦ τὰ μετὰ ποικιλίας σοφίσματα, δεδιὼς μήπου λεληθότως λοχήσας τινὰ ἑαυτῷ ποιήσοιτο θήραμα, ἠγωνία καὶ ἤσχαλλεν καὶ ταῖς εὐχαῖς ἐκτενέστερον νύκτωρ καὶ μεθ᾽ ἡμέραν ἀπεχρᾶτο πρὸς Κύριον, "Μὴ παραδῷς τοῖς θηρίοις, ὦ Δέσποτα," λέγων, "ψυχὰς ἐξομολογουμένας σοι [Psalm 73(74):19], ἀλλὰ φιλόψυχος ὢν ὡς διὰ σὲ τῷ κόσμῳ ἀποταξαμένους φύλαξον αὐτοὺς ὑπὸ τὴν σκέπην τῶν ἀηττήτων πτερύγων [see Psalm 16(17):8] σου· προσλαβοῦ αὐτοὺς ὑπὸ τὴν περιοχὴν τῆς σῆς ἐπαύλεως· τήρησον αὐτοὺς ἐκ τοῦ Πονηροῦ· ἁγίασον αὐτοὺς τῷ ἁγίῳ σου ὀνόματι· σόφισον αὐτοὺς κατὰ τῶν μεθοδειῶν τοῦ πολυμηχάνου δυσμενοῦς· δός μοι ἐπὶ σοῦ μετὰ παρρησίας καυχήσασθαι ὑπὲρ αὐτῶν, ὅτι οὓς δέδωκάς μοι ἐφύλαξα καὶ οὐδεὶς ἐξ αὐτῶν ἀπώλετο [see John 17:12]· τεύξομαι θυμηδίας μετὰ πάντων τῷ σῷ παριστάμενος βήματι, ὥστε ἔχειν ἱκανῶς ἀνακράζειν· Ἰδοὺ ἐγὼ καὶ τὰ παιδία, ἅ μοι δέδωκας, Κύριε'" [Isaiah 8:18].

Chapter 32

But although these items, dedicated for different reasons and at different times, allowed the monastery to expand, extending its land holdings, the most honorable elder Euthymios saw that most of the people who had renounced and were renouncing the world in his monastery were novices and untrained in asceticism, and he knew clearly the various devices of the Enemy. So, fearing that the Enemy would set up a secret ambush for someone and make him his victim, he was distressed and worried and used to pray at length night and day to the Lord, saying, "Master, *do not deliver unto the wild beasts souls who have made confession to you,* but, since you are a lover of souls, protect them *under the shelter of* your invincible *wings* as people who have renounced the world for your sake. Bring them into the enclosure of your estate. Preserve them from the Evil One. Sanctify them with your holy name. Instruct them about the wiles of our very devious enemy. Allow me to boast confidently to you on their behalf, that *I have protected* those whom *you gave to me and none of them has been lost.* Standing beside your altar I will be gladdened with them all, so as to be able to cry out, *'Behold, I and the children whom you have given to me, Lord.'"*

33

Τοιαῦτα μέν (ὡς ὀλίγα ἐκ πλειόνων ἐν τύπῳ περιελά-
βομεν) ὁ πρεσβύτης ἐβόα πρὸς Κύριον· ὁ δὲ Θεὸς αὐτῷ
ἀδιαλώβητον συνετήρει τὸ ποίμνιον· αὐτὸς δ᾽ οἷα ποιμὴν
γνήσιος θηρῶν αὐτῷ ἐλπιζομένης ἐφόδου τοῖς θρέμμασιν
ἐναγώνιος ἦν, καὶ διδασκαλίαις ἀνενδότοις προκαταρτίζειν
ἐπειρᾶτο τὸ ποίμνιον, "Ὁ ἀντίδικος ἡμῶν, ἀδελφοί, Διάβολος," προμαρτυρούμενος, "ὡς λέων περιέρχεται ὠρυόμενος
καὶ ζητῶν τίνα ἐξ ἡμῶν καταπίῃ [1 Peter 5:8]. Ἀσφαλισώ-
μεθα οὖν ἑαυτοὺς καί, δι᾽ ὃ ἐξήλθομεν, δι᾽ αὐτὸ καὶ
ἀγωνισώμεθα· εἰ τῷ κόσμῳ ἀπεταξάμεθα, ταῖς κοσμικαῖς
ἐπιθυμίαις [see Titus 2:12] μὴ ὑποπίπτωμεν· εἰ τὸ σῶμα
ἐσταυρώσαμεν καὶ τὸν θάνατον τοῦ Κυρίου ἐπενδυσάμεθα, Πνεύματι περιπατῶμεν καὶ ἡδονὴν σαρκὸς οὐκ ἐπι-
τελέσωμεν· εἰ διὰ τὴν βασιλείαν τῶν οὐρανῶν τὸ ἀγγε-
λικὸν ἐπενδυσάμεθα πρόσχημα, ὡς ἄγγελοι ἐπὶ γῆς
πολιτευσώμεθα· καὶ γὰρ τὸν θεῖον πόθον καὶ τὴν πρὸς τὰ
κρείττω ἐμβίβασιν δύο ταῦτα ἀπογεννᾶν πεφύκασιν, ἢ
ἔρως δόξης ἢ φόβος κολάσεως. Εἰ οὖν ἀγαπῶμεν τὸν
Κύριον, τὰς ἐντολὰς αὐτοῦ τηρήσωμεν καὶ τῆς δόξης
αὐτοῦ οὐ διαμαρτήσομεν· εἰ δ᾽ οὖν, ἀλλὰ τήν γε κόλασιν
φοβηθῶμεν (καλὸν γὰρ ἀμφοτέρωθεν σωφρονίζεσθαι),
καὶ τάχα καὶ οὕτως οὐ μακρὰν τῆς βασιλείας τῶν οὐρανῶν
ἐσόμεθα, φόβῳ τοῦ μὴ παθεῖν τὸ κακῶς ποιεῖν ἀπαρνού-
μενοι.

2   "Ἐργαζώμεθα ταῖς οἰκείαις χερσίν [see 1 Corinthians

Chapter 33

Such words (of which I have included a few out of many as an example) the elder cried out to the Lord; and God preserved his flock unharmed for him. But he, like a true shepherd, was anxious about the attack of wild beasts that he expected against his sheep, and tried to prepare his flock with constant instruction, saying: "Brethren, our *adversary the Devil* comes like *a lion roaring and seeking to devour one* of us. Let us therefore safeguard ourselves and, for whatever reason we have come out here to the wilderness, let us fight for that. If we have renounced the world, let us not yield to *worldly desires.* If we have crucified the body and clothed ourselves in the death of the Lord, let us walk in the Spirit and not be subject to the pleasure of the flesh. If we have clothed ourselves in the angelic habit for the sake of the kingdom of heaven, let us live like angels upon earth. For these two things, either love of glory or fear of punishment, can engender divine yearning and embarkation on the better course. So if we love the Lord, let us keep His commandments and let us not fail to achieve His glory. Otherwise, let us fear punishment (for it is good to be prudent on both accounts), and perhaps thus we will not be far from the kingdom of heaven, renouncing evil deeds through fear of suffering.

"*Let us work with our own hands,* so that we may not suffer   2

4:12], ἵνα μὴ ἀκαρπίαν νοσήσωμεν· ὁ γὰρ ὀκνηρὸς καὶ ἄερ-
γος συνάγει ἀκάνθας [see Proverbs 15:19] καὶ ὁ μὴ συμπεριφερόμενος τῷ ἑαυτοῦ οἴκῳ κληρονομεῖ ἀνέμους [Proverbs
11:29], καθὼς Σολομὼν διαγορεύει, ὁ ἐν βασιλεῦσι σοφώτα-
τος· Παῦλος δὲ ὁ ἀπόστολος καὶ τροφῆς ἀνάξιον τὸν μὴ
ἐργαζόμενον διορίζεται· 'Ὁ ἀργὸς γάρ,' φησί, 'μηδὲ ἐσθι-
έτω' [see 2 Thessalonians 3:10], καὶ αὖθις· Ἐργαζόμενοι ταῖς
οἰκείαις χερσὶν [1 Corinthians 4:12] εἰς τὸ μὴ ἐπιβαρῆσαί
τινα' καὶ 'ταῖς χρείαις μου καὶ τοῖς οὖσι μετ᾽ ἐμοῦ ὑπηρέτησαν
αἱ χεῖρες αὗται' [Acts 20:34], ὡς ἂν μὴ μόνον ἑαυτῷ ἐπαρκῇ
ὁ ἐργαζόμενος, ἀλλὰ καὶ τῷ δεομένῳ τῶν ἀδελφῶν τὰ
πρὸς τὴν χρείαν παρέχοιτο. Πάντα μὲν ὅσα ἂν ποιῆτε,' ὁ
αὐτός φησιν ἀπόστολος, 'εἰς δόξαν Θεοῦ ποιεῖτε, εἴτε ἐσθίετε
εἴτε πίνετε εἴτε τι ἄλλο ποιεῖτε' [1 Corinthians 10:31].

3   ''Ἐγὼ δὲ πρὸς τοῖς εἰρημένοις καὶ τοῦτο λέγω ὑμῖν ἐκ
τῆς Γραφῆς ἀναλεγόμενος· Ταπεινώθητε ὑπὸ τὴν κρα-
ταιὰν χεῖρα τοῦ [1 Peter 5:6] Χριστοῦ καὶ σώσει ὑμᾶς· τῇ
τιμῇ ἀλλήλους προηγούμενοι, τῇ σπουδῇ μὴ ὀκνηροί, τῷ
Πνεύματι ζέοντες, τῷ Κυρίῳ λατρεύοντες [Romans 12:10–
11]· πᾶσα κραυγὴ καὶ βλασφημία σὺν πάσῃ κακίᾳ ἀρθήτω ἀφ᾽
ὑμῶν [Ephesians 4:31]· αἱ χεῖρες ὑμῶν χωρὶς ὀργῆς καὶ διαλογισμῶν πρὸς τὸν Θεὸν αἱρέσθωσαν [see 1 Timothy 2:8]·
οἱ πόδες ἐν ἑτοιμασίᾳ τοῦ εὐαγγελίου τῆς εἰρήνης κινείσθω-
σαν [see Ephesians 6:15]· ἡ ἀγάπη ἀνυπόκριτος· ἀποστυ-
γοῦντες μὲν τὸ πονηρόν, κολλώμενοι δὲ τῷ ἀγαθῷ [Romans
12:9], πείθεσθε τοῖς ἡγουμένοις ὑμῶν καὶ ὑπείκετε· αὐτοὶ γὰρ
ἀγρυπνοῦσιν ὑπὲρ τῶν ψυχῶν ὑμῶν' [Hebrews 13:17].

4   ''Συγχωρεῖτε ἀλλήλοις τὰ εἰς ἑαυτοὺς ἁμαρτήματα,

the disease of unfruitfulness. For the idler and *sluggard* gathers *thorns* and *he that deals not graciously with his own house shall inherit the wind,* as Solomon, the wisest of kings, declares. And Paul the apostle declares the man who does not work unworthy of food; for he says, 'The lazy man *should not eat,*' and again, '*Those who work with their own hands* so as not to burden anyone,' and '*these hands ministered to my necessities and to those who were with me,*' so that he who works is not only sufficient unto himself, but also provides the necessities to one who is needy among our brethren. The same apostle says, '*Whatever you do, do it all to the glory of God, whether you eat or drink, or do anything else.*'

"In addition to what has already been said, I say this to you, quoting from the Scriptures: '*Humble yourselves therefore under the mighty hand* of Christ, and He will save you. *Outdoing one another in showing honor, never flag in zeal, be aglow with the Spirit, serve the Lord. Let all clamor and slander be put away from you, with all malice; let* your *hands be lifted* to God *without anger or quarreling. Let your feet* be moved *with the equipment of the gospel of peace; let love be genuine; hating what is evil, holding fast to what is good, obey your leaders and submit to them, for they are keeping watch over your souls.*' 3

"Forgive each other your sins against yourselves, since *it is* 4

ἐπειδὴ ἀνάγκη ἐστὶν ἐλθεῖν τὰ σκάνδαλα [Matthew 18:7], καθὼς ὁ Κύριος προηγόρευσεν, ἐξαγορεύετε ἀλλήλοις τὰ ἁμαρτήματα, ὡς ἂν ὑπὲρ ἀλλήλων προσεύχησθε [James 5:16], ἐξαιρέτως τῷ προεστῶτι, ὅπως ὑμῖν ἐκεῖνος θεόθεν ἐξαιτῆται τὴν ἄφεσιν, ἐπείπερ, ὡς τὰ θεῖα διδάσκουσι λόγια, μώλωπες θριαμβευόμενοι οὐ προκόψουσιν ἐπὶ τὸ χεῖρον, ἀλλ᾽ ἰαθήσονται [see 1 Peter 2:24; 2 Timothy 3:13]· ὥσπερ καὶ ἐν τῷ εἰς μετάνοιαν κηρυττομένῳ τοῦ Προδρόμου βαπτίσματι ἐξαγορευόμενοι ἕκαστος τὰς ἁμαρτίας αὐτῶν ἐβαπτίζοντο [see Mark 1:4–5]· καὶ γὰρ ὥσπερ τὰ ᾠὰ ἐν κόλπῳ θαλπόμενα ζῳογονεῖται, οὕτως καὶ λογισμοὶ κρυπτόμενοι εἰς ἔργα προβαίνουσιν."

5 Ὑπεμίμνησκε δὲ αὐτοὺς συνεχῶς καὶ τοῦ κοινοβίου, οὗπερ Ἰωάννης ὁ τῆς Κλίμακος τὰ κατορθώματα ἀναγράφεται, ἐν ᾧ πᾶσαν ἀρετῶν ἰδέαν ὡς ἐν ἀρχετύπῳ πίνακι περιλαβὼν ἐζωγράφησε· καὶ ἁπλῶς διδασκαλίαν παλαιάν, πᾶσαν δὲ νέαν ὡς ἐπὶ γλώσσης φέρων ἀκωλύτως ἐχορήγει τοῖς ἀκούουσιν, ὥστε θαυμάζειν πάντας τὸ εὐφυὲς τοῦ ἁγίου γέροντος καὶ ἐκπληττομένους λέγειν θείαν αὐτῷ ἐπιπνέεσθαι, ὡς τοῖς ἀποστόλοις ποτὲ ὑπὸ τοῦ ἁγίου Πνεύματος, χάριν ἐν ἀνοίξει τοῦ στόματος [Ephesians 6:19].

necessary that temptations come, as the Lord proclaimed; confess *your sins to one another,* so that *you may pray for one another,* especially for your superior, so that he may request forgiveness for you from God, since, as the divine scriptures teach, *wounds* that are revealed *do not go from bad to worse,* but *are healed,* just as, at the baptism of John the Forerunner, which was preached for repentance, each of them was baptized after confessing his sins. For just as eggs nurtured in the womb generate life, so concealed thoughts progress to deeds."

He used to remind them continuously about the communal life, the achievements of which are recounted by John of the Ladder, in a work in which he included every idea of virtue and described it as in an archetypal painting. For, bearing the teachings of old and every new teaching as if on the tip of his tongue, Euthymios would provide them in simple language to his listeners without impediment, so that everyone was amazed at the skill of the holy elder and in their astonishment said that *when he opened his mouth* he was inspired with divine grace, just as the apostles were once by the Holy Spirit.

34

Ἐν ταύταις οὖν ταῖς θεοπνεύστοις καὶ μελιρρύτοις διδασκαλίαις καὶ ἡμᾶς καταθέλξας οἷά τις Ὀρφεὺς ὀπαδοὺς
ἐπηγάγετο, ἔτος ἤδη ἐν τῇ θεοσυστάτῳ μονῇ διαπεραι-
ούμενος τέταρτον, ἀποκείρας μὲν ἡμᾶς ἐν τῇ Σερμιλίᾳ
λεγομένῃ κώμῃ, ἐν τῷ Δημητρίου ναῷ τοῦ κοσμοποθήτου
μεγαλομάρτυρος, καὶ πρὸς βραχὺ τάξας ἐν τοῖς ἀναχωρη-
τικοῖς αὐτοῦ κελλίοις ἔξω κατοικεῖν· ἔρως γὰρ ἡμᾶς εἶχε
τῆς ἡσυχίας τέως διάπυρος (κἂν φιλοδοξίᾳ νικηθέντες
τοὺς θορύβους καὶ τὰς ἐν ἄστει διατριβὰς μετὰ ταῦτα προ-
ετιμήσαμεν), ὅτε ζήλῳ θείῳ κινούμενοι καὶ τὴν μανιχαϊκὴν
βίβλον Ἀντωνίου τοῦ ἐν Κρανέαις πεπλανημένου μοναχοῦ
εὐχαῖς τοῦ ἱεροῦ ποιμένος πυρὶ καύσαντες ἠφανίσαμεν, ἢ
"Τὰ ἀπόκρυφα" μὲν "τοῦ εὐαγγελίου" ἐπεγέγραπτο, πᾶσαν
δὲ βλασφημίαν καὶ πᾶσαν αἱρέσεως ἀπαρχὴν ἐν ἑαυτῇ
ἐπεφέρετο.

2 Βούλομαι μὲν ἐνταῦθα τοῦ λόγου γενόμενος καὶ τὰς εἰς
ἡμᾶς προρρήσεις τοῦ διορατικωτάτου ἡμῶν πατρὸς ἀνα-
γράψασθαι καὶ ἔτι μᾶλλον τὰς ἐν διαφόροις καιροῖς καὶ
τόποις προφητείας αὐτοῦ· δέδοικα δὲ μὴ ἀμετρίαν ἐνδίκως
ἐγκληθήσωμαι ὑπὸ τῶν ἐπαινούντων τὴν συμμετρίαν ἐν
τοῖς συγγράμμασιν· ὅμως οἷον ἥδυσμά τι τῷ λόγῳ τὰ
ἡμέτερα μόνα διὰ βραχέων ἐνταῦθα συνάψαντες, τὰ πλείω
τοῖς βουλομένοις διηγεῖσθαι παραχωρήσωμεν.

Chapter 34

Enchanting me, too, with these divinely inspired and mellifluous teachings, like another Orpheus, he made me one of his followers; and, during his fourth year in the monastery at Peristerai established by God, he tonsured me in the town called Sermylia, in the church of Demetrios the great martyr loved by the world, and ordered me to live outside the monastery for a short time in his anchoritic cells. For an ardent love of spiritual tranquility held me fast (even though later on, defeated by vainglory, I preferred the clamor and distractions of a city), at a time when, moved by divine zeal, with the blessing of the holy shepherd I consigned to the flames and destroyed the Manichaean book of the deluded monk Antony of Kraneai, which was entitled *The Apocrypha of the Gospel,* and contained every blasphemy and every source of heresy.

Now that I am at this point in my narrative, I would like 2 also to record the predictions made to us by our most clairvoyant father and especially his prophecies at different times and places. But I fear that I may be justly accused of a lack of proportion by those who praise balanced proportions in compositions. And so, after attaching only my own stories about Euthymios to the account, in brief and as a kind of seasoning, let me leave any further stories to those who wish to tell them.

35

Τίνα οὖν τὰ ἡμέτερα; Ἀποκαρθέντων ἡμῶν ἐν τῷ Δημητρίου νεῴ, ὡς ἤδη καὶ προλελέχαμεν, καὶ τρίτην ἡμέραν διαννόντων ἐν τῇ παρεδρεύσει τούτου, ὡς ἔθος ἐστὶ τοῖς μονάζουσιν, ὁ ἀληθῶς τοῦ Θεοῦ ἄνθρωπος καὶ τῇ ἀγαθῇ πράξει τῇ θεωρίᾳ ἐπιβεβηκὼς καὶ ὡς ὑποβάθρᾳ ταύτῃ πρὸς τὴν τῶν μελλόντων γνῶσιν ἀποχρώμενος, τὰ καθ᾽ ἡμᾶς ἐμπνευσθεὶς τῇ φωταυγίᾳ τοῦ Πνεύματος περὶ μέσην ἡμέραν ἐν μιᾷ τῶν τοῦ ναοῦ στοῶν μόνους ἀπὸ τῶν ἄλλων μεθ᾽ ἑαυτοῦ προσλαβόμενος, ταῦθ᾽ ἡμῖν ἐμφανίζειν διέγνωκεν.

2 "Ἐγώ," φησίν, "ὦ Βασίλειε, ἀνάξιός εἰμι θείας φωταυγίας ἀξιοῦσθαι ἢ προρρήσεως· ταῦτα γὰρ τῶν μεγάλων ἐστὶ πατέρων καὶ οἷς ὁ βίος τὴν κάθαρσιν προεθησαύρισεν· ἐπειδὴ δὲ ὑμεῖς εἴτε πλανηθέντες ἢ καὶ καλῶς εἰς τὴν ἐμὴν κατεδράμετε ἀναξιότητα διὰ τὴν ὑμῶν ὠφέλειαν, ὡς ἂν μὴ πάντῃ ἀδόκιμοι δόξητε, εὐδόκησεν ὁ Θεὸς καὶ ἐν ἐμοὶ ἐπιστάξαι τῆς οἰκείας ἀπορροὴν χάριτος, ὅπως τὰ τῶν ἰδίων φοιτητῶν προγινώσκων ἄγω ταῦτα ῥυθμίζων, ἐν οἷς τὸ θεῖον ἀρέσκεται. Καὶ σὺ οὖν, τέκνον, γίνωσκε, Θεοῦ μοι τὰ κατὰ σὲ φανερώσαντος, μαθημάτων ἔρωτι τάχιον τῆς μονῆς ἀναχωρεῖς καὶ ἀρχιερεὺς γίνῃ, ὅπου τὸ θεῖον προεθέσπισε βούλημα. Ἀλλ᾽ ὅρα," φησί, "καὶ ἡμῶν ὡς γεννητόρων μνημόνευε, καὶ τῆς μονῆς καὶ τῶν ἐν αὐτῇ ἀδελφῶν μηδέποτε λήθην παρασκευάσῃς ἐπιγίνεσθαί σοι." Ταῦτ᾽ εἰπὼν καὶ ἀνέκφορα πᾶσιν ἕως τῆς ἐκβάσεως

Chapter 35

What then are my stories about Euthymios? After I was tonsured at the church of Demetrios, as I have already recounted, and was spending the third day in devotion to this saint there, as is customary for those who become monks, this true man of God, who attained the contemplative life through good deeds and used it as the foundation for his knowledge of future events, received inspiration about my future career through the illumination of the Spirit. Around midday he took me alone apart from the others into one of the church aisles, and decided to reveal the following to me.

"Basil," he said, "I do not deserve to be deemed worthy of 2 divine illumination or prophecy; for this is the prerogative of the great fathers and those in whom their life has stored up purity. But since you have come to my unworthy self, either at random or for good purpose, for your benefit, so that you might not seem completely worthless, God has seen fit to instill in me a stream of His grace, so that through foreknowledge of the fate of my disciples I may lead them, guiding them in ways that are pleasing to God. You should thus know, my child, that God has revealed this to me about you: on account of your love of learning you will soon depart from the monastery and become a bishop at a place which the divine will has foreordained. But look upon me," he said, "and remember me as your parent, and do not ever permit yourself to forget your monastery and the brethren within it." After saying these words and bidding me keep them se-

φυλάττειν διακελευσάμενος ἐπὶ νουθεσίαν ἱερὰν τὸν λόγον ἡμῖν πεπεράτωκεν.

36

Ἦν μὲν οὖν ἀκόλουθον ἐνταῦθα καὶ τὸν διὰ προσευχῆς τοῦ ἁγίου ἐπιχορηγηθέντα ἡμῖν ἄρτον κατὰ τὴν ἔρημον ἐν ἀβάτῳ καὶ οὐχ ὁδῷ [Psalm 106(107):40] ἀνατάξασθαι, ὅταν σὺν τῷ Ἰωάννῃ τῷ Τζάγαστῃ λεγομένῳ βαδίζοντες πείνῃ καὶ ὁδοιπορίᾳ ἐκλυθέντες ἤδη θανεῖν ἐβιαζόμεθα, καὶ ὅπως ἐξ αὐτοῦ διατραφέντες νεαροὶ καὶ πρόθυμοι τὸ λεῖπον τῆς ὁδοῦ διηνύσαμεν· αὖθις δὲ τὴν περὶ τοῦ αὐτοῦ Ἰωάννου καὶ Ἀντωνίου πρόορασιν, ὅταν βαδιζόντων ἡμῶν κατὰ τὴν Κορωνίαν λεγομένην λίμνην, ἐκείνων διὰ φιλονεικίαν τῆς μονῆς ὑποχωρούντων, αὐτὸς ὡς ὁρῶν τὸ πόρρωθεν αὐτοῖς ἀνυόμενον αὐθωρὸν ἡμῖν διηγόρευσεν, ὡς σημειωσάμενοι τὸν καιρὸν μετὰ τοῦτο μαθεῖν ἠδυνήθημεν.

2   Πρὸς δὲ τούτοις ἔδει προσκεῖσθαι τῇ τάξει τῆς γραφῆς τὴν ἐν Θεσσαλονίκῃ ἐν τῇ πρώτῃ εἰς τὸν στύλον ἀναβάσει τοῦ δαιμονιῶντος ἀνθρώπου διὰ προσευχῆς ἱερᾶς καὶ χρίσεως ἐλαίου ἀποκάθαρσιν, καὶ τὴν Ἱλαρίωνος τοῦ μοναχοῦ ἐν Περιστεραῖς διὰ θείας ἐντεύξεως ἴασιν καὶ τοῦ συμπνίγοντος αὐτὸν δαιμονίου δραπέτευσιν, ὅπως τε αὐτῷ πάλιν κακῶς διατεθέντι πρὸς τὸν ἅγιον μετὰ πλείονος τῆς παρασκευῆς τὸ πονηρὸν πνεῦμα ἐπεπήδησεν εἰς

cret from everyone until they should come to pass, he concluded his speech of holy admonition to me.

Chapter 36

I should next describe the bread provided to us through the holy man's prayer in the wilderness when we were in *an untrodden and trackless place.* This happened while I was walking with John, who is called Tsagastes. We were faint with hunger and exhaustion from the journey and were near death, but, after Euthymios provided us with nourishment, we finished the rest of the journey with renewed energy and eagerness. Then I should recount his prophetic vision about the same John and Antony, made while we (that is, Basil and Euthymios) were walking beside the lake called Koroneia. Those two, John and Antony, were leaving the monastery because of a dispute; the holy man saw from afar what they were doing and immediately revealed this to me. I noted the time and was able to verify the incident afterward.

In addition I must add to the sequence of my account his 2 exorcism of the demoniac through holy prayer and anointing with oil at the time when he first ascended the column in Thessalonike; his healing of the monk Hilarion at Peristerai as a result of divine intercession and the flight of the demon who was choking him; and how, when Hilarion was again ill disposed toward the holy one, the evil spirit attacked him

σωφρονισμὸν καὶ διόρθωσιν τῶν κατεπαιρομένων τοῖς ἡγήτορσι καὶ ὕβρεσι τούτους κατατολμώντων ἀμύνεσθαι, οὓς ἀμφοτέρους αὐτοὶ ἡμεῖς τεθεάμεθα καὶ ὑπὸ Θεῷ μάρτυρι τὸ βέβαιον ἐπιστώθημεν.

3   Πρὸς δ' ἀμφοτέροις καὶ τὸ πολυθρύλλητον ἐκεῖνο θαῦμα μικροῦ καὶ ἄπιστον τοῖς μικροψυχίᾳ κακῶς τὰ θεῖα ταλαντεύουσιν, ὅταν, πρὸ τούτου ἐν τῷ Ἄθωνι τῶν περὶ αὐτὸν ἀδελφῶν τῇ κορυφῇ τοῦ Ὄρους ἀνελθεῖν προαιρουμένων, αὐτὸς τὴν ἄνοδον ὡς ἀσύμφορον διεκώλυεν, ἰδιορρυθμίᾳ δὲ τὴν ὁδὸν ἐκείνων διανύειν ἐπιχειρούντων, χιόνος αὐτοῖς ἐπιπεσούσης, κινδυνεύειν ἔμελλον, εἰ μὴ φθάσας ὁ φιλόστοργος πατὴρ ὡς προκατοπτεύων τῷ Πνεύματι τοὺς ἀνηκόους μαθητὰς τοῦ ἐκ τοῦ κρύους θανάτου διεσώσατο· ἔνθα καί, ὥς φασιν οἱ αὐτόπτως θεασάμενοι, πυρὸς αὐτοῖς μὴ ὑπόντος καὶ πυρέμβολον μηδενὸς ἐξ αὐτῶν ἐπιφερομένου, ὁ τῇ θέρμῃ τοῦ Πνεύματος πυρσὸς ἤδη χρηματίζων πατὴρ ἡμῶν φρυγάνων σωρείαν συστρέψας καὶ τούτοις ἐπιφυσᾶν σχηματισάμενος (ὦ τοῦ θαύματος!), πῦρ ἀνῆψε παράδοξον. Τἆλλά τε ὅσα διηγουμένων ἀκούειν ἔστιν, ὅσοι πείρᾳ ταῦτα παρειλήφασιν. Ἀλλ' ἐπεί, ὡς προέφαμεν, πολλὰ ταῦτα καὶ τῇ τοῦ λόγου συμμετρίᾳ ἀντίθετα, ἄγε δῆτα τοῖς ἄλλοις χαίρειν εἰπάμενοι, αὐτοὶ τὰ καθεξῆς ἡμῖν τῷ λόγῳ προσανατάξωμεν.

more forcefully in order to chasten and correct those who are arrogant toward their leaders and dare to retaliate with insults. I saw both of these miracles myself and assured myself of their veracity, with God as my witness.

And in addition to both of these I should add that most 3 celebrated miracle which those who wickedly hesitate concerning divine affairs as the result of faintheartedness find almost unbelievable. This was when, at a previous time on Athos, his brethren proposed to climb to the peak of the Mountain. He tried to prevent them from making the ascent as being inappropriate, but, when they followed their own course and attempted to make the journey, snow fell upon them and they would have been endangered, if their affectionate father had not been forewarned by the Spirit and caught up with his disobedient disciples and saved them from freezing to death. As eyewitnesses report, since they did not have fire and none of them was carrying a flint, our father, who was already a torch on account of the heat of the Spirit, collected a pile of firewood and, after pretending to blow upon the wood (oh, what a marvel!), kindled a miraculous fire. As for the other stories one can hear told about him, it is for those who have experienced them to narrate them. But since, as I already said, they are numerous and incompatible with the proportions of my narrative, let me pass over the other tales now and add the following to my tale.

37

Ὁ μὲν οὖν ἅγιος ἐν τούτοις τεσσαρεσκαίδεκα ἐνιαυτῶν ἀγνωρίστως ποιμάνας τὸ ποίμνιον, τοῖς συγγενεῦσι καὶ ἰδίοις μετὰ δύο καὶ τεσσαράκοντα ἔτη ὡς Ἰωσὴφ ὑπαναγνωρίζεται. Προσκαλεῖται δὲ τούτους καὶ ὡς ἐκεῖνος φιλοφρονεῖ καὶ τόπον αὐτοῖς ὠνησάμενος, ταῖς μὲν γυναιξὶ μοναστήριον γυναικῶν συνιστᾷ πάντοθεν εὐθηνούμενον, τοῖς δ᾽ ἀνδράσι τὴν οἰκείαν ἐγχειρίζει διοίκησιν.

2 Καὶ δὴ Μεθόδιον τὸν ἱερὸν τῆς Θεσσαλονίκης ἀρχιεπίσκοπον ἀμφοτέραις ταῖς μοναῖς προσκαλεσάμενος, λείψανά τε ἁγίων καὶ θυσιαστήριον ἱερὸν ἱδρύσαι ἐν αὐτοῖς πεποιηκώς, ἀμφότερα Θεῷ ἀφιεροῖ τὰ μοναστήρια, ἐν οἷς μετ᾽ οὐ πολὺ Μεθοδίῳ μὲν τῷ υἱωνῷ καὶ τῇ τούτου ὁμαίμονι Εὐφημίᾳ ἀμφοτέρας τὰς μονὰς παραθέμενος καὶ ἡγουμενεύειν ἐν αὐταῖς παρασκευάσας, αὐτὸς τὴν περὶ αὐτῶν μέριμναν ὥσπερ ἀποφορτισάμενος εἰς τὸν στύλον ἀνέρχεται, ἔνθα καὶ πρώην ἀνεληλυθὼς ἐγινώσκετο.

3 Μηδόλως οὖν ἐν αὐτῷ ἡσυχάζειν ἐώμενος, τὰ τοῦ Ἄθωνος πάλιν ἐπικαταλαμβάνει ἀκρωτήρια. Ὡς δὲ κἀκεῖσε διοχλοῦντας αὐτῷ τοὺς μοναχοὺς ἔβλεπεν καὶ μάλιστα τοὺς ἰδίους, οὓς καὶ ὡς ἄχθος ἀποσκευαζόμενος τὴν ἐρημίαν ἠσπάζετο, προγνοὺς τὴν ἡμέραν τῆς ἰδίας ἐξοδεύσεως, καὶ βουλόμενος ἐν ἀταραξίᾳ νοὸς ὡς δὲ καὶ ἀνθρώπων παρενοχλήσεως ἄνευθε ταύτην ποιήσασθαι, τῇ ἑβδόμῃ τοῦ Μαΐου μηνὸς τὴν ἀνακομιδὴν τοῦ λειψάνου τοῦ ὁσίου πατρὸς ἡμῶν Εὐθυμίου ἐπιτελεῖν σχηματισάμενος καὶ

Chapter 37

After shepherding his flock for fourteen years without revealing his identity, the holy one made himself known to his relatives and family after forty-two years, just like Joseph. And, like him, Euthymios summoned them and looked after them and, after buying a plot of land for them, he established a nunnery for the women, one that prospered in every way, and entrusted the administration of his monastery to the men.

Then he invited Methodios, the holy archbishop of Thessalonike, to both monasteries, and arranged for the installation of saints' relics and a holy altar in them, and dedicated both monasteries to God. Not long after, he handed over the two monasteries to his grandson Methodios and the latter's sister Euphemia, having prepared them to be superiors in them. He himself, as if having cast off the burden of his care for them, went up on the pillar where he had previously been. 2

But since it was impossible for him to have any spiritual tranquility on it, he went back again to the heights of Athos. But there, too, he saw that the monks were distracting him, especially his own monks, so he rid himself of them, considering them a burden, and embraced the wilderness, foreseeing the date of his own departure from life, and desiring to experience this in peace of mind and without human disturbance. On the 7th of May he made a show of celebrating the translation of the relic of our blessed father Euthymios the 3

πάντας τοὺς σὺν αὐτῷ ἀδελφοὺς συνεστιαθῆναι αὐτῷ προτρεψάμενος, λεληθότως αὐτοῖς συνταξάμενος, τῇ ἐπαύριον πάντας διαλαθὼν τῇ Ἱερᾷ λεγομένῃ νήσῳ λέμβῳ ἐπιβὰς διαπορθμεύεται, Γεώργιόν τινα μοναχὸν ὑπηρετεῖν αὐτῷ μονώτατον προσλαβόμενος. Ἔνθα διαρκέσας μέχρι τρισκαιδεκάτης τοῦ Ὀκτωβρίου μηνὸς τῆς δευτέρας ἐπινεμήσεως, μικρὰ νοσήσας (ὅσον ἄνθρωπον ὄντα ὑποπεσεῖν τοῖς τῆς φύσεως ἰδιώμασιν), τῇ ιε΄ τοῦ αὐτοῦ Ὀκτωβρίου μηνὸς ἐν εἰρήνῃ ἐπὶ τὸ αὐτὸ *ἐκοιμήθη καὶ ὕπνωσε* [3 Kings 19:5], τῶν μακρῶν ἱδρώτων καὶ τῆς πολυχρονίου ἀσκήσεως τοῦτο λαβὼν ἀνταπόδομα, *τὸ ἀναλῦσαι καὶ σὺν Χριστῷ εἶναι* [Philippians 1:23], ᾧ ζῶν καὶ πολιτευόμενος νεκρὸς τῷ βίῳ ἐδείκνυτο, πᾶσαν θανατώσας ἐπιθυμίαν καὶ σαρκὸς κίνησιν ἀντιστρατευομένην τῷ πνεύματι.

4   Προσετέθη δὲ τοῖς πρὸ αὐτοῦ μεγάλη προσθήκη καὶ ἐπέραστος, τοῖς πατριάρχαις ὡς ζηλώσας αὐτῶν τὸ ὁμότροπον, τοῖς ἀποστόλοις ὡς τῆς διδασκαλίας τηρητὴς καὶ τῆς πράξεως συμμέτοχος, τοῖς προφήταις ὡς διορατικώτατος ὑπάρξας καὶ προβλεπτικώτατος, τοῖς ἀρχιερεῦσιν ὡς ἱερεύς, τοῖς διδασκάλοις ὡς πρακτικὸς καὶ θεωρητικὸς διδάσκαλος, τοῖς ὁσίοις καὶ δικαίοις ὡς ὁσίως καὶ δικαίως πολιτευσάμενος, καὶ πᾶσιν ἁπλῶς τοῖς ἁγίοις ὡς ἅγιος, χορεύει τε περὶ Θεὸν καὶ τῶν ἐν ἐπαγγελίαις ἀγαθῶν ἀποκληροῦται τὴν κατάσχεσιν.

Great and invited all his brethren to dine with him; and then, secretly taking his leave of them, on the next day, without anyone's knowledge, he embarked on a boat and crossed over to the island called Hiera, taking along only a monk named George to serve him. He remained there until the 13th of the month of October of the second indiction, and then, after a short illness (since, being human, he was subject to the realities of nature), *he fell asleep* peacefully on the 15th of the same month of October *and went to his repose* at the same time. The reward Euthymios received for his long hard labor and many years of asceticism was *to depart and to be with Christ,* to whom, while he was alive and conducting his life, he showed himself dead to life, having killed every desire and urge of the flesh that militated against the spirit.

He made a great and desirable addition to his precursors: 4 to the patriarchs inasmuch as he strove to achieve a way of life similar to theirs; to the apostles as a preserver of their teaching and a fellow participant in their actions; to the prophets as being most clairvoyant and most foreseeing; to the bishops as a priest; to the teachers as a practical and contemplative teacher; to the blessed and righteous as one who conducted his life in a blessed and righteous manner; and, in short, to all the saints as a saint; and he is part of the choir that surrounds God and inherits the possession of the promised blessings.

38

Διαγνωσθείσης οὖν ὀψὲ τοῦ καιροῦ ὑπό τινος μοναχοῦ τῆς αὐτοῦ ἐν Κυρίῳ κοιμήσεως, οἱ τῆς αὐτοῦ μονῆς, πόθῳ τοῦ καὶ μετὰ θάνατον ἔχειν αὐτὸν φρουρὸν καὶ ὑπερασπίζοντα, διὰ Παύλου μοναχοῦ καὶ Βλασίου πρεσβυτέρου ἐν ξυλίνῃ λάρνακι τοῦτον ἑαυτοῖς ἀνακομίζουσι, σῷον εὑρημένον καὶ ἄρτιον, οἷον ἔστιν ἰδεῖν τὸν αὔθωρον καὶ αὐθήμερον τελευτήσαντα, καὶ ταῦτα μέχρι Δεκεμβρίου εἰκάδος δευτέρας ἐν τῷ σπηλαίῳ χρονίσαντος καὶ τῇ τρισκαιδεκάτῃ τοῦ Ἰανουαρίου μηνὸς ἐν τῇ μαρτυροπλουτίστῳ τῶν Θεσσαλονικέων πόλει τοῖς μαθηταῖς ἐπιφοιτήσαντος.

2   Καὶ νῦν ἡμῖν ὁ πολὺς καὶ μέγας Εὐθύμιος, εὐλογίας ἀπαρχή, νεκρὸς ζωηφόρος, διδάσκαλος πρακτικός, σιωπῶν παραινέτης, μᾶλλον δὲ καὶ μεγάλα βοῶν ἐν τοῖς θαύμασιν, ἐπόπτης τῶν πρακτέων, σωφρονιστὴς τῶν πλημμελουμένων, συντηρητὴς τῶν κατορθουμένων, φύλαξ τῶν μετὰ πεποιθήσεως αὐτῷ προσανεχόντων, ῥύστης τῶν ἀνιώντων, περιποιητὴς τῶν εὐθύμων, πάντων ἀγαθῶν ἐν τῇ πρὸς Θεὸν μεσιτείᾳ ἐπιχορηγῶν, ἐκ τῆς Ἱερᾶς νήσου μετακομίζεται, ὕμνοις ἐξ ὕμνων παραπεμπόμενος, μοναχῶν ὤμοις ἀνακλινόμενος, ἀρχιερέων χερσὶ μυριζόμενος, ἀσκητῶν δήμοις ἐπευφημούμενος, κληρικῶν ἱερᾷ προπομπῇ τιμώμενος, λαοῦ εὐσεβοῦς καὶ θεοφιλῶν γυναίων κηροφανείαις καταπυρσευόμενος καὶ τῇ ἱερᾷ ταύτῃ ἐναποτιθέμενος λάρνακι, ἔνθα ὡς ζῶν ἡμῖν καθορώμενος σώματι

Chapter 38

Sometime later, when his falling asleep in the Lord was made known by a monk, the monks of his monastery at Peristerai, in their desire to retain him even after his death as their guardian and defender, and, through the agency of the monk Paul and the priest Blasios, used a wooden coffin to bring his body back to them. It was discovered to be intact and whole, such as one might see in the case of someone who had died at that same hour or on that very day, in spite of the fact that it had remained in the cave until December 22 and came to his disciples in the martyr-rich city of Thessalonike on January 13.

And now our famous and great Euthymios, the source of 2 blessing, the life-bearing corpse, the one who teaches through actions, the one who exhorts in silence, or rather cries out loudly through his miracles, the supervisor of what should be done, the chastiser of those who sin, the preserver of those who succeed, the guardian of those who confidently devote themselves to him, the savior from grievous troubles, the provider of joy, the one who supplies all manner of good things through his mediation with God, is transferred from the island of Hiera, escorted with a succession of hymns, resting on the shoulders of monks, anointed with perfumed oil by the hands of bishops, acclaimed by crowds of ascetics, honored with a holy procession of clerics, illuminated by the candles of pious men and God-loving women, and lying in this holy coffin, where, still looking to us as though he is alive, he delivers us from the sufferings of the

μὲν ἡμῶν ἀποκαθαίρει τὰ πάθη τοῦ σώματος, ψυχῇ δὲ
πρεσβεύει βελτιοῦσθαι ἡμῶν τῆς ψυχῆς τὰ κινήματα.

39

ʽΗμῖν μὲν ἐπὶ τοσοῦτον ἀποχρώντως τόδε σοι προσ-
ανατέθειται τὸ ἐφύμνιον· σὺ δὲ ἡμᾶς ἐποπτεύοις ἄνωθεν,
ὦ θεία καὶ ἱερὰ κεφαλή, καὶ ὡς ἀμέσως τανῦν προσομιλῶν
Θεῷ καὶ βλέπειν τοῦτον σὺν ἀγγέλοις καταξιούμενος,
μέμνησο Βασιλείου τοῦ σοῦ, ἐκεῖνο Θεὸν ἀντιδοῦναι ἡμῖν
ἐξαιτούμενος, ὃ καὶ ἐν τῷ βίῳ περιὼν πολλάκις ὑπὲρ ἡμῶν
καθικέτευσας, ἀξίως ἡμᾶς τῆς κλήσεως καὶ τοῦ ἐπαγγέλμα-
τος πολιτεύεσθαι.

2   Ὁρᾷς τὸ ἐπισφαλὲς τοῦ ἀξιώματος καὶ ὡς μεγάλων
ἐγκλημάτων αἴτιον τοῖς ἀμελήσασιν· ἐπάρηξον ἡμῖν περιτραπῆναι κινδυνεύουσι· *πολλὰ ἰσχύει δέησις δικαίου ἐνερ-
γουμένη* [James 5:16], καὶ ταῦτα πατρός, ᾧ τὸ ἀνύειν ὑπὸ
Θεοῦ πολλαχόσε προκατεπήγγελται. Ἔχεις συνεργὸν
ὑπὲρ ἁμαρτωλῶν τὴν Θεοτόκον συνικετεύουσαν· συναγω-
νιεῖταί σοι καὶ ὁ *τῆς παλαιᾶς καὶ καινῆς μεσίτης ὡς τὴν μετάνοιαν κηρύξας* [see Mark 1:4], ὑπὲρ διορθώσεως ἀνθρώπου
τὴν ἱκεσίαν προσάγοντι· ἀποδέξεται καὶ Θεὸς αὐτὸς τὸ
τῆς προθέσεως εὐσυμπάθητον, ὁ *πάντας θέλων σωθῆναι
καὶ εἰς ἐπίγνωσιν ἀληθείας ἐλθεῖν* [1 Timothy 2:4]· μόνον
αὐτὸς εἰς ἱκεσίαν τὴν παρρησίαν ἐπιτάχυνον.

body through his body, and intercedes for the betterment of our souls through his soul.

Chapter 39

This eulogy, such as it is, has been my offering to you, Euthymios; may you watch over me from above, O divine and holy head, and since you now address God directly and are deemed worthy to see Him together with the angels, remember your Basil, asking God to reward me with that for which you, while still alive, often entreated Him on my behalf, that is, to conduct my office in a manner worthy of my calling and my vows.

You see the peril of my position and that for the negligent it can be the cause of serious allegations. Help me when I am in danger of going astray; for *the prayer of a righteous man has great power in its effects,* and this is true of a father to whom the accomplishment of this in many ways was previously promised by God. You have as your assistant the Mother of God who makes supplication together with you on behalf of sinners. When you offer supplication for the correction of mankind, you also have as a fellow contender *the interceder of the Old and New Testaments* (that is, John the Baptist), as one who has *preached repentance.* And God Himself, *He who desires all men to be saved and to come to the knowledge of the truth,* will accept your compassionate intention; only make haste to utter confident supplication.

3   Προσλαβοῦ Πέτρον, Ἀνδρέαν τὸν πρωτόκλητον συμ-
πρεσβευτὴν ἀποκλήρωσαι· ἔχεις ἀφορμὰς εὐπορίστους
τὰς ἰσχυούσας αὐτοὺς ἐκβιάζεσθαι, Πέτρον μὲν ὡς τῆς
ἐκκλησίας ἀρωγὸν καὶ θεμέλιον, ἧς ὀρθοδοξούσης ὡς
ἀρχιερεῖς ἐξηρτήμεθα, Ἀνδρέαν δ᾽αὖθις ὡς τῆς ποίμνης
ἐξάρχοντα καὶ ὑπ᾽αὐτὸν ἡμᾶς τεταγμένους ἀποκληρωσά-
μενον, ὡς ἂν μεθ᾽ ὑμῶν κἀκεῖθεν, εἰ καὶ παρ᾽ἀξίαν καὶ μέγα
τὸ αἰτούμενον, ἐν ἐσχάτοις τεταγμένοι τοῦ φωτισμοῦ Κυρίου μεταλάβοιμεν, οὗ καὶ ἐνταῦθα τῶν ἰνδαλμάτων ὑπο-
δεχθείημεν τὴν λαμπρότητα ἐν αὐτῷ Χριστῷ τῷ Κυρίῳ
ἡμῶν, ᾧ ἡ δόξα σὺν τῷ ἀνάρχῳ Πατρὶ καὶ τῷ συμφυεῖ καὶ
ἁγίῳ Πνεύματι, νῦν καὶ εἰς τοὺς ἀτελευτήτους αἰῶνας τῶν
αἰώνων, ἀμήν.

Take as your helper Peter, and choose Andrew, the first-   3
called disciple, as your fellow intercessor. You have plausible
reasons for insisting on their intervention, in the case of Peter as the helper and foundation of the Church, upon which
I, as a bishop, depend as the teacher of correct doctrine; and
in the case of Andrew again as the leader of the flock and
as the one allotted me by my appointment under him. So,
<with them, make supplication that>, when I receive my assignment in the last days, I may share the illumination of
the Lord with you from that time forward, even if what I
ask is great and undeserved; and may I receive from him in
this life the brightness of the reflections of that illumination
in Christ Himself our Lord, to whom be glory together with
the Father who is without beginning and the Holy Spirit
which is of one nature with Him, now and unto the unending ages of ages, Amen.

LIFE OF ATHANASIOS OF ATHOS, VERSION B

Βίος καὶ ἀγῶνες καὶ μερικὴ θαυμάτων διήγησις τοῦ ὁσίου πατρὸς ἡμῶν Ἀθανασίου τοῦ ἐν τῷ Ἄθῳ

I

Οἱ τῶν ἀρίστων ἀνδρῶν ἀνάγραπτοι βίοι καὶ τοῖς παλαιοῖς μὲν ἀναγκαῖοι ὑπῆρχον διὰ τὸ ἐκ τούτων τοῖς ἀνθρώποις προσγινόμενον ὄφελος· τῇ δέ γε καθ᾽ ἡμᾶς ὀψιγόνῳ γενεᾷ, εἰς ἣν τὰ τέλη τῶν αἰώνων κατήντησαν [1 Corinthians 10:11], καὶ λίαν ἀναγκαιότεροι καθεστήκασι, τοῦτο μὲν ὅτι μὴ τὰς τῆς ἀρετῆς ἐμψύχους εἰκόνας καθάπερ ἐκεῖνοι πολλὰς κεκτήμεθα, τοῦτο δὲ καὶ διὰ τὴν ἐνοῦσαν ἡμῖν ῥαθυμίαν· μόλις γὰρ ἂν καὶ πολλὰ καὶ μεγάλα τὰ παραδείγματα πρὸς βραχεῖαν ἡμᾶς κινήσωσι τοῦ βίου διόρθωσιν.

2   Διά τοι ταῦτα τὸν τοῦ τρισμάκαρος Ἀθανασίου βίον τοῦ ἐν τῷ Ἄθῳ ἀσκήσαντος εἰς διήγησιν προτίθημι καὶ τοῖς προλαβοῦσι προστίθημι διηγήμασιν, οὐκ ἐξ ἀκοῆς μόνης τοῦτον παραλαβών, ἀλλὰ πολλοῖς ἐντυχὼν τοῖς περὶ ἐκείνου συγγράμμασιν, ἅπερ οἱ αὐτοῦ φοιτηταὶ τοῖς μετ᾽ ἐκείνους κατέλιπον, ὡς κλήρου τινὰ διαδοχὴν καὶ θησαυρὸν πολύολβον τῇ ἐκείνου ποίμνῃ παραπέμψαντες.

Life and trials and a partial narration of the miracles of our
blessed father Athanasios of Athos

Chapter 1

The biographies of the most excellent of men were certainly necessary for those in olden days because of the benefit that people derived from them, but they have become
even more necessary for our present generation, *upon* whom
the end of the ages has come, on the one hand because we do not
have as many living icons of virtue as they did, and on the
other because of our inherent indolence. For even a large
number of great examples would barely nudge us toward a
modest improvement in our way of life.

For these reasons I am setting forth in narrative form the $\quad$ 2
life of the thrice-blessed Athanasios who was an ascetic on
Athos, adding it to those earlier narratives. I have ascer-
tained information concerning this not only from hearsay,
but also by reading many works about him, which his disciples left for their successors, transmitting them as a legacy
and spiritually valuable treasure for his flock. My account

Προβήσεται δὲ ἡμῖν ὁ λόγος οὐκ ἐγκωμιαστικός, ἀλλ' ἀφηγηματικὸς μᾶλλον, διὰ τὴν τῶν ἀναγινωσκόντων ὠφέλειαν πλέον καὶ οὐ διὰ τὴν τοῦ ἀνδρὸς εὐφημίαν γενόμενος.

3 Ἀνενδεής τε γὰρ ἐκεῖνος τῶν ἀνθρωπίνων ἐπαίνων, τῶν θείων πλήρης τυγχάνων καὶ ἀγγελικῶν, καὶ ἄλλως οὐδὲ ὁ φιλοσοφώτατος νοῦς καὶ πρὸς λόγων γένεσιν πορ” μώτατος πρὸς τὸ τοιοῦτον ἔργον ἀποδύσαιτο ἄν, μὴ ὅτι γε ἡμεῖς, οἷς ὁ νοῦς μὲν ἐμπαθὴς καὶ ἀκάθαρτος καὶ ἄπορος ἐννοιῶν σοφωτάτων, ὁ δὲ λόγος ἀνάσκητος πάντῃ καὶ ἀπαίδευτος καὶ ὡς εἰπεῖν βάρβαρος. Πλὴν ἐπεὶ καὶ Θεῷ καὶ ἀνθρώπων τοῖς εὐγνωμονεστέροις φίλον τὸ κατὰ δύναμιν, ἀρξόμεθα τῆς διηγήσεως· ἀρξόμεθα δὲ ὅθεν ἄρχεσθαι ἄμεινον· ἄμεινον δὲ ὅθεν ὁ μέγας ἤρξατο τῆς εἰς τὸν βίον παραγωγῆς καὶ τῆς πρώτης γεννήσεως.

2

Τοῦτον τοιγαροῦν ἤνεγκε μὲν ἡ μεγαλόπολις Τραπεζοῦς, ηὔξησε δὲ λογικῶς ἡ Βυζαντίς, Κυμινᾶς δὲ καὶ Ἄθως ἐκαρποφόρησαν τῷ Θεῷ [Romans 7:4]. Ἀλλ' ἡ μὲν ἐνεγκαμένη τοῦτον θαυμαστή τις οἵα ἐστίν, οὐ μόνον ὅτι εὐφορωτάτη τυγχάνει τῶν πρὸς τρυφὴν καὶ ἀπόλαυσιν, ἀλλ' ὅτι καὶ ἄνδρας φέρει χρηστοὺς καὶ ἐραστὰς τοῦ καλοῦ καὶ ἐργάτας τῆς ἀρετῆς. Οἱ δὲ τούτου γεννήτορες γεγέννην-

will be couched not in the form of an encomium, but rather as a narrative, being produced more for the benefit of its readers than for the good repute of its hero.

For Athanasios has no need of human praise, since he has quite enough of divine and angelic praise. Moreover, not even the most erudite mind, one most fertile in literary production, would endeavor to undertake such a work, let alone myself, whose mind is subject to passions and impure and lacking in wise thoughts, and whose speech is in every way unpracticed and untrained and, one might almost say, barbarous. But since *to do one's best is pleasing to God and the more sensible of men,* we will begin our narrative, and *we will begin at the point where it is best to begin; for it is best to begin at the point where* the great one was first brought to life and his first birth.

Chapter 2

Thus the great city of Trebizond gave birth to him, while the city of Byzantion nurtured him intellectually, and Mounts Kyminas and Athos *offered him as fruits to God.* But it is his native city that is most wondrous, not only because it is most fertile in products that lead to delight and enjoyment, but because it gives birth to worthy men, lovers of the good and workers of virtue. His parents had also been born

ται μὲν καὶ αὐτοὶ ἐκ τῆς εἰρημένης πόλεως· πλὴν ὁ μὲν ἐξ Ἀντιοχείας τῆς μεγάλης εἷλκε τὸ γένος, ἡ δὲ ἐκ Κολχίδος τῆς ἐπαινετῆς καὶ θαυμαστῆς πόλεως· οἵτινες εὐγενεῖς ὄντες καὶ πλούσιοι καὶ πᾶσι περίβλεπτοι, εὐγενέστεροι καὶ τὴν γνώμην ἐτύγχανον καὶ τὴν ἀρετὴν πλουσιώτεροι καὶ μακάριοι, ὅτι πατέρες γεγόνασι τοιούτου παιδός.

2   Ἀλλ' ὁ μὲν πατὴρ σπείρας τοῦτον, πρὸ τοῦ τεχθῆναι αὐτόν, τὴν ζωὴν ἐξεμέτρησεν· ἡ δὲ μήτηρ τέξασα καὶ γαλακτοτροφήσασα καὶ Ἀβραάμιον ὀνομάσασα, εἶτα χρόνον ὀλίγον ἐπιβιώσασα, ἐπαπῆλθε καὶ αὐτὴ τῷ ἀνδρί. Ὁ Ἀβραάμιος δέ, εἰ καὶ τοῦ πατρὸς ἀπωρφανίσθη καὶ τῆς μητρός, ἀλλὰ τῆς τοῦ Θεοῦ κηδεμονίας, τοῦ πατρὸς τῶν ὀρφανῶν [Psalm 67(68):5], οὐκ ἀπωρφανίζετο· γυνὴ γάρ τις τῶν εὐγενῶν καὶ πλουσίων, παρθένος οὖσα καὶ μοναχή, γνώριμος καὶ προσφιλὴς ἐτύγχανε τῇ μητρὶ τοῦ παιδός, ἥτις ἀλγήσασα τὴν καρδίαν ἐπὶ τῇ ὀρφανίᾳ αὐτοῦ καὶ μονώσει ἀνέλαβε πρὸς αὐτὸν στοργὴν φυσικῆς μητρὸς καὶ ἀνεδέξατο τοῦτον καὶ ἀνέτρεφε καὶ ἀνῆγεν εὐγενῶς τε καὶ εὐσεβῶς.

3   Οὕτω τοίνυν τὸ εὐγενέστατον τοῦτο γέννημα ἀναγόμενον, οὐκ εἶχεν ἦθος ἄκοσμόν τε καὶ ἄτακτον, οὐ λίχνος τὴν γαστέρα ἐτύγχανεν, οὐ πρὸς φαῦλα καὶ ἄσεμνα ἔνευεν, ἀλλ' ἐν ἅπασιν ἐδείκνυ συνετὸν καὶ σῶφρον καὶ ἀβραμιαῖον ἀληθῶς φρόνημα. Ὅταν δὲ ἔπαιζε, προεφητεύετο ὑπὸ Θεοῦ ὅπερ ἔπαιζε· συναρπάζοντες γὰρ αὐτὸν εἰς παίγνιον οἱ ἡλικιῶται αὐτοῦ, σπήλαιόν τι τῶν ἐγχωρίων κατελάμβανον, καὶ οὐκ ἐψήφιζον τοῦτον βασιλέα ἢ στρατηγὸν ἢ νυμφίον ἐποίουν, ὅπερ ὡς τὰ πολλὰ τοῖς παισὶν

in the aforementioned city, although his father's family originated from Antioch the Great, and his mother's from the renowned and marvelous city of Kolchis. They were noble people, who were wealthy and prominent in all respects, but they became even nobler in purpose and richer in virtue and blessed because they were the parents of such a child.

The father who sired him, however, completed the span 2 of his life before he was born, while his mother, after giving birth and breastfeeding him and naming him Abraamios, lived a short time longer, but then departed to join her husband in death. Abraamios, however, even if he was orphaned of father and mother, was not deprived of the guardianship of God, *the father of orphans.* For a noble and wealthy woman, who was a virgin and nun, and had been a dear friend of the boy's mother, grieving in her heart at his orphaned and solitary state, developed for him the love of a natural mother; and so she took him in and nurtured him and raised him in a noble and pious way.

So this most noble child, being raised in this way, exhibited no inappropriate or disorderly behavior, nor was he 3 greedy, nor did he have vulgar or ignoble inclinations, but in all things displayed an intelligent and prudent attitude, truly worthy of his namesake Abraham. And even when he played, his playacting was actually a prophecy from God. For when his companions took him along to play and they went to a local cave, they did not choose him as an emperor or general or make him a bridegroom, as children usually do, but they

εἴθισται, ἀλλ᾽ ἀρχηγὸν καὶ νομοθέτην βίου μονήρους προεχειρίζοντο· καὶ ἦσαν μὲν οἱ παῖδες αὐτῷ ὑποκείμενοι, αὐτὸς δὲ ἐθεωρεῖτο ἐν τούτοις ἐν τάξει καθηγητοῦ. Πάντως δὲ προεδείκνυεν αὐτὸν ὁ Θεὸς καθηγεμόνα καὶ προστάτην ποιμνίων πολλῶν, ὅπερ καὶ γέγονεν, ἀποκαρέντων ὕστερον καὶ αὐτῶν τῶν παίδων τῶν συμπαιζόντων αὐτῷ.

3

Ἐπεὶ δὲ ἡ μητρικῶς ἀνατρέφουσα τὸν Ἀβραάμιον μοναχὴ προσευχαῖς καὶ νηστείαις ἐνδελεχῶς προσέκειτο, ὁρῶν ταύτην οὗτος οὕτω πράττουσαν, ξένον τι ἐδόκει ὁρᾶν καὶ πειρώμενος τὴν αἰτίαν μαθεῖν ἠρώτα αὐτήν· ἡ δέ φησιν· "Ὦ τέκνον, ἡμεῖς οἱ φοροῦντες τοῦτο τὸ ἔνδυμα ὀφείλομεν γρηγορεῖν ἐν νηστείαις καὶ προσευχαῖς, ὅτι ὁ ἐχθρὸς ἡμῶν Διάβολος περιέρχεται καθεκάστην ὡς λέων ζητῶν τίνα καταπίῃ [1 Peter 5:8] Χριστιανόν." Ὁ δὲ ἀκούσας εὐφράνθη λίαν, καὶ ἔθετο ἔκτοτε τὰ παιδικὰ πάντα καταλιπεῖν καὶ ζῆν ἐν σωφροσύνῃ καὶ ἐγκρατείᾳ.

2   Ἐντεῦθεν οὖν ὁ παῖς ἀρχὴν σοφίας ἐλάμβανε τὸν τοῦ Θεοῦ φόβον [see Proverbs 1:7], καὶ τὸν πόθον αὐτοῦ συνελάμβανε, καὶ ἐπελαμβάνετο τῆς θείας ὁδοῦ καὶ ἐκραταιοῦτο τῇ τοῦ Πνεύματος χάριτι. Εὐθὺς οὖν γραμματιστῇ παραδιδόμενος τῆς τῶν βίβλων ἀναγνώσεως ἕνεκεν,

appointed him as a leader and legislator of monastic life. And the children would obey him, and he would be treated by them as if he were in the position of their spiritual instructor. Surely God thus revealed in advance that he would be a spiritual leader and a guardian of many flocks, something which came to pass, for later on even the very boys who used to play with him received the tonsure.

Chapter 3

Since the nun who raised Abraamios like a mother used to engage in assiduous prayer and fasting, he was puzzled when he saw her acting in this way and, seeking to find the reason, asked her. She replied, "My child, we who wear this habit need to be vigilant in fasting and prayer, because *our* enemy *the Devil* goes around every day like a *lion seeking to devour* a Christian." When he heard these words he was very happy, and decided to abandon all childish things from that moment on and to live in prudence and self-control.

So, from then on, the child received the *fear* of God as *a beginning of wisdom,* realized what it was he desired, and set forth upon the divine path, fortified by the grace of the Spirit. He was thus immediately entrusted to a teacher of grammar to learn to read books, and he was a source of as-

ἔκπληξις ἦν τῷ τε διδάσκοντι καὶ τοῖς συμμανθάνουσι, φύσιν ἔχων ἐπιτηδείαν καὶ ἀγῶνα περὶ τὸ μανθάνειν πολύν.

4

Ὡς δὲ τὴν παιδικὴν ἡλικίαν παρῆλθεν ἤδη, ἐν τοσούτῳ ἐτελεύτησε τὸν βίον καὶ ἡ θαυμαστὴ ἐκείνη γυνή, ἡ θετὴ μήτηρ τοῦ Ἀβρααμίου. Καὶ λοιπὸν δι᾽ ἐπιθυμίας εἶχεν ὅτι πολλῆς ὁ καλὸς οὗτος παῖς πρὸς τὴν βασιλίδα γενέσθαι καὶ τῆς γραμματικῆς ἐπιστήμης πεῖραν λαβεῖν· καὶ ταύτης τῆς ἐπιθυμίας οὐδέν τι τοῦτον ἐχώριζεν, οὐκ ἀπορία ἀνθρωπίνης προνοίας, οὐκ ὀρφανίας λύπη, οὔτε ἄλλη στέρησις τῆς ἀναγκαίας χρείας τοῦ σώματος, ἀλλὰ ἀμηχανία εἶχεν αὐτόν, πῶς ἂν αὐτοῦ τὸ καταθύμιον γένοιτο.

2 Ὁ δὲ Θεός, ὁ πόρον ἐν ἀπόροις διδούς, συνήργησε καὶ τούτῳ δι᾽ οἰκονομίας τινὸς πρὸς τὸ τελεσθῆναι αὐτοῦ τὸ κατὰ σκοπόν· βασιλεύοντος γὰρ τῷ τότε τοῦ ἀοιδίμου Ῥωμανοῦ (ὃς ἐν συγκρίσει τοῦ νέου γέρων ὠνόμαστο), πέμπεταί τις εὐνοῦχος κομμερκιάριος ἐν Τραπεζοῦντι, ὅστις ἰδὼν τὸν παῖδα σώφρονά τε καὶ συνετώτατον καὶ τῷ ὄντι φυτὸν τοῦ Θεοῦ, ἠγάπησε λίαν καὶ γνησίως ἐνηγκαλίσατο τοῦτον καὶ συνόντα εἶχεν αὐτῷ καὶ συνεσθίοντα. Ἐπεὶ δὲ οὗτος ὁ κομμερκιάριος ἀνακάμπτειν ἐβούλετο πρὸς τὴν βασιλεύουσαν, ἐλάμβανε καὶ τὸν παῖδα μεθ᾽ ἑαυτοῦ διὰ τὴν ἐνοῦσαν αὐτῷ ἀρετήν· ὁ δὲ παῖς ἠκολούθει αὐτῷ, τῷ πόθῳ τῶν γραμμάτων ἀγόμενος.

tonishment to both his teacher and fellow pupils, since he had natural aptitude and much engagement in learning.

Chapter 4

A braamios had already passed childhood when that wondrous woman, his foster mother, reached the end of her life. Then this fine boy developed a great desire to go to the Queen of Cities to be trained in grammatical knowledge; and nothing would thwart his desire, neither his lack of human protection, nor the grief of orphanhood, nor any other absence of physical necessities, but he was uncertain as to how to achieve his desire.

But God, *Who provides a way for those in difficulty,* supported him through some divine dispensation to achieve his purpose. For at that time, during the reign of the celebrated Romanos (the one who is called the Elder in contrast with the Younger), a eunuch *kommerkiarios* was dispatched to Trebizond. At first sight of the boy, who was well-behaved and very intelligent and truly a scion of God, he conceived a great affection for him, received him with open arms, and took the boy to live with him and share his table. When this *kommerkiarios* decided to return to the imperial city, he took the boy along as well, on account of his innate virtue, and the boy followed him, led by his desire for learning.

2

3   Εἰσελθόντων τοίνυν ἀμφοτέρων εἰς τὴν βασιλεύουσαν,
ἐφεῦρεν ὁ κομμερκιάριος τῷ παιδὶ διδάσκαλον, Ἀθανάσιον
τοὔνομα, ἄνδρα τήν τε γνῶσιν καὶ τὸν λόγον καὶ τὴν
πρᾶξιν τοῦ βίου ἀσύγκριτον· ὁ δὲ παῖς, ὀξέως νοῶν καὶ
ἀνενδότως πονῶν περὶ τὰ μαθήματα, οὐδὲ τῆς ἀρετῆς
ἠμέλει, ἀλλ' ἤσκει ἐπιμελῶς ἐπιτεταμένην ἐγκράτειαν καὶ
πολλὴν σκληραγωγίαν· ὅσῳ γὰρ ἔτρεφε τὸν νοῦν τοῖς τῆς
σοφίας μαθήμασι, τοσούτῳ τὴν σάρκα ἐλιμοκτόνει καὶ
ἐξεπίεζεν· ἠπίστατο γάρ, κατὰ τὸν Παῦλον, ὅτι πάντα μὲν
ἔξεστιν, ἀλλ' οὐ πάντα συμφέρει [1 Corinthians 10:23], καὶ
ἔσπευδεν ὁ καλὸς μαθητὴς ἐξισωθῆναι κατὰ πάντα τῷ
καλῷ διδασκάλῳ.

5

Ἦν δέ τις ἀνὴρ ἐν Βυζαντίδι, Ζεφιναζὲρ τὴν κλῆσιν,
τὴν ἀξίαν δὲ στρατηγός, ὅστις συγγενίδα τοῦ Ἀβρααμίου
ἐνυμφεύσατο εἰς τὸν τούτου υἱόν. Ὑπὸ τούτου τοῦ στρα-
τηγοῦ ἀναγνωρισθείς, ἔνδον τῆς οἰκίας αὐτοῦ γίνεται· ἡ
δὲ νύμφη τούτου, ὡς ἀνεγνώρισε τὸ αἷμα τὸ ἴδιον, ἐχάρη
τῇ ψυχῇ καὶ φαιδροῖς ἑώρακε τοῦτον τοῖς ὀφθαλμοῖς, εἶτα
καὶ παρεκάλει αὐτὸν ἅμα τῷ ἀνδρὶ καὶ τῷ πενθερῷ συνοι-
κεῖν αὐτοῖς τοῦ λοιποῦ· ἔλεγον γὰρ αὐτῷ· "Ὦ γλυκύτατε,
οὐ προτιμότερον ἄρα τὸ γένος τὸ σὸν εἰς δουλαγωγίαν σοι
ὑπὲρ τὸ ἀλλότριον;" Ἐπείσθη οὖν ἐκεῖνος μετὰ τὴν πολλὴν
ἐκείνων παράκλησιν.

And so when they both arrived at the imperial city, the ₃ *kommerkiarios* found a teacher for the boy, a man named Athanasios, who was peerless in knowledge, learning, and manner of life. And the boy, while exercising his sharp intellect and working ceaselessly at his studies, also did not neglect the pursuit of virtue, but assiduously practiced intense abstinence and great physical mortification. For he starved and oppressed his flesh to the same extent that he nourished his mind with the study of wisdom. For he knew that, in the words of Paul, *all things are lawful but not all things are helpful,* and the good student strove to emulate his good teacher in all things.

Chapter 5

There was a man in Byzantion named Zephinazer, a general in rank, who had arranged his son's marriage to a kinswoman of Abraamios. After coming to the attention of this general, Abraamios was invited to his house. When the bride recognized that they were related by blood, she rejoiced in her soul and gazed at him with shining eyes, and then, together with her husband and father-in-law, she begged him to live with them from that moment on. For they said to him, "Dearest boy, isn't it better for your own kin to look after you rather than another family?" And so he was persuaded after their many entreaties.

6

Ἀλλὰ τὴν μὲν ἐγκράτειαν ἤδη καὶ τὴν ἄλλην ἄσκησιν ἐκ ψυχῆς ἀσπασάμενος, ἰδιάζουσαν καὶ τὴν διαγωγὴν ἔχειν ἤθελεν· οἱ δὲ συγγενεῖς αὐτῷ χαλεπῶς καὶ λυπηρῶς τοῦτο ἔφερον· οὐδὲ γὰρ ἐπείθετο συνεσθίειν αὐτοῖς· καὶ ποῦ γὰρ ἄξιον τὸν ἐγκρατῆ συνεσθίειν τοῖς τρυφηταῖς; Δύο δὲ τῶν δούλων αὐτοῖς ἔταξαν εἰς ὑπηρεσίαν αὐτοῦ· καὶ ἐχορηγεῖτο αὐτῷ διὰ τῶν τοιούτων ἡ ἡμερήσιος τροφή, ἄρτος τε καθαρώτατος καὶ ἰχθύες καὶ ὀπῶραι καὶ εἴ τι ἄλλο τοὺς ἀγνοφαγοῦντας παραμυθεῖται. Καὶ οἱ μὲν συγγενεῖς ἐνόμιζον ἄρα αὐτὸν ἐσθίειν τὰ ἀποστελλόμενα, ὁ δὲ σώφρων οὗτος καὶ ξένος ἐγκρατευτὴς τῶν μὲν ἄλλων ἁπάντων τοῖς οἰκέταις παρεχώρει, τὸν δὲ καθαρώτατον ἄρτον ἀποδοκιμάζων, παρεκάλει αὐτοὺς πωλεῖν καὶ ἐξωνεῖσθαι αὐτῷ ἄρτον κρίθινον ἑνὸς φόλεως, ὃν καὶ μόνον ἤσθιε δι᾽ ἡμερῶν δύο. Εἰ δέ ποτε καὶ ἔδει παραμυθήσασθαι τὸ σῶμα, ὠμοῖς λαχάνοις καὶ ὀπώραις ἐπλήρου αὐτῷ τὴν παράκλησιν· τὸ δὲ ἴαμα τοῦ δίψους αὐτῷ τὸ νηφάλιον ὕδωρ ἦν· ἐχορτάζετο γὰρ ἀεὶ τὴν διηνεκῆ ἐγκράτειαν, ἐνετρύφα δὲ πολλάκις καὶ νηστείαις μακραῖς, καὶ ἐλογίζετο τὴν ἀλουσίαν ἀπόλαυσιν καὶ τὴν γυμνιτείαν ἐν τῷ τοῦ χειμῶνος καιρῷ ἐδόκει θερμότητα.

2   Οὕτω δὲ τὴν σάρκα ἐτυράννει καὶ ἐβασάνιζεν ὥστε, ἡνίκα κατεπονεῖτο τῇ τοῦ ὕπνου φυσικῇ τυραννίδι, ἀντετυράννει ταύτην μακροτάτῃ ὑπομονῇ ἐν τοιούτῳ ἐπινοήματι· λεκάνην γὰρ πληρῶν ὕδατος, ἤντλει τὸ ἑαυτοῦ

Chapter 6

Although he had already spiritually embraced abstinence and other forms of ascetic discipline, Abraamios also wished to lead a life of solitude. But his relatives were upset and saddened by this; for he would not eat with them. For how is it proper for an abstemious person to dine with gourmands? So they assigned two of their slaves to serve him, and these men provided him with his daily food, the finest bread and fish and fruit and whatever else may be of comfort to those who eat pure food. His relatives thought that he was eating what was sent to him, but this man of temperate behavior and remarkable abstemiousness gave all the other food to the servants, and, also refusing the highly refined bread, asked them to sell it and buy him one *follis* worth of barley bread, which, even then, he ate only every other day. If ever he needed to offer some comfort to his body, he satisfied his craving with raw vegetables and fruits, and to quench his thirst he drank plain water unmixed with wine. For he always felt well fed by his constant abstemious regimen, often took pleasure in lengthy fasts, considered it enjoyable to forego bathing, and viewed lack of clothing in wintertime as warmth.

Thus he disciplined and tormented his flesh to such an 2 extent that, when he was overwhelmed by the natural need to sleep, he resisted it with lengthy endurance, using the following stratagem: he would fill a basin with water, empty it

πρόσωπον καὶ τοῦ ὕπνου εὐθὺς ἀπηλλάττετο· τοῦτο δὲ ποιοῦντος αὐτοῦ καὶ ἐν τῷ τοῦ χειμῶνος καιρῷ, ἀπεκρυσταλλοῦτο αὐτῷ καὶ τὸ πρόσωπον ὑπὸ τοῦ παγετοῦ· ὕπνου δὲ βραχέος ἀπογευόμενος, οὐκ ἐπὶ κλίνης ἀλλ᾽ ἐπὶ θρόνου ὕπνωττεν.

3   Οὕτω τοίνυν τῇ ἑαυτοῦ σαρκὶ ἐχθρὸς ὢν ἄσπονδος, τοῖς πένησιν ἱλαρὸς ἐγίνετο καὶ συμπαθέστατος καὶ ἐλεήμων, εἴτε εἶχεν, εἴτε καὶ μή· ἃ γὰρ ἐδίδοτο τούτῳ παρά τε φίλων καὶ συγγενῶν, εἰς τὰς χεῖρας ἐτίθει τῶν πενήτων καὶ τῶν πτωχῶν· ὅτε δὲ οὐκ εἶχεν, εἴ τις τῶν ἐνδεῶν συναντήσας ἐδέετο τούτου, ἐκεῖνος φλεγόμενος σφόδρα τῷ πρὸς αὐτὸν οἰκτιρμῷ, ἐχώρει εἰς μέρος ἀπόκρυφον καὶ ἐξεδιδύσκετο τῷ ἐνδεεῖ τὰ ἱμάτια, κἂν χειμέριος ἦν ὁ καιρός, μόνον ὑποκρατῶν τὸ ἐπανωφόριον διὰ τὴν ἀναγκαίαν σκέπην τοῦ σώματος· ὅπερ οἱ δοῦλοι διαγινώσκοντες ἐδήλουν τῇ κυρίᾳ αὐτῶν. Οἱ συγγενεῖς δὲ ἐλεοῦντες αὐτόν, καὶ μάλιστα διὰ τὸν τοῦ ψύχους καιρόν, ἐδίδουν μὲν αὐτῷ ἱμάτιον, διὰ πολλῆς δὲ ἀνάγκης ἔπειθον αὐτὸν καὶ βίας τοῦτο ἐνδύσασθαι. Βασιλικῶς οὖν ὑποτάσσων τὴν σάρκα, ὡς εἴρηται, καὶ τὴν ψυχὴν λαμπρυνόμενος καὶ τὸν νοῦν φωτιζόμενος τοῖς τῆς σοφίας μαθήμασι, πρὸ τοῦ σχήματος τῆς μοναδικῆς πολιτείας μοναστὴς ἐγνωρίζετο, καὶ πρὸ τῆς ποιμαντικῆς τελειότητος ποιμὴν τελειότατος.

over his face, and immediately be relieved from drowsiness. When he did this even in the wintertime, his face would be encrusted with ice. If he did indulge in a little sleep, he did not doze upon a bed, but on a chair.

Although in this way Abraamios was an implacable foe of 3 his own flesh, he was cheerful and most compassionate and merciful to the poor, whether or not he had something to give. For whatever was given to him by friends and relatives, he would place in the hands of the poor and beggars. And when he did not have anything, if he encountered a needy person who entreated him, becoming inflamed with pity for the man, he would go somewhere private and remove his clothes to give to the needy person; even if it was wintertime, he would keep only his outer garment as the necessary covering for his body. When the slaves saw this, they would tell their mistress. And his relatives would take pity on him, especially because of the cold weather, and give him a tunic, but would only persuade him to put it on with much pressure and force. Thus splendidly subduing his body, as has been said, as well as illuminating his soul and enlightening his mind through the lessons of wisdom, he was recognized as a monk even before he adopted the habit of the monastic way of life, and as a most perfect shepherd even before his period of pastoral perfection.

7

Ἐπεὶ δὲ τὸ ἐνάρετον τοῦ βίου αὐτοῦ καὶ τὸ πραότατον ἦθος καὶ ἡ πολλὴ χρηστότης καὶ τὸ γλυκὺ τῆς ὁμιλίας καὶ ὁ πλοῦτος τῆς σοφίας αὐτοῦ καὶ τῆς γνώσεως ἔντιμον καὶ ἀγαπητὸν καὶ ποθητὸν ἐποίουν αὐτὸν τοῖς πᾶσι, διὰ ταῦτα σφόδρα φιλοῦντες τοῦτον οἱ συμμαθηταὶ καὶ πίστιν πολλὴν περὶ αὐτὸν κτησάμενοι, διδάσκαλον ἐψηφίσαντο, καὶ προσελθόντες τῷ βασιλεῖ ἐδέοντο κράζοντες· "Ὁ θαυμαστὸς Ἀβραάμιος, δέσποτα, πολλὴν ἔχων τὴν γνῶσιν καὶ τὴν ἀρετήν, ἄξιός ἐστι διδάσκαλος χειροτονηθῆναι ἡμῖν." Καὶ ὁ μὲν αὐτοκράτωρ τοιοῦτον εἶναι αὐτὸν ἀκούσας, διδάσκαλον εὐθὺς ἐχειροτόνησεν· ὁ δὲ παντοκράτωρ Θεὸς διὰ τῆς ἀφορμῆς τοῦ διδασκαλικοῦ ἀξιώματος ἤδη μετ᾽ ὀλίγον μαθητὴν αὐτοῦ προσελάμβανεν.

2 Ὡς γὰρ ἐπέβη τοῦ θρόνου τῆς διδασκαλίας, ὁ μὲν Ἀθανάσιος, ὁ τοῦ Ἀβρααμίου διδάσκαλος, ὁρῶν τὸν αὐτοῦ μαθητὴν προκαθεσθέντα διδάσκαλον, ἐγκαλλώπισμα τοῦτον εἶχε καὶ καύχημα· ἐπεὶ δὲ ὁ Ἀβραάμιος γραμματικώτατος ἦν καὶ σοφώτατος, πλῆθος μὲν παίδων πολλῶν τούτῳ προσήρχοντο, ἦσαν δὲ οὐκ ὀλίγοι καὶ ἐκ τῶν μαθητῶν τοῦ διδασκάλου αὐτοῦ. Ἐκεῖνος δὲ οὐ θέλων σκανδαλίσαι τὸν διδάσκαλον ἀνέκοπτε τούτους καὶ ἀπετρέπετο, οἱ δὲ οὐκ ἤθελον ἀποσπᾶσθαι αὐτοῦ· καὶ ὁ μὲν κοινὸς διδάσκαλος, ὁρῶν τοὺς αὐτοῦ μαθητὰς παραγινομένους πρὸς τὸν Ἀβραάμιον, ἀγανακτῶν ἐφαίνετο καὶ ἠγνόηκεν ὅτι πολλὴν τὴν ἀγάπην εἶχε περὶ αὐτόν. Ἐπεὶ δὲ ἐνίσταντο

Chapter 7

Abraamios's virtuous lifestyle, his most gentle manner, his great goodness, the sweetness of his discourse, and the abundance of his wisdom and knowledge made him honored and beloved and dear to everyone. For this reason his fellow students, who loved him very much and had great confidence in him, nominated him as a teacher. They approached the emperor, and appealed loudly to him: "Master, the wondrous Abraamios, who possesses much knowledge and virtue, is worthy to be appointed our teacher." The emperor, hearing that he was such a person, immediately appointed him as a teacher. But it was actually almighty God who would soon take him on as His disciple, using the occasion afforded by his elevation as a teacher.

When Abraamios ascended to the teacher's chair, Athanasios, his teacher, seeing his pupil presiding as a teacher, at first considered him an adornment and a source of pride. But since Abraamios was extremely learned in letters and very wise, he attracted a large number of boys, many of whom were the students of his own teacher. Because Abraamios did not wish to offend his teacher, he stopped them and turned them away, but they did not want to leave him. And now, when their common teacher saw his pupils going to Abraamios, he appeared to be annoyed, and had forgotten how much love he had for Abraamios. And when

οἱ μαθηταὶ τοῦ Ἀθανασίου μὴ ἀποστῆναι τῆς διδασκαλίας τοῦ Ἀβρααμίου, τοῦτο δὲ μάχῃ ἐδόκει τῷ κοινῷ διδασκάλῳ, ἀναγκαῖον ἦν ὥστε ὑπομνησθῆναι περὶ τούτου καὶ τὸν βασιλέα καὶ οὕτω λυθῆναι τὸ φιλονείκημα. Ὁ δὲ βασιλεὺς ὑπομνησθεὶς περὶ τούτου καὶ μὴ δυνηθεὶς ἀποσπάσαι αὐτοὺς ἐκ τοῦ Ἀβρααμίου, τὸ διδασκαλεῖον τούτου μετέθετο πόρρωθεν· οἱ δὲ παῖδες οὐδὲ οὕτως ἀφίσταντο. Τότε τοίνυν ὁ Ἀβραάμιος οὐκ ἀνεχόμενος λυπεῖσθαι κατ᾽ αὐτοῦ τὸν διδάσκαλον, καταβέβηκε μὲν τοῦ διδασκαλικοῦ θρόνου, πάντα δὲ τὰ τοῦ κόσμου κατέλιπε καὶ καταμόνας ἔζη τῷ Θεῷ. Ἔνθέν τοι καὶ μέγας ἐδόκει παρὰ πᾶσι καὶ ἐπαινούμενος καὶ δόξαν εἶχεν ἐξ ἀνθρώπων πολλήν.

8

Ἀλλ᾽ ἐκεῖνος τὸ δοξάζεσθαι ὡς αἰσχύνην καὶ ἁμάρτημα λογιζόμενος, διὰ φροντίδος εἶχε πολλῆς παντελῶς τὸν κόσμον φυγεῖν καὶ δουλεῦσαι Θεῷ. Ὁ δέ γε στρατηγὸς ἐκεῖνος, τὴν τοῦ Αἰγαίου πελάγους στρατηγίδα ἐγχειρισθεὶς καὶ πολλὴν ἔχων τὴν στοργὴν περὶ τὸν Ἀβραάμιον, μεθ᾽ ἑαυτοῦ καὶ τοῦτον ἐξερχόμενος ἔλαβεν· οἳ καὶ εἰς Ἄβυδον καταπλεύσαντες ἐκεῖθεν εἰς τὴν Λῆμνον ἐξώρμησαν, τοῦ Θεοῦ πάντως οἰκονομοῦντος τοῦτο καὶ προδεικνύοντος τῷ Ἀβρααμίῳ τὴν μέλλουσαν τούτῳ κατάπαυσιν· ἐκ

Athanasios's students refused to give up Abraamios's instruction, their common teacher took this as a declaration of war, and it became necessary for the emperor to be notified about this so that the rivalry might thus be resolved. When the emperor was notified about this and was unable to make the students leave Abraamios, he moved his school far away; but the boys still did not stay away. Then Abraamios, who could not bear for his teacher to be upset with him, resigned his teacher's chair, abandoned all worldly things, and lived in solitude with God. As a result, however, he seemed great and praiseworthy to all and received much glory from men.

Chapter 8

But since Abraamios considered glorification a disgrace and a sin, he gave much thought to how he might flee the world completely and serve God. At this point, the general Zephinazer, who had been given command of the Aegean Sea and had great affection for Abraamios, took him along when he set out. They sailed to Abydos and from there set forth for Lemnos, for God was, as always, arranging this and revealing to Abraamios in advance his future abode. For af-

ταύτης γὰρ κατασκοπήσας τὸν Ἄθω ὁ Ἀβραάμιος, ἠγάπησε λίαν τὴν ἐν αὐτῷ κατασκήνωσιν. Ὑποστρέψαντες δὲ
ἐκεῖθεν, ἐπανῆλθον πρὸς τὴν βασιλίδα.

2   Ἔτυχε δὲ κατά τινα θείαν πρόνοιαν ἐκεῖσε παρεῖναι
τὸ τηνικαῦτα καὶ τὸν ἁγιώτατον Μιχαὴλ ἐκεῖνον τὸν
Μαλεῖνον, ἀπὸ τῆς τοῦ Κυμινᾶ μονῆς εἰσελθόντα. Ὁ δὲ
Ἀβραάμιος, ἀκούσας μέγαν εἶναι τὸν ἄνδρα κατὰ ἀρετὴν
καὶ παρὰ πάντων ᾀδόμενον, καὶ ἐπιθυμῶν ἀπολαῦσαι παρ'
αὐτοῦ λόγων ψυχωφελῶν καὶ εὐχὰς κομίσασθαι, παρέβαλε
πρὸς τὸν γέροντα, καὶ θεασάμενος τοῦτον καὶ τῇ ὁμιλίᾳ
αὐτοῦ προσεσχηκώς, θερμότερον πόθον ἐδέχετο τῆς τοῦ
κόσμου ἀποστροφῆς, καὶ εὐθὺς ἀνεκάλυπτεν αὐτῷ τὸν
περὶ τῆς ἀποταγῆς λογισμόν.

3   Ὁ δὲ γέρων, ἅμα τῷ ἀκοῦσαι περὶ τούτου, ἔγνω τὸν
Ἀβραάμιον, ὅτι μέλλει γενέσθαι σκεῦος τοῦ Πνεύματος
τοῦ ἁγίου, καὶ ἐγλυκαίνετο τὴν καρδίαν ἐπὶ τῇ γνώσει
αὐτοῦ καὶ τῇ ἀρετῇ καὶ τῇ καλλίστῃ βουλῇ. Τοῦτο δὲ
πάντως οὐκ ἄνευ Θεοῦ, ἀλλ' ἔργον ἦν τῆς ἐκείνου προ-
νοίας· ἔτι γὰρ ὁμιλούντων αὐτῶν, ἦλθε πρὸς τὸν μέγαν
ἐκεῖνον γέροντα καὶ ὁ τῶν Ἀνατολικῶν στρατηγός, ὁ
περιφανὴς τὰ πάντα Νικηφόρος, ὁ ἀνεψιὸς αὐτοῦ, ὁ καὶ
βασιλεὺς ὕστερον· ἀπὸ γὰρ τοῦ μεγάλου ἐκείνου γέροντος ἐγνωρίσθη ὁ ἅγιος ἐκείνῳ τῷ βασιλεῖ. Ὁ οὖν
Ἀβραάμιος, ὡς εἶδε τοῦτον, αὐτίκα ὥρμησεν ὑπανα-
χωρῆσαι· ὁ δὲ γέρων ἀποδεχόμενος αὐτὸν οὐκ ἤθελεν
ἀπολῦσαι ταχέως· ὀλίγον δὲ προσκαρτερήσας ὁ Ἀβραάμιος,
μετὰ τοῦτο μετάνοιαν βαλὼν ὑπεχώρησεν. Ὁ δὲ καλὸς
Νικηφόρος βαθύτατον ἔχων φρόνημα, ὁρῶν τοῦ

ter catching a glimpse of Athos from this island, Abraamios developed a strong desire to settle there. But for now they returned from there, and came back to the Queen of Cities.

It so happened that at that very time, by divine providence, the most holy Michael Maleinos was there, having come from the monastery of Kyminas. Abraamios, who had heard that the man had great virtue and was celebrated by all, wished to enjoy his words of spiritual benefit and receive his blessing, and so went to visit the elder. When he saw Michael and had conversed with him, he developed an even more ardent desire to retire from the world, and immediately revealed to him his idea of renouncing it. 2

As soon as the elder heard about this, he recognized that Abraamios was destined to be a vessel of the Holy Spirit, and his heart was sweetened by his knowledge and his virtue and most excellent intention. And surely this did not take place without God, but was the work of His providence. For while they were still conversing, the military governor of the Anatolikon came to that great elder; this was his nephew, the most remarkable Nikephoros, the future emperor. Thus it was through the great elder Michael that the holy one became acquainted with that emperor. As soon as Abraamios saw Nikephoros, he immediately hastened to withdraw, but the elder, now that he had received Abraamios, did not want to dismiss him so quickly. So Abraamios remained a while longer, and then prostrated himself and departed. The good Nikephoros, who was a man of deep understanding, 3

Ἀβρααμίου τό τε βλέμμα καὶ τὸ ἦθος καὶ τὴν ὅλην κατάστασιν, θαυμαστόν τινα καὶ οὗτος κατενόει αὐτόν, καὶ "Τίς ἐστι, πάτερ, οὗτος ὁ ἀνήρ," τῷ θείῳ αὐτοῦ ἔλεγε, "καὶ πόθεν καὶ τίνος χάριν ἐλήλυθε;" Καὶ μαθὼν παρὰ τοῦ μεγάλου πάντα τὰ τοῦ Ἀβρααμίου καὶ ὅτι μοναχὸς γενέσθαι ἐπιθυμεῖ, διὰ μνήμης εἶχεν αὐτόν.

9

Ἀλλ᾽ ὁ μὲν θεῖος ἐκεῖνος Μιχαὴλ ὁ Μαλεῖνος ἤδη ὑπεξῆλθε τῆς Βυζαντίδος καὶ πρὸς τὸν Κυμινᾶν ἐπανῆλθε· ὁ Ἀβραάμιος δὲ τὸ τῶν μοναχῶν σχῆμα περιβαλέσθαι ποθῶν καὶ φλεγόμενος ὑπὸ τῆς τοιαύτης ἐπιθυμίας, οὐκ ἦν βραδύνων, ἀλλ᾽ εὐθέως ἐχώρει πρὸς τὸν μέγαν ἐκεῖνον γέροντα, καὶ προσελθὼν αὐτῷ ᾐτεῖτο περιβαλέσθαι τὸ μοναχικὸν ἔνδυμα. Ὁ δὲ γέρων γινώσκων τοῦτον ὁποῖός ἐστιν, οὐ παρεπέμπετο αὐτὸν εἰς καιρὸν δοκιμῆς, ἀλλὰ ταχέως πάντα τὰ νενομισμένα τελέσας ἐπ᾽ αὐτῷ, τὸ θεῖον καὶ μακάριον ἀμφιέννυσι σχῆμα, Ἀθανάσιον ὀνομάσας ἀντὶ Ἀβρααμίου.

2 Ἔθους δὲ μὴ ὄντος ἐν τῷ τοῦ Κυμινᾶ ὄρει τρίχινα περιβάλλεσθαι τοὺς μοναχούς, ὁ μέγας ἐκεῖνος πατὴρ πολεμικώτατον στοχασάμενος τὸν Ἀθανάσιον, τὸ βαρύτερον ὅπλον, τὸ τρίχινον, αὐτὸν ἐνέδυσε καὶ Χριστοῦ στρατιώτην παρεσκεύασεν. Ἀξιοῦντος δὲ τοῦ Ἀθανασίου ἅπαξ

observing Abraamios's look and manner and his entire bearing, realized also that he was a remarkable individual, and said to his uncle, "Father, who is this man? Where is he from and why has he come here?" And when he learned all about Abraamios from the great man and that he wanted to become a monk, he kept him in his thoughts.

Chapter 9

After that divine Michael Maleinos had already departed from Byzantion and returned to Kyminas, Abraamios, who yearned to don the monastic habit and was inflamed by the desire to do so, did not delay, but immediately went to visit that great elder. He approached him and asked to be garbed with the monastic habit. The elder, realizing what sort of a person he was, did not refer him for a trial period, but quickly performed all the customary rituals for him, garbed him with the divine and blessed habit, and gave him the name of Athanasios instead of Abraamios.

Although it was not customary at Mount Kyminas for the monks to wear hair garments, that great father, surmising that Athanasios was very well suited for ascetic combat, garbed him with the heaviest armor, a hair shirt, and prepared him to be a soldier for Christ. But when Athanasios

τῆς ἑβδομάδος μεταλαμβάνειν τροφῆς, ὁ γέρων κόπτων αὐτοῦ τὸ θέλημα, διὰ τριῶν ἡμερῶν ἐσθίειν ἐκέλευε, καὶ θέλοντος αὐτοῦ ἐπὶ θρόνου ὑπνώττειν, ἐπὶ ψιάθῳ κατὰ γῆς ἐκεῖνος κλίνεσθαι προσέταττεν. Οὐ μόνον δὲ ταῦτα ἐποίει Ἀθανάσιος, ἀλλὰ καὶ διηκόνει ἐν ταῖς ὑπουργίαις τῆς ἐκκλησίας, ὅτε παρὰ τοῦ ἐκκλησιάρχου προσετάττετο, καὶ τὸν λοιπὸν τῆς σχολῆς καιρὸν διετέλει καλλιγραφῶν κατὰ τὴν ἐντολὴν τοῦ μεγάλου ἐκείνου πατρός, καὶ οὕτως ἀπετελεῖτο τέκνον ὑπακοῆς [1 Peter 1:14] καὶ παρὰ πάσης τῆς συνοδίας τῶν ἀδελφῶν εὐλογεῖτο καὶ ἐθαυμάζετο. Τοίνυν καὶ διὰ τεσσάρων ἐνιαυτῶν πᾶσαν ἀσκητικὴν πολιτείαν κατώρθωσε καὶ πᾶν εἶδος ἀγώνων διήνυσε δι' ἐγκρατείας διηνεκοῦς καὶ πολλῶν νηστειῶν, ἀγρυπνίας τε καὶ στάσεως καὶ ὁλονύκτων γονυκλισιῶν καὶ πόνων νυκτερινῶν καὶ ἱδρώτων ἡμερινῶν καὶ πάσης ὑπακοῆς καὶ ὑποταγῆς.

10

Ἐνθέν τοι καὶ τὴν διάνοιαν καλῶς καθαρθεὶς καὶ θείων θεωρημάτων γευσάμενος, ἀπελύθη παρὰ τοῦ μεγάλου ἐκείνου γέροντος καὶ εἰς τὸ μέγα τῆς ἡσυχίας στάδιον· ἦν δὲ τοῦτο ἐν τόπῳ ἀπέχοντι τῆς λαύρας μίλιον ἕν. Ἐξερχομένῳ δὲ ἐκεῖσε τῷ Ἀθανασίῳ ἐνετείλατο ὁ γέρων μηκέτι διὰ τριῶν ἡμερῶν ἐσθίειν, ὥσπερ εἴθιστο, ἀλλὰ διὰ δύο

requested to take nourishment only once a week, the elder sought to restrain his will, and ordered him to eat every three days, and when he wanted to sleep on a chair, he ordered him to lie down on the ground on a straw mat. Not only did Athanasios do these things, but he also served in various church ministries, whenever he was ordered to do so by the sacristan, and he spent the rest of his spare time copying manuscripts at the bidding of that great father. In this way he was perfected as a *child of obedience* and was praised and admired by the whole community of the brethren. Thus over a period of four years he mastered every form of ascetic conduct, and accomplished every sort of spiritual contest through constant abstinence, numerous fasts, vigils and standing vigils, genuflections throughout the night, nocturnal labors, diurnal endeavors, and total submission and obedience.

Chapter 10

When his mind had been well purified in this way and he had gained a taste of divine contemplation, he was granted permission by that great elder to enter the great arena of spiritual tranquility. This was at a place about one mile distant from the *lavra*. As Athanasios was leaving for that place, the elder instructed him to no longer eat every three days, as was his wont, but to eat some dry bread and drink a little

ἄρτον ξηρὸν καὶ ὀλίγον ὕδωρ, ἐν ταῖς τρισὶ δὲ τεσσαρα-
κοσταῖς δι᾽ ἡμερῶν πέντε σιτίζεσθαι, καθεύδειν δὲ μὴ κατὰ
γῆς ἐν ψιάθῳ, ἀλλ᾽ ἐπὶ θρόνου πάλιν ὡς πρότερον, καὶ ἐν
πάσαις ταῖς δεσποτικαῖς ἑορταῖς καὶ ἐν αὐταῖς δὴ ταῖς τῶν
ἑβδομάδων κυριακαῖς ἀπὸ ὀψὲ ἕως τρίτης ὥρας διανυκτε-
ρεύειν ἐν προσευχαῖς καὶ δοξολογίαις. Ταῦτα δὲ ἐντελλόμε-
νος αὐτῷ ὁ γέρων, ἐχώριζε τοῦτον πάλιν ἐκ τοῦ ἰδίου
θελήματος, καὶ διὰ τῆς αὐτοῦ γενναιότητος διήγειρεν εἰς
ἀγῶνας καὶ τοὺς λοιποὺς μοναχούς.

11

Καὶ οὕτω μὲν εἶχε ταῦτα· ὁ δὲ τῶν Ἀνατολικῶν στρατηγὸς Νικηφόρος, περὶ οὗ προλαβόντες εἴπομεν, τὸν Κυμινᾶν καταλαβὼν καὶ τῷ θείῳ αὐτοῦ παραβαλών, οἷα ἐξ
ἔθους ἔχων τοῦτο ποιεῖν, ὡμίλει τῷ μεγάλῳ γέροντι καὶ
ὁμιλῶν ἠρώτα περὶ τοῦ Ἀθανασίου· ὁ δὲ γέρων αὐτίκα διηγεῖτο αὐτῷ τοὺς ἄθλους τε καὶ τὰς κατὰ τοῦ Διαβόλου
ἀριστείας αὐτοῦ. Ὁ δὲ Νικηφόρος ἀκούσας ταῦτα ἠτεῖτο
τὸν γέροντα ἀπελθεῖν πρὸς τὸν Ἀθανάσιον· ἔτυχε δὲ κατὰ
ταῦτα παραγενόμενος ἐκεῖσε καὶ ὁ πατρίκιος Λέων καὶ
δομέστικος τῶν σχολῶν τῆς Δύσεως, ὁ αὐτάδελφος τοῦ
προρρηθέντος Νικηφόρου.

2   Ἰδὼν οὖν ὁ γέρων καὶ τοῦτον ἐλθόντα, εἶπε πρὸς
αὐτούς· "Εὐκαίρως ἐπεδημήσατε, ὦ φίλτατοι, ἵνα ἐπιδείξω

water every two days, and during the three periods of Lent every five days. He also ordered him not to sleep on the ground on a straw mat, but on a chair again, as previously, and to keep vigil with prayer and words of praise on all the dominical feast days and every Sunday from sunset until the third hour. By giving Athanasios these instructions, the elder was again separating him from his own will, and through Athanasios's valor was encouraging the other monks as well to spiritual combat.

Chapter 11

So this was the situation. Nikephoros, the military governor of the Anatolikon, about whom we have previously spoken, came to Kyminas; he met with his uncle, as was his custom, and conversed with the great elder. During the conversation he asked him about Athanasios, and the elder immediately told him about his exploits and his prowess against the Devil. When Nikephoros heard these words, he asked the elder for permission to visit Athanasios. At that moment the *patrikios* Leo, who was Domestic of the Schools of the West, and the aforementioned Nikephoros's brother, also happened to arrive there.

When the elder saw him come as well, he said to them, 2 "You have arrived at an opportune moment, my dearest

ὑμῖν οἷον ἔχω θησαυρὸν τὸν ἐμὸν Ἀθανάσιον." Τούτων
οὖν προθύμων ὄντων ἀπελθεῖν πρὸς ἐκεῖνον, ὁ πατὴρ ἔλε-
γεν· "Ἀλλ' οὐ βούλομαι οὕτως ἐγώ, ἐκεῖνος δὲ μᾶλλον
ἐλθέτω πρὸς ὑμᾶς." Ὡς δὲ ἐκεῖνοι ἐνίσταντο ἀπελθεῖν
πρὸς αὐτόν, ἐπένευσεν ὁ γέρων, καὶ οἱ μὲν ἀπῆλθον πρὸς
τὸν Ἀθανάσιον, ὁ δὲ ἐξελθὼν ἐκ τῆς ἡσυχίας ἤρξατο ὁμιλεῖν αὐτοῖς, καὶ ἤκουσαν ῥήματα τὰ πολλοῖς μὴ λεγόμενα
καὶ λόγους ἔμαθον οὓς οὐδέποτε ἤκουσαν· ὑπὸ γὰρ τῆς
ἡδονῆς τῶν ἐκείνου λόγων τοσοῦτον ἐθηρεύθησαν εἰς τὴν
ἀγάπην αὐτοῦ ὥστε μόλις ἀποσπασθῆναι τούτους τῆς
ὁμιλίας αὐτοῦ.

3 Ἐκεῖθεν οὖν ἀναστρέψαντες, εἶπον τῷ γέροντι· "Χάριν
ὁμολογοῦμέν σοι, πάτερ, ὅτι ἔδειξας ἡμῖν οἷον ἔχεις θη-
σαυρόν." Ὁ γέρων δὲ προσέταξεν εὐθὺς κατελθεῖν πρὸς
αὐτὸν καὶ τὸν Ἀθανάσιον· καὶ ἐλθόντος ἀμφοτέρων τῶν
αὐταδέλφων τὰς χεῖρας ἐνέβαλεν εἰς τὰς τούτου, εἰπὼν
πρὸς αὐτούς· "Ἀπὸ τοῦ παρόντος ἀνάθεσθε τοὺς ἑαυτῶν
λογισμοὺς τούτῳ τῷ μοναχῷ καὶ πείθεσθε αὐτῷ τοῦ λοιποῦ ὡς πατρὶ κατὰ πάντα." Πεισθέντος δὲ τῷ γέροντι καὶ
τοῦ Ἀθανασίου, προσεκύνησαν κἀκεῖνοι τῷ θείῳ αὐτῶν
καὶ ἀπεδέξαντο λίαν τὴν τοιαύτην οἰκονομίαν καὶ κηδε-
μονίαν, καὶ εὐχαριστήσαντες σφόδρα τῷ γέροντι εἶπον
αὐτῷ· "Ἀπό γε τοῦ νῦν, πάτερ, οὐκέτι σοι ἐνοχλήσομεν
περὶ ψυχικῆς ὠφελείας." Ἔπειτα ἰδίᾳ καὶ καθ' ἑαυτοὺς
γενόμενοι, ἐξεῖπον τῷ Ἀθανασίῳ τοὺς ἑαυτῶν λογισμούς·
ὑπ' αὐτοῦ δὲ λόγοις παραινετικοῖς περιαντληθέντες τὰς
ἀκοάς, ἤδη τῆς μετανοίας τὰ κέντρα ἐδέχοντο καὶ
ἐξεπλήττοντο λίαν ἐπὶ τῇ διδασκαλίᾳ αὐτοῦ.

kinsmen, so that I can show you what a treasure I have in my Athanasios." When they were eager to go visit him, the father said, "That is not my wish; rather he should come to you." But when they insisted on going to him, the elder agreed. So they went to Athanasios, and, leaving his pursuit of spiritual tranquility, he began to converse with them, and they heard speech that few could utter, and learned words which they had never heard. They were so captivated with affection for him through their pleasure in his words that they could barely tear themselves away from conversation with him.

When they had returned from there, they said to the elder, "We want to thank you, father, for having shown us what a treasure you have." The elder immediately ordered Athanasios to join him, and, when he had arrived, he placed the hands of both brothers in those of Athanasios, saying to them, "From this moment on entrust your thoughts to this monk, and in future obey him as your father in all respects." When Athanasios had himself been persuaded by the elder, the brothers did obeisance to their uncle and eagerly accepted such guidance and protection. Thanking the elder effusively, they said to him, "From now on, father, we will no longer trouble you for our spiritual assistance." Then withdrawing to a private place, they each confessed their thoughts to Athanasios. After their ears were completely filled with his words of encouragement, they accepted the goads of repentance and continued to be amazed by his teaching.

3

4   Ὁ Νικηφόρος δὲ ἰδιαζόντως παραλαβὼν τὸν Ἀθανάσιον, ἀνεκάλυπτεν αὐτῷ ἐν μυστηρίῳ τὸν θεάρεστον αὐτοῦ σκοπόν, λέγων αὐτῷ· "Ποθῶ, πάτερ, ἡσυχάσαι ἀπὸ τῆς κοσμικῆς ζάλης, καὶ ἐθέμην ἀποτάξασθαι πᾶσι τοῖς τοῦ κόσμου καὶ τῷ Θεῷ δουλεῦσαι, ὡς δυνατόν, καὶ εἴπέρ μοι δίδως συνθήκην, ἀπὸ τῆς σήμερον εἰς σὲ τὰ τῆς ἐλπίδος μου ταύτης ἀνατίθημι." Ὁ δὲ Ἀθανάσιος· "Τῷ Θεῷ, τέκνον, ἀνάθου τὸ πᾶν καὶ αὐτὸς φροντιεῖ περὶ τούτου." Ταῦτα εἰπὼν καὶ ἐπευξάμενος ἀπέλυσεν αὐτούς, καὶ οὗτοι μὲν ἔκτοτε σέβας καὶ τιμὴν καὶ πίστιν ἄπειρον περὶ τὸν Ἀθανάσιον ἐκτήσαντο, ὅσην οὐδὲ εἰς τὸν θεῖον αὐτῶν.

12

Ἐπεὶ δὲ ὁ μακαριώτατος ἐκεῖνος Μιχαήλ, ὁ τοῦ Ἀθανασίου πατήρ, τοὺς ἀπερχομένους πρὸς αὐτὸν μεγιστάνας συγκλητικοὺς χάριν εὐχῆς ἐξέπεμπε πάντας καὶ πρὸς τὸν Ἀθανάσιον, ὥστε εὐλογεῖσθαι καὶ παρ' αὐτοῦ καὶ ὠφέλειαν ψυχικὴν κομίζεσθαι, ὁ Ἀθανάσιος, μισόδοξος ὢν καὶ τὴν ἐντεῦθεν ὄχλησιν φεύγων, ἀκούσας δὲ ὅτι καὶ ὁ μέγας ἐκεῖνος γέρων βούλεται ἐμπιστεῦσαι αὐτῷ τὴν ἡγουμενείαν τῆς ποίμνης αὐτοῦ, ἐμελέτα ἀπολιπεῖν τὸ ἡσυχαστήριον καὶ πρὸς τὸν Ἄθων χωρῆσαι, τὸν πάλαι τούτῳ ἐράσμιον. Ὁ γὰρ μακάριος ἐκεῖνος γέρων ἀπὸ τοῦ ἐλλάμποντος αὐτῷ πνεύματος ἐπιγνοὺς τὸν Ἀθανάσιον

Nikephoros took Athanasios aside and secretly revealed   4
to him his pious goal, saying to him, "Father, I desire to live
in spiritual tranquility away from the storms of the world,
and I have decided to renounce all worldly things and serve
God, to the best of my ability. If you agree, from today on I
will entrust to you the realization of this hope of mine." But
Athanasios replied, "My child, entrust everything to God
and He will take care of it." Saying these words and giving
his blessing he dismissed them, and from then on they had
reverence and honor for Athanasios and boundless faith in
him, even more than they had for their uncle.

Chapter 12

That most blessed Michael, Athanasios's spiritual father,
then began to send all the senatorial magnates who came to
him for a blessing to Athanasios as well, so that they might
also be blessed by him and acquire spiritual benefit. But
when Athanasios, who despised glory and sought to avoid
the disturbance that arises from it, heard that that great elder also wanted to entrust to him the leadership of his flock,
he began to think about leaving his place of spiritual tranquility and going to Athos, beloved to him from of old. That
blessed elder, realizing from the spirit that shone in him
that Athanasios was already advancing in virtue and

προκόψαντα ἤδη κατὰ ἀρετὴν καὶ εἰς ὕψος θεωρημάτων ἀνελθόντα καὶ τὴν χάριν τοῦ Θεοῦ πρὸς αὐτὸν ἐλθοῦσαν, εἰπέ ποτε πρός τινα τῶν αὐτῷ γνωρίμων λόγον τοιοῦτον περὶ τοῦ Ἀθανασίου· "Ἰδοὺ καὶ ὁ διάδοχός μου." Ἀλλ᾽ ἐκεῖνος οὕτω λέγων, οὐ περὶ ἡγουμενείας τῆς ἐν τῇ ποίμνῃ αὐτοῦ ἔλεγεν, ὡς ὑπενόησαν οἱ ἀκούσαντες, ἀλλ᾽ ἐδήλου ὅτι τοῦ ὁμοίου αὐτῷ χαρίσματος ἠξιώθη καὶ ὁ Ἀθανάσιος, καὶ ἔμελλε ποιμὴν προβάτων ἀναδειχθῆναι ἐν ἑτέρῳ τόπῳ καὶ μέγας κληθῆναι καὶ παρὰ ἀνθρώπων, ὥσπερ ἐνομίσθη καὶ τῷ Θεῷ.

2   Καὶ ὁ μὲν θεῖος Μιχαὴλ ἤδη εἰς γῆρας ἦλθε βαθὺ καὶ νόσοις συχναῖς προσεπάλαιεν· οἱ δὲ πρόκριτοι τῶν μοναχῶν τῆς τοῦ Κυμινᾶ μονῆς ποιμένα ἑαυτῶν προχειρισθῆναι τὸν Ἀθανάσιον ὅσον οὔπω ἐλπίζοντες, ἀνήρχοντο πολλάκις εἰς αὐτὸν καὶ τιμὰς καὶ κολακείας προσέφερον αὐτῷ καὶ ἐπαίνους καὶ θεραπείας, ὃ πρότερον οὐκ ἐποίουν. Ἀθανάσιος δέ, ὀξὺς ὢν περὶ τὸ νοεῖν, οὐκ ἄνευ αἰτίας τοῦτο ἔλεγεν εἶναι· ὅμως ἐν τῷ θαυμάζειν καὶ ἀπορεῖν περὶ τούτου ἔμαθε παρά τινος ἀδελφοῦ εἰπόντος αὐτῷ ὅτι "Ὁ πατὴρ διάδοχον αὐτοῦ ὀνομάζει σε."

3   Καὶ πιστεύσας τῷ λόγῳ τοῦ ἀδελφοῦ καὶ ἀνάξιον κρίνας ἑαυτὸν ποιμένα γενέσθαι ψυχῶν, μισῶν δὲ καὶ τὸ πρᾶγμα διὰ τὸ πολύφροντι, φυγὰς ἐκεῖθεν ἐγένετο, οὐχ ἕτερόν τι ἐπιφερόμενος ἢ μόνα βιβλία δύο, ἅπερ αὐτοχείρως ἔγραψε, τό τε τετραευάγγελον καὶ τὸν Πραξαπόστολον, καὶ τὸ ἱερώτατον κουκούλιον τοῦ πατρὸς αὐτοῦ, ὅπερ καὶ ἐν τῷ βίῳ ὥσπέρ τι φυλακτήριον ψυχωφελὲς ἐπεφέρετο, καὶ τελευτῶν καλὸν ἑαυτῷ ἐντάφιον ἐποιήσατο.

ascending to the heights of contemplation and that the grace of God was upon him, once remarked about Athanasios to an acquaintance something like, "Here is my successor." But when he spoke these words, he was not speaking about leadership of *his* flock, as those who heard him thought, but was indicating that Athanasios was also considered worthy of the same spiritual gift as he was, and that he was going to be revealed as a shepherd of sheep in another place, and men would also call him great, just as he was considered great by God.

The divine Michael had already reached extreme old age 2 and was contending with many illnesses. The preeminent monks of the Kyminas monastery, hoping that Athanasios would soon be appointed their shepherd, began to visit him often and offered him honors and flattery and praise and veneration, which they had not done previously. But Athanasios, who had a quick grasp of things, realized that there must be a reason for this. While he was wondering and puzzled about this, he learned what was going on from a monk who remarked to him, "The father is naming you as his successor."

Athanasios believed the monk's words and, judging himself unworthy to become a shepherd of souls and hating the idea because it would entail many practical concerns, he made his escape from there. He took nothing with him except for two books which he had copied with his own hand, a gospel book and the Praxapostolos, as well as his spiritual father's most holy cowl. This he kept with him throughout his life as a spiritually beneficial amulet, and at his death used it as a fine burial shroud for himself.

13

Διαπεράσας οὖν πρὸς τὸν πάλαι φίλον αὐτῷ Ἄθων καὶ ἐμπεριπατήσας αὐτῷ καὶ περιελθὼν πανταχόθεν, περισκοπήσας δὲ καὶ τὸ πλῆθος τῶν ἐν αὐτῷ ἀσκουμένων μοναχῶν καὶ τὴν τραχυτάτην ἀγωγὴν αὐτῶν ἀνιχνεύσας καὶ τὸν ἐρημικὸν βίον καὶ ἀπερίσπαστον, ἐθαύμαζε καὶ εὐφραίνετο καὶ ᾠκοδομεῖτο κατὰ ψυχήν, ὡς τοιούτων ἐπιτυχὼν ἀνθρώπων καὶ τοιαύτης ἐλευθερίας καὶ καταστάσεως, οἵας καὶ πρὸ τούτου ἐγλίχετο. Οἱ γὰρ καλοὶ πατέρες ἐκεῖνοι οὐκ ἐργασίαν εἶχον γεωργίας, οὐ πράγμασι συνεπλέκοντο, οὐ μερίμναις περιεσπῶντο σωματικαῖς, οὐχ ὑποζύγιον εἶχον οὐδὲ ὀνάριον οὔτε κυνάριον, ἀλλὰ καλύβας ἀπὸ χόρτου κατασκευάζοντες, ἐν ταύταις διεκαρτέρουν θέρους τε καὶ χειμῶνος, ἡλίῳ φλεγόμενοι καὶ τῷ ψύχει πηγνύμενοι.

2   Εἰ δέ ποτε καὶ γέγονέ τις χρεία αὐτοῖς τοῦ μετακομίσαι τι εἴς τινα τόπον, αὐτοὶ δι᾽ ἑαυτῶν τοῦτο ἐποίουν· στρώματα γὰρ ἐπιτιθέντες τοῖς ὤμοις αὐτῶν, ἐβάσταζον τὸ εἶδος καὶ μετεκόμιζον ὅπου ἐβούλοντο. Ἡ δὲ τροφὴ αὐτοῖς ἀκρόδρυα ἦν καὶ ἑτέρων δένδρων καρποί. Εἴ ποτε δέ τινες προσωρμίζοντό ποθεν τῷ Ὄρει διὰ πλοίου χάριν εὐχῆς, ὥσπερ εἴθιστο πολλάκις τισί, τότε σῖτον λαμβάνοντες παρ᾽ αὐτῶν ἢ κέγχρον ἢ ἕτερον εἶδος σπέρματος, ἀντιπαρεῖχον αὐτοῖς ὀπώρας· καὶ τοῦτο οὐκ ἀδεῶς οὐδὲ διόλου ἐγίνετο, ἀλλὰ καὶ βραδέως καὶ ἐν παρατηρήσει πολλῇ διὰ τὴν πάλαι συνήθη καταδρομὴν τῶν ἀθεωτάτων Κρητῶν, οἵτινες

Chapter 13

Crossing over then to Athos, dear to him from of old, he walked about on the Mountain and wandered all around. Observing the multitude of monks who were practicing asceticism there and investigating their very harsh way of life and their solitary existence free from distractions, Athanasios marveled and rejoiced and was spiritually edified to encounter such men and such freedom and conditions as he had yearned for even before. For those good fathers did not engage in agricultural work, nor were they entangled in business affairs, nor were they distracted by bodily concerns, nor did they own a beast of burden nor an ass nor a dog, but constructed huts of wild grasses and lived in these summer and winter, scorched by the sun and frozen by the cold.

If they ever needed to transport something somewhere, 2 they did this themselves. For they would place pads on their shoulders and, carrying the object, would transport it wherever they wished. Their food was nuts and the fruit of other trees. And if ever people came by ship from somewhere to anchor at the Mountain for the sake of a blessing, as some often used to do, then the monks would take wheat or millet from the visitors or some other kind of grain, and in return would provide them with fruit. This would not happen without precautions or frequently, but with due deliberation and careful observation on account of the attacks of the most godless Cretans which used to occur in the old

ταῖς κοιλότησι τῶν πετρῶν ἐνεδρεύοντες, ἐληΐζοντο τοὺς παράγοντας καὶ πολλοὺς τῶν μοναχῶν τοῦ Ὄρους ἐφόνευον.

14

Ἐνταῦθα τοίνυν γενόμενος ὁ Ἀθανάσιος, ἔμαθε προβληθῆναι δομέστικον ἁπάσης τῆς Δύσεως τὸν μάγιστρον Λέοντα καὶ αὐτάδελφον τοῦ ἀοιδίμου Νικηφόρου, καὶ δεδοικὼς μήποτε ψηλαφώμενος διαγνωσθῇ, Βαρνάβαν ἑαυτὸν ἀντὶ Ἀθανασίου ὠνόμασε. Γενόμενος δὲ ἐν τῇ τοῦ Ζυγοῦ μονῇ, γέροντί τε περιτυχὼν ἁπλουστάτῳ καὶ ἀπράγμονι, ἔξωθεν ταύτης ἡσυχάζοντι, προσέρχεται τούτῳ μετὰ ταπεινοῦ καὶ εὐτελοῦς σχήματος. Ὁ δὲ γέρων ἀπεριέργως ἰδὼν αὐτὸν ἠρώτα· "Τίς εἶ, ἀδελφέ, καὶ πόθεν καὶ τίνος χάριν εἰσῆλθες ἐνταῦθα;" Ὁ δὲ Ἀθανάσιος ἀπεκρίνατο· "Πλώϊμος ἤμην, ὦ πάτερ, καὶ κινδύνῳ περιπεσών, ὑπεσχόμην Θεῷ πάντων χωρισθῆναι τῶν κοσμικῶν καὶ κλαῦσαι τὰς ἁμαρτίας μου, καὶ διὰ τοῦτο ἐνεδυσάμην καὶ τοῦτο τὸ ἅγιον ἔνδυμα· τοῦ Θεοῦ δὲ ὁδηγοῦντός με, ἦλθον ὧδε εἰς τὴν ἁγιωσύνην σου, ποθήσας συνεῖναί σοι καὶ χειραγωγεῖσθαι παρὰ σοῦ ἐπὶ τὴν τῆς σωτηρίας ὁδόν." Ὁ γέρων δὲ πιστεύσας ἀκάκως καὶ ἀπονήρως τῷ σοφῷ ἐκείνῳ πλάσματι, προσεδέξατο τὸν πλαστὸν Βαρνάβαν, καὶ τοῦ λοιποῦ συνῆν τῷ γέροντι καὶ ἠκολούθει αὐτῷ ὡς

days, for they would lurk in rocky inlets and rob passersby and murder many monks on the Mountain.

Chapter 14

When Athanasios arrived here, he learned that the *magistros* Leo, the brother of the celebrated Nikephoros, had been appointed Domestic of the entire West, and in fear of being sought out and recognized, he called himself Barnabas instead of Athanasios. When he came to the monastery of Zygos, he met an elder, who was very simple and free from worldly cares, and was living a life of spiritual tranquility outside its walls, and approached him in his poor and shabby habit. The elder looked at him without suspicion and asked him, "Who are you, my brother? Where are you from and why have you come here?" Athanasios replied, "My father, I was a sailor, and once, when I fell into danger, I vowed to God that I would separate myself from all worldly things and weep for my sins, and for this reason I have donned this holy habit. With God's guidance, I have come here to your holiness, desiring to live with you and to be guided by you on the road of salvation." The elder, innocently and naively believing that clever fabrication, received the supposed Barnabas, who from then on lived together with the elder and followed him as if he were his own father. Athanasios yielded

ἰδίῳ πατρὶ καὶ ὑπετάσσετο ἐν πᾶσι τῷ αὐτοῦ θελήματι καὶ σὺν αὐτῷ εἰργάζετο τὰς ἐντολὰς τοῦ Κυρίου. Ἀλλ' ὁ μὲν γέρων, οἷα γέρων, ἀδύνατος ἦν κοπιᾶν· ὁ δὲ νέος τὸ ὑστέρημα ἀνεπλήρου τοῦ γέροντος.

15

Ἐπεὶ δὲ μετὰ τοὺς πολλοὺς καμάτους καὶ ἄθλους καὶ τὰς κατὰ ψυχὴν προκοπὰς πᾶσαν διακονίαν καὶ ὑπηρεσίαν ἄτιμον καὶ εὐτελῆ κατορθώσας, ἐπόθει κατορθῶσαι καὶ τὸ μεῖζον τῆς ταπεινοφροσύνης (ἐνταῦθά μοι σκόπει τὴν μεγίστην ἐργασίαν καὶ τὸ μέγα φρόνημα τοῦ ἀνδρός)· εἰδὼς γὰρ ὅτι κατὰ τὴν εὐαγγελικὴν φωνὴν "ὁ ταπεινώσας ἑαυτὸν ὡς παιδίον μείζων ἔσται ἐν τῇ βασιλείᾳ τῶν οὐρανῶν" [Matthew 18:4], ἔσπευσε καὶ αὐτὸς ὅλον ἑαυτὸν ἐκδοῦναι τοῖς ἔργοις τῆς ταπεινώσεως· ἐπιμείνας γὰρ χρόνον τινὰ τῇ διακονίᾳ τοῦ γέροντος, προσῆλθεν αὐτῷ λέγων· "Ποίησόν μοι ἀρχὴν γραμμάτων, ἀββᾶ μου, ὅπως μάθω ἀναγινώσκειν τὸ ψαλτήριον· ἐν γὰρ τῷ κόσμῳ ὤν, ἐκτὸς τῆς κώπης οὐδὲν πλέον μεμάθηκα." Ἤκουσεν ὁ γέρων, καὶ λαβὼν πινακίδιον, χαράττει αὐτῷ τὰ στοιχεῖα· οὗτος δὲ ὁ πολὺς τὴν σοφίαν καὶ ποτὲ διδάσκαλος λαβὼν τὸ πινακίδιον γεγραμμένον καὶ βαλὼν μετάνοιαν, ὡς ἀρχάριος ἐδείκνυτο καὶ ὡς μαθητὴς ἤγετο. Εἶχε μὲν οὖν ἐν χερσὶ

to his will in all matters, and together with him accomplished the commandments of the Lord. But the elder, who was an old man, was unable to perform physical labor; and the young man made up for the elder's need.

Chapter 15

When, after many toils and trials and spiritual progress, Athanasios had carried out every task and lowly and mean service, he yearned to attain even greater humility (pay attention now to the man's great accomplishment and great purpose!). For knowing that, in the words of the Gospel, "whoever *humbles himself like a child is greater in the kingdom of heaven,*" he strove to give himself over entirely to works of humility. After remaining for some time in the elder's service, he came to him and said, "Start to teach me my letters, my *abbas,* so that I may learn to read the psalter. For when I was in the world, I learned nothing except how to row." The elder heard him and, taking a tablet, scratched the letters on it. And so Athanasios, who possessed much wisdom and had once been a teacher, took the tablet with letters written on it, and prostrating himself, acted like a beginner and behaved like a pupil. He held the tablet in his hands, and labored at

τοὺς πίνακας καὶ τῇ μελέτῃ διεπονεῖτο, προσεποιεῖτο δὴ μὴ δύνασθαι καταλαβεῖν τοῦτό τε κἀκεῖνο τὸ γράμμα, καὶ τοῦτο μέχρι πολλοῦ ὑπεκρίνετο.

2 Ὁ γέρων δὲ ὁρῶν αὐτὸν οὕτως ἔχοντα, ἐδυσφόρει καὶ ἠγανάκτει καὶ ἐχόλα καὶ μακρὰν ἀπεδίωκε τοῦτον μετ' ὀργῆς. Ὁ δὲ θαυμαστὸς Ἀθανάσιος ἔλεγε· "Μὴ ἀποδοκιμάσῃς με, πάτερ, τὸν ἄνουν καὶ χωρικόν, ἀλλὰ μακροθύμησον· μᾶλλον δὲ διὰ τὸν Κύριον, εἴ τι δύνασαι καὶ σὺ διὰ τῶν εὐχῶν σου, βοήθει μοι." Ὁ δὲ γέρων οὐδὲ προσεῖχεν αὐτῷ, ἀλλὰ καθάπαξ ἀπεγίνωσκε τοῦ μαθεῖν αὐτόν· καὶ παραιτούμενος ἦν λοιπόν· ὁ δὲ Ἀθανάσιος οὐκ ἠμέλει τοῦ σκοποῦ· πείθει δὲ ὅμως ὀψέ ποτε τὸν γέροντα εὔξασθαι ὑπὲρ τούτου. Καὶ ὁ μὲν γέρων ηὔχετο, ὁ δὲ Ἀθανάσιος ἤρξατο κατὰ μικρὸν προκόπτειν· καὶ ἰδὼν αὐτὸν ὁ γέρων ταχέως προκόπτοντα καὶ βεβαίως ἐλπίσας, ἐσπούδαζε προάγειν αὐτὸν ἐπὶ τὰ ἔμπροσθεν. Καὶ ὁ μὲν σοφὸς Ἀθανάσιος ἐμάνθανε τὴν ἀλφάβητον, ὁ δὲ ἄσοφος γέρων ἐδίδασκε τὸν σοφώτατον.

16

Νικηφόρος δὲ ὁ ἀοίδιμος ἤδη τὴν ἀρχὴν ἐμπεπιστευμένος τῆς ἁπάσης Ἀνατολῆς, ἐπειδὴ διέγνω τὰ κατὰ τὸν πατέρα Ἀθανάσιον, τήν τε φυγὴν αὐτοῦ καὶ τὴν μετανάστασιν, οὐκ εἶχεν ὅλως φέρειν τὴν αὐτοῦ στέρησιν, ἀλλ'

his studies, and pretended that he could not understand this or that letter, and he continued this pretense for a long time.

The elder, seeing how he was having these problems, was impatient and irritated and enraged and kept angrily sending him away. But the wondrous Athanasios said, "Father, don't reject me for being a stupid country bumpkin, but be patient. Rather, for the Lord's sake, help me, if you can, through your prayers." The elder paid no attention to Athanasios, however, but despaired once and for all that he would ever learn, and flatly refused to pray for this. But Athanasios did not give up his goal, and finally persuaded the elder to pray for this. So the elder prayed, and Athanasios began to make progress bit by bit. When the elder saw him advancing quickly, he became really hopeful and strove to lead him to further progress. Thus the wise Athanasios learned the alphabet, while the elder who lacked wisdom taught this very wise man.

Chapter 16

When the celebrated Nikephoros, who had now been entrusted with the command of all the East, learned the news about his spiritual father Athanasios, about how he had taken flight and moved away, he really could not bear to

ἐν κατηφείᾳ καὶ λύπῃ καὶ ἀπορίᾳ διετέλει, οὐκ ἔχων ὅτι καὶ πράξοι καὶ ὅπως ἀναζητήσει περὶ αὐτοῦ.

2　Ἐπεὶ δὲ ἐμνήσθη τοῦ Ἄθω (ἦσαν γὰρ κοινολογησάμενοι περὶ τούτου πρὸς ἀλλήλους), γράμμασι παρακλητικοῖς πρὸς τὸν κριτὴν Θεσσαλονίκης ἐχρήσατο, γράψας οὕτως· "Δέομαι καὶ ἱκετεύω σε θερμῶς, πνευματικὲ ἀδελφέ, μή μου παρόψει ταύτην τὴν δέησιν, μὴ δὲ ὀκνήσῃς ἢ καταρραθυμήσῃς πράγματος καλοῦ καὶ κέρδος φέροντος τῇ ἀγάπῃ σου· ἀλλὰ τάχει δραμὼν πρὸς τὸν Ἄθω, ἐρεύνησον ἀκριβῶς περὶ τοῦ μοναχοῦ Ἀθανασίου τοῦ τιμιωτάτου πατρός μου, καὶ δός μοι χάριν, ἧς μείζων ἄλλη οὐκ ἔστιν ἐμοί· διὰ γὰρ τούτου τοῦ μικροῦ σοι κόπου ὅλον ἐμαυτὸν δίδωμι δοῦλόν σου, ἄχρις ἂν ζῶ, καὶ τὴν ὁμολογίαν ταύτης τῆς χάριτος οὐ διακόψει οὐδὲ τάφος αὐτός." Καὶ ταῦτα μὲν οὕτως· προσέθετο δὲ καὶ τὰ τούτου γνωρίσματα, τό τε εἶδος καὶ τὴν γνῶσιν καὶ τῆς ἀρετῆς τὸ ἐξαίρετον.

3　Ὁ δὲ κριτὴς τὸ γράμμα δεξάμενος καὶ δυσωπηθεὶς τοῦ ἀνδρὸς τὴν ἀξίωσιν, ἐτρέπετο πρὸς τὴν περὶ τοῦ Ἀθανασίου ἔρευναν. Αὐτίκα τοίνυν εἰς τὸ Ὄρος ἐχώρησε, καὶ τὸν πρῶτον τοῦ Ὄρους προσκαλεσάμενος, ἠρώτα τοῦτον περὶ αὐτοῦ. Ὁ δὲ διεβεβαιοῦτο λέγων ὅτι "τοιοῦτος ἀνὴρ οἷον ἡ ἐνδοξότης σου ζητεῖ, ἐν τῷ Ὄρει οὐκ ἐπεδήμησεν· ὅμως εἰ καὶ ἀγνοῶ, ἀλλ' ἐπειδὴ καταλαμβάνει ὁ καιρὸς τῆς συνάξεως, ὅστις ἂν εἴη καὶ οὗτος, μετὰ τῶν ἄλλων πάντως συναθροισθήσεται." Ἐδόκει ταῦτα τούτοις· καὶ ὁ μὲν ἄρχων ὑπέστρεψεν, ὁ δὲ πρῶτος διελογίζετο ἐν ἑαυτῷ τοῦ ἄρχοντος τὸ παράγγελμα.

be deprived of his presence, but fell into sorrowful despair and uncertainty about what to do and how to search for him.

But when he remembered Athos (for they used to talk to 2 each other about it), he wrote a letter to the judge of Thessalonike, asking for his help in the following words: "I beg and ardently beseech you, my spiritual brother, do not disregard my request, and do not hesitate or neglect a good deed that will also benefit you, my dear friend. Go quickly to Athos, and make careful inquiries about the monk Athanasios, my most venerable spiritual father; do me this favor which is more important to me than anything else. For in return for this small labor I will give myself completely to you as your servant, as long as I shall live, and not even the grave itself will interrupt my gratitude for this favor." This is what he wrote; and he also added Athanasios's distinctive characteristics, his appearance and his knowledge and his exceptional virtue.

When the judge received the letter, out of respect for 3 Nikephoros's rank he undertook a search for Athanasios. He immediately set out for the Mountain and, summoning the *protos* of the Mountain, asked him about Athanasios. The *protos* assured him, "Such a man as your excellency seeks has not taken up residence on the Mountain. However, even if I am mistaken, when the time for the *synaxis* comes, whoever this man may be, he will surely assemble with the others." This seemed a good idea to them, and the official returned to Thessalonike, while the *protos* pondered the official's information.

17

Ἐπεὶ τοίνυν σύναξις ἐτελεῖτο τρὶς τοῦ ἐνιαυτοῦ, πάντων συνερχομένων ἐν τῇ τῶν Καρεῶν οὕτω λεγομένῃ λαύρᾳ καὶ τὰς συνήθεις τρεῖς ἐπιτελούντων ἑορτάς, ἐπί τε τῷ μεταλαμβάνειν τῶν ἁγίων μυστηρίων καὶ συνεσθίειν ἀλλήλοις (προσεκτέον μοι ὧδε, ὦ ἱερώτατον σύστημα, ἵν᾽ εἰδῆτε πρᾶγμα θαύμαστόν τε καὶ χαριέστατον καὶ εὐφροσύνης μεστόν), ἐπέστη ἡ ἡμέρα τῆς τῶν πατέρων συναγωγῆς (αὕτη δὲ ἦν ἡ πρώτη καὶ κυριωτάτη καὶ λαμπροτάτη, ἡ τοῦ Χριστοῦ γέννησις), καὶ συνηθροίσθησαν ἅπαντες πάντοθεν· πατέρες οὗτοι, εὐπρεπεῖς καὶ τῇ τάξει καὶ τῇ πολιτείᾳ καὶ τῇ πολιᾷ, ὕμνουν, ἔψαλλον ἅπαντες, καὶ ἐν μέσοις τούτοις ὁ ζητούμενος ἐγνωρίζετο οὐκ ἄλλῳ τινὶ ἀλλ᾽ ἢ τῷ πρώτῳ τῶν ἄλλων καὶ ἀπὸ τῶν γνωρισμάτων ὧν παρηγγέλλετο.

2   Εἶτα τί; Κατέλαβε καὶ τῆς ἀναγνώσεως ὁ καιρός, προτίθεται βίβλος ἡ σεβασμία τοῦ Θεολόγου, τάττεται ἀναγνῶναι ὁ Ἀθανάσιος παρὰ τοῦ τεταγμένου εἰς τοῦτο τῇ νεύσει τοῦ πρώτου, παραιτεῖται ἐκεῖνος ἐπειπὼν τοῦτο δὴ τὸ "συγχώρησον," τάσσεται καὶ πάλιν οὐχ ἁπλῶς, ἀλλὰ μετὰ τοῦ δέοντος ἐπιτιμίου· καὶ τούτων τελουμένων ὁ δῆθεν διδάσκαλος καὶ παιδευτὴς αὐτοῦ ὁ γέρων ἐξίστατο, καὶ ἡσύχως πως ὑπογελῶν ἀπεδίωκε διὰ τοῦ σχήματος τῆς χειρὸς τὸν αὐτὸν τάττοντα, λέγων· "Ἄπελθε, ἀββᾶ, μὴ εἰδὼς τὴν ἀγροικίαν καὶ ἀγνωσίαν τοῦ ἀδελφοῦ· ἄρτι γὰρ διδάσκεται συλλαβίζειν τὴν τοῦ ψαλτηρίου ἀρχήν."

Chapter 17

The *synaxis* took place three times a year, when everyone assembled at the so-called *lavra* of Karyes and celebrated the three customary feast days, by partaking of the holy mysteries and dining together. (Pay attention to me now, O most holy congregation, so that you may learn about a wondrous and most pleasing and joyous incident!) So the day came for the assembly of the fathers (this one was the first and most important and most splendid feast day, the Nativity of Christ), and everyone gathered together from all over. These fathers, who were distinguished in rank and conduct and old age, were all singing and chanting, and in their midst was the man who was being sought, unrecognized by anyone except for their *protos* from the distinctive characteristics about which he had been informed.

And then what happened? The time for the reading arrived, and the venerable book of the Theologian was set out, and Athanasios was assigned to read by the man in charge of this by a nod from the *protos*. When Athanasios refused, adding the words "forgive me," he was not just ordered again to read, but was threatened with punishment if he did not. When this happened, the elder, his supposed teacher and instructor, was astonished. Smiling gently to himself, with a gesture of his hand he dismissed the one who gave this order, saying, "Forget it, my *abbas*. You are unaware of the brother's rustic ignorance; for he is just now learning to read the beginning of the psalter by sounding out each syllable."

2

3   Τί οὖν ἡ ταπεινόφρων καὶ δικαία ψυχή; Οὐ γὰρ εἶχεν
ἀντιπίπτειν ὑπὲρ τὸ μέτρον καὶ ἀθετεῖν τὴν σύνοικον
αὐτῷ ὑπακοήν. Ἀνίσταται μὲν καὶ ποιεῖ τὸ ἐπίταγμα,
ἀνεγίνωσκε δὲ ὡς παιδίον ἀρχὴν ἔχον τοῦ συλλαβίζειν·
κατὰ μίαν γὰρ συλλαβὴν τὴν φωνὴν ἐπέκοπτε καὶ τὴν
λέξιν εἰς πολλὰ κατέτεμνεν. Ὁ πρῶτος τοίνυν ὡς ἑώρα
τοῦτον οὕτως ἀναγινώσκοντα καὶ μεγάλως παραταξάμε-
νον ἐπὶ τὸ κρύψαι τὴν γνῶσιν αὐτοῦ, ἐξανέστη ἀπὸ τοῦ
θρόνου αὐτοῦ καὶ ἐπιτιμίῳ καθυποβάλλει φρικτῷ, ὥστε
ὑπαναγνῶναι καθὼς ἐπίσταται. Τότε δὴ ἡ εὔλαλος ἐκείνη
γλῶσσα, ἡ δεσμουμένη πρότερον, τῷ ἐπιτιμίῳ τῆς ταπεινώσεως ἐλύετο, καὶ ἐδείκνυ τὴν τέχνην αὐτῆς καὶ τὸ
κάλλος τῆς σοφίας καὶ τῆς ἀρετῆς αὐτοῦ τὸ μέγεθος.

4   Καὶ ὁ μὲν χορὸς ἅπας τῶν γερόντων ὁρῶντες αὐτὸν
ἐπιστημόνως ἀναγινώσκοντα, ἐξίσταντο καὶ ἐθαύμαζον,
πρᾶγμα ὁρῶντες οἷον οὐδέποτε εἶδον οὔτε ἤκουσαν· ὁ
γέρων δὲ ὁ τούτου παιδευτὴς μικροῦ καὶ ἀπεπάγη· αὐτίκα
γὰρ καὶ δακρύων ἐπληροῦντο οἱ ὀφθαλμοὶ αὐτοῦ, ὅστις
καὶ τὰ τοῦ Θεοῦ μεγαλεῖα ἐδόξαζε καὶ πολλὰς ὄντως εἶναι
τὰς πρὸς σωτηρίαν ὁδοὺς ἐδιδάσκετο, καὶ ἀντὶ τῆς μικρᾶς
ἐκείνης διδαχῆς μέγαν μισθὸν ἀντελάμβανεν, ὅτι ἔφθασεν
ὀνομασθῆναι διδάσκαλος τοιούτου διδασκάλου σοφίας
καὶ ἀρετῆς, καὶ εὐχαριστεῖ τῷ Θεῷ λέγων· "Εὐχαριστῶ τῇ
οἰκονομίᾳ σου, Δέσποτα, ὅτι ἔδειξάς μοι τῆς ταπεινοφροσύνης τὴν πρώτην ὁδὸν διὰ τούτου τοῦ σοφωτάτου
ἀδελφοῦ."

So what did that humble and righteous soul do then? For 3 he could not unduly resist and set aside his inherent obedience. He stood up and did as he was told, and read like a child who was just beginning to sound out the syllables; for he halted his speech at each syllable and divided the word into many parts. When the *protos* saw Athanasios reading in this way and so obstinately trying to conceal his knowledge, he rose from his chair and threatened to subject him to a horrific punishment to make him read aloud as he well knew how to do. Then that eloquent tongue, which had previously been bound fast, was loosed from its humility on account of the threatened penalty, and revealed its skill and the beauty of his wisdom and the magnitude of his virtue.

When they saw him reading so knowledgeably, the whole 4 assembly of elders was astounded and marveled, for they were seeing something the like of which they had never seen or heard before. But the elder who had been his teacher was all but struck dumb. His eyes immediately filled with tears, and he glorified the splendors of God and was taught that there are indeed many ways that lead to salvation. And he received great compensation for the little teaching he had done, because he ended up being known as the teacher of such a teacher of wisdom and virtue. He gave thanks to God, saying, "I give thanks for your dispensation, my Lord, because you have shown me the foremost path to humility through this most wise brother."

18

Λέγεται δὲ καὶ τοῦτο περὶ τοῦ Ἀθανασίου, ὅτι ἐν τῇ τῶν πατέρων συνάξει καὶ οὗτος συναθροιζόμενος, ἔβαλε μετάνοιαν τούτοις καθεζομένοις· οἱ δὲ εὐθέως ὑπανέστησαν αὐτῷ καὶ μετάνοιαν ἔβαλον ἄχρι καὶ τοῦ ἐδάφους τῆς γῆς, ὅπερ δὴ καὶ αὐτοὺς ἐκείνους ἐξέπληξεν· οὐκ ᾔδεισαν γὰρ ὅτι προφητικῶς τοῦτο ἐποίουν ὑπὸ τῆς ἐνοικούσης αὐτοῖς χάριτος, ὥστε καὶ Παῦλος ἐκεῖνος ὁ Ξηροποταμίτης, ὁ τὰ πρῶτα φέρων ἐν τούτοις, ἰδὼν αὐτοὺς οὕτως ἐκ πρώτης ταπεινωθέντας αὐτῷ καὶ ὑποκλιθέντας, τοιοῦτόν τι περὶ αὐτοῦ ἔφη προφητικῶς· "Οὗτος, ἀδελφοί, ὁ ὀπίσω ἡμῶν γεγονὼς ἐν τῷ Ὄρει, ἔμπροσθεν ἡμῶν ἐστι κατὰ ἀρετήν, ὅτι καὶ πρῶτος ἡμῶν [see John 1:15] φανήσεται ἐν τῇ βασιλείᾳ τῶν οὐρανῶν· ἔσται γάρ τις ἀρχηγὸς ἐν τῷ Ὄρει, καὶ μάνδραι πολλαὶ δι' αὐτοῦ φυτευθήσονται ἐν αὐτῷ, καὶ ἅπαντες τούτῳ ὑποταγήσονται."

19

Οὕτω μὲν οὖν ὁ Ξηροποταμίτης. Ἐπεὶ δὲ ἤδη διεγνώσθη ὁ Ἀθανάσιος, ἀνιχνεύει ὁ πρῶτος πάντα τὰ κατ' αὐτόν, ἀνακαλύπτει δὲ τούτῳ καὶ τὴν γενομένην περὶ αὐτοῦ ἀναζήτησιν, καὶ ὅτι, φησί, "Πολλὴν ἔχουσι τὴν περὶ σοῦ φροντίδα καὶ ἔρευναν ὁ τῶν Ἀνατολικῶν στρατηγὸς

Chapter 18

It is also said about Athanasios that, when he joined the *synaxis* of the fathers, he prostrated himself before them as they were seated; but they immediately stood up and did obeisance to him, even prostrating themselves on the ground. This astonished them, for they did not know that they were doing so prophetically through the grace that resided in them. Even Paul of Xeropotamou, who was preeminent among them, when he saw them humbling themselves before Athanasios right from the start in this way and bowing to him, prophetically said something of this sort about him: "Brethren, this man, *who* came *after* us on the Mountain, *ranks before* us in virtue, *because* he will appear *first* among us in the kingdom of heaven; for he will be a leader on the Mountain, and will establish many sheepfolds on it, and everyone will be obedient to him."

Chapter 19

These then were the words of Paul of Xeropotamou. Since Athanasios had now been recognized, the *protos* sketched out the whole story with regard to him. He let him know about the ongoing search for him, and that, as he said, "The military governor of the Anatolikon, Kyr Nikephoros,

κῦρις Νικηφόρος καὶ ὁ τούτου αὐτάδελφος." Ὁ δὲ Ἀθανάσιος ἐδυσώπει αὐτὸν λέγων· "Ἀλλὰ μὴ ἐξείποις, πάτερ, τὰ κατ᾽ ἐμὲ τοῖς ζητοῦσί με, ἵνα μὴ ἀναγκασθῶ μεταβῆναι ἐντεῦθεν καὶ κόπον οὐ μικρὸν προξενήσῃς μοι." Ὁ πρῶτος δὲ ζημίαν τὴν ἐσχάτην ἡγούμενος τῷ Ὄρει τὴν ἐκείνου στέρησιν, ἐν μυστηρίῳ μὲν κατέχειν ἐπηγγείλατο τὴν ἐκείνου εὕρεσιν, συμβουλεύει δὲ αὐτῷ ἡσυχάσαι ἔν τινι μονοκέλλῃ τῶν Καρεῶν τρισὶ μιλίοις ἀπεχούσῃ. Ὃ δὴ καὶ ποιήσας ὁ Ἀθανάσιος, προσωμίλει μὲν ἀπερισπάστως τῷ Θεῷ, ἐλάνθανε δὲ καὶ οὓς ἐβούλετο.

2   Ἐπεὶ δὲ ἄνθρωπος ἦν καὶ ἀπαραίτητον εἶχε τὴν τοῦ ἄρτου μικρὰν τροφήν, ἠναγκάσθη καὶ ἐργοχείρου ἅψασθαι, ἵνα διὰ τούτου τρέφηται. Καὶ ἐφανεροῦτο ἤδη σὺν τῇ γνώσει αὐτοῦ καὶ τὸ γράφειν ὡραίως τε καὶ ταχέως· καὶ τὸ μὲν κάλλος τῶν γραμμάτων αὐτοῦ δῆλόν ἐστιν ἐκ τῶν ἔτι περιόντων αὐτοχείρως αὐτῷ γραφέντων βιβλίων, τὸ δὲ τάχος τὸ κάλλος ἐνίκησε· διὰ γὰρ ἓξ ἡμερῶν ὅλον συνεπλήρου τὸ ψαλτήριον, οὐδὲ τοῦ συνήθους αὐτῷ κανόνος ὑστερήσαντός ποτε πολλοῦ ὄντος. Ἵνα δὲ καὶ τὸ ἀπερίκοπον ἔχῃ ἐν ἅπασι, κέχρηταί τινι τῶν εὐλαβῶν γερόντων καὶ τῆς τροφῆς ὑπουργῷ καὶ τῆς γραφῆς συνεργῷ, Λουκίτζῃ ὀνομαζομένῳ· αὐτὸς γὰρ πᾶσαν τὴν ἐν ταῖς βίβλοις ὑπουργίαν εἰσέφερε τούτῳ, καὶ ἐκ τοῦ ἐντεῦθεν μισθοῦ ἄρτον ὀλιγοστὸν διηκόνει αὐτῷ, καὶ πλέον οὐδέν.

and his brother are very concerned about you and are searching for you." But Athanasios begged him, saying, "Father, don't tell those who are searching for me where I am, so that I won't be forced to move away from here and you don't cause me great trouble." The *protos,* believing that being deprived of him would be the worst possible loss for the Mountain, promised to keep his discovery of Athanasios a secret, but he advised him to retire to a solitary cell, which was three miles distant from Karyes. Athanasios did this, and conversed uninterruptedly with God, while escaping the notice of those he wanted to elude.

But since he was human and needed a little nourishment 2 from bread, he was forced to undertake some manual labor so as to feed himself. And so now, along with his knowledge, his beautiful and rapid handwriting became known. But while the beauty of his calligraphy is apparent from the books which still survive, copied in his own hand, his speed eclipsed the beauty. For he would complete an entire psalter in six days, but still never lag behind in his customary spiritual regimen, despite its length. So as not to be at all distracted, he used one of the pious elders named Loukitzes as a helper with his meals and as a collaborator in his copying work. For Loukitzes used to offer him every assistance with the books, and as payment for this <Athanasios> would give him a tiny amount of bread and nothing else.

20

Ἀλλὰ γὰρ τηλικοῦτος ὢν ἐργάτης τῆς ἀρετῆς ὁ Ἀθανάσιος, οὐκ εἶχεν εἰς τέλος λαθεῖν, ὥσπερ οὐδὲ πόλις κρυβῆναι ἐπάνω ὄρους κειμένη [Matthew 5:14]. Ὁ γὰρ μάγιστρος Λέων, ὃν πρῴην εἴπομεν ἄρχειν τῶν τῆς Ἑσπέρας ταγμάτων, νίκην λαμπρὰν ἀράμενος κατὰ τῶν νομάδων Σκυθῶν, ὑπέστρεφε μὲν ἐκεῖθεν, εἰς δὲ τὸν Ἄθω παραγέγονε, τοῦτο μὲν ἵνα καὶ εὐχαριστήσῃ τῇ μητρὶ τοῦ Θεοῦ ἕνεκεν τῆς κατὰ τῶν βαρβάρων νίκης, τοῦτο δὲ ἵνα καὶ τὰ κατὰ τὸν Ἀθανάσιον ἀκριβῶς ἐρευνήσῃ. Ἐπεὶ δὲ εἰσελθὼν εἰς τὸ Ὄρος τὰ κατ᾽ αὐτὸν ἐμάνθανεν, εὐθὺς ἐζήτει θεάσασθαι καὶ αὐτὸν τὸν ποθούμενον· ὃν καὶ εὑρὼν καὶ περιπλακείς, πολλῆς ἐπληροῦτο χαρᾶς.

2 Ὡς δ᾽ οὖν ἐγνώκεισαν οἱ τοῦ Ὄρους μοναχοὶ πολλὴν τοῦ μαγίστρου τὴν πίστιν καὶ τὸ σέβας περὶ τὸν Ἀθανάσιον, παρεκάλεσαν αὐτὸν περὶ ἀνοικοδομῆς τοῦ ναοῦ τῶν Καρεῶν· βραχὺς γὰρ ὤν, πολλὴν παρεῖχε τὴν στενοχωρίαν ἐν ταῖς συνάξεσιν. Ὁ δὲ Ἀθανάσιος αἰτησάμενος τοῦτον, οὐκ ἠστόχησε τῆς αἰτήσεως· αὐτίκα γὰρ ἱκανὰ τούτοις δέδωκε χρήματα καὶ ἐκέλευσεν ἐκ βάθρων αὐτῶν ἀνοικοδομῆσαι τὸν ναὸν καὶ περικαλλῆ ἀπαρτίσαι, ὅπερ καὶ γέγονεν. Εἶτα τοῦτον μὲν παρέπεμψεν, αὐτὸς δὲ εἰς τὸ ἑαυτοῦ καταγώγιον ἐπανῆλθε καὶ τῆς συνήθους διαγωγῆς εἴχετο.

Chapter 20

But since Athanasios was such a practitioner of virtue, in the end he could not escape notice, just as a *city set on a hill cannot be hid*. For the *magistros* Leo, who, as we said previously, commanded the troops of the West, won a brilliant victory over the nomadic Scythians, and came to Athos on his way back from there. He did this to offer thanks to the Mother of God for his victory over the barbarians, but also to make detailed inquiries about Athanasios. And so, when Leo arrived at the Mountain and learned about him, he immediately asked to see this man who was the object of his desire. And after finding him and embracing him, he was filled with much joy.

When the monks of the Mountain recognized the great 2 faith of the *magistros* and his reverence for Athanasios, they asked him about rebuilding the church at Karyes. For since it was small, it was very crowded during the monastic assemblies. And when Athanasios requested this, he did not fail to gain his request. For Leo immediately gave them a lot of money and told them to rebuild the church from its foundations and to furnish it beautifully, which indeed happened. Then Athanasios bade him farewell, went back to where he lived, and resumed his customary lifestyle.

21

Ἔνθέν τοι καὶ ἄπασιν ἐξάκουστος γέγονε καὶ εἰς πάντας διεφημίζετο, καὶ πολλοὶ πρὸς αὐτὸν διαπαντὸς χάριν ὠφελείας συνέτρεχον· ἀλλ᾽ αὐτὸς θερμότατος ἐραστὴς τῆς ἡσυχίας τυγχάνων καὶ πάντοθεν φεύγων τὰς πρὸς τὴν κενὴν δόξαν ἀφορμάς, πρὸς τὰ τοῦ Ὄρους ἐχώρει ἐνδότερα· ὁ γὰρ Θεός, ἀποκαθιστῶν αὐτῷ τὴν κληρονομίαν [Psalm 15(16):5], ὡδήγησεν αὐτὸν ἐπ᾽ αὐτὸ τὸ ἀκρωτήριον τοῦ Ἄθω, Μελανὰ μὲν προσαγορευόμενον καὶ πολλὴν τὴν ἐρημίαν ἔχον, πολὺ δὲ ἀπέχον καὶ τῶν ἄλλων ἀσκητικῶν καταγωγίων. Ἐν δὲ τῷ μεσαιτάτῳ τόπῳ τοῦ τοιούτου ἀκρωτηρίου καλύβην πηξάμενος ὡς ἄλλο ἀρετῆς ἐργαστήριον, πρὸς πόνους μείζονας καὶ ἀγῶνας ἀσκητικοὺς διηγείρετο.

2   Ἀλλ᾽ ὁ μελανὸς τῷ ὄντι καὶ ἀκοίμητος Πολεμήτωρ ἡμῶν, ὁρῶν τοὺς μεγάλους καὶ ἀνενδότους ἐκείνους ἀγῶνας τοῦ Ἀθανασίου καὶ τὴν ἐπιπονωτέραν αὐτοῦ ἄσκησιν, καὶ δείσας μὴ καὶ παντελῶς τοῦ τόπου ἐξελάσῃ αὐτόν, παρεσκευάζετο πρὸς τὸν κατ᾽ αὐτοῦ πόλεμον, καὶ τὰ βέλη τῆς ἀκηδίας πέμπων, ἐτόξευε τὸν ἀκαταγώνιστον καὶ ἐποίει αὐτὸν μισεῖν τὸν τόπον τῆς καλῆς κατοικίας, καὶ σφόδρα ἐπολέμει αὐτὸν ἐν τοῖς λογισμοῖς τῆς ἀναχωρήσεως. Ἀλλ᾽ ἔλαθε τὸν Πονηρὸν ὅτι θεία οἰκονομία ἦν ἡ τοῦ τοιούτου πολέμου παραχώρησις· ἐδίδασκε γὰρ ὁ Θεὸς τὸν Ἀθανάσιον διὰ τῆς πείρας τοῦ τοιούτου πολέμου, ἵνα καὶ αὐτὸς γινώσκῃ βοηθεῖν τοῖς ἐμπιστευθησομένοις αὐτῷ θρέμμασιν ὕστερον, ὅτε καὶ οὗτοι πειράζονται.

Chapter 21

In this way Athanasios came to be celebrated by everyone and was praised in every way, and many people kept flocking to him for their personal benefit. But since he was a most ardent lover of spiritual tranquility and always fled occasions for vainglory, he withdrew to the interior of the Mountain; for God, *restoring his inheritance to him,* guided him to the Athonite promontory that is known as Melana. This was extremely desolate, and a long way from the abodes of the other ascetics. Right in the middle of this promontory he built a hut as another *workshop of virtue,* and roused himself to even greater labors and ascetic struggles.

But when our Enemy, who is truly black and never sleeps, saw Athanasios's immense and relentless struggles and his even more arduous ascetic regime, he grew fearful that the holy man would drive him away completely from that place, and so prepared for battle against him. Unleashing the arrows of despondency, he struck the invincible one and made him hate the location of his fine dwelling, and he attacked Athanasios vigorously with thoughts of abandoning it. But the Evil One failed to realize that it was divine dispensation that permitted this battle; for God taught Athanasios through the trial of this battle, so that later on he might know how to help those nurslings who were entrusted to him, when they too were being tempted.

3   Οὕτως οὖν ἰσχυρῶς πολεμηθεὶς ὑπὸ τῆς ἀκηδίας καὶ τοῖς λογισμοῖς τῆς ἐκεῖθεν ἀναχωρήσεως τυραννούμενος, μὴ ἔχων δὲ γνῶναι εἰ καὶ Θεὸς βούλεται ἐξελθεῖν αὐτὸν ἐκεῖθεν, μήτε δὲ συμβούλῳ χρήσασθαι δυνάμενος, μήπως διαγνωσθῇ ὁποῖός ἐστι τὴν ἀρετήν, καὶ εἰς ἀπορίαν περιϊστάμενος, βουλὴν βουλεύεται γενναίαν τε καὶ συνετήν· εἶπε γὰρ πρὸς ἑαυτόν· "Ὑπομείνω τοῦτον τὸν πόλεμον ἄχρις ἐνιαυτοῦ ὅλου, καὶ τούτου πληρουμένου, εἰ μὲν ὁ Θεὸς ἐπισκέψεταί με καὶ λύσει μοι τοῦτον τὸν πειρασμόν, δῆλον ἔσται πάντως ὅτι Θεοῦ βουλή ἐστι τὸ εἶναί με ἐνταῦθα· εἰ δὲ τοῦτο μὴ γένηται, τηνικαῦτα ὑπαναχωρήσω ἐντεῦθεν." Καὶ οὗτος μὲν ἄπαυστον εἶχε τὸν πόλεμον· ἡ δὲ προθεσμία ἤδη ἐπληροῦτο.

4   Καταλαβούσης δὲ τῆς τελευταίας ἡμέρας τοῦ ἐνιαυτοῦ καὶ τοῦ πειρασμοῦ μὴ ἐνδιδόντος, ἐμελέτα τὴν ἐπαύριον ἐξελθεῖν ἐκεῖθεν καὶ εἰς τὰς Καρέας ἀπελθεῖν καὶ τὸν πόλεμον τοῦ λογισμοῦ ἐξαγγεῖλαι τοῖς ἀδελφοῖς καὶ βαλεῖν αὐτοῖς μετάνοιαν καὶ ἀναχωρῆσαι. Κατ᾽ αὐτὴν δὲ τὴν ἡμέραν ἐν τῷ ποιεῖν αὐτὸν τὴν τῆς τρίτης ὥρας εὐχήν, ἐχύθη φῶς οὐράνιον ἐπ᾽ αὐτὸν καὶ περιήστραψε καὶ φωτοειδῆ ἀπειργάσατο· καὶ τὸ μὲν νέφος τοῦ πολέμου ἔφυγεν ἀπ᾽ αὐτοῦ, αὐτὸς δὲ εὐφροσύνης ἀρρήτου καὶ χαρᾶς πληρωθείς, πόθον τε θεῖον ἐλάμβανε καὶ γλυκὺ δάκρυον ἔσταζεν· ἔκτοτε γὰρ ὁ πατὴρ τὸ τῆς κατανύξεως ἔλαβε χάρισμα, καὶ ὅτε ἐβούλετο, ἀπόνως ἐδάκρυε. Λοιπὸν οὖν καὶ τὸν τόπον τῶν Μελανῶν τοσοῦτον ἠγάπησεν ὅσον ἐμίσει τὸ πρότερον.

So, bitterly attacked by despondency, oppressed by 3
thoughts of abandoning the site, unable to know if even
God wanted him to leave that place, and unable to resort to
a counselor, lest his virtue be recognized, Athanasios fell
into perplexity. But then he resolved upon an excellent and
sensible plan. For he said to himself, "I will endure this
struggle for an entire year, and at the end of that time, if
God visits me and releases me from this temptation, it will
surely be clear that it is God's will that I remain here; but if
this does not happen, then I will go away from here." And
thus his struggle was relentless, but the allotted period of
time was eventually fulfilled.

When the last day of that year arrived and the tempta- 4
tion did not cease, he made plans to leave that place on the
very next day, return to Karyes, confess to the brethren his
struggle with temptation, prostrate himself before them,
and go away. But on that very day, while he was saying his
prayer at the third hour, a heavenly light poured over him
and flashed all around and made him luminous. The cloud of
struggle fled from him, he was filled with ineffable happiness and joy, received divine yearning, and shed a sweet tear.
For from that time on the father received the gift of contrition and was able to weep effortlessly, whenever he wished.
Thus from then on he came to love the site of Melana as
much as he had previously hated it.

22

Καὶ οὗτος μὲν ἐν τούτοις ἐτύγχανεν· ὁ δὲ κράτιστος Νικηφόρος, τοῦ παντὸς στρατεύματος τὴν ἐξουσίαν πεπιστευμένος ὑπὸ τῆς ἀνακτορικῆς μεγαλειότητος καὶ εἰς Κρήτην ἐξαποσταλείς, οὐκ ἦν θαρρῶν τῇ ρωμαϊκῇ δυνάμει, ἀλλὰ τὰς τῶν πατέρων εὐχὰς ἐλάμβανεν εἰς βοήθειαν. Καὶ ἐπειδὴ ἔφθασε μαθὼν παρὰ τοῦ αὐταδέλφου αὐτοῦ τοῦ πατρικίου Λέοντος ἐν τῷ Ἄθῳ ἡσυχάζειν τὸν Ἀθανάσιον, ἐξέπεμψέ τινας τῶν ὑπ᾽ αὐτὸν διὰ χελανδίου ἐκεῖσε, τοῦτο μὲν αἰτούμενος τὴν γερουσίαν εὐχὰς βοηθούσας αὐτῷ εἰς τὸν κατὰ τῶν Κρητῶν πόλεμον, τοῦτο δὲ σταλῆναι αὐτῷ καὶ τὸν Ἀθανάσιον ἐξάπαντος μετὰ ἑνὸς ἢ δύο γερόντων.

2   Οἱ δὲ μοναχοί, δεξάμενοι τὴν γραφὴν αὐτοῦ καὶ ἀναγνόντες αὐτήν, πρῶτον μὲν ἐθαύμαζον καὶ ὑπερεξεπλήττοντο τὴν πολλὴν περὶ τὸν Ἀθανάσιον φιλίαν καὶ τὸ σέβας τοῦ καλοῦ Νικηφόρου· συναχθέντες δὲ ἅπαντες, ἐπέτρεπον αὐτῷ ἀπελθεῖν πρὸς τὸν στρατηγικώτατον Νικηφόρον. Αὐτὸς δὲ ἐκ πρώτης οὐδόλως ἐπείθετο, οἱ δὲ ἐπέκειντο ἀναγκάζοντες αὐτὸν εἰς τοῦτο μετ᾽ ἐπιτιμίων φρικτῶν. Ἐπεὶ δὲ μόλις ἐπείσθη, ἔκριναν ἀπελθεῖν μετ᾽ αὐτοῦ καὶ ἕνα τῶν γερόντων, ᾧτινι καὶ ἀκολουθῶν ὁ Ἀθανάσιος ἐν τάξει μαθητοῦ, ἐπιβὰς τοῦ χελανδίου ἅμα αὐτῷ, ἐπὶ τὴν Κρήτην ἐξέπλευσεν.

3   Ὁ γοῦν εὐσεβέστατος Νικηφόρος, καταλαβόντων αὐτῶν, ἰδὼν τὸν Ἀθανάσιον, ἠσπάσατο μὲν καὶ ὡς πατέρα

Chapter 22

While Athanasios was in this situation, the most mighty Nikephoros, who had been entrusted by his imperial majesty with command of the entire army and dispatched to Crete, did not have confidence in the military strength of the Romans, but was receiving the prayers of the fathers in support. Since he had just learned from his brother, the *patrikios* Leo, that Athanasios was practicing spiritual tranquility on Athos, he sent some of his men there in a boat, partly to ask the council of elders for prayers to assist him in his war against the Cretans, and partly also to request that Athanasios be sent to him without fail with one or two elders.

When the monks received his message and read it, they 2 were initially amazed and totally astonished at the good Nikephoros's great love and veneration for Athanasios. Then, when they had all assembled, they ordered Athanasios to go to the supreme commander Nikephoros. At first there was no way he could be persuaded, but they put pressure on him, forcing him to do so with threats of frightful penalties. When he had been persuaded with difficulty, they decided that one of the elders should accompany him, and Athanasios, following him in the role of a disciple, boarded the boat with him, and sailed off to Crete.

When they arrived, and the most pious Nikephoros saw 3 Athanasios, he embraced him and honored him as his

ἐτίμησεν αὐτοῦ πνευματικόν· μαθὼν δὲ ὅτι καὶ ὡς μαθητὴς ἐγένετο τῷ γέροντι, ἐξεπλάγη ἐπὶ τῇ ταπεινώσει καὶ μισοδοξίᾳ αὐτοῦ. Εὐθὺς οὖν πάντων καθάπαξ ἀφέμενος, τῆς τε νίκης τοῦ πολέμου καὶ τῶν κατὰ τῶν πολεμίων ἀνδραγαθημάτων, τῶν παλαιῶν ὑποσχέσεων αὐτὸν ἀνεμίμνησκε λέγων· "Ὁ φόβος, ὦ πάτερ, ὃν εἶχον οἱ μοναχοὶ ἐκ τῶν κακωνύμων Ἀγαρηνῶν, ἤδη ἀπηλάθη τοῦ Ὄρους διὰ τῶν εὐχῶν ὑμῶν· ἐπέστη δὲ καιρός, οὗ ἔκπαλαι ἐπεθύμουν, πρὸς τὸ φυγεῖν τὰ τοῦ κόσμου, καὶ οὐδέν ἐστιν ἡμῖν ἄρτι εἰς τοῦτο ἐμπόδιον, εἰ μὴ μόνον τὸ οἰκοδομηθῆναι ἡμῖν οἰκητήρια· καὶ δέομαί σου τῆς ὁσιότητος πρῶτον μὲν οἰκοδομῆσαι ἡμῖν κελλία ἡσυχαστικά, θεμελιῶσαι δὲ καὶ ναὸν καὶ ἀπαρτίσαι αὐτὸν εἰς κοινόβιον, ὡς ἂν ἐγὼ μὲν καὶ σὺ μετὰ καὶ ἑτέρων τριῶν ἀδελφῶν ἐν τοῖς ἡσυχαστικοῖς κελλίοις μονάζωμεν, τῇ δὲ κυρίᾳ ἡμέρᾳ κατερχώμεθα ἅμα εἰς τὴν λαύραν καὶ τῶν θείων ἁγιασμάτων μεταλαμβάνωμεν καὶ συνεσθίωμεν τοῖς ἀδελφοῖς καὶ τῷ ἡγουμένῳ, καὶ πάλιν ἀνερχώμεθα."

4   Καὶ ταῦτα μὲν ὁ Νικηφόρος ἐξαιτούμενος, ἐπεδίδου αὐτῷ καὶ χρυσίον πρὸς τὴν τῶν οἰκοδομηθησομένων καταβολήν· ὁ δὲ πατὴρ Ἀθανάσιος τὸν ἀπράγμονα καὶ ἀθόρυβον βίον ποθῶν, οὔτε τὸ χρυσίον ἐλάμβανεν, οὔτε ὅλως τῷ Νικηφόρῳ ἐπείθετο· "Ἀλλὰ σὺ μέν, ὦ τέκνον," ἔλεγε, "τὸν τοῦ Θεοῦ φόβον ἔχε διὰ παντὸς καὶ πρόσεχε ἀεὶ σεαυτῷ, ὡς ἐν μέσῳ πολλῶν πορευόμενος παγίδων τῶν κοσμικῶν πραγμάτων· τὸν δὲ τοιοῦτόν σοι σκοπόν, ἐὰν καὶ ὁ Θεὸς εὐδοκῇ, τὸ πρᾶγμα δείξει πάντως καὶ ἀποτελεσθήσεται."

spiritual father. But when he learned that he was acting as a disciple to the elder, he was astonished at his humility and disregard for glory. Immediately then, setting everything aside, his victory in battle and his brave exploits against the enemy, Nikephoros reminded Athanasios of his old vow, saying, "Father, the monks' earlier fear of the ill-named Agarenes has already been banished from the Mountain through your prayers. The time has come, for which I have long been yearning, to flee the affairs of this world; all we need to do now is to build a place for us to live. So I beg your holiness first of all to build us cells in which to pursue spiritual tranquility, and to establish a church and fit it out for a cenobitic community. There, you and I, together with three other brethren, may live the solitary life in cells designed for the pursuit of spiritual tranquility, but on Sundays we may come together in the *lavra* to partake of the divine sacraments and eat together with the brethren and the superior, and then leave again."

As Nikephoros made this request, he gave him gold as a 4
down payment on the construction. But the father Athanasios, yearning for an undistracted and untroubled life, would neither accept the gold, nor was he persuaded by Nikephoros in any way. "My child," he said, "fear God in everything and always take heed for yourself, as long as you continue to live in the midst of the many snares of worldly affairs. But if God approves such a purpose for you, He will let you know it and it will come to pass."

23

Τ αῦτα εἰπὼν ὁ πατὴρ σφόδρα τὸν Νικηφόρον ἐλύπησε. Χρόνον δέ τινα ὀλίγον τῆς κατὰ φιλίαν ὄψεως ἀπολαύσαντες, ἐχωρίσθησαν ἀπ᾽ ἀλλήλων· καὶ ὁ μὲν Ἀθανάσιος ἐπὶ τὸν Ἄθων ἀνέκαμψεν, ὁ δὲ κράτιστος Νικηφόρος θερμότερος γεγονὼς ἐπὶ τῷ σκοπῷ τῆς οἰκοδομῆς καὶ μὴ ἀνεχόμενος ἐπιπολύ, πέμπει τινὰ τῶν οἰκειοτάτων αὐτῷ πρὸς τὸν Ἀθανάσιον, Μεθόδιον ὀνομαζόμενον καὶ ἡγούμενον γεγονότα μετ᾽ ὀλίγον ἐν τῇ τοῦ Κυμινᾶ μονῇ, χρυσίνους κομίζοντα αὐτῷ λίτρας ἓξ καὶ τῆς οἰκοδομῆς ἀπάρξασθαι κατεπείγοντα. Ἐντεῦθεν οὖν ὁ σοφώτατος Ἀθανάσιος πολὺν τοῦ Νικηφόρου τὸν θεῖον πόθον στοχασάμενος καὶ θερμὴν τὴν ἐπιθυμίαν, καὶ Θεοῦ βουλὴν τὸ πρᾶγμα τεκμηράμενος, δέχεται τὸ χρυσίον καὶ ὡς ἐπίταγμα θεῖον τοῦτο λογίζεται καὶ ἀναδέχεται τὴν ἐπὶ τὰς οἰκοδομὰς φροντίδα.

2   Νικηφόρος δέ, ὁ περιώνυμος τὴν ἀνδρείαν καὶ τὴν ἀρετήν, τροπαιοφόρος καὶ νικητὴς κατὰ τῶν ἀθέων Ἀγαρηνῶν ἀνεδείκνυτο, πορθήσας τὴν Κρήτην καὶ δουλωσάμενος ἐν ἔτει τῷ ἑξακισχιλιοστῷ τετρακοσιοστῷ ἑξηκοστῷ ἐνάτῳ, ἐν μηνὶ Μαρτίῳ καὶ ἰνδικτιῶνι τετάρτῃ. Ἐν δὲ τῇ αὐτῇ ἰνδικτιῶνι τοῦ αὐτοῦ ἔτους ἀπάρχεται τοῦ οἰκοδομεῖν καὶ ὁ πατὴρ ἡμῶν Ἀθανάσιος. Καὶ πρῶτον μὲν τὸν ὑλώδη τόπον τῆς πολλῆς ἐκείνης ὕλης ἀνακαθάρας καὶ τὸ τραχὺ ἐξομαλίσας διὰ πόνων καὶ ἱδρώτων πολλῶν, σεμνότατον ἡσυχαστήριον κατεσκεύασεν εἰς κατασκήνωσιν Νικηφόρου τοῦ πάνυ καὶ οἶκον εὐκτήριον χάριν αὐτοῦ

Chapter 23

With these words the father caused Nikephoros great sorrow. After enjoying each other's friendly company for a short while, they took their leave of one another. Athanasios returned to Athos, but the most mighty Nikephoros, who had become even more enthusiastic about his proposed construction project, without much delay sent one of his closest retainers to Athanasios. This man, who was named Methodios and shortly after became superior at the monastery of Kyminas, brought him six pounds of gold pieces and urged him to begin construction. From this the most astute Athanasios understood the extent of Nikephoros's divine yearning and his ardent desire, and decided that the project was the will of God. So he accepted the gold and, considering this as a divine commandment, assumed responsibility for the construction.

Nikephoros, who was celebrated for his valor and virtue, 2 proved to be a champion and victor over the godless Agarenes by ravaging Crete and subduing it in the year 6469, in the month of March and the 4th indiction. And, in the same indiction of the same year, our father Athanasios began to build. First of all he cleared the wooded area of its dense forest and smoothed the rough ground with much toil and sweat; he prepared a most holy place of spiritual tranquility as a dwelling for the great Nikephoros, and

ᾠκοδόμησε, κλῆσιν φέροντα τοῦ πανενδόξου Προδρόμου. Ἔπειτα καὶ ναὸν τῇ Θεοτόκῳ ἀνεγείρει περὶ τοὺς πρόποδας τοῦ Ὄρους κάλλιστόν τε καὶ ἀσφαλέστατον, ἔνθα δηλονότι τὴν ἀσκητικὴν καλύβην ἐπήξατο, ὅπου δὴ καὶ τῆς θείας ἔτυχε χάριτος.

24

Πλὴν ἀλλ᾽ ὥσπερ πρὸ τῆς χάριτος ταύτης βαρὺν τῷ πατρὶ τὸν πόλεμον ὁ μελανώτατος ἤγειρεν, οὕτω καὶ πρὸ ταύτης τῆς οἰκοδομῆς τοῦ ναοῦ ἐν δεινῷ τῷ πειρασμῷ τοὺς οἰκοδομοῦντας ἐπείρασε. Συνήχθησαν μὲν γὰρ οἱ τοιοῦτοι τεχνῖται καὶ ὅσοι ἔμελλον τούτοις συμβοηθεῖν καὶ τῆς ἐκκλησίας τὸ σχῆμα ἐχάραττον· ἀλλ᾽ ὁ τῆς κακίας δημιουργὸς καὶ τοῦ φθόνου πατὴρ τῶν οἰκοδόμων τὰς χεῖρας ἀκινήτους παντελῶς ἀπειργάσατο, τοσοῦτον ὥστε μηδὲ τῷ στόματι ταύτας προσφέρειν δύνασθαι. Καὶ ταῦτα μὲν ὁ Πονηρὸς καὶ ἄδικος· ὁ δὲ δίκαιος τί ἐποίησε [Psalm 10(11):4]; Τὴν τοῦ τρισαγίου εὐχὴν ποιησάμενος, τὰς χεῖρας αὐτῶν ἔλυσε καὶ τὸν Πονηρὸν κατησχυμμένον ἀπέδειξεν.

2 Αὕτη ἡ ἀπαρχὴ τῶν θαυμάτων τοῦ μεγάλου πατρός, τοῦτο τοῖς τεχνίταις ἀρχὴ σωτηρίας ἐγένετο· εὐθὺς γὰρ ὁ πατὴρ ὀρυκτῆρος λαβόμενος ἤρξατο πρῶτος ἐκεῖνος διορύσσειν· εἶτα καὶ τοῖς μέλλουσι κτίζειν εἰς τοῦτο

constructed a chapel for him, bearing the name of the all-glorious Prodromos. Then he erected a most beautiful and sturdy church to the Virgin near the foot of the Mountain, at the place where he had established his ascetic hut, and where he had also received the gift of divine grace.

Chapter 24

But just as that blackest Devil had stirred up a violent battle against the father before his gift of grace, so also before this construction of the church he subjected the builders to a terrible trial. For when the craftsmen and all their assistants were assembled and were marking out the plan of the church, that skilled *worker of evil* and father of envy completely paralyzed the builders' hands, so that they could not even raise them to their mouths. This was the work of the Evil and unjust One, but as for *the righteous one, what did he do?* After saying the *trisagion* prayer, he released their hands and put the Evil One to shame.

This was the beginning of the great father's miracles, and 2 it was also the beginning of the craftsmen's salvation. For straightaway the father took up a shovel and was the first to begin to dig. Then he urged those who were going to do the

προέτρεπε, καὶ ὡρῶντο αὐτίκα οὗτοι ἀκωλύτως ἐργαζόμε-
νοι· οἳ καὶ ξενισθέντες ἐπὶ τῷ θαύματι καὶ παραχρῆμα
μεγάλην τὴν πίστιν κτησάμενοι περὶ τὸν θαυματουργὸν
Ἀθανάσιον, προσέπεσον τοῖς ποσὶν αὐτοῦ καὶ καθικέτευον
προσδέξασθαί τε καὶ ἀποκεῖραι αὐτούς. Ὃ δὴ καὶ πεποίηκεν ὁ πατήρ, καὶ τὸ θαῦμα ξένον· πρὸ γὰρ τοῦ κτισθῆναι
τὸν οἶκον, οἱ μέλλοντες οἰκῆσαι προσελαμβάνοντο. Λοιπὸν
οὖν οἱ τοιοῦτοι οὐχ ὡς μίσθιοι ἀλλ᾽ ὡς δεσπόται τὴν ἰδίαν
κατοικίαν καὶ ἀνάπαυσιν ἔκτιζον, καὶ διὰ τῆς πολλῆς
αὐτῶν σπουδῆς προέκοπτε τὸ ἔργον καὶ ηὔξανεν.

3   Ἐπεὶ δὲ ἡ τοῦ πατρὸς ἀρετὴ ἐδημοσιεύετο καὶ τὸ θεῖον
τοῦτο ἔργον εἰς ἅπαντας ἐξηκούετο, πολλοὶ συνέτρεχον
πρὸς αὐτὸν ἐκ διαφόρων χώρων καὶ πόλεων, διψῶντες τὴν
μετ᾽ αὐτοῦ συνοίκησιν, καὶ τὸ συνεργάζεσθαι καὶ συμ-
πονεῖν τοῖς λοιποῖς εἰς τὴν τοῦ ἔργου κατασκευὴν προ-
τιμῶντες τῆς ἀναπαύσεως, εἰ καὶ ἑώρων τὴν δίαιταν τῶν
σὺν αὐτῷ ἄρτον οὖσαν ξηρὸν καὶ ἀγρίων δένδρων καρ-
ποὺς καὶ ὕδωρ· ὁρῶντες γὰρ ἐκεῖνον τοῖς αὐτοῖς τρεφό-
μενον εἴδεσι διὰ τριῶν ἢ τεσσάρων, τρυφὴν ἡγοῦντο τὸ
καθεκάστην ἐσθίειν. Ἐκεῖνος δὲ τὸν Χριστὸν μιμούμενος
οὐκ ἐξέβαλεν ἔξω τὸν αὐτῷ προσερχόμενον [John 6:37],
ἀλλὰ καὶ προσεδέχετο καὶ πρὸς ἀρετὴν ἐπαίδευε καὶ ἐκ
τοῦ κατ᾽ αὐτὸν βίου ἐπὶ τὴν ἐργασίαν τῆς ἀρετῆς διήγειρε.

construction to get on with it, and immediately they could be seen working away without any impediment. They were so astonished at the miracle and right away acquired such great faith in the miracle-working Athanasios that they fell at his feet and entreated him to accept them as monks and to tonsure them. The father did so, and the miracle was a strange one, for even before the building was constructed, its future inhabitants were enrolled. So these people built their own dwelling and residence not as employees but as masters, and the work advanced and prospered on account of their great enthusiasm.

Since word of the father's virtue was spread abroad and this divine activity came to everyone's attention, many people flocked to him from different places and cities, thirsting to dwell with him. Rather than resting, these people preferred to join in the labor and toil together with the others in the construction work, even if they saw that the diet of Athanasios's associates was dry bread, the fruit of wild trees, and water. For since they saw Athanasios eating the same food as they did only every third or fourth day, they considered it a luxury to eat on a daily basis. And Athanasios, in imitation of Christ, *did not cast out the one who came to him,* but accepted him and trained him in virtue and from the example of his own lifestyle spurred him to virtuous work. 3

25

Τούτων οὖν οὕτως συγκαμνόντων καὶ συνεργαζομένων ἀλλήλοις, συνεργούσης ἄνωθεν τῆς θείας δυνάμεως ταῖς εὐχαῖς τοῦ μεγάλου, ἀπηρτίσθη ὡς κάλλιστα ὁ σταυροειδῶς κατασκευασθεὶς ναὸς ἐπ᾽ ὀνόματι τῆς δεσποίνης ἡμῶν παναγίας τοῦ Κυρίου μητρός, δομηθέντων καὶ τρουλοειδῶν δύο μικρῶν ναῶν ἐξ ἑκατέρων τῶν πλευρῶν αὐτοῦ συνημμένως ἐν τάξει εὐκτηρίων, τοῦ μὲν ἑνὸς ἐπ᾽ ὀνόματι τῶν ἁγίων τεσσαράκοντα μαρτύρων, τοῦ δὲ ἑτέρου ἐπ᾽ ὀνόματι τοῦ θαυματουργοῦ Νικολάου. Ἐπεὶ δὲ ὁ ψυχικὸς ναὸς τοῦ πατρὸς τέλειος ἦν κατὰ ἀρετήν, τὸ δὲ σχῆμα τῆς τελειότητος οὐκ ἦν περιτεθειμένον αὐτῷ διὰ ταπεινοφροσύνης ὑπερβολήν, πρῶτον μὲν αὐτὸς ἐτελειώθη τῷ μεγάλῳ σχήματι διὰ μοναχοῦ τινος, τὸ τοῦ προφήτου Ἡσαΐου ἔχοντος ὄνομα καὶ τὸ χάρισμα καὶ ἐν τοῖς βαθυτέροις τόποις τοῦ Ὄρους κατοικοῦντος, ἔνθα δὴ φροντιστήριον ὕστερον ἤγειρεν ὁ πατήρ· λοιπὸν δὲ ἀπέκειρε καὶ οὗτος τοὺς οἰκοδόμους ἐκείνους, οὓς καὶ πρώτους προσεδέξατο, περὶ οὓς καὶ πρώτους ἐθαυματούργησε.

2 Καὶ μετὰ τοῦτο τῆς τῶν κελλίων ἀπαρξάμενος οἰκοδομῆς, κύκλῳ ταῦτα τῆς ἐκκλησίας κατεσκεύασεν ἐν τετραγώνῳ τῷ σχήματι, κελλίον τῷ κελλίῳ συνάψας, ὧντινων μέσον ἵσταται ἡ ἐκκλησία ὥσπέρ τις ὀφθαλμὸς βλεπόμενος πάντοθεν. Εἶτα καὶ τὸ ἀριστήριον κατασκευάζει, ἔχον ἔσωθεν τραπέζας εἴκοσι πρὸς τῇ μιᾷ ἐκ πλακὸς μαρμάρου λευκῆς, μιᾶς ἑκάστης ἀνὰ δυοκαίδεκα

Chapter 25

So, as they labored and worked alongside each other, with the assistance from above of divine power through the great man's prayers, the cross-shaped church, dedicated to our Lady the all-holy Mother of the Lord, was completed in the most beautiful fashion. Two small domed chapels were also built attached on each side of it to form oratories, the one dedicated to the Forty Holy Martyrs of Sebaste, the other to the miracle-worker Nicholas. Although the father's spiritual temple was perfect in virtue, the vestment of perfection had not yet been conferred on him on account of his extreme humility. So first of all he was initiated into the great habit at the hands of a monk who had the name and the grace of the prophet Isaiah and lived in the innermost reaches of the Mountain, at a site where the father later built a monastic complex. Then he tonsured those construction workers whom he had first accepted, and for whom he had first wrought a miracle.

After this, beginning the construction of the cells, he built them around the church on a rectangular plan, attaching cell to cell, and at the center stood the church like an eye visible from all sides. Then he also built the refectory, which had twenty-one tables inside made of white marble slabs, each accommodating twelve diners. Next he constructed a

χωρούσης τοὺς ἀριστοῦντας. Ἔπειτα καὶ νοσοκομεῖον καὶ ξενοδοχεῖον οἰκοδομεῖ καὶ λοετρὸν σὺν τούτοις διὰ τὴν χρείαν τῶν ἀσθενῶν. Ἐπεὶ δὲ ἀπορία ἦν ἀφθόνων ὑδάτων ἐν τῷ τόπῳ τῆς Λαύρας, πόρον ἐξ ἀπόρων σοφίζεται καὶ δείκνυσι τὸ μέγεθος τῆς μεγαλοφυΐας καὶ σοφίας αὐτοῦ· πολλὰ γὰρ μέρη τοῦ Ἄθω διελθὼν ἐπὶ τὸ εὑρεῖν ἄφθονον πόρον ὕδατος καὶ πολλὰ ταλαιπωρήσας, εὗρε τόπους ὑψηλοὺς καὶ δυσβάτους, ἔχοντας μὲν ὕδωρ, ἀπέχοντας δὲ τῆς Λαύρας ἐπέκεινα τῶν ἑβδομήκοντα σταδίων. Ἐκεῖθεν δὲ διορύσσειν ἀρξάμενος, διασκάπτων τε καὶ αὐτοὺς τοὺς διὰ μέσου κρημνώδεις τόπους καὶ ὑψηλούς, καὶ σωλῆνας ταῖς διωρυχίαις ὑποβαλών, ποταμὸν ὑδάτων ἐκ διαφόρων πόρων ἐπὶ τὸ μοναστήριον κατήγαγε.

3   Καὶ τὸ μὲν τούτων διαπορεύεται ἔσωθεν καὶ ἐπὶ πάσης διακονίας χρείαν ἀδιαλείπτως μερίζεται καὶ πᾶσι τοῖς κελλίοις παραρρέει ἀστάτως καὶ πᾶν μέρος τῆς Λαύρας πλουσίως κατάρδεται ὑπ’ αὐτοῦ· τὸ δὲ διὰ σωλήνων ἐν πύργῳ ἐγχορήγῳ ἐπεισρέον δύο μύλους κινεῖ ὑφ’ ἑνὶ πέτωνι· δι’ οὗ καὶ τὰ κάρπιμα δένδρα ποτίζονται καὶ οἱ κῆποι ἀρδεύονται καὶ αἱ πλυνοὶ τῶν ἱματίων τῶν ἀδελφῶν πληροῦνται· ὅθεν καὶ τὸ ποτὸν τὰ ζῷα ἀρύονται.

4   Περὶ δὲ τῶν λοιπῶν χρειωδῶν οἰκημάτων καὶ ἐκκλησιῶν, φυτεύσεώς τε ἀμπελώνων καὶ δένδρων, καὶ ἑτέρας ἀνοικοδομῆς ἡσυχαστηρίων καὶ κελλίων τῶν ἐν τοῖς μετοχίοις τοῖς ἐν τῷ Ὄρει, τῶν τε ἐν τῷ λιμένι καταγωγίων καὶ τῶν λοιπῶν αὐτουργημάτων αὐτοῦ, οὐκ ἔστι δυνατὸν διηγεῖσθαι· ἱστορίας γὰρ ἔργον τοῦτο καὶ οὐχὶ βίου διήγησις. Ἐκεῖνο δὲ πῶς ἂν σιωπήσω, ὅτι καὶ οὗτος συνεμόχθει

hospital and a guesthouse, and along with them a bathhouse, for the use of the sick. But since there was a lack of abundant water on the site of the Lavra, he devised a way out of his difficulties and demonstrated the greatness of his genius and cleverness. For, after traversing many parts of Athos with great effort in order to find an abundant source of water, he found some places which were high up and hard to access, but which had water, even though they were more than seventy stades distant from the Lavra. He began to dig from that point and, cutting through the steep and high places which lay in between the spring and the Lavra, and placing pipes in the trenches, he brought a stream of water to the monastery from different channels.

One of these streams passes through the interior of the 3 monastery and is distributed continuously for every purpose; it flows uninterrupted to all the cells, and every part of the Lavra is abundantly watered by it. The other, flowing through pipes in a tower built with mortar, sets in motion two millstones beneath a millrace. By this means also the fruit trees are watered, the gardens are irrigated, and the washtubs for laundering the brethren's clothes are filled; the animals, too, get their drinking water from it.

I cannot describe in detail the rest of the service build- 4 ings and churches, the planting of vineyards and trees, other construction of hermitages and monastic cells in the *metochia* on the Mountain, the lodgings at the harbor, and the rest of his projects. For this would be a work of history and not the narrative of someone's life. But how also can I keep silent about this, since Athanasios himself labored and

καὶ συνεκοπία πολλὰ τοῖς οἰκοδόμοις τε καὶ ἐργάταις; Τοσοῦτον γὰρ ἦν ἀνδρεῖος καὶ ἀδαμάντινος, ὅτι πολλάκις ἕλκοντος αὐτοῦ τὸν τῆς ἁμάξης ζυγὸν ἐν τῷ ἑνὶ μέρει, μόλις ἴσχυον ἐν τῷ ἑτέρῳ τρεῖς ἄνδρες συνελκύσαι αὐτῷ τὸν φόρτον τῆς ἁμάξης. Οὕτως οὖν ἔχοντος αὐτοῦ, πλῆθος λαοῦ ἁπανταχόθεν πρὸς αὐτὸν παρεγένετο, οἱ μὲν εὐλογίας τυχεῖν, οἱ δὲ καὶ ἐρωτῆσαι περὶ ὧν εἶχον ἀγνοημάτων, οἱ δὲ καὶ λύσεις ἐπιζητοῦντες διαφορῶν τινων· καὶ πάντα ἔλυε καὶ πάντα ἡρμήνευε καὶ πάντας εὐλόγει καὶ οὐδένα κενὸν ἀπέλυεν.

26

Ἐπεὶ δὲ ταῦτα καλῶς εἶχεν αὐτῷ, ἤρξατο τιθέναι καὶ τοὺς τῆς ἐκκλησίας θεσμοὺς καὶ τύπους εἰς εὐταξίαν τε καὶ κατάστασιν καὶ νόμον κανόνος ψυχωφελοῦς, ἐν ποίᾳ δεῖ τῇ γρηγόρσει ὑμνεῖν τὸν Θεὸν ἕν τε ταῖς ἡμεριναῖς καὶ νυκτεριναῖς ἀκολουθίαις. Ἐπέστησε μὲν οὖν καθ᾽ ἕκαστον τῶν χορῶν ἕνα ἀδελφόν, ἐπιστημονάρχην καλέσας τοῦτον, τοῦ πρὸς εὐκοσμίαν αὐτὸν εἶναι τῶν ψαλλόντων καὶ ψυχικὴν ἐπιμέλειαν, καὶ πρὸς τὸ τοὺς ἀπολιμπανομένους ποτὲ μὲν δι᾽ ἑαυτοῦ, ποτὲ δὲ διὰ καταμηνύσεως αὐτοῦ τῆς πρὸς τοὺς θυρωρούς, ἐπισυνάγειν ἐν τῇ τοῦ Θεοῦ ἐκκλησίᾳ, καὶ τοῦ μὴ ἐᾶν τινα συντυγχάνειν ἐν ταῖς δοξολογίαις ἢ ἀργεῖν καὶ μὴ ψάλλειν, ἀλλ᾽ οὐδὲ ἀδεῶς εἰσέρχεσθαί τε καὶ

toiled hard alongside the construction workers and laborers? For he was so strong and tough that many times when he was pulling the yoke of a wagon on one side, three men on the other side could barely drag the wagonload together with him. While he was engaged in this construction project, a horde of people came from all over to visit him, some to attain a blessing, others to ask him about questions that they had, and yet others seeking solutions to different problems; and he solved all of them and explained everything and blessed everyone and sent no one away empty-handed.

Chapter 26

Since this project was going well for him, Athanasios also began to establish the ordinances and rules for the church in order to promote good order and proper conditions and regulation of a discipline beneficial to the soul, prescribing the state of vigilance necessary to sing praise to God in the offices during the day and at night. He appointed one monk in each choir, called an *epistemonarches,* to be responsible for both the harmony and spiritual diligence of the singers, and to gather up the monks who were missing and assemble them in the church of God, doing this either himself, or through his instructions to the doorkeepers. He was not to permit anyone to chat during the doxologies, or to be idle and not sing, or to come in and go out whenever he wanted,

ἐξέρχεσθαί τινα ὁπότε καὶ βούλεται, ἀλλὰ μέτρῳ καὶ καιρῷ τῷ ὡρισμένῳ ποιεῖν ταῦτα, ἵνα μὴ κόπον ἀλλήλοις παρέχωσιν οἱ ἐν τοῖς χοροῖς τῷ συχνῶς προσκυνεῖν καθ᾽ ἕνα τῶν εἰσιόντων.

2   Ἐν δὲ τοῖς ἀναγνώσμασιν ἕνα προσέταξεν ἀφυπνίζειν τοὺς ἀδελφοὺς δι᾽ ὅλης τῆς ἐκκλησίας, καθ᾽ ἑκάστην ἀνάγνωσιν ὑπαλλαττόμενον τοῦτον, ἤτοι τὸν μὲν ἐπὶ τῆς πρώτης τεταγμένον ἀναγνώσεως ἐν τῇ δευτέρᾳ ἀναπαυόμενον, τὸν δὲ ἐπὶ τῆς δευτέρας ἐν τῇ τρίτῃ, ἄλλον δὲ ἐν ταύτῃ διακονεῖν, μὴ συγχωρουμένου τοῦ ἐπιστημονάρχου περικόπτειν ἢ ἐμποδίζειν αὐτοῖς τὸ καθόλου ἢ συμβοηθεῖν αὐτοῖς ἀφ᾽ ἑαυτοῦ δίχα προτροπῆς τοῦ πατρός, μήτε πάλιν κἀκείνους ἐν ταῖς ὑμνολογίαις περικόπτειν τὸν ἐπιστημονάρχην ἢ περισσοπρακτεῖν, ἀλλ᾽ ἕκαστον ἐν τῷ ἰδίῳ καιρῷ χρῆσθαι τῇ τῆς ἰδίας διακονίας ἐξουσίᾳ.

3   Ἐν δὲ ταῖς πύλαις τοῦ νάρθηκος ἑτέρους ἔστησε δύο τῶν ἀδελφῶν, θυρωροὺς καλέσας αὐτούς, ὅπως τοὺς ἀπολιμπανομένους τῶν χορῶν διὰ τῆς καταμηνύσεως τῶν ἐπιστημοναρχῶν ἄγωσιν ἐν τῇ ἐκκλησίᾳ, οὐ μὴν δὲ ἀλλὰ καὶ ἐπιτηρῶσι πάρεξ τῶν χορῶν τοὺς λοιποὺς πάντας τοὺς ἐν τῇ ἐκκλησίᾳ, ὥσπερ οἱ ἐπιστημονάρχαι τοὺς ἐν τοῖς χοροῖς, εἰ ἐν ἀρχῇ τοῦ "Δόξα ἐν ὑψίστοις" εἰσῆλθον ἢ ἐν τῷ μέσῳ ἢ ἐν τῷ τέλει ἢ μὴ καθόλου, καὶ εἰ μήτε ἀσθενοῦντες μήτε εἰς διακονίαν πεμφθέντες διὰ ῥαθυμίαν ἀπελείφθησαν τῆς ἐκκλησίας, ἵνα δηλοποιῶνται οἱ τοιοῦτοι δι᾽ αὐτῶν τῶν θυρωρῶν τῷ πατρί, καὶ ὡς αὐτὸς θελήσει, οἰκονομήσῃ τὰ περὶ αὐτῶν.

4   Ὁμοίως δὲ ἐπιτηρεῖν καὶ τοὺς εἰσιόντας καὶ ἐξιόντας

but rather to make sure the monks did these things in moderation and at the appointed time, so that those in the choirs would not disturb each other by the necessity for frequent obeisance to each monk as he entered.

He ordered that during the readings one monk should 2 make sure the brethren throughout the whole church stayed awake. This person was to be changed at each reading, that is, the one assigned for the first reading would rest during the second reading, the one assigned to the second reading would rest during the third, and another person would serve during this reading; also the *epistemonarches* should not be permitted to interrupt or impede them at all or help them of his own accord without the father's permission, nor again should they interrupt the *epistemonarches* during the singing of hymns or do more than was prescribed, but each should use the authority of his own ministry at the appropriate time.

Athanasios appointed two additional brothers, called 3 doorkeepers, to stand at the narthex doors to bring those monks who were missing from the choirs into the church at the instructions of the *epistemonarchai.* Furthermore they were to monitor everyone else in the church, except for the choirs, just as the disciplinarians were to do with those in the choirs, to see if they entered at the beginning of the "Glory in the Highest" or in the middle or at the end or not at all, and if they were absent from church on account of laziness (but not if they were ill or sent on an errand), so that such delinquents might be pointed out to the father by the doorkeepers, and he might deal with them as he decided.

In the same way he instructed them to monitor all those 4

πάντας προετρέψατο αὐτούς, καὶ μετὰ μίαν ἐξέλευσιν μηκέτι ἐᾶν τὸν περαιτέρω τολμῶντα προϊέναι, ἀλλ᾽ ἐρωτᾶν καὶ διερευνᾶν, καὶ εἰ κατὰ χρείαν ἀναγκαίαν τοῦτο ποιεῖ, συγχωρεῖν αὐτῷ ἀκωλύτως, εἰ δὲ μή γε, μὴ ἐᾶν ἐξελθεῖν ἀλλὰ προτρέπεσθαι εἰσελθεῖν αὐτὸν ἐν τῇ ἐκκλησίᾳ· ὡσαύτως δὲ καὶ περὶ τῆς βραδυτῆτος τῶν ἐξερχομένων ἀκριβολογεῖσθαι τὰς αἰτίας πλεῖον παρὰ πάντα, μήτε δὲ διακονητὴν ἢ ἄλλον τινὰ δύνασθαι εἰσέρχεσθαι ἐν τῇ ἐκκλησίᾳ καὶ ἐκκαλεῖσθαι ἔξω τινὰ διὰ δουλείαν ἢ ἰδίαν ἢ τοῦ κοινοῦ, ἀλλ᾽ οὐδὲ αὐτὸν τὸν οἰκονόμον τοῦτο ποιεῖν, εἰ μὴ διὰ τῶν θυρωρῶν καὶ μόνων γίνεσθαι τοῦτο.

5 Ἐπὶ τούτοις ἡγεῖσθαί τινα καὶ προέχειν ἠθέλησεν οὐ μόνον τῶν προρρηθέντων, ἀλλὰ καὶ αὐτῶν τῶν ἱερέων καὶ τῶν διακόνων καὶ πάντων τῶν ἐν τῇ τοῦ Θεοῦ ἁγίᾳ ἐκκλησίᾳ παντοίως διακονούντων, ἐκκλησιάρχην τοῦτον καλέσας, λόγῳ καὶ βίῳ τετιμημένον καὶ δυνάμενον πρὸς ταῦτα πάντα τὰ τῆς ἐκκλησίας θεαρέστως καὶ καλῶς διοικεῖν, ἔγγραφον ἔχοντα πᾶσαν αὐτῆς τὴν ἀκολουθίαν, ὑπὸ πάντων τε ἀκουόμενον τῶν ἐν τῇ ἐκκλησίᾳ διαφόρους ἐχόντων διακονίας καὶ τιμώμενον.

27

Ἐπειδὴ δὲ ὁ διακριτικώτατος ποιμὴν καὶ σοφὸς τὰ θεῖα ἐγίνωσκε τοὺς ἀλάστορας δαίμονας ἐν παντὶ μὲν

who came in and went out, and, after a monk had left once, not to allow him to proceed if he dared to do this again, but to question and interrogate him. If he was doing this out of urgent necessity, they should give him permission to leave without any hindrance; otherwise they were not to allow him to leave, but tell him to go back into the church. In the same way they were, in particular, to closely question the reasons for the slow return of those who went out; nor were they to allow a servant or anyone else to enter the church and call someone outside for some task, whether it was personal or for the community. Not even the steward himself was to do this; this should be done by the doorkeepers alone.

In addition he wanted someone to lead and supervise not 5 only the aforementioned monks, but also the priests themselves and the deacons and all those who serve in any way in the holy church of God. This person, called the sacristan, was to be someone respected for his learning and lifestyle who could manage in addition, in a good and God-pleasing manner, all ecclesiastical matters, a man who had all the liturgical offices in written form, and was heeded and respected by all those who held different ministries in the church.

Chapter 27

As a most discerning shepherd, wise in divine things, Athanasios knew that pernicious demons are always

ἐπιτιθεμένους διὰ ποικίλων πολέμων τοῖς ἐν κοινοβίοις καὶ λαύραις, μάλιστα δὲ ἐν ταῖς ἐκκλησίαις, ὥσπερ τοῖς ἐν ἡσυχίᾳ ἐν ταῖς κέλλαις, δεῖν ᾠήθη βοήθειαν ἐπινοήσασθαι τοῖς πειραζομένοις ἐγγύθεν· καὶ μέντοι ὡς ἐπιστήμων τῆς πάλης καὶ τροπαιοφόρος κατ' αὐτῶν ὑπὸ Θεοῦ ἀποδει-χθείς, ἐφεῦρεν. Ἐφ' ἑνὸς τῶν εὐκτηρίων, ἐν τῷ τῶν ἁγίων τεσσαράκοντα, ἐπενόησε μετὰ τὴν ἐσχάτην ἀνάγνωσιν εἰσέρχεσθαι, εἶτα τοὺς ἀδελφοὺς ἐν αὐτῷ ἕνα καθ' ἕνα εἰσιέναι καὶ διηγεῖσθαι τὰ τοῦ Πειράζοντος ἔνεδρα καὶ τοξεύματα καὶ παμπληθῆ θήρατρα, τά τε καθ' ὕπαρ ἐν τῇ ὀρθρινῇ δοξολογίᾳ καὶ τὰ καθ' ὕπνους.

2   Εἰ δέ τι συνέβη τινὶ τῶν ἀδοκήτων καὶ μεθ' ἡμέραν, οὐκ ἴσχυσε δὲ δι' ὅλης αὐτῆς ἐξαγορεῦσαι αὐτό, ἐξωμολογεῖτο κἀκεῖνο τῷ πατρί, πλὴν μετὰ αἰδοῦς· παραγγελία γὰρ ἦν τοῖς πᾶσι, μηδὲν ἀνεξαγόρευτον ἔχοντας τῶν ἐν τῇ ἡμέρᾳ συμβάντων, οὕτω τὴν ἑσπέραν καταλαμβάνειν. Ὁ δὲ τοῦ Θεοῦ ἄνθρωπος ἀνθοπλίζων αὐτοὺς τῇ εἰς Θεὸν πίστει καὶ πεποιθήσει καὶ τῇ ὑπομονῇ, ἔτι δὲ πρὸς τούτοις καὶ τῇ καταλλήλῳ θεραπείᾳ τῶν αὐτοῦ εἰσηγήσεων θεραπεύων ἕνα ἕκαστον, καθὼς ἄν τις διὰ τῆς ἐξαγορεύσεως ἐδείκνυε τὴν ἑαυτοῦ ψυχικὴν νόσον, ἀπέλυε πάντας χαίροντας καὶ ἀγαλλιωμένους καὶ καταθαρροῦντας τῆς τῶν δαιμόνων πάλης.

3   Οὕτως ἦν αὐτῷ ἔργον καὶ κανὼν ἀπαράβατος καθ-εκάστην εἰσιέναι ἐν τῷ εὐκτηρίῳ τῶν ἁγίων τεσσαράκοντα καὶ τοὺς πειραζομένους τῶν ἀδελφῶν παραμυθεῖσθαι καὶ παραθαρρύνειν πρὸς ἀγῶνας. Οὐκ ἐν τῇ ἐκκλησίᾳ δὲ μόνη ἦν αὐτοῖς—καὶ ἔτι ἐστί—τὸ τῆς ἐξαγορίας καλόν, ἀλλὰ

inflicting a variety of assaults on those who live in cenobitic monasteries and *lavrai,* and that they do this especially in church, just as they attack those who live in spiritual tranquility in their cells. He thus decided he should devise a method to assist those who were being tempted right there; and since he had been shown by God to be an expert in battle and a champion over demons, he discovered a way. He decided to go into one of the chapels, that of the Holy Forty Martyrs, after the last reading, and then have the brethren come in one by one and recount the traps and bowshots and innumerable snares of the Tempter, those they experienced in their waking hours during the matins service and those in their sleep.

If anything untoward had happened to someone in the daytime, and he had no opportunity to confess it during that day, he should confess that as well to the father, but with shame; for they were all instructed to confess everything that had occurred during the day before evening arrived. And the man of God would send them all on their way, joyful, happy, and encouraged in their struggle with the demons, after arming them with faith in God and confidence and endurance, and moreover healing each one with the appropriate therapy of his exhortations, in accordance with the spiritual malady he might have revealed through his confession. 2

Thus it was his work and unbreakable rule to go each day into the chapel of the Holy Forty and to console those brethren who were suffering from temptation and encourage them in their struggles. They had—and still have—the benefit of confession not only in church, but all day long, 3

καὶ δι' ὅλης τῆς ἡμέρας καὶ αὐτῆς ἑσπέρας ὁ βουλόμενος ἀκωλύτως εἰσῄει πρὸς τὸν πατέρα ἐν τῷ κελλίῳ αὐτοῦ, θριαμβεύων τοὺς αὐτοῦ διαλογισμοὺς καὶ τὴν ὠφέλειαν καρπούμενος· ἅπερ καὶ νῦν εἰσέτι πάντα τὰ καλὰ ταῦτα παρὰ τῶν αὐτοῦ καὶ τῆς ἀρετῆς καὶ τοῦ θρόνου κληρονόμων καὶ διαδόχων ἐκδιδάσκονται καὶ διατηροῦνται καὶ διαφυλάττονται.

28

Τῆς τοίνυν τοσαύτης ἀκριβείας, ἣν περὶ τὴν ἐκκλησίαν ἐνεδείξατο ὁ πατήρ, ὁρᾶτε οἷον δρέπεται καὶ τρυγᾷ τὸν καρπόν, ὡς ἡδὺν καὶ λίαν ἥδιστον καὶ ὃν προσήκει πατράσι καὶ διδασκάλοις παρὰ παίδων πνευματικῶν ἐπιζητεῖν καὶ ἀπεκδέχεσθαι, τὸ ἀρέσαι Θεῷ ἐν πολιτείᾳ σεμνῇ καὶ βίῳ ἐπαινουμένῳ καὶ τὸ τὴν ἐν Χριστῷ κεκρυμμένην ζωὴν [see Colossians 3:3] βιοῦν τε καὶ ζῆν αὐτοὺς καὶ πολιτεύεσθαι. Δέδεικται δὲ τοῦτο προδήλως καὶ φανερῶς ἀφ' ἧς ἠξίωται θεωρίας ὁ καθαρὸς τῇ καρδίᾳ καὶ τὸν νοῦν πεφωτισμένος, ὁ μακαρίτης Ματθαῖος.

2   Οὗτος, τὸν ὀρθρινὸν ὕμνον τῷ Θεῷ τελούντων τῶν ἀδελφῶν σὺν τῷ πατρὶ μετὰ φόβου καὶ προσοχῆς πολλῆς, ἐν μιᾷ ἀνοιχθέντων τῶν ἔνδοθεν τῆς ψυχῆς αὐτοῦ ὀφθαλμῶν, ὁρᾷ ἱστάμενος ἐν τῷ νάρθηκι γυναῖκα ὀψικευομένην παρὰ δύο εὐνούχων λευκοφόρων, τὸν μὲν ἕνα μετὰ

and in the evening anyone who wished could approach the father in his cell without any hindrance, divulging his wicked thoughts and reaping the benefit from doing so. Even now all these good traditions are still taught and preserved and maintained by the heirs and successors to his virtue and his abbatial office.

Chapter 28

See, then, the fruit plucked and harvested by the father as a result of the strict observance which he demonstrated with regard to the church! How sweet, indeed how very sweet it was, a fruit which fathers and teachers should seek and expect from their spiritual children: to please God through reverent conduct and a praiseworthy lifestyle and to live and experience and practice the life concealed in Christ. This was clearly and manifestly revealed by the vision which was granted to the blessed Matthew, who was pure in heart and enlightened in his mind.

While the brethren and the father were completing the 2 matins hymn to God with fear and full attention, suddenly the inner eyes of Matthew's soul were opened. As he was standing in the narthex, he saw a woman escorted by two eunuchs dressed in white, one in front with a blazing torch

λαμπάδος πυρὸς ἔμπροσθεν προπορευόμενον ἀνὰ πᾶσαν τὴν ἐκκλησίαν, τὸν δὲ ἕτερον ἐπακολουθοῦντα ὄπισθεν τῆς ἐν γυναικείῳ φανείσης τῷ σχήματι, αὐτὴν δὲ τὴν δορυφορουμένην δωρεὰς προτείνουσαν καὶ διανέμουσαν, τοῖς μὲν ἐν τοῖς χοροῖς ἱσταμένοις τῶν ἀδελφῶν ἀνὰ μιλιαρήσιον ἕν, τοῖς δὲ ἔνδον πρὸς ταῖς πύλαις ἀνὰ φόλεις δυοκαίδεκα, τοῖς δὲ ἐν τῷ νάρθηκι ἀνὰ φόλεις ἕξ, τισὶ δὲ τῶν ἀδελφῶν ἐδίδου καὶ ἀνὰ μιλιαρήσια ἕξ. Ταῦτα ἰδών, ἅμα δὲ καὶ αὐτὸς λαβὼν φόλεις ἕξ, ὡς ἀπέστη τὰ τῆς θεωρίας, ὡς εἶχε τάχους πρὸς τὸν πατέρα ἡμῶν γέγονεν ἐν τῷ χορῷ ἱστάμενον, καὶ τόπον καθικέτευε δοῦναι αὐτῷ πρὸς τὸ καὶ αὐτὸν ἐν τῷ χορῷ τῶν ψαλλόντων ἵστασθαι, ἐξειπὼν τὴν ὀπτασίαν ἣν ἑώρακεν.

3 Ὁ δὲ πατὴρ ἔγνω ἀληθῆ εἶναι ταύτην ἀφ᾽ ὧν προσώπων λαβόντων εἶδε τὸ τῶν ἓξ μιλιαρησίων ποσόν· καὶ γὰρ τοὺς ἑκάστου γινώσκων ἀπαραλογίστως λογισμούς, ἔγνω κατ᾽ αὐτὸ ἀναλόγους λαβεῖν καὶ τὰς δωρεάς. Τὸ δὲ καὶ τὸν τῆς τοιαύτης θείας ἀξιωθέντα θεωρίας ἴσην λαβεῖν τὴν διανομὴν μετὰ τῶν ἐσχάτων δικαίως διαπορήσειέ τις· ἀλλ᾽ ὁ διακρινόμενος πρὸς τοῦτο ἀκουέτω εὐπειθῶς· οἶμαι, ἵνα μὴ ἀμέριμνος γεγονὼς ὡς μετὰ τῶν τὰ πρῶτα φερόντων καὶ αὐτὸς ἀξιωθεὶς τῆς μεγαλοδωρεᾶς σιωπήσῃ ταπεινοφρονῶν, τοῦτο γέγονεν οἰκονομικῶς, ἵνα τῇ ὑστερήσει λυπηθείς, καὶ τὴν θεωρίαν ἐξείποι καὶ ἐπὶ τῆς αὐτῆς ἧς μετεῖχε, μᾶλλον δὲ πολλῷ πλείονος, διαμείνῃ τῆς ταπεινοφροσύνης.

leading the way through the entire church, the other following behind the female apparition. The woman under escort was offering and distributing gifts, one *miliaresion* to each of the brethren standing in the choirs, twelve *folles* each to those inside by the doors, and six *folles* to those in the narthex; to some of the brethren she even gave six *miliaresia* each. Matthew witnessed this and at the same time himself received six *folles*. As soon as the vision vanished, he went as quickly as possible to our father, who was standing in the choir, and begged him to give him a place to stand in the choir with the singers, recounting the vision he had seen.

The father realized that this was a true vision from the identity of those whom he saw receiving the sum of six *miliaresia*. For since he had accurate knowledge of each monk's thoughts, he knew that they were receiving appropriate gifts. One might rightly wonder why a person considered worthy of such a divine vision would receive the same sum of money as the least of the monks. But anyone who is trying to decide about this should listen with an open mind. I think this happened on purpose so that he would not become complacent, as one deemed worthy to receive the larger gift together with the first ranked, and therefore remain silent about the vision out of humility. This happened out of divine dispensation so that, in his distress at receiving the lower sum, he would both recount the vision and remain in the same state of humility which he already had, or rather in even greater humility.

29

Ἀλλὰ τὰ μὲν περὶ τῆς ἐκκλησιαστικῆς εὐταξίας καὶ τοῦ περὶ αὐτὴν γενομένου θαύματος οὕτως ἔχει. Οὐκ ἀπεικὸς δὲ καὶ περὶ τῆς ἐν τραπέζῃ καταστάσεως καὶ ἑτέρων τινῶν βραχέα διαλαβεῖν· τοὺς γὰρ κατὰ μέρος βουλομένους μαθεῖν περὶ πάντων τῷ παρὰ τοῦ ἁγίου γραφέντι τυπικῷ παραπέμπω. Ἐπέστησε τοίνυν καὶ τοῖς ἐστιωμένοις ἐπιτηρητὰς δύο, ἵνα ἐν σιωπῇ καὶ φόβῳ Θεοῦ τὸν ἄρτον αὐτῶν ἐσθίωσιν, ὁμοίως δὲ καὶ οἱ παριστάμενοι τούτοις ἐν σιγῇ καὶ εὐταξίᾳ διακονῶσιν αὐτοῖς, καὶ ἐπιβλέπωνται οἱ ἐσθίοντες μὴ ποιεῖν τι ἄτακτον μήτε διδόναι τὸ παράπαν τινὶ τὸ ἑαυτοῦ κρασοβόλιον, μήπως ἐμβάλῃ μέθη τὸν ἀδελφόν, ἣν αὐτὸς φεύγει.

2 Ἵνα δὲ ἀνακρίνωνται καὶ οἱ ἀπολειφθέντες τῆς τραπέζης, καὶ εἰ μὲν εὐλόγως ἀπελείφθησαν, συγχωρεῖσθαι αὐτοὺς ἐν τῇ δευτέρᾳ τραπέζῃ· εἰ δὲ ἀργοῦντες ἐν τοῖς κελλίοις αὐτῶν ἀπελείφθησαν, μὴ συγχωρεῖσθαι αὐτούς, ἕως ἂν ὑπομνησθῇ περὶ αὐτῶν ὁ πατήρ. Ἀλλὰ καὶ εἴ τις τῶν διακονούντων ἐν ταῖς τραπέζαις ἢ ἐν ἄλλαις διακονίαις σκεῦός τι συντρίψει εἴτε ἑκὼν εἴτε ἄκων, ἵστασθαι ἔγγιστα τοῦ ἀναγνώστου καὶ ὑψοῦ τὴν χεῖρα αἴρειν καὶ τὸ σύντριμμα τοῦ σκεύους φέρειν, καὶ οὕτω συγχωρεῖσθαι παρὰ τῶν πατέρων, ἵνα διὰ τῆς μικρᾶς ταύτης αἰσχύνης προσεκτικὸς γένηται.

Chapter 29

So these were Athanasios's prescriptions with regard to the orderly organization of church matters and the miracle which occurred concerning it. I think it would also be appropriate to say a few words about the arrangements in the refectory and some other matters. But I refer those who wish to learn in detail about all these matters to the monastic rule that was written by the holy one. Thus he also appointed two monitors for those who were eating to ensure that they ate their bread in silence and fear of God; likewise, those who were waiting on them were to perform their service for them in silence and in an orderly way. The monks who were eating were to be supervised so that they did not act in an inappropriate manner, and also so that no one might give anyone his wine ration as an extra serving, lest he lead the monk into the drunkenness which he himself was avoiding.

The monitors were also to question those who were absent from the refectory and, if they were absent for a good reason, they were to permit them to eat at a second sitting; but if they were absent because they were lazing around in their cells, they were not to permit them to eat until the father was informed about them. And if one of the monks who was serving at the tables or in the course of other duties were to break a dish, either deliberately or by accident, he was to stand next to the reader and raise his arm up high and hold the broken fragment of the dish, and thus receive forgiveness from the fathers, so that he would become more careful on account of this small act of humiliation. 2

3   Μετὰ δὲ τὸ ἀριστῆσαι καὶ δειπνῆσαι, περιεργάζεσθαι
καὶ ἐπιτηρεῖν (ὅπερ καὶ ὁ πατὴρ ἐποίει πολλάκις), μή τινα
παραβάλλειν ἑτέρου κελλίῳ, μήτε παρασυνάξεις ποιεῖν ἐν
τοῖς κελλίοις αὐτῶν, μήτε δὲ περιέρχεσθαι καὶ ἀναπατεῖν,
μήτε ἵστασθαι καὶ ἀργολογεῖν· εἰ δέ γε καὶ τύχοι ἀπο-
λεσθῆναι ῥαφίδιον εἴτε γραφίδιον ἢ μάχαιραν εἴτε χειρο-
μάνδηλον ἤ τι τῶν τοιούτων, μὴ περιέρχεσθαι τὰς κέλλας
καὶ τοῦτο ζητεῖν (τοῦτο γὰρ ἀπηγορευμένον ἐδόκει τῷ
πατρί), ἀλλ᾽ εἰς τὴν ἐκκλησίαν ἀπέρχεσθαι καὶ ἐν τῇ πύλῃ
τοῦ ναοῦ ἀτενίζειν, κἀκεῖ εὑρίσκειν τὸ ἀπολεσθὲν κρεμάμε-
νον εἰς τὸ χαλκοῦν κρεμαστήριον. Καὶ μή τινα ἴδιόν τι
ἔχειν μήτε πολιτεύεσθαι ἐν αὐτοῖς τὸ "τοῦτο ἐμόν, ἐκεῖνο
σόν," τὸ ψυχρὸν τοῦτο ῥῆμα καὶ τῆς ἀγάπης χωρίζον
ἡμᾶς.

4   Ἐν πᾶσι δὲ τυγχάνων ὁ πατὴρ γλυκύς τε καὶ συμπαθὴς
καὶ ἕως τέλους μὴ ὀργιζόμενος, ἐν τούτῳ μόνῳ τῷ ἁμαρτήματι τοῦ τολμᾶν τινα ὀνειδίζειν ὡς ξενοκουρίτην, καὶ
λίαν ἦν αὐστηρὸς καὶ σφόδρα σκληρὸς καὶ ἀσυμπαθής.
Δόγμα γὰρ ἔθετο τοῦτο· εἴ τις τολμήσει χεῖρα ἐπᾶραι κατὰ
τοῦ ἀδελφοῦ ἢ ξενοκουρίτην ὑβρίσαι, αὐτίκα, εἰ μὲν κατά
τινα συναρπαγὴν τούτῳ περιέπεσε τῷ ἁμαρτήματι, ἀφορί-
ζεσθαι τοῦτον τῆς ἐκκλησίας καὶ ἐπὶ τρισὶν ἑβδομάσι τῶν
ἁγιασμάτων ἀπέχεσθαι καὶ δίχα οἴνου καὶ ἐλαίου εἶναι αὐτῷ
τὴν τροφήν· καὶ εἰ μὲν διορθώσεται, τῷ Θεῷ χάρις· εἰ δὲ μή,
διώκεσθαι παντελῶς τῆς μονῆς ὡς μέλος τι σεσηπὸς καὶ
ἄχρηστον, ἵνα μὴ καὶ ἑτέρους διδάξῃ τοῦτο.

5   Ὅταν γὰρ ὁ μέγας Παῦλος φησίν, "Εἷς Θεός, μία πίστις,
ἓν βάπτισμα [Ephesians 4:5–6], λαὸς εἷς, ἐκκλησία μία, ἐν

After the conclusion of the morning meal and supper, the 3
monitors were to make sure to watch carefully (which the
father also did frequently), that no one went to another's
cell or held clandestine meetings in their cells, or wandered
around and paced back and forth, or stood about talking
idly. And, if a monk should happen to lose a needle or a pen
or a knife or a towel or any such item, they were to watch
that he did not go around the cells looking for it (for this
was forbidden by the father), but went to the church and
looked on the door of the nave, to find the lost item hanging
on the bronze hook there. They were also to make sure that
no one had any private property, and that the chilling phrase
that separates us from charity, "this is mine, that is yours,"
never became part of their lives.

The father was sweet-tempered and compassionate in all 4
things and never got angry while he was alive, but, in the
case of this one offense, if a monk should dare to reproach
another monk as an "outsider," he was strict and extremely
harsh and unsympathetic. For this was his judgment: if
someone should dare to lift a hand against a brother or insult him by calling him an "outsider," then, if he had committed this offense *on impulse,* he was to *be expelled from the
church* and *abstain from the sacraments for three weeks* and have
his food without *wine and olive oil. And if he mended his ways,
thanks be to God;* otherwise, he was to be expelled uncondi-
tionally from the monastery as a *festering* and useless *limb,* so
that he would not teach this to *others.*

For when the great Paul says, *"There is one* God, *one faith,* 5
one baptism, one people, one church, one name of Christ, and

τὸ ὄνομα τοῦ Χριστοῦ καὶ ἓν τὸ σχῆμα τὸ ἅγιον," πῶς τολμᾷ τις κατατέμνειν τὸ τοῦ Χριστοῦ ὄνομα καὶ τοὺς ἐνδυσαμένους αὐτόν [see Romans 13:14], ὡς τὸν μὲν ὀνομάζεσθαι "*τοῦ Παύλου,*" ἄλλον δὲ "*τοῦ Κηφᾶ*" καὶ ἄλλον "*τοῦ Ἀπολλώ*" [see 1 Corinthians 1:12]; Ἐκεῖνοι γὰρ ξενόκουροι εἶεν, οὓς ὁ Σατανᾶς τῇ ψαλίδι τῆς κακοδοξίας ἐκούρευσε.

6   Καὶ ταῦτα μὲν ἐκ πολλῶν τῶν διατάξεων αὐτοῦ ὀλίγα. Σὺν ἅπασι δὲ καὶ ταύτην τὴν ἐντολὴν ἔθετο ὥσπέρ τινα κλεῖδά τε καὶ σφραγίδα καὶ δεσμὸν ἄλυτον· "*Ἐπὶ πᾶσι,*" γάρ φησι, "*τούτοις, ἐπισκήπτω τοῖς πατράσι καὶ ἀδελφοῖς καὶ πνευματικοῖς μου τέκνοις καὶ παρακαλῶ πάντας διὰ τὴν ἐν Χριστῷ ἀγάπην καὶ ὅρκοις καθυποβάλλω ἀπὸ Θεοῦ καὶ τῆς ὑπεραγίας Θεοτόκου ἡμῶν, ὑπείκειν καὶ ὑποτάσσεσθαι τῷ καθηγουμένῳ ὡς αὐτῇ τῇ ἐμῇ ταπεινώσει.*"

30

Ἀλλὰ ταῦτα μὲν ὕστερον. Ἔτι δὲ τῶν κτισμάτων ἐχομένῳ τῷ ἁγίῳ τούτῳ πατρὶ καὶ τῇ κατὰ Θεὸν πολιτείᾳ ἐνευδοκιμοῦντι, παραγέγονέ τις λέγων ἀναγορευθῆναι βασιλέα τὸν ἐπιφανῆ καὶ μεγαλώνυμον Νικηφόρον. Καὶ εἰ μὲν ἦν ἕτερος, μεγάλως ἂν ἐπεχάρη τῷ πράγματι ὡς λαμβάνων ἤδη καιρὸν εὐτυχίας· ὁ δὲ πατὴρ καὶ σφόδρα

one holy habit," how can someone dare to divide the name of Christ and those who have garbed themselves in Him, so that one is called "*of Paul,*" another "*of Kephas,*" and another "*of Apollos*"? For those monks would be the real outsiders, whom Satan tonsured with the scissors of wicked belief.

These are a few of his many ordinances. Together with all of these, he also issued this ordinance as a key and seal and unbreakable bond; for he says, "*In all these matters I adjure the fathers and brothers and my spiritual children, and by the love of Christ I exhort all of you and I place you under oath before God and our all-holy Mother to yield and subject yourselves to the superior just as you did to my humble self.*" 6

Chapter 30

But these things happened later. While this holy father was still involved with the construction project and was gaining glory in his godly way of life, someone came to tell him that the illustrious and renowned Nikephoros had been proclaimed emperor. Any other person would have been very pleased by this development as if he had now received good fortune, but the father Athanasios was very upset by

ἐσκυθρώπασεν ἐπὶ τούτῳ· διὰ τοῦτον γὰρ ὁ πατὴρ τῇ οἰκοδομῇ τῆς μονῆς ἐπεχείρησεν, ὡς ἐκείνου ὑποσχομένου αὐτῷ τοῖς κοσμικοῖς ἀποτάξασθαι πράγμασι καὶ μετ᾽ αὐτοῦ ἡσυχάζειν. Ἀλλ᾽ ἐπειδήπερ ἤκουσεν ὃ μὴ ἐβούλετο, ἔθετο παρ᾽ ἑαυτῷ μηκέτι προσμεῖναι τῷ τόπῳ τοῦ Ὄρους, ἀλλὰ φυγῇ χρήσασθαι.

2   Πρὸς τοῦτο οὖν παρασκευαζόμενος, πλάττεται πρόφασιν τοῦ βούλεσθαι ἀπελθεῖν εἰς τὸν βασιλέα χάριν προνοίας καὶ ὠφελείας τῆς μονῆς. Λαβὼν οὖν τοὺς πλείους τῶν ἀδελφῶν, διαπεραιοῦται ἕως Ἀβύδου, καὶ τοὺς μὲν ἄλλους ἀπέπεμψεν ἀναστρέφειν εἰς τὴν μονήν, τρεῖς δὲ μόνους κρατήσας, "Ἀρκεῖν ἡμῖν," ἔλεγε, "μετὰ τούτων καὶ μόνων ἀπελθεῖν εἰς τὴν βασιλεύουσαν." Τούτων ἑνὶ τῶν τριῶν ἐπιστολὰς ἐγχειρίσας, ἐπὶ τὴν βασιλίδα τοῦτον ἐξέπεμψεν, ἀποκρυψάμενος αὐτῷ τὸν νοῦν τῆς γραφῆς· τὰ δὲ βασιλεῖ γραφέντα ἀθέτησίν τε ὧν πρὸς Θεὸν ἔθετο συνθηκῶν ἐνεκάλει καὶ τὴν ἐπιζήμιον ἀνταλλαγὴν ἐπεμέμφετο καὶ ὡς ἀνηνύτοις αὐτὸν περιέβαλε κόποις· καὶ τελευταῖον, "Ἐγὼ μέν," φησι, "τὴν ἐμαυτοῦ, τὴν τοῦ Χριστοῦ δὲ μᾶλλον εἰπεῖν, ἄπειμι· τὴν δέ γε ποίμνην Θεῷ καὶ σοὶ παρατίθημι," προσθεὶς εἶναί τινα τῶν ἐκεῖσε ἀξιόλογον, Εὐθύμιον μὲν ὀνομαζόμενον, βίῳ δὲ καὶ λόγῳ λαμπρυνόμενον ἀρίστῳ, ᾧ καὶ τὴν τῶν μοναχῶν προστασίαν ὡς ἀξίῳ ταύτης ἐπεψηφίζετο. Καὶ ὁ μὲν μοναχὸς ἐξώρμα πρὸς τὴν βασιλεύουσαν· ὁ δὲ πατὴρ ἐξέπεμψεν εἰς τὸ μοναστήριον καὶ τὸν ἕτερον μοναχόν, Θεόδοτον ὀνομαζόμενον, ὥστε ἐπισκέψασθαι μὲν καὶ τοὺς ἀδελφούς, ἰδεῖν δὲ εἰ ἄρα ποιεῖται πρόνοιαν ὁ βασιλεὺς τῆς μονῆς· ἐγίνωσκε δὲ καὶ

this. For the father had undertaken the construction of the monastery because of this Nikephoros, since that man had promised him to renounce worldly affairs and live with him in spiritual tranquility. Thus when Athanasios heard this unwelcome news, he decided not to remain on the Mountain any longer, but to prepare his flight.

Making preparations for this, he devised the excuse that 2 he wanted to go to the emperor for the welfare and benefit of the monastery. Taking along most of the brethren, he thus crossed over to Abydos; then he sent the others back to the monastery, keeping with him only three monks, and saying, "These alone suffice to accompany me to the imperial city." He entrusted one of these three with letters and sent him to the Queen of Cities, concealing from him the content of the message. His letter to the emperor accused him of renouncing the promises he had made to God and criticized his hurtful change of plan and the fact that he had saddled Athanasios with pointless labors. Lastly, Athanasios wrote, "But I am going my own way, or rather that of Christ, and I entrust my flock to God and to you." He added that one of the brethren there at the monastery, named Euthymios and distinguished by his lifestyle and great knowledge, was deserving of special mention, and to him he assigned the leadership of the monks as a man worthy of this responsibility. So the monk set out for the imperial city, while the father sent the other monk, named Theodotos, back to the monastery, to check on the brethren and see if the emperor was indeed looking after the welfare of the monastery. And this

οὗτος τὴν τοῦ πατρὸς φυγὴν καὶ τὴν περίληψιν τῆς πρὸς τὸν βασιλέα γραφῆς.

3 Ὁ δὲ πατὴρ μετὰ τοῦ Ἀντωνίου μόνου περιλειφθείς, σὺν αὐτῷ ἐπὶ Κύπρον ἐκπλεῦσαι ἠθέλησε· καὶ πλοίου ἐπιβάντες τῆς θαλασσοπορίας εἴχοντο. Ὁμιλούντων οὖν αὐτῶν ἐν τῷ πλοίῳ, τὸν μέγαν ἠρώτησε μετ᾽ ἐκπλήξεως· "Πῶς, πάτερ, ἐν τῷ Γεροντικῷ γέγραπται, ὅτι τοῦ ἐν ἁγίοις Ἰσιδώρου ἀπελθόντος ἀπὸ Σκήτεως πρὸς τὸν ἐν Ἱεροσολύμοις πάπαν καὶ ἐρωτηθέντος μετὰ τὴν ὑποστροφὴν παρὰ τῶν μαθητῶν αὐτοῦ· 'Πῶς οἱ ἐν τῇ πόλει, πάτερ;' ἔφη πρὸς αὐτούς, 'Φύσει, τέκνα, οὐκ εἶδον ἄλλον ἄνθρωπον, εἰ μὴ μόνον τὸ πρόσωπον τοῦ πάπα.'" Ὁ δὲ πατὴρ χαριέντως φησί· "Καὶ ἐγὼ εἶδον ἕτερον εἰρηκότα μοι ὅτι διῆγε μετὰ γυναικῶν χρόνους ἱκανοὺς καὶ συνωμίλει αὐταῖς καὶ οὐκ εἶδε τὸ πρόσωπον αὐτῶν πώποτε." Ὁ δὲ Ἀντώνιος τοῦτο ἀκούσας ἔφη· "'Ἰδού, πάτερ, ἡ ἀπορία αὕτη μείζων τῆς προτέρας· ἀλλά, δέομαί σου, λῦσόν μοι τὴν δευτέραν καὶ ἀρκεσθήσομαι." Ὁρῶν οὖν αὐτὸν παρακαλοῦντα ἐπιπολύ, ὁ πατὴρ ἔφη· "Ἐγώ εἰμι ὁ ἁμαρτωλός, καὶ διὰ τὴν ἀσθένειάν μου ἐσκέπασέ με ὁ Θεός· πλὴν ἐξορκῶ σε μηδενὶ τοῦτο ἐξειπεῖν, ἕως ἂν ἐν τοῖς ζῶσίν εἰμι."

man was aware of the father's flight and the content of his letter to the emperor.

Then the father, now left alone with Antony, decided to 3 sail with him to Cyprus; and they boarded a ship and began their voyage. As they were conversing on the ship, Antony asked the great one in some perplexity, "How is it written in the *Gerontikon*, father, that when the holy Isidore went from Sketis to the patriarch in Jerusalem and was questioned by his disciples after his return, 'What are those people in the city like, father?' he replied to them, '*Actually*, children, *I saw no* other *man, except the face of the* patriarch.'" The father said with a smile, "And I saw another man who told me that he spent many years with women and conversed with them and never saw their faces." When Antony heard this, he said, "Look, father, this conundrum is even greater than the previous one. But, please, resolve the second one for me and I'll be satisfied." Seeing that he kept on asking him, the father said, "I am that sinner, and because of my weakness God shielded me; but I ask you to swear to tell this to no one, as long as I shall live."

31

Κ̲αὶ τοῦτο μὲν οὕτως. Ἐν Κύπρῳ δὲ τῇ νήσῳ προσ-
ορμίσαντες, τῇ μονῇ τῶν Ἱερέων οὕτω καλουμένῃ παρέβα-
λον· καὶ τῷ καθηγητῇ τῆς τοιαύτης μονῆς προσελθόντες
καὶ μετάνοιαν βαλόντες αὐτῷ, αἰτοῦσιν αὐτὸν χορηγεῖν
αὐτοῖς τὴν ἀναγκαίαν διατροφὴν καὶ τὰ ἐργόχειρα τούτων
λαμβάνειν· "Πόθος γὰρ ἔλαβεν ἡμᾶς," ἔλεγον, "ἀπελθεῖν
εἰς προσκύνησιν τοῦ Ἁγίου Τάφου, καὶ διὰ τὸν φόβον τῶν
Ἀγαρηνῶν δειλιῶμεν ὁδεῦσαι τὴν ἐκεῖ φέρουσαν." Καὶ
οὗτοι μὲν ταῦτα ἠξίωσαν· ὁ δὲ χαίρων τούτους ἐδέξατο καὶ
ἐν τοῖς παρακειμένοις αὐτῷ ὄρεσιν ἀπένειμε τούτοις οἴκη-
σιν, ἕως ἐβούλοντο. Καὶ ἦσαν μὲν διακαρτεροῦντες ἐκεῖσε.

2   Ὁ δὲ πρὸς τὴν βασιλίδα πεμφθεὶς μοναχὸς τὸ γράμμα
ἐνεχείρισε τῷ αὐτοκράτορι· ὁ δὲ βασιλεὺς πρὸ μὲν τοῦ
ἀναπτύξαι τὸ γράμμα χαρᾶς ἐπίμπλατο καὶ Θεοῦ λόγους
ἔλεγε δέξασθαι· μετὰ δὲ τὸ ἀναγνῶναι τοῦτο, εἰς λύπην
σφοδρὰν καὶ πένθος ἐτρέπετο, καὶ πολλὰ ἑαυτῷ ἐπεμέμφετο. Γνοὺς δὲ τὸ πρᾶγμα καὶ ὁ μοναχός, ἀπήρχετο
ὀδύρεσθαι ὡς ἀπολέσας ἤδη τὸν πατέρα ἐκ τῶν χειρῶν.
Ἀλλ' ὁ μὲν βασιλεὺς τὸν δηλωθέντα αὐτῷ παρὰ τοῦ πατρὸς
μοναχὸν Εὐθύμιον προεστῶτα τῆς μονῆς αὐτίκα πρου-
βάλετο· αὐτὸς δὲ ἐν παντὶ τόπῳ τῆς δεσποτείας αὐτοῦ
διατάγματα καὶ γράμματα πέμπει διὰ τὴν τοῦ πατρὸς
ἀναζήτησιν. Ταῦτα οὖν τὰ βασιλικὰ γράμματα πανταχοῦ
φθάσαντα ἔφθασε καὶ μέχρις αὐτῆς τῆς Κύπρου, καὶ ζήτη-
σις ἦν πολλὴ τούτου καὶ ἐν αὐτῇ.

Chapter 31

So much for this. When they arrived at the island of Cyprus, they went to the so-called Monastery of the Priests. They approached the superior of this monastery, made obeisance to him, and asked him to give them the food they needed and to accept their handwork in return. "For," they said, "we were seized by the desire to go venerate the Holy Sepulcher, but now, because of our fear of the Agarenes, we are hesitant to travel the route that leads there." So Antony and Athanasios made this request, and the superior gladly received them and assigned to them a place to live in the nearby mountains, for as long they wished. And so they took up residence there.

As for the monk who had been sent to the Queen of Cities, he delivered the letter to the emperor. Before he opened the letter, the emperor was filled with joy and said that he was receiving the words of God; but after he read it, he sank into deep sorrow and grief and severe self-reproach. When the monk also realized what was going on, he went off to lament for having already let the father slip from his grasp. But the emperor immediately appointed as superior of the Lavra monastery the monk Euthymios, who had been pointed out to him by the father; and he sent orders and letters to every part of his realm to search for the father. Thus these imperial letters, which went everywhere, reached even Cyprus as well, and there was much searching for him here too. 2

3   Ὁ γοῦν τῆς μονῆς τῶν Ἱερέων καθηγούμενος ἀκούσας ταῦτα, πεῖραν ἐποιεῖτο καὶ δοκιμὴν πρὸς τὸν πατέρα, ὡς ἂν γνῷ τίνες εἰσὶν ἀμφότεροι καὶ πόθεν· τὸν δὲ πατέρα ἐρωτώμενον παρὰ τοῦ καθηγουμένου οὐκ ἔλαθε τίνος χάριν ἠρώτα αὐτόν, ἀλλ᾽ ὡς εἶχε τάχους ἀναστρέφει πρὸς τὸν Ἀντώνιον καὶ ἀπαγγέλλει αὐτῷ τὴν ἐρώτησιν τοῦ ἡγουμένου καὶ [ὅτι] φησὶν "οὐ δυνησόμεθα, Ἀντώνιε, λαθεῖν ἕως τέλους, εἰ μὴ τάχος ἐντεῦθεν ἀποπλεύσαιμεν."

32

Καὶ ἅμα τῷ λόγῳ πρὸς τὸν αἰγιαλὸν ἐχώρουν, καὶ σκάφει ταχυναυτοῦντι περιτυχόντες κατὰ θείαν πρόνοιαν, ἐνέβησαν εἰς αὐτό, καὶ τυχόντες ἐπιτηδείου πνεύματος, εἰς τὸ πέραν γίνονται καὶ σκοποῦσι πρὸς ποίαν ἄρα τὴν ὁδὸν ἐφορμήσουσιν· ἡ μὲν γὰρ φέρουσα πρὸς τοὺς Ἱεροὺς Τόπους ἄβατος ἦν διὰ τὴν τότε τῶν ἀθέων Ἀγαρηνῶν ἐκεῖσε καταδρομήν· ἐν δὲ τῇ φερούσῃ πρὸς τὰ ρωμαϊκὰ μέρη ἐκωλύοντο διὰ τὴν περὶ τοῦ πατρὸς βασιλικὴν ἔρευναν, καὶ οὐκ εἶχον ποίαν ὁδὸν ὁδεύσουσι. Νυκτὸς οὖν ἐγκείμενος τῇ εὐχῇ ὁ πατὴρ καὶ τοῦ Θεοῦ δεόμενος βουλὴν δοῦναι αὐτῷ τί ἄρα καὶ πράξει, ὄψιν ἐθεάσατο θείαν κατεπείγουσαν αὐτὸν πρὸς τὴν οἰκείαν ἐπανελθεῖν μονήν, προφητεύουσάν τε αὐτῷ τὸν πλατυσμὸν ταύτης

When the superior of the Monastery of the Priests heard 3
this, he quizzed the father to find out who they both were
and where they had come from. But when the father was
questioned by the superior, he realized on whose behalf he
was questioning him. As fast as he could he returned to
Antony, told him about the superior's questioning and said,
"Antony, we will not be able to avoid detection in the end,
unless we sail away from here quickly."

Chapter 32

As soon as he said this, they went to the seashore, and by
divine providence came across a swift-sailing vessel and
boarded it. Obtaining a fair wind, they crossed over to the
other side and considered which route they should take. For
the road which led to the Holy Places was impassable at that
time on account of the incursion of the godless Agarenes in
that region, and they were prevented from taking the road
that led to Roman territory on account of the imperial
search for the father, and so they did not know which road
to follow. At nightfall, when the father devoted himself to
prayer and entreated God to advise him as to what he should
do, he saw a divine vision urging him to return to his own
monastery, and prophesying its expansion and embellish-

καὶ καλλωπισμόν. Τὴν τοιαύτην οὖν προαγγελίαν δεξάμενος ἐκ Θεοῦ, ἐδήλωσε καὶ τῷ Ἀντωνίῳ, καὶ αὐτίκα τῆς ὁδοιπορίας ἀπήρξαντο.

2 Ὡς δὲ πολλὰς ἡμέρας ὡδοιπορήκασι καὶ ἱκανῶς ἐκοπίασαν, πόνος ἐγενήθη τῷ τοῦ Ἀντωνίου ποδί, συνήθης μέν, διὰ δὲ τὸν τῆς ὁδοιπορίας κόπον σφοδρότερον προσβαλών, ὥστε καὶ τὴν ζωὴν ἀπολέγεσθαι. Ὁ δὲ πατὴρ ὁρῶν αὐτὸν λίαν κακῶς ἔχοντα, ἔπασχε τὴν ψυχὴν οἷα πατὴρ ἀληθής· ὅθεν καὶ μικρὸν ἀφεστηκὼς ἀπ᾽ αὐτοῦ καὶ τὰς χεῖρας σὺν τῷ ὄμματι ἐπάρας πρὸς τὸν Θεὸν καὶ τῇ προσευχῇ ἐμβραδύνας, εἶτα ἐπιστραφεὶς καὶ παραστὰς τῷ ἀλγοῦντι, εἶπεν ὑπογελώσῃ τῇ ὄψει· "Ἆρα, τέκνον Ἀντώνιε, σὺ ἰατρὸς ὢν οὐκ ἐπίστασαι θεραπεῦσαι σαυτόν;" Ὁ δέ φησιν· "Οἶδα, πάτερ, ἀλλ᾽ ἀπορίας οὔσης καθάπαξ, τί ἂν ὠφεληθείην; Οὐδὲν γὰρ ἡμῖν πλέον τῆς πλατάνου ταύτης καὶ τῆς ἀπόρου καὶ στενοτάτης ζωῆς."

3 Ὁ δὲ πατὴρ βοτανῶν τῶν παραφυομένων λαβόμενος καὶ ταύτας ἐπὶ πλακὸς τρίψας καὶ τῷ πάσχοντι ποδὶ περιθεὶς καὶ φύλλα ἐπιθεὶς τῆς πλατάνου ὑφ᾽ ἣν ἐκάθηντο, περιεδέσμησεν αὐτὸν ἐν τῷ ἐγχειρίῳ αὐτοῦ, ἐν ᾧ ἀπεκάθαιρεν ἀεὶ τὸ καταρρέον τῶν ὀφθαλμῶν αὐτοῦ δάκρυον· εἶτα τοῦτον κρατήσας τῆς χειρός, ἀνίστησιν ὁ σοφὸς ἰατρός, καὶ παραχρῆμα ἐξεβόησεν ὁ Ἀντώνιος· "Δόξα σοι, ὁ Θεός, ὅτι ἐκουφίσθην τοῦ πόνου." Καὶ περιεπάτει λοιπὸν ὡς τὸ πρότερον.

4 Ὁδεύειν οὖν ἀρξαμένων, πάλιν ἐπῆλθε νόσος τῷ Ἀντωνίῳ ἡ λεγομένη δυσεντερία· ὅντινα σφοδρὸς πυρετὸς ἡμιτριταῖος ἐπαναφθεὶς εἰς παραφροσύνην ἤγαγε καὶ

ment. After receiving this prediction from God, he revealed it to Antony, and they started off on their journey at once.

But after they had traveled for many days and were very 2 tired, Antony developed a pain in his foot. This was chronic, but affected him more severely on account of the tiring journey, to the point that he was despairing of life itself. When the father saw him in such great distress, he suffered in his soul like a true father. So he moved a little ways off from him and, raising his arms and his eyes to God, remained for a long time in prayer. Then he came back and, standing next to the afflicted monk, said to him with a smile on his face, "Antony, my child, even though you're a doctor, don't you know how to heal yourself?" And he replied, "I know how, father, but since I have absolutely nothing, what help is that? For we have nothing except this plane tree and our poor and meager provisions."

But the father picked some of the plants growing there 3 and crushed them on a flat stone. These he placed around the afflicted foot and put on top of them leaves from the plane tree beneath which they were sitting, and he bound the foot with his handkerchief with which he always wiped away the tears that flowed from his eyes. Then the skillful physician took his hand and raised him up, and immediately Antony cried out, "Glory be to Thee, O God, for I am relieved of my pain." And afterward he was able to walk as he had previously.

So, after they had resumed their journey, Antony was 4 again afflicted by illness, by what is known as dysentery. Moreover he was burning up with a raging semi-tertiary

οὕτως κατειργάσατο ὡς νεκρὸν νομισθῆναι· οὐδὲ γὰρ πρὸς τὴν ἐπείγουσαν αὐτὸν χρείαν ἠδύνατο τοῖς ποσὶν αὐτοῦ χρήσασθαι, ἀλλ' ὑπὸ τοῦ πατρὸς βασταζόμενος πρὸς ταύτην ἀπήγετο, ὥστε πολλάκις παραιτεῖσθαι αὐτὸν εὐλαβούμενον τὴν τοῦ πατρὸς ὑπηρεσίαν. Ἀλλ' ὁ πατὴρ ἐδείκνυε τὸ φιλόστοργον· θνήσκοντα γὰρ τοῦτον ἤδη ἀνέστησε πάλιν διὰ τῆς ὁλοκαρδίου αὐτοῦ προσευχῆς.

33

Καὶ οὗτοι μὲν ἐν τοιούτοις τοῖς συναντήμασιν ἐπανήρχοντο. Ὁ δὲ Θεόδοτος ὁ πρότερον ὑπὸ τοῦ πατρὸς πεμφθεὶς ἐπὶ τὸ Ὄρος, ὡς ἄνωθεν προειρήκαμεν, ἀναστρέψας εἰς τὴν μονὴν καὶ πάντας εὑρὼν κυμαινομένους ἐπὶ τῇ τοῦ πατρὸς ὀρφανίᾳ, ἐν πολλῇ τε τῇ στενώσει διάγοντας, ἅμα δὲ καὶ τὸν προεστῶτα τῆς Λαύρας παραιτούμενον τὴν ἡγουμενείαν, ἐδάκνετο τὴν καρδίαν καὶ τὴν στέρησιν τοῦ πατρὸς οὐχ ὑπέφερεν. Ἐπιμείνας οὖν τῷ Ὄρει χρόνον ὀλίγον, ἐπὶ Κύπρον ἐχώρει καὶ τὸν ποιμένα ἐζήτει.

2   Ἀλλὰ τὸ μὲν πλοῖον ὅπερ ἔφερε τοῦτον μέχρι μὲν τῆς Ἀτταλείας ἀκωλύτως ἐφέρετο· ἐπεὶ δὲ τῆς ἐπὶ τὰ ἔμπροσθεν πορείας ἐκωλύετο ὑπὸ τῆς πολλῆς τοῦ ἀνέμου ἐναντιότητος, ἐκβέβηκε τούτου καὶ πεζοπορῆσαι ἐβούλετο, καὶ ἐντὸς τῆς Ἀτταλείας γενόμενος, εἰς χεῖρας εἶχε τὸ θήραμα· περιέτυχε γὰρ ἐκεῖ τῷ πατρὶ ἀπροσδοκήτως κατά τινα

fever that made him delirious and made him look as though he were dead; for he could not use his legs to go to relieve himself, but had to be supported by the father in order to do this, so that he often had to discreetly request the father's assistance. But the father showed his affection; for through his wholehearted prayer he revived him again when he was already at death's door.

Chapter 33

So they continued their return journey with such incidents. As for Theodotos, whom the father had previously sent back to the Mountain, as we have already mentioned above, he returned to the monastery. There he found everyone agitated at the loss of their father, and living under severely straitened circumstances, and he also discovered that the superior of the Lavra, Euthymios, had renounced his position. As a result he was heartbroken and could not bear his father's absence. Thus after remaining on the Mountain for a short time, he left for Cyprus to search for their shepherd.

The boat which was carrying him made its way to Attaleia 2 without any hindrance, but when he was prevented from continuing his journey by severe adverse winds, he disembarked from this boat and decided to proceed on foot. Once he entered Attaleia, he had his quarry in his hands; for there, by some divine providence, he unexpectedly ran into the

θείαν οἰκονομίαν. Ὡς δὲ ἀλλήλους ἐθεάσαντο, σφόδρα
ἠγαλλιῶντο τῷ Πνεύματι [Luke 10:21]· ἐπεὶ δὲ ὁ πατὴρ τε-
ταραγμένους ἐμάνθανεν εἶναι τοὺς ἀδελφοὺς καὶ τὸ ὅλον
ἀποιμάντους καὶ διεσκορπισμένους, ἀπὸ χαρᾶς εἰς κατ-
ήφειαν καὶ λύπην μετεβάλλετο· καὶ τότε δὴ τὸν μὲν Θεόδοτον εὐθὺς εἰς τὴν Λαύραν ἐξέπεμπεν, ὡς ἂν δηλώσῃ τοῖς
ἀδελφοῖς τὴν ἔλευσιν αὐτοῦ· αὐτὸς δὲ ὁ πατήρ, εἰς τὴν τοῦ
Διουγκίου μονὴν ἀπελθὼν τὴν ἐν τῇ Λάμπῃ διακειμένην,
καὶ τοῖς ἀδελφοῖς παραβαλὼν χάριν εὐχῆς, καὶ τὸν τοῦ
καθηγουμένου τῆς τοιαύτης μονῆς αὐτάδελφον τῷ τῆς
παραφροσύνης κατεχόμενον πνεύματι θεασάμενος, καὶ
τὴν χεῖρα ἐπιθεὶς αὐτῷ καὶ παραχρῆμα ἰασάμενος, εὐθὺς
ἐπὶ τὸν Ἄθων ἀνέκαμψε καὶ ἐντὸς τῆς μονῆς γέγονεν.

3   Ὃν ἰδόντες οἱ ἀδελφοί, ἐδόκουν ἥλιον βλέπειν ἀπὸ
χειμῶνος καὶ ἔαρ καὶ ζωῆς εὕρεσιν, καὶ ἦν ἀκούειν συχνῶς
τὸ "Δόξα σοι, ὁ Θεός," καὶ πάντας βλέπειν τὸν μὲν τὰς
χεῖρας αὐτοῦ φιλοῦντα, τὸν δὲ τοὺς πόδας, τὸν δὲ τὸ
ράκος αὐτοῦ κατασπαζόμενον. Ἔχαιρε μὲν οὖν καὶ ὁ
καλὸς πατὴρ τὰ γεννήματα τῆς ἀρετῆς αὐτοῦ βλέπων καὶ
τὰ διεσκορπισμένα σεσυνηγμένα ἤδη ἀπολαμβάνων. Οἱ
δέ γε γειτνιάζοντες τῇ Λαύρᾳ καὶ ὅσοι τῶν πλησιοχώρων
σέβας εἶχον καὶ πίστιν πρὸς τὸν πατέρα εἰλικρινῆ, ὁμοίως
καὶ οὗτοι ἔχαιρον καὶ ἐδόξαζον τὸν Θεὸν ἀκούσαντες τὸν
πατέρα ἐπανακάμψαντα, καὶ τὴν χαρὰν ἐξ ἔργων ἐδείκνυον·
ἤρχοντο γὰρ ἰδεῖν τοῦτον καὶ εὐλογηθῆναι παρ' αὐτοῦ οὐ
κεναῖς ταῖς χερσίν, ἀλλ' ὁ μὲν σῖτον ἔφερεν, ὁ δὲ οἶνον,
ἄλλος δέ τι τῶν ἀναγκαίων, ἐκεῖνα δὲ πάντως ἕκαστος
ἅπερ ᾔδει ἐπιλείπειν τοῖς ἀδελφοῖς· οὐδὲ γὰρ κἂν γοῦν

father. As soon as they saw each other, *they rejoiced* exceedingly *in the Spirit*. But when the father learned that the brethren were upset and totally unshepherded and starting to disperse, he turned from joy to dejection and sorrow, and sent Theodotos straight back to the Lavra to let the brethren know he was coming. As for the father himself, he left for the monastery of Dioungiou located at Lampe. When he joined the brethren for prayer, he observed that the brother of this monastery's superior was afflicted by the spirit of insanity, and, after laying hands upon him, immediately healed him; he then headed straightaway for Athos and arrived at the monastery.

When the brethren saw him, it was like seeing the sun after the winter and like the arrival of spring and the renewal of life. One could frequently hear the words, "Glory be to Thee, O God," and everywhere one could see someone kissing Athanasios's hands, another his feet, and yet another his habit. The good father also rejoiced when he saw the fruits of his virtue and welcomed back those who had been dispersed, but were now rounded up. Those who lived near the Lavra and those from nearby places who also revered and had sincere trust in the father, these too rejoiced in the same way and glorified God upon the news of the father's return. They demonstrated their joy through their deeds; for when they came to see Athanasios and receive his blessing, they did not come empty-handed, but one brought grain, another wine, and yet another some necessity, each one bringing those items in particular which he knew the brethren were lacking. For otherwise they would not have had even a

τεμάχιον εἶχον ἄρτου εἰ μὴ τὴν ζύμην, ἣν εἶχον τότε, ὡς ἐξηγεῖτο ὁ Λαρισσαῖος Παῦλος, ἀνὴρ εὐλαβής τε καὶ τίμιος καὶ ἀρχαῖος ὢν τοῦ πατρὸς μαθητὴς καὶ πάντα ἰδὼν καὶ εἰδώς.

34

Ἐν ὀλίγῳ δὲ χρόνῳ ἀνακτησάμενος τὴν μονὴν καὶ πάντα καλῶς διαθέμενος, ἐπὶ τὸν βασιλέα ἀνέρχεται. Ὁ βασιλεὺς δὲ μαθὼν τοῦτον ἐρχόμενον, ἔχαιρε μὲν ὅτι ἐπόθει τοῦτον θεάσασθαι, ἠσχύνετο δὲ ὡς μέλλων ὀφθῆναι αὐτῷ ἐν βασιλικῇ τῇ στολῇ· διὸ καὶ ὑπήντησε τούτῳ οὐχ ὡς βασιλεὺς ἀλλ' ὡς εἷς τῶν πολλῶν· καὶ τῆς χειρὸς αὐτοῦ λαβόμενος μετὰ τὸν ἀσπασμὸν καὶ πρὸς τὸν ἴδιον κοιτῶνα ἀπαγαγών, συγκαθεσθεὶς αὐτῷ καταμόνας ἔφη· "Οἶδα, πάτερ, ὡς πασῶν σου τῶν θλίψεων καὶ κόπων ἐγώ εἰμι ὁ αἴτιος, τὸν τοῦ Θεοῦ φόβον περιφρονήσας καὶ τὰς πρὸς αὐτὸν συνθήκας ἀθετήσας καὶ καταπατήσας· πλὴν ἀντιβολῶ καὶ δέομαι μακροθυμῆσαι ἐπ' ἐμοὶ ἀναμένοντα τὴν ἐπιστροφήν μου, ἕως οὗ δῴη μοι ὁ Θεὸς ἀποδοῦναι αὐτῷ τὰς εὐχάς μου."

2 Τούτοις τοῖς φιλοθέοις ῥήμασιν εὐφρανθεὶς ὁ πατήρ, καίπερ εἰδὼς μὴ εἰς τέλος ἐκβησόμενα, ὁρῶν τε τὴν πολλὴν αὐτοῦ συντριβὴν καὶ μετάνοιαν, οὐ καλὸν ἔκρινε *κάλαμον κατεάξαι συντετριμμένον* [see Matthew 12:20], ὅπερ οὐδὲ ὁ

piece of bread except for the sourdough starter which they had then, as Paul of Larissa explained, a pious and venerable man who was an old disciple of the father and saw and knew everything.

Chapter 34

After restoring the monastery in a short time and putting everything in good order, Athanasios went to visit the emperor. When the emperor learned of his arrival, he rejoiced because he yearned to see him, but at the same time he was ashamed since Athanasios would see him in his imperial robes. And so he went to meet him not dressed as an emperor, but as an ordinary person. After their embrace he took Athanasios's hand and led him to his own bedchamber; there Nikephoros sat down with him privately and said, "Father, I know that I am the cause of all your sorrows and troubles, since I have disregarded my fear of God and set aside and trampled upon my covenants with Him. But I beg you and plead with you to be patient with me while you wait for me to change my way of life, at such time as God permits me to offer Him my vows."

The father was pleased by these pious words, even though 2 he knew that they would not come to pass in the end, and, seeing his great contrition and repentance, decided it was not right *to break a bruised reed,* something which not even

Νάθαν πρὸς τὸν Δαυῒδ ἐποίησεν, ἀλλ᾽ εὐθὺς συνεχώρει τε καὶ παρήνει ἑαυτὸν ὥσπερ ἰδιώτην ἡγεῖσθαι καὶ ζῆν λιτῶς καὶ ἐν ταπεινώσει, ἐξομολογεῖσθαί τε καὶ μετανοεῖν τῷ Θεῷ καθεκάστην ἐπί τε ταῖς λοιπαῖς αὐτοῦ ἁμαρτίαις καὶ ἐφ᾽ ᾧ ἐψεύσατο αὐτῷ, καὶ πρὸς τούτοις παρήγγελλεν εἶναι καὶ συμπαθῆ τοῖς πταίουσιν εἰς τὸ κράτος αὐτοῦ καὶ ἐλεημοσύνας ποιεῖν διαπαντός. Καὶ τοῦτον μὲν ἐνουθέτει ἐν τούτοις· πρὸς δέ γε τοὺς γνωρίμους αὐτῷ προέλεγεν ὅτι ἐν τῇ βασιλείᾳ τὴν ζωὴν καταλύσει.

3   Ὁ γοῦν βασιλεὺς τῆς οἰκείας φροντίζων μονῆς, ἐξέθετο τῷ πατρὶ χρυσοβούλλιον ἐπιβραβεῦον τῇ μονῇ σολεμνίου ποσότητα διακοσίων τεσσαρακοντατεσσάρων νομισμάτων, καὶ εἰς ἐπίδοσιν προσετίθει αὐτῷ καὶ τὴν ἐν Θεσσαλονίκῃ μονήν, ἢ Μέγα παρ᾽ αὐτοῖς ἔστι τε καὶ ὀνομάζεται Μοναστήριον. Ἐπεὶ δὲ καὶ οἱ μοναχοὶ τοῦ Ὄρους ἠτήσαντο τὸν πατέρα ἀξιῶσαι τὸν βασιλέα περὶ τοῦ ναοῦ τῶν Καρεῶν, τοῦ τυπωθῆναι καὶ τούτῳ παροχὴν σολεμνίου, ὑπήκουσε καὶ ἠξίωσε, καὶ προσετέθησαν τῷ παλαιῷ σολεμνίῳ τῶν τριῶν λιτρῶν ἕτεραι λίτραι τέσσαρες.

35

Ταῦτα διαπραξάμενος ὁ πατὴρ καὶ τῷ βασιλεῖ συνταξάμενος, ἐπὶ τὸ Ὄρος κάτεισι, τῶν ἑξῆς νεανικώτερον ἐχόμενος πόνων. Ὁ δὲ ἀριθμὸς τῶν μοναχῶν προσετίθετο·

Nathan did to David. Instead he forgave him straightaway and encouraged him to conduct himself as an ordinary person, to live simply and humbly, and to make confession to God and repent every day for his other sins and for not remaining true to his promises. In addition the father told him to show compassion toward those who offended against his might, and always to give alms. So he gave him advice along these lines, but to his acquaintances he predicted that Nikephoros would lose his life while he was still emperor.

Then the emperor, providing for his own monastery, issued for the father a chrysobull awarding to the monastery the sum of 244 gold coins as an annual stipend, and also granted to it as an additional endowment the monastery in Thessalonike which both is and is called the "Great Monastery." When the monks of the Mountain asked the father to petition the emperor about the church of Karyes, that it also might be provided with an annual stipend, he agreed to do so and made the petition, and another four pounds of gold were added to the previous stipend of three pounds. 3

Chapter 35

After the father had concluded these negotiations and bade farewell to the emperor, he returned to the Mountain, and energetically undertook the following labors. For the

ὅσῳ δὲ προσετίθετο, τοσούτῳ καὶ ὁ ταμίας τῶν ἀγαθῶν ἐπεχορήγει τὰ ἐπιτήδεια· ὅσῳ δὲ τὰ προσφερόμενα τῇ μονῇ ἐπληθύνετο, τοσούτῳ τὰ τῆς φιλοξενίας ἐπηύξανεν· οὐδεὶς γὰρ τῇ μονῇ παραβαλὼν κεναῖς ταῖς χερσὶν ὑπεχώρει.

2   Εἰ δὲ καὶ ζάλη τις ἢ χειμὼν ἐπεκράτει ἐν τῷ λιμένι τοὺς προσορμιζομένους, ὅσον ἂν καιρὸν ἐκεῖσε διήγαγον, πᾶσιν αὐτοῖς ἐχορηγεῖτο τὰ πρὸς τροφὴν ἀπὸ τῆς μονῆς· ἀλλὰ καὶ ὅσα πλοῖα ἐθραύετο καὶ διερρήγνυτο ἐν ταῖς τῆς θαλάσσης πέτραις, ἐκεῖ προσορμιζόμενα καὶ αὐτὰ τῆς ἁρμοζούσης ἐπιμελείας ἐτύγχανεν, ὅπερ ἐξ ἐκείνου τυπωθὲν ἄχρι τοῦ νῦν γίνεται. Ἐπεὶ δὲ ἡ γειτνιάζουσα τῇ μονῇ θάλασσα, ἀλίμενος οὖσα παντελῶς καὶ ἀπόκρημνος, οὐκ εἴα προσορμισθῆναι τά τε τῆς μονῆς πλοῖα καὶ τὰ παραβάλλοντα πάντοθεν κατὰ χρείαν τινά, ἀλλ᾽ ἀεὶ φόβον παρεῖχε κινδύνου, ὁ φιλόξενος ἐκεῖνος καὶ θεῖος ἀνήρ, τὸ μὲν διὰ τὴν τῆς μονῆς ἀναγκαίαν χρείαν, τὸ δὲ καὶ τῶν παραβαλλόντων ξένων κηδόμενος, πρὸς κατασκευὴν λιμένος ἐχώρησεν.

3   Ἀλλ᾽ ὅρα μοι τὸν μισόκαλον Ἐχθρὸν καὶ βάσκανον τί τεχνάζεται· ὁρῶν γὰρ τὰ τελούμενα ὑπὸ τοῦ πατρὸς καὶ προορῶν ἑαυτὸν ὅσον οὔπω τῶν ἐκεῖσε παντελῶς ἀπελαθησόμενον, παρατάσσεται ἀνδρικώτερον ἢ μᾶλλον εἰπεῖν θρασύτερον, ὡς πρὸς ἀνταγωνιστὴν ἰσχυρὸν ἀντιτασσόμενος, καὶ πειρασμὸν ἐπεγείρει τῷ πατρὶ ἀφόρητον ὡς εἰπεῖν καὶ ἀνύποιστον. Τοῦτον δὲ προεῖδέ τις γέρων τῶν τῆς μονῆς ἀδελφῶν δι᾽ ἐκστάσεως, ἣν καὶ ἐξηγήσατο αὐτῷ·

number of monks kept increasing and, to the extent that their numbers increased, so to the same degree God, *the steward of blessings,* continued to provide the necessary resources. Moreover, to the extent that the offerings to the monastery kept multiplying, to the same degree its hospitality increased. For no one who came to the monastery departed empty-handed.

If a squall or a storm forced those who were anchored in 2 the harbor to remain there, they were all provided with food by the monastery, whatever the duration of their stay. Furthermore, any ships that had been damaged and smashed by rocks in the sea received the appropriate repairs if they anchored there, a rule ordained by Athanasios and observed until the present day. Since the sea coast near the monastery lacked any natural harbor whatsoever and was precipitous, it did not permit anchorage either for the monastery's ships, or for those that came from elsewhere for some purpose, but always threatened terrible danger. For this reason that hospitable and divine man set about constructing a harbor, partly because of the urgent need of the monastery and partly out of concern for the visitors who arrived there from afar.

But let me show you what the envious Enemy who hates 3 the good wrought next. For when he saw the father's accomplishments, he foresaw that he himself would soon be driven entirely out from there. In a rather bold or, better, a rather audacious manner he drew up his battle line, as if preparing to confront a mighty opponent, and stirred up a torment for the father that one might describe as intolerable and unbearable. Indeed, an elder, who was one of the brethren of the monastery, foresaw this torment in an ecstatic vision,

"Ἑώρων γάρ," φησι, "καὶ ἰδοὺ εἷς χιλίαρχος τὸ Ὄρος εἰσήρχετο, μεγάλην πνέων τὴν ἀπειλὴν καὶ πολλὴν ἐνδεικνύμενος ἐξουσίαν καὶ σοβαρότητα, ὃς καὶ διεμέριζε τὴν πονηρὰν ἐκείνην λεγεῶνα, προστάσσων ἑκατὸν μὲν εἰς ἅπαν τὸ ὄρος ἀναστρέφεσθαι καὶ τοὺς μοναχοὺς ἐνεδρεύειν, αὐτὸς δὲ ὁ παμμέλανος ἄρχων εἰς τὰ Μελανὰ προσέβαλε σὺν τοῖς ἐννακοσίοις μετὰ πολλοῦ τοῦ φρυάγματος." Καὶ τοιαύτη μὲν ἡ ὅρασις· πρὶν ἢ δὲ ταύτην ἀπαγγεῖλαι τὸν γέροντα, εἰς ἔργον προέβαινεν.

4   Ὡς γὰρ εἴθιστο ὁ πατὴρ συγκάμνειν τοῖς κάμνουσι, μᾶλλον δὲ καὶ πρῶτος αὐτὸς τὴν χεῖρα ἐπιβάλλειν τοῖς ἔργοις, μετεκομίζετο μὲν εἰς τὸν λιμένα ξύλον ὑπερμέγεθες, συνεβοήθει δὲ καὶ οὗτος εἰς τὴν τούτου καταγωγήν· καὶ αὐτὸς μὲν εἰς τὸ κάτω μέρος ἵστατο, οἱ δὲ τεχνῖται εἰς τὸ ἄνω· καὶ οἱ μὲν ὤθουν τὸ ξύλον ἐπὶ τὸ κάταντες, ὁ δὲ πατήρ τινι τῶν παραλίων πετρῶν ἐπερείδων τὸν πόδα μετὰ τῶν κάτω ἱσταμένων κατ᾽ εὐθεῖαν εἷλκε τὸ ξύλον. Συνεπωθήσαντος δέ, ὡς ἔοικε, καὶ τοῦ πονηροῦ στίφους ἐκείνου μετὰ τοῦ αὐτῶν χιλιάρχου (ὦ τῶν πικρῶν αὐτοῦ βελῶν καὶ ἐπιβουλῶν!), ἀθρόον παρασύρεταί πως τὸ ξύλον καὶ καταχθὲν συντρίβει τὸν ἀστράγαλον αὐτοῦ μετὰ τοῦ σκέλους.

5   Ἴσχυσεν οὖν ὁ Πονηρός· ὁ δὲ πατὴρ ἐπὶ τρισὶν ἔτεσι κλινήρης γενόμενος καὶ δριμείαις ταῖς ὀδύναις βαλλόμενος, οὐδὲ οὕτως ἠνείχετο ἀργεῖν, ἀλλ᾽ ἐν τεσσαράκοντα μὲν ἡμέραις γράφων τὸ Γεροντικὸν συνετέλεσεν ἅπαν· τὸ δὲ τῆς ψυχῆς ἔργον πολλῷ μᾶλλον ἐπολυπλασίασε· τῶν γὰρ ἐκτὸς ἀπεχόμενος ἔργων διὰ τὸν ἐπενεχθέντα αὐτῷ

which he described to Athanasios: "I saw a military commander arrive at the Mountain," he said, "giving off an immensely threatening air and putting on a great show of authority and arrogance. He divided up his wicked legion, ordering one hundred men to explore the entire mountain and lay ambushes for the monks, while he himself, the pitch-black commander, took nine hundred men to Melana with a lot of haughty posturing." Such was his vision; but before the elder could relate it, it actually happened.

For since the father used to work alongside the workmen, 4 or rather he himself was the first to set his hand to the construction work, one day he was helping in the transport of a very large log that was being transferred to the harbor. He was standing at the lower end, and the workmen at the upper end. While the latter were pushing the log downhill, the father, planting his foot on one of the rocks along the seashore, was dragging the log straight down together with those standing below. It seems, however, that that wicked gang of demons was also pushing together with their commander (alas for his bitter arrows and plots!), and the log was somehow violently diverted to one side and crashed down, breaking his ankle and his leg.

Thus the Evil One prevailed, and the father lay bedridden for three years, afflicted by severe pain. Not even in this state could he bear to remain idle, however, but over a period of forty days he completed an entire *Gerontikon*. And he multiplied even more his spiritual labors; for, being unable to work outside on account of the trial that had befallen

πειρασμόν, ἑαυτῷ μόνον ἐσχόλαζε καὶ τῷ Θεῷ, ἔστι δὲ ὅτε καὶ τῷ παρέργῳ.

36

Τὸν μὲν οὖν εἶχεν ἡ κλίνη διὰ τὴν ἀλγηδόνα τῆς ἐκ τοῦ πειρασμοῦ πληγῆς, ὁ δὲ τάφος εἶχε τὸν ἀοίδιμον βασιλέα Νικηφόρον διὰ τὴν ἐπιβουλὴν ἣν πάντες γινώσκουσι, κἂν ἐγὼ σιωπήσωμαι. Ὁ δὲ ἄρχων τοῦ σκότους ἀφορμῆς δραξάμενος τῆς βασιλείας τοῦ μετ᾽ αὐτὸν κεκρατηκότος Ἰωάννου, ἐπανίσταται πάλιν κατὰ τοῦ πατρός· ἁπλουστά-τους γὰρ εὑρὼν τοὺς τότε γέροντας τοῦ Ὄρους καὶ ζῆλον πνευματικὸν ἔχοντας καὶ μὴ θέλοντας παρεξελθεῖν τοῦ παλαιοῦ ἔθους αὐτῶν, περιῆλθεν ἅπαντας καὶ ὑπεποιήσα-το ἕκαστον, κλέπτων αὐτῶν τὴν ἁπλότητα καὶ συμβου-λεύων αὐτοῖς ταῦτα· "Τί ὅτι περιείδετε τὸν Ἀθανάσιον καταδυναστεύοντα τοῦ Ὄρους καὶ τοὺς ἀρχαίους τύπους καὶ τὰ ἔθιμα καταλύοντα; Οἰκοδομὰς γὰρ ἀνήγειρε πολυ-τελεῖς καὶ ναοὺς καὶ λιμένας ἐνεούργησεν, ἐπιρροάς τε ὑδάτων κατήγαγε καὶ ζεύγη βοῶν ὠνήσατο καὶ εἰς κόσμον ἤδη τὸ Ὄρος μετεποίησεν. Ἢ οὐχ ὁρᾶτε ὅτι καὶ *ἀγροὺς ἔσπειρε καὶ ἐφύτευσεν ἀμπελῶνας καὶ καρπὸν γενήματος ἐποίησεν*" [Psalm 106(107):37];

2   Ὁ ἀλιτήριος γὰρ καὶ Γραφῶν ἐστιν ἔμπειρος· ἀλλ᾽ οὐκ εἶπεν ὁ σοφιστὴς τῆς κακίας καὶ τὸ λοιπόν, ὅτι *καὶ εὐλόγη-σεν αὐτοὺς καὶ ἐπληθύνθησαν σφόδρα* [see Psalm 106(107):38],

him, he focused solely on himself and on God, except for incidental business.

Chapter 36

While Athanasios was confined to his bed on account of the pain from the injury sent to him as a trial, the celebrated emperor Nikephoros went to his grave on account of the conspiracy with which everyone is familiar, even if I will keep silent about it. Then the archon of darkness, seizing the opportunity provided by the reign of Nikephoros's successor on the throne, John, rose up again against the father. After discovering that the elders of the Mountain were extremely simple men who, in their spiritual zeal, did not wish to diverge from their old traditions, he went to visit all of them and deceived each one, taking advantage of their simplicity and giving them this advice: "Why have you disregarded the fact that Athanasios is lording it over the Mountain and destroying the ancient rules and customs? For he has erected luxurious buildings and has constructed churches and harbors, and channeled streams of water and bought teams of oxen, and has already transformed the Mountain into a worldly place. Don't you see that *he has sown fields and planted vineyards and made them to yield fruit of increase?*"

For the wicked one is also well acquainted with the Scriptures, but that clever deviser of evil thus did not say the rest of the verse, that he *also blessed them and they multiplied*

ἀλλὰ τοῦτο ὑπερπηδήσας ὡς καταδικάζον αὐτόν, εἰς φονικὴν συμβουλὴν ἔκλινε· "Πλὴν ἀλλὰ δεῦτέ," φησιν, "ἐξολοθρεύσωμεν αὐτὸν ἀπὸ τῶν ὧδε ταχέως, καὶ ἅπερ ᾠκοδόμησε καταβαλώμεθα καὶ τὰς ἐπαύλεις αὐτοῦ κατασκάψωμεν, καὶ οὐ μὴ μνησθῇ τὸ ὄνομα αὐτοῦ [Psalm 82(83):4]· ἢ γοῦν δεήθητε τοῦ βασιλέως Ἰωάννου, καὶ ἐπὶ κεφαλὴν ἐξώσει αὐτὸν ἀπὸ τῶν ὧδε."

3 Τούτοις τοῖς λογισμοῖς ἐξαπατήσας ὁ πανοῦργος τοὺς γέροντας, οἰκειοῦται τὴν αὐτῶν ἁπλότητα καὶ πόλεμον ἐγείρει ἐμφύλιον, κατὰ τοῦ πατρὸς κινήσας αὐτούς, καὶ ἐνθύμησιν ἐμβάλλει τούτοις προσελθεῖν τῷ βασιλεῖ καὶ δέησιν φέρειν αὐτῷ αἰτίας κατὰ τοῦ Ἀθανασίου περιέχουσαν, ὅτι τε "Τοὺς ἀρχαίους ἡμῶν ὅρους παρακινεῖ καὶ μεταποιεῖ τὰ παλαιὰ ἔθη τοῦ Ὄρους." Οὗτοι μὲν οὖν τοιαῦτα τῷ βασιλεῖ ἀνήνεγκαν· ὁ δὲ βασιλεὺς γράφει τῷ Ἀθανασίῳ ταχέως ἀναπλεῦσαι εἰς τὴν βασιλεύουσαν. Ἐπεὶ δὲ ἀνῆλθε καὶ ὡμίλησε τῷ βασιλεῖ, αὐτίκα τὸν πρὶν ὠργισμένον αὐτῷ βασιλέα ἡ τοῦ Θεοῦ χάρις, ἡ συνοδεύουσα αὐτῷ καὶ ἀντιλαμβανομένη τούτου ἀεί, οὐ μόνον προσφιλῆ ἐποίησε τότε, ἀλλὰ καὶ φιλοφροσύνης καὶ εὐεργεσίας βασιλικῆς ἠξίωσεν.

4 Ἐδωρήθη γὰρ τῇ μονῇ παρὰ τοῦ βασιλέως Ἰωάννου διὰ χρυσοβούλλου δωρεᾶς σολεμνίου ποσότης διακοσίων τεσσαρακοντατεσσάρων χρυσίνων, ὅση δηλονότι καὶ παρὰ τοῦ ἀοιδίμου βασιλέως κυροῦ Νικηφόρου δεδώρητο. Θεασάμενοι δὲ οἱ γέροντες τὸ παράδοξον τοῦτο καὶ μηδαμῶς ἀγνοήσαντες τὴν ἐπισκιάζουσαν χάριν τῷ Ἀθανασίῳ, αἴσθησιν ἔλαβον τῆς δαιμονικῆς κακοτεχνίας ὑφ'

exceedingly, but omitting this in order to condemn him, he turned to some murderous advice: *"Come and let us* quickly *root him out* of here, and let us cast down what he has built, and let us destroy his farm buildings, and *let his name be remembered no more.* Or else make a petition to the emperor John and he will throw him out of here headlong."

The crafty one deceived the elders with these thoughts, 3 and then, taking advantage of their simplicity, stirred up a civil war, inciting them against the father. He gave them the idea of approaching the emperor and bringing him a petition containing charges against Athanasios, that "He is transgressing our ancient rules and transforming the old customs of the Mountain." So they reported this to the emperor. The emperor wrote to Athanasios, asking him to sail immediately to the imperial city. When he arrived and spoke with the emperor, the grace of God, which always accompanied Athanasios and assisted him, not only immediately mollified the emperor who was previously enraged against him, but made him consider the father worthy of imperial benevolence and benefaction.

For the emperor John granted to the monastery by 4 chrysobull a sum of 244 gold pieces as a stipend, which is the same amount that had been granted also by the emperor Kyr Nikephoros, of blessed memory. When the elders saw this strange turn of events and no longer had doubts about the grace that overshadowed Athanasios, they perceived the evil demonic ruse by which they had been tricked. They re-

ἧς ἐκλάπησαν, καὶ πολλὰ μεταμεληθέντες καὶ μεταγνόντες, προσπίπτουσι τούτῳ καὶ αἰτοῦνται συγχώρησιν· ὁ δὲ πατὴρ τοῦτο ποιήσας εἰς τὴν ἀγάπην αὐτοῦ καὶ πίστιν πάντας ἐδούλωσεν.

37

Ὁ τοίνυν μισόκαλος Ἐχθρὸς ἀποτυχὼν τῆς κατὰ τοῦ πατρὸς ἐπιβουλῆς καὶ αὖθις νικηθεὶς ὑπ᾽ αὐτοῦ καὶ καταισχυνθείς, πάλιν ἐπωρύετο κατ᾽ αὐτοῦ καὶ διηγείρετο ἔτι πρὸς πόλεμον ἰσχυρότερον, οὐκέτι δι᾽ ἑτέρου τινός, ἀλλὰ δι᾽ ἑαυτοῦ προσβαλεῖν αὐτῷ πειρώμενος. Διὸ καὶ συμμάχους ἐκάλει καὶ πόλεμον ἐκρότει φρικτόν· καὶ ὅπως, ἄκουε. Ὥρα μὲν ἦν τρίτη τῆς ἡμέρας, καί τις τῶν ἱερῶν γερόντων, Θωμᾶς ὀνομαζόμενος, καθαροὺς ἔχων τοὺς τῆς ψυχῆς ὀφθαλμούς, εἰς ἔκστασιν ἐλθὼν μετὰ τοὺς ὕμνους τῆς τρίτης ὥρας, εἶδε, καὶ "Ἰδοὺ πάντα τὰ ὄρη καὶ οἱ βουνοί, νάπαι τε καὶ ἄλση μεστὰ πάντα αἰθιόπων πιθήκων, οἵτινες δεινῶς ἐμαίνοντο, ἀπειλοῦντες, ὑβρίζοντες, φόνου πνέοντες, ἀλλήλοις ἐγκελευόμενοι ὡς ἐν πολέμῳ καὶ παρατάξει καὶ μετ᾽ ὀργῆς κράζοντες· 'Τί βραδύνομεν, ὦ φίλοι; Τί μὴ σπαράσσομεν διὰ τῶν ὀδόντων; Τί μὴ ταχέως ἐξολοθρεύομεν ἀπὸ τῶν ὧδε τὸν δεινότατον ἡμῶν ὀλοθρευτήν; Μέχρι τίνος ὑπομενοῦμεν; Οὐχ ὁρᾶτε ὅπως ἀθλίως διέθηκεν ἡμᾶς καὶ τὴν γῆν ἡμῶν

pented deeply and had a change of heart, falling at his feet and begging forgiveness. And the father, in granting this, subjected them all to love of and faith in him.

Chapter 37

Therefore the Enemy, who hates everything good, because he had failed in his plot against the father and had once again been defeated by him and put to shame, began again to howl against him and was roused to an even mightier war, trying to attack him directly himself, and no longer through someone else. So he summoned allies and launched a frightful battle. And hear how it turned out. It was the third hour of the day, and one of the holy elders, named Thomas, who had pure spiritual insight, went into an ecstatic trance after the hymns of the third hour. He had a vision, which he described as follows: "All the mountains and hills, woodland valleys and groves were all filled with black dwarves, who raged terribly, uttering threats, casting insults, breathing murder, encouraging each other as if arrayed for battle. And they shouted angrily: 'What are we waiting for, my friends? Why don't we tear them apart with our teeth? Why don't we quickly root out from here our most terrible destroyer? How long are we going to put up with him? Don't you see how he has reduced us to this miserable state and

ἔλαβεν;' Οἱ μὲν δὴ ταῦτα ἔλεγον· ὁ δὲ πατήρ," φησιν, "ἐξῆλθε τῆς κέλλης, ῥάβδον κατέχων ἐν τῇ χειρί· οἱ δὲ Αἰγύπτιοι οὗτοι πίθηκες ἰδόντες αὐτὸν εὐθὺς ἐπτοήθησάν τε καὶ ἐταράχθησαν, οἷστισι καὶ τεταραγμένοις ἐπεισπεσών, τοὺς μὲν ἐμάστιζε, τοὺς δὲ καὶ ἐδίωκε, καὶ οὐκ ἐπαύσατο ἕως ἐξώρισεν αὐτοὺς ἐκ τῶν Μελανῶν καὶ παντελῶς ἐξετόπισε τῇ τοῦ Χριστοῦ χάριτι."

38

Οὗτος ὁ ἀκοίμητος Ἐχθρὸς ἀδελφόν τινα τῆς συνοδίας εἰς μῖσος ἔβαλε τῆς ἀσκητικῆς καὶ τεθλιμμένης ζωῆς καὶ κατὰ τοῦ πατρὸς ἐξέμηνεν, ὡς δῆθεν αὐτοῦ πρὸς ἀγῶνας βιάζοντος· ὅθεν καὶ εἰς φόνον τὸν κατ' αὐτοῦ τοῦτον παρώρμησεν. Ὁ γοῦν μάταιος ἐκεῖνος στιλβώσας τοῦ φόνου τὴν μάχαιραν καὶ καιρὸν ἐπιτηρήσας τὸν τῆς νυκτός (ὅτε δηλονότι τὸν πατέρα γρηγόρως ἔχειν ἠπίστατο), ἐπέστη τῇ κέλλῃ αὐτοῦ. Ψάλλοντος οὖν καὶ ὑπὲρ αὐτοῦ εὐχομένου (αὐτοὶ γάρ, φησιν, ἀγρυπνοῦσιν ὑπὲρ τῶν ψυχῶν ὑμῶν [Hebrews 13:17]) ἀκροασάμενος, "Εὐλόγησον, πάτερ," εἶπε, τάχα νομίζων ὁ ἀτυχὴς ἐκεῖνος ἐχθρὸς ἅμα τῇ φωνῇ ἐξελθεῖν τὸν πατέρα καὶ ἀδεῶς τὸν φόνον ἐργάσασθαι. Καὶ ἡ μὲν φωνὴ ἦν φωνὴ Ἰακώβ, αἱ δὲ χεῖρες χεῖρες Ἡσαῦ [Genesis 27:22]· ὁ δὲ πατήρ, Ἄβελ δίκαιος ὤν, οὐκ ᾔδει ὅτι Κάϊν ἵστατο ἔξω, ἀλλ' ἔνδοθεν τῆς κέλλης

taken our land?' These were their words, but the father," he continued, "came out of his cell, holding his staff in his hand. And these Egyptian dwarves were immediately scared and terrified at the sight of him, and he fell upon them in their confusion, flogging some, and chasing others away, and he did not stop until he had driven them away from Melana and completely removed them through the grace of Christ."

Chapter 38

This sleepless Enemy caused a monk of the community to develop a hatred of the grueling ascetic lifestyle and enraged him against the father, because he was supposedly forcing him into ascetic struggles. And in this way the Devil even incited him to attempt to murder Athanasios. Thus that foolish monk, polishing his murderous knife and waiting for nighttime (when, that is, he knew the father would be awake), came to his cell. Hearing Athanasios singing psalms and praying on his behalf (*for,* Paul says, *they are keeping watch over your souls*), his unfortunate assailant said, "Give me your blessing, father," thinking perhaps that the father would come out at the sound of his voice and he could carry out the murder with impunity. And *the voice was Jacob's voice, but the hands were the hands of Esau.* The father, being a righteous Abel, did not know that it was Cain standing outside, but

θαρραλέα τῇ φωνῇ ἠρώτα αὐτόν, "Σὺ τίς εἶ;" καὶ τὴν θύραν παρήνοιξεν.

2   Ὁ δὲ ξιφηφόρος ἐκεῖνος, τῆς τοῦ ποιμένος ἀκούσας φωνῆς, ἐπατάχθη τῷ ἤχῳ ταύτης, καὶ ὡσεὶ νεκρὸς τῷ τρόμῳ καὶ τῷ φόβῳ γενόμενος, ἐξελύετο τὰς χεῖρας, καὶ ἡ μάχαιρα κατὰ γῆς ἔρριπτο, καὶ αὐτὸς εἰς τοὔδαφος κατὰ πρόσωπον ἔπιπτε καὶ πρὸ τῶν ποδῶν τοῦ πατρὸς ἐκυλίετο, καὶ ἐλεειναῖς φωναῖς αὐτὸν καθικέτευεν· "Ἐλέησον, πάτερ μου, τὸν σφαγέα σου· συγχώρησον ταύτην τὴν ἀνομίαν μου καὶ ἄφες τὴν ἀσέβειαν τῆς καρδίας μου." Ἅψας οὖν φῶτα ὁ πατὴρ καὶ τὴν μάχαιραν ἰδὼν κατὰ γῆς *ἠκονημένην ὡσεὶ ξυρὸν* [Psalm 51(52):2] καὶ τὸν σκοπὸν αὐτοῦ γνούς, φησίν· "*Ὡς πρὸς λῃστὴν ἐξῆλθες ἐμέ, ὦ τέκνον, μετὰ τοιαύτης μαχαίρας* [see Matthew 26:55; Mark 14:48; Luke 22:52]; Ἀλλὰ παῦσαι τῶν ὀδυρμῶν, κλεῖσον τὸ στόμα, κρύψον τὸ πρᾶγμα, μὴ θριαμβεύσῃς σαυτόν, μὴ δὲ πρός τινα ἐξαγγείλῃς τὸ γεγονὸς καθ' οἰονδήτινα καιρόν· ὁ γὰρ Θεὸς ἀφεῖλέ σου τὸ ἁμάρτημα, καὶ δεῦρο ἀσπάσομαί σε τὸ ἐμὸν τέκνον."

3   Καὶ ὁ μὲν πατὴρ οὐ μόνον τοῦτο ἐποίησεν, ἀλλ' ἔκτοτε καὶ πλείονα τὴν στοργὴν πρὸς αὐτὸν ἐδείκνυε καὶ πολλῶν ἠξίου τῶν σωματικῶν ἀγαθῶν. Ἀλλ' ὁ ἀδελφὸς ἐκεῖνος, τὴν ἁμαρτίαν αὐτοῦ ἀναλογιζόμενος καὶ τῆς τοῦ πατρὸς συμπαθείας ἀναμιμνησκόμενος, καὶ εἰς αἴσθησιν ὢν ἠξίωτο παρ' αὐτοῦ ἀγαθῶν ἐρχόμενος καὶ ὅτι οὐκ ἀπεκηρύχθη ὡς ἐπίβουλος, τὴν παραγγελίαν τοῦ σιωπῆσαι φυλάσσειν οὐκ ἠδύνατο, ἀλλὰ τὴν ἁμαρτίαν αὐτοῦ φαυλίζων τὴν τοῦ πατρὸς ἀνεξικακίαν ἐδημοσίευε. Λέγεται δὲ ὅτι καὶ μετὰ

from inside his cell asked him in a confident voice, "Who is it?" and opened the door a little.

But when that knife-wielding monk heard his shepherd's 2 voice, he was stricken at the sound. In his terror and fear he became like a dead man, and relaxed his grip. The knife dropped to the ground and he himself fell to the floor on his face and groveled at the father's feet, entreating him with pitiful words: "My father, have mercy on your murderer; forgive my transgression and forgive the impiety of my heart." The father then struck a light and, when he saw the knife on the ground, *like a sharpened razor,* and realized the monk's intention, he said, "My child, *have you come out against* me *as against a robber with* such *a sword?* But stop this wailing, close your mouth, keep this affair secret, don't make a spectacle of yourself, and never ever tell anyone what happened. For God has remitted your sin; come now, I will embrace you as my child."

The father not only did this, but from that time on 3 showed even greater affection for him and considered him worthy of many material blessings. But that brother, reflecting upon his sin and remembering the father's compassion, and comprehending the blessings of which he had considered him worthy and that he did not denounce him as a conspirator, could not abide by the instruction to remain silent, but disparaged his sinful act and publicized the father's

τὸ ἀποθανεῖν ἐκεῖνον τὸν ἀδελφόν, τοσοῦτον ἐθρήνησεν
ὁ πατὴρ ὅσον οὐδένα τῶν ἄλλων.

39

Καὶ τοῦτο μὲν οὕτως. Ἕτερος δέ τις ἀδελφὸς πολλαῖς
γοητείαις τὸν πατέρα, ὅσον τὸ ἐπ᾽ αὐτῷ, κατεργασάμενος
καὶ ὁρῶν μηδαμῶς ὑπ᾽ αὐτῶν βλαπτόμενον, ἐξενίζετο μὲν
καὶ πρότερον· τότε δὲ ἀκούσας παρὰ τοῦ ἀδελφοῦ τὸ φο-
νικὸν ἐκείνου τόλμημα καὶ καταπλαγεὶς ἐπὶ τῇ τοῦ πατρὸς
ἀνεξικακίᾳ καὶ ὅτι τοσοῦτον αὐτὸν εὐηργέτησε, μετενόει
καὶ κατενύγετο καὶ ἑαυτοῦ κατεμέμφετο ἐπὶ τῷ τῶν γοη-
τειῶν ἁμαρτήματι. Καὶ ἐπεὶ ἔτυχέ τις ἐρωτῶν αὐτὸν τότε,
οἷα συμβαίνει ἐν ταῖς ὁμιλίαις παρεμπίπτειν, "Ἆρα, ἀδελφέ,
θανατοῦσιν αἱ γοητεῖαι ἄνθρωπον ἐὰν τοῦτο ἤκουσας;"
ἀπεκρίνατο ἐκεῖνος· "Οὐδεμίαν δύναμιν ἔχουσιν αὗται
πρὸς θεοσεβῆ ἄνθρωπον." Ἐπιστοῦτο δὲ τοῦτο ἀφ᾽ ὧν τὸν
πατέρα ἐπεβουλεύσατο· καὶ θαρρήσας τῇ τούτου ἀνεξικακίᾳ, ἀπελθὼν πρὸς αὐτὸν ἐξωμολογεῖτο τούτῳ τὴν κατ᾽
αὐτοῦ ἐπιβουλήν, καὶ προσέπιπτεν αὐτῷ ἐν θρήνοις καὶ
δάκρυσι συγχωρηθῆναι αὐτῷ τὸ ἁμάρτημα. Ὁ δὲ πατὴρ
κατακλασθεὶς τὴν ψυχὴν ἐπὶ τῇ τούτου θερμῇ μετανοίᾳ,
ἐδείκνυ καὶ πρὸς αὐτὸν παραχρῆμα τὸ συμπαθὲς αὐτοῦ
καὶ φιλόστοργον.

forbearance. And it is said that, after that monk's death, the father mourned for him more than for any other.

Chapter 39

And that's how this happened. Another monk attacked the father with many spells, as best he could. When he saw that they caused no harm at all to Athanasios, he was at first astonished; but then, when he heard from the brother about his murderous attack, he was astounded at the father's tolerant attitude and how he had treated him so well. So he repented, was filled with contrition, and blamed himself for his sin of casting magic spells. When someone asked him by chance at that time, as happens in conversations, "Brother, have you heard whether spells kill people?" he replied, "They have no power over a pious person." This was confirmed by what he had plotted against the father; and so, taking confidence in Athanasios's tolerant attitude, he went to him and confessed his plot against him, and prostrated himself before him with lamentation and tears, begging forgiveness for his sin. And the father, moved in his soul by the monk's ardent repentance, immediately showed him his compassion and affection too.

40

Τοιοῦτος ἦν πρὸς τοὺς ἁμαρτάνοντας, ἵνα μόνον κερδήσῃ τὰς ἐκείνων ψυχάς. Τὸ δὲ συμπαθὲς ὅπερ εἶχε πρὸς τὸ ὁμόφυλον, πόσα ἄν τις εἰπὼν ἐπαινέσοι ἀξίως; Εἴ τινα γὰρ εὕρισκεν ἀπερριμμένον καὶ πάρετον καὶ ἀπηγορευμένον καὶ φίλαργον, ἄρρωστον τυχόν, εἴτε λωβὸν εἴτε φιλομέθυσον ὄντα ἢ βίον ἄλλως διεφθαρμένον ἔχοντα, πάντας προσεδέχετο καὶ ἀντελαμβάνετο καὶ ἄριστα ᾠκονόμει τούτοις τήν τε σωματικὴν καὶ ψυχικὴν πρόνοιαν.

2 Ἔλεγε γὰρ ἀεὶ ὅτι τοῦτό ἐστι τὸ ζητούμενον παντὶ ἀνθρώπῳ δυναμένῳ, τὸ περιποιεῖσθαι σῶμα καὶ ἀνακαλεῖσθαι ψυχὴν ἐκ βυθοῦ καὶ ἐξ ἀναξίων ἐξάγειν τίμιον [see Jeremiah 15:19]· εἰδὼς γὰρ ὅτι ἡ ἀργία πάθη πολλὰ κινεῖ τῇ ψυχῇ, οὐκ ἠφίει αὐτοὺς ἐσθίειν καὶ ἀναπαύεσθαι, ἀλλ᾽ οἷα σοφὸς ἰατρὸς τοὺς μὲν αὐτῶν ἐν τῷ μαγειρείῳ προσέταττεν εἶναι, ὥστε συγκόπτειν λάχανα, τοὺς δὲ ἐν τῇ τραπέζῃ διαθρύπτειν τὸν ἄρτον, τοὺς δὲ εἰς τὸ χαλκεῖον παρέπεμπεν, ἵνα τοὺς φυσητῆρας κατέχωσι καὶ ὑπηρετῶσι τοῖς ἐργαζομένοις, ὡς ἂν ἀπὸ τοῦ προσέχειν ἐκεῖ λυτρῶνται τῶν πονηρῶν λογισμῶν καὶ εἰς μετάνοιαν ἔρχωνται.

3 Ταῦτα πράττων ἐκεῖνος καὶ οὕτως ἰατρεύων, ἐπαίδευε τοὺς ὑπ᾽ αὐτὸν ἀδελφοὺς τῆς ἀρετῆς τὴν ἀλήθειαν καὶ ἐδίδασκεν ὅπως δεῖ ἰατρεύειν τοὺς τὴν ψυχὴν ἰατρεύειν ἐθέλοντας, καὶ τὴν τοιαύτην ἐπιμέλειαν τῶν ἐν Χριστῷ ἀδελφῶν ἐνομοθέτει φυλάττεσθαι, ὥσπερ καὶ τὰ οἰκεῖα μέλη περιποιούμεθα, "μήποτε καὶ ἡμεῖς," φησι, "τῶν

Chapter 40

He treated sinners in this way with the sole purpose of winning their souls. As for the compassion which he had for his fellow human beings, what words could one use to praise it sufficiently? For if he came across anyone who was an outcast, or apathetic, worn out, or indolent, perhaps because they were sick or maimed or an alcoholic or had had their life ruined in some other way, he would welcome them all and help them, and provide them with the best physical and spiritual care.

For he always used to say that this is the goal for every 2 person who can do so: to take care of the body, recall the soul from the depths of despair, and *bring forth the precious from the worthless*. For in the knowledge that idleness stirs up many passions in the soul, he did not let them merely eat and relax, but like a wise physician he assigned some of them to the kitchen to cut up vegetables, and he sent some to the refectory to slice the bread, and some to the smithy to hold the bellows and assist the workers, so that, by being forced to focus their attention there, they would be delivered from wicked thoughts and come to repentance.

By doing this and healing them in this way, he trained the 3 brethren under him in the truth of virtue, and taught them how one should heal those who are intent on healing their souls. He also made it a rule that the brethren in Christ should receive the same care, just as we take care of our own

ὁμοίων κακῶν πεῖραν λάβωμεν· τὸ γὰρ ποιεῖν καλὸν
κρεῖσσον ἄγαν ὑπὲρ τὸ πάσχειν κακῶς."

4   Ὥσπερ δὲ ἐκείνους διὰ τὸ μὴ ἀργεῖν καὶ βλάπτεσθαι
ψυχικῶς εἰς τὰς εἰρημένας διακονίας καθίστα, οὕτω καὶ
τοὺς ἐργαζομένους ἐν τοῖς ἐργοχείροις ἀδελφούς, εἴτε ἐν
ζύμη διακονοῦντας, εἴτε ἐν τῷ μαγειρείῳ, εἴτε ἐν ἀμπελῶνι,
εἴτε ἐν ἄλλη διακονίᾳ δουλεύοντας, οὐκ ἀφῆκε μετὰ ἀργο-
λογίας τοῦτο ποιεῖν, ἀλλὰ διάταγμα ἔθετο ἀκατάλυτον
ψαλμολογεῖν τούτους καὶ μὴ ἀργολογεῖν, ἵνα καὶ τὸ ἔργον
εὐλογοῖτο καὶ ἡ ψυχὴ ἁγιάζοιτο, τοῦτο δὲ ποιεῖν καὶ ἐν
ταῖς μετακομιδαῖς τῶν εἰδῶν τῶν ἀπὸ τῶν πλοίων ἀποθη-
σαυριζομένων εἰς τὴν ἀποθήκην, ὡς ἂν ψαλλόντων καὶ
τῶν μετακομιζόντων αὐτὰ εὐχαριστῆται Θεὸς ὁ τρέφων
ἡμᾶς.

41

Τοὺς μὲν οὖν ἐν διαφόροις νόσοις καὶ ἀρρωστίαις ἐτα-
ζομένους, τούς τε τῆς ποίμνης μοναχοὺς καὶ τοὺς ἐν
Χριστῷ ἀδελφοὺς τῷ νοσοκομείῳ παρέπεμπεν ἐπιμελη-
θήσεσθαι, τοὺς δέ γε πάντη λελωβημένους παρεδίδου τοῖς
ἐπιτηδείως ἔχουσιν ἀδελφοῖς, ὡς παρακαταθήκην τινὰ ἢ
θησαυρὸν ἄσυλον· ἣν γὰρ οἰκοδομήσας καὶ νοσοκομεῖον
καὶ λοετρὸν διὰ τὴν χρείαν τῶν ἀσθενῶν, καὶ ὡς φιλόπο-
νος ἰατρὸς νοσοκόμον τε ἔταξε καὶ ἑτέρους ἀδελφοὺς

limbs, "so that," he said, "we too may not experience similar ills; for to do good is certainly better than to suffer ill."

Just as he assigned those people to the above-mentioned 4 duties so that they would not be idle and suffer spiritual harm, so also he did not permit the brethren who were engaged in manual labor, whether they were assisting with the leavened dough, or working in the kitchen, or in the vineyard, or at some other task, to accompany their labors with idle chitchat, but he made it an unbreakable rule that they were to sing psalms and not engage in idle conversation, so that their work would be blessed and their souls hallowed. He also charged them to do this while transporting to the warehouse goods that had been stowed on the ships, so that God who nourishes us would be thanked, as those transferring the goods chanted psalms.

Chapter 41

As for those who were afflicted by different diseases and illnesses, he used to send both the monks of his flock and the brethren in Christ to the infirmary for care, and as for those who were totally incapacitated he entrusted them to the appropriate brethren, as a valuable deposit or inviolate treasure. For he built both an infirmary and a bath for the use of the sick, and like a conscientious physician he appointed an infirmarian and other brethren to assist him in

συμπονοῦντας αὐτῷ εἰς τὴν χρείαν τῶν θεραπευομένων ἀρρώστων καὶ ὑπουργίαν. Ἁπάντων δὲ τούτων αὐτὸς ἦν ἀρχηγός, πάντας ἐπιβλέπων καὶ πρῶτος τὴν χεῖρα ἐπιβάλλων τοῖς τραύμασιν· εἴπερ γὰρ οἱ δουλεύοντες τούτοις οὐκ ἠδύναντο φέρειν τὴν δυσοσμίαν τῶν τραυμάτων ἢ ἀηδίαν εἶχον ἐν τοῖς ἕλκεσιν, αὐτὸς οἰκείαις χερσὶ τούτων τὰ ἕλκη ἐκάθαιρε, τὰ σεσηπότα μέλη θερμοῖς ἐπαντλῶν ὕδασι, καταδεσμῶν τε καὶ διὰ τῆς προσψαύσεως μόνης κουφίζων τὰς ὀδύνας καὶ θεραπεύων.

2 Ἐν οἷς καὶ πολλὰ μὲν λανθάνειν ἐσπούδαζεν· ἡ δύναμις δὲ τῆς αὐτοῦ ἀρετῆς τοῦτον ἐδημοσίευε διὰ τῶν ἰάσεων. Τίς γὰρ οὐκ οἶδε τὸν λεπρὸν ὂν τότε ἰάσατο; Ὅν ἔπαισε μὲν ὁ Πονηρὸς *ἕλκει πονήρῳ* [see Job 2:7], ὁ δὲ θεραπευτής, καὶ αὐτὸν τοῦτον τὸν τεθεραπευμένον διαλαθεῖν μηχανώμενος, τῆς ὑπ᾽ αὐτὸν συνοδίας ἐχώρισε καὶ ἰδίᾳ πόρρω που κατοικίαν ἔνειμε κἀκεῖσε τῆς παντελοῦς ἀπώνατο καθάρσεως.

3 Ἡνίκα δέ τις τῶν πασχόντων τῇ χρονίᾳ κατακλίσει ἐδαπανᾶτο καὶ οὐκ ἦν ὑγείας ἐλπὶς ἐπ᾽ αὐτῷ, ἀπήγγελλε μὲν ὁ νοσοκόμος αὐτῷ τὴν περὶ τὸν ἀσθενῆ ἀπαγόρευσιν· οὗτος δὲ πρὸς τὸν κείμενον ἀπερχόμενος, ἠρώτα τοῦτον· "Πῶς ἔχει, τέκνον, τὰ κατὰ ψυχήν;" Τοῦ δὲ ἀσθενοῦς, εἴτε ἐν ὑγείᾳ ψυχῆς ἦν, εἴτε καὶ μή, ἐξαγγέλλοντος, ὁ πατὴρ τὰ πρὸς ὑπομονὴν καὶ καρτερίαν παραινῶν αὐτῷ ὑπεχώρει.

4 Ἐπειδὰν δὲ ὁ χρόνος τῆς κατακλίσεως ἐπετείνετο καὶ οἱ διακονοῦντες οὐκ ἠδύναντο ὑπομένειν λοιπὸν τὸ ἐκ τῆς νόσου βάρος καὶ τὴν ἀηδίαν, προσήρχοντο πάλιν τῷ πατρὶ καὶ ἐδέοντο αὐτοῦ λέγοντες· "Δεήθητι, πάτερ, τοῦ Θεοῦ

the care and service of the sick people who were undergoing treatment. He himself headed the entire staff, overseeing everyone and being the first to lay hands upon the wounds. For if those who ministered to these patients could not bear the foul stench of the wounds or were disgusted by the suppurating sores, he himself with his own hands would clean their sores, pouring warm water over their gangrenous limbs and applying bandages, and through his touch alone he would soothe their pains and heal them.

In these endeavors Athanasios tried hard not to attract attention; but the power of his virtue made him known through his healings. For who did not know about the leper whom he cured at that time? During his treatment his healer tried to conceal this man, whom the Evil One *smote with sore boils;* he thus removed him from the community that was under his direction and assigned him to a private dwelling somewhere far away, and there the man happily experienced a complete recovery. 2

If one of the patients was worn out by lengthy confinement to bed and there was no hope of his recovery, the infirmarian would report to Athanasios his despair about the patient; and Athanasios would go to the bedridden man, and ask him, "My child, how is your spiritual state?" After the sick man declared whether or not he was in good spiritual health, the father would exhort him to patience and endurance and depart. 3

If the period of his confinement to bed was prolonged and the attendants could not endure any longer the severity and the disgusting symptoms of the disease, they would again approach the father and entreat him, saying, "Father, 4

ἐλευθερωθῆναι καὶ τὸν ἀδελφὸν ἐκ τῶν ὀδυνῶν καὶ ἡμᾶς ἐκ τῶν κόπων." Ὁ δὲ παρήνει αὐτοῖς, "Ἔτι ὑπομείνατε, τέκνα," λέγων, "ἵνα καὶ ὁ στέφανος ὑμῶν μείζων ἔσται." Εἰ δέ γε ἄλλην πληροφορίαν εἶχε παρὰ Θεοῦ περὶ τοῦ πάσχοντος, τότε δὴ ἐτελεῖτο παννυχὶς ὑπὲρ τοῦ ἀδελφοῦ, καὶ ἐδέετο τοῦ Θεοῦ, καὶ τῆς εὐχῆς ἐπιτελεσθείσης ἀπηλλάττετο τοῦ βίου ὁ ἀδελφός· δι᾿ ὑπερβολὴν δὲ ταπεινοφροσύνης οὐχ ἑαυτοῦ ἔλεγεν εἶναι, ἀλλὰ τῆς τῶν μοναχῶν προσευχῆς τὴν τοῦ θανάτου ταχύτητα.

5 Μετὰ γοῦν τὸ θανεῖν τὸν ἀδελφόν, οὗτος μὲν ἐφίστατο τῷ νεκρῷ, οἱ δὲ τῆς ἐκκλησίας διακονηταὶ ἐτίθουν παρὰ τοὺς πόδας αὐτοῦ τὸ πτυστήριον· ὁ δὲ κύπτων περὶ αὐτό, τοσαῦτα κατέχεεν ὑπὲρ τοῦ τελευτήσαντος δάκρυα, ὡς καὶ λιμνάζεσθαι τὸ δακρυοδόχον ἀγγεῖον· ἐξ ἐκείνου δὲ ἀνανεύων, ἐρυθρὸν ἐδείκνυ τὸ πρόσωπον ὥσπερ ἀπὸ πυρός. Καὶ οὐκ ἦσαν πενθοῦντος τὰ δάκρυα, ἀλλ᾿ εὐχαριστοῦντος τῷ Θεῷ, ὅτι προσέφερεν αὐτῷ τὸν ἀπελθόντα ὥσπερ θυσίαν τινά· μετὰ γὰρ τὸ τελεσθῆναι τὴν ἐπιτάφιον ὑμνῳδίαν προσήγγιζε μὲν τῷ νεκρῷ, ἔπιπτε δὲ κατὰ γῆς ἐπὶ πρόσωπον· εἶτα ἀνιστάμενος τὰς χεῖρας ἐξέτεινε, καὶ ἱκανῶς τῷ Θεῷ εὐχαριστήσας, ἠσπάζετο τοῦτον τὰ τελευταῖα καὶ τῷ τάφῳ παρέπεμπεν, εἰς πάντας τοῦτο ποιῶν καὶ ὑπὲρ πάντων εὐχαριστῶν τῷ Θεῷ.

pray to God that the brother be delivered from his suffering and we from our labors." But he would advise them, "My children, endure a while longer, so that your martyr's wreath may be even larger." But if he had some other indication from God about the patient, then a night vigil would be celebrated on the brother's behalf, and Athanasios would pray to God, and when the prayer was accomplished the brother would depart from this life. But on account of his excessive humility Athanasios used to say that the swiftness of death did not result from his own prayer, but from that of the monks.

After the brother had died, Athanasios would station 5 himself by the corpse, and the church attendants would place a spittoon at his feet. He would lean over it, and shed so many tears on behalf of the deceased that the receptacle of his tears would overflow; and when he raised his head up from it, he would reveal a face reddened as if by fire. These tears were not those of someone who was grieving, but of one giving thanks to God, because he was offering Him the departed as a sacrifice. For after the funeral hymnody was concluded, he would approach the corpse and prostrate himself on the ground. Then, rising to his feet, he would stretch out his arms, offer many thanks to God, give him the final kiss and entrust him to the grave, doing this for every monk, and giving thanks to God on behalf of all.

42

Ὅσῳ τοιγαροῦν ἐμεγεθύνετο ἡ ποίμνη αὐτοῦ, τοσούτῳ καὶ ἀγώνων μειζόνων εἴχετο, ἐγκρατείᾳ διηνεκεῖ προσκείμενος καὶ γρηγόρσει μείζονι καὶ νηστείᾳ πενταημέρῳ τὰς τρεῖς διατελῶν τεσσαρακοστάς· καὶ σχεδὸν εἰπεῖν ἡ πᾶσα αὐτῷ ζωὴ νηστεία ἦν· ὅτε γὰρ ἔνδον τῆς τραπέζης καὶ οὗτος μετὰ τῶν ἀδελφῶν ἐγίνετο, τούτοις μὲν τὰ παρατιθέμενα διένεμεν, αὐτὸς δὲ σχῆμα ἐσθίοντος δεικνύων, ἐλάνθανε τὰς ὄψεις αὐτῶν, καὶ οὐδὲ αὐτὴν ὁλόκληρον ἐδαπάνα τὴν διανεμομένην μετὰ τὴν λειτουργίαν εὐλογίαν. Ἡ ἀγρυπνία δὲ αὐτῷ ἡμέραν ἐποίει τὴν νύκτα, καὶ οἱ πόδες αὐτῷ κίονες ἐδόκουν ὑπὸ τῆς πολλῆς στάσεως· εἰ δὲ καὶ ἔδει ὀψέ ποτε ὕπνου μετρίου ἀπογεύσασθαι, δέρμα μόνον ἦν αὐτῷ ἡ στρωμνὴ καὶ ἡ χρεία τῆς σκέπης μόνον τὸ παλλίον αὐτοῦ.

2   Ἔνθέν τοι καὶ ἀνέκλειπτον εἶχεν ἐν αὐτῷ τὴν τοῦ Θεοῦ χάριν καὶ ἐν πᾶσι συμπράττουσαν· τίς γὰρ ἀγνοεῖ ὅσα κατώρθωσε διὰ τῶν αὐτοῦ διδαχῶν τε καὶ παραινέσεων, ἑκάστῳ νομοθετῶν ἰδίᾳ καὶ κοινῶς, κατηχήσεις ποιῶν, *ἐπιτιμῶν τε καὶ παρακαλῶν* [see 2 Timothy 4:2] καὶ διεγείρων κατὰ τοῦ ἀοράτου Ἐχθροῦ, *τὰ βάρη πάντων βαστάζων* [see Galatians 6:2] καὶ τῷ ἑαυτοῦ αὐχένι ἐπιτιθέμενος, *τοῖς πᾶσι πάντα γινόμενος* [see 1 Corinthians 9:22] καὶ σῴζων τούτους διὰ τῶν παραινέσεων αὐτοῦ καὶ τοῦ τῆς ἀρετῆς ὑποδείγματος;

Chapter 42

Therefore, to the extent that his flock increased, so Athanasios endured greater ascetic struggles, devoting himself to constant abstinence and greater vigilance and observing five-day fasts during the three lenten periods. In fact, almost his entire life was spent in fasting; for when he was in the refectory with the brethren, he used to distribute to them the food that was set out, while he himself only pretended to eat, avoiding attracting attention, and he did not even completely consume the blessed bread distributed after the liturgy. His vigils turned night into day, and his legs came to resemble columns as a result of so much standing. And if he ever needed to take a short nap late at night, a leather hide alone served as his mattress and his cloak was his only covering.

Thus he had God's grace perpetually within him, supporting him in all his endeavors. For who is unaware of how much he accomplished through his teachings and exhortations, establishing rules for each monk in private and publicly, giving catechetical instruction, *rebuking and exhorting* and inciting them against the invisible Enemy, *bearing the burdens* of all and carrying them around his own neck, *becoming all things to all men,* and saving them through his exhortations and the example of his virtue?

3   Ὅσην δὲ σπουδὴν εἶχε περὶ τὸ λανθάνειν θαυματουρ-
γῶν, ἐντεῦθεν δῆλον· ἄλλοις μὲν γὰρ τὰς χεῖρας ἐπιτιθεὶς
ἀσθενοῦσιν, ὡς δῆθεν τοῦ πάθους ἁπτόμενος, ἰᾶτο αὐτούς·
ἄλλοις λέγων, "Οὐδὲν κακὸν ἔχεις, ἀδελφέ," ἀκόλουθον
τῷ λόγῳ τὸ ἔργον εἶχε διὰ τῆς χάριτος· ἄλλους πλήττων
ἐν τῇ ἁγιαστικῇ αὐτοῦ ῥάβδῳ ἐθεράπευεν. Εἴ τις δὲ εἶχε
καὶ πάθος θυμοῦ ἢ μίσους ἢ φθόνου καὶ ἐξήγγελλε τοῦτο
τῷ πατρί, ἐνουθετεῖτο μὲν ἀγάπην ἔχειν πρὸς τὸν πλήσιον
[see Matthew 5:43; Mark 12:31, 33], ἐπετίθετο δὲ καὶ ἡ τοῦ
πατρὸς βακτηρία ἐν τῇ κεφαλῇ αὐτοῦ εἴτε τῷ στήθει, καὶ
"Ἄπελθε ἐν εἰρήνῃ," ἀκούων, "οὐδὲν κακὸν ἔχεις," ἐπαύετο
τοῦ θυμοῦ καὶ τοῦ μίσους ἀπηλλάττετο καὶ τὸν φθόνον εἰς
ἀγάπην μετέβαλλε. Πλὴν οὐκ ἐπὶ πᾶσιν οὕτω ταχὺς ἦν
ἰατρός, ἀλλὰ ἄλλοις μὲν ὑπισχνεῖτο μετ᾽ ὀλίγον ἀπαλ-
λαγὴν τῆς νόσου, ἄλλους ὀλίγον ἐκούφιζεν, ἑτέρους δέ γε
καὶ παντελῶς, ἑτέρων τὴν πρᾶξιν τοῦ κακοῦ ἐκκόπτων
ἠφίει μόνον κατὰ τοῦ λογισμοῦ ἀγωνίζεσθαι, καὶ ὡς
ἑκάστῳ συμφέρειν ἠπίστατο.

43

Ἐντεῦθεν καὶ μέγας ἦν παρὰ πᾶσιν, ἐντεῦθεν κοινὸς
κηδεμὼν καὶ προστάτης παρὰ τῆς ἄνωθεν προνοίας πρου-
βάλλετο, καὶ διὰ τῆς αὐτοῦ ἀρετῆς τὸ Ὄρος ἅπαν ᾠκίσθη
καὶ ἐν τοσούτῳ πλήθει ἐμεγαλύνθη τῶν εὐαρεστούντων

His determination to avoid attention when he performed   3
miracles is evident from the following: for he would lay
hands on some sick people, as though he were grabbing hold
of their suffering, and would heal them; but to others he
would say, "There's nothing wrong with you, brother," and
through his grace he would make his words actually come to
pass. Others again he would heal by striking them with his
sanctifying staff. If someone was afflicted with anger or hatred or envy and confessed this to the father, he would first
admonish him to *have love for his neighbor,* and then he would
also lay his staff on his head or his chest. And when the person heard him say, "Depart in peace; there's nothing wrong
with you," he would cease from his anger and hatred and
transform the envy into love. Athanasios was not always
such a swift healer, however. To some he promised relief
from their illness after a short time, to others he gave some
slight relief, and yet others he healed completely; for others
again he would excise the practice of evil and only let them
struggle against wicked thoughts, knowing what was beneficial for each one.

Chapter 43

Athanasios was thus great in the eyes of all, thus he was
set forth as a *common guardian and protector* by heavenly providence, and through his virtue the entire Mountain was
inhabited and magnified by such a multitude of monks

δὴ τῷ Θεῷ· ὅθεν καὶ ὁ σύμπας χορὸς τῶν γερόντων τὸν ἡσυχαστικὸν βίον καὶ ἐρημικὸν καταλιμπάνοντες αὐτῷ προσήρχοντο, ὠφελιμώτερον κρίνοντες τὸ συνεῖναι αὐτῷ καὶ τυποῦσθαι πρὸς ἀρετὴν καὶ κανονίζεσθαι ὑπ᾽ αὐτοῦ. Τινὲς δὲ καὶ τοὺς μαθητὰς αὐτῶν νοσοῦντας τὸ ἀνυπότακτον καὶ ἀδιόρθωτον προσέφερον αὐτῷ, καὶ ἰᾶτο καὶ τούτους διὰ τῆς σοφῆς αὐτοῦ παραινέσεως· ἄλλοι δὲ καὶ τὰ προσόντα τούτοις κελλία καὶ ἑαυτοὺς συμπαρεδίδοσαν, ὥστε ὑπ᾽ αὐτοῦ ποιμαίνεσθαι.

2 Ἤδη δὲ καὶ πλῆθος πολὺ συνέτρεχε πρὸς αὐτὸν ἐκ παντοδαπῶν ἐθνῶν, ἀπό τε Ῥώμης αὐτῆς, Ἰταλίας, Καλαβρίας, Ἀμάλφης, Ἰβηρίας καὶ Ἀρμενίας, οὐ τῶν ἀγενῶν μόνον καὶ κοινῶν, ἀλλὰ καὶ τῶν εὐγενῶν καὶ πλουσίων· καὶ οὐ μόνον οὗτοι, ἀλλὰ καὶ κοινοβίων ἡγούμενοι καὶ ἐπίσκοποι τοὺς ἑαυτῶν παραιτούμενοι θρόνους, προσήρχοντο καὶ οὗτοι αὐτῷ καὶ τῇ τούτου ὑποταγῇ ἑαυτοὺς ὑπεστρώννυον· ἐξ ὧν ἦσαν καὶ οὗτοι, ὅ τε μέγας ἐν πατριάρχαις Νικόλαος, ὁ περιβόητος Χαρωνίτης καὶ ὁ σοφώτατος καὶ ἐν ἀσκήσει πολὺς Ἀνδρέας ὁ Χρυσοπολίτης, Ἀκάκιός τε ὁ ἐν πολλοῖς ἔτεσιν ἀσκητικῶς διαλάμψας.

3 Ἀλλὰ καί τινες ἐρημῖται καὶ σιδηροφόροι ἀναχωρηταὶ τῇ πολυχρονίῳ ἀσκήσει ἐγγηράσαντες, κατά τινα θείαν οἰκονομίαν τούτῳ προσήρχοντο καὶ παρ᾽ αὐτοῦ ποιμαίνεσθαι ἐδέοντο· ὧν εἷς ἦν καὶ ὁ μακαριώτατος Νικηφόρος ὁ ἐν τοῖς ὄρεσι τῆς Καλαβρίας συνδιαιτώμενος τῷ ἐν ἁγίοις Φαντίνῳ· ἐκεῖ γὰρ συνδιάγοντες ἄμφω, θεῖον χρησμὸν ἐδέξαντο κελεύοντα τούτοις τὸν μὲν ἀπελθεῖν εἰς Θεσσαλονίκην, ὡς ἐκεῖ τελευτᾶν ὀφείλοντα, τὸν δὲ Νικηφόρον

pleasing unto God. As a result the entire band of elders abandoned the contemplative and eremitic lifestyle and came to him, judging it more profitable to associate with him and be modeled in virtue and trained by him. Some elders also brought him their disciples who were disobedient and incorrigible, and he cured these too through his wise exhortation. And yet others gave up their hermitages and themselves to Athanasios so as to be shepherded by him.

Already, a great multitude of people from all sorts of different origins was flocking to him, from Rome itself, from Italy, Calabria, Amalfi, Iberia, and Armenia, not only ordinary and common people, but wellborn and wealthy men as well; and not only these, but also the superiors of cenobitic monasteries and bishops renounced their thrones and came to him and subjected themselves in obedience to him. Among these were the following: the great patriarch Nicholas, the celebrated Charonites and the most wise and great ascetic Andrew of Chrysopolis, and Akakios who was distinguished for his asceticism over many years.

In addition some hermits and anchorites who wore irons and had grown old in lengthy labors of asceticism came to him through some divine dispensation and begged to be shepherded by him. One of these was the most blessed Nikephoros who lived in the mountains of Calabria together with the holy Phantinos. While the two of them were living together, they received a divine prophecy bidding Phantinos to go to Thessalonike, since he was destined to die

καταλαβεῖν τὸν Ἄθων καὶ τῷ ἀρχηγῷ τοῦ Ὄρους Ἀθανασίῳ προσελθεῖν καὶ ὅλον αὐτοῦ τὸ θέλημα ἐκείνῳ δοῦναι
καὶ ὑπ' ἐκείνου ποιμαίνεσθαι, ὅπερ δὴ καὶ πεποίηκε. Καὶ
τὰ μὲν πρῶτα δεξάμενος αὐτὸν ὁ πατὴρ οὐκ ἐκώλυεν ἀπὸ
τῆς εἰθισμένης αὐτῷ διαγωγῆς· ἦν γὰρ περιβεβλημένος
μὲν τριχίνην μόνην σινδόνα, ἐσθίων δὲ πίτυρα βρεκτὰ ἐν
χλιαρῷ ὕδατι καὶ ὀλίγῳ ἅλατι μετὰ τὸ δῦναι τὸν ἥλιον·
ὀλίγου δὲ παρελθόντος χρόνου, τήν τε σινδόνα ἐξέδυσεν
αὐτὸν καὶ τὴν ὅλην αὐτοῦ διαγωγὴν εἰς τὴν τῶν κοινο-
βιακῶν κατήλλαξεν.

4 Ὁ δὲ τοιοῦτος Νικηφόρος ἱκανὸν καιρὸν τῇ καλῇ
ταύτῃ ὑποταγῇ ἐπιζήσας, εἰς τοσαύτην ἀρετὴν ἔφθασεν
ὡς καὶ θείου ἁγιασμοῦ τυχεῖν· ἀλλὰ καὶ μετὰ τὸ θανεῖν
μετατεθεὶς ἐν ἑνὶ τῶν καινουργηθέντων τάφων παρὰ τοῦ
πατρός (ὢ τῶν τοῦ Θεοῦ παραδόξων!), θρόμβους μύρων
ἐδείκνυ ἐπιπολάζοντας τοῖς ξηροῖς ὀστέοις αὐτοῦ εὐω-
δεστέρους παντὸς ἀρώματος. Εἰ τοίνυν δείκνυσιν ὁ καρπὸς
τὸ δένδρον καὶ τὸ δένδρον τὴν ῥίζαν, δείκνυται καὶ ὁ
Ἀθανάσιος οἷος ἦν ἀπὸ τοῦ καρποῦ τῶν παιδευμάτων
αὐτοῦ.

44

Ἀλλὰ καὶ τὸ τοῦ μακαρίτου Νικολάου τοῦ μαγείρου
κατόρθωμα τίς ἂν ἀκούσας οὐκ ἐκπλαγείη; Ὁ μακαριώτατος γὰρ Θεοδώριτος, ὁ χρηματίσας καὶ αὐτὸς μαθητὴς

there, and Nikephoros to go to Athos and approach Athanasios, the leader of the Mountain, and entrust to him his entire personal volition and be shepherded by him, which indeed he did. When the father first received him, he did not prevent him from following his customary regimen; for he was wearing only a piece of hair cloth, and used to eat bran husks soaked in warm water and a little salt after sunset. But after a short time passed, Athanasios took the cloth away from him and transformed his whole way of life to a cenobitic one.

This Nikephoros, after spending a long time in this fine 4 condition of obedience, attained such a degree of virtue as to achieve divine sanctification; and thus after his death, when he was transferred into one of the tombs newly created by the father (oh, the marvels of God!), drops of perfumed oil, sweeter smelling than any fragrance, were revealed on the surface of his dry bones. If, then, the fruit reveals the tree and the tree the root, the nature of Athanasios is demonstrated by the fruit of his nurslings.

Chapter 44

But who would not be astonished at hearing about the feat of the late Nicholas the cook? For the most blessed Theodoritos, who was himself a disciple of the father, asked

τοῦ πατρός, ἠξίωσε τὸν εἰρημένον Νικόλαον φθέγξασθαι πρὸς αὐτὸν λόγον τινὰ περὶ ὑπομονῆς· ὁ δὲ εἶπεν αὐτῷ· "Γίνωσκε, ἀδελφὲ Θεοδώριτε, ὅτι πασῶν τῶν ἀρετῶν ἡ ῥίζα καὶ ὁ θεμέλιος ἡ ὑπομονή ἐστι, καὶ χωρὶς αὐτῆς οὐδεμία τῶν ἀρετῶν τελειοῦται." Εἶτα ἠρώτα πάλιν ὁ Θεοδώριτος· "Ἐγὼ δέ, τιμιώτατε πάτερ, πλέον τῶν ἄλλων ἀπορῶ, πῶς δῆτα ἡ ὁσιωτάτη Εὐπραξία, νέα οὖσα καὶ ἁπαλωτάτη κόρη, τοιούτου ἠξιώθη χαρίσματος τῆς τηλικαύτης στάσεως καὶ νηστείας τῶν τεσσαρακονταπέντε ἡμερῶν· οἶμαι γὰρ μὴ δίδοσθαί τινι νῦν τοιοῦτον χάρισμα."

2 Ὁ δὲ ἀποκριθεὶς ἔφη ἐν μειδιῶντι προσώπῳ· "Μὴ λέγε, ἀδελφέ, ὅτι οὐ δίδωσιν ὁ Θεὸς νῦν τοιαύτας δωρεάς, ἀλλὰ μᾶλλον εἰπὲ ὅτι οὐ θέλομεν ἄρτι οὕτως ἑαυτοὺς βιάσασθαι ὥσπερ οἱ ἅγιοι καὶ ἀξιωθῆναι τοιούτων χαρισμάτων." Τοῦ δὲ Θεοδωρίτου ἀντιτείνοντος μὴ εἶναι δυνατὸν ἄρτι τοιοῦτόν τι γενέσθαι, ἐκεῖνος ἀντέφησεν· "Ἐπεὶ ὁρῶ σε ἐπιθυμοῦντα ἀκοῦσαι λόγον ὠφελείας, οὐκ ἀποκρύψομαί σοι τὰ μεγαλεῖα τοῦ Θεοῦ, ἅπερ ἡ πεῖρά με ἐδίδαξε διὰ τῶν πρεσβειῶν τοῦ ὁσίου πατρὸς ἡμῶν Ἀθανασίου καὶ τοῦ ἀθλοφόρου βασιλέως τοῦ ἀοιδίμου Νικηφόρου. Πλὴν οὖν καθορκῶ σε φυλάξασθαι τὸ λεχθησόμενόν σοι μέχρι τέλους ζωῆς μου."

3 Καὶ ἐπεὶ συνέθετο ὁ Θεοδώριτος τοῦτο ποιῆσαι, ἤρξατο τοιαύτης διηγήσεως πρὸς αὐτὸν ὁ μακαρίτης Νικόλαος· "Ἐξεπληττόμην καὶ ἐγὼ ἀεί, ἀδελφέ, ἐπὶ τῇ τοσαύτῃ καρτερίᾳ τῆς μακρᾶς στάσεως τῆς μακαριωτάτης Εὐπραξίας, καὶ πολὺν διοχλούμενος χρόνον ὑπὸ τῶν λογισμῶν κατ᾽ αὐτὴν ἀγωνίσασθαι, ἐν μιᾷ τῶν ἡμερῶν πλήρης

this Nicholas to give him a word of advice about perseverance. Nicholas replied to him, "Brother Theodoritos, you
should know that perseverance is the root and the foundation of all virtues, and without it none of the virtues is
achieved." Then Theodoritos asked him again, "Most venerable father, more than anything I wonder how the most
blessed Eupraxia, even though she was a young and tender
girl, was considered worthy of the grace of such a long standing vigil and fasting for forty-five days. For I do not think
that such a gift of grace has been given to anyone in the
present day."

Nicholas replied with a smile on his face, "Brother, don't   2
say that God does not grant such gifts nowadays, but rather
say that these days we don't want to exert ourselves like the
saints of old and be considered worthy of such gifts of
grace." When Theodoritos objected that such a feat could
not be accomplished now, Nicholas responded, "Since I see
that you're eager to hear something beneficial, I won't conceal from you the greatness of God which experience has
taught me through the intercessions of our blessed father
Athanasios and the victorious emperor, the late Nikephoros. But I ask you to swear that until the end of my life you'll
keep secret what I'm about to say."

When Theodoritos made this promise, the late Nicholas   3
began to tell him the following story: "I too was always astonished, brother, at the great endurance manifested by the
lengthy standing vigil of the most blessed Eupraxia. After
being troubled for a long time by thoughts of undertaking a

γενόμενος τῆς τοιαύτης ἐπιθυμίας καὶ μηκέτι δυνάμενος
ὑπερβιβάσαι, εἶπον ἐν ἑαυτῷ· Ἄρξομαι τοῦ πράγματος
ἤδη· τί γὰρ ὀφείλω δαπανᾶσθαι ταῖς φροντίσι ματαίως;'
Τοίνυν καὶ τὴν εὐχὴν τοῦ ὁσίου πατρὸς ἡμῶν ἐπικαλεσάμενος εἰς βοήθειαν, ἠρξάμην ἵστασθαι, τὴν μὲν ἡμέραν
ὅλην διατελῶν ἐν τῷ μαγειρείῳ, τὴν δὲ νύκτα ἱστάμενος
ἐπὶ τῆς κοίτης μου, ὅπως μὴ διαγνωσθῶ τοῖς συγκελ-
λιώταις μου (οὐκ εἴχομεν γὰρ φῶτα ἐν τῷ κελλίῳ, ἵνα μέ
τις ὁρᾷ τί ποιῶ, ἀλλ᾽ οὐδὲ εἰκόνας διὰ τὸ ἀπερίσπαστον)·
ἐν τῷ τῆς ἀναγνώσεως δὲ καιρῷ ἔξω ἤμην ἱστάμενος.

4   "Τῇ γοῦν τρισκαιδεκάτῃ νυκτὶ λογισμός μοι ἐπῆλθε
περὶ τοῦ μάρτυρος Νικηφόρου, ἐὰν ὡς μάρτυρα ὀφείλω-
μεν ἔχειν αὐτόν, εἴτε καὶ μή· πολλοὶ γὰρ τοῦτο κάκεῖνο
διϊσχυρίζοντο· ἐγὼ δὲ τῷ λόγῳ τοῦ πατρὸς πειθόμενος,
ἐπεκαλεσάμην αὐτὸν ὡς μάρτυρα *ποιῆσαι μετ᾽ ἐμοῦ σημεῖον εἰς ἀγαθόν* [see Psalm 85(86):17]· ἤμην γὰρ κατωφερής. Ἀρκούντως οὖν παρακαλέσας μετὰ γονυκλισιῶν,
ἐπαυσάμην, καὶ τηνικαῦτα ἔγνων ὅτι μοι τὰ ἔγκατα ἅπαντα
ἄχρι καὶ τῶν γονάτων ἐχάλασεν· ἐβιαζόμην δὲ ἐμαυτὸν
ἰδεῖν τί συνέβη μοι· ἀλλ᾽ ἐγὼ οὐκ ἐπείσθην τῷ λογισμῷ,
ἀλλ᾽ εἶχον ἀμετατρέπτως ἐν τῷ νοΐ μου ὅτι πάντως θερα-
πεύσει με ὁ μάρτυς. Καὶ μετὰ παραδρομὴν πέντε νυχθη-
μέρων πάλιν ἤμην ἐπικαλούμενος τὸν μάρτυρα, καὶ ἔτι
τῆς εὐχῆς οὔσης ἐν τῷ στόματί μου ἔγνων ὅτι ἀνῆλθε
πάντα τὰ ἐντός μου καὶ γέγονα ὑγιής. Καὶ ἕως διῆλθον αἱ
τεσσαρακονταπέντε ἡμέραι τῆς στάσεώς μου, οὐκ ἐπείσθην
τῷ λογισμῷ ψηλαφῆσαι καὶ γνῶναι τί μοι συμβέβηκε."

feat like hers, one day, when I was filled with such a desire that I could no longer overcome it, I said to myself, 'I'm going to start doing this right now; for why should I be consumed with worries to no purpose?' So, after calling upon the prayers of our blessed father for assistance, I began my standing vigil, spending the entire day in the kitchen, and at night standing on my bed, so that I should not be discerned by my cellmates. (For since we did not have lights in the cell, no one could see what I was doing, nor did we even have icons lest they serve as a distraction.) At the time of the readings in church I stood outside.

"On the thirteenth night I had a troubling thought about 4 the martyr Nikephoros, wondering whether or not we ought to consider him a martyr; for many people assert one thing, others another. But persuaded by the father's words, I called upon Nikephoros as a martyr *to show me a sign for good,* for I had grown weak. After making many supplications with genuflections, I stopped, and then I realized that all my internal organs had dropped as far as my knees. I was tempted to see what had happened to me, but I did not yield to this thought; rather, I remained firmly convinced in my mind that the martyr would cure me completely. After the passage of five days and nights I again called upon the martyr, and while my prayer was still on my tongue I realized that all my internal organs had returned to their normal position and I was healed. And during the entire forty-five days of my standing vigil, I did not yield to the thought of touching myself and finding out what had happened to me." This was

Καὶ ταῦτα μὲν ὁ Νικόλαος. Εἴπερ δὲ καὶ ἤσθιε τὰς τοσ-
αύτας ἡμέρας, λέληθε τὸν Θεοδώριτον ἐρωτῆσαι αὐτόν.

45

Οὕτω καταρτίζων ὁ πατὴρ τὰ τέκνα αὐτοῦ καὶ τοιούτους ἀποτελῶν αὐτούς, οὐδὲ τοῦτο ἀτελὲς κατελίμπανε·
τινῶν γὰρ ἀδελφῶν ἀγραμμάτων ὄντων, πονούντων δὲ
καὶ ἀγωνιζομένων ἀσκητικῶς, ἐμπόδιον ἦν αὐτοῖς πρὸς
τὸν δρόμον τῆς ἀρετῆς τὸ μὴ νοεῖν τὰς Γραφάς. Διατοῦτο
καὶ κελλία οἰκοδομηθῆναι αὐτοῖς ᾠκονόμησε, κοιμητήρια
καὶ παιδευτήρια ὀνομάσας αὐτά· ἐπέστησε δὲ τούτοις καὶ
διδασκάλους, οἳ καὶ μετὰ τὴν ἀποπλήρωσιν τῶν ἀπο-
δείπνων τὰς βίβλους κατέχοντες ὑπανεγίνωσκον αὐτοῖς
τὰ ψυχωφελέστερα λόγια, καὶ ταῦτα ἡρμήνευον τούτοις
καὶ εἰς φόβον θεῖον καὶ ἀρετῆς ἐπιμέλειαν διήγειρον.

2   Εἴ τις δὲ θυμώδης οὐκ ᾐσθάνετο τοῦ πάθους αὐτοῦ ἀλλ᾽
ἦν ἀδιόρθωτος, πρῶτον μὲν παρῄνει τούτῳ καὶ τὰ ἐκ τοῦ
θυμοῦ τικτόμενα σφάλματα τῇ ψυχῇ πολλὰ εἶναι ἐδίδασκε,
καὶ ὅτι τοῖς ἀνταγωνιζομένοις κατὰ τούτου τοῦ πάθους
πολὺς ὁ μισθὸς ἀπόκειται· εἴπερ δὲ καὶ ἑώρα αὐτὸν δικαίως ὀργίζεσθαι λέγοντα, τότε ἰᾶτο τοῦτον ἐν ἔργῳ
σοφῷ· ἐπέτρεπε γὰρ λεληθότως ἅπασιν ἔκδοτον λαμβάνειν
αὐτὸν εἰς τὸ σκώπτειν, καὶ ἄλλος μὲν ἱστάμενος κατὰ
πρόσωπον αὐτοῦ ἔσκωπτεν αὐτὸν ἀδεῶς, ἕτερος δὲ

Nicholas's tale. And Theodoritos forgot to ask him whether he ate anything during these days.

Chapter 45

While the father was thus training his children and perfecting them, he did not leave unfinished the following endeavor. For some of the brethren, who were illiterate, found their inability to understand Scripture an obstacle on the path of virtue, as they labored and pursued their ascetic struggle. For this reason Athanasios arranged for cells to be constructed for them, calling them dormitories and school buildings. And he appointed teachers for them who, after the completion of compline, would take books and read aloud to them the most beneficial passages, explaining these to them and instilling in them divine fear and concern for virtue.

If a monk had a hot temper and did not realize what was 2 wrong with him but was incorrigible, Athanasios would first advise him and instruct him that the faults engendered in the soul by anger are numerous, and that a great reward lies in store for those who struggle against this affliction. If Athanasios observed him saying that he had good reason to be angry, then he would heal him by a clever device. For he would secretly allow him to be made the butt of everyone's mockery; one person would stand in front of him and mock him with impunity, and another one passing by would mock

διερχόμενος ἐπέσκωπτε, καὶ ἄλλος ἀντιδιερχόμενος προσεπέπληττεν. Οὗτος δὲ τῷ πλήθει τῶν σκωμμάτων πληττόμενος διερρήγνυτο τὴν καρδίαν, καὶ τὰς χεῖρας ἐκτείνας πρός τινα τῶν διερχομένων, βοηθὸν ἐξεκαλεῖτο, οὐκέτι λοιπὸν ἐπιπλέον φέρειν δυνάμενος· ὁ δὲ καὶ αὐτὸς ἔσκωπτε τοῦτον, καὶ ἄλλος ἑτέρωθεν.

3   Ὁ δὲ ἀπορῶν καὶ πάσης βοηθείας ἀπογινώσκων ἄλαλος ἔμενε, πρὸς δὲ τὸν πατέρα καταφεύγων ἀπωδύρετο τὰ τῆς συμφορᾶς· καὶ τότε παραλαμβάνων αὐτὸν ὁ πατὴρ καλῶς πλυθέντα καὶ ἱκανῶς ἀποστυφθέντα, παρεμυθεῖτο αὐτὸν λόγοις θεραπευτικοῖς, προσεποιεῖτο δὲ μέμφεσθαι καὶ τοὺς ἀποσκώψαντας εἰς αὐτόν, ἀδιακρίτους εἶναι λέγων καὶ ἀπηνεῖς. Ὅτε δὲ ἔγνω αὐτὸν ἐνδόντα μικρὸν ἀπὸ τοῦ θυμοῦ, τότε ἤρχετο παραινεῖν αὐτὸν λέγων· "Οὐ δεῖ, τέκνον, τὸν μοναχὸν ὀργίζεσθαι ἢ παροργίζειν· ἀμφότερα γὰρ μεγάλα νοσήματα τῆς ψυχῆς· καὶ εἰ μὴ ἦν δαιμονιῶδες πάθος τὸ θυμοῦσθαι ἀκρατῶς, οὐκ ἂν εἶχόν σε σκώπτειν οἱ ἀδελφοί. Δεῖ οὖν σε πείθεσθαι τῇ τῶν πολλῶν κρίσει καὶ μὴ στοιχεῖν τῇ οἰκείᾳ ἀπειθείᾳ." Ταῦτα λέγων κατεπράϋνεν αὐτοῦ τῆς λύπης τὴν φλεγμονὴν καὶ πρὸς τὴν ὁδὸν ἐπανῆγε τῆς ἀρετῆς.

4   Εἴ τινες δὲ πάλιν ἐτύγχανον οὐ πολὺν χρόνον ἔχοντες ἐν τῇ ἀποταγῇ, φιλοκαλίαις τε καὶ βλακείαις καὶ μύρων εὐωδίαις προσκείμενοι, τούτοις ἀνακαθαίρειν ἐπέταττε τοὺς ὑποδεχομένους τόπους τὰ τῶν ἀδελφῶν περιττώματα, ἔστι δὲ ὅτε καὶ τὴν κηπεύσιμον κόπρον μετακομίζειν· τοὺς δέ γε σφάλλοντας καθ᾽ ἕτερόν τι εἰς τὸν τοῦ νάρθηκος τόπον ἵστα καὶ μετὰ τὴν ἀπόλυσιν μετάνοιαν βάλλειν

him as well, and yet another passing by in the other direction would add to the abuse. This monk, assailed by all the mockery, would be cut to the heart, and would stretch out his arms to one of the passersby and ask his help, unable to endure the abuse any longer. But then that man would mock him as well, and someone else from another quarter.

The monk, who was now at a loss and despairing of any 3 help, would remain speechless, before taking refuge with the father to complain of his mistreatment. The father would then take him in hand, well washed and completely receptive; he would console him with healing words, and pretend to find blame with those who had mocked him, calling them undiscriminating and cruel. When he perceived that the monk's anger was abating a bit, Athanasios would begin to exhort him, saying, "My child, a monk should not be angry or provoke another to anger; for both are great illnesses of the soul. And if unbridled anger were not a demonic affliction, the brethren would not be able to mock you. Therefore you must be persuaded by the judgment of the majority and not persist in your own disobedience." With these words he would alleviate the sting of his grief and lead him back to the path of virtue.

Again, if certain monks who had not renounced the world 4 very long retained an attachment to nice things and luxuries and fragrant perfumes, he would assign them to clean the latrines for the brethren's excrement, and sometimes to transport the manure for the garden. As for those who erred in other ways he would make them stand in the narthex, and after the dismissal would order them to prostrate

ἑκάστῳ τῶν ἀδελφῶν ἐκέλευε καὶ τὸ "συγχώρησον" λέγειν, ὥστε καὶ οἱ μηδὲν σφαλλόμενοι, ὁρῶντες τὴν τούτων ὠφέλειαν, ἐπόθουν καὶ αὐτοὶ καὶ ἐζήτουν εἰς τὸν τόπον τῶν καταδίκων ἵστασθαι καὶ ὁμοίως ἐκείνοις τὸ "συγχώρησον" λέγειν.

5 Οὗτος οὖν ὁ σοφώτατος ἰατρὸς τὸν τυχόντα ἐν τῇ Λαύρᾳ ἀρχάριον καὶ σφάλματί τινι περιπίπτοντα ὡς ἄπειρον τῆς μοναδικῆς καταστάσεως, οὐκ ἔσκωπτε τοῦτον ὁ πατήρ, μὴ δυνάμενον φέρειν ἔλεγχον ἐπιστάμενος, ἀλλ᾽ οὔτε πάλιν ἠφίει αὐτὸν ἀδιόρθωτον, ἑτέρῳ δέ τινι τῶν γνωστικῶν γερόντων καὶ *βάρος ἀδελφοῦ δυναμένων βαστάσαι* [see Galatians 6:2] τὸ τούτου περιτιθεὶς ἁμάρτημα, ἔσκωπτέ τε καὶ κατεγίνωσκε καὶ ἐπὶ πάντων ἔλεγεν· "Οὐκ αἰσχύνη, γέρον, ἔτι σφάλλεσθαι τὰ τῶν ἀρχαρίων, ἤδη παλαιωθεὶς ἐν τῷ μοναχικῷ βίῳ;" Ὁ δὲ καλὸς ἐκεῖνος γέρων τὴν σοφίαν οὐκ ἀγνοῶν τοῦ πατρός, συνωμολόγει, λέγων ὅτι "Ναί, πάτερ, ὡς ἀληθῶς ἥμαρτον, καὶ συγχώρησόν μοι."

6 Τότε ὁ πταίσας ἀρχάριος, ὁρῶν τοῦ ἀναιτίου τὴν ταπείνωσιν καὶ ὑπότρομος γινόμενος διὰ τὴν αὐτοῦ συνείδησιν, ἔβαλλε μετάνοιαν τῷ πατρὶ καὶ ἐξωμολογεῖτο τὸ ἁμάρτημα τούτου μετὰ φόβου καὶ κατανύξεως· ὁ δὲ πατὴρ ἔλεγε τούτῳ· "Οὐ διὰ σὲ ἐπετιμήθη ὁ γέρων, τέκνον, ἀλλὰ διὰ τὸ ἴδιον σφάλμα, ὅτι γέρων ὤν, τὰ τῶν νέων ποιεῖ καὶ ἀρχαρίων· σὺ δὲ πρόσεχε σεαυτῷ τοῦ λοιποῦ." Ἐντεῦθεν δύο τὰ κάλλιστα κατώρθου· οἵ τε γὰρ ἀρχάριοι διωρθοῦντο τῇ ὑπομονῇ τῶν τελείων, οἱ τέλειοι δὲ τὰ *βάρη τῶν*

themselves before each of the brethren, saying, "Forgive me." In this way even those who had done nothing wrong, seeing the benefit that accrued to these sinful monks, would themselves yearn and request to stand in the place of those who were being punished and, like them, say, "Forgive me."

Thus, when a novice at the Lavra fell into error since he 5 was inexperienced in the monastic routine, the father, that most clever physician, would not rebuke him, knowing that he could not endure criticism, but neither would he allow him to go uncorrected. Rather, he would attribute his offense to one of the enlightened elders who could *bear* a brother's *burden,* and he would rebuke and criticize him and say in front of everyone, "Aren't you ashamed, elder, to still be making the errors of a novice, even though you have long grown old in monastic life?" And that good elder, realizing the father's clever stratagem, would confess, saying, "Yes, father, I truly have sinned. Forgive me."

Then the novice who had made the error, seeing the hu- 6 mility of the guiltless one and becoming afraid because of his conscience, would prostrate himself before the father and confess his fault with fear and contrition. The father would say to him, "The elder was not punished on your account, but on account of his own fault, because, although he is an elder, he acts like those who are young and novices; but you should watch out for yourself in the future." In this way he achieved two very fine results: for the novices were corrected through the patient endurance of the perfected ones,

ἀδυνάτων ἐβάσταζον καὶ οὕτως ἀνεπλήρουν τὸν νόμον τοῦ Χριστοῦ [Galatians 6:2].

46

Ἐπεὶ δὲ ἀνάγκη καὶ ἑτέρων τοιούτων οἰκονομιῶν καὶ διακρίσεων τοῦ μεγάλου ἐπιμνησθῆναι διὰ τὴν τῶν πολλῶν ὠφέλειαν, μικρὸν τοῖς τοιούτοις ἐνδιατρίψαντες, ἐπὶ τὴν τῶν θαυμάτων διήγησιν τὸν λόγον τρέπομεν. Τὸ δ᾽ οὖν παρὸν λεγέσθω τι τῶν παρομοίων. Χρείας γενομένης ποτὲ ἰχθύων ἔν τινι τῶν μεγάλων ἑορτῶν, ἐπέτρεψεν ὁ πατὴρ τοῖς τεταγμένοις ἐπὶ τὸ ἁλιεύειν ἀδελφοῖς τὴν ἄγραν, γνωρίσας αὐτοῖς καὶ τὸν τόπον ὅπου ἔδει βαλεῖν τὸ δίκτυον. Ἐκεῖνοι δὲ τῆς μὲν ἄγρας ἐπεμελήθησαν, τὸν δὲ ὁρισθέντα τόπον καταλιπόντες, ἐν ἑτέρῳ ἐπιτηδειοτέρῳ τὸ ἀμφίβληστρον βαλόντες, πλῆθος ἰχθύων εἵλκυσαν.

2 Ὡς δὲ ἐπανῆλθον εἰς τὴν μονὴν καὶ ἐθεάσατο ταῦτα ὁ πατήρ, εὐφράνθη λίαν· ἦν γὰρ ἡ χρεία ἀπαραίτητος· ἐπεὶ δὲ διωμολόγουν καὶ τὸν τόπον ὅθεν τὸ πλῆθος τῶν ἰχθύων ἤγρευσαν, ὡς ἐμπειρότερόν τι φρονήσαντες, οὐκ ἠνέσχετο ὁ πατὴρ ἀκόλαστον καταλιπεῖν τὸ τῆς παρακοῆς τόλμημα, καίτοι οὐκ ἐκ ῥαθυμίας ἢ καταφρονήσεως τοῦτο ποιησάντων. Παραχρῆμα τοίνυν ὁ φόρτος ἐκεῖνος, προστάξαντος τοῦ πατρός, κατὰ γῆς ἔρριπτό τε καὶ ἐσκορπίζετο,

and the perfected ones *bore the burdens* of the weak *and thus fulfilled the law of Christ.*

Chapter 46

Since I should mention other such dispensations and discernments of the great one because they are beneficial for the many, I will spend a short while on matters of this sort before shifting my account to the narration of miracles. So now let me tell you a similar tale. Once, when fresh fish were needed for one of the great feast days, the father told the monks who were appointed as fishermen to go fishing, even indicating to them the spot where they should cast the net. They busied themselves with fishing, but left their assigned spot, cast the net in another more suitable place, and hauled in a multitude of fish.

When they returned to the monastery and the father saw ₂ them, he was very happy; for they had urgent need of the fish. But when they revealed the place where they had caught the multitude of fish, as though they considered themselves more experienced, the father could not bear to leave their bold disobedience unpunished, even though they had not done this out of laziness or contempt. Thus, at the father's orders, that haul of fish was immediately cast to the

σωφρονίζοντος ἐν τούτῳ καὶ τοὺς λοιποὺς ἅπαντας, ὥστε μηδέποτε παρακούειν τῶν ἐπιταγμάτων μὴ δ᾽ ἐπ᾽ εὐλόγοις προφάσεσιν.

47

Οὐδὲ τοῦτο μικρὸν πάντως εἰς εὐφημίαν, εἰ καὶ περὶ μικρῶν ὁ λόγος, οὐδὲ τῆς αὐτοῦ σοφίας ἀνάξιον. Ἦλθόν ποτε πρὸς τὸν πατέρα τινὲς τῶν Ἀμαλφηνῶν γερόντων, γάρον αὐτῷ φέροντες δῶρον. Ὁ πατὴρ δὲ ἀποδεξάμενος τοῦτον καὶ ὡς εὐλογίαν λογισάμενος παραδέδωκε τῷ ἀποθηκαρίῳ ὥς τι τίμιον, ἐντειλάμενος αὐτῷ ἀπ᾽ αὐτοῦ μόνου παρατιθέναι αὐτῷ ἐν καιρῷ χρείας· τοῦτο γὰρ ἠξίουν οἱ γέροντες. Ἐκεῖνος δὲ καταφρονήσας τοῦ παραγγέλματος, ἐκ τοῦ προτέρου, οὗπερ αὐτὸς ἐσκεύαζε, παρετίθει αὐτῷ.

2   Τινῶν δὲ παρόντων καὶ συνεσθιόντων αὐτῷ καὶ ἐπαινούντων τὸν γάρον ὡς ἄριστον, ὁ πατὴρ σκευασίαν εἶναι αὐτὸν ἔλεγε τῶν Ἀμαλφηνῶν γερόντων· ὁ ἀποθηκάριος δὲ οὐκ ἤνεγκεν ἐκείνους ἐπαινεθῆναι εἰς τὸν ἴδιον ἔπαινον, ἀλλ᾽ ἑαυτὸν εἶναι ἔλεγε τὸν τοῦτον κατασκευάσαντα. Ὁ δὲ πατὴρ προστάσσει κατὰ γῆς ἐκχυθῆναι ὅσον ἂν γάρον ὁ ἀποθηκάριος κατεσκεύασε, τήν τε παρακοὴν τοῦ οἰκείου μαθητοῦ διορθούμενος καὶ τὸ τοῦ τύφου πάθος ἐκδιώκων.

ground and scattered, as he chastened all the others in this way as well, so that they would never disobey his orders, not even for good reasons.

Chapter 47

Neither is the following tale undeserving of praise, nor unworthy of his wisdom, even if the story concerns small matters. Some Amalfitan elders once came to the father, bringing him a gift of garum. The father accepted it, considering it as a blessed gift, and handed it over to the storeroom keeper as a valuable commodity, instructing him to serve him from this jar alone when it was time to use it; for the elders had made this specific request. But the storeroom keeper disregarded his instructions, and served him from the previous batch, which he himself had prepared.

When some of the company dining with him praised the 2 garum as being of excellent quality, the father remarked that it was the Amalfitan elders' recipe. But the storeroom keeper could not stand the latter receiving the praise that was actually due him, and said that he was the one who had made this garum. The father then ordered that all the garum prepared by the storeroom keeper should be poured out on the ground, and in this way he corrected his own disciple's disobedience and chased away the sin of arrogance.

48

Λεκτέον οὖν ἤδη καὶ περὶ τῆς ζύμης. Ἐκάλει μὲν ὁ ταύτης καιρὸς τὸν ταύτην ἐγκεχειρισμένον τὴν διακονίαν πρὸς ἑτοιμασίαν ταύτης· ὁ δὲ συμφύρας τὸ ἄλευρον ἐκάλει καὶ τοὺς ὀφείλοντας συμβοηθῆσαι αὐτῷ εἰς τὸ τοιοῦτον ἔργον. Τότε δὲ δεσποτικῆς ἑορτῆς λαμπρᾶς τελεσθείσης ἐν ἀγρυπνίᾳ μεγάλῃ, οἱ ἐπὶ τὸ ζυμῶσαι καλούμενοι διὰ τὸν ἐκ τῆς ἀγρυπνίας κόπον οὐ παρεγένοντο, ἀλλ᾽ ἄζυμον τὸ φύραμα εἴασαν. Ὁ δὲ διακονητὴς προσῆλθε τῷ πατρὶ καὶ τὸ ἀνήκοον αὐτῶν ἀπήγγελλεν. Ὁ δέ γε πατὴρ κολάζων σοφῶς καὶ τὸ τοιοῦτον ἁμάρτημα ἐκέλευσε σχολάσαι πάσας τὰς διακονίας σὺν αὐτῇ τῇ ζύμῃ, αἰνιττόμενος τάχα ὅτι οὐ χρήζουσι τροφῆς οἱ ἀδελφοί. Καὶ τοῦτο γέγονεν ἐπὶ τρισὶν ἡμέραις, πάντων ἐν ἀσιτίᾳ μεινάντων καὶ αὐτοῦ τοῦ πατρὸς ἀπεσφαλισμένου ἔνδον τῆς κέλλης αὐτοῦ.

2 Τῶν δὲ ἀδελφῶν ἐνοχλουμένων ὑπὸ τῆς πείνης καὶ ἐπικειμένων τῇ θύρᾳ τῆς κέλλης αὐτοῦ καὶ κρουόντων, ἐξέρχεται μόλις ὀψέ ποτε, καὶ πάντων συναθροισθέντων τῶν ἀδελφῶν, ἀναβὰς ἐπὶ τὴν ἀναβάθραν, ἐπέπλησσε τούτους διὰ τραχέων καὶ αὐστηρῶν ῥημάτων· ἔπειτα προσέταξε συγκομισθῆναι τὸ ἀζύμωτον φύραμα καὶ πρὸ τοῦ πυλῶνος τεθῆναι, ὡς ἂν ἐκφαυλίσῃ καὶ δημοσιεύσῃ τοὺς παρακούσαντας καὶ εἰς τὰς μετέπειτα γενεάς.

3 Οὗτοι δὲ τὴν αἰσχύνην οὐ φέροντες ἔρριψαν ἑαυτοὺς εἰς τοὺς πόδας τοῦ πατρὸς καὶ ἐν συντριβῇ πολλῇ τοῦτον καθικετεύοντες ἔλεγον· "Συγχώρησον τοῖς τέκνοις σου,

Chapter 48

So now I must also tell the story about the leavened dough. It was time for the monk entrusted with this job to prepare it; after mixing the flour paste, he also summoned those who were supposed to help him with this job. But since an important dominical feast had just been celebrated with a great vigil, those whom he summoned to prepare the leavened dough did not come due to their fatigue from the vigil, but left the flour paste unleavened. The responsible official approached the father and reported their disobedience to him. So the father, devising a clever punishment for this kind of sin as well, told the monks to take a break from all their jobs, including that of preparing the leavened dough, perhaps hinting that the brethren did not need food. This went on for three days, while everyone went hungry and the father himself remained enclosed in his cell.

When the brethren, tormented by hunger, pressed up 2 against his cell door and knocked, he emerged only after a long delay. And when all the brethren had assembled, he ascended the *bema,* and rebuked them with harsh and severe words. Then he ordered that the unleavened flour paste be brought and placed before the monastery gate so that it might reproach and disgrace the disobedient monks even to later generations.

Unable to bear the shame, these monks threw themselves 3 at the father's feet. With much contrition, they begged him, saying, "Forgive your children, holy father, forgive us, and do

πάτερ ἅγιε, συγχώρησον καὶ μὴ ἐάσῃς παραδειγματίζε-
σθαι τὸ ἀνήκοον ἡμῶν τῆς μιᾶς ἡμέρας ἐπιπολύ· ἡμεῖς δὲ
εἰς τιμωρίαν ἐπιτιμίας τὴν ὀξώδη ζύμην δαπανήσομεν ἀντὶ
ἄρτου, αἱρετώτερον τοῦτο ἡγούμενοι ὑπὲρ πολυχρόνιον
ὄνειδος."

4   Καὶ ὁ μὲν πατήρ, καμφθεὶς ἐπὶ τῇ ἑκουσίῳ τιμωρίᾳ
αὐτῶν, συνεχώρησεν αὐτοῖς· ἐκεῖνοι δὲ τὸν ἀηδῆ τοῦτον
καὶ ἄβρωτον ἤσθιον ἄρτον. Οὐ μέχρι δὲ τῆς ἐπιτιμίας ὁ
συμπαθέστατος ἵσταται, ἀλλὰ καὶ πρὸς τὴν θεραπείαν τοῦ
πράγματος διανίσταται· τὸν γὰρ πόνον τῆς διακονίας
πολὺν ὄντα κουφίζων τοῖς ἀδελφοῖς, σοφίζεται μηχανήν,
ἣν βόες εὐτέχνως στρέφουσι, δι'ἧς τελεσιουργεῖται ἡ ζύμη,
ἔργον ὁμοῦ συμπαθείας καὶ εὐτεχνίας τὸ κάλλιστον.

49

Τῆς αὐτῆς ἐστιν οἰκονομίας καὶ κρίσεως καὶ τὸ νῦν ῥη-
θησόμενον. Συνήθως ἔχων ὁ πατὴρ παραβάλλειν τῷ Μυλοποτάμῳ, παραγέγονεν ἐκεῖσε χάριν τοῦ ἐπισκέψασθαι
τὸ τοιοῦτον φροντιστήριον τῆς μονῆς. Ἀναστρέφων δὲ
ἐκεῖθεν, ὡς εἰς Βελᾶς ἤγγισε, τοὺς μὲν σὺν αὐτῷ ἀδελφοὺς
διὰ τοῦ πλοίου εἰς τὴν Λαύραν χωρεῖν ἐκέλευσεν, αὐτὸς δὲ
πεζῇ τὴν πορείαν ἐποιεῖτο· καὶ πορευόμενος περιτυγχάνει
γέροντί τινι τῶν ἐν Χριστῷ ἀδελφῶν.

2   Ὁ δὲ πατὴρ τὸν προσαίτην καὶ αὐτὸς προσποιούμενος,
ἠσπάσατο τὸν γέροντα καὶ ἐρωτᾷ αὐτὸν εἰ μακρὰν ἔτι τῆς

not let our single day of disobedience be set forth as an example for such a long time; as punishment we will eat the sourdough mix instead of bread, since we think this would be preferable to long term reproach."

The father, swayed by their willingness to submit to punishment, forgave them, and they ate this disgusting and inedible bread. But that most compassionate man did not stop with their punishment, but also set out to resolve the problem; thus to lighten the great labor of this work for the brethren, he devised a contraption, easily turned by oxen, by which the leavened dough is finished off, a very fine deed combining compassion and ingenuity.

Chapter 49

The story I will now tell also demonstrates the same qualities of accommodation and judgment. Since the father was accustomed to visit Mylopotamos, he went there once to visit this training facility for the monastery. On his way back, as he neared Belas, he ordered the brethren with him to go to the Lavra by boat, and said he would make the journey on foot. As he continued his journey, he met an elder of the brethren in Christ.

The father, pretending that he himself was also a mendicant, embraced the elder and asked him if he was still far

Λαύρας ἐστὶ καὶ εἰ φιλοξενοῦσιν ἄρα ἐν τῇ τοιαύτῃ μονῇ·
"Εἰ γὰρ σὺ ἔτυχές," φησιν, "εὐποιΐας ἐκεῖσέ τινος, εὐθύμως
κἀγὼ ἀπελεύσομαι." Ὁ δὲ γέρων διηγεῖτο, λέγων ὅτι "Καὶ
πολλή ἐστιν ἡ φιλοξενία καὶ ἡ χάρις ἐκεῖ, πατήρ μου· κἀγὼ
γὰρ πολλῶν ἠξιώθην ἐκεῖ τῶν ἀγαθῶν· ἄλλος γὰρ μανδύαν
μοι δέδωκε καὶ ἄλλος κουκούλλιον καὶ ἄλλος ἄλλο. Εἰ δὲ
καὶ σὺ ἀπέλθῃς ἐκεῖ καὶ θεάσονται τοιοῦτον γέροντα οἷον
σέ, πλείονά σοι ἀγαθὰ ποιήσουσι."

3   Ταῦτα ἀκούσας ὁ πατὴρ καὶ ἐντὸς τῆς μονῆς γενόμενος, μετὰ τὸν ἑσπερινὸν ὕμνον ἐπὶ τῆς ἀναβάθρας στάς,
ἠγανάκτει πολλὰ κατ' αὐτῶν καὶ κατηγόρει πικρῶς καὶ
ᾐτιᾶτο αὐτοὺς οὐκ ὀλίγα, τοιαῦτα λέγων· "Ἐγὼ θαυμάζω
ὑμᾶς, ἀδελφοί, πῶς ἠγνοήσατε ὅτι κλέπτεσθε ὑπὸ τοῦ
Διαβόλου, καταλύοντες τὸν νόμον τῆς ὑποταγῆς· ὅταν
γάρ τις ἑαυτοῦ ἐξουσίαν οὐκ ἔχῃ, πῶς τὰ μὴ ὄντα αὐτοῦ
δωρήσεται τοῖς πένησιν; Ὁ γὰρ ἑαυτὸν ἅπαξ ἀρνησάμενος
[see Luke 9:23] σὺν πᾶσιν αὐτοῦ τοῖς θελήμασι καὶ τῷ
Χριστῷ δεδουλωμένος, εἶτα κατὰ τὸ οἰκεῖον περιπατῶν
θέλημα, τί ἄλλο ποιεῖ ἢ τὴν δικαιοσύνην φεύγων δεδούλω-
ται τῇ ἁμαρτίᾳ; Ποῖος δὲ μισθὸς ἢ φιλοξενία, ὅταν τις τὰ
παλαιὰ παρέχων ἄλλα καινὰ ζητῇ; Κινδυνεύει γὰρ μὴ δὲ
φιλοξενίαν ἐργάζεσθαι ἀλλ' ἀνταλλαγὴν πράττειν ἐπι-
κερδῆ.

4   "Εἰ δὲ καὶ ποθεῖτε οὕτως ποιεῖν, δέον ἐστὶ μὴ ζητεῖν
ἕτερα, ἀλλὰ ῥιγᾶν τὴν σάρκα καὶ ὑπομένειν τὴν γυμνιτείαν, ἵνα καὶ ἑαυτόν τις πληροφορῇ καὶ τὸν ποιμένα ὅτι
πάσχει ὑπὲρ τῆς τοῦ πλησίον ἀγάπης· εἰ δὲ καὶ τοῦτό ἐστι
καλόν, ἀλλὰ τῷ ἀρνησαμένῳ τὸ ἑαυτοῦ θέλημα ἀνοίκειον

from the Lavra and if they offered charity to strangers in that monastery; "For if you received charity there, I too will happily go there." The elder replied to him, "There's lots of hospitality to strangers and generosity there, my father; for even I was considered worthy of many good things there. One monk gave me a cloak and another a cowl, and another one something else. But if you go there and they see such an elder as yourself, they will give you even more good things."

Upon hearing this, the father went inside his monastery. 3 After the vespers hymns he stood on the *bema,* and gave vent to his great indignation with the monks. He bitterly reproached them and criticized them harshly, saying something like this: "I am surprised by you, brethren, how you didn't realize that you are being deceived by the Devil, when you break the rule of obedience. For how can someone who doesn't have his own property give away to the poor something he doesn't possess? For if he *has* once and for all *denied himself* together with all his desires, and has made himself a servant of Christ, but then lives according to his own will, what else is he doing but fleeing righteousness and enslaving himself to sin? What reward is there or charity to strangers, when someone gives away old things and then seeks new replacements? For he runs the risk of not practicing charity, but engaging in profitable exchange.

"But if one of you really wants to do this, he must not 4 seek replacements, but freeze his flesh and endure nakedness, so that he and his shepherd may be assured that he is suffering for the sake of his love for his neighbor. Anyway, even if this type of charitable behavior is admirable, for a monk who has renounced his own will it is inappropriate

καὶ ἀνάρμοστόν ἐστι καὶ ἄμισθον. Δεῖ δὲ μᾶλλον ἐν πᾶσιν ἄγεσθαι καὶ πείθεσθαι τῷ ποιμαίνοντι, καὶ ὅπερ οὗτος κρίνει καὶ δοκιμάσει, τοῦτο στέργειν καὶ ἐμμένειν, καὶ αὐτὸν μόνον εἶναι νόμον καὶ ἐντολὴν καὶ τύπον, καὶ τούτου δοκεῖν τὸ πρόσταγμα ὡς θείαν βουλήν, καὶ μὴ κλέπτεσθαι καὶ ἀγνοεῖν τὰ τοῦ Πονηροῦ νοήματα· κοινὴ γὰρ ἡ φιλο-ξενία καὶ κοινῶς ὑπὲρ πάντων τὰ πάντα δίδοται." Τοιαῦτα εἰπὼν ὡς ἐν κατηχήσει αὐτοῖς, διωρθώσατο τούτους καὶ πρὸς τὸν ἀκριβῆ τῆς ὑποταγῆς βίον ἐπανήγαγεν.

50

Ὅρα δέ μοι καὶ ἑτέραν σοφωτάτην διάκρισιν. Ἡμέρα ἦν ἑόρτιος τοῦ μεγάλου Ἀθανασίου· ὁ δὲ ἀποθηκάριος ὁ τότε, Ἀθανάσιος ὀνομαζόμενος, ἠξίου τὸν πατέρα συγ-χωρῆσαι αὐτῷ ἐκτελέσαι ταύτην τὴν ἑορτήν· ὁ δὲ πατήρ, εἰ καὶ πρόχειρος οὐκ ἦν ἐπινεύειν ἐν τοῖς τοιούτοις, ὅμως ὑπήκουσεν. Ὁ γοῦν ἀποθηκάριος, συνεργούμενος ὑπὸ τῆς διακονίας αὐτοῦ, προήχθη ἑτοιμάσαι τὴν παράκλησιν φι-λοτιμότερον, παραθέμενος ἐσχάτως μελίπηκτα καὶ πλα-κοῦντας.

2 Ἅπερ ἰδὼν ὁ μέγας καὶ τῷ ἀσυνήθει ξενισθεὶς θεάματι, ἠγανάκτει κατὰ τοῦ πεποιηκότος καὶ καινὸν εὑρετὴν ἀσω-τίας ἐκάλει καὶ ἀκρασίαν ταῦτα ἐνόμιζε, καὶ τηνικαῦτα,

and unsuitable and brings no reward. You should instead be guided by and obey your shepherd in everything, and gladly accept and abide by whatever he decides and approves. You should believe that he alone is the law and commandment and model, and should consider his command as the divine will, and you should not be deceived by and fail to recognize the Evil One's designs. For charity to strangers is a communal endeavor and all donations are made jointly on everyone's behalf." By offering them such instructions, he corrected their behavior and led them toward the strict life of obedience.

Chapter 50

Now let me show you yet another very clever act of discernment. It was the feast day of the great Athanasios of Alexandria, and the storeroom keeper at that time, who was called Athanasios, asked the father's permission to celebrate this feast day. The father, even though he was not usually keen on this sort of thing, nevertheless agreed. Thus the storeroom keeper, assisted by his staff, set about preparing a quite splendid meal, setting out honey cakes and flat cakes for dessert.

When the great Athanasios saw these cakes, he was disturbed at the unaccustomed sight and grew angry at the man who had done this. He called him a new deviser of 2

προστάξαντος αὐτοῦ, ἐξέρριπτο τῆς τραπέζης τὰ τοιαῦτα ἅπαντα. Εἷς δέ τις τῶν ἀδελφῶν κάτω που περὶ τὰ τελευταῖα τῆς τραπέζης καθήμενος, ὡς εἶδεν αἰρόμενα τὰ γλυκύσματα, νικηθεὶς ὑπὸ τῆς τούτων ἐπιθυμίας, αὐτός τε παρωρμήθη ἅψασθαι τούτων καὶ τοὺς συγκαθημένους αὐτῷ παρεκίνησεν εἰς τοῦτο.

3 Ἀλλ᾽ οὗτοι μὲν ταῦτα· ὁ δὲ πατὴρ διὰ τῆς τῶν ἐπιτηρητῶν ὑπομνήσεως τὸ πρᾶγμα διαγνούς, ἐκάλει αὐτίκα τὸν προκατάρξαντα καὶ τοὺς συμφαγόντας αὐτῷ καὶ πρὸς αὐτοὺς ἔλεγε· "Πῶς δῆτα εἰς τοσαύτην παραφροσύνην ἤλθετε ὥστε καταφρονῆσαι τῶν πατρικῶν παραδόσεων καὶ καταναισχυντῆσαι τῆς κοινῆς καταστάσεως καὶ προπετῶς ἀπογεύσασθαι τούτων; Οὐκ οἴδατε ὅτι καὶ ὁ προπάτωρ ἡμῶν διὰ τὴν προπετῆ βρῶσιν τοῦ ξύλου τὴν πολύμοχθον κατεκρίθη ζωήν;"

4 Ταῦτα εἰπὼν προσέταξεν ἀφορισθῆναι αὐτούς· οἱ δὲ πεσόντες εἰς τοὺς πόδας αὐτοῦ ἱκετεύοντες ἔλεγον· "Συγχώρησον ἡμῖν, πάτερ, ἡμάρτομεν ἀληθῶς." Ὁ δὲ πατὴρ ἀσυμπαθὴς ἦν αὐτοῖς λέγων· "Ἀλλ᾽ οὐ τοῦτο προστάσσουσιν ἡμῖν οἱ ἱεροὶ κανόνες." Ὁ δὲ πρωταίτιος ἀπελογεῖτο αὐτῷ μετὰ πολλῆς ταπεινώσεως, λέγων· "Ἀλλὰ σὺ ὡς πατὴρ ἡμῶν ἐξουσίαν ἔχεις συγχωρῆσαι ἡμῖν." Ὁ δὲ πατήρ, "Ἐξουσίαν," φησίν, "ἔχω εἰς τὸ μὴ ἀνακρίνεσθαι ὑπό τινος τῶν ποιμαινομένων· ἀνάγκη δὲ πᾶσι τοῖς ποιμέσιν ἐπίκειται μὴ παραβαίνειν τοὺς νόμους· ὅμως ὁ Κύριος συγχωρήσοι ὑμῖν, πλὴν τῆς τιμωρίας τὸ ἐπιτίμιον ἐγὼ βαστάσω· οὔτε γὰρ διὰ τὸ ἐμὸν ὄνομα ἑορτασθήσεταί ποτε ὁ ἅγιος οὗτος, οὔτε δι᾽ ἑτέρου, μήπως καὶ εἰς ἕτερον χρόνον ἢ

profligacy and considered it an act of intemperance, and then, at his command, all these delicacies were thrown off the table. One of the brethren, who was sitting somewhere near the far end of the table, was overcome by his desire for the sweets when he saw them being taken away, and rushed to grab them, prompting those who were sitting with him to do this as well.

That's what they did. But the father, realizing what was happening after being alerted by the refectory supervisors, immediately summoned the instigator and his fellow gluttons and said to them, "How on earth have you gone so crazy that you disregard our ancestral traditions and bring disgrace on our communal way of life by impulsively seeking to eat these sweets? Don't you know that our forefather Adam was condemned to a life of toil on account of his impulsive eating from the tree?" 3

After saying this, he ordered that the monks be placed in confinement; but they fell at his feet and begged him, saying, "Forgive us, father, truly we have sinned." But the father had no sympathy for them, saying, "But the holy canons don't permit me to do so." The primary instigator spoke in their defense with much humility, saying, "But you, as our father, have the authority to forgive us." But the father replied, "I have the authority not to be interrogated by one of my flock; and it's mandatory that no shepherds should transgress the laws. So even if the Lord should forgive you, I will bear the penalty of punishment; for even though he is my namesake, or someone else's, this saint will never be celebrated, so that such a feast day should not become the 4

τοιαύτη ἑορτὴ ἀφορμὴ σκανδάλου καὶ ἁμαρτίας γένηται. Ὁ δὲ νῦν ἑορτάσας αὐτὸν καὶ αἴτιος σκανδάλου γεγονὼς ἄχρις ἑσπέρας οὐ μεταλάβῃ τροφῆς."

51

Οὕτως δὲ μὴ εὐκαταφρόνητος ὢν τὸ ἦθος, ἀλλ' ἀρχικός τις καὶ μετὰ θαύματος ἀγαπώμενος, ἐν ταῖς καταμόνας ὁμιλίαις καὶ λίαν χαρίεις ἦν καὶ εὐόμιλος· εἰ γάρ ποτε συνέβη ἀποδημῆσαι αὐτὸν εἴς τινα χρείαν μετά τινων ἀδελφῶν, πολλὴν εἶχε τὴν συγκατάβασιν καὶ ὅμοιος ἦν τοῖς ἄλλοις ἐν ταῖς ὑπουργίαις τῆς κοινῆς χρείας καὶ σχεδὸν ὑπουργὸς καὶ θεραπευτής, ξύλα συλλέγων, ὕδωρ μετακομίζων καὶ τὰ πρὸς τὴν ὑπουργίαν τῆς βρώσεως ἐνεργῶν καὶ ὅλος χαρά τε καὶ ἡδονὴ καὶ παρηγορία πολλή.

2 Καὶ ταῦτα ποῦ; Ἔνθα τυχὸν προσορμίζοντες τὸ πλοῖον ἐξέβαινον πρὸς ὀλίγον διαναπαύσασθαι εἴς τινα τόπον ἰδιάζοντα· "Δεῦτε, τέκνα," λέγων, "ἀγαλλιασώμεθα σήμερον καὶ παρακληθῶμεν, ἐλευθερίαν ἔχοντες ἀπὸ τῶν βιαστῶν ἐπιτηρητῶν· οὐκέτι γὰρ νῦν πτοούμεθα ἐκείνους τοὺς καθεκάστην ἡμᾶς βιάζοντας." Ὅτε δὲ πόλει τινὶ ἢ χωρίῳ παρέβαλεν, ἀπεδύετο τὴν χαρίεσσαν ἐκείνην ὄψιν καὶ τὸ γλυκύτατον ἦθος καὶ ἐξηλλάττετο πάλιν εἰς τὸ φοβερώτατον καὶ στυγνόν.

3 Ὁ δὲ πάντων ἐπέκεινα καὶ ὃ παρελθεῖν ζημία πολλὴ

cause of scandal and sin at another time. And the monk who has celebrated him now and has become the cause of scandal is forbidden to partake of food until evening."

Chapter 51

Thus Athanasios was by no means weak in character, but someone who was authoritative as well as held in love and awe, and in his private dealings with people he was extremely pleasant and affable. For if he ever happened to go on a trip for some reason with some of the brethren, he was most accommodating and shouldered an equal burden in carrying out tasks for the common good. In fact, he was virtually a laborer and servant, gathering wood, carrying water, preparing food, and was always a source of joy and pleasure and comfort.

And where could you see an example of this? If they happened to anchor their ship and disembarked for a while to rest in an isolated spot, he would say, "Come, children, let's enjoy ourselves today and relax, since we're free of our overbearing supervisors; for now we needn't worry about those who push us so hard every day." But when he arrived at some city or village, he would shed that pleasant aspect and most delightful manner and would change back into a most fearful and harsh individual.

And above all, something it would be most detrimental to

τοῖς τῶν καλῶν ζηλωταῖς, ὅτι μὴ δὲ αὐτὸς αὐτοῖς συγκακοπαθεῖν ἀπηξίου· εἰ γάρ ποτε κοινῇ πάντας συνέβη ἐπιτιμηθῆναι, καὶ ἑαυτὸν αὐτοῖς ὁ ἀναίτιος συγκατεδίκαζε, τοῦτο μὲν καὶ δι᾽ ἐγκράτειαν, τοῦτο δὲ καὶ Χριστὸν τὸν ἑαυτοῦ ποιμένα μιμούμενος, ὃς θανάτῳ τὸν ἄνθρωπον διὰ τὴν παράβασιν ἐπιτιμήσας, ἐβάστασε καὶ αὐτὸς ἐν τῇ ἑαυτοῦ σαρκὶ τὸ ἐπιτίμιον ὁ μόνος ἀνεύθυνος καὶ ἀναμάρτητος.

52

Ταῦτα μὲν οὖν ἐκ πολλῶν ὀλίγα τῶν ἐκείνου σοφωτάτων οἰκονομιῶν· καιρὸς δὲ λοιπὸν τῆς τῶν θαυμάτων καὶ αὖθις μετασχεῖν τραπέζης, ἑνὸς πρότερον ἐπιμνησθέντας διηγήματος τὸ διορατικὸν αὐτοῦ δηλοῦντος χάρισμα.

2 Χειμὼν ἦν βαρύτατος καὶ δριμύς, καὶ ὁ πατὴρ ἔτυχεν ἱστάμενος πρὸ τῆς κέλλης αὐτοῦ· διήρχετο δὲ καθ᾽ ἕτερον μέρος ὁ μοναχὸς Ἰωάννης καὶ δοχειάριος τῷ τότε, ὃς καὶ κληθεὶς ὑπὸ τοῦ πατρὸς παρέστη αὐτῷ μετὰ τοῦ συνήθους δουλοπρεποῦς σχήματος. Ὁ πατὴρ δὲ οὐκ ἀπήγγελλεν αὐτῷ τὴν αἰτίαν τῆς κλήσεως, ἀλλ᾽ ἦν σύννους ὅλος καὶ ἐξεστηκὼς καὶ πρὸς ἑαυτὸν συννενευκὼς ἐπιπολύ.

3 Ὀψὲ δέ ποτε ἀνανεύσας, "Κάλει μοι," φησί, "τὸν κυνηγὸν Θεόδωρον." Καὶ τούτου παραστάντος, "Ἄπελθε,"

omit for those who are concerned with the good, is the fact that he himself did not disdain to share in the sufferings of his fellow monks. For if ever all the monks happened to be punished in common, even though he was innocent, he would condemn himself as well, along with the others. He did this on the one hand for the sake of self-control, and on the other in imitation of Christ, his own shepherd, who, in punishing man with death on account of his transgression, Himself bore the punishment in His own flesh, He who alone was innocent and without sin.

Chapter 52

These then are a few of the many examples of his most wise acts of accommodation. But now it is time to partake in turn of the banquet of his miracles, first calling to mind a story that reveals his gift of clairvoyance.

During one very severe and harsh winter, the father happened to be standing in front of his cell. The monk John, who was then treasurer, was passing by on the other side; when he was called by the father, he stood before him in his usual manner, at his service. But the father did not tell him why he had called him, but was completely lost in thought and in a trance and inwardly focused. 2

Finally he raised his head and said, "Call Theodore the hunter for me." When this man appeared, the father said, 3

φησὶν ὁ πατήρ, "ἀρίστησον· εἶτα τροφὰς ἀναλαβόμενος, δράμε τὸ τάχος ἐπὶ τὸν τῆς Κερασέας τόπον· ἐπὰν δὲ ἐξεναντίας γένῃ τῶν Χαλασμάτων, πρὸς τῇ θαλάσσῃ γενοῦ καὶ εὑρήσεις ἄνδρας τρεῖς λειποψυχοῦντας τῷ ψύχει τε καὶ τῇ πείνῃ, ὧν ὁ εἷς μοναχὸς τυγχάνει. Σπούδασον οὖν καταλαβεῖν αὐτοὺς ζῶντας καὶ ἄρτου μεταδοῦναι αὐτοῖς καὶ παντοίως παραμυθήσασθαι, πρινὴ ἀποψύξωσι παντελῶς, καὶ μετὰ τὸ ἐνδυναμωθῆναι αὐτούς, ἐλθέτωσαν καὶ αὐτοὶ μετὰ σοῦ."

4   Ὁ κυνηγὸς οὖν τὰ ἐντεταλμένα ποιῶν εὗρε πάντα καθὼς ὁ πατὴρ εἶπε προφητικῶς, καὶ θρέψας τοὺς τοιούτους καὶ κορέσας ὧν ἐπεφέρετο καὶ παντοίως ἀνακτησάμενος, διατάχους μεθ᾽ ἑαυτοῦ ἤγαγεν εἰς τὴν μονήν, τῷ Θεῷ καὶ τῷ τούτου θεράποντι τὰ σωτήρια θύσοντας.

53

Διακονίας τινὸς κατεπειγούσης τῶν ἀναγκαιοτάτων, εἰς πλοῖον ἐμβὰς ὁ πατὴρ μετά τινων ἀδελφῶν ἀπέπλευσεν· ἔφερε δὲ αὐτοὺς γαληνιῶσα θάλασσα καὶ μέτριος ἄνεμος. Ἐπεὶ δὲ ἐπὶ τοῦ πελάγους ἐγένοντο, ἔσπευδεν ὁ Ἐχθρὸς τὸν πατέρα καταποντίσαι σὺν τοῖς ἀδελφοῖς. Ἐγείρας οὖν σφοδρὸν καὶ βίαιον ἄνεμον καὶ συνταράξας τὴν θάλασσαν, συστρέψας τε τὸ πλοῖον, ἀνέτρεψεν εὐθὺς καὶ πάντας ἐκάλυψε καὶ ὑπὸ τὸ ὕδωρ ὑπήγαγεν.

"Go and have your midday meal; then take some food and run as fast as you can to Kerasea. When you're opposite Chalasmata, head toward the sea and you'll find three men faint from cold and hunger, one of whom is a monk. So hurry to reach them while they're still alive, and give them bread and care for them in every way, before they die from exposure; and after they recover their strength, bring them back here with you."

When the hunter carried out his instructions, he found   4 everything just as the father had predicted. After he had fed these men and given them their fill of the provisions he was carrying and revived them in every way, he quickly led them back with him to the monastery, as they gave thanks for their salvation to God and His servant.

Chapter 53

Once, when he had some urgent business of a most pressing nature, the father embarked on a ship and sailed off with some of the brethren; and they were carried along by a calm sea and moderate wind. But when they reached the open sea, the Enemy endeavored to drown the father together with the brethren. He thus stirred up a violent and blustery wind and threw the sea into tumult, causing the ship to roll, so that he soon capsized the ship and buried them all under the waves and plunged them beneath the water.

2   Ἀλλ᾽ ὦ τῶν τοῦ Θεοῦ θαυμασίων! Ὁ μὲν γὰρ πατὴρ ἅμα
τῷ ἀνατραπῆναι τὸ σκάφος εὑρέθη ἐν τῇ τρόπει καθήμενος, θαρσοποιῶν τε τοὺς ἀδελφοὺς καὶ παντοίως ἀνακαλούμενος, οὓς καὶ καθ᾽ ἕνα συναγαγὼν τοῦ ὕδατος πάντας
ἀνείλκυσε καὶ διέσωσεν. Εἷς δὲ τούτων, Πέτρος ὀνομαζόμενος, Κύπριος τὸ γένος, ὥσπερ ὁ Πέτρος ἀπιστίαν νοσήσας αὐτίκα κατεποντίζετο· ἀλλ᾽ ὁ πατήρ, τῶν ἄλλων συλ-
λεγομένων, ἐκεῖνον μὴ θεασάμενος, ἐπλήγη τὴν καρδίαν
καὶ μέγα ἀνέκραξε· "Τέκνον Πέτρε, ποῦ εἶ;" Καὶ ἅμα τῇ
βοῇ ἀνήγετο ὁ Πέτρος ἐκ τοῦ βυθοῦ.

3   Καὶ ἦν μὲν καὶ ταῦτα μεγίστη καὶ ξένη θαυματουργία·
τὸ δὲ μηδέν τι καταπεσεῖν ἀφ᾽ ὧν τῷ πλοίῳ συνεσκευάζετο,
τοῦτο παραδοξότερον καὶ ὑπερεκπλῆττον τὸν νοῦν. Οἱ
οὖν ἐν τῇ Λαύρᾳ ἀδελφοὶ προπέμψαντες τὸν πατέρα ἄχρι
τοῦ λιμένος κἀκεῖ ἱστάμενοι καὶ ὁρᾶν ἐθέλοντες τοῦτον ἐκ
πόθου, ἄχρις ἂν καὶ δύναιντο, ἐπειδήπερ ἔβλεπον ἀκριβῶς
τὰ γινόμενα, παραχρῆμα εἰς ἕτερον πλοῖον ἐμβάντες καὶ
διὰ τάχους πολλοῦ φθάσαντες, τό τε σκάφος ἀνώρθωσαν
καὶ ἀνεβίβασαν ἅπαντας καὶ σύναμα ἀνέστρεψαν καὶ ἣν
εἶχον πίστιν περὶ τὸν πατέρα ἐπολυπλασίαζον.

54

Μοναχός τις ποθὲν ἥκων, χαλκοτύπος τὴν τέχνην,
Ματθαῖος τὸ ὄνομα, δαίμονι κάτοχος, προσελθὼν τῷ

But, oh, the marvels of God! For the moment the ship 2
capsized, the father found himself sitting on the keel; encouraging the brethren and calling out to them, he gathered them together one by one, dragged them all out of the water, and saved them. One of them, named Peter, a Cypriot in origin, who just like Saint Peter was afflicted with lack of faith, sank momentarily; when the father could not see him, after the others were gathered together, he was stricken in his heart and called out loudly, "My child Peter, where are you?" And at the moment he let out this shout, Peter rose up from the depths.

This was a very great and extraordinary miracle; but even 3
more marvelous and amazing was the fact that none of the cargo which had been stowed on the ship sank. The brethren in the Lavra had escorted the father as far as the harbor and had remained standing there, wanting in their love to keep him in sight as long as they could. When they saw precisely what was happening, they immediately boarded another vessel and, arriving very quickly, they righted the ship, embarked everyone upon it, and returned together; and their faith in the father was greatly increased.

Chapter 54

A monk called Matthew, who came from somewhere or other and was a coppersmith by trade, became possessed by

πατρί, βοηθείας τυχεῖν παρεκάλει, οὐχ ὥστε ἀπαλλαγῆναι τοῦ πάθους (πόθεν γὰρ ἂν ἤλπισε τοῦτο;), ἀλλὰ μικρὰν σκέπην καὶ παρηγορίαν τῆς νόσου λαβεῖν.

2 Καὶ ὁ μὲν ταῦτα. Ὁ δὲ μέγας τῆς οἰκείας ἀρετῆς οὐκ ἐπελανθάνετο, ἀλλὰ δέχεται τοῦτον ὥς τι τῶν τιμίων καὶ ὡς οἰκεῖον ἀσπάζεται μέλος· εἶτα καὶ καλεῖ τινα τῶν ἀδελφῶν, ὃν ἐργάτην ἐγίνωσκε δόκιμον, καὶ τόν τε πάσχοντα παρατίθησιν αὐτῷ ὥς τινα παραθήκην πολύτιμον καὶ τὰ περὶ αὐτοῦ ἀνατίθησιν ἐν μυστηρίῳ, εἰπὼν αὐτῷ ὅτι "Πολλὴν ἐντεῦθεν ἕξεις τὴν ὠφέλειαν καὶ τὸ κέρδος." Ὁ δὲ ἐργάτης ἐκεῖνος δέχεται εἰς τὸ κελλίον αὐτοῦ τὸν δαιμονῶντα ἀδελφὸν ὥσπέρ τινα θησαυρὸν πολύτιμον.

3 Ἐπεὶ δὲ μὴ οἷός τε ἦν ὑπενεγκεῖν ἐπιπολὺ τὴν τοῦ δαίμονος ἀγριότητα, προσῆλθε τῷ πατρὶ μετ᾽ εὐλαβείας καὶ κατηφείας, λέγων αὐτῷ· "Συγχώρησόν μοι, πάτερ· ὑπὲρ γὰρ τὴν δύναμίν μου ἐστὶ τὸ ἔργον ὅ μοι δέδωκας." Ὃν ὡς ἀκαρτέρητον ἐκεῖνος αἰτιασάμενος, ἕτερον ἀδελφὸν καλεῖ δοκιμώτερόν τε καὶ γενναιότερον· ὁ δὲ καὶ αὐτὸς ὁμοίως τῷ προτέρῳ μὴ δυνάμενος ὑπομεῖναι τὴν αὐτοῦ ὑπηρεσίαν, παρῃτεῖτο τὸν ἀδελφόν· ὁ δὲ πατὴρ οὐδὲ οὕτως ἠμέλει αὐτοῦ, ἀλλ᾽ ἕτερον ἐκάλει τὸν ἐν τοῖς τοιούτοις καρτερικώτερον, λέγων αὐτῷ· "Ἐν συντόμῳ σοι λέγω, Ἀμβρόσιε" (τοῦτο γὰρ ἐκαλεῖτο), "παραλαβὼν τὸν ἀδελφόν, εἴπερ οὐκ ἐκκακήσεις πρὸς τὸν κλύδωνα τοῦ πάθους αὐτοῦ ἀλλ᾽ ὑπομενεῖς ἐπιπολύ, ἐγὼ ἐγγυῶμαι καὶ διαβεβαιοῦμαί σοι ἐκ ταύτης μόνης τῆς ὑπομονῆς κληρονόμον γενέσθαι σε τῆς βασιλείας τῶν οὐρανῶν."

4 Ὁ δὲ Ἀμβρόσιος ὥσπέρ τι εὕρεμα ἡγησάμενος τὸ

a demon. He approached the father and begged to receive his assistance, not so as to be delivered from his affliction (for how could he hope for this?), but simply to receive some small protection and relief from his illness.

This was his situation. As for the great one, he did not 2 forget his innate virtue, but received the monk as something precious and embraced him as though he was one of his own limbs. Then he called one of the brethren whom he knew to be a reliable worker, and entrusted the demoniac to him like a valuable deposit. In private he described the monk's condition, saying to him, "You will derive much benefit and profit from this." And that worker took the demoniac brother into his cell like some valuable treasure.

But since he was unable to endure for long the ferocity of 3 the demon, he anxiously approached the father in a dejected frame of mind, saying to him, "Forgive me, father; for the task which you have given me is beyond my ability." After the father accused him of lack of perseverance, he summoned another brother who was even more reliable and of even better character; but, just like the previous monk, he too was unable to endure his assignment, and gave up on the brother. But the father did not cease in his care of the demoniac, but summoned yet another monk who was even more steadfast in such duties, saying to him, "I tell you in short, Ambrosios," (for this was his name), "if you take charge of the brother and do not lose heart when faced by the rough waters of his affliction, but persevere for a long time, I guarantee and assure you that as a result of this perseverance alone you will inherit the kingdom of heaven."

Ambrosios, believing the assignment to be a godsend, 4

ἐπίταγμα, τὸ μέτωπον τῇ γῇ προσερείσας, τὰ ἴχνη τοῦ πατρὸς κατησπάσατο, καὶ τὴν ὑπόσχεσιν πρὸ ὀφθαλμῶν θέμενος, γενναίως κατὰ τοῦ δαίμονος καθωπλίζετο· ἀλλ᾽ ἤλεγξε καὶ τοῦτον ἀσθενῆ τοῦ πονηροῦ πνεύματος ἡ θρασύτης. Ὃς δὴ καὶ ἡττηθείς, οἷά τις φυγοπόλεμος πρὸς τὸν πατέρα δραμών, τὴν οἰκείαν ὡμολόγει ἀσθένειαν, προ-αιρούμενος ἄλλό τι δεινὸν παθεῖν ἢ παραμένειν τοιούτῳ κακῷ.

5   Ὁ δὲ πατήρ, δειλὸν τοῦτον ἀποκαλέσας καὶ ἄνανδρον, ἔτι ἅπαξ προσέταξεν ὑπομεῖναι εἰπών· "Ἡνίκα πάλιν ἐπ-έλθῃ τῷ ἀδελφῷ ἡ τοῦ δαίμονος τυραννίς, ἐλθὲ πρός με ταχέως, μηδὲν εὐλαβηθείς, μήτε ἀωρίαν καιροῦ, μήτε τόπου ἀνοικειότητα." Ὑπήκουσεν ὁ Ἀμβρόσιος, καὶ εἰς μανίαν ἐλθόντος πάλιν τοῦ ἀδελφοῦ, δρομαῖος πρὸς τὸν πατέρα ἄπεισι, καὶ τὴν θύραν κρούσας ἀθρόως, ἐκάλει τὸν πατέρα, ὡς προσετάχθη· καὶ ὁ πατὴρ ὥσπερ ἐπιλαθόμενος διελοιδορεῖτο αὐτὸν καὶ ἀπεδίωκεν, "Ἐσκοτισμένε," λέ-γων, "ἱνατί με περιέκοψας;" Τί οὖν τὸ ἐντεῦθεν; Ὑποστρέφει μὲν ὁ γέρων, ὁ δὲ πάσχων ἀπηλλάττετο τοῦ πάθους καὶ ὑγιὴς ἐγίνετο.

55

Καὶ τοῦτο μὲν τοιοῦτον. Μοναχὸς δέ τις ἕτερος τῶν τεταγμένων ὑπὸ τῷ μεγάλῳ τούτῳ πατρὶ δεινήν τινα

pressed his forehead to the ground, and kissed the father's feet. After making his promise in his sight, he prepared himself nobly to fight against the demon; but the vehemence of the evil spirit proved him to be weak as well. After suffering defeat, he ran to the father like a deserter, and confessed his weakness, saying that he preferred to suffer any fate rather than to remain in the presence of such an evil spirit.

The father, calling him cowardly and unmanly, ordered 5 him once more to persevere, saying, "When the demon takes control of the brother again, come quickly to me, and don't worry about how late it is or how unsuitable the place may be." Ambrosios obeyed him, and when the brother again began to rave, he ran quickly to the father, and knocking loudly on the door, called the father as he had been instructed. But the father, as if he had forgotten his previous instructions, rebuked him and sent him away, saying, "You dimwit, why have you disturbed me?" What happened then? The elder returned, and the patient was relieved of his affliction and restored to health.

Chapter 55

And that's what happened in this case. Another monk who was under the authority of this great father suffered

νόσον ἔπασχε καὶ ἀπόρρητον· τὸ γὰρ οὖρον αὐτοῦ ὑπνοῦντος ἀνεπαισθήτως ἐκενοῦτο. Οὐκ εἶχε τοιγαροῦν ὅτι καὶ δράσει· ἐποίει γὰρ αὐτῷ παντελῶς τὸ πάθος ἀφόρητον τὸ μὴ δύνασθαι αὐτὸ ἐξαγγεῖλαι ἀλλ᾽ ἐπαισχύνεσθαι τὴν ἐξαγόρευσιν. Ὡς οὖν πολλὰ καμὼν καὶ πᾶσαν ἐπίνοιαν ἐπελθὼν καὶ μηχανήν (ἦν γὰρ τῶν ἄγαν ἀσκητῶν καὶ ἀγωνιστῶν ὁ ἀνήρ) οὐχ εὕρισκε τοῦ πάθους ἀπαλλαγήν, τέλος (ὦ τῶν ὀλεθρίων βουλευμάτων τοῦ Πονηροῦ!) βουλεύεται (οἴμοι) ἀπαγχονήσασθαι καὶ ἑαυτὸν θανατῶσαι.

2   Ἀλλ᾽ οὐ παρεῖδεν ἡ τοῦ Θεοῦ ἀγαθότης τὰς τοῦ θεράποντος αὐτοῦ προσευχάς, ἃς ἐποιεῖτο ὑπὲρ τοῦ ποιμνίου αὐτοῦ, ἀλλ᾽ ἥψατο τῶν φρενῶν αὐτοῦ ἀφανῶς καὶ φρόνησιν καὶ σύνεσιν ἐνέθηκεν αὐτῷ. Θαρρήσας οὖν ἐκκαλύπτει τὸ τόλμημα τῷ πατρὶ καὶ τὸν βρόχον δείκνυσιν· ὁ δὲ τῷ παραδόξῳ ἐκθαμβηθείς, ἠρώτα τὴν αἰτίαν. Ἔτι δὲ κρύπτειν οὗτος τὴν νόσον πειρώμενος ὑπ᾽ αἰσχύνης, ἀθυμίαν καὶ λύπην δαιμονικὴν εἶναι ἔλεγεν ἁπλῶς τὴν αἰτίαν τοῦ τοσούτου κακοῦ.

3   Ὁ δὲ πατὴρ ἐπέκειτο ἐρωτῶν· "Μήτι τοῦτό ἐστι, τέκνον; Μήτι γε ἐκεῖνο;" Οἷος ἐκεῖνος τὰ τοιαῦτα· ὁ δὲ ἀδελφὸς παντάπασιν ἀπηρνεῖτο· ὁ δὲ οὐκ ἠφίει αὐτὸν ἀλλ᾽ ἐπεζήτει τὸ αἴτιον. Κατανυγεὶς οὖν ἐκεῖνος καὶ βύθιόν τι στενάξας, ἀπεκάλυψεν αὐτῷ τὸ τῆς νόσου μυστήριον. Ὁ δὲ δεινὸν ἐμβλέψας αὐτῷ· "Ἐσκοτισμένε," φησί (τοῦτο γὰρ εἴθιστο λέγειν), "καὶ διατί μὴ προπολλοῦ εἶπάς μοι τοῦτο; Ἄπελθε, μηκέτι τοῦτο τολμήσῃς ποιῆσαι." Καὶ παραυτίκα ἡ ἐπιτίμησις εἰς ἔργον ἐξέβαινε, καὶ τῷ τοῦ πατρὸς λόγῳ ἡ τοῦ Θεοῦ χάρις ἐπηκολούθει.

from an awful and unspeakable affliction; for while he slept, his urine would flow without his realizing it. He did not know what to do; for what made the affliction completely unbearable was that he could not tell anyone, but was ashamed to admit to his incontinence. After he suffered a great deal and came up with every kind of idea and device (for he was one of the great ascetics and spiritual combatants), and did not find any relief from his affliction, finally (oh, the pernicious plots of the Evil One!) he decided (oh, woe is me!) to hang himself and commit suicide.

But the goodness of God did not disregard the prayers of His servant, which he made on behalf of his flock, for it touched the monk's mind imperceptibly and instilled good sense and understanding in him. Thus, taking courage, the monk revealed his rash plan to the father and showed him the noose. And Athanasios, taken by surprise, asked the reason. The monk, in his shame still trying to conceal his affliction, said that the reason for such a wicked plan was simply despondency and demonic depression.

But the father persisted in his questioning, asking, "Is this really the reason, my child? Is there not another reason?" The father kept pressing him in this way, but the monk steadfastly denied it. The father would not leave him in peace, however, but continued seeking the cause for his depression. At last the monk, stricken with contrition and with a deep sigh, revealed to him the secret of his affliction. And the father, looking fiercely at him, said, "You dimwit!" (for this was one of his customary retorts), "Why didn't you tell me this long ago? Go away, and don't ever dare do this." The rebuke was immediately effective, and God's grace followed upon the father's words.

56

Οὐκ ἄξιον δὲ τὸ τοῦ μοναχοῦ Θεοδώρου παραδραμεῖν· τούτῳ γὰρ πάθους ἐνσκήψαντος ὅπερ καρκῖνος λέγεται, βαρείας καὶ ἀφορήτους ὀδύνας ἐνεποίει καὶ ἀπόγνωσιν ἐνετίθει, ἐπεὶ πάντες οἱ θεασάμενοι αὐτὸν ἰατροὶ ἀπηγόρευσαν τὴν ἴασιν· ἀλλ᾽ οὗτος, ἐπὶ τῷ πατρὶ μόνῳ τὰς ἐλπίδας σαλεύων, προσῆλθεν αὐτῷ οὐχ ὡς γινώσκοντι ἰατρεῦσαι ἀλλ᾽ ὅπως ἀναθήσει αὐτὸν Τιμοθέῳ τῷ ἰατρῷ τῆς Λαύρας· "Εἰ γάρ," φησι, "μόνον θελήσει, πάτερ, τὸ πάθος θεραπευθήσεται."

2 Αὐτίκα γοῦν μετεκαλεῖτο ὁ Τιμόθεος. Γνοὺς δὲ οὗτος τίνος χάριν ἐκλήθη, δῆλος ἦν ἀγανακτῶν ἐπὶ τούτῳ, ὡς ἐπιστάμενος οἷον τὸ πάθος ἦν. Ὁ δὲ πατὴρ φησὶ πρὸς αὐτόν· "Τιμόθεε, τὸ πάθος τοῦ ἐμοῦ τέκνου ἐμόν ἐστι γίνωσκε· καὶ τὴν θεραπείαν ἐμοὶ προσφέρεις." Ὁ δὲ Τιμόθεος, μὴ ἔχων ἀντιτείνειν εἰς ἅπαν, τοῦ ἰατρεύειν ἀπήρχετο. Καὶ οὗτος μὲν ἐπὶ πολλαῖς ἡμέραις τὸ πάθος μετήρχετο διὰ παντοίας ἐπινοίας, ἐκεῖνο δὲ ἀνίατον ἔμενε· καὶ τί γὰρ ἢ καρκῖνος μὴ δ᾽ ἐπ᾽ ὀλίγον ὀρθοποδῶν;

3 Ἐπεὶ δὲ ὁ μέγας ἰατρὸς ἀφίκετο εἰς ἐπίσκεψιν τῶν ἐν τῷ Μυλοποτάμῳ ἀδελφῶν, ἐπεσκέψατο σὺν τούτοις καὶ τὸν Θεόδωρον (ἐκεῖ γὰρ συνῆν τούτῳ καὶ ὁ Τιμόθεος), καὶ ἐρωτήσας πῶς ἔχει αὐτῷ τὰ τοῦ πάθους, διακελεύεται ἐκκαλύψαι αὐτό, καὶ δῆθεν ἰλιγγιάσας, ἐπεσφράγισεν αὐτὸ τρὶς τῇ χειρὶ ἐπειπών· "Ὁ Θεὸς καταργήσαι σε."

4 Αὕτη δὲ ἡ ἐπιτίμησις ἴασις μετ᾽ ὀλίγον ἐγένετο· ὡς γὰρ

Chapter 56

It would not be right to pass over the story of the monk Theodore. When he was afflicted with the disease called cancer, it caused him severe and unbearable pain and made him despondent, since all the doctors who saw him had no hope of a cure. But this monk anchored his hopes on the father alone, and approached him, not as someone who would know how to cure him, but so that he might entrust him to Timothy, the physician of the Lavra. "For," he said, "if Timothy only wills it, father, the disease will be cured."

So Timothy was summoned immediately. But when he 2 learned the reason for his summons, he was clearly vexed at this, since he understood the nature of the disease. But the father said to him, "Timothy, you should realize that my child's suffering is mine as well, and you are offering your healing to me." And Timothy, who could not possibly refuse, went off to treat Theodore. For many days he tackled the disease in all sorts of ways, but it remained incurable. For what disease besides cancer does not get better in a short time?

But when the great physician Athanasios came to visit 3 the brethren at Mylopotamos, he also visited Theodore (for Timothy was also there with him). After asking him how his disease was, Athanasios told him to uncover the tumor, and, as if reeling with dizziness, made the sign of the cross over it three times with his hand while saying, "May God render you powerless!"

And this rebuke soon became a cure. For since Theodore 4

προετράπη λούσασθαι, αὐτὸς μὲν ὁ ἐπιτάξας τοῦτο πατὴρ πρῶτος εἰσῆλθε, τὰ δὲ τῶν ποδῶν αὐτοῦ ἀρτάρια κατα-λέλοιπε τῷ Θεοδώρῳ, ὡς ἂν τὰς ψύλλας ἀποτινάξοι· ὁ δὲ κρατῶν ταῦτα καὶ εἰς ὑπέρθερμον πίστιν τοῦ πατρὸς ἐλθών, ἐπετίθει αὐτὰ τῷ τραύματι ὡς ἰατρείας ἐπίθεμα, καὶ τὴν ἐπίκλησιν ἐκείνου καὶ τὴν εὐχὴν ὡς ἐπίπασμα ἰατρικὸν προσεπετίθει. Ὡς δὲ τοῦ λουτροῦ ὁ πατὴρ ἐξήρχετο καὶ τὸν Θεόδωρον ἐκάλει εἰσελθεῖν (ὢ Θεοῦ θαυμασίων!), αὐτίκα τό τε πάθος ἐξερράγη καὶ ἕλκος ἐξέρρευσε, καὶ ὁ παθὼν ἀπολουσάμενος ὑγιὴς ἐδείκνυτο.

57

Ἀλλὰ μεταβατέον καὶ ἐφ' ἕτερα τοῦ μεγάλου θαυμα-τουργήματα. Ἡ τῶν Νέων νῆσος μία ἐστὶ καὶ αὐτὴ τῶν πρὸς τὴν Λαύραν δωρεῶν τῶν κρατίστων καὶ ἀοιδίμων βασιλέων· οὕτω δὲ ἐπωνομάσθη διὰ τὸ φροντιστήριον γεγονέναι ἐν αὐτῇ καὶ προγυμνάζεσθαι ἐκεῖσε τοὺς νεω-τέρους τῶν μοναχῶν. Αὕτη ξηρὰ μὲν τὴν φύσιν ἐστίν, ἀγαθὴ δὲ τἆλλα καὶ βοσκημάτων εὔφορος· αὐτόθεν γὰρ καὶ τὰ φορτηγὰ ζῷα τῇ Λαύρᾳ κεχορήγηται. Ἐν ταύτῃ τῇ νήσῳ πλῆθος ἀκρίδων ἐπιστρατεῦσαν πᾶσι μὲν σπορίμοις ἐπελυμαίνετο, παντὸς δὲ χόρτου χλωροῦ τὴν γῆν ἀπ-εγύμνου, ὡς μὴ δὲ τοῖς ἐκεῖσε ζῴοις ὑπολείπεσθαι κἂν γοῦν βραχεῖαν τροφήν· ὅθεν καὶ πρὸς ἑτέρους τόπους μετ-ετέθησαν αἱ τὸ κάλλιστον ἔριον φύουσαι αἶγες.

had been told to bathe himself, the father, who had ordered this, went in first, but left his slippers for Theodore, so that he might shake off the fleas. While holding these slippers, Theodore was overcome by ardent faith in the father, placed them on his cancerous sore like a medical remedy, and added to this, like a medicinal powder, an invocation of Athanasios and a prayer. And when the father was coming out of the bath and called Theodore to enter (oh, the marvels of God!), the tumor suddenly burst and pus flowed out. After washing himself off, the patient was seen to be healed.

Chapter 57

But now we must pass on to other miracles of the great man. The island of the Neoi is one of the gifts to the Lavra from the most mighty emperors of blessed memory. It received its name on account of the school that was on it and the fact that the younger monks received their early training there. This island is naturally arid, but good in other respects and able to support grazing animals; it has thus also supplied the pack animals for the Lavra. On this island a horde of locusts was attacking all the crops and damaging them, stripping the earth of every green plant, so that there was not even a shred of fodder left for the animals there. As a result the goats which yielded the finest wool had been transported to other locations.

2   Οἱ οὖν ἐν τῇ τοιαύτῃ νήσῳ μὴ δυνάμενοι φέρειν ταύτην
τὴν βάσανον, προσῆλθον τῷ πατρί, τὰ συμβάντα ἐκδιη-
γούμενοι καὶ τὴν ἑαυτῶν συμφορὰν ἀποδυρόμενοι· "Ἐξέλιπον γάρ," φησιν, "ἀπὸ βρώσεως πρόβατα καὶ βόες ἐν φάτναις
οὐχ ὑπάρχουσιν [Habakkuk 3:17]· ἀλλὰ διαβὰς βοήθησον
ἡμῖν" [Acts 16:9]. Ἐπιστὰς τοίνυν τῇ νήσῳ ὁ θαυματουργὸς
οὗτος πατὴρ εὗρε τὰ μὲν ἄλλα πάντα κατανεμομένην τὴν
ἀκρίδα, τῶν ἀμπέλων δὲ μόνων ἀπεχομένην· οὗ καὶ τὴν
αἰτίαν ἐρωτηθείς, οἰκονομίαν εἶναι Θεοῦ τοῦτο ἔλεγε, τὴν
ἡμετέραν ἀσθένειαν παραμυθουμένου καὶ ὑποστηρίζον-
τος· οἱ δὲ φυσικῶς ἀπέχεσθαι τούτων ἀντέλεγον.

3   Ὁ δὲ πατήρ, τὴν ἐσφαλμένην αὐτῶν ὑπόνοιαν διορθούμενος, φύλλα κοπῆναι τῆς ἀμπέλου καὶ τῶν ὁρίων
ταύτης ἐκτὸς ῥιφῆναι προσέταξεν. Ὡς δὲ τοῦτο γέγονε,
θᾶττον ἢ λόγος ταῦτα κατήσθιον αἱ ἀκρίδες. Ἐπευξάμενος τοίνυν σὺν τοῖς λοιποῖς ἀδελφοῖς, ἔστησε τὴν πληγὴν
καὶ τὴν θραῦσιν ἐκόπασε [see Numbers 16:48; Psalm
105(106):30]· πλῆθος γὰρ ὀρνέων ἀκορέστων, εἴτε τοῦτο ὁ
σελευκὶς λέγεται εἴτε ἄλλο γένος ὀρνίθων, ἀθρόως ἐπελ-
θὸν κατήσθιε ταύτας ἐν τάχει.

58

Ἀλλ᾽ ἀφηγητέον ἡμῖν καὶ ἕτερόν τι καινότερον. Τινὲς
τῶν τοῦ Ὄρους ἡγουμένων, φιλαρχίας ἔρωτι κρατηθέντες,

The inhabitants of this island, who were unable to bear this disaster, approached the father, explaining what had happened and lamenting their misfortune. "For," they said, "*the sheep have failed from the pasture,* and *there are no oxen at the cribs; come over and help us.*" Thus, when this wonderworking father arrived on the island, he found that the locusts had ravaged everything else, but had spared only the grapevines. When he was asked the reason for this, he said it was a dispensation of God, to console us and support us in our weakness, but they responded that the locusts had avoided them for natural reasons.

The father, seeking to correct their mistaken assumption, ordered vine leaves to be cut and thrown outside the vineyard's boundaries. When this happened, the locusts ate them more quickly than words can tell. So then, Athanasios prayed with the remaining brethren, and stopped the infestation and *made the plague to cease;* for a large flock of insatiable birds, either the ones called rose-colored pastors, or some other kind of bird, swooped down and quickly devoured the locusts.

Chapter 58

But now I must tell yet another more recent tale. Some of the superiors from the Holy Mountain, possessed by a greed

οὐκ ἠνείχοντο δεύτεροι τῶν παλαιῶν γερόντων δοκεῖν τε καὶ ὀνομάζεσθαι, ἀλλ᾽ ἐπίσης ἐκείνοις τιμᾶσθαι καὶ προκαθέζεσθαι ἐπεζήτουν· οὗ μὴ τυγχάνοντες, οὐκ εὐδοκίαν τοῦτο εἶναι Θεοῦ ἐλογίζοντο, ἀλλ᾽ ἠτιῶντο τὸν πατέρα, ἀδοξίας αἴτιον εἶναι αὐτοῖς τοῦτον νομίζοντες.

2   Διὸ καὶ προσελθόντες τῷ τότε πρώτῳ, ὃς ἦν ὁ Φακηνὸς Ἰωάννης, τοιαῦτα ἔλεγον ἐν φιλικῷ σχήματι· "Ἱνατί σὺ μὲν τὸ ὄνομα τοῦ πρώτου φέρεις, ὁ δὲ τῆς Λαύρας ποιμὴν τὸ ἔργον κέκτηται; Ἀλλ᾽ εἴπερ οὐ καταφρονήσεις τῆς ἡμετέρας συμβουλῆς, ἀνασώσεις τῇ ἀρχῇ σου τὸ δύνασθαι." Ὁ δὲ γέρων, ἁπλούστατον ἔχων φρόνημα, οὐκ ἐπέγνω τὴν ἐξαπάτην, ἀλλ᾽ ἐπείθετο τούτοις ὥσπερ συμβούλοις ἀγαθοῖς.

3   Ἐπεὶ οὖν τότε ὁ ἀοίδιμος ἐν βασιλεῦσι Βασίλειος, κατὰ τῶν βαρβάρων ἐκστρατευσάμενος, ἐν Μακεδονίᾳ τότε διανέπαυε τὸν στρατόν, οἱ μοναχοὶ ἐκεῖνοι βουλεύονται προσελθεῖν τῷ βασιλεῖ καὶ ἐντυχεῖν αὐτῷ κατὰ τοῦ πατρός, ἐπαγόμενοι καὶ τὸν πρῶτον ὥσπερ προκάλυμμα τῆς ἰδίας κακίας. Ἀπερχόμενοι οὖν πρὸς τὸν βασιλέα, συνήντησαν τῷ πατρὶ ἐκεῖθεν ὑποστρέφοντι, ᾧ καὶ τὴν συνήθη πρόσρησιν καὶ τιμὴν ἀπονείμαντες, ἐρωτῶνται παρ᾽ αὐτοῦ ποῦ τε ἀπέρχονται καὶ τίνος χάριν. Καὶ οἱ μὲν προφάσεις τινὰς καὶ αἰτίας ἐπλάσαντο· ὁ δὲ γέρων τῆς ἁπλότητος αὐτοῦ μὴ ἐπιλαθόμενος, "Κατὰ σοῦ," φησι, "πάτερ, πρὸς τὸν βασιλέα ἀπερχόμεθα." Ὁ δὲ πατὴρ καὶ αὐτὸς τῇ συνήθει ἁπλότητι χρησάμενος μετὰ χαρᾶς ἀντέφησε· "Πατέρες, ἀπέλθετε."

4   Καὶ ὁ μὲν πρῶτος, αἰδεσθεὶς τὸν πατέρα, αὐτίκα

for power, could not bear to appear to be and actually be called secondary to the traditional elders, but sought to be honored and assigned precedence equal to them. When they did not achieve this, they did not consider it to be God's will, but blamed the father, holding him responsible for their lack of honor.

For this reason they approached the *protos* at that time, 2 who was John Phakenos, and said the following to him in a seemingly friendly way: "Why is it that you bear the name of *protos,* but the shepherd of the Lavra actually holds this position? But if you don't disdain our advice, you'll regain real power for your position." That elder, who was very naive, did not realize their deceitful design, but was persuaded by them as if they were good advisors.

Since at that time Basil, celebrated among emperors, was 3 then resting his army in Macedonia after his campaign against the barbarians, those monks planned to approach the emperor and to speak with him against the father, bringing along the *protos* as well, as a cover for their iniquity. So, as they were on their way to the emperor, they met the father returning from a visit with him. After they had accorded Athanasios the customary salutation and honor, he asked them where they were going and for what reason. They concocted some excuses and pretexts; but the elder, persisting in his naïveté, said, "Father, we're going to the emperor to complain about you." And the father, also demonstrating his own customary simplicity, happily responded, "Off you go then, fathers."

But the *protos,* out of respect for the father, immediately 4

ἐξαιτεῖται συγχώρησιν· ἐκεῖνοι δὲ τότε μὲν ἡσύχασαν, ἐκείνου παρόντος· ἐπεὶ δὲ διΐσταντο, ἀφελῆ καὶ κοῦφον ἀπεκάλουν τὸν γέροντα καὶ τὰ μεγάλα κατητιῶντο καὶ ὑποκλέπτειν ἐπειρῶντο καὶ ὑποσπᾶν καὶ παραφθείρειν τὸ ἀγαθὸν ἦθος αὐτοῦ. Ὁ δὲ γέρων, τὸ μετ' αὐτῶν ἀπελθεῖν παραιτησάμενος, παρήνει καὶ αὐτοὺς παύσασθαι τῆς πρὸς τὸν πατέρα ἐπιβουλῆς· "Αὐτὸν μὲν γάρ," φησιν, "οὐδόλως βλάψετε, καθ' ἑαυτῶν δὲ τὸν βόθρον ὀρύξετε" [see Ecclesiastes 10:8; Ecclesiasticus 27:26]. Οἱ δὲ ὡς οὐδὲν ἡγησάμενοι τοῦτον, τῆς αὐτῆς ἦσαν βουλῆς καὶ πάλιν τῆς πρὸς τὸν βασιλέα ὁδοῦ ἐπελαμβάνοντο.

5   Καὶ ὅρα μοι τὸν Θεὸν ὅπως ἐκδικεῖ τὸν αὐτοῦ θεράποντα· ἐν γὰρ τῷ ἀπέρχεσθαι κινδύνῳ περιπίπτουσιν ἀδοκήτῳ, οὐ πολεμίοις περιπεσόντες ἔθνεσιν, ἀλλὰ ταῖς τῶν Τούρκων χερσὶν εἰρήνην ἐχόντων τὸ τηνικαῦτα μεθ' ἡμῶν καὶ τὸν βασιλέα φοβουμένων· οἵτινες ἀποδύσαντες αὐτοὺς καὶ εἰς θανάτου φόβον ἐμβαλόντες γυμνοὺς παντελῶς ἀφῆκαν, τὴν αἰσχύνην αὐτῶν μόνην φέροντας. Ἐκεῖνοι δὲ τῆς τοῦ σώματος σκέπης δεόμενοι καὶ ἀποροῦντες, ὑπέστρεφον μὲν κατῃσχυμμένοι, ἐθάρρησαν δὲ τῇ ἀνεξικακίᾳ καὶ χρηστότητι τοῦ πατρὸς καὶ ἐνεφανίσθησαν τούτῳ. Ὁ δὲ ἰδὼν αὐτοὺς οὕτως ἔχοντας καὶ ὡς οἰκεῖα μέλη κατοικτειρήσας, διένειμεν αὐτοῖς ἱμάτια, ἀφ' ὧν ἐφόρουν οἱ ὑπ' αὐτὸν μοναχοί, καὶ τὴν τῆς ὁδοῦ χρείαν παρέσχεν αὐτοῖς, καὶ οὕτως ὑπέστρεψαν ἅπαντες εἰς τὰς οἰκείας μονάς.

asked his forgiveness. The other monks kept quiet while Athanasios was present, but as soon as they parted, they called the elder silly and foolish; and they reproached him harshly and tried by subterfuge to corrupt his good character. But the elder refused to go with them, and urged them to end their plot against the father. "For," he said, "you're not going to hurt him at all, but *you will dig a pit* for yourselves." But the monks, disregarding the *protos,* adhered to their plan and resumed their journey to the emperor.

See how God avenges His servant! For, as they were leaving, they fell into unexpected danger, not falling in with hostile peoples, but into the hands of the Turks who at that time had peaceful relations with us and were in awe of the emperor. These Turks stripped them and frightened them to death, leaving them completely naked, clothed only in their shame. Since they needed some covering for their bodies and were otherwise at a loss, they returned shamefaced, but took courage from the forbearance and goodness of the father and revealed themselves to him. When he saw them in this condition, he took pity on them as if they were the limbs of his own body, and gave them cloaks out of the supply of cloaks worn by the monks under him, and provided them with what they needed for their journey. And thus they all returned to their own monasteries.

59

Ἐγένετο ἀποπλεῦσαί ποτε τὸν πατέρα ἐπί τινι διακονίᾳ τῆς μονῆς μετά τινων ἀδελφῶν, καὶ συνέβη αὐτοῖς ὕδατος στέρησις· εἷς δὲ τούτων, καταπονηθεὶς τῇ παντελεῖ δίψῃ, ἀπελέγετο τὴν ψυχήν. Ὁ οὖν φιλότεκνος πατὴρ οἰκτείρας αὐτὸν ἐπελάβετο τοῦ κεραμίου καὶ ἔπλησεν αὐτὸ θαλασσίου ὕδατος, καὶ εὐλογήσας δέδωκε πιεῖν τῷ φλεγομένῳ ἀδελφῷ, εἰπών· "Ἐν ὀνόματι τοῦ Κυρίου ἡμῶν Ἰησοῦ Χριστοῦ λάβε καὶ πίε εἰς κόρον ἐξ αὐτοῦ καὶ μετάδος καὶ τοῖς χρείαν ἔχουσιν ἀδελφοῖς." Ὁ δὲ λαβὼν καὶ γευσάμενος ἐθαύμασε τὴν τούτου γλυκύτητα, καὶ κορεσθεὶς μετέδωκε καὶ τοῖς ἑτέροις ἀδελφοῖς.

60

Ἕτερος ἀδελφός, ὁ μοναχὸς Γεράσιμος, πλήρης ὢν καὶ αὐτὸς τῶν τοῦ πατρὸς θαυματουργιῶν, γενναίαν ποτὲ ἄμπελον καὶ περιμήκη ἠθέλησεν αὐτοχειρὶ ἐκ τῶν τῆς γῆς κόλπων ἀνασπάσαι, ἅτε ῥώμῃ σωματικῇ πολὺ κατισχύων· καὶ γὰρ ἦν πεπηγὸς αὐτῷ τὸ σῶμα ἐκ στερεῶν ὀστῶν τε καὶ νεύρων. Οὗτος ταῖς χερσὶ τῆς ἀναδενδράδος κρατήσας καὶ δὶς καὶ τρὶς διασείσας καὶ ταύτην ἐκσπάσαι μὴ δυνηθείς, τὰ ἔγκατα αὐτοῦ κατὰ τῶν αἰδοίων καὶ ἄκων κατέσπασε. Τῷ αὐτῷ καὶ νόσος ἄλλοτέ ποτε ἐπιγενομένη κατὰ τῶν

Chapter 59

Once, when the father was sailing off on some monastery business with some of the brethren, they happened to run out of water; and one of them, overwhelmed by his consuming thirst, had given himself up for dead. The father, who loved his children, thus took pity on him, grabbed a jar and filled it with seawater. After blessing it, he gave it to drink to the brother who was burning up with thirst, saying, "In the name of our Lord Jesus Christ, take and drink your fill of this, and share it with your brethren who have need of it." The monk took it and tasting it, marveled at its sweetness; and after drinking his fill, he shared it with the other brethren.

Chapter 60

Another brother, the monk Gerasimos, was also someone replete with the father's wonderworking. He once wanted to pull a tough and very long grapevine out of the ground with his bare hands, because he had great physical strength; for his body was well built with strong bones and sinews. But when this man grasped the grapevine in his hands and yanked hard on it two or three times, he could not pull it out, and accidentally gave himself a hernia which extended down to his genitals. At another time the same

γονάτων, πολὺν ἤδη χρόνον κλινοπετῆ πεποίηκεν. Ἀλλ᾽ ἐξ ἑκατέρων ἐν καιροῖς ἰδίοις δι᾽ εὐχῶν καὶ ἐπαφῆς τοῦ πατρὸς καὶ τῇ τοῦ σωτηρίου σταυροῦ χαράξει ἐλεύθερος γέγονε, καὶ σωτηρίας καὶ ἰάσεως παραδόξου παρὰ πᾶσαν ἀνθρωπίνην ἐλπίδα τετύχηκεν.

2   Ὁ αὐτός, εἰς τὸν σωτήριον τοῦ Κυρίου ἡμῶν Ἰησοῦ Χριστοῦ τάφον ἐν Ἱεροσολύμοις ἐπιθυμήσας ἀπελθεῖν χάριν εὐχῆς καὶ προσκυνήσεως, ἅμα δὲ καὶ διακονίαν τινὰ τῆς Λαύρας τελέσαι, παρὰ τοῦ πατρὸς ἀπελύθη. Μετὰ οὖν τὸ ἐκπληρῶσαι τὴν ὁρισθεῖσαν αὐτῷ παρὰ τοῦ πατρὸς διακονίαν, ἅμα δὲ καὶ τὰς εὐχὰς ἀποδοῦναι τῷ Κυρίῳ, ὑπέστρεψε πάντοθεν ἀβλαβής, τῇ τοῦ πατρὸς εὐχῇ περιφυλαχθείς.

3   Ἐξεῖπε δὲ καὶ τόδε, μάρτυρα τὸν Θεὸν προβαλλόμενος, ὅτι "Μετὰ τὴν ὑποστροφὴν μιᾷ τῶν ἡμερῶν ἠθέλησα συντυχεῖν τῷ πατρὶ ἐξ ἀναγκαίου· ἦν γὰρ τότε τὴν τοῦ ἀρτοκοπείου ἐκτελῶν διακονίαν. Ἔτυχε δὲ τότε εἶναι τὸν πατέρα ἐν τῷ ναῷ τῶν Ἁγίων Ἀποστόλων· ἀπῆλθον οὖν ἐκεῖσε, καὶ τῆς πύλης ἐγγὺς γενόμενος, εἶδόν," φησι, "τὸ πρόσωπον αὐτοῦ ὡσεὶ φλόγα πυρός· εἶτα ἀναχωρήσας μικρόν, πάλιν προέκυψα ἰδεῖν τοῦτον, καὶ θεωρῶ ἐξαστράπτον αὐτοῦ τὸ πρόσωπον καί τινα ὁμοίωσιν ἀγγελικὴν πύρινον περικυκλοῦσαν αὐτόν, καὶ ἀπὸ τοῦ φόβου ἔκραξα· 'Ὦ πάτερ.' Ὁ δὲ ἰδών με ἔμφοβον, ἔφη ἐν πραείᾳ φωνῇ· 'Ὥραν ἔχεις εἰσελθών;' Ἐγὼ δὲ ἀφέμενος τοῦ ἀποκριθῆναι πρὸς τὴν ἐρώτησιν, διηγούμην αὐτῷ τὸ ὁραθὲν καὶ ὅπως ἤλπιζον ἐντεῦθεν ἀποθανεῖσθαι. Ὁ δὲ πατὴρ ἔφη μοι· 'Μὴ φοβοῦ, τέκνον· πλὴν ἐντολήν σοι δίδωμι ἀπὸ

man suffered an affliction in his knees, which confined him to bed for a long time. But he was delivered from both afflictions at separate times through the father's prayers and healing touch and his making the sign of the salvific cross, and contrary to any human expectation he received deliverance and miraculous healing.

The same man yearned to go to the salvific tomb of our 2 Lord Jesus Christ in Jerusalem so as to pray and worship there, as well as to perform some business for the Lavra, and he was given permission by the father to depart. So, after he completed the business the father had assigned him, and rendered up his prayers to the Lord, he returned, completely protected from harm by the father's prayers.

Gerasimos also told this story, offering God as his wit- 3 ness, that "One day after my return I wanted to speak with the father on an urgent matter; for I was then working in the bakery. The father happened to be in the church of the Holy Apostles at that time. So I went there, and when I was close to the door," he said, "I saw his face like a fiery flame. I withdrew a bit and then peeked in again to see him, and I observed his radiant face and something like angelic fire surrounding him, and in my fear I cried out, 'O father!' When he saw me in such a fright, he said in a gentle voice, 'Have you been here long?' I did not answer his question, but told him what I had seen and how I expected to die at that moment. But the father said to me, 'Fear not, my child; but I give you a commandment from the Lord almighty, not to

Κυρίου παντοκράτορος, μὴ ἐξειπεῖν τινι τὸ ὁραθέν σοι, ἄχρις ἂν ἐν τοῖς ζῶσίν εἰμι,᾽ ὃ καὶ ἐτήρησα."

61

Ἀδελφός τις, ἐπὶ διακονίαν τινὰ ἀποσταλεὶς παρὰ τοῦ πατρὸς καὶ καταρραθυμήσας τῆς αὐτοῦ ψυχῆς, ἐναυάγησε, φεῦ, ἐν τῷ κλύδωνι τῆς πορνείας· ἀναστρέψας δὲ εἰς τὴν μονὴν ἐξηγόρευσε τῷ πατρὶ τὴν ἁμαρτίαν καὶ τὸν ἐντεῦθεν ἐνοχλοῦντα τῆς ἀπογνώσεως λογισμόν. Ὁ δὲ συγκεχωρηκὼς αὐτῷ παρήνει καὶ ἐπεστήριζε καὶ ἔσω τῶν ἐλπίδων τῆς σωτηρίας ἐποίει, καὶ τῶν προτέρων ἀγώνων ἄρξασθαι παρεσκεύαζε καὶ τῆς τοῦ Θεοῦ μὴ ἀπογνῶναι φιλανθρωπίας.

2 Τοῦτο μὴ συνιείς τις τῶν ἀδελφῶν κατεβόα τοῦ πατρὸς καὶ τοῦ πεσόντος ἀδελφοῦ κατὰ πρόσωπον, ὡς οὐ δίκαιόν ἐστι λέγων συμπαθεῖν αὐτῷ, ἀλλ᾽ ἐπεξέρχεσθαι διὰ ποικίλων βασάνων, ἐπαρώμενος τῷ ἀδελφῷ καὶ καταθεματίζων αὐτόν, ὡς τοιούτου μιαροῦ πράγματος κατατολμήσαντα. Ὁ οὖν πρᾶος ἡμῶν πατήρ, μετὰ στυφότητος ἀπιδὼν πρὸς τὸν ἐγκαλοῦντα, ἔφη· "Ὦ Παῦλε" (τοῦτο γὰρ ὄνομα τῷ γέροντι), "πρόσεχε τί ποιεῖς."

3 Ἔκτοτε οὖν τοξεύειν τοῦτον ἤρξατο ὁ Πονηρὸς τοῖς βέλεσι τῆς πυρώσεως ἐφ᾽ ὅλοις τρισὶ νυχθημέροις, ὥστε ἀπογινώσκειν αὐτὸν τὴν ἰδίαν σωτηρίαν, καὶ τὸ χεῖρον ὅτι

tell anyone what you have seen, as long as I am alive,' and I've kept this commandment."

Chapter 61

A brother, who had been sent out on some business by the father, was neglectful of his soul and, alas, was shipwrecked in the stormy waves of fornication. When he returned to the monastery, he confessed to the father his sin and the despairing thoughts which troubled him as a result. Athanasios forgave him, gave him encouragement and support, made him hopeful of salvation, and thus prepared him to begin anew his previous spiritual contests and not to despair of God's compassion.

One of the brethren, who did not understand this, loudly 2 decried the father and the fallen brother to their faces, saying that it was not right to have compassion on him, but that he should be punished by various torments; he also cursed the brother and condemned him for daring to commit such an abominable act. Then our mild-mannered father, staring sternly at the accuser, said, "Paul," (for this was the elder's name), "watch what you're doing."

From that moment the Evil One began to shoot arrows of 3 burning desire at Paul for three entire days and nights, so that he despaired of his own salvation, and the worst was

καὶ ᾐσχύνετο ἐξαγγεῖλαι τὸν πόλεμον τῷ πατρί· ἀλλ᾽ οὗτος, ἕλκων αὐτὸν πρὸς ἐξαγόρευσιν τοῦ οἰκείου πάθους, ὡμίλει τούτῳ συχνῶς περί τινων δουλειῶν τῆς μονῆς. Ὁ Παῦλος τοίνυν θάρσος λαβών, ὡς τυχὼν τῆς τοῦ πατρὸς ὁμιλίας, προσπίπτει τούτῳ καὶ τὸν πειρασμὸν ἀπαγγέλλει, καὶ κουφισμὸν ἐξαιτεῖται καὶ ἀπαλλαγήν, καὶ τῆς αἰτήσεως οὐκ ἀστοχεῖ.

4   Τῶν γὰρ ἀδελφῶν ἐν τῷ λεγομένῳ τόπῳ τῆς Κερασέας κοπιώντων καὶ συνταλαιπωροῦντος τούτοις καὶ τοῦ πατρός, ηὐτρέπιζεν ὁ Παῦλος τὴν διακονίαν αὐτῶν ὡς κελλαρίτης. Ἤδη δὲ καταλαβούσης τῆς τοῦ ἀρίστου ὥρας, ἐκέλευεν αὐτοῖς ὁ πατὴρ μεταλαμβάνειν τροφῆς· αὐτὸς δὲ εἰς προσευχὴν ἐτρέπετο ὑπὲρ τοῦ πειραζομένου Παύλου. Ἔγνω οὖν ὁ ἀδελφὸς ἐν αὐτῇ τῇ ὥρᾳ ψυχρότητά τινα εὐθέως χεθεῖσαν ἀπὸ κεφαλῆς ἄχρι τῶν ποδῶν αὐτοῦ καὶ κατασβέσασαν τὸν βρασμὸν τῆς σαρκὸς αὐτοῦ· ὃς καὶ τὴν ὥραν σημειωσάμενος καὶ ἐρωτήσας περὶ τούτου τοὺς ἀδελφούς, εὗρεν ὅτι ἐν αὐτῇ τῇ ὥρᾳ προσηύξατο ὁ πατὴρ ἐν ᾗ καὶ οὗτος τοῦ πολέμου ἀπηλλάγη.

62

Ἀλλὰ καὶ ὁ ἀποθηκάριος Ἀθανάσιος ἐν ἀρχῇ τῆς ἀποταγῆς αὐτοῦ ἐν τῷ Μυλοποτάμῳ τυγχάνων καὶ ἀκαίρῳ ὑδροποσίᾳ χρησάμενος ὑδέρῳ περιέπεσεν· ὃν ἰδὼν ὁ

that he was ashamed to tell the father about his struggle. Athanasios, however, seeking to persuade him to confess his own suffering, would chat with him frequently about certain jobs that needed to be done at the monastery. Then Paul summoned up his courage and, when he happened to be engaged in conversation with the father, fell down before him and confessed his temptation; he begged for some relief and deliverance, and did not fail to receive his request.

For when the brethren were laboring in the place called 4
Kerasea and the father was toiling alongside them, Paul had prepared their provisions, since he was cellarer. When it was time for the midday meal, the father told them to eat some food, while he himself turned to prayer on behalf of the tormented Paul. Then, at that very hour, the brother felt a cold chill envelop him from head to feet and quench the burning of his flesh. He noted the hour and, when he asked the brethren about this, he found out that the father had made his prayer at the very hour in which he was delivered from his struggle.

Chapter 62

The storeroom keeper Athanasios, who was at Mylopotamos at the beginning of his monastic renunciation, was afflicted by dropsy after drinking an inordinate amount of

πατὴρ ἐξωγκωμένον καὶ διαρρήγνυσθαι μέλλοντα, προσέταξεν ἰατρευθῆναι αὐτὸν ἀπελθόντα εἰς τὴν Λαύραν. Ὡς δὲ ἀπελθὼν ἀπηγορεύθη παρὰ τῶν ἰατρῶν, σπλαγχνισθεὶς ὁ πατὴρ ἥψατο τῆς κοιλίας αὐτοῦ τῇ ἰδίᾳ χειρί, εἰπών· "Ὕπαγε, τέκνον, οὐδὲν κακὸν ἔχεις." Αὐτίκα οὖν λυθείσης αὐτοῦ τῆς γαστρός, ἐξεφυσήθη πᾶσα ἡ ὄγκωσις καὶ ὑγιὴς γέγονεν.

63

Ὁ Λαμψακηνὸς μοναχὸς Μάρκος, ἀδελφὸς τυγχάνων καὶ αὐτὸς τῆς μονῆς, ἐχειμάζετό ποτε χαλεπῶς τῇ ἐπαναστάσει τοῦ πορνικοῦ κλύδωνος· τῷ πατρὶ δὲ προσελθὼν καὶ τῶν ποδῶν αὐτοῦ ἁψάμενος καὶ τὰ καθ' ἑαυτὸν ἐξειπών, εἰς οἰκτιρμὸν τὸν συμπαθέστατον ἔκαμψε, καὶ μετ' ὀλίγας ἡμέρας ἔδοξεν ἰδεῖν κατ' ὄναρ αὐτὸν λέγοντα· "Πῶς τὰ κατὰ σέ, ὦ Μάρκε;" Ὁ δέ φησι· "Λίαν κακῶς, ὦ πάτερ." Καὶ ὁ πατήρ· "Ἔκτεινον σεαυτὸν κατὰ τοῦ ἐδάφους ἐπὶ πρόσωπον." Τοῦ δὲ ὑφαπλώσαντος ἑαυτὸν κατὰ γῆς, ἔθηκεν ὁ πατὴρ τὸν πόδα αὐτοῦ ἐπὶ τῶν νεφρῶν αὐτοῦ· ὁ δὲ τῷ βάρει τοῦ ποδὸς αὐτοῦ ἔξυπνος γεγονώς, ἔγνω αὐτίκα γαλήνην καὶ κουφισμὸν καὶ λύτρωσιν τῆς τοῦ πάθους ὀχλήσεως.

water. When the father saw him all swollen up and about to burst, he ordered him to go to the Lavra for medical treatment. When he went, the doctors despaired of him, but the father, out of compassion, touched his belly with his own hand, saying, "Go home, my child, there is nothing wrong with you." And immediately his belly was relieved, all the swelling was reduced, and he was healed.

Chapter 63

The monk Mark, from Lampsakos, who was also a brother at the monastery, was once wretchedly buffeted by the onset of a storm wave of fornication. Approaching the father, he clasped his feet, told him about his predicament, and persuaded that most compassionate man to take pity on him. A few days later Mark seemed to see him in a dream saying, "How are you, Mark?" And he said, "In a very bad way, father." And the father replied, "Stretch yourself out face down on the ground." When he had laid himself flat on the ground, the father placed his foot on his kidneys; Mark was awakened by the weight of his foot, and immediately experienced calm and relief and deliverance from the torment of his suffering.

64

Τοιαῦτα τὰ τοῦ πατρὸς ἀγωνίσματα, τοιαῦτα τὰ κατορθώματα, τοιαῦτα τὰ πνευματικὰ χαρίσματα· ὅσα δὲ καὶ εἴη τῷ πλήθει, γραφῇ παραδοῦναι ἀδύνατον. Ἐπεὶ δὲ τοιοῦτος ἐκεῖνος ἀνωμολόγηται, φέρε δὴ λοιπόν, συγκρίνωμεν τοῦτον καὶ τοῖς πάλαι βεβοημένοις ἐπ᾽ ἀρετῇ καὶ σοφίᾳ, ἵν᾽ εἰδῶμεν εἴπερ ὡς ἀληθῶς οὐδέ τινος τῶν ἐξαιρέτων ἐλείπετο.

2 Τὴν σωφροσύνην τοῦ Ἰωσὴφ καὶ τὸ ἄπλαστον τοῦ Ἰακὼβ ἐκέκτητο καὶ τοῦ Ἀβραὰμ τὸ φιλόξενον. Κατὰ τὸν μέγαν Μωυσῆν καὶ τὸν μετ᾽ ἐκεῖνον Ἰησοῦν δημαγωγὸς ἐχρημάτισε καὶ ποιμὴν λαοῦ πολλοῦ καὶ νομοθέτης καὶ κληροδότης τῆς βασιλείας τῶν οὐρανῶν τοῖς ποιμαινομένοις καὶ κανονιζομένοις παρ᾽ αὐτοῦ. Σοφὸς ἦν ὁ μέγας Ἀρσένιος καὶ τὸ κρυπτὸν εἶχε καὶ ἀνεπίδεικτον, ἀλλὰ καὶ οὗτος σοφώτατος ἦν, εἰ καὶ τὴν αὐτοῦ σοφίαν ἀπέκρυπτε.

3 Περιβόητος ἦν ὁ μέγας Σάβας ὡς οἰκιστὴς καὶ κοσμήτωρ τῆς ἐρήμου. Οὗτος δὲ οὐ ποίμνην ἐκτήσατο πολυάνθρωπον; Οὐ τὸν Ἄθων ἐπλήρωσε φροντιστηρίων πολλῶν; Οὐκ ἔσχε καὶ οὗτος τὸ διακριτικόν τε καὶ οἰκονομικὸν κατὰ τοὺς πάλαι βεβοημένους ἐπὶ τούτῳ; Καὶ ὥσπερ μὲν τὸν Παχώμιον, οὕτω καὶ τοῦτον ἄνωθεν ὁ Θεὸς προεχείρισεν· ὥσπερ δὲ τὸν Ἀντώνιον, οὐκ ἐπηγγείλατο μὲν *ποιῆσαι ὀνομαστόν* [see Deuteronomy 26:19], πεποίηκε δέ, καὶ τὴν φήμην τῆς ἀρετῆς αὐτοῦ μέχρι καὶ βασιλέων

Chapter 64

Such were the contests of the father, such his achievements, such his spiritual gifts, but there is such a host of them that it would be impossible to commit them all to writing. But, come now, since he is agreed to be such a man, let us compare Athanasios with those men of old who were acclaimed for virtue and wisdom, so that we may see how he was truly not inferior to any of the exceptional figures of the past.

He possessed the moderation of Joseph, the natural simplicity of Jacob, and the hospitality of Abraham. Like the great Moses and his successor Joshua he was a popular leader and a shepherd of many people, a lawgiver and an executor of the inheritance of the kingdom of heaven for those who were shepherded and given rules by him. The great Arsenios was wise, even though he kept this hidden and did not reveal it, but this man too was most wise, even if he concealed his own wisdom.

The great Sabas was celebrated as one who settled and adorned the monastic desert. But did not this shepherd, Athanasios, acquire a populous flock? Did he not fill Athos with many monastic complexes? Did not this man also have the gift of discernment and dispensation like those celebrated of old for this? Just as with Pachomios, did not God also appoint this man from heaven above? Just as with Antony, He not only promised *to make him famous,* but actually made him so, conveying the report of his virtue even to

παρέπεμψεν. Ἀλλὰ τί ἔτι; Χρέος γὰρ ἡμᾶς διηγήσασθαι καὶ ἐν ποίῳ τέλει τῶν ἀγώνων ὑπεξῆλθε τὸ στάδιον.

65

Ἐπειδὴ γάρ, ὡς ἄνω μοι λέλεκται, πολλοὶ τούτῳ προσήρχοντο ἐκ παντὸς μέρους τῆς οἰκουμένης, ὥστε δι' αὐτοῦ χειραγωγεῖσθαι πρὸς ἀρετὴν καὶ σωτηρίας τυχεῖν ψυχικῆς, ἐκεῖνος ἀνάγκην ἔχων ἀναλόγως τῷ πλήθει τῶν μοναχῶν κατασκευάσαι καὶ τοῦ ναοῦ τὸ εὐρύχωρον, πρὸς τὸ ἔργον εὐθὺς διανέστη, καὶ ὁ ναὸς ἐπλατύνετο. Ἐπεὶ δὲ μόνης ἐδεῖτο τῆς κατακλειδώσεως τὸ τοῦ ναοῦ θυσιαστήριον, ἡτοιμάζετο ἀνελθεῖν ἐπὶ τὸ ἔργον, ὡς ἂν κατασκέψηται τοῦτο.

2   Καὶ πρῶτον μὲν συνέλεξε πᾶσαν τὴν ἀδελφότητα καὶ κατήχησιν αὐτοῖς ἐκ τοῦ μακαριωτάτου Θεοδώρου τοῦ Στουδίτου ἐποιήσατο· εἶτα καὶ νουθεσίαν προσέθετο οἴκοθεν, "Ἀδελφοί μου," λέγων, "καὶ τέκνα, προσέχωμεν ἑαυτοῖς καὶ τῆς γλώσσης κρατῶμεν· κρεῖσσον γὰρ ἀφ' ὕψους ἢ ἀπὸ γλώσσης πεσεῖν. Προσδοκῶμεν δὲ ἀεὶ καὶ πειρασμόν, ὅτι διὰ πειρασμῶν καὶ θλίψεων δεῖ ἡμᾶς εἰσελθεῖν εἰς τὴν βασιλείαν [Acts 14:22] τῶν οὐρανῶν. Ἐπὶ δὲ τῷ μέλλοντι ἀπευκταίῳ μηδόλως σκανδαλισθήσεσθε, ἀλλὰ καὶ λίαν συμφέρον ὑμῖν τοῦτο νομίσατε· ἄλλως γὰρ τοῖς ἀνθρώποις νοοῦνται τὰ ὁρώμενα καὶ ἄλλως τῷ Θεῷ ᾠκονόμηται."

emperors. But what else is left to tell? We must narrate with what sort of a death he left the arena of spiritual contests.

Chapter 65

Since, as I have said above, many people flocked to this man from every part of the world so as to be guided to virtue by him and achieve spiritual salvation, he had to enlarge the church in proportion to the great number of monks. He set about the work directly, and the church was widened. When the sanctuary of the church was finished except for the keystone, he prepared to climb up onto the construction site in order to inspect it.

But first he assembled all the brotherhood and delivered 2 a catechetical instruction to them from the most blessed Theodore the Stoudite; then he added some advice of his own, saying, "My brothers and children, let us take heed for ourselves and control our tongues; for *it is better to fall from a height than to fall from a slip of the tongue.* And let us always expect trials, since it is *through* trials and *tribulations that we must enter the kingdom* of heaven. And as for the unwelcome event that's about to happen, don't be upset by it at all, but treat it instead as something that's extremely helpful to you. For the things that we witness are understood by human beings in one way, but are planned by God in another."

3 Τοιαύτην τὴν κατήχησιν αὐτοῖς ποιησάμενος, ἀπορίαν καὶ φροντίδα πολλὴν ἐνεποίησε περὶ οὗ προεῖπε συμβήσεσθαι. Περιβαλόμενος δὲ τὸ ἱμάτιον καὶ τὸν μανδύαν, ἔτι δὲ καὶ τὸ ἱερώτατον κουκούλιον τοῦ μακαριωτάτου αὐτοῦ πατρὸς τοῦ Μαλεΐνου, ἅπερ εἴθιστο περιβάλλεσθαι ἐν ταῖς τῶν μεγάλων καὶ δεσποτικῶν ἑορτῶν ἡμέραις (ὅτε δηλονότι μετελάμβανε τῶν ἁγίων τοῦ Χριστοῦ μυστηρίων), καὶ φαιδρὸν καὶ χάριεν δείξας τὸ πρόσωπον, ἐξένισε πάντας ἐπὶ τῷ ἀσυνήθει τούτῳ θεάματι.

66

Ἔνδον δὲ καὶ τῆς κέλλης αὐτοῦ γενόμενος καὶ εὐξάμενος ἐπιπολὺ καὶ ἑτέρους ἓξ ἀδελφοὺς συμπαραλαβὼν ἑαυτῷ, ἐπὶ τὸ ἔργον ἀνῆλθον. Τὸ δὲ ἅμα τῷ αὐτοὺς ἀνελθεῖν (ὢ πικρᾶς καὶ δεινῆς ἀνελεύσεως! Ὦ ὑπακοῆς καθαρᾶς τῶν συναναβάντων αὐτῷ!) συγκατέσπασεν αὐτίκα καὶ συγκατήνεγκεν ἅπαντας. Ἀλλ᾽ οἱ μὲν πέντε αὔθωρον τὰς ψυχὰς τῷ Θεῷ παρέθεντο· ὁ δέ γε πατὴρ καὶ εἷς ἀδελφός, Δανιὴλ ὁ οἰκοδόμος, ζῶντες τῇ ὕλῃ ἐναπελείφθησαν, ὡς καὶ τὸν πατέρα ἐξακούεσθαι παρὰ πάντων μέχρι τριῶν ὡρῶν ἢ καὶ πλεῖον κράζοντα τὸ "Κύριε, Ἰησοῦ Χριστέ, βοήθει μοι· δόξα σοι, ὁ Θεός."

2 Θορύβου δὲ γενομένου αὐτίκα καὶ τῶν ἀδελφῶν πάντων συναθροισθέντων καὶ χερσὶ καὶ ποσὶ καὶ ὄνυξιν,

This catechetical instruction caused anxiety and much 3
concern about the event that he predicted would happen.
He put on his outer garment and cloak, as well as the most
holy cowl of his most blessed father Maleinos, which he
used to wear on great dominical feast days (when he partook
of the holy mysteries of Christ), and, with a bright and
cheerful countenance, he astonished everyone with this unaccustomed sight.

Chapter 66

He went into his cell and prayed for a long time, and
then took six other monks with him and they climbed up to
the construction site. But while they were climbing up (oh,
bitter and terrible ascent! Oh, the pure obedience of those
who climbed up with him!), all of a sudden the scaffolding
collapsed and brought them all tumbling down. Five of them
immediately delivered their souls to God; but the father and
one brother, Daniel, the mason, were left still alive amid the
debris, so that everyone could hear the father calling out for
three hours or more, "Lord, Jesus Christ, help me; glory be
to Thee, O God."

Immediately there was a commotion and all the brethren 2
gathered around, digging with their hands and feet and

ὡς ὁ λόγος, ὀρυσσόντων καὶ διὰ τῶν παρατυχόντων ὀργάνων ἐκφορούντων τὴν ὕλην καὶ δάκρυσι ταύτην κιρνώντων καὶ ὀλοφυρομένων καὶ θρήνοις κοπτομένων, εὗρον τὸν πατέρα ἐν Κυρίῳ ἤδη τελειωθέντα καὶ τὴν ἱερὰν μὲν κεφαλὴν κάτω ἔχοντα ἐγγίζουσαν τῷ ἁγίῳ συνθρόνῳ, τὰς δὲ χεῖρας σταυροειδῶς ἐσχηματισμένας καὶ τοὺς πόδας δὲ ὑψοῦ ὡς πρὸς οὐρανὸν βαδιοῦντας, σῶον μέντοι καὶ ὑγιῆ, τοῦ δεξιοῦ αὐτῷ ποδὸς μόνον ἐπιξεσθέντος ὑφ᾽ ὦν παρελήφθη ξύλων.

3　Ἄραντες τοίνυν αὐτὸν ἐκεῖθεν καὶ τῇ κλίνῃ ἐπιθέντες, τὸν ὀδυρμὸν ἀνενέωσαν καὶ δακρύειν ἀπήρχοντο ἅπαντες, τὸν κυβερνήτην ζημιούμενοι, τὸν ἰατρὸν ἀφαιρούμενοι, τοῦ παιδαγωγοῦντος στερούμενοι, καὶ ἑαυτοὺς ταλανίζοντες ὅτι δι᾽ αὐτοὺς ὁ δίκαιος πέπονθε θάνατον τὸν ἁγίοις ἀνάξιον· ἀλλὰ τοῦτον καὶ λίαν ἄξιον οἶδα τῆς ἐκείνου ψυχῆς.

4　Ἐνταῦθα γὰρ τὸν ἀθλοθέτην αὐτοῦ Χριστὸν ἐμιμήσατο, τὸν ἑκουσίως θανατωθέντα ὑπὲρ τῶν ἑκουσίως ταῖς ἁμαρτίαις νεκρωθέντων. Τὸ δὲ τοιοῦτον τέλος οὐ μόνον ἐν τῇ κατηχήσει ἐπεσημήνατο, ἀλλὰ καὶ τῷ μοναχῷ Ἀντωνίῳ τῷ οἰκειοτάτῳ αὐτοῦ μαθητῇ προεῖπε φήσας· "Τὴν προκειμένην ὁδὸν ἐπὶ τὴν βασιλεύουσαν τῆς ἐπικειμένης ἡμῖν διακονίας, Ἀντώνιε, σὲ δέον ποιῆσαι ἐξ ἀνάγκης· ἡμᾶς γὰρ οὐκέτι λοιπὸν δοκεῖ τῷ Θεῷ βασιλέα θεάσασθαι."

fingernails, as the saying goes, and carrying away the debris with any handy implements, mixing with it their tears, wailing aloud, and beating their breasts with lamentations. They found the father already deceased in the Lord, with his holy head upside down near the holy *synthronon,* his arms arranged in the form of a cross, and his feet up high as if he were walking toward heaven; he was intact and unscathed, except that his right leg was scraped by the wooden beams by which he had been brought down.

So they lifted him up from there and laid him on the bier, 3 and they all renewed their lamentation and began to weep, saying that they had lost their steersman, had been separated from their physician, and deprived of their teacher. They thought themselves unfortunate because for their sake the righteous one had suffered a death unworthy of the saints, but I know that it was indeed most worthy of his soul.

For here he imitated Christ, his judge in the contest, who 4 was of His own accord put to death for the sake of those who of their own accord gave themselves to death through their sins. Not only did he allude to such a death in his catechetical teaching, but he also foretold it to the monk Antony, his closest disciple, saying, "Antony, you will of necessity have to make the upcoming journey to the imperial city for our pressing business, for it is God's will that I should not see the emperor again."

67

Ἐπεὶ δὲ καὶ τριήμερον καιρὸν προέκειτο ἄταφος (ἀνέμενε γὰρ τὴν παρὰ πάντων ὀφειλομένην αὐτῷ ἐπιτάφιον ὑμνῳδίαν), ἀναλλοίωτος ἦν, οὐκ ὄγκον, οὐ μελανίαν, οὐκ ἀηδίαν φέρων. Ἡ δὲ τοῦ Ὄρους γερουσία τὴν κοινὴν ταύτην συμφορὰν μαθοῦσα καὶ ταραχθεῖσα ἐπὶ τῷ πάθει, ἀπήντησαν διὰ τριῶν ἡμερῶν, ὥστε τὴν ἐπιτάφιον αὐτῷ ᾇσαι ᾠδήν. Πάντων δὲ παρισταμένων καὶ ᾀδόντων, γέρων τις ὁρᾷ τὸν ἱερώτατον νεκρὸν τοῦ πατρὸς αἷμα σταλά-ζοντα ἀπὸ τοῦ τραυματισθέντος ἐκείνου ποδός, καὶ τὸ θαῦμα ὡς μέγα καὶ ὑπερφυέστατον. Τίς γὰρ νεκρὸς καὶ ταῦτα τριήμερος αἵματος ῥανίδας ἐστάλαξε πώποτε; Τοῦτο γὰρ ἐπὶ μόνου τοῦ ἐμοῦ Χριστοῦ γέγονεν. Οὐ μόνον δὲ τοῦτο, ἀλλὰ καὶ τὸ πρόσωπον αὐτοῦ ἐδοξάσθη αὐτῇ τῇ ὥρᾳ καὶ γέγονεν ὡσεὶ χιών.

2 Ὁ γέρων οὖν ἐγκύψας τῷ ἱερωτάτῳ ποδὶ καὶ ἰδὼν τὸ τραῦμα ὅθεν τὸ αἷμα ἐπήγαζε, καὶ ἐκμάξας αὐτὸ διὰ τοῦ ἐγχειριδίου οὗ ἐπεφέρετο, πηγὴν εὐθὺς ἀπὸ σταγόνος ἑώρα, καὶ αὐτίκα πάντες ἠρύοντο καὶ ἐχρίοντο εἰς ψυχῶν καὶ σωμάτων ἴασιν. Ἔνθέν τοι καὶ τὴν ἐπιτάφιον ὑμνῳδίαν αὐτῷ ἀποφλήσαντες μετὰ πολλῆς τῆς φαιδρότητος, ἔκρυ-ψαν ὑπὸ γῆν τὸ πολύαθλον ἐκεῖνο σῶμα καὶ σκεῦος τοῦ πνεύματος.

Chapter 67

During the three days that he was laid out unburied (for he was awaiting the funeral service that was owed to him by all), he remained unaltered in appearance, suffering neither any distention, nor discoloration, nor foul odor. When the assembly of elders of the Mountain learned that he had met our common fate, they were distressed by this event and came over a period of three days to sing his funeral hymns. When everyone had arrived and sung the hymns, one elder saw the father's most holy corpse dripping blood from his injured leg. What a great and most extraordinary miracle! For what corpse ever dripped drops of blood, especially after three days? For this happened only to my Christ. And this was not all, but also his face was glorified at that time and was like snow.

So, when the elder looked closely at that most holy leg 2 and saw the wound from which the blood was flowing, he wiped it off with a handkerchief he was carrying, and straightaway saw a fountain of blood instead of a drop; and everyone immediately drew some of it for themselves and anointed themselves for the healing of their souls and bodies. Then, after they had paid their respects to him with a splendid funeral service, they laid in the earth that sorely tried body and spiritual vessel.

68

Τῶν μέντοι πέντε ἀδελφῶν τὰ σώματα ἐκφορήσαντες συντετριμμένα καὶ κατηλεσμένα, ἐξήγαγον ζῶντα τὸν μοναχὸν Δανιὴλ καὶ οἰκοδόμον, τραυματισθέντα καὶ αὐτὸν οὐ μετρίως· ὅστις, ἀνὴρ τυγχάνων τιμιώτατος καὶ πνευματικώτατος, ὄψεως νυκτερινῆς ἠξιώθη περὶ τοῦ τοιούτου πάθους. Ἔτι γὰρ οἰκοδομῶν τῷ καλλιγράφῳ Ἰωάννῃ τὰ προσταχθέντα αὐτῷ κελλία παρὰ τοῦ πατρός, ἠκούετο παρ᾽ αὐτοῦ στενάζων βύθιον καὶ οἰκτρόν τινα στεναγμόν, καὶ τὴν αἰτίαν ἐρωτηθεὶς παρὰ τοῦ Ἰωάννου, τὴν ὄψιν ἐξηγεῖτο.

2   "Ἑώρων γάρ," φησι, "καὶ ἰδού τις παρὰ βασιλέως στελλόμενος ἐκάλει τὸν πατέρα, καὶ αὐτίκα ἐξελθὼν οὗτος τῆς Λαύρας ἠκολούθει τῷ σταλέντι μετὰ καὶ ἑτέρων ἓξ ἀδελφῶν, ἀφ᾽ ὧν εἷς ὑπῆρχον κἀγώ. Ὡς οὖν προσηγγίσαμεν τῇ πύλῃ δι᾽ ἧς ἐμέλλομεν εἰσελθεῖν πρὸς τὸν βασιλέα, αὐτὸς μὲν ἅμα τοῖς πέντε εἰσῆλθεν εἰς τὸ παλάτιον, ἐγὼ δὲ ἔξω ἀπολειφθεὶς ἐθρήνουν σφόδρα καὶ γοερῶς ἔκραζον· ὁ γὰρ τοῦ πατρὸς χωρισμὸς καὶ ἡ στέρησις τῆς μετ᾽ αὐτοῦ εἰσελεύσεως ἐξέπινέ μου τὸ αἷμα [see Job 6:4] καὶ τὸν μυελὸν ἐξέτηκεν. Ἤκουσα δέ τινος ἔνδοθεν λέγοντος ὡς ‘εἰς κενόν σοι πᾶς θρῆνος, ἄνθρωπε, καὶ ἄβατά σοι καὶ ἀθέατα πάντῃ τὰ ἐνταῦθα εἰς τὸ παντελές, εἰ μὴ χαρίσει σοι τὴν εἴσελευσιν ἐκεῖνος μεθ᾽ οὗ παραγέγονας.'

3   "Ὡς δὲ πάλιν ὠλοφυρόμην καὶ θρῆνον ἐπὶ θρῆνον προσετίθουν, ἰδοὺ καὶ ὁ πατήρ, τὸ γλυκὺ καὶ φαιδρὸν

Chapter 68

After they had removed the crushed and bruised bodies of the five brethren, they brought out the monk Daniel, the mason, who was alive, but seriously injured. He was a most venerable and spiritual man who had been deemed worthy of a nocturnal vision about the accident. For while he was building the cells that the father had ordered for the calligrapher John, John heard Daniel uttering a deep and piteous groan. When John asked him the reason, he described his vision.

"I was having a vision," he said, "and, lo and behold, 2 someone who'd been sent by the emperor was summoning the father. He went straight out of the Lavra and followed the emissary along with six other brethren, of whom I was one. When we reached the doorway through which we were supposed to enter for our audience with the emperor, Athanasios went into the palace together with the five monks, but I was left outside, bitterly lamenting and crying out miserably. For separation from the father and being refused entrance alongside him *drank up my blood* and *melted my marrow*. And I heard someone inside say, 'Mister, there's no point in all your complaining. Everything in here is totally off limits and secret, unless the man you came with gives you permission to come in.'

"When I began to wail loudly again and lamented over 3 and over, lo and behold, *the father, sweet and* gleaming *in both*

337

πρᾶγμα καὶ ὄνομα, καὶ λαβόμενός μου τῆς δεξιᾶς εἰσήγαγέ με εἰς τὸν βασιλέα καὶ ἠξιώθην τοῦτον ἰδεῖν καὶ προσκυνῆσαι." Ταῦτα τοῦ οἰκοδόμου ἰδόντος, γέγονε καὶ ἡ ἔκβασις· εἰσῆλθε γὰρ εἰς τὴν τῶν οὐρανῶν βασιλείαν ὁ πατὴρ καὶ οἱ πέντε ἀδελφοὶ καὶ μετ᾽ ὀλίγον σὺν τούτοις καὶ ὁ οἰκοδόμος.

69

Οὕτω τοίνυν τῆς ποίμνης ἀπορφανισθείσης τοῦ μεγάλου πατρός, καὶ τοῦ μοναχοῦ Ἀντωνίου ἐν τῇ βασιλευούσῃ ἀποδημοῦντος διὰ τὴν ἀναγκαίαν ἐκείνην διακονίαν τῇ μονῇ, ἀνήρχοντο ἐπὶ τὴν μεγαλόπολιν οἱ ἀδελφοὶ καταγαγεῖν αὐτὸν καὶ καθηγούμενον ἐπιστῆσαι τῇ Λαύρᾳ κατὰ τὴν τοῦ μεγάλου διάταξιν· καὶ ἐν τῷ ἀνέρχεσθαι προσώρμισαν τοῖς τοῦ Γάνου μέρεσιν. Ἦν δέ τις ἐκεῖσε ποιμὴν υἱὸν ἕνα ἔχων καὶ τοῦτον ἤδη ὑπὸ τῆς κυνάγχης ἀφαιρούμενος, ἐφ᾽ ᾧ καὶ δακρύων ἦν καὶ θρηνῶν καὶ κοπτόμενος. Ἰδὼν δὲ τοὺς μοναχούς, ἐφιλοξένησε τούτους ἐν ᾧ εἶχε γάλακτι· οἵτινες καὶ τὴν ἐν τοσούτῳ πένθει προαίρεσιν αὐτοῦ θαυμάσαντες καὶ ἀποδεξάμενοι καὶ κατελεήσαντες, ἀπῆλθον ἰδεῖν καὶ τὸν ὑπὸ τῆς κυνάγχης πνιγόμενον υἱὸν αὐτοῦ. Ἐπεὶ δὲ εἶδον αὐτόν, εἷς τούτων, ὁ μοναχὸς Συμεών, ἐγχείριόν τι ἐξενεγκὼν αἵματι τοῦ πατρὸς βεβαμμένον, περιέθηκε τοῦτο τῷ τοῦ παιδὸς

reality and name, took me by my right hand and led me in to the emperor, and I was thought worthy to see him and prostrate myself before him." And what the mason saw did indeed come to pass; for the father and the five brethren entered into the kingdom of heaven, and the mason joined them a little while later.

Chapter 69

Since the flock was thus orphaned of its great father, and the monk Antony was away in the imperial city on account of that urgent business for the monastery, the brethren went up to the great city to bring him back and install him as superior of the Lavra in accordance with the great one's instructions. While they were en route, they anchored in the region of Mount Ganos. There was a shepherd there who had one son, whom he was about to lose to the disease of quinsy, and he was weeping for him and lamenting and striking himself. When he saw the monks, he offered them some of the milk that he had as an act of hospitality. They were amazed at his attitude in the midst of such great grief and, accepting his offer and taking pity on him, went off with him to see his son who was choking to death with croup. When they saw the boy, one of them, the monk Symeon, took out a handkerchief dipped in the father's blood, and placed it on the child's neck. Immediately the child slept

τραχήλῳ, καὶ παραυτίκα ὕπνωσε τὸ παιδίον δι᾽ ὅλης νυκτός, καὶ ἅμα πρωῒ ὑγιὲς ὡρᾶτο καὶ τροφῆς μετελάμβανε.

70

Προσθετέον τοῖς εἰρημένοις καὶ ἑτέρων τινῶν θαυμάτων ἐκ πολλῶν ὀλίγα διηγήματα, δι᾽ ὧν ὁ Θεὸς ἐδόξασε καὶ μετὰ θάνατον τὸν αὐτοῦ θεράποντα Ἀθανάσιον. Μοναχός τις, ἀπὸ Ὡρεοῦ ὁρμώμενος, πονηρῷ πνεύματι κατάσχετος γεγονὼς καὶ ἄκων τῇ παραφροσύνῃ συνελαθεὶς ἐνταῦθα παραγέγονε. Προσπελάσας οὖν τῇ ἱερᾷ σορῷ τοῦ πατρὸς καὶ ἔλαιον ἀρυσάμενος ἐκ τῶν προσκαιομένων ἐν αὐτῇ καὶ ἐπιχρίσας ἑαυτόν, ἤρξατο ἐνεργεῖσθαι καὶ σπαράττεσθαι ὑπὸ τοῦ ἀκαθάρτου καὶ πονηροῦ πνεύματος· μετὰ ταῦτα ἤμεσεν ὥσπέρ τινα ζωΰφια μετὰ αἵματος καὶ εὐθὺς ἀπηλλάγη τοῦ δεινοῦ καὶ φθονεροῦ δαίμονος. Τριάκοντα δὲ μετὰ τὴν ἴασιν ἐν τῇ Λαύρᾳ προσκαρτερήσας ἡμέρας καὶ μηκέτι ἐνοχληθεὶς ὑπὸ τοῦ τυραννήσαντος αὐτὸν ἀγρίου καὶ πονηροῦ πνεύματος, ὡς ἤδη τελείαν τὴν πληροφορίαν σχὼν τῆς ἰδίας ἐπισκέψεως, ἀνεχώρησε χαίρων καὶ αἰνῶν καὶ δοξάζων τὸν Θεὸν τὸν δόντα τοιαύτην χάριν τῷ ὁσίῳ πατρί.

through the whole night, and by morning was seen to be well and partaking of food.

Chapter 70

I should add to those I have already recounted a few tales from the many other miracles by which God glorified His servant Athanasios even after death. A monk who came from Oreon was afflicted by a wicked spirit, and, driven involuntarily by his madness, arrived here at the Lavra. He approached the father's holy tomb and, taking oil from the lamps that were burning there and anointing himself, he began to be afflicted by that impure and wicked spirit and suffer convulsions. Then he vomited something like tiny insects and blood and was immediately delivered from the terrible and envious demon. He remained in the Lavra for thirty days after his cure and was no longer troubled by the cruel and wicked spirit that had tyrannized him. As he now had full satisfaction from his visit, he departed, rejoicing and praising and glorifying God who had granted such grace to the holy father.

71

Εὐστράτιος ὁ μετὰ τὴν πρὸς Κύριον ἐκδημίαν τοῦ πατρὸς τὰς ἡνίας τῆς καθ' ἡμᾶς εὐαγεστάτης Λαύρας προσβραχὺ διαδεξάμενος, καὶ δι' εὐλάβειαν ἐμφρόνως ὡς τάχιστα τὸ ταύτης βάρος ἀποσεισάμενος, ἔτι περιόντος τοῦ πατρός, ἐν τῇ νήσῳ τῶν Νέων διακονῶν καὶ τὰ ὑπὲρ τῆς μονῆς πονούμενος, ῥεύματος καταφορᾷ τοὺς νεφροὺς δεινῶς ἐπλήγη. Ἐκ τούτου οὖν τὸ προχωροῦν ὕδωρ ἐξ αὐτοῦ ἐναλλαγὴν ἐδέξατο, καὶ ἀντὶ τῶν κατὰ φύσιν οὔρων αἷμα μονοειδὲς ἐξ αὐτοῦ μετ' ὀδύνης ὅτι πλείστης ἀπέρρει.

2   Τοῦτο μαθὼν ὁ πατὴρ καὶ μέσην ὀδυνηθεὶς τὴν καρδίαν ἐπὶ τῷ δυσαχθεῖ τοῦ πάθους καὶ βαρυτάτῳ, δηλοῖ αὐτῷ ἀνελθεῖν ἐν τῇ πόλει καὶ περιοδευθῆναι. Ὁ δὲ τοῖς πόνοις νυττόμενος ὡς ὑπὸ κέντρων καὶ τῆς ὑγείας ἱμειρόμενος, ἀνῆλθε προσδοκῶν ἐπιτυχεῖν ἰάσεως. Ὡς δὲ τοῖς πρώτοις τῶν ἰατρῶν ἐντυχὼν καὶ πλεῖστα παρ' αὐτῶν περιοδευθεὶς οὐδεμίαν εὗρεν ἐξ αὐτῶν τὴν ὠφέλειαν, μᾶλλον δὲ καὶ προσέθεντο αὐτῷ βλάβην οὐ τὴν τυχοῦσαν, ὑπέστρεψεν ἐν τῇ νήσῳ, μετὰ πλείονος τοῦ πόνου ἐπιφερόμενος τὸ πάθος καὶ ἐλεεινῶς κατατρυχόμενος ὑπ' αὐτοῦ ἐπὶ χρόνοις ἑπτά.

3   Ὡς δὲ ἀνωτέρω εἴρηται ὅτι μετὰ τὴν ἀποβίωσιν τοῦ πατρὸς προεχειρίσθη εἰς προεστῶτα, ἔχων πίστιν πολλὴν πρὸς τὸν πατέρα, ἠντιβόλει, καθικέτευεν, ἐδυσώπει αὐτὸν ὅπως ἴασιν εὕρῃ τοῦ δεινοτάτου πάθους. Καὶ δὴ μιᾷ τῶν νυκτῶν ἔδοξεν ὁρᾶν καθ' ὕπνους ἐλθόντα τὸν πατέρα

Chapter 71

After the father's departure to the Lord, Eustratios took over for a short time the reins of our most holy Lavra, but very quickly and sensibly shook off this burden on account of his piety. But while the father was still alive, and Eustratios was serving on the island of the Neoi and laboring on the monastery's behalf, he was severely afflicted by a flux in the kidneys. As a result the urine he excreted underwent a change in character, and instead of normal urine he was passing pure blood, accompanied by terrible pain.

When the father learned this, he was deeply troubled at 2 the painfulness and severity of the illness, and he told Eustratios to sail up to the city for medical treatment. And so, stabbed with pains as if by sharp spikes and yearning for health, he went up to the city, expecting to find a cure. But although he consulted with the leading physicians and received extensive treatment from them, he derived no benefit from them, but rather they significantly increased his suffering. So he returned to the island, enduring his affliction with even greater pain and being pitifully oppressed by it for seven years.

But when, as has been said above, he was appointed supe- 3 rior after the father's death, since he had much faith in the father, he entreated, he supplicated, he implored him that he might find a cure from this most terrible affliction. And then one night in his sleep he seemed to see the father

μετά τινων τιμίων γερόντων καὶ αὐτῶν τυγχανόντων μοναχῶν, προτρεπόμενόν τε αὐτοὺς δῆθεν εἰσελθεῖν ἐν τῇ
τραπέζῃ. Ὡς δὲ μετὰ τοῦ πατρὸς συνεισῆλθε καὶ ὁ μοναχὸς Εὐστράτιος, οἷα δὴ προεστὼς καὶ καθηγούμενος,
ὁρᾷ κείμενον ἐν τῇ τραπέζῃ ποτήριον πλῆρες ὕδατος καὶ
ῥόδα ἐπὶ πίνακος. Λαβὼν οὖν ὁ πατὴρ τῶν ῥόδων καὶ
ἐμβαλὼν τῷ ποτηρίῳ, δέδωκε τῷ Εὐστρατίῳ πιεῖν· ὁ δὲ
δεδιττόμενος καὶ ὑπονοῶν μή τι τῶν συνήθων βοηθη-
μάτων ἢ φαρμάκων ἐστίν, ἀνένευε τοῦ λαβεῖν καὶ πιεῖν. Ὁ
δὲ πατήρ φησι· "Μὴ φοβοῦ, ἀλλὰ λαβὼν πίε· εἰς ὑγείαν
γάρ σοι γενήσεται."

4   Λαβὼν τοίνυν καὶ πιὼν εὐθὺς διυπνίσθη, καὶ ἐξελθὼν
πρὸς ὕδωρ καὶ διερευνήσας, βλέπει αὐθωρὸν ὅτι τὰ οὖρα
αὐτοῦ πρὸς τὸ κατὰ φύσιν ἦλθον. Σιωπήσας οὖν κατ᾽
ἐκείνην τὴν ὥραν, μετὰ τὴν συμπλήρωσιν τοῦ ὀρθρινοῦ
κανόνος ἀνεκήρυξε πᾶσι τὰ μεγαλεῖα τοῦ Θεοῦ, ἃ διὰ τῆς
τοῦ πατρὸς ἐπισκοπῆς καὶ θερμῆς ἀντιλήψεως εἰργάσατο
εἰς αὐτόν.

72

Χρεία τις γέγονεν ἀνελθεῖν πρὸς Σμύρναν ἀδελφούς.
Τῇ οὖν εὐχῇ τοῦ πατρὸς ἡμῶν οὐρίου πνεύματος ἐπι-
τυχόντες, αἰσίως τε πάνυ εὐπλοήσαντες, προσώρμισαν τῷ
λιμένι καὶ τὴν ἐγχειρισθεῖσαν αὐτοῖς δουλείαν διήνυον

coming with some venerable old men, who were also monks, and ordering them to go into the refectory. When the monk Eustratios also went in along with the father, as he was superior and abbot, he saw a cup full of water and a plate of roses sitting on the table. Then the father took the roses and, putting them in the cup, gave it to Eustratios to drink. But he was afraid and suspected that it was not a usual medicament or drug, and refused to take the cup and drink from it. And the father said, "Don't be afraid, but take it and drink; for you'll be restored to health."

Then, after taking it and drinking it, Eustratios immediately woke up. When he went out to urinate and inspected his urine, he saw immediately that it had returned to its normal state. He said nothing at the time, but at the end of the matins hymns he announced to everyone the greatness of God which was worked in him through the visitation and fervent assistance of the father.

4

Chapter 72

Some of the brethren had to go to Smyrna. After opportunely attaining a favorable wind through our father's prayer and making a very good voyage, they cast anchor in the harbor and accomplished without difficulty the business they

ἀπροσκόπως. Συνέτυχον δέ τινι φιλοχρίστῳ, ὃς καὶ ἠξίωσεν αὐτοὺς ἀνελθεῖν εἰς τὸν οἶκον αὐτοῦ τοῦ φαγεῖν ἄρτον·
ὡς δὲ ἀνῆλθον, βλέπουσι πολλὴν φωταγωγίαν καὶ θυμιαμάτων πλῆθος καὶ τὴν γυναῖκα τοῦ αὐτοὺς κεκληκότος
περὶ πολλοῦ ποιουμένην ἄσβεστον τηρεῖσθαι τὴν φωταύ-
γειαν καὶ ἀκατάπαυστον τὴν τοῦ θυμιάματος ἀναπέμπε-
σθαι εὐωδίαν. Ὡς οὖν εἶδον ταῦτα ἐν ἡμέρᾳ μέσῃ πιστῶς
ἐκτελούμενα, οὐκ ἔχοντες ὅπως κρίνωσι τὸ ὁρώμενον,
ἠρώτησαν τοὺς τοῦ οἴκου δεσπότας, "Τίς ἡ τοσαύτη ἔκ-
καυσις," λέγοντες, "τῶν τε κηρῶν καὶ θυμιαμάτων καὶ τοῦ
ἐλαίου;"

2   Ἡ δὲ γυνή φησιν· "Ἐγώ, πατέρες, ἀδελφὴν ἔχω συνοι-
κοῦσαν ἀνδρί· αὕτη αἱμόρρους γεγονυῖα, χρόνον ἐφ᾽
ἱκανὸν κλινοπετὴς ὑπὸ τοῦ ὀλεθρίου τούτου γέγονε
πάθους. Ἔτυχε δέ τινα κατὰ σύμβασιν ἐν τῷ οἴκῳ αὐτῆς
ὑποδέξασθαι μοναχόν· ἰδὼν δὲ αὐτὴν ἐκεῖνος οὕτως ὀδυ-
νωμένην καὶ δεινῶς βασανιζομένην, ἐλεήσας καὶ συμ-
παθήσας αὐτῇ τῆς συμφορᾶς, ἠρώτησε τὴν αἰτίαν, καὶ
μαθὼν ἔφη· Ἔχω αἷμα ἐν ῥακίῳ τοῦ ἁγίου Ἀθανασίου τοῦ
ἐν τῷ Ἄθῳ· εἰ θέλεις, ἀπομυρίσω ἐν ὕδατι τὸ ἡμαγμένον
ῥάκος, καὶ πιοῦσα εὑρήσεις βοήθειαν.᾽

3   Ἡ δὲ ἀσθενὴς ἅμα τῷ ἀκοῦσαι μετὰ δακρύων καθικέτευε τοῦτο ὡς τάχιστα γενέσθαι. Ἑτοιμάσαντος δὲ τοῦ
μοναχοῦ τὸ πόμα καθὼς ἔδει, κἀκείνης μετὰ πίστεως ζε-
ούσης καὶ πολλῶν δακρύων ἐπιβοωμένης τὸ ῾Ἅγιε Ἀθανάσιε, βοήθει μοι,᾽ λαβούσης τε τὸ ἔκπωμα καὶ χανδὸν
ἐκπιούσης τῇ τῆς ὑγείας ἐπιθυμίᾳ καὶ τῇ ἐλπίδι, εὐθὺς
ἔγνω ἑαυτὴν ἀπολυθεῖσαν τῆς μάστιγος. Τοῦτο οὖν τὸ

had been assigned. They happened to meet a devout Christian, who invited them to come to his home for a meal; when they arrived, they saw many lights and an abundance of incense and observed that their host's wife was devoting much attention to keeping the lamps lit and assuring that the fragrance of the incense rose up continually. When they saw her doing this with much faith in the middle of the day, they were unsure what to make of what they were seeing, and asked the householders, "Why so much burning of candles and incense and oil?"

The wife replied, "Fathers, I have a married sister; she 2 was afflicted with a hemorrhage, and was bedridden for a long time due to this life-threatening malady. It so happened that by coincidence she welcomed a monk into her house; and when he saw her in such pain and suffering so terribly, he took pity on her and felt sympathy for her affliction. He asked her about the cause of her illness and, when he learned it, he said, 'I have some blood of the holy Athanasios of Athos on a cloth; if you like, I will dip the bloodstained cloth in water and, when you drink it, you will find relief.'

"As soon as my ailing sister heard this, she begged him 3 tearfully to do so as quickly as possible. After the monk had properly prepared the potion, she made the invocation, 'Holy Athanasios, help me,' with ardent faith and many tears. Then she took the potion and swallowed it in one gulp in the desire for and hope of restored health. Immediately, she realized that she had been delivered from the scourge of

παράδοξον θαῦμα καὶ ὑπὲρ φύσιν ἀνθρωπίνην διὰ τῶν αὐτῆς γραμμάτων πληροφορηθεῖσα ἄρτι, εὐχαριστοῦσα τῷ ἁγίῳ ποιῶ ταῦτα, ἅμα δὲ καὶ εὐχομένη ὅπως ὁ Θεὸς ἐλεήσῃ κἀμὲ δι᾽ αὐτοῦ."

73

Νεανίας τις δύο νόσους εἶχε μεγάλας, πενίαν ἐσχάτην καὶ ἐλεφαντίαν λέπραν, καὶ διὰ ταύτην τὴν νόσον ἐβδελύττοντο τοῦτον καὶ ἀπεδίωκον οἱ πλείους τῶν ἀνθρώπων, ὅσοι ἄσπλαγχνοι καὶ ἀπάνθρωποι ἦσαν καὶ θηριώδεις τὴν γνώμην, καὶ ἐκινδύνευεν ὁ ἄνθρωπος τῷ λιμῷ ἀπολέσθαι ἐκ τοῦ μισεῖσθαι καὶ ἀποδιώκεσθαι διὰ τὸ ἕλκος καὶ τὴν σηπεδόνα τῆς περικεχυμένης αὐτῷ λέπρας.

2   Οὗτος ἀκούσας τὰ ἐξαίσια θαύματα τοῦ μεγάλου θαυματουργοῦ Ἀθανασίου, ἔδραμεν ἐπὶ τὸ ἄμισθον ἰατρεῖον, καὶ ἐγγὺς γενόμενος τοῦ ἁγίου τάφου αὐτοῦ ἔκλινε τὰ γόνατα εἰς τὸ ἔδαφος, καὶ ἐπὶ πολλὴν ὥραν κείμενος ἱκέτευε τοῦτον μετὰ δακρύων καὶ στεναγμῶν μεγάλων καὶ τεταπεινωμένου πνεύματος, ταῦτα διαλεγόμενος πρὸς αὐτόν· "Ἐγὼ μέν, ὦ ἰσάγγελε πάτερ καὶ τοῦ Θεοῦ ἄνθρωπε, δύο ἀρρωστίας ἔχων μεγάλας, τὴν μὲν πενίαν ἄξιός εἰμι ἔχειν, ἵνα πάσχω καὶ παιδεύωμαι δι᾽ αὐτῆς· τὸν δὲ αἰσχρὸν χιτῶνα τῆς λέπρας μου, δέομαι καὶ παρακαλῶ, διάρρηξον καὶ ἔκδυσόν με τοῦτον καὶ ἴασαί με τῇ θερμῇ σου πρεσβείᾳ,

her affliction. So, since I've just been informed by her letter about this extraordinary, supernatural miracle, I'm doing this in thanksgiving to the saint, and I'm praying at the same time that God may also have mercy on me through him."

Chapter 73

A young man suffered from two great afflictions, extreme poverty and elephant leprosy. Because of this disease most people, who were heartless and inhumane and brutal in their attitude, were repulsed by him and shunned him. The man was thus in danger of perishing from starvation because he was despised and shunned on account of his sores and the putrefaction of the leprosy that had engulfed him.

When he heard about the extraordinary miracles of the great miracle worker Athanasios, he hurried to that medical facility where no payment was required and, when he drew near to his holy tomb, knelt on the ground. After lying there for a long time, he begged Athanasios with tears and great groans and a humble spirit, saying these words to him: "O father and man of God, equal of the angels, I have two great illnesses. I deserve to be afflicted by poverty so that I may suffer and be edified by it, but please, I beg you, tear off the shameful tunic of my leprosy, strip me of it and heal me

ὅτι οὐ φέρω τὴν τῶν ἀνθρώπων ἀποστροφὴν καὶ τὸ ὄνειδος." Τούτοις τοῖς ῥήμασιν ἐκδυσωπήσας τὸν μέγαν καὶ ἀπὸ τῆς κανδήλας αὐτοῦ ἔλαιον λαβὼν ἅγιον καὶ καταχρίσας ἑαυτὸν μετὰ πολλῆς πίστεως, τὴν πᾶσαν λεπίδα ἀπεδύσατο καὶ ὑγιὴς ὅλος γέγονεν.

74

Ἀνήρ τις Ἀθανάσιος, υἱὸν ἔχων ὡσεὶ ἐτῶν ὀκτώ, τοὺς ὀφθαλμοὺς μὲν ἀνεῳγμένους ἔχοντα, ἐστερημένους δὲ ὁράσεως, λαβὼν τοῦτον, ὥσπερ εἰς ἰατρεῖον κοινὸν τὴν ὑπὸ τοῦ ἁγίου ἐκτισμένην Λαύραν κατέλαβε, καὶ τῷ ξενοδοχείῳ παραμένων μετὰ τοῦ παιδὸς αὐτοῦ, τῇ ἁγίᾳ θήκῃ τοῦ μεγάλου πατρὸς καθεκάστην προσήρχετο, καὶ ἔλαιον ἅγιον ἀρυόμενος ἀπὸ τῆς κανδήλας τοῦ τάφου αὐτοῦ καὶ χρίων τοὺς ὀφθαλμοὺς τοῦ παιδὸς αὐτοῦ, παρεκάλει μετὰ δακρύων καὶ ἱκεσίας καὶ ῥημάτων ἐλεεινῶν, τοιαῦτα προσφθεγγόμενος· "Σὺ μέν, πάτερ ὁσιώτατε, ἔρωτα σαρκὸς μὴ γνωρίσας, ἀμύητος εἶ τῆς ἀγάπης τῆς φύσεως· ἐγὼ δὲ ὁ γεννήσας, τὴν περὶ τὸν παῖδα ἔμφυτον στοργὴν βαστάζων ἐν τῇ καρδίᾳ μου καὶ οὐκέτι φέρων ὁρᾶν μου τὸν παῖδα ἐλεεινὴν ζῶντα ζωὴν καὶ ὄνειδος παρὰ ἀνθρώπων ἔχοντα, δέομαι καὶ προσπίπτω τῇ ἀντιλήψει σου, ἵνα φωτίσῃς τοὺς αἰσθητοὺς ὀφθαλμοὺς τοῦ δυστυχοῦς καὶ μονογενοῦς μου παιδός."

through your fervent intercession, because I cannot endure people's aversion and scorn." After he had supplicated the great man with these words and taken holy oil from the lamp and anointed himself with much faith, he shed all his leprous scales and became completely healthy.

Chapter 74

A man called Athanasios had a son about eight years old, whose eyes were wide open, but who could not see. He took the boy and came to the Lavra built by the holy man as if to a public medical facility. While he was staying at the guesthouse with his child, he used to go every day to the great father's holy reliquary. He would draw holy oil from the lamp at the tomb and anoint his child's eyes, while calling on the holy man with tears and supplication and pitiful words, uttering words of this sort: "Most blessed father, because you did not know fleshly passion you are unfamiliar with natural love; but I, who have fathered this boy, carry in my heart innate affection for the child and can no longer bear to see him living a pitiful life and being scorned by people. I beg you and implore your help, that you may give light to the corporeal eyes of my unfortunate only child."

2 Ταῦτα λέγων καὶ ἀνενδότως ἐκδυσωπῶν τὸν ἅγιον ἄχρι καὶ μιᾶς ἑβδομάδος, ἔκαμψε καὶ οὗτος τὰ σπλάγχνα τοῦ συμπαθεστάτου πατρὸς καὶ ἀπέλαβε τὸν υἱὸν αὐτοῦ πεφωτισμένους ἔχοντα τοὺς ὀφθαλμούς· καὶ ἦν ἰδεῖν ἐπὶ τούτοις τὸ προφητικὸν ἐκεῖνο πληρούμενον λόγιον, πατέρα ἐπὶ τέκνῳ εὐφραινόμενον [see Ecclesiasticus 25:7].

75

Ὁ προειρημένος μοναχὸς Παῦλος ὁ κελλαρίτης μετὰ δέκατον ἔτος τῆς ἐκδημίας τοῦ πατρὸς παρεκινήθη ὑπὸ τοῦ δαίμονος καὶ προσέκρουσε τῷ καθηγουμένῳ (Θεόκτιστος δὲ οὗτος ἦν), καὶ μέχρις ἀντιλογίας αὐτῆς ἐχώρησε καὶ συγχώρησιν οὐκ ἠτήσατο. Καταλαβούσης δὲ τῆς ἑσπέρας, τῷ θυμῷ διεπρίετο, καὶ τὰ μὴ διαφέροντα αὐτῷ κατὰ διάνοιαν μελετῶν μόλις ὕπνωσε, καὶ ἔδοξε κατ' ὄναρ τὸν σημειοφόρον ἡμῶν ὁρᾶν πατέρα κατηχητικῶς προσδιαλεγόμενον τοῖς ἀδελφοῖς καί τινα τῶν ἀδελφῶν ἀντιλέγοντα αὐτῷ. Ὁ δὲ Παῦλος οἷα δῆθεν χαριζόμενος τῷ πατρί, ἅμα δὲ καὶ τὸ αἰδέσιμον αὐτῷ διαφυλάττων, ἤρξατο σκωπτικῶς ἐπιλέγειν τῷ ἀδελφῷ· "Πῶς σὺ τολμᾷς ἀντιλέγειν τῷ ἁγίῳ πατρί;" Ὁ δὲ ὅσιος ἡμῶν πατήρ, δριμὺ καὶ βλοσυρὸν αὐτῷ ἐνιδών, δέδωκεν αὐτῷ κόσσον κατὰ τῆς παρειᾶς αὐτοῦ, εἰπών· "Ναί, σὺ καλῶς ὑποτάσσῃ καὶ

As he said these words and implored the holy man un- ² ceasingly for an entire week, he softened the heart of the most compassionate father, and took his son away with eyes that could see the light; and in these people one could see fulfilled the words of the prophet, a father *that has joy in his child.*

Chapter 75

Ten years after the father's death, the aforementioned monk Paul the cellarer was incited by the Devil and had a falling out with the superior (this was Theoktistos), going so far as to contradict him and not seek his forgiveness. When evening came, Paul was still furious and, mulling over in his mind things that should have been of no importance to him, he fell asleep only with difficulty. In a dream he seemed to see our miracle-working father engaged in instructional discussion with the brethren and one of the brethren arguing with him. As if seeking to please the father, and at the same time pretending to show proper respect for him, Paul began to say mockingly to the brother, "How dare you contradict the holy father?" But our holy father gave him a fierce and grim look, and slapped him on the cheek, saying, "Yes indeed, you should be properly submissive and thus teach

δίδασκε ἑτέρους." Καὶ παρευθὺ γέγονεν αὐτοῦ ἡ δεξιὰ παρειὰ ὅλη τραῦμα ἕν, ἑλκώδη ὑγρότητα αὐθωρὸν ἀποστάζον.

2 Ὡς δὲ ἔξυπνος γέγονε καὶ τὸ παράδοξον τοῦ θαύματος τῇ πείρᾳ ἐπέγνω, κατέγνω εὐθὺς ἑαυτοῦ, καὶ προσελθὼν ἅμα πρωῒ τῷ καθηγεμόνι, προσέπεσέ τε τοῖς ποσὶν αὐτοῦ, τὴν συγχώρησιν ἐξαιτούμενος ὧν εἰς αὐτὸν ἐξ ἀφροσύνης ἐτόλμησε, καὶ τῆς φοβερᾶς ἐκείνης πληγῆς τε καὶ μάστιγος τὸ παράδοξον ἀπεκάλυψε. Τῆς μὲν οὖν συγχωρήσεως τῆς ἀπὸ τοῦ καθηγουμένου παραυτίκα τετύχηκε, τῆς δὲ ἰάσεως μόλις ἐπὶ τριάκοντα ἡμερῶν μετὰ στεναγμῶν καὶ δακρύων πολλῶν καθικετεύων τὸν σημειοφόρον ἡμῶν πατέρα ἠξιώθη.

76

Ὁ μοναχὸς Συμεὼν καὶ ὁ μοναχὸς Γεώργιος, ἀποστελλόμενοί ποτε διὰ πλοίου εἰς διακονίαν, προσώρμισαν τῷ λιμένι τῶν Πευκίων· φωνὰς δὲ γοερὰς καὶ ὀδυρμοὺς ἀκούοντες ἠρώτων τὴν αἰτίαν. Ναυτικοὶ δὲ παρόντες τὸν τοῦ συνναυτίλου θάνατον τοῦ πένθους ἔφασκον αἴτιον· "Ὀγδόην ἤδη ταύτην ἡμέραν ἀφώνου προκειμένου καὶ ὡς ἀπεγνωσμένου, θρηνοῦμεν ἐπ' αὐτῷ."

2 Ἠθέλησαν οὖν οἱ μοναχοὶ ὄψεσιν αὐταῖς ἰδεῖν τὸν νοσοῦντα. Ἀπελθόντες οὖν καὶ ἰδόντες αὐτὸν οὕτως ἔχοντα, ἤλγησαν καὶ αὐτοὶ τὴν ψυχήν, καὶ ὁ μὲν Γεώργιος

others." And straightaway his entire right cheek became one large sore, instantly oozing purulent fluid.

When Paul awoke, he realized the extraordinary charac- 2 ter of the miracle from what had happened to his cheek, and immediately condemned himself. As soon as day broke, he went to the superior and fell at his feet, begging forgiveness for the foolish remarks he had dared to make to him; and he revealed the miracle of that terrible lesion and affliction. He received the superior's forgiveness right away, but was deemed worthy of healing only after entreating our miracle-working father for thirty days with groans and copious tears.

Chapter 76

The monks Symeon and George were once dispatched by boat on business and anchored in the harbor of Peukia. When they heard piteous cries and lamentations, they asked the reason. Some sailors who were there said that the reason was their sorrow at the imminent death of their shipmate: "Since this is already the eighth day he's been laid out without speaking and, as he's not expected to live, we're mourning for him."

The monks then wanted to see the ailing man with their 2 own eyes. So they went off, and when they saw him in this condition, they were deeply grieved. George advised

συνεβούλευε τῷ Συμεὼν περιθεῖναι τῷ τραχήλῳ τοῦ θνήσκοντος τὸ ἡμαγμένον ῥάκος· ὁ δὲ Συμεὼν ἀνένευε, "μὴ καὶ γέλωτα ὄφλωμεν," λέγων, "τοῖς παροῦσιν." Ὁ δὲ Γεώργιος, ἀδίστακτον ἔχων τὴν εἰς τὸν ἅγιον πίστιν, παρεβιάσατο αὐτὸν περιάψαι τῷ τραχήλῳ τοῦ παρὰ μικρὸν νεκροῦ τὸ ῥηθὲν ῥάκος.

3   Ὡς δὲ τοῦτο γέγονε, τὰ ὅμοια τοῖς προλαβοῦσι καὶ ἐπ' αὐτῷ ἐτελεῖτο· οὕτως γὰρ αἰφνίδιος καὶ παράδοξος γέγονεν ἡ τούτου παντελὴς ὑγεία, ὡς δοκεῖν αὐτὸν ἐξ ὕπνου ἀναστῆναι καὶ τοῖς συμπλωτῆρσιν ἐπιμέμφεσθαι ὅτι μὴ τάχιον ἀποπλέουσι, τήν τε αἰτίαν τοῦ πένθους τὸν ἀδελφὸν αὐτοῦ πυνθάνεσθαι. Ἀλλὰ τοῦτο μὲν τοιοῦτον· ἐγὼ δὲ ἐφ' ἕτερον μεταβήσομαι τῶν εἰρημένων οὐκ ἔλαττον.

77

Πολίχνη τίς ἐστιν, Ἐρισὸς καλουμένη, ἔνθα καὶ μοναχοὺς καὶ μοναστήριον (ὃ καλοῦσι μετόχιον), ὑφ' ἑαυτὴν εἶχεν ἡ Λαύρα, οἷς καὶ μοναχός τις οἰκονόμος ἐτύγχανε, τὴν κλῆσιν Ἰωαννίκιος. Οὗτος ἀπέπλευσεν ἐπὶ Στρυμμόνα διακονίας τινὸς χάριν μετὰ καί τινων τοῦ μετοχίου ἀδελφῶν. Ἀπερχόμενοι δὲ ἤδη τῆς ἑσπέρας καταλαβούσης, ἐξῆλθον τοῦ πλοίου διαναπαύσασθαι καὶ βρώσεως μεταλαβεῖν· οἱ δὲ τότε τοῖς ἐκεῖσε μέρεσιν ἐπιχωριάζοντες βάρβαροι ἄφνω ἐπεισπεσόντες κατέσχον αὐτούς. Ὁ δὲ

Symeon to place the blood soaked cloth on the neck of the dying man; but Symeon refused, "so that we don't make ourselves a laughing stock for those who are there," he said. But George, who had unwavering faith in the holy man, forced Symeon to place the above-mentioned cloth around the neck of the man who was at death's door.

When this happened, the same thing occurred with him 3 as in the previous cases: for his health was so suddenly and miraculously completely restored, that he seemed to awaken from sleep and reproach his fellow sailors for not sailing away more quickly, and he asked his brother why he was grieving. But so much for this; I will now move on to *another miracle no lesser than those already described.*

Chapter 77

There is a small town called Erisos, where the Lavra had under its supervision monks and a monastery (what they call a *metochion*), and a monk named Ioannikios served as their steward. This man sailed off to the Strymon on business with some of the brethren of the *metochion*. In the course of their voyage, as dusk had already fallen, they disembarked from the boat to rest and eat some food; but the barbarous people who were then living in that region suddenly fell upon them and took them captive. But Ioannikios secretly

Ἰωαννίκιος λαθὼν αὐτοὺς ἔρριψε κατὰ τῆς θαλάσσης ὅπερ ἐπεφέρετο χρυσίον τῆς διακονίας χάριν, ἵνα μὴ πρόφασις αὐτοῖς θανάτου ὁ θανάτου ῥύεσθαι λεγόμενος γένηται.

2 Ἐκεῖνοι δὲ περιαγκωνίσαντες αὐτοὺς ὡς αἰχμαλώτους, πρὸς τὸν ἄρχοντα αὐτῶν ἀπήρχοντο, καὶ νυκτὸς μὲν δεδεμένους εἶχον αὐτούς, ἡμέρας δὲ ἔλυον οὐ διὰ φιλανθρωπίαν (πῶς γάρ, φύσις ὄντες βάρβαρος καὶ ἀπάνθρωπος;), ἀλλ᾽ ἵνα ταχέως τὴν ὁδὸν διανύωσιν. Ὡς οὖν αἱ χεῖρες αὐτῶν τῶν δεσμῶν ἀνείθησαν, τῷ μοναχῷ Ἰωαννικίῳ εὐθὺς ἐπῆλθε λογίσασθαι ὡς οὐκ ἀθεεὶ τοῦτο οἱ βάρβαροι ἔδρασαν· ἔπειτα καί τινα ἔννοιαν τῶν τοῦ μεγάλου θαυμάτων ἐλάμβανε· καὶ δὴ θάρσους πλησθεὶς καὶ τὴν τοῦ ἁγίου βοήθειαν ἐπικαλεσάμενος, μεγάλῃ τῇ φωνῇ ἀνεβόησεν· "Ἰδοὺ καὶ οἱ ἡμέτεροι!" Καὶ ἅμα τῇ βοῇ τὰς χεῖράς τε ἐκρότει καὶ πρὸς τοὺς ἑαυτοῦ δῆθεν ἀπέτρεχεν. Οἱ δὲ βάρβαροι, ἀθρόον δειλίας ἐμπλησθέντες καὶ τρόμου πολλοῦ, φυγάδες ἐφέροντο· οἱ δὲ περὶ Ἰωαννίκιον, ὡς εἶδον ταῦτα καὶ τοὺς βαρβάρους φεύγοντας ἀκρατῶς, καὶ αὐτοὶ κατόπιν αὐτοῦ ἔτρεχον καὶ πρὸς τὴν Λαύραν ἅμα πάντες ἐχώρουν, τοῦ μεγάλου θαύματος τούτου καὶ τῆς ἑαυτῶν κήρυκες σωτηρίας.

3 Καὶ τότε μὲν ηὐχαρίστησαν τῷ Θεῷ ἅπαντες· μικρὸν δὲ ὕστερον καὶ ἕτερον θαῦμα τῷ προλαβόντι συνήφθη· διακονίας γάρ τινος πρὸς ἀποδημίαν ἀδελφοὺς καλούσης, ἐγένετο τούτους κατὰ τοὺς τόπους ἐκείνους γενέσθαι, ἐν οἷς τὸ χρυσίον ἐρρίφη· συνέβη δὲ συνεῖναι τοῖς ἀδελφοῖς καί τινα τῶν τῷ Ἰωαννικίῳ τηνικαῦτα συνόντων, ὃς δὴ καὶ

threw into the sea the gold he was carrying for his business, so that what is said to save one from death might not be a pretext for their death.

The barbarians tied their hands behind their backs like 2 captives, and headed off toward their leader. They kept the monks bound at night, but removed their bonds during the day, not through any human compassion (for how would this be possible, since they were barbarian and inhumane by nature?), but so that they might accomplish their journey more quickly. When their hands were thus released from their bonds, it immediately occurred to the monk Ioannikios that the barbarians had not done this without divine intervention. He then called to mind the great man's miracles and, plucking up courage and calling upon the holy man's assistance, he yelled out in a loud voice, "Look, there are some of our men!" At the same time as he shouted, he clapped his hands and ran off as if toward his own people. The barbarians, who were suddenly filled with fear and much trembling, turned to flight; and when Ioannikios's companions saw this development and the barbarians in headlong flight, they also ran after him and all went to the Lavra together, as heralds of this great miracle and their own deliverance.

Then they all gave thanks to God. But a short time later 3 another miracle was added to the previous one. For when some business prompted the brethren to go on a journey, they chanced to be in the area where the gold had been thrown into the sea. It so happened that one of Ioannikios's companions on that previous trip was with the brethren,

τὸν τόπον ἐδείκνυε τοῖς ἀδελφοῖς, λέγων· "Ἐνταῦθα ὁ μοναχὸς Ἰωαννίκιος ἐπαφῆκε τὸ χρυσίον." Καὶ σὺν αὐτῷ
πάντες χαριεντιζόμενοι ἔφασκον· "Εἰ Θεοῦ διδόντος
εὕροιμεν τοῦτο, τότε ἂν ἀληθῶς ἔγνωμεν οἵας ὁ πατὴρ
ἡμῶν ἠξίωται χάριτος καὶ δυνάμεως."

4   Οὕτως εἶπον καὶ σὺν τῷ λόγῳ τὸν βυθὸν διηρεύνων,
καὶ δὴ πολύπους ἐν τῇ θαλάμῃ αὐτοῦ προεκάθητο· οἱ δὲ
ἄγκιστρον ἐπεζήτουν, τὸν πολύπουν ἀνάξοντες. Ὡς δὲ
τοῦτον ἀνείλκυσαν, ὡρᾶτο ξένον μυστήριον· ὁ γὰρ πολύπους ταῖς ἰδίαις πλεκτάναις τὸ χρυσίον ἐφείλκετο. Καὶ
τοῦτο μὲν οὕτως παραδόξως καὶ ἐξαισίως τὴν ἔκβασιν
εἴληφεν.

78

Ἐπεὶ δὲ πάντων τῶν τοῦ μεγάλου πατρὸς θαυμάτων
μιμνήσκεσθαι ἴσον ἐστὶ καὶ ἀστέρας ἀπαριθμεῖν ἢ τὸ τῆς
θαλάσσης ὕδωρ ἢ τὴν ψάμμον ἐπιμετρεῖν, ἑτέρου ἑνὸς
τῶν ἐκείνου ἐπιμνησθέντες τέλος τῷ λόγῳ δώσομεν, τὴν
ἀμετρίαν ἐκκλίνοντες.

2   Κοσμᾶς, ὁ ποτὲ τῆς Λαύρας ἐκκλησιάρχης, εἴωθει, ὅτε
τῇ βασιλευούσῃ διά τινα χρείαν ἐπεδήμει, παραβάλλειν τῇ
τοῦ Παναγίου μονῇ διὰ τὸ ταύτης καθηγεμόνα τυγχάνειν
τὸν μοναχὸν Ἀντώνιον, τὸν γνησιώτατον μαθητὴν τοῦ
ἁγίου ἡμῶν πατρός. Ἀπελθὼν οὖν ποτε ἐκεῖσε, εἶδεν

and he showed the place to the brethren, saying, "Here's where the monk Ioannikios left the gold." And they all joked with him, saying, "If God were to let us find it, then we would truly know how much grace and power our father is thought worthy of."

These were their words and, as they spoke, they searched 4 the seabed, and saw an octopus sitting in its rocky chamber. So they looked for a hook to bring up the octopus. But when they hauled it up, a strange mystery was seen. For the octopus was holding the gold in its tentacles. And this was the marvelous and extraordinary conclusion to this incident.

Chapter 78

If I were to mention all of the great father's miracles, it would be tantamount to enumerating the stars or measuring the water in the sea or the sand of the seashore. Thus, after describing one more of his miracles, I will bring my narrative to an end, avoiding excessive length.

Whenever Kosmas, the former sacristan of the Lavra, 2 visited the imperial city on business, he used to stay at the Panagiou monastery because its superior was the monk Antony, our holy father's closest disciple. Once when he went there, he saw an icon of the great father that was a

εἰκόνα τοῦ μεγάλου πατρὸς ἀπαράλλακτον οὖσαν ἐκτύπωμα τῆς ἁγίας ἐκείνου μορφῆς, καὶ παρεκάλει τοῦτον δοῦναι ταύτην αὐτῷ· ὁ δὲ Ἀντώνιος ἐκ πόθου ταύτην καὶ πίστεως πολλῆς κτησάμενος, "Ἀδύνατον," ἔλεγεν, "ἀδελφέ, ὅλως στερηθῆναί με ταύτης." Ὁ δὲ ἐπέκειτο αἰτούμενος ταύτην, αὐτὸν τὸν ἅγιον ἀντὶ μεσίτου προβαλλόμενος· καὶ τέλος ἐκβιάζεται τοῦτον τῇ συνεχείᾳ τῆς αἰτήσεως ἐκβῆναι τῆς οἰκείας προθέσεως καὶ συνθέσθαι τούτῳ παρασχεῖν ταύτην· "Πλὴν," ἔλεγεν, "εἰ βούλει τοῦ ποθουμένου τυχεῖν, μεῖνον ἄχρι τριῶν ἡμερῶν, ὡς ἂν ἀρχετύπῳ ταύτῃ χρησάμενοι ἑτέραν ἐξεργασώμεθα, καὶ μετὰ τοῦτο παρέξομέν σοι ταύτην ἀλύπως." Πείθεται τούτοις ὁ γέρων καὶ μένει τὴν προθεσμίαν.

3   Ὁ δὲ μοναχὸς Ἀντώνιος περὶ τοὺς ἑωθινοὺς ὕμνους ἀναστάς, ἄπεισι πρὸς τὸν τῆς εἰκόνος ἐργάτην, ὄνομα Παντολέοντα, καὶ τὰ τοῦ πράγματος εἰσηγεῖται καὶ πρὸς τὸ ἔργον ἐπείγει, καὶ "Εἴ μοι βούλει," φησί, "ποτὲ καταθέσθαι χάριν, μὴ ἀποκνήσῃς ἐργάσασθαί μοι ὁμοίαν ταύτης εἰκόνα· πλὴν μὴ βραδέως· τοῦτο γὰρ ἡ χάρις." Ὁ δὲ Παντολέων πρὸς τὴν πολλὴν τούτου ἔπειξιν ἐδυσχέραινε, καὶ "Ἱνατί," ἔλεγε, "πάτερ, σὺ αὐτὸς παραγέγονας πρὸς ἡμᾶς; Ἀφοῦ γὰρ χθὲς περὶ δείλην ὀψίαν ἐμηνύθη μοι τὰ τοῦ πράγματος διὰ τοῦ σοῦ μαθητοῦ, πᾶν εἴ τι πρὸς τοῦτο φέρει τὸ ἔργον ἡτοίμασα, καὶ ἰδού, ὡς ὁρᾷς, μέλλω τούτου κατάρξασθαι."

4   Ὁ δὲ ἔκπληκτος γέγονε, μὴ συνιεὶς τῶν λεγομένων τὴν δύναμιν, καὶ τὸν ἀδελφόν, ὃν ὁ Παντολέων ἔλεγε χθὲς παραγενέσθαι, ἐκεῖ παρόντα πρὸς πίστιν ἐκάλει· ὁ δὲ καὶ

perfect likeness of his holy appearance, and he asked Antony to give it to him. But Antony, who had acquired it out of love and great faith, said, "My brother, I can't possibly be totally deprived of this icon." But Kosmas kept on asking for it, suggesting the holy man himself as an arbitrator. Finally, as a result of his continuous demands, he persuaded Antony to abandon his original position and agree to hand the icon over to him. "But," said Antony, "if you want to have your wish, wait three days, so that we may use this archetype to make another icon, and then I'll happily hand this one over to you." The elder Kosmas was persuaded by these words and awaited the deadline.

Meanwhile the monk Antony arose around the time for the matins hymns, and went off to the icon maker, whose name was Pantoleon. He explained the matter to him and urged him on to the work, saying, "If you ever want to do me a favor, don't delay in making me a copy of this icon; just don't be slow about it, and that will be your favor to me." Pantoleon was annoyed at the monk's urgent insistence, and said, "Why did you come to me yourself, father? For since your disciple informed me about the matter late yesterday evening, I've made all the preparations to do the job, and look, as you can see, I am just about to start painting it." 3

Antony was astonished, not understanding the import of his words, and summoned the brother who, according to Pantoleon, had come the previous day, to verify the story, 4

αὐτὸς ἠρνεῖτο παντελῶς τὴν ἄφιξιν. Ἔγνωσαν οὖν ἅπαντες ὅτι ἐπισκίασις ἦν τοῦ ἁγίου. Ἐντὸς οὖν τριῶν ἡμερῶν ἑτέρας ἀντιτύπου γενομένης, ἔλαβεν ὁ μοναχὸς Κοσμᾶς τὴν πρωτότυπον μετὰ θαύματος ὅτι πολλοῦ καὶ πρὸς τὴν ἁγίαν Λαύραν ἤνεγκεν, ἐκδιηγούμενος πᾶσι τοῖς ἀδελφοῖς τὴν γενομένην τοῦ ἁγίου θαυματουργίαν· ἥτις καὶ μέχρι τῆς σήμερον προσκυνεῖται παρὰ πάντων ἐν τῷ ἁγίῳ αὐτοῦ τάφῳ, τὸν ἀκριβῆ χαρακτῆρα τῆς ἁγίας αὐτοῦ μορφῆς ἀποσῴζουσα.

79

Ἀλλὰ τὰ μὲν τοῦ βίου σου καὶ τοῦ τέλους, ὦ μακάριε πάτερ, καὶ ὅσα μετὰ τὸ τέλος, τοιαῦτα καὶ οὕτως ἔχοντα· ἡμεῖς δὲ οἱ τῇ ἱερᾷ σου ποίμνῃ προσεδρεύοντες καὶ περὶ γῆν ἔτι στρεφόμενοι καὶ ταῖς καθ᾽ ἑκάστην ἡμέραν προσβολαῖς τῶν δαιμόνων καὶ ἐπηρείαις τῶν πονηρῶν ἀνθρώπων βαλλόμενοι, χρῄζομέν σου τῆς χάριτος καὶ τῆς ἀντιλήψεως, χρῄζομέν σου τῆς πρὸς Θεὸν πρεσβείας καὶ μεσιτείας, καὶ ἀντιβολοῦντες καθικετεύομεν, μὴ διαλίποις τοῦ πρεσβείαν ποιεῖσθαι πρὸς τὸν φιλάνθρωπον Θεὸν ὑπὲρ τῆς σῆς ποίμνης, ἣν ἐκ ψυχῆς ἠγάπησας, ὑπὲρ ἧς πολλοὺς ἱδρῶτας καὶ πόνους ὑπέμεινας, ὑπὲρ ἧς τὸ αἷμά σου ἐξέχεας καὶ μέχρι θανάτου ἠγωνίσω, ὅπως ῥύσηται

but he absolutely denied that he had gone to Pantoleon. Thus everyone realized that it was an apparition of the holy one. So within three days another copy was finished, and the monk Kosmas took the original with much wonder and brought it to the holy Lavra, recounting to all the brethren the holy one's miracle working. And to this day the icon is venerated by everyone at his holy tomb, since it preserves the precise features of his holy appearance.

Chapter 79

O blessed father, this is the story of your life and death, and what happened after your death; but we who belong to your holy flock and still wander the earth, and are victims of the daily assaults of demons and the abuses of wicked people, need your grace and assistance, we need your intercession and mediation with God. We entreat you with supplication not to cease making intercession with the compassionate God on behalf of your flock, which loved so dearly, on behalf of which you endured many toils and labors, and on behalf of which you shed your blood and struggled until your death, so that He may save us from the

ἡμᾶς ἀπὸ τοῦ σκότους τῶν παθῶν καὶ πάσης τῆς ἐπικρατείας τῶν πονηρῶν δαιμόνων καὶ ἀνθρώπων.

2   Καὶ γὰρ οἶδας τὸν ἐξ ἑκατέρων ἐπηρτημένον ἡμῖν ἀεὶ
φόβον, οἶδας τὸν ἀκατάλλακτον τῶν δαιμόνων πρὸς ἡμᾶς
πόλεμον, οἶδας τὸ τοῦ σώματος δυσάγωγον καὶ δυσήνιον,
οἶδας τὸ τῆς προαιρέσεως ἡμῶν ῥάθυμον καὶ εὐόλισθον
καὶ πρὸς κακίαν ὀξύρροπον. Διατοῦτο δυσωποῦμέν σε, ἵνα
ὡς ἐν τῷ μοχθηρῷ τούτῳ καὶ πολυωδύνῳ καὶ ἀπατεῶνι καὶ
πλάνῳ βίῳ, ἕως παρῇς, ὁδηγὸς καὶ καθηγητὴς ἡμῶν
ὑπῆρχες σωτήριος, οὕτω πολλῷ πλειόνως νῦν, ὡς τῇ
Τριάδι παριστάμενος καὶ ταῖς ἐκεῖθεν φεγγοβόλοις ἀκτῖσι
καταστραπτόμενος, *ἐποπτεύοις ἡμᾶς ἄνωθεν καὶ διεξ-
άγοις,* ὅπως ἤρεμον καὶ γαλήνιον τὸν τῆς παροικίας ἡμῶν
μικρὸν χρόνον βιώσαντες, ἵλεων καὶ εὐμενῆ τὸν κριτὴν
εὕρωμεν ἐν τῇ ἡμέρᾳ τῇ φοβερᾷ τῆς δίκης· ᾧ πρέπει δόξα
καὶ μεγαλοπρέπεια σὺν τῷ ἀνάρχῳ αὐτοῦ Πατρὶ καὶ τῷ
συναϊδίῳ Πνεύματι, νῦν καὶ ἀεὶ καὶ εἰς τοὺς αἰῶνας τῶν
αἰώνων, ἀμήν.

darkness of the passions and all the dominion of wicked demons and people.

For you understand the fear of both that always hangs 2 over us, you understand the irreconcilable war of the demons against us, you understand the difficulty of guiding and reining in the body, you understand the indifference and unsteadiness of our free will and how quickly it turns to evil. For this reason, just as you were our saving guide and teacher while you were present in this wretched and very painful, deceitful and fickle life, so now we entreat you even more, as you stand in the presence of the Trinity and are brilliantly illuminated by its shining rays, that *you watch over us from above and guide us,* so that after living out the short time of our sojourn on earth in a tranquil and peaceful way, we may find the Judge merciful and gracious on the terrible day of judgment; to Whom be glory and majesty together with His eternal Father Who is without beginning and His coeternal Spirit, now and forever and unto the ages of ages, Amen.

LIFE OF MAXIMOS THE HUTBURNER BY NIPHON

Βίος καὶ πολιτεία τοῦ ὁσίου πατρὸς ἡμῶν Μαξίμου τοῦ Ἀθωνίτου καὶ Καυσοκαλύβη λεγομένου, συγγραφεὶς παρὰ τοῦ ὁσίου πατρὸς ἡμῶν Νίφωνος ἱερομονάχου

1

"Μὴ σιγήσῃς," λέγοντι τῷ προφήτῃ ἐκ Πνεύματος ἁγίου, "μηδὲ καταπραΰνῃς, ὁ Θεὸς ἡμῶν" [Psalm 82(83):1], ὁ ἐν Τριάδι ἁγίᾳ προσκυνούμενος καὶ ὑπὸ τῶν Χερουβεὶμ δοξαζόμενος καὶ ὑπὸ τῶν Σεραφεὶμ ἀνυμνούμενος, καὶ ὁ ἄγγελος εἶπε τῷ Τωβήτ, "Τὰ ἔργα τοῦ Θεοῦ ἀνακηρύττειν ἔνδοξον" [see Tobit 12:11], καὶ πάλιν ὁ προφήτης Δαβὶδ καὶ θεοπάτωρ, "Οὐκ ἔκρυψα ἐν τῇ καρδίᾳ μου τὴν ἀλήθειάν σου καὶ τὸ σωτήριόν σου εἶπα· οὐκ ἔκρυψα τὸ ἔλεός σου καὶ τὴν ἀλήθειάν σου ἀπὸ συναγωγῆς πολλῆς" [Psalm 39(40):10]· διὰ τοῦτο οὐκ ἔστι καλὸν σιγῇ παραδοῦναι τὰ τοιαῦτα μυστήρια καὶ θαυμαστὰ τέρατα ὑπὸ τῶν ἐκλεκτῶν τοῦ Θεοῦ γενόμενα καὶ οἰκείων δούλων αὐτοῦ· καὶ εἰς ὠφέλειαν τῶν ἀκουόντων γενήσονται, ὅτι καὶ οἱ ζηλοῦντες τοὺς βίους τῶν ἁγίων πρόξενον σωτηρίας ὑπάρχει.

2   Ἐξ ἀρχῆς ἐγένοντο φωστῆρες φωστήρων ἐν τῷ Ἁγίῳ Ὄρει τούτῳ τοῦ Ἄθωνος καὶ ποιμένων ποιμένες καὶ ὁδηγοὶ

The life and conduct of our holy father Maximos the Athonite also called the Hutburner, written by our holy father the hieromonk Niphon

Chapter 1

"*Do not keep silent,*" says the prophet through the Holy Spirit, "*do not keep your peace, O our God,*" you who are venerated in the Holy Trinity, glorified by the Cherubim, and celebrated in song by the Seraphim. The angel also said to Tobit, "*It is glorious to reveal the works of God*"; and again the prophet and ancestor of God, David, said, "*I have not hidden your truth in my heart and I have spoken of your salvation; I have not hidden your mercy and your truth from the great congregation.*" For this reason it is not good to remain silent about such mysteries and wondrous marvels as are performed by God's elect and His own servants; and they will be of benefit to those who hear them, because those who emulate the lives of the saints find this is a way of securing salvation.

From the beginning there were luminaries among luminaries on this Holy Mountain of Athos and shepherds

2

ἀπλανεῖς πλανωμένων καὶ ἀστέρες φαεινοὶ τῶν θελόντων σωθῆναι, καθὼς ἠκούσαμεν καὶ εἴδομεν τοὺς βίους αὐτῶν καὶ πολιτείας ἐν ἰδίοις καιροῖς καὶ χρόνοις γενόμενα καὶ πληρούμενα. Ἐν ὑστέροις δὲ καιροῖς καὶ χρόνοις ἐπέλαμ-ψεν ὡς ἥλιος ὑπέρλαμπρος ἐκ τῶν αὐτοῦ κατορθωμάτων ἐν τῷ Ἁγίῳ Ὄρει τούτῳ ὁ ὅσιος πατὴρ ἡμῶν Μάξιμος ὁ Καυσοκαλύβης, καθὼς ἄνωθεν εἴρηται, φωστὴρ φωστήρων καὶ ὁδηγὸς ἀπλανὴς πλανωμένων καὶ ἀστὴρ φαεινότατος καὶ παράκλησις τῶν μοναζόντων τοῦ Ἄθωνος, πάντων [τῶν] πρὸς αὐτὸν μετὰ πίστεως φοιτώντων· οὐ μόνον δὲ τῶν μοναχῶν, ἀλλὰ δὴ καὶ βασιλέων καὶ ἀρχόντων στή-ριγμα καὶ ὁδηγὸς πρὸς ὠφέλειαν, καθὼς καὶ ὁ λόγος δη-λῶσαι ἐπείγεται.

3   Ἔπρεπε γὰρ τοὺς λέγοντας καὶ γράφοντας βίους ἁγίων, ἵνα καὶ αὐτοὶ ὦσι κεκοσμημένοι ἀρετῶν καὶ κατορθω-μάτων, ὅπως καὶ ἐκ τῶν ἀρετῶν κοσμοῦνται οἱ λόγοι αὐ-τῶν. Ἐγὼ δὲ ὁ εὐτελὴς Νίφων ζήλῳ θείῳ πυρούμενος ἐπι-χείρησα γράψαι τὰ ὑπὲρ τὴν ἐμὴν δύναμιν, ἀλλὰ κατ᾽ ἐπίγνωσιν ἔγραψα καὶ ἐπέμνησα τοῦ ὁσίου πατρὸς ἡμῶν Μαξίμου τὸν βίον· πόθῳ γὰρ θείῳ, ὡς εἴρηται, κινηθεὶς καὶ ἅπερ ἤκουσα ἐκ τοῦ ἁγίου αὐτοῦ στόματος καὶ ἀπὸ εὐλαβῶν καὶ πεφωτισμένων ἁγίων πατέρων· ἤκουσα καὶ τῆς θείας φωνῆς τοῦ κρύψαντος τὸ τάλαντον τὴν κατάκρι-σιν, "Φοβήθητι, ψυχή, μὴ κρύπτε λόγον Θεοῦ·" ταῦτα κἀμὲ ἠρέθισαν πρὸς ὑπόμνησιν τοῦ θείου πατρὸς γράψαι, ἵν᾽ ὅπως ὁδηγηθῇ τις ἐκ Θεοῦ τῶν φιλοθέων γραμματεὺς νουνεχὴς συγγράψαι βίον καὶ λόγον αὐτοῦ εἰς ὠφέλειαν τῶν ἐντυγχανόντων· αὐτὸς μὲν τὰς εὐχὰς τούτων καὶ

among shepherds, unerring guides for those who went astray, and brilliant stars for those who wished to be saved, as we have heard from the lives they lived, and as we have seen from the way they conducted themselves in their own seasons and times. But in recent seasons and times our blessed father Maximos the Hutburner shone out like an exceptionally bright sun, as a result of his accomplishments on this Holy Mountain, being, as is said above, a luminary among luminaries, an unerring guide for those who went astray, a most brilliant star, and a comfort for all those who lived the monastic life on Athos and visited him with faith. And not only for the monks, but also indeed a support and beneficial guide for emperors and officials as well, as this narrative will hasten to explain.

Those who tell and write saints' lives should themselves 3 be adorned with virtues and achievements so that their words may be adorned by their virtues. And so I, the worthless Niphon, burning with divine zeal, have attempted to write what is beyond my ability, but I have written from my personal knowledge and have recalled from memory the life of our holy father Maximos. For, being moved by divine fervor, as I say, I have also included whatever I heard from his holy mouth and from other pious and enlightened holy fathers. And I have heard also the divine Scripture's *condemnation of the man who hid the talent,* "Be fearful, *O soul, and do not hide the word of God.*" And this aroused me to write down my recollections of the divine father so that some intelligent scholar from among the devout might be guided by God to compose a life and account of him for the benefit of its readers. He, then, with their prayers, will enjoy double garlands,

διπλοῦς τοὺς στεφάνους ἀπολαύσει, ἐκεῖ δὲ ἕξει ἐπόπτην καὶ συνόμιλον τὸν ὅσιον πατέρα.

2

Οὗτος ἦν ἐκ πόλεως Λαμψάκου· ἐμυήθη δὲ τὴν ἄσκησιν καὶ τὴν ἀκτημοσύνην ἀπὸ Θεοῦ παντοκράτορος ἐκ νεότητος. Ὅτε τὰ ἱερὰ γράμματα ἐμάνθανεν, ἔφευγεν εἰς τὰς ἐρήμους καὶ σπήλαια, καὶ ὅσον οἱ γονεῖς αὐτοῦ ἔπειθον μένειν μετ᾽ αὐτῶν, τοσοῦτον αὐτὸς ἔφευγε. Καὶ ὅτε ἐνόησε τὸ κρεῖττον, ἠμφιάσθη τὸ μοναχικὸν σχῆμα εἰς ὑποταγὴν πνευματικοῦ πατρός. Καὶ ποιήσας ἐκεῖ καιρὸν οὐκ ὀλίγον, ὡς ἤκουσε διὰ τὸ περιβόητον Ἅγιον Ὄρος τοῦ Ἄθωνος, ἠθέλησεν εἰς θεωρίαν τούτου ἐλθεῖν. Καὶ δὴ λαβὼν συγγνώμην ἐκ τοῦ πατρὸς αὐτοῦ καὶ ἐφοδιασθεὶς ὑπὸ τῶν εὐχῶν αὐτοῦ, ἐξῆλθε. Καὶ εὑρών τινα μοναχὸν Ἀθηναῖον συνοδίτην, Θεοῦ ὁδηγοῦντος ἔφθασαν εἰς τὸ Ὄρος. Οὐ πολὺ τὸ ἐν μέσῳ, καὶ ὁ ἅγιος ἦλθεν εἰς τὴν σεβασμίαν Λαύραν καὶ ποιήσας ἐκεῖ μετάνοιαν, ὡς σύνηθες ἦν τῶν θελόντων προσμεῖναι, ἔμεινε παρὰ τὴν θείαν Λαύραν ὡρολόγος καιρὸν ὀλίγον. Μετὰ ταῦτα ἀνῆλθεν εἰς τὴν Κωνσταντινούπολιν εἰς προσκύνησιν τῶν ἁγίων Παθῶν καὶ τῶν ἁγίων λειψάνων. Καὶ πάλιν ὑπέστρεψεν εἰς τὸ Ἅγιον Ὄρος καὶ ηὐλίζετο εἰς τὰς ἐρήμους τοῦ Ἄθωνος, ἄστεγος, ἄοικος, ὡς ἄλλος Ὀνούφριος καὶ Πέτρος ὁ Ἀθωνίτης. Καὶ ποτὲ μὲν ἐπλησίαζε πρὸς τοὺς ὁσίους

and in the world to come will have the blessed father to watch over him and be his associate.

Chapter 2

This man came from the city of Lampsakos. He was initiated into asceticism and poverty by almighty God from his youth. When he had learned the holy Scriptures, he used to run away into the wilderness and to caves and, as often as his parents tried to persuade him to remain with them, so often would he run away. And, when he knew better, he put on the monastic habit in obedience to a spiritual father. And after he had spent a long time there, when he heard about the famous Holy Mountain of Athos, he wished to go and see it. And getting permission from his spiritual father, and provided for through his blessings, he set out. And finding an Athenian monk as a traveling companion, with God's guidance they reached the Mountain. Soon after, the holy one came to the venerable Lavra. And after he had made obeisance there, as was the custom for those who wished to stay, he remained at the divine Lavra as timekeeper for a short time. After this he went up to Constantinople for the veneration of the relics of the Holy Passion and the saints. And then he returned to the Holy Mountain and dwelt in the wilderness of Athos, with no roof over his head, with no home, like another Onouphrios and Peter the Athonite. And sometimes he used to visit the blessed fathers who

πατέρας τῶν ἐν ταῖς ἐρήμοις ἐκείναις οἰκούντων καὶ ἐπαραμυθεῖτο μικρᾶς τροφῆς· ἐπὶ τὸ πλεῖστον δὲ ἐν ταῖς ἐρήμοις διῆγεν, ἀρκούμενος βοτάνων καὶ βαλάνων καὶ καστάνων καὶ ἄλλα τινὰ πρὸς παραμυθίαν. Εἶχε δὲ αὐτὸν ἡ ἔρημος αὕτη ἐνιαυτῶν δέκα περίοδον.

2   Καὶ οὕτω μετὰ ταῦτα ἦλθεν εἰς τὸν τόπον τῆς ἁγίας Λαύρας, πλησίον τῆς Παναγίας· καὶ πήξας ἐκεῖσε μικρὸν καλύβιον ἐκαθέζετο· καὶ ἐξήρχετο μίαν τῆς ἑβδομάδος διὰ μικρὰν παραμυθίαν. Ὅτε δὲ γνωστὸς ὑπό τινος ἐγένετο, καύσας τὴν καλύβην ἀνεχώρει ἀλλαχόθεν διὰ τὸ ἀτάραχον καὶ ἥσυχον καὶ ἀπαρρησίαστον. Καὶ ὅσον αὐτὸς ἔφευγε τὴν δόξαν καὶ τὸ λανθάνειν τοὺς ἀνθρώπους ποῦ καὶ πόθεν κατοικεῖ, τοσοῦτον ὁ Θεὸς κατὰ τὴν αὐτοῦ φωνήν, τό, "Οὐ δύναται πόλις κρυβῆναι" [Matthew 5:14] καὶ τό, "Οὐ καίουσι λύχνον" [Matthew 5:15] καὶ τὰ ἑξῆς, ἐφανέρωνεν αὐτόν. Καὶ οἱ γινώσκοντες τοῦτον μεγάλως ηὐχαρίστουν τὸν Θεὸν τὸν διδόντα τοῖς δούλοις αὐτοῦ τοσαύτην ὑπομονὴν ἔν τε σκληραγωγίαις καὶ μονώσεσι καὶ τὸ ἀπέριττον καὶ τὸ ὑπομένειν τὸν καύσωνα τῆς ἡσυχίας καὶ τὸν παγετὸν τῆς κακοπαθείας, ἐν ὑλικῷ σώματι ἄϋλον πολιτείαν ὁρῶντες τοῦ ὁσίου πατρὸς τὸν βίον. Οἱ δὲ ἀνόητοι καὶ ἀσύνετοι οἱ μὴ γινώσκοντες αὐτὸν ἔλεγον ὅτι ἐξέστη καὶ ἐπλανήθη, καὶ εἰς πρόσωπον ὠνείδιζον αὐτόν. Αὐτὸς δὲ ὡς μαθητὴς τοῦ Χριστοῦ καὶ μιμητὴς γενναίως πάντα ὑπέμενε διὰ τὸν λέγοντα, "Ὁ ὑπομείνας εἰς τέλος οὗτος σωθήσεται" [Matthew 10:22, 24:13] καὶ "Μακάριοί ἐστε, ὅταν ὀνειδίσωσιν ὑμᾶς οἱ ἄνθρωποι" [Matthew 5:11] καὶ τὰ ἑξῆς.

lived in that wilderness and would be sustained with a little food; but for the most part he lived in the wilderness, surviving on wild plants, acorns and chestnuts and other things for sustenance. And that wilderness supported him for a period of ten years.

And so, after this, he went to the area of the holy Lavra, near the Panagia. And after he had built a tiny hut there, he settled down and would only go out once a week for a little sustenance. But when he was discovered by someone, he would burn the hut and go away somewhere else for peace and quiet and to be free of human conversation. And as often as he ran away from fame and tried to conceal from people where he was living, so often would God reveal him, in accordance with His words, *"A city cannot be hidden . . . ,"* and *"Men do not light a lamp . . ."* and so on. And those who came to know him would give great thanks to God who has given His servants such endurance in both austerity and solitude, and such simplicity and the ability to endure the burning heat of spiritual tranquility and the freezing cold of mortification, seeing, in the life of the blessed father, immaterial conduct in a material body. But the unintelligent and stupid people who did not understand him said that he was crazy and deranged, and they used to insult him to his face. But he, as a disciple and imitator of Christ, bore everything nobly according to the One who said, *"He who endures to the end will be saved,"* and *"Blessed are you when men revile you,"* and so on.

3

Τῆς φήμης δὲ αὐτοῦ πανταχοῦ διαθεούσης καὶ τὸ ὄνομα αὐτοῦ ἐν ταῖς τῶν ἁπάντων γλώσσαις ἀδόμενον, οὐ μόνον ἐν τῷ Ὄρει τοῦ Ἄθωνος, ἀλλὰ καὶ εἰς πᾶσαν τὴν γῆν (προφητικῶς εἰπεῖν) ἐξῆλθεν ὁ φθόγγος [Psalm 18(19):4] αὐτοῦ. Συνέτρεχον οὖν πρὸς αὐτὸν οἱ ἐν τοῖς μοναστηρίοις κατοικοῦντες, ἀναρίθμητον πλῆθος, καὶ οἱ ἐν ταῖς σκήταις. Καὶ μετ᾽ ὀλίγον συνέρρεον καὶ πλῆθος ἐκ τοῦ κόσμου, βασιλεῖς καὶ ἄρχοντες καὶ ὄχλος πολὺς ἀπὸ τῶν πόλεων, καὶ μεγάλως ὠφελοῦντο· ἕκαστος κατὰ τὴν πίστιν αὐτοῦ καὶ εὐλάβειαν καὶ κατὰ τὸν σκοπὸν ὃν εἶχεν ὠφελεῖτο. Ἦν δὲ πεφωτισμένος ὁ πατήρ· ὁμιλοῦντος γὰρ αὐτοῦ αἰσθητῶς, ἑτέρα τις φωνὴ ἠκούετο ἐκ τοῦ λογιστικοῦ αὐτοῦ· καὶ οἱ ἀκούοντες μεγάλως ηὐφραίνοντο. Καὶ οὐ μόνον ἔλαβεν ἀπὸ τῆς ἄνωθεν σοφίας καὶ χάριτος τὸ προορᾶν τοῖς ἐγγύς, ἀλλὰ καὶ τοῖς μακράν. Καὶ ὅσα ἔλεγε τοῖς ἀνθρώποις, ἄλλα μὲν διὰ συντόμως ἐπληροῦντο, ἄλλα δὲ μετὰ καιρόν.

2 Ἦν δὲ σπήλαιον μικρὸν ἐπάνωθεν τῆς καλύβης αὐτοῦ. Ἐν μιᾷ γοῦν τῶν ἡμερῶν εἰσῆλθεν εἰς τὸ σπήλαιον καὶ ἀφύπνωσε· καὶ ἀναστὰς ἐκάθισε, καὶ θεωρεῖ γύναιον κεκοσμημένον ἔμπροσθεν τοῦ σπηλαίου· καὶ γνοὺς τὴν ἐπίνοιαν τοῦ παμπονήρου δαίμονος καὶ ποιήσας ἐκ τρίτου τὸ σημεῖον τοῦ ζωοποιοῦ σταυροῦ, ἄφαντος ἐγένετο. Καὶ ὀλίγων ἡμερῶν παρελθουσῶν, ἔλεγεν ὁ μέγας ὅτι "Μοναχός τις ἦλθεν ἡμέρᾳ δευτέρᾳ καὶ ἐκάθητο ἔμπροσθεν τοῦ σπηλαίου, ὃν οὐκ εἶδά ποτε· ἦν δὲ κατάξηρος ἀπὸ τῆς

Chapter 3

His fame spread everywhere, and his name was celebrated on everyone's tongue, not only on Mount Athos but (to speak like the prophet) "*word* of him *went out to all the earth.*" Those who lived in the monasteries thus hastened to meet him, forming a countless multitude, along with those in the hermitages. And after a short time a multitude from the outside world also streamed to him, emperors and officials and a whole crowd from the cities, and they received great benefit. Each was helped in accordance with his faith and piety, and the purpose he had. But the father was illuminated, for although he would converse through the senses, a different voice could be heard coming from his intellect. And those hearing it would be made very happy. And he received foresight, by means of heavenly wisdom and grace, not only into things that were close, but also into things that were far off. And, whatever things he said to people, some were fulfilled immediately, others only after some time.

There was a small cave above his hut. One day, then, he went into the cave and fell asleep; when he woke up and was sitting there, he saw a finely adorned woman in front of the cave. And after he realized that this was a device of the most evil demon, he made the sign of the life-giving cross three times, and she disappeared. And a few days later, as the great man said, "A monk, whom I had never seen before, came on Monday and sat in front of the cave. He was all withered up 2

πολλῆς ἐγκρατείας. Καὶ τῇ τρίτῃ ἡμέρᾳ πρωΐ ἦλθε πρός
με καὶ ὡμιλήσαμεν ἀλλήλοις· καὶ μὴ ἔχοντες ἄρτον τοῦ
φαγεῖν ἀμφότεροι ἢ ἄλλο τι τοῦ συνεσθιαθῆναι, ἐξῆλθε
καὶ ἐκάθητο ἄνωθεν ἕως τῇ Πέμπτῃ πρωΐ, καὶ πάλιν ἦλθε
καὶ ὡμιλήσαμεν· καὶ πάλιν ἀνέβη ἐκ τρίτου καὶ ἐκάθητο
ἕως τῷ Σαββάτῳ πρωΐ. Τότε ἐξῆλθον κἀγὼ διὰ σωματικὴν
παράκλησιν καὶ ἔκτοτε οὐκ εἶδον αὐτόν."

3   Ἐτῶν οὖν δεκατεσσάρων διανύσας ἐν τῷ προειρημένῳ
σπηλαίῳ πλησίον τῆς Παναγίας διάστημα, ἐξῆλθεν ἐκεῖθεν καὶ ἐλθὼν κατῴκησε πλησίον τῆς ἁγίας Λαύρας, ὅσον
καὶ τὰ πνευματικὰ ὄργανα ἠκούοντο· καὶ πήξας πάλιν
καλύβιον ἐκάθητο, ἐν ᾧ καὶ ἐτελειώθη. Ἐκείνη δὲ τῇ
καλύβῃ παρεχώρησεν ἐμοί.

4

Ἡμερῶν δὲ οὐκ ὀλίγων παρελθουσῶν, ἠβουλήθησαν
οἱ βασιλεῖς, ὁ Καντακουζηνὸς καὶ Ἰωάννης ὁ Παλαιολόγος, ἐλθεῖν εἰς ἐπίσκεψιν τοῦ ἁγίου· καὶ πρὸ τοῦ ἀκουσθῆ-
ναι ἢ λεχθῆναι ἡ παρουσία τούτων, φησὶν ὁ πατήρ,
"Γινώσκετε, ὦ πατέρες, ὅτι οἱ βασιλεῖς Καντακουζηνὸς καὶ
Παλαιολόγος ἀφικνοῦνται ἐνταῦθα εἰς ἐπίσκεψιν ἡμῶν."
Καὶ καθὼς προεῖπεν, οὕτω καὶ ἐγένετο· ἦλθον ἀμφότεροι
οἱ βασιλεῖς εἰς τὴν ἁγίαν Λαύραν καὶ προσεκύνησαν. Εἶτα
μετὰ πολλῆς τῆς εὐλαβείας καὶ ταπεινότητος ἦλθον καὶ εἰς

from his great asceticism. On Tuesday morning he came to me and we talked with each other; and since neither of us had any bread to eat nor any other food, he went out and sat up above until Thursday morning. And he came again and we talked, and he got up a third time and sat there until Saturday morning. Then I went out to relieve myself, and from that time I did not see him."

After spending a period of fourteen years in the previously mentioned cave near the Panagia, he left it and came and settled nearer the holy Lavra, where its spiritual instruments could be heard. He again built a small hut there and remained in it until his death. This hut he passed on to me.

Chapter 4

After many days had passed the emperors Kantakouzenos and John Palaiologos wanted to come to visit the holy one, and, before their presence had been heard or spoken of, the father said, "You know, fathers, the emperors Kantakouzenos and Palaiologos are coming here to visit us." And just as he foretold, so it happened. Both the emperors came to the holy Lavra and made obeisance there. Then with much piety and humility they also came to the blessed father. And

τὸν ὅσιον πατέρα· καὶ ἰδόντες αὐτὸν προσέπεσον τοῖς ποσὶν αὐτοῦ, δεόμενοι ἀκοῦσαι λόγον παρ' αὐτοῦ καὶ διδαχθῆναι τὰ πρὸς σωτηρίαν ὠφέλιμα ῥήματα. Καὶ ἀνοίξας τὸ ἅγιον αὐτοῦ στόμα καὶ πολλὰ πρὸς σωτηρίαν λέξας αὐτούς, καὶ ἀκούσαντες μετὰ πολλῆς τῆς εὐλαβείας ηὐφράνθησαν ἐκ τῆς γλυκύτητος τῆς ἐκπορευομένης ἐκ τοῦ στόματος αὐτοῦ, καὶ μάλιστα ὅτε διελέγετο πρὸς αὐτοὺς ταῦτα· "Ἀπέχεσθαι δεῖ ἀπὸ ἀδικίας καὶ πλεονεξίας καὶ τοὺς πταίοντας συγχωρεῖν καὶ τοὺς πένητας ἐλεεῖν καὶ τοῖς μοναχοῖς ἐπαρκεῖν τὰ πρὸς τὴν χρείαν τοῦ σώματος, ὅπως καὶ αὐτοὶ θερμοτέρως ὑπὲρ αὐτῶν ὑπερεύχωνται." Καὶ ἄλλα πολλὰ εἰπὼν πρὸς αὐτοὺς οἴκαδε ἀπέπεμψε. Αὐτοὶ δὲ εὐχαριστήσαντες ἀνεχώρησαν.

5

Ἀλλ', ὦ φιλόθεοι καὶ φιλήκοοι ἀκροαταί, ἀκούσατε καὶ θαυμάσατε καὶ δοξάσατε τὸν Θεὸν τὸν δοξάζοντα τοὺς αὐτὸν γνησίως δοξάζοντας [see 1 Kings 2:30], καὶ διορατικοὺς καὶ θαυματουργοὺς αὐτοὺς ἀναδείκνυσι, καθὼς ὁ θεοπάτωρ καὶ προφήτης Δαβὶδ λέγει, "Ἐγὼ εἶπα· θεοί ἐστε καὶ υἱοὶ ὑψίστου πάντες" [Psalm 81(82):6]. Παρέβαλόν ποτε μοναχοὶ ἐκ τῆς ἁγίας Λαύρας πρὸς αὐτὸν τοῦ ποιῆσαι αὐτὸν παράκλησιν· καὶ καθημένων αὐτῶν ἐπὶ τοῦ ἀρίστου, ἦλθον δύο κοσμικοί, ὁ εἷς ἔχων δαιμόνιον καὶ δεόμενος

when they saw him they fell at his feet, asking him to speak to them and to teach them things that would be beneficial for their salvation. And he opened his holy mouth and said many things concerning their salvation; and after they had heard this with great piety, they were delighted by the sweetness that issued from his mouth, especially when he said to them, "You must refrain from injustice and greed, and must forgive those who stumble, and show mercy to the poor, and supply the monks with their physical needs, so that they may also pray more earnestly on your behalf." And, after saying much else to them, he sent them home. And they left after offering their thanks.

Chapter 5

But, devout and attentive listeners, hear, wonder, and then glorify God who glorifies those who truly glorify Him, and reveals them as possessors of foresight and as miracle workers, just as the ancestor of God and prophet, David, says, "*I say, 'You are gods and all sons of the Most High.'*" Some monks from the holy Lavra once went to him to take him some refreshment. And while they were sitting down with him for the midday meal, two laymen came, one of whom was possessed by a demon; and he begged the blessed one to

τοῦ ὁσίου, ὅπως ἰαθῇ. Καὶ εὐθέως ἀνέστη καὶ εἶπε τὸν μοναχὸν Μερκούριον τὸν παρατυχόντα τότε ἐν τῇ τραπέζῃ, "Εὐλόγησον αὐτόν, ἵνα ἰαθῇ." Καὶ εὐλόγησεν αὐτὸν ὁ Μερκούριος, καὶ εἶπεν αὐτόν, "Πορεύου ἐν εἰρήνῃ [see 1 Kings 1:17; Luke 7:50, 8:48]· καὶ γυναικὸς μὴ ἅψῃ καὶ κρέα μὴ φάγῃς." Καὶ ἰάθη ἀπὸ τῆς ὥρας ἐκείνης ὁ ἄνθρωπος.

2   Ἕτερος μοναχὸς νεώτερος εἶχε δαιμόνιον, καὶ ἀπεστάλη πρός τινα γέροντα ἰάσασθαι αὐτόν. Ἐρχομένου δέ, καὶ μὴ θέλων συνήντησε τὸν μέγαν· καὶ ἐρωτηθεὶς παρ' αὐτοῦ ποῦ πορεύεται καὶ ἀποκριθεὶς ὅτι εἰς τὸν ὁδεῖνα γέροντα, εἶπε δὲ αὐτῷ ὁ ὅσιος, "Μὴ ἀπέλθῃς ἐκεῖ πειράσαι θέλων τὸν γέροντα, ὅτι καὶ ὁ τόπος ἐστὶ κρημνώδης καὶ κινδυνεῦσαι ἔχεις· ἀλλ' ὑπόστρεψαι εἰς τὸν γέροντά σου καὶ ἔχε ὑπακοὴν καὶ ταπείνωσιν, καὶ τυρὸν μὴ ἐσθίης." Καὶ ποιήσας αὐτὸν εὐχήν, ἀπέλυσεν αὐτὸν καὶ εἶπε, "Πορεύου ἐν εἰρήνῃ" [see 1 Kings 1:17; Luke 7:50, 8:48]. Καὶ ἰάθη ἀπὸ τῆς ὥρας ἐκείνης. Τινὲς δὲ φθόνῳ τηκόμενοι ἐλοιδόρουν τὸν ἅγιον· ἡ ἀρετὴ γάρ, καθὼς γέγραπται, δῆλον αὐτὸν ἐποίει πανταχόθεν, καθάπερ λαμπὰς τὸν φέροντα, κἂν πολὺ τὸ τοῦ φθόνου περιθέῃ σκότος.

6

Παρέβαλόν ποτε μοναχοί τινες μετὰ κοσμικοῦ τινος· καὶ πρὸ τοῦ πλησιάσαι τοῦ ὁσίου, ἔτι πόρρω αὐτοὶ ὄντες,

heal him. And immediately Maximos stood up and told the monk Merkourios, who was present at the table then, "Bless him, so that he may be healed." And Merkourios blessed him and told him, "*Go in peace;* and do not touch a woman or eat meat." And the man was healed from that time.

Another young monk had a demon, and he was sent to an elder to be healed. But, while he was on the way, he met the great one by chance. When he was asked by Maximos where he was going, and he replied that it was to this particular elder, the blessed one said to him, "Don't go there to bother the elder, because the place is craggy and you'll be in danger. Go back to your own elder and maintain your obedience and humility; and don't eat cheese." After Maximos had said a prayer for him, he sent him away and said, "*Go in peace.*" And he was healed from that time. But some who were consumed by envy reviled the holy one, *for virtue,* just as it has been written, *makes everything around the person who possesses it visible, just as a lamp does the person who carries it, even if the darkness of envy deeply envelops it.*

Chapter 6

Some monks once approached Maximos along with a layman; and before they had come near the blessed one, while

ἐλάλησεν ὁ γέρων πρὸς τὸν κοσμικόν, λέγων, "Ἀκινδυνᾶτος εἶ, καὶ στῆθι μακράν, ὅτι οὐχ ὑποφέρω τὸν πλη-
σιασμόν σου καὶ τῆς σῆς ὁμιλίας τὴν δυσωδίαν." Καὶ πάλιν
ἦλθον ἕτεροι μοναχοί, καὶ γνοὺς τὸν ἕνα, ἐλάλησεν ἀπὸ
μακρόθεν, "Ἀκινδυνᾶτος εἶ καὶ σύ, στῆθι ἀπὸ μακρόθεν,
μὴ πλησιάσῃς ἐνταῦθα." Καὶ οὕτως ἐγίνωσκε τὸν καθ' ἕνα
καὶ ἕκαστον τί ἐστι καὶ τί διαλογίζεται.

2 Καὶ τί πλέον ἔχω λέγειν περὶ τοῦ ὁσίου; Ἐπιλείψει γάρ
με διηγούμενον ὁ χρόνος ὑπὲρ τὸ καθ' ἓν ἐξετάζειν· ἀλλ'
ὅμως ὡς ἀμαθὴς καὶ ἀμελὴς καὶ πένης τῶν ἀρετῶν, ἀπὸ
τῶν πολλῶν καὶ μεγάλων κατορθωμάτων καὶ ἀρετῶν τοῦ
ὁσίου πατρὸς οὐκ ἀμελήσω λέγειν καὶ γράφειν ὅσα ἐπίστα-
μαι.

7

Ἦλθέ ποτε ὁ οἰκουμενικὸς πατριάρχης Κωνσταντι-
νουπόλεως Κάλλιστος μετὰ τοῦ κλήρου αὐτοῦ πρὸς αὐ-
τόν· καὶ μετὰ τῆς συνομιλίας καὶ τοῦ ἀρίστου, ἐν τῷ ἐξελθεῖν αὐτούς, διὰ λόγου βραχέος ἐσήμανεν αὐτοὺς τὸν ἐπὶ
τῶν Σερρῶν ἄδικον θάνατον· καὶ διὰ δηλητηρίου ἐτε-
λειώθησαν, καὶ πάλιν τούτου μείζων ἡ ῥύμη τοῦ λόγου
συνέβαλεν.

they were still a long way off, the elder called to the layman and said, "You too are an Akindynatos; so stay well away because I can't stand you near me and the stench of your company!" And again some other monks came, and he recognized one of them and called from far away, "You too are an Akindynatos, stay well away; don't come near here!" And thus he knew what sort of person each and every one was and what he was thinking.

And what more can I say about the blessed one? For I 2 don't have time in my account to go through everything one by one; but nevertheless, although I'm unlearned and negligent and poor in virtue, I will not neglect to tell and write as many as I can of the blessed father's many great accomplishments and virtues.

Chapter 7

The ecumenical patriarch of Constantinople, Kallistos, once came to him with his clergy. And, after they had had their conversation and the midday meal, as they were leaving, Maximos predicted to them in a brief statement their unjust demise at Serres; and they were indeed killed with poison, so again the power of his words turned out to be immense.

8

Ἦλθέ τις Μεθόδιος μοναχὸς εἰς θεωρίαν τοῦ γέροντος, καὶ εἶδεν αὐτὸν ἔσωθεν τῆς καλύβης· καὶ λέγει πρὸς αὐτὸν ὁ πατήρ· "Δεῦρο πλησίον." Αὐτὸς δὲ ἀπὸ τὴν λαμπρότητα ἣν εἶδεν, οὐκ ἠδύνατο πλησιάσαι. Καὶ μικρᾶς ὥρας διάστημα, ἀλλοιωθέντος τοῦ φωτὸς ἐκείνου, ἐπλησίασε καὶ συνωμίλουν ἕως τὸν καιρὸν τοῦ ἀρίστου.

2 Καὶ πάλιν ἄλλοτε ἦλθεν Ἀρσένιός τις μοναχὸς πρὸς αὐτόν· καὶ εἶδεν αὐτόν, ὡς φλόγα πυρὸς ἐξερχομένη ἀπ᾽ αὐτοῦ καὶ ἀνέβαινεν ἕως τὴν κορυφὴν τῆς καλύβης αὐτοῦ, ὡς νομίζειν ὅτι ἐπυρπολήθη ἡ καλύβη· καὶ ἐξέστη ἐπὶ τούτου. Γενομένης δὲ ἀλλοιώσεως τοῦ πυρὸς ἐκείνου, ἠρώτησεν αὐτόν· "Τί ἐστι τοῦτο, πάτερ;" Ἀποκριθεὶς εἶπεν, "Οὐκ οἶδα τί λέγεις."

3 Καὶ πάλιν ὁ αὐτὸς Ἀρσένιος εἶπε, "Φόβον ἤκουσα ἀπὸ τῶν Ἰσμαηλιτῶν καὶ ἐλθὼν ἀνήγγειλα τῷ γέροντι, καὶ λέγω αὐτῷ, ᾽Ποίησον εὐχὴν περὶ τούτου.᾽ Καὶ λέγει μοι, ᾽Ὕπαγε ἐν εἰρήνῃ.᾽ Ἐγὼ δὲ ὡς πονηρὸς ἔδειξα ὅτι ὑπάγω. Καὶ ἱσταμένου μου κρυφίως, ὁρῶ αὐτὸν ἱστάμενον καὶ τὰς χεῖρας αὐτοῦ ἐκτείναντα εἰς ὕψος ἐπὶ πολλὴν ὥραν. Καὶ ἐγένετο νεφέλη κύκλῳ αὐτοῦ, καὶ ὑψώθη τοῦ πυρὸς ἡ φλὸξ ἐπάνω τῆς κεφαλῆς αὐτοῦ καὶ ἕως τῶν κλάδων τῶν δένδρων, ὡς νομίζειν με κατακαίεσται τοὺς κλάδους· καὶ φοβηθεὶς ἔφυγον εἰς τὸ κελλίον μου ἐξιστάμενος καὶ θαυμάζων. Καὶ τῷ πρωῒ ἦλθον καὶ ἠρώτησα αὐτόν, ῾Τί

Chapter 8

A monk called Methodios went to visit the elder and he saw him inside the hut. And the father said to him, "Come closer." But Methodios was unable to go any closer on account of the brilliant light that he saw. After a short while, when the light had faded from Maximos, he approached him and they talked together until it was time for the midday meal.

And again, another time, a monk called Arsenios went to 2 him, and when he saw Maximos it looked as though flames of fire were coming from him and reaching up to the roof of his hut, so that he thought that the hut had caught fire. And he was astounded by this. But when Maximos's fire had faded, Arsenios asked him, "What is this, father?" And he answered, "I don't know what you're talking about."

And again, the same Arsenios said, "I heard there was a 3 panic over the Ishmaelites and I went and told the elder. And I said to him, 'Say a prayer about this.' And he said to me, 'Go in peace.' But I, acting wickedly, only pretended to leave. And while I was standing in hiding, I saw him standing with his hands stretched up to heaven for a long time. And a cloud formed around him and flames of fire rose up above his head as far as the branches of the trees, so that I thought they would burn the branches. And, being terrified, I fled to my cell, astounded and filled with wonder. And in the morning I went and asked him, 'What were you doing,

ποιεῖς, πάτερ;' Καὶ ἀποκριθεὶς εἶπεν, "Ὡς με εἴρηκας διὰ τοὺς Ἰσμαηλίτας, ἐφοβήθην πολλὰ τῇ νυκτὶ ταύτῃ.'"

9

Ἀναγκαῖόν ἐστι καὶ τοῦτο εἰς μέσον ἀγαγεῖν. Πρὸ ἐτῶν οὐκ ὀλίγων ἠκούετο περὶ τοῦ ἁγίου πατρὸς ὅτι ἄρτον οὐράνιον δέχεται· καὶ τοῦτο πολλοὶ οὐκ ἐπίστευον. Ὁ νοσοκόμος δὲ τῆς ἁγίας Λαύρας Γρηγόριος ἦλθεν ἐν καιρῷ χειμῶνος μετὰ καὶ ἑτέρου μοναχοῦ. Δεξάμενος οὖν ὁ πατὴρ αὐτοὺς εἶπεν, "Ἐγὼ ἄρτον ἔχω ζέοντα καὶ ὕδωρ." Καὶ ἔδωκεν αὐτοῖς ἐξ αὐτοῦ καὶ ἔφαγον, καὶ εἶπε, "Δέομαι ὑμῶν, μὴ εἴπητε τοῦτο πρὸ τοῦ τέλους μου." Ἐξέστημεν δὲ ἐπὶ τὸ ὁρώμενον καὶ ἐθαυμάσαμεν. Μετὰ δὲ τὴν κοίμησιν αὐτοῦ ἦσαν ἀναβαίνοντες εἰς τὴν ἁγίαν κορυφὴν τοῦ Ἄθωνος εἰς προσκύνησιν τοῦ Σωτῆρος Χριστοῦ, καὶ ἔλεγον περὶ τούτου καὶ εἶπον ὅτι "Ἐπὶ τοῦ χιόνος οὔτε μαλαγὴν εὕρομεν ἄλλου τινός, οὔτε πῦρ ἐν τῇ καλύβῃ, ἀλλὰ ἄρτον εὔοσμον ζέοντα, ὃν καὶ ἡμᾶς ὁ ὅσιος ἔδωκεν εἰπών· 'Φάγετε καὶ ὑμεῖς, ὡς ἔτυχεν.'" Ἀλλὰ καὶ τοῦτο γνωστὸν πολλοῖς ἐγένετο ὅτι καὶ ὕδωρ θαλάσσιον εἰς γλυκύτητα μετέβαλεν, ἐξ αὐτοῦ δὲ ἔπιε.

father?' And he answered, 'When you told me about the Ish-maelites, I was very frightened last night.'"

Chapter 9

I need to bring this up too. Many years ago it was rumored about the holy father that he used to receive heavenly bread; and many would not believe this. But Gregory, the infirmarian of the holy Lavra, went in wintertime with another monk. So when the father greeted them, he said, "I've got hot bread and water." And he gave some of it to them and they ate, and he said, "Please, don't speak of this before my death." We were astounded at the sight and were filled with wonder. But after his death, when they (that is, Gregory and the other monk) were going up to the holy summit of Athos to worship at Christ the Savior, they spoke about this and said, "We found neither the tracks of anyone else in the snow, nor fire in the cell, but fragrant piping hot bread which the blessed one gave to us, saying, 'You eat too, as it's here.'" And it was also common knowledge that he used to change sea water into fresh water and drink it.

10

Καὶ πάλιν ὁ καθηγητὴς τοῦ ἐνδόξου Προδρόμου τοῦ Μικροαθωνίτου, λαβὼν τὰ πρὸς τροφὴν ἐπιτήδεια, εἶπεν ἐν ἑαυτῷ, "Καρτέρει με, Καυσοκαλύβη, νὰ φάγωμεν." Ἐλθόντος οὖν ἐκείνου, πρὸ τοῦ ἰδεῖν αὐτὸν ὁ μέγας ἐλάλησε πρὸς αὐτόν, "Δεῦρο, παπᾶ, καρτερῶ σε."

2   Ἄλλος πάλιν ἀπὸ τὴν λαύραν τῶν Καρεῶν ἦλθεν, ἀλγῶν τὴν χεῖρα αὐτοῦ· ἐβούλετο δὲ ἀπελθεῖν εἰς τὴν Πόλιν. Καὶ πρὸ τοῦ εἰπεῖν αὐτὸν τὸν λογισμὸν αὐτοῦ καὶ τὸ ἄλγος τῆς χειρός, λέγει ὁ ὅσιος, "Εἰς τὴν Πόλιν βούλεσαι ἀπελθεῖν· καὶ προσέχου, μὴ ἀπέλθῃς, ὅτι οὔτε ἡ χείρ σου ἰαθήσεται, οὔτε ἄλλον τι ἀγαθὸν συναντήσεταί σοι· ἐδόθη σοι γὰρ σκόλοψ τῇ σαρκί [see 2 Corinthians 12:7], κατὰ τὸν ἀπόστολον, καὶ ὑπόμεινον. Ἔχεις καὶ ἀργύρια ὑπέρπυρα τέσσαρα, καὶ διάδος πτωχοῖς [Luke 18:22] καὶ κτῆσαι φίλον τὸν Κύριον· τὰ μὲν ἀνάλωσαι διὰ τὴν σὴν χρείαν, τὰ δὲ ὡς εἴρηται δὸς τοῖς πτωχοῖς [Matthew 19:21; Mark 10:21], ἵνα εὖ σοι γένηται." Ταῦτα ἀκούσας ἐκεῖνος ἐθαύμασε· καὶ προσκυνήσας τὸν ἅγιον ὑπέσχετο, ἵνα οὕτως ποιήσῃ. Καὶ ἀναχωρήσας οἴκαδε, εὐχαρίστει τὸν Κύριον καὶ τὸν θεράποντα αὐτοῦ Μάξιμον.

3   Καὶ ἄλλος τις ἦλθεν ἐκ πόλεως Σερρῶν, ὃν οὐδέποτε εἶδε, καὶ λέγει πρὸς αὐτόν, "Ὁ πατέρας σου δέεται διορθώσεως· καὶ θᾶττον πεῖσον αὐτόν, ἵνα διορθωθῇ."

4   Παρέβαλέ ποτε ὁ ὅσιος πρός τινα μοναχόν, ὀνόματι Μάρκον, καὶ εὗρεν ἐκεῖ ἕτερον μοναχόν· καὶ ἰδὼν αὐτὸν

Chapter 10

And again, the teacher of the famous monastery of the Prodromos on Little Athos, when he was taking some food to Maximos, said to himself, "Wait for me, Hutburner, so we can eat." So when he went, before Maximos saw him, the great one called out to him, "Here, *papas,* I'm waiting for you."

Another man again, from the *lavra* of Karyes, went to Maximos with a pain in his hand; and he wanted to go to the city of Constantinople. But before he told him his intention and about the pain in his hand, the blessed one said, "You want to go to the City. But take care, don't go, because your hand will not be healed, nor will any other good come to you. For *a thorn in the flesh has been given* to you, in the words of the apostle, and you must endure. You also have four silver *hyperpyra* coins, *distribute these to the poor* and make yourself a friend of the Lord. Spend some on your own need, but the rest *give to the poor,* as it has been said, so that it may go well for you." When the man heard this he was filled with wonder; and after he had prostrated himself before the holy one, he promised that he would do so. And as he went back home, he thanked the Lord and His servant Maximos.

And another man, whom Maximos had never seen, came from the city of Serres. And he said to the man, "Your spiritual father needs setting straight; you must persuade him of this soon, so that he may be set straight."

The blessed one once went to visit a monk called Mark, and he found another monk there. And when Maximos saw

ἀπὸ μακρόθεν ἐλάλησε, "Τί ποιεῖ ἐνταῦθα ὁ ἀσεβὴς οὗτος; (Αὐτὸς γὰρ ἦν αἱρετικὸς Μασ<σ>αλιανός.) Καὶ οὐχ ὑποφέρω τοῦ ἰδεῖν αὐτόν." Καὶ ἐτράπη ὁ μέγας εἰς φυγήν. Καὶ ταῦτα ἰδὼν ὁ Μάρκος ἐδίωξε τὸν ἀσεβῆ· καὶ τότε ὑπέστρεψεν ὁ πατὴρ πρὸς τὸν Μάρκον. Ἄλλοτε πάλιν ὁ αὐτὸς Μάρκος καὶ ἕτερος μοναχὸς παρέβαλον πρὸς αὐτόν, καὶ εἶπεν ὁ μοναχός, "Τριάντα δουκᾶτα ἔχω."—"Ναί, ἔχεις καὶ ἄλλα τριάντα καὶ ἄλλα τριάντα." Καὶ ὁ Μάρκος εἶπεν, "Ἀλλ᾽ ἐγὼ οὐδὲν ἔχω." Καὶ ὁ γέρων εἶπε, "Λέγεις, 'οὐκ ἔχω.' Δώδεκα ὑπέρπυρα ἔχεις, καὶ συντόμως διαβήσονται." Καὶ ἐγένετο οὕτως· ἐποίησε μετάνοιαν εἰς τὸ μοναστήριον καὶ ἔδωκεν αὐτά.

II

Καὶ πάλιν παρέβαλεν ὁ γέρων πρός τινα μοναχόν, Δαμιανὸν ὄνομα, καὶ λέγει αὐτῷ ὁ Δαμιανός, "Ἔχομεν εἰς τὸ μοναστήριον μοναχὸν ὑπερβαίνοντά σου τὴν ἀρετήν, τὸν ὁδεῖνα." Ὁ δὲ γέρων λέγει, "Καλὸς ἔνι, ἀλλὰ ἔχει ξ′ ὑπέρπυρα." Τοῦ Δαμιανοῦ δὲ τοῦτο μὴ πειθομένου, δι᾽ ὀλίγων ἡμερῶν ἐκοιμήθη ὁ μοναχός, καὶ εὑρέθησαν καθὼς εἶπεν ὁ ἅγιος. Καὶ ἀκούσας ὁ Δαμιανός, ἐλθὼν ἔβαλε μετάνοιαν λέγων, "Συγχώρησόν μοι, τίμιε πάτερ, ὅτι ὡς εἴρηκας οὕτως εὑρέθησαν τὰ ἀργύρια τοῦ ἀδελφοῦ."

2   Παρέβαλε Θεόδουλός τις μοναχὸς πρὸς τὸν ὅσιον· καὶ

him a long way off, he called out, "What's this impious man doing here? (For he was a Messalian heretic.) I can't even bear to set eyes on him." And the great one turned and fled. And when he saw this, Mark chased away the impious man, and then the father returned to Mark. Another time again the same Mark and another monk went to visit Maximos and the monk said, "I have thirty ducats."—"Yes, and you have another thirty too and yet another thirty." And Mark said, "But I haven't got any." And the elder replied, "You say, 'I don't have any,' but you have twelve *hyperpyra*. And they're going to be spent very soon!" And this happened, for he prostrated himself in repentance in the monastery and donated this money.

Chapter 11

And again the elder went to visit a monk, called Damianos, and Damianos said to him, "In our monastery we have a monk, so-and-so, who surpasses you in virtue." But the elder said, "He may be a good man, but he has sixty *hyperpyra!*" Damianos was not convinced of this, but a few days later the monk died, and the coins were found, just as the holy one had said. And when Damianos heard, he came and prostrated himself, saying, "Forgive me, venerable father, because the brother's coins were found, just as you said."

A monk, Theodoulos, went to visit the blessed one. And   2

τὸν οἶνον, ὃν ἐβάσταζεν, ἔκρυφεν αὐτὸν ἔξωθεν. Καὶ λέγει ὁ γέρων, "Φέρε καὶ τὸ περσικάριον, ἐὰν ἔφερες, καὶ ἄρτον." Καὶ εἶπεν, "Οὐκ ἔφερον ἄρτον, διὰ τὸ εἶναι αὐτὸν ξηρόν." Καὶ εἶπεν ὁ πατήρ, "Τρεῖς ἡμέρας ἔχω οὕτως." Καὶ ἐξελθὼν ἔφερε τὸ περσικάριον. Καὶ μετ᾽ ὀλίγον ἦλθον ἄλλοι τινὲς κομίζοντες τροφὰς καὶ ποτούς· καὶ φαγόντες ηὐφράνθημεν, ὥστε καὶ ἐπερίσσευσεν ἐκ πάντων ὧν ἔφερον.

3 Ἕτερος δὲ Καλλίνικος μοναχὸς ἡλίευσεν ἰχθύας· καὶ χωρίσας τοὺς ἐλάττονας, ποιήσας ἔδεσμα ἦλθεν εἰς τὸν ὅσιον. Καὶ λέγει αὐτῷ ὁ πατήρ, "Τοὺς μείζονας ἔκρυψας καὶ τοὺς ἐλάττονας ἔφερες." Καὶ ἀναστὰς ἔβαλε μετάνοιαν λέγων, "Συγχώρησόν μοι, πάτερ, ὅτι οὕτως ἐποίησα."

4 Ἄλλος τις Κασσιανὸς μοναχὸς ποιήσας πίτα, εἰπών, "Δεῦρο, Καυσοκαλύβη, ἵνα φάγῃς πίτα" (ἦν γὰρ τὸ μῆκος τῆς ὁδοῦ ὡσεὶ μίλιον ἓν καὶ πλέον), καὶ δι᾽ ὀλίγην ὥραν ἔφθασεν εἰπών, "Ἐλάλησάς μοι καὶ ἦλθον. Φέρε καὶ οἶνον τοῦ πιεῖν ἡμᾶς." Τοῦ δὲ Κασσιανοῦ μὴ βουλομένου δεῖξαι τὸν οἶνον, λέγει αὐτῷ ὁ ἅγιος, "Λέγεις, 'οὐκ ἔχω.' Ἀναστὰς ἀκολούθει μοι." Καὶ ἐπορεύθησαν ἐν τῷ τόπῳ οὗ ἦσαν ξύλα, καὶ λέγει αὐτὸν ὁ πατήρ, "Ἄνοιξον ἐνταῦθα καὶ φέρε οἶνον, ὅπως πίωμεν· καὶ μὴ λέγε ψεῦδος, ὅτι οἱ ἀγαπῶντες τὸ ψεῦδος ἀπολοῦνται." Ταῦτα ἰδὼν ὁ Κασσιανὸς ἔντρομος ἐγένετο ὅλος ἐξιστάμενος, καὶ βαλὼν μετάνοιαν λέγων, "Συγχώρησόν μοι, ἅγιε, τὸν ψεύστην."

he hid outside the wine he was carrying. And the elder said, "Bring in the bag if you brought it, and bread." And he said, "I didn't bring bread, because it was dry." And the father said, "I've been like this for three days." And Theodoulos went out and brought in the bag. And a little while later some others came bringing food and drink. And we ate and were content, as there was more than enough from all that they brought.

Another monk, Kallinikos, caught some fish. And after 3 separating out the smaller ones, he made a dish from them and came to the blessed one. And the father said to him, "You've hidden the larger ones and brought the smaller ones!" And Kallinikos got up and prostrated himself saying, "Forgive me, father, because that's just what I did."

Another monk, Kassianos, made *pita* bread and said, 4 "Come here, Hutburner, so that you can eat some *pita*." The length of the path which separated them was over a mile, but a short time later he arrived, saying, "You called me and I've come. Bring some wine for us to drink too." But, when Kassianos didn't want to show him the wine, the holy one said to him, "You say you haven't got any. Get up and follow me." And they walked to the place where the wooden barrels were, and the father said to him, "Open this one here and bring some wine, so that we may drink! And don't tell lies, because lovers of falsehood will perish." When he saw this, Kassianos started to tremble and was completely astounded, and prostrating himself said, "Forgive me, holy one, for being a liar."

12

Βαρλαάμ τις μοναχός, πορευόμενος εἴς τινα χρείαν καὶ ὑποταγὴν Ἰωαννικίου τοῦ Ἐξυπολύτου, εἶδεν αὐτὸν ὁ ἅγιος καὶ λέγει πρὸς αὐτόν, "Ἴσθι, ἀδελφέ, ὅτι αὐτόθι, οὗ βούλεσαι ἀπελθεῖν, ἔχεις τελειωθῆναι ὑπὸ κρημνοῦ." Καὶ ἐγένετο οὕτως. Καὶ ἄλλον Ἀθανάσιον τὸν Κροκᾶν, εἶπεν αὐτῷ, "Ὦ πάτερ Ἀθανάσιε, ὑπὸ Ἰσμαηλιτῶν μέλλεις τελει-ωθῆναι." Καὶ ἐγένετο οὕτως. Νικόδημος δέ τις μοναχὸς ἦλθε πρὸς αὐτόν· καὶ ἰδὼν αὐτὸν λέγει, "Νικόδημε, διὰ συντόμως μέλλω ἐξελθεῖν τοῦ κόσμου τούτου." Εἶπε δὲ καὶ <τὰ ὀνόματα> τῶν παρατυχόντων πατέρων εἰς τὴν κη-δείαν αὐτοῦ.

13

Καὶ πληρουμένων ἐτῶν ἑπτὰ καὶ μηνῶν ε΄ μετὰ τὴν κοίμησιν τοῦ ὁσίου, ἐσυνεβουλεύσαντο δύο μοναχοί, Νίφων καὶ Γεράσιμος, τοῦ ἀνοῖξαι τὸν τάφον καὶ ἀπὸ τῶν ἁγίων αὐτοῦ ἁγιασθῆναι λειψάνων. (Ἦν δὲ προετοι-μασμένος ὁ τάφος ἀπὸ Θεοῦ ἐπάνω πέτρας· καὶ καθαρίσας αὐτὸν ἐκεῖνος, ἵστατο ἕτοιμος· καὶ ὅταν ἐκοιμήθη, ἔθηκαν αὐτὸν ἐκεῖ.) Ἐλθόντες οὖν οἱ ῥηθέντες μοναχοὶ ἐν μιᾷ ἑσπέρᾳ ὤρυξαν· καὶ οὐδὲν εὗρον ἐκ τῶν ἁγίων λειψάνων αὐτοῦ, μόνον ὠσφράνθησαν ἀπὸ τῆς κόνεως, ὡς ὀσμὴν

Chapter 12

When a monk called Barlaam was going on some business and service for Ioannikios from Exypolytos, the holy one saw him and said to him, "Know this, brother, that right there, where you want to go, you're going to die by falling off a cliff." And that's what happened. And when he saw another man, Athanasios Krokas, Maximos said to him, "Father Athanasios, you're going to be killed by Ishmaelites." And that's what happened. A monk called Nikodemos came to him, and when Maximos saw him, he said to him, "Nikodemos, I'm going to leave this world very soon." And he spoke the names of the fathers who would be present at his funeral.

Chapter 13

Seven years and five months after the holy one's death, two monks, Niphon and Gerasimos, agreed to open the grave and be sanctified by his holy remains. (The grave had been prepared in advance by God on top of a rock, and, after Maximos had cleaned it out, it stood ready; and when he died, they buried him there.) So the two previously mentioned monks came one evening and dug; and they did not find any of the holy one's remains, but only detected an odor from the dirt like the scent of the most fragrant perfume.

μύρου εὐωδεστάτου. Καὶ τῷ πρωὶ ἐλθόντες καὶ ἐξορύξαν-
τες εὗρον τὸ τίμιον αὐτοῦ λείψανον καὶ ἐπλήσθησαν εὐωδίας, ὥσπερ ἀρωμάτων πολλῶν τε καὶ θυμιαμάτων. Καὶ
λαβόντες μερίδα ἀπὸ τοῦ ἁγίου αὐτοῦ λειψάνου, ἐποίησαν
ἀπομύρισμα καὶ ἡγιάσθησαν καὶ ἔπιον ἐξ αὐτοῦ. Αὖθις δὲ
ἔθηκαν τὴν μερίδα τοῦ ἁγίου λειψάνου ἐν τῷ τόπῳ ἔνθα
ἔλαβον αὐτήν· καὶ τὸν τάφον κατασφαλίσαντες ἀνεχώρησαν.

2   Ὁ Διονύσιος, οὗ τὸ ἐπίκλην Κοντοστέφανος, εἶχε κεφαλαλγίαν μακροχρόνιον· καὶ πολλὰ καταναλώσας τοῖς ἰατροῖς, οὐδὲν ἤνυσεν. Τέλος δὲ ἦλθε καὶ ἐν τῇ σορῷ τοῦ
ἁγίου καὶ προσπεσὼν μετὰ πολλῶν δακρύων καὶ στεναγμῶν, ἐκλιπαρῶν τὸν ἅγιον καὶ λέγων, "Ἅγιε τοῦ Θεοῦ,
μὴ παρίδῃς δάκρυα οἰκέτου σου, μὴ ἀπώσῃ δέησιν ἀναξίου
δούλου σου." Καὶ ἀφυπνώσας μικρὸν ἐπάνω τοῦ τάφου,
ὑγιὴς ἐγένετο, ὡς οὐδέποτε ἀλγήσας μηδὲ αἰσθανόμενος
ὅτι ἤλγησέ ποτε. Ἐξελθὼν οὖν ἐκεῖθεν ἀνεχώρησεν, εὐχαριστῶν τὸν Θεὸν καὶ τὸν αὐτοῦ θεράποντα.

14

Παρέβαλεν ὁ ἀββᾶς Δανιὴλ ἀπὸ τῆς ἁγίας Λαύρας
πρὸς τὸν μέγαν ποτέ. Εὑρὼν αὐτὸν ἔξωθεν τῆς καλύβης,
"Τίς εἶ ὁ ἐλθών," ἀπεκρίνατο ὁ ἅγιος πρὸς αὐτὸν ἅμα τοῦ
ἰδεῖν αὐτόν, "καὶ οὐκ εἰσῆλθες πρωΐ, ἀλλὰ πρὸς ἑσπέραν;"

And they came back in the morning and, when they dug again, they found his venerable corpse and were surrounded by a fragrance like many aromatic herbs and incenses. And after they had taken a small piece from his holy corpse, they made a holy infusion and were sanctified and drank from it. Then they replaced the piece of the holy one's corpse in the place from which they had taken it. And they left after filling in the grave.

Dionysios, whose surname was Kontostephanos, had a headache for a long time and had spent a lot on doctors with no results. In the end he too came to the holy one's tomb and fell down with many tears and moans and implored the holy one, saying, "Holy one of God, do not overlook the tears of your servant, do not reject the entreaties of your unworthy slave." And after he had slept for a short time on top of the grave, he recovered his health so that he never had the pain again or felt that he had once been in pain. So he left there and went away, giving thanks to God and His servant.

Chapter 14

*A*bbas Daniel from the holy Lavra once came to the great one. He found him outside his hut. "Who's that who's come," the holy one replied to him when he saw him, "and why didn't you come in the morning instead of in the

Ἦν γὰρ πρωῒ τότε ἀνατείλαντος τοῦ ἡλίου. Ἀποκριθεὶς ὁ ἀββᾶς Δανιὴλ εἶπεν, "Πρωῒ ἐστι, πάτερ, νῦν ἀνέτειλεν ὁ ἥλιος." Ἀπὸ τούτου ἐγνώρισαν οἱ πατέρες, ὅτι καὶ τὰς νύκτας ὡς ἡμέρας διεβίβαζε, καθὼς γέγραπται· "Φῶς δικαίοις διὰ παντός [Proverbs 13:9]· οἱ γὰρ ἅγιοι ἐν σοὶ φωτισθέντες καταλάμπουσιν ὡς φωστῆρες" [see Philippians 2:15].

15

Διηγήσατο ἡμῖν Νίφων ὁ ἱερομόναχος ἐκ τῆς ἁγίας Λαύρας, ὅτι "Ἤμην κανονάρχης εἰς τοῦ Δωροθέου· καὶ ἦλθόν τινες μοναχοὶ τότε εἰς τὸν ὅσιον πατέρα. Ἦν δὲ καιρὸς τοῦ τρυγητοῦ καὶ γαλήνη μεγάλη καὶ ἥλιος ὑπέρλαμπρος καὶ διαυγής. Καὶ λαβὼν ὁ ἅγιος εἰς τὰς χεῖρας αὐτοῦ ἕν παξιμᾶν ἐπέδωκεν ἑνὸς τῶν εὑρεθέντων ἀδελφῶν εἰπών, Λαβὲ τοῦτο τὸ ψωμίον καὶ δὸς αὐτὸ τοῦ ἱερέως εἰς τοῦ Δωροθέου εἰς τὰς χεῖρας αὐτοῦ. Καὶ προσέχεσθε, μὴ ἐξέλθετε ἐκεῖσε, ὅπως μὴ κινδυνεύσετε· μέλλει γὰρ γενέσθαι χειμὼν βαρύτατος.' Ἐλθόντες οὖν τότε ἐκεῖ, καὶ μετὰ τὸ λαβεῖν ὁ ἱερεὺς τὸν παξαμᾶν εἰς χεῖρας αὐτοῦ, εὐθέως ἐγένοντο ἀστραπαὶ καὶ βρονταὶ καὶ νεφέλαι καὶ γνόφος καὶ χάλαζαι, ὥστε ἐξαπορηθῆναι οἱ ἀδελφοὶ καὶ γενέσθαι ἔντρομοι καὶ θαυμάσαι τοῦ ἁγίου τὴν προφητείαν. Καὶ ὡς εἶδον ταῦτα, ἀνήγγειλαν τῶν πατέρων περὶ

evening?" For it was then morning and the sun had risen. *Abbas* Daniel said in reply, "It is morning, father, and the sun has risen." The fathers realized from this that he spent his nights in the same way as his days, just as it has been written, "*There is always light for the righteous.* For the holy ones, being enlightened by you, shine *like lights.*"

Chapter 15

The hieromonk Niphon from the holy Lavra told us, "I used to be the precentor at Dorotheou. And some monks had come to the blessed father then. It was the time of the grape harvest and it was very calm and the sun was shining brightly and it was a clear day. And the holy one took a rusk in his hands and gave it to one of the brethren who were there, saying, 'Take this piece of bread and place it in the hands of the priest at Dorotheou. And take care that you don't leave there, so that you're not in danger, for there's going to be a very severe storm.' So when they went there, and after the priest had taken the rusk in his hands, immediately there was lightning and thunder and storm clouds and darkness and hail, so that the brethren were stunned and shaken and amazed by the holy one's prophecy. And when they saw this, they told the fathers about the blessed one and said,

τοῦ ὁσίου ὅτι 'Οὕτως εἶπε· καὶ ἐγενήθησαν, ὡς ὁρᾶτε.' Καὶ ἀκούσαντες οἱ πατέρες ἐξέστησαν. Καὶ τὰς ἀμπέλους τοὺς εὑρεθέντας τότε ἀτρύγους πάντας ἠφάνισεν ὁ χειμών· καὶ μιᾷ φωνῇ ἅπαντες ἔλεγον τὸ 'Κύριε ἐλέησον.' Καὶ ἀπὸ τὴν βίαν τοῦ χειμῶνος ἐκείνου εἰσήλθομεν εἰς τὸν ναὸν καὶ ἀπεκλείσθημεν· καὶ ποιήσαντες ἐκεῖσε ἱκαναῖς ἡμέραις, ἕως οὗ παρῆλθεν ἡ ὀργὴ τοῦ Θεοῦ, ἐξήλθομεν ἐκεῖθεν, εὐχαριστοῦντες τὸν Θεὸν καὶ τὸν αὐτοῦ δοῦλον."

2   Πάλιν ὁ αὐτὸς εἶπεν, "'Ελθόντος μου μιᾷ πρὸς τὸν ὅσιον καὶ ὁμιλήσας μετ' αὐτοῦ, εἶπον ἵνα φάγωμεν. Αὐτὸς δὲ εἴρηκε πρός με, 'Κερατάδες ἔρχονται· καὶ ὅταν ἐξέλθωσι, τότε θέλομεν φάγειν.' Καὶ ἔτι μιᾶς στιγμῆς οὔπω παρελθούσης, ἦλθον κοσμικοί τινες τρεῖς καὶ λέγουσιν ὅτι "Ὑπὸ τῶν γυναικῶν ἡμῶν ἠδικήθημεν, ὦ πάτερ, ὅτι ὁδὸν ἐβάδισαν κακήν· καὶ εἴ τι ἡμᾶς κρίνεις, οὕτω καὶ ποιήσομεν.' Καὶ λέγει πρός με ὁ ἅγιος, ''Επίδος αὐτοῖς ἄρτον καὶ ἀπὸ ἑνὸς ποτηρίου οἶνον.' Καὶ μετὰ τὸ φαγεῖν αὐτούς, ἐλάλησε πρὸς αὐτοὺς ῥήματα ψυχωφελῆ καὶ ἀπέλυσεν ἐν εἰρήνῃ."

3   Πάλιν ὁ αὐτὸς εἶπεν ὅτι "Ποιήσαντός μου ἐδέσματα πρὸς τὸ φαγεῖν, ἀπῆλθον εἰς τὸν ἀββᾶ Χαρίτωνα. Καὶ λέγει ὁ μέγας, ''Ώρα ἦλθε τοῦ φαγεῖν ἡμᾶς· καὶ δεῦτε, καθίσαντες εὐφρανθῶμεν.' Καὶ μετὰ τοῦ ἀρίστου λέγει, 'Φέρετε βότρυας.' Ὁ δὲ ἀββᾶς Χαρίτων ἔλεγεν, 'Οὐκ ἔχομεν.' Καὶ πάλιν λέγει, 'Φέρετε, ἵνα φάγωμεν, ὅτι ἔρχονται ἄλλα καὶ ἄλλα.' Καὶ παρευθὺς ἦλθέ τις μοναχὸς φέρων βότρυας κοφίνιον πλῆρες. Ἰδὼν δὲ τὴν διπλῆν ἐξήγησιν τοῦ ἁγίου, ὁ Χαρίτων ἐξέστη ἐπὶ τούτῳ καὶ ἀναστὰς ἔβαλε μετάνοιαν."

'It's happened just like he said it would, as you see.' And when the fathers heard this, they were astounded. And the storm stripped the vines that were there of all their fruit. And with one voice everyone called out, 'Lord have mercy.' And because of the violence of that storm we went into the church and shut ourselves in. And after we had spent several days there, until the wrath of God had passed, we came out of there, giving thanks to God and His servant."

The same man said again, "One day I went to the blessed 2 one and, after I had talked with him, I said that we should eat. But he said to me, 'Some cuckolds are coming; and when they've left, then we'll eat.' And not even a minute later three laymen came and said, 'We've been wronged by our wives, father, because they've gone a bad way; and we'll do whatever you decide.' And the holy one said to me, 'Give them some bread and a cup of wine each.' And after they had eaten, he said some spiritually beneficial words to them and sent them away in peace."

The same man said again, "After I'd made some food to 3 eat, I went to *abbas* Chariton. And the great one said, 'The time's come for us to eat. Come here, then, and sit down and let's enjoy ourselves.' And after the meal Maximos said, 'Bring some grapes!' But *abbas* Chariton said, 'We don't have any.' And again he said, 'Bring them so that we can eat, because there are lots more coming.' And straight away a monk came, carrying a basket full of grapes. When he understood the holy one's double insight, Chariton was astounded by it and, getting up, prostrated himself."

4   Παρέβαλεν ἐν μιᾷ Θεόδουλος μοναχὸς Βεροιώτης
πρὸς τὸν ὅσιον· εὗρε δὲ καὶ ἕτερον μοναχὸν ἐκ τῆς Λαύρας
ἐσθίοντα μετ' αὐτοῦ. Λαβὼν ὁ πατὴρ ποτήριον οἴνου ἐν
τῇ χειρὶ αὐτοῦ εἶπε, "Ῥάπτης εἶμαι ἀπὸ τὸ Προσφόριν· καὶ
κρατῶ χύτραν ἰχθύας, καὶ βρεμένος ἕως τὴν μέσην." Καὶ
μιᾶς στιγμῆς παρελθούσης, ἔφθασέ τις κοσμικός, καὶ ἐρωτηθεὶς παρ' αὐτοῦ εἶπε, "Ῥάπτης ὢν ἀπὸ τὸ Προσφόριν
καὶ κρατῶ χύτραν ἰχθύας· καὶ ἐξελθόντος μου ἐκ τοῦ σκά-
φους, ὅλος ἐβράχην παρ' ὀλίγον· καὶ Θεοῦ εὐδοκοῦντος,
μόνον ὡς τὴν μέσην ἐβράχηκα." Τοῦτον ἰδόντες οἱ πατέρες
καὶ ἀκούσαντες τὸ ταχὺ τῆς προοράσεως ἐξέστησαν, καὶ
σύντρομοι γεγονότες τὰς ὄψεις ἠλλοιώθησαν, καὶ παρ'
ὀλίγον εἰς ἔκστασιν φρενῶν ἤγγισαν· καὶ ἐπὶ πολὺ τὸ
"Κύριε ἐλέησον" ἐν ἑαυτοῖς ἔλεγον, δοξάζοντες τὸν Θεὸν
καὶ τὸν αὐτοῦ θεράποντα.

16

Ὁ ἀββᾶς Καλλίνικος εἶπε τῷ ἀδελφῷ αὐτοῦ Μελετίῳ,
"Ποίησον, ἀδελφέ, ἔδεσμα, ἵνα ἀπέλθωμεν εἰς τὸν Καυσοκαλύβην, ὅτι πολλὰς ἡμέρας ἔχει τοῦ φαγεῖν." Ἦν δὲ καιρὸς τοῦ τρύγους. Καὶ πάλιν εἶπε, "Τρυγήσαντες πρότερον
καὶ φάγωμεν· ὕστερον ἀπελθόντες πληρώσομεν τὸ καταθύμιον πρὸς τὸν ὅσιον." Καὶ τοῦτο τοῦ μεγάλου μὴ ἐπι-
λανθανομένου, ἐλθὼν εὗρεν αὐτοὺς συλλέγοντας τοὺς

One day, Theodoulos, a monk from Berrhoia, came to the   4
blessed one. And he found another monk from the Lavra
eating with him. The father took a cup of wine in his hand
and said, "I'm a tailor from Prosphorin, and I'm holding a
pot of fish and I'm soaked to the waist." And a minute later a
layman appeared, and when he was questioned by Maximos
he said, "I'm a tailor from Prosphorin and I'm holding a pot
of fish; and as I got out of the boat, I was almost drenched
completely, but with God's help I've only been drenched to
the waist." When the fathers saw this man and heard the
speed with which the holy one's foresight was fulfilled, they
were astounded; they started to shake and their faces were
changed, and they almost lost their minds. And they said
"Lord have mercy" to themselves many times, glorifying
God and His servant.

Chapter 16

*A*bbas Kallinikos said to his brother Meletios, "Make
some food, brother, so that we may go to the Hutburner,
because he hasn't eaten for many days." But it was the time
of the grape harvest. So then he said, "Let's harvest first and
then eat; later we can go and fulfill our intention for the
blessed one." Even this did not escape the notice of the
great one, for he came and found them picking the grapes,

βότρυας, καὶ ἔδωκαν αὐτῷ φαγεῖν. Ὁ δὲ λέγει πρὸς αὐτούς, "Εἶπον ἵνα ἔλθωσιν οἱ πατέρες· καὶ διὰ τοῦ τρύγους ἠμποδίσθησαν." Καὶ ὅσα ἐλάλησαν καὶ ὅσα εἶπον ἐν ἑαυτοῖς, πάντα ἀνήγγειλεν αὐτοῖς. Ἐκράτει δὲ ὁ πατὴρ κεράμιον, ὅπως ἄρῃ ὕδωρ· καὶ λαβὼν αὐτὸ ὁ Μελέτιος ἀπῆλθε τοῦ κομίσασθαι τὸ ὕδωρ. Ἀπερχόμενος δὲ ἐλογίζετο ἐν ἑαυτῷ, ἵνα ἐκ τῆς ἄνωθεν πηγῆς ἀντλήσῃ. Γνοὺς δὲ ὁ πατὴρ τοὺς διαλογισμοὺς αὐτοῦ εἶπε, "Μὴ ἐκ τῆς ἄνωθεν, ἀλλ᾽ ἐκ τῆς κάτωθεν γεμίσας τὸ κεράμιον φέρε." Ἰδόντες δὲ ταῦτα οἱ πατέρες ἐθαύμασαν, ὅτι οὐδὲν ἔλαθεν αὐτῷ· δοξάζοντες ἦσαν τῷ Θεῷ ποιοῦντι θαυμαστὰ τέρατα ἐν τοῖς δούλοις αὐτοῦ.

17

Ἦλθέ ποτε ἀπὸ τὰς νήσους πλοῖον ἐν τῷ λιμένι τῆς Λαύρας. Ἦν δὲ ἐν τῷ πλοίῳ ἄνθρωπος ἔχων δαιμόνιον ἀπληστίας· ἐὰν ἤσθιεν ἡμέρας τε καὶ νυκτός, οὐκ ἐκορέννυτο. Ἀναστὰς οὖν τῷ πρῶῒ ὁ ναύκληρος ἔλαβε μετ᾽ αὐτοῦ τὸν ἄνθρωπον καὶ ἄλλους ἀπὸ τοῦ πλοίου καὶ ἤρχοντο εἰς τὸν μέγαν. Καὶ ὁ ἄνθρωπος μὴ δυνάμενος περιπατεῖν, ὅτι οὐκ ἔδωκαν αὐτὸν φαγεῖν, ὅπως νῆστις ἀπέλθῃ εἰς τὸν ἅγιον, ὑπέμεινεν ἐν τῇ ὁδῷ. Καὶ ἰδὼν αὐτοὺς ὁ πατὴρ ἐρχομένους, φησὶ πρὸς αὐτούς, "Καὶ ὁ ἄλλος ποῦ; Εἰ μὴ φέρετε κἀκεῖνον, οὐδὲ ὑμᾶς δέξομαι." Στραφέντες δὲ

and they gave him some to eat. But he said to them, "The fathers said they would come, and then they were prevented by the harvest." And whatever they spoke aloud and whatever they said to themselves, he reported it all to them. And the father was holding a pot, so that he could get some water. Taking this, Meletios went off to fetch the water, and as he was leaving he thought to himself that he would draw it from the upper spring. But the father knew what he was thinking and said, "Bring the pot back when you've filled it from the lower one, not the upper one!" When they saw this, the fathers were amazed because nothing escaped him, and they gave glory to God who performs such wonderful miracles through His servants.

Chapter 17

A ship once came into the harbor of the Lavra from the islands. And in the ship there was a man who had a demon of insatiability; even if he ate day and night, he was never full. So when he got up in the morning, the captain took with him the man and some others from the ship and they went to the great one. And the man, who was unable to walk because they had not given him anything to eat, so that he might go fasting to the holy one, stayed put on the path. When the father saw them coming, he said to them, "Where's the other one? If you don't bring him, I won't see

ὀπίσω, ἤγαγον αὐτὸν μετὰ βίας. Καὶ ποιήσας εὐχὴν ὁ ἅγιος, ἐκάθισαν ἐπὶ τοῦ ἀρίστου· καὶ λαβὼν ὁ πατὴρ ἄρτον δέδωκε τῷ ἀπληστίας δαίμονα ἔχοντι, καὶ εἶπεν αὐτόν, "Τόσον ἄρτον ἔσθιε καὶ χορτάζου, καὶ εἰρήνευε ἐν Κυρίῳ." Καὶ ἰδὼν ὁ ἄνθρωπος ὅτι ἐνεπλήσθη ἀπὸ τοῦ ἄρτου διὰ τῆς εὐχῆς τοῦ ὁσίου, ἀναστὰς ἔπεσεν ἔμπροσθεν αὐτοῦ, μετὰ δακρύων λέγων, "Ἐνταῦθα οὐκ ἐξέρχομαι· ἀλλὰ καὶ ὁδήγησόν με, δοῦλε τοῦ Θεοῦ, πῶς σωθῶ." Δεξάμενος οὖν αὐτὸν ὁ πατὴρ ὡδήγησεν αὐτὸν εἰς τὸν μονήρη βίον. Καὶ τοὺς συνοδοιπόρους αὐτοῦ εἶπεν, "Πορεύεσθε ἐν εἰρήνῃ [see 1 Kings 1:17; Luke 7:50, 8:48]· καὶ τὸ γύναιον αὐτοῦ μηδὲν ἀδικήσετε ἀπὸ τὴν μερίδα αὐτοῦ τὸ τυχόν." Καὶ ποιήσας εὐχὴν ἀπέλυσεν αὐτοὺς μετ᾽ εἰρήνης.

18

Διηγήσατο ὁ ἡγούμενος τοῦ ἐνδόξου Προδρόμου τοῦ Μικροαθωνίτου ὅτι "Παρέβαλε πρός με γέρων πάνυ ἀσκητικώτατος· ἐπεθύμει δὲ τοῦ προσκυνῆσαι εἰς τὴν ἁγίαν κορυφὴν τοῦ Ἄθωνος καὶ ἀπολαῦσαι καὶ τὸν ἅγιον· ἐγὼ δὲ σπλαγχνισθεὶς αὐτὸν συνώδευσα μετ᾽ αὐτοῦ. Ἠθέλησα οὖν λαβεῖν καὶ ἄρτον εἰς παραμυθίαν, αὐτὸς δὲ οὐκ ἔασε, ἀλλ᾽ ἐπορεύθημεν ἄνευ τινὸς βρωτοῦ καὶ ποτοῦ. Πορευθέντες δὲ ἀμφότεροι ἤλθομεν εἰς τὴν Παναγίαν, μέσον τοῦ Ἄθωνος· ἠσθένησε γὰρ ὁ γέρων ἐκ τῆς

you." So they went back and brought him by force. After the holy one had said a prayer, they sat down for the meal, and the father took some bread and gave it to the man who had the insatiable demon, saying to him, "Eat that much bread and be full, and find peace in the Lord." When the man realized that he had been satisfied by the bread through the blessed one's prayer, he stood up and then prostrated himself before him, saying tearfully, "I'm not going to leave here. Show me how I may be saved, servant of God." So the father received him and guided him toward the monastic life. And Maximos said to the man's fellow travelers, "*Go in peace,* and don't cheat his wife out of any of his share." And after he had said a prayer, he dismissed them in peace.

Chapter 18

The superior of the glorious monastery of the Prodromos on Little Athos recounted this story. "An extremely ascetic elder came to me. He was eager to worship at the holy summit of Athos and also to benefit from a visit to the holy one. And I took pity on him and accompanied him. I also wanted to take bread to sustain us, but he would not allow it and we set out without any food or drink. On our way we both went to the Panagia, halfway up Athos, for the elder was very

ὁδοιπορίας πάνυ· καὶ εὕρομεν ἐκεῖ παξαμάτας καὶ ὕδωρ· γευσάμενος οὖν ὁ γέρων ἐδυναμώθη. Καὶ τῇ νυκτὶ ἀνεκλίθημεν· καὶ τῷ πρωῒ ἤθελον πάλιν λαβεῖν ἄρτους, καὶ ὁ γέρων οὐκ εἴασεν. Ἐλθόντες δὲ ἀνέβημεν μετὰ πολλοῦ κόπου· ὁ γέρων γὰρ ἐν τῇ ὁδῷ ἐλιγοθύμησε. Καὶ πάλιν ὅταν ἀνέβημεν εἰς τὴν ἁγίαν κορυφὴν καὶ προσεκυνήσαμεν, τοσοῦτον ἐλιγοθύμησεν, ὥστε πεσεῖν ἐπὶ τῆς γῆς καὶ μὴ δυνάμενος ἀναστῆναι, ὥστε λέγειν ἐγὼ ὅτι ἀπέθανεν. Λυπούμενος δὲ πάλιν ἐγὼ ἕως θανάτου καὶ μὴ ἔχοντός μου τί ποιῆσαι ἢ τί διαπράξασθαι καὶ ἐν πολλῇ ἀδημονίᾳ ὄντος μου, ἐξῆλθον ὄπισθεν τοῦ βήματος· καὶ θεωρῶ ἐπάνω τῆς δεξαμενῆς τοῦ ὕδατος μῆλα τέσσαρα μεγάλα, εὔοσμα καὶ τῷ εἴδει ὡραῖα. Καὶ ταῦτα ἰδών, φοβούμενος τὴν ἀπάτην τοῦ Πολεμήτορος, ἐποίησα εὐχὴν καὶ τὸ σημεῖον τοῦ σταυροῦ ἐκ τρίτου, καὶ εἶδα ὅτι τὰ μῆλα οὐκ ἐξέλιπον. Λαβὼν αὐτὰ ὡς ἐκ τοῦ Θεοῦ, τὸν παράδεισον εἰσῆλθον πρὸς τὸν γέροντα καὶ εὗρον αὐτὸν ἔτι ἐμπνέοντα· καὶ συγκόψας ἀπὸ τὰ μῆλα ἔδωκα τῷ γέροντι, καὶ φαγὼν ἐνεδυναμώθη· καὶ πάλιν ἔφαγε καὶ ἐκραταιώθη, καὶ ἀναστὰς ἐκάθισε· καὶ πάλιν φαγὼν ἐστάθη εἰς τοὺς πόδας αὐτοῦ καὶ ἐπεριεπάτει.

2 "Καὶ περιπατοῦντες ἀμφότεροι, εἶπεν ὁ γέρων, Καυσοκαλύβη, ἑτοίμασον ἡμῖν πολύποδας καὶ ἄρτον καὶ οἶνον· ὅταν ἔλθωμεν, παραθήσῃς ἡμῖν τράπεζαν.' Καὶ οὕτως οἰκονόμησεν ὁ Θεὸς ἀμφοτέρων τῶν ἁγίων τὴν αἴτησιν. Ἀκούσας τὴν φωνὴν ἐκεῖνος τοῦ γέροντος ἀοράτως καὶ νοερῶς, ἐποίησεν εὐχὴν περὶ τούτου, καθὼς αὐτὸς ἡμῖν ὕστερον ἔλεγεν, Ἦλθε μοναχός τις, ὃν ἡμεῖς οὐκ οἴδαμεν,

weak from the journey. We found rusks and water there, so the elder regained some strength after he had eaten. And during the night we lay down. And in the morning I again wanted to take along some bread, but the elder would not allow it. We set off and made our way up with great effort, for the elder kept feeling faint on the way. And again, when we had made our way up to the holy summit and worshipped, he was so faint that he fell to the ground and was unable to get up, and I thought he was dead. But while I was worrying myself to death and had no idea what I could do or get for him and was completely distraught, I went out behind the sanctuary and saw on top of the water cistern four big, fragrant and nice looking apples. When I saw them I feared a trick of the Enemy, so I said a prayer and made the sign of the cross three times, and saw that the apples did not disappear. Taking them as a gift from God, I went into the enclosure to the elder and found that he was still breathing. I cut a piece from one of the apples and gave it to the elder, and when he ate it he regained some strength. And he ate again and became stronger, and getting up from the ground, he was able to sit; and when he had eaten again, he stood on his feet and started walking about.

"While we were both walking around, the elder said, 2 'Hutburner, prepare some octopus and bread and wine for us; set the table for us when we get there!' And this is how God arranged to fulfill the request of both his holy ones: when Maximos heard the voice of that elder, invisibly and intellectually, he said a prayer about this, and, as he said to us later, 'A monk, whom we didn't know, came carrying bread

βαστάζων ἄρτους καὶ οἶνον καὶ πολύποδας χύτραν μίαν μεστήν.' Ἦλθον ἐγὼ μετὰ τοῦ γέροντος, καὶ πρὸ τοῦ ἰδεῖν ἡμᾶς, ἐλάλησε λέγων, 'Δεῦτε, πατέρες, ὅτι ὑπὲρ ὑμῶν ἑτοίμασα τράπεζαν καὶ ἀναμένω προσδεχόμενος ὑμᾶς.' Καὶ ποιήσαντες εὐχὴν καὶ μετάνοιαν, ἀπολαύσαμεν τῆς θεωρίας καὶ ὁμιλίας τοῦ γέροντος· καὶ ηὐφράνθημεν καὶ σώματι καὶ πνεύματι. Καὶ καθήμενοι ἐπὶ τοῦ ἀρίστου, εἶπεν ὁ γέρων, ''Εσθίετε, πατέρες, ὅτι ἠγγαρεύσατέ με.' Ἀνηγγείλαμεν δὲ αὐτῷ καὶ τὰ συμβάντα ἐν τῇ ὁδῷ, ἣ ἐποιήσαμεν, καὶ πῶς τὰ μῆλα, εἰ μὴ ἦν ἐκ Θεοῦ, οὐκ ἂν ὁ γέρων ἀνέστη. Ταῦτα ἀκούσας ὁ μέγας μεγάλως τῷ Θεῷ ηὐχαρίστησε· καὶ ἡμεῖς ἰδόντες τὴν ἑτοιμασίαν τοῦ ἀρίστου, ὅπως διὰ τὴν ἡμετέραν ἀσθένειαν οἰκονομεῖ ὁ Θεὸς ταῦτα πάντα, μεγάλως τῷ Θεῷ ἐδοξάσαμεν."

19

Διηγήσατο ἡμῖν ὁ ἀββᾶς Γεράσιμος ἀπὸ τὴν ἁγίαν Λαύραν, ὅτι παρέβαλέ ποτε ὁ ἐκκλησιάρχης αὐτῆς πρὸς τὸν ὅσιον πατέρα ἡμῶν μετὰ καὶ ἑτέρων μοναχῶν. Καὶ ὁμιλούντων αὐτῶν μετ' αὐτοῦ, εἶπε πρὸς αὐτούς, "Καὶ ὁ Κανάκης ποῦ;" Καὶ οἱ πατέρες εἶπον, "Εἶπεν ὅτι ἔρχομαι.'" Καὶ ὁ πατὴρ εἶπε, "Καὶ νὰ φάγη ὁ Κανάκης ἰχθύας." Καθίσαντες δὲ ἐπὶ τοῦ ἀρίστου, πάλιν εἶπε τὸν αὐτὸν λόγον· καὶ ἰδοὺ ἔφθασεν ὁ Κανάκης, καὶ καθίσας ἤσθιε.

and wine and a dish full of octopus.' Then I came with the elder and, before he saw us, Maximos called out, 'Come here, fathers, because I've prepared the table for you and I'm waiting to welcome you.' And after we had said a prayer and prostrated ourselves, we enjoyed the sight and company of the elder, and we were content in both body and spirit. And when we sat down for the meal, the elder said, 'Eat, fathers, because you've put me to work!' Then we told him what had happened on the journey which we had made, and how, unless God had provided the apples, the old man would not have been able to get up again. When he heard this, the great one gave great thanks to God; and we, seeing in the way the meal had been prepared how God had arranged everything on account of our frailty, glorified Him greatly."

Chapter 19

*A*bbas Gerasimos from the holy Lavra told us that the sacristan of the monastery once went to our blessed father with some other monks. And while they were talking with him, Maximos said to them, "And where's Kanakes?" And the fathers said, "He said he was coming." And the father said, "Kanakes is going to eat fish!" When they had sat down for the meal, he said the same thing to them again. And, lo and behold, Kanakes arrived and sat down and ate. And

Καὶ δι᾽ ὀλίγην ὥραν ἤκουσαν ὁμιλίαις ἀνθρώπων· καὶ πρὸ
τοῦ ἰδεῖν αὐτοὺς ὁ πατὴρ εἶπε, "Ράπτης εἶμαι ἀπὸ τὸ Λουπάδι, καὶ πηδῶ καὶ ἐμπρὸς καὶ ὀπίσω." Καὶ ἰδοὺ ἔφθασαν
δύο κοσμικοὶ βαστάζοντες ἰχθύας πολλούς· καὶ ἠρώτησεν
αὐτούς, καὶ εἶπεν ὁ εἷς, "Ράπτης εἶμαι ἀπὸ τὸ Λουπάδι,
μᾶλλον δὲ καὶ καλὸς ράπτης." Καὶ ἀκούσας ταῦτα ὁ ἐκκλησιάρχης καὶ οἱ παρατυχόντες μοναχοί, ὅτι προεῖπε καὶ
τῶν ἰχθύων τὴν ἐπέλευσιν καὶ τὸν ράπτην καὶ τὸ Λουπάδι,
ἐξέστησαν ἐπὶ τὰ λεγόμενα καὶ γενόμενα παρὰ τοῦ ὁσίου
πατρός· καὶ τῷ Θεῷ μεγάλως ἐδόξαζον τῷ ποιοῦντι θαυμάσια μεγάλα μόνῳ.

20

Ὁ αὐτὸς εἶπεν ὅτι παρέβαλέ τις μοναχὸς πρὸς τὸν ὅσιον πατέρα καὶ λέγει αὐτόν, "Συγχώρησόν με, ὅτι βούλομαι
ἀπελθεῖν εἰς τὴν Πόλιν." Καὶ εἶπεν αὐτῷ ὁ πατήρ, "Ἐὰν
ὑπάγῃς, πάλιν διὰ συντόμως ὑπόστρεψον. Ὕπαγε δὲ εἰς
τὸν Καντακουζηνὸν τὸν βασιλέα καὶ ἐπίδος αὐτῷ ταῦτα,
παξαμᾶν καὶ σκόροδον καὶ κρόμμυον." Ἀπελθὼν δὲ ὁ μοναχὸς εἰς τὸν βασιλέα, καὶ δεξάμενος αὐτὰ ὁ βασιλεὺς
μετὰ πολλῆς τῆς εὐλαβείας ὡς ἀπὸ χειρὸς τοῦ ἁγίου,
μεγάλως ἐδόξασε τὸν Θεόν. Ἐπυνθάνετο οὖν μετὰ τῆς
δεσποίνης, τί ἂν εἴη τοῦτο. Τὸ δὲ σημεῖον προσφόρως τὰ
ὑπὸ τοῦ ὁσίου πέρας ἔλαβον γενόμενα καὶ λεγόμενα περὶ
τῆς μοναδικῆς πολιτείας.

after a short time they heard people talking, and before he saw them the father said, "I'm a tailor from Loupadion, and I'm jumping backward and forward." And, lo and behold, two laymen arrived carrying many fish. And he questioned them and one said, "I'm a tailor from Loupadion, actually a good tailor." When the sacristan and the monks who were there heard that he had foretold the arrival of the fish and the tailor and Loupadion, they were astounded at what the blessed father had said and done; and they greatly glorified God by whom alone great miracles are done.

Chapter 20

The same man said that a monk came to the blessed father and said to him, "Give me permission, because I want to go to the City of Constantinople." And the father said to him, "If you go, you must come straight back again. But go to the emperor Kantakouzenos and give these to him: a rusk, and a head of garlic, and an onion." The monk went off to the emperor and the emperor received these things with great piety as they came from the holy one's hand, and he greatly glorified God. So he asked the empress what this might be about. And in the end they rightly understood the things that the blessed one had done and said as being a sign of the monastic life.

21

Ἐγὼ δὲ ὁ εὐτελὴς Νίφων, εἰς τὴν μνήμην τῶν ἁγίων ἀποστόλων, ἐν ἡμέρᾳ ἕκτῃ, ὥρᾳ δ' τῆς ἡμέρας, ὅταν ἔβαλα ἀρχὴν γράφειν τὸ προειρημένον κεφάλαιον, πῶς ἐθαύμαζεν ὁ βασιλεὺς διὰ τὰ σταλέντα ὑπὸ τοῦ ὁσίου, ὑπέθηκα τὴν χάρτην, ἵνα μικρὸν ἀναπαύσωμαι ἀπὸ τῆς ἀσθενείας μου. Καὶ ὑπνώσαντός μου μικρόν, καὶ ἰδοὺ ἐφάνη μοι ὡς τὸν ὅσιον πατέρα καὶ τῇ χειρὶ αὐτοῦ τῇ δεξιᾷ πλήττοντά μου τὴν πλευρὰν καὶ λέγοντα, "Ἀνάστα. Αἴ, αἴ, ὅλον ὑπνοῖς;" Ἀναστὰς οὖν ἐγὼ ὁ ἀνάξιος, καὶ ἀπὸ τοῦ λόγου αὐτοῦ ηὐφράνθη μου τὸ πνεῦμα καὶ ἡ ψυχή, καὶ τὸ σῶμα ὑγιὲς ἐγένετο καὶ ἐρρωμένον, ὥστε μὴ αἰσθάνεσθαι ὅτι εἶχά ποτε ἀσθένειαν. Καὶ οὕτω λοιπὸν σὺν Θεῷ ἐτελείωσα τὸ λοιπὸν τοῦ κεφαλαίου εἰς δόξαν Πατρὸς καὶ Υἱοῦ καὶ ἁγίου Πνεύματος, καὶ διὰ πρεσβειῶν τοῦ ὁσίου πατρὸς ἡμῶν.

22

Πάλιν ἦλθέ ποτε ἀπὸ τὴν Κωνσταντινούπολιν εἰς τὴν ἁγίαν Λαύραν γραμματεὺς λόγιος καὶ νουνεχής. Εἶχε γοῦν ἀμφιβολίαν πολλὴν ἐν τῷ νοῒ αὐτοῦ τοιαύτην, ὅτι οἱ ἅγιοι κατὰ καιρὸν ὁποῦ ἐγένοντο ὀλίγα τίποτε ἐποίησαν, οἱ δὲ συγγράψαντες ταῦτα ἐποίησαν προσθήκην εἰς ταῦτα, εἰς

Chapter 21

But I, the worthless Niphon, on the feast day of the Holy Apostles, on Friday at the fourth hour of the day, when I had begun to write the previous chapter, about how the emperor was amazed by the things the blessed one had sent him, I set aside the paper so that I could take a little rest, due to my sickness. And after I had been asleep for a little while, lo and behold, someone like the blessed father appeared to me and hit me in the side with his right hand and said, "Get up! Hey, hey, are you always fast asleep?" So I got up, unworthy as I am, and my spirit and my soul were happy at his words, and my body was healthy and I was vigorous, so that I felt as though I had never been sick. And so, then, with God's help I finished the rest of the chapter to the glory of the Father, the Son and the Holy Spirit, and through the intercessions of our blessed father.

Chapter 22

Again, a learned and intelligent scholar once came from Constantinople to the holy Lavra. In fact, he had much doubt in his mind in this regard, namely that the saints, at the time they lived, did almost nothing, but that those who wrote about these things made these additions to their

τοὺς βίους καὶ εἰς τὰ μαρτύρια αὐτῶν. Ἀναστὰς οὖν μιᾷ τῶν ἡμερῶν ἦλθε πρὸς τὸν ὅσιον πατέρα· καὶ ἰδὼν αὐτὸν ἀνήγγειλεν αὐτῷ ὅσα ἐκεῖνος διελογίζετο περὶ τῶν ἁγίων τὰ συγγράμματα. Ἀκούσας δὲ ταῦτα ἐκεῖνος ἐξέστη, θαυμάζων καὶ ἐκπληττόμενος ἐπὶ τοῖς λόγοις τοῖς ἐκπορευομένοις ἐκ τοῦ στόματος αὐτοῦ, ηὐφράνθη δὲ τῷ πνεύματι ἐπὶ τοῖς θεοπνεύστοις λόγοις αὐτοῦ. Καὶ πάλιν ὅταν ἐξῆλθεν, εἶπεν αὐτῷ ἄλλα μειζότερα, ἅπερ ἐκεῖνος οὐδέπω ἤκουσεν. Ὑπέστρεψε δὲ εἰς τὴν ἁγίαν Λαύραν καὶ ἀνήγγειλε τὰ περὶ τοῦ ὁσίου τῷ ἀββᾷ Ἰγνατίῳ τῷ ἡσυχαστῇ, μαρτυρῶν αὐτὸν ἐπίγειον ἄγγελον καὶ οὐράνιον ἄνθρωπον, δοξάζων τὸν Θεόν, ὑμνολογῶν καὶ τὸν ὅσιον ἐν τοῖς θαυμαστοῖς αὐτοῦ λόγοις καὶ διδάγμασιν.

23

Ἀρσένιός τις μοναχὸς ἀπὸ τὴν ἁγίαν Λαύραν ἠβουλήθη ἀπελθεῖν εἰς τὴν Πόλιν· καὶ εἶπεν αὐτῷ ὁ πατήρ, "Μὴ ἀπέλθῃς, ὅτι τὸ πλοῖον αὐτὸ ἔχει κινδυνεῦσαι." Καὶ ἐγένετο οὕτως· μετὰ τρίτην ἡμέραν, ἠκούσθη, τὸ Θεσσαλονικαῖον πλοῖον ἐπνίγη. Καὶ πάλιν ἕτερος μοναχὸς Ἰάκωβος ἀπὸ τὴν ἁγίαν Λαύραν ἦλθε μετὰ τοῦ ἀδελφοῦ αὐτοῦ, καὶ εἶπεν ὁ ἀδελφὸς αὐτοῦ πρὸς τὸν ὅσιον, "Ἐγώ, πατήρ μου, εἶμαι αἰχμάλωτος, καὶ ἦλθα νά με γράψῃς χαρτίν, νὰ διακονιστῶ, νὰ ξαγοραστῶ." Καὶ ταῦτα ἀκούσας ὁ ἅγιος

Lives and to the accounts of their martyrdom. So one day he got up and came to the blessed father. And when Maximos saw him, he told that man what he had been thinking about what was written about the saints. And when the man heard this, he was totally astounded and was astonished by the words issuing from Maximos's mouth; and he rejoiced in his spirit at his divinely inspired words. And again when the man was leaving, Maximos said other even better things to him, of a kind the man had never heard before. And he returned to the holy Lavra and he told *abbas* Ignatios the hesychast all about the blessed one, testifying that he was an earthly angel and a heavenly man, glorifying God and praising the blessed one for his wondrous words and teachings.

Chapter 23

A monk from the holy Lavra, Arsenios, wanted to go to the city of Constantinople and the father said to him, "Don't go, because that ship is going to be in danger." And that's what happened: three days later it was learned that the Thessalonican ship had sunk. And again, another monk from the holy Lavra, Iakobos, came with his brother; and his brother said to the blessed one, "I, my father, am a captive, and I've come to ask you to write a note for me so that I may use it to get my ransom." When he heard this, the holy

ἐσιώπησε μικρόν· καὶ ἀποκριθεὶς μετὰ πολλῆς τῆς αὐστηρότητος λέγει, "Ἐσὺ ἔχεις ξ′ ὑπέρπυρα εἰς τὸν πύργον εἰς
τὸ τεῖχος, καὶ ἦλθες νά σε γράφω; Ὕπαγε καὶ ἐξαγοράσου
μὲ τὰ ἄσπρα σου." Καὶ ἀναστάντες ἔβαλον μετάνοιαν καὶ
ἐξῆλθον. Πορευομένων δὲ αὐτῶν ἐν τῇ ὁδῷ, ἐρώτησεν ὁ
Ἰάκωβος τὸν ἀδελφὸν αὐτοῦ, εἰ ἀληθῶς εἶπεν ὁ γέρων.
Καὶ εἶπε, "Ναί, ἀληθῶς εἶπε." Καὶ ἐξέστησαν ἐπὶ τοῦτο καὶ
τῷ Θεῷ μεγάλως ἐδόξασαν.

24

Ἀπὸ τὴν εὐαγεστάτην μονὴν τοῦ Ἀλυπίου ἦλθέ τις
μοναχός, ὄνομα Ἰωσήφ, πρὸς τὸν ὅσιον· καὶ ὁμιλούντων
αὐτῶν εἶπε πρὸς αὐτὸν ὁ πατήρ, "Εἰς τὸ μοναστήριόν σου
τοῦ Ἀλυπίου ἐν ταύτῃ τῇ ὥρᾳ ψάλλουσι τὸ Μακάριοι οἱ
ἄμωμοι" [Psalm 118(119):1]. Καὶ μετὰ τὸ πληρῶσαι τὴν
πρώτην στάσιν τοῦ Ἀμώμου πάλιν εἶπεν, "Εἰς τὸ μοναστήριόν σου ψάλλουσιν." Ἐσημειώσατο οὖν τὴν ὥραν ὁ
Ἰωσήφ· καὶ ἐπιστρέψας εἰς τὸ μοναστήριον ἐπυνθάνετο
διὰ τὴν ὥραν ἐκείνην, καὶ εὗρεν ὅτι ἐκοιμήθη Ἰωσήφ
γραμματεὺς ἐν ἐκείνῃ τῇ ὥρᾳ. Καὶ ἀνήγγειλε τοῖς πατράσι
τὰ προειρημένα ὑπὸ τοῦ μεγάλου πατρός· καὶ ἀκούσαντες
οἱ πατέρες, ὅτι οὐ μόνον τοῖς ἐγγὺς προορᾷ, ἀλλὰ καὶ τοῖς
μακράν, τῷ Θεῷ μεγάλως ἐδόξαζον τῷ ποιοῦντι θαυμάσια
τοῖς φοβουμένοις αὐτῷ.

one was silent for a while; and then he responded with great severity, "You have sixty *hyperpyra* in the wall in the tower and you come here asking me to write for you? Go and pay the ransom with your own money!" They got up and prostrated themselves and left. And while they were on their way Iakobos asked his brother if the elder had spoken the truth. And he said, "Yes, he spoke the truth." And they were astounded at this and glorified God greatly.

Chapter 24

A monk, named Joseph, came to the blessed one from the most holy monastery of Alypios. And, while they were talking, the father said to him, "At this moment they're singing the *'Blessed are the blameless'* at your monastery of Alypios." And after finishing the first section of the Blameless psalm he again said, "They're singing it at your monastery." Joseph noted the time and, after he returned to the monastery, asked about that time and discovered that Joseph the scholar had died at that very hour. He told the fathers about the great father's prediction; and, when the fathers heard that he foresaw not only things that were close at hand but also those far away, they greatly glorified God who works miracles for those who fear Him.

25

Ἦλθέ τις μοναχὸς Ματθαῖος ἀπὸ τὴν Πόλιν καὶ εἶπεν ἡμῖν ὅτι "Ἦλθά ποτε μὲ κοσμικοὺς ἀνθρώπους, καὶ μὴ εἰδὼς ἡμᾶς εἶπεν, 'Ἐδῶ καὶ οἱ Πολῖται, οἱ Ἁγιορωμανῖται.' Καὶ εἶπε καὶ τὰ ὀνόματα ἡμῶν. Καὶ πάλιν εἶπε, 'Καὶ σύ, κῦρι Μοδινέ, ἀπὸ πολλῶν ἡμερῶν ἐβούλεσο νὰ ἔλθῃς νά με εἰδῇς, καὶ ἰδοὺ ἐπλήρωσας τὸ σὸν καταθύμιον.' Καὶ ὁ Μοδινὸς εἶπεν, 'Ἀληθῶς, ναί, πατήρ μου, ἀληθῶς εἶπεν ἡ σὴ ἁγιωσύνη.'" Ἦλθέ ποτε κοσμικός τις πρὸς τὸν ὅσιον, καὶ ἰδὼν αὐτὸν εἶπεν, "Ἰωάννη, μέλλεις γενέσθαι ἱερεὺς καὶ ἡγούμενος· ἀγωνίσου δὲ νὰ γένῃς καὶ καλόγερος." Καὶ καιροῦ προϊόντος ἐγένετο μοναχός, καὶ ἐλθὼν ἔν τινι τῶν μονῶν τοῦ Ἁγίου Ὄρους ἐγένετο καὶ ἱερεὺς καὶ ἡγούμενος.

26

Μηνᾶς, ἱερεὺς καὶ ἡγούμενος τοῦ Ἀλυπίου, εἶπεν ὅτι "Παρεβάλομέν ποτε ἐγὼ καὶ ὁ μαθητὴς τοῦ ἐν ἁγίοις Γρηγορίου τοῦ Παλαμᾶ, ὁ ἱερομόναχος Γρηγόριος, πρὸς τὸν ὅσιον Καυσοκαλύβην. Εὕρομεν δὲ ἐκεῖ καὶ δύο ἄρχοντας κοσμικούς. Καὶ εἶπε πρός με ὁ ὅσιος, 'Εἰπὲ ἡμῖν ἀπὸ τῶν θαυμάτων τοῦ Θεσσαλονίκης.' Ἐμοῦ δὲ ἀντιλέγοντος μὴ εἰδέναι, καὶ πάλιν εἶπεν, 'Λέγε, εἰπέ.' Ἐγὼ δὲ ἀντέλεγα, 'Οὐ

Chapter 25

Amonk Matthew from the city of Constantinople came and said to me, "I once came with some laymen and, although he did not know us, Maximos said, 'And here are the men from the City, the Hagioromanitai.' And he said our names. And he said again, 'And you, Kyr Modinos, you've been wanting to come see me for a long time, and now, look, you've fulfilled your desire.' And Modinos said, 'Yes, it's true, my father; your holiness is telling the truth.'" Once a layman came to the blessed one and, when he saw him, Maximos said, "John, you're going to be a priest and a superior; strive to be a good monk too." And when some time had passed, he became a monk and, coming to one of the monasteries on the Holy Mountain, he became both a priest and a superior.

Chapter 26

Menas, a priest and the superior of Alypios, said, "I and the hieromonk Gregory, the disciple of Saint Gregory Palamas, once went to the blessed Hutburner. And we found two lay officials there. And the blessed one said to me, 'Speak to us about the miracles of the bishop of Thessalonike.' But, when I denied knowing them, he said again, 'Tell me, speak!' I told him, 'I don't know them.' But I had a book

γινώσκω.' Ἦν δὲ ἐν τῷ κόλπῳ μου τόμος γεγραμμένος περὶ τῶν θαυμάτων τοῦ Θεσσαλονίκης. Καὶ τότε μόλις ἔδειξα αὐτὸν λέγων, ''Εδῶ πού εἰσι γεγραμμένα.' Καὶ εἶπεν ὁ ὅσιος, 'Ταῦτά σοι λέγω νὰ λέγῃς, καὶ σὺ ἀντιλέγεις.' Ἡμεῖς δὲ οἱ παρατυχόντες ἐξέστημεν, θαυμάζοντες τὴν πρόορασιν τοῦ ἁγίου καὶ τῷ Θεῷ μεγάλως ἐδοξάσαμεν."

27

Ὁ ἀρχιερεὺς Τραϊανουπόλεως ἐρχόμενος πρὸς τὸν ὅσιον μετὰ τοῦ μαθητοῦ αὐτοῦ, ἦλθον ἔν τινι λάκκῳ. Καὶ ὁ μὲν ἀρχιερεὺς ἦν ὀλιγογένης, ὁ δὲ μαθητὴς αὐτοῦ ἐπλούτει ἐν ταύτῃ. Συμβούλιον δὲ λαβόντες [see Matthew 12:14], ἐγένετο ὁ ἀρχιερεὺς ὡς μαθητὴς καὶ ἐνέδυσεν αὐτὸν τὸν μανδύαν μὲ τὰ πώματα· καὶ αὐτὸς ἔβαλε τοῦ μαθητοῦ τὸν μανδύαν καὶ ἦλθεν εἰς τὸν ὅσιον πρὸς ὑπόμνησιν. Ὁ δὲ ὅσιος προγνοὺς τὸ δρώμενον ἀπὸ τῆς χάριτος ἐξῆλθεν εἰς ἀπάντησιν αὐτοῦ. Καὶ βαλόντες μετάνοιαν ἀμφότεροι, εἶπεν ὁ ἀρχιερεὺς πρὸς τὸν ὅσιον, "Ὁ δεσπότης μου ἀρχιερεὺς Τραϊανουπόλεως ἦλθε· καὶ ἂν κελεύῃς, νὰ ἔλθῃ νά σε ἴδῃ." Καὶ εἶπεν ὁ ὅσιος, "Σὺ εἶ ὁ ἀρχιερεύς· καὶ εὐλόγησόν με." Ὁ δὲ εἶπεν, "Οὐκ εἰμὶ ἐγώ, ἀλλ' ὁ ἀρχιερεὺς ὀπίσω ἵσταται· ἂν κελεύῃς, νὰ ἔλθῃ." Καὶ πάλιν ὁ ὅσιος εἶπε, "Σὺ εἶ ὁ ἀρχιερεύς· καὶ εὐλόγησόν με,

written about the miracles of the bishop of Thessalonike in the folds of my habit. So I then reluctantly showed him this and told him, 'Here, this is where they've been written down.' And the blessed one said, 'I told you to tell them and you told me you couldn't.' And those of us who were there were totally astounded, marveling at the holy one's clairvoyance, and we greatly glorified God."

Chapter 27

When the archbishop of Traianoupolis was coming with his disciple to the blessed one, they went aside into a dry cistern. And the archbishop had only a light beard, while his disciple's was thick. After *they had planned* this *together,* the archbishop switched roles with his disciple, and clothed him in his episcopal mantle with its rectangular embroidered panels, while he put on his disciple's mantle and went to the blessed one to inform him <of the archbishop's impending arrival>. But the blessed one, who already knew what had occurred through the grace that was in him, went out to meet him. And after both of them prostrated themselves, the archbishop said to the blessed one, "My master, the archbishop of Traianoupolis, has arrived and, if you tell him to, he would like to come and see you." And the blessed one retorted, "You're the archbishop, and should be blessing me!" But he said, "No, I'm not. The archbishop is standing back there, and, if you tell him to, he wants to come." And again the blessed one said, "You're the archbishop!

καὶ μὴ ὑποκρίνῃ ὡς κλέπτης· ἐπεὶ ἐκεῖ ἤμην ἐγὼ ἐπάνωθεν τοῦ λάκκου, ὅταν ἐβουλεύσασθε καὶ ἠλλάξατε τοὺς μανδύας. Καὶ εὐλόγησόν με." Καὶ ἰδὼν καὶ ἀκούσας ταῦτα, ὁ ἀρχιερεὺς εὐλόγησεν αὐτόν, καὶ ἀσπασμὸς ἐγένετο ἐν ἁγίῳ Πνεύματι. Ηὐφράνθησαν δὲ καὶ ὁ ἀρχιερεὺς καὶ ὁ μαθητὴς αὐτοῦ ἀπὸ τῆς ὁμιλίας τοῦ ὁσίου πατρὸς καὶ ἠγαλλιάσαντο καὶ σώματι καὶ πνεύματι· καὶ ἐδόξασαν τὸν Θεόν, ὑμνοῦντες καὶ θαυμάζοντες καὶ τὸν αὐτοῦ θεράποντα.

28

Ἦλθόν ποτε δύο μοναχοὶ ἀπὸ τὴν εὐαγεστάτην μονὴν τοῦ Βατοπαιδίου πρὸς τὸν ὅσιον. Καὶ ἦν ἔξω τῆς καλύβης· καὶ ἤρχετο ὡς ὑπόπτερος ἐπάνω τῶν κλάδων τοῦ ἄλσους πρὸς τὴν καλύβην. Καὶ ἰδόντες τοῦτον ἐξέστησαν, καὶ φόβος μέγας ἔλαβεν αὐτούς, καὶ σύντρομοι ἐγένοντο ἀπὸ τοῦ φόβου. Καὶ μεθ᾽ ὥραν ἐπορεύθησαν πρὸς τὸν ὅσιον καὶ ποιήσαντες μετάνοιαν ἐκάθισαν, λαβόντες παρ᾽ αὐτοῦ εὐχήν. Καὶ ἠρώτησεν αὐτούς, "Πόθεν ἐστέ;" Καὶ ἀπεκρίθησαν, "Ἀπὸ τὸ Βατοπαίδι· καὶ ἤλθομεν ἵνα εὐλογηθῶμεν καὶ λάβωμεν εὐχὴν παρὰ τῆς σῆς ἁγιότητος· καὶ εὐχαριστοῦμεν τὸν Θεόν, ὅτι σε εἴδαμεν." Πάλιν ἠρώτησεν αὐτούς, "Μὴ νὰ εἴδατέ τί ποτε;" Καὶ εἶπον, "Οὐκ εἴδαμεν." Τότε ὡμίλησαν μετὰ τοῦ ὁσίου, καὶ ἐδίδαξεν αὐτοὺς τὰ

Bless me and don't be deceitful like a thief. I was there myself above the cistern when you planned this and traded your mantles. So bless me!" When the archbishop saw and heard this, he blessed him and they kissed in the Holy Spirit. And the archbishop and his disciple took pleasure in the blessed father's conversation and rejoiced in body and spirit. And they glorified God, and also praised and marveled at His servant.

Chapter 28

Two monks from the most holy monastery of Vatopedi once went to the blessed one. And he was away from his hut; but he came to his hut, as though on wings, above the branches of the forest. When they saw this, they were astounded, and a great fear took hold of them, and they started trembling with fear. After some time they approached the blessed one and, after prostrating themselves, sat down, receiving his blessing. And he asked them, "Where did you come from?" And they replied, "From Vatopedi; and we came to be blessed and to receive a blessing from your holiness; and we thank God that we've seen you." He asked them again, "You didn't see anything, did you?" And they said, "We didn't see anything." Then they conversed with the blessed one and he taught them about their salvation.

πρὸς σωτηρίαν αὐτῶν. Καὶ ποιήσαντες μετάνοιαν, ἀπέλυσεν αὐτοὺς μετ' εἰρήνης. Καὶ αὐτοὶ ἐδιηγοῦντο ἐν τῇ ὁδῷ
ἃ εἶδον οἰκείοις ὀφθαλμοῖς, θαυμάζοντες τοῦ ἁγίου τὴν
παρρησίαν ἣν ἔχει πρὸς τὸν Θεόν.

29

Εἶπε δὲ καὶ ὁ ἱερομόναχος Μακάριος ἀπὸ τὴν ἁγίαν
Λαύραν, οὗ τὸ ἐπίκλην Χαμνός, ὅτι ἐν καιρῷ χειμῶνος
ἠβουλήθη ἀπελθεῖν πρὸς τὸν ὅσιον, καὶ "Ποιήσαντός
μου," φησίν, "ἔδεσμα καὶ λαβὼν μετ' ἐμοῦ καὶ ἕτερον
ἀδελφὸν ἐπορεύθημεν· καὶ κρούσαντες τὴν θύραν, οὐκ
ἀπεκρίθη. Ἦν γὰρ ἀπὸ τὴν ψύχραν, καὶ λαβὼν πλοκοτήν,
ἣν εἶχε κατασκευασμένην ἀπὸ καλάμων, ἐσκεπάστη καὶ
ὕπνωσε. Ὡς οὖν εἶδα ὅτι οὐχ ἀποκρίνεται, ὑπέλαβα ὅτι
ἀπὸ τῆς ψυχρότητος ἐζάρωσε καὶ κοιμᾶται. Καὶ εἰσῆλθα
καὶ ὁρῶ τὸν ὅσιον, ὅτι ὑπνοῖ κεκαλυμμένος μετὰ χρυσοῦ
ὑπαπλώματος· καὶ ἔλαμπεν ἡ καλύβη, ὡς ἐνόμισα, ἀπὸ τοῦ
ὑπαπλώματος. Καὶ τοῦτο ἰδὼν ἐθαύμασα· καὶ ἐξῆλθα καὶ
ἀνήγγειλα τῷ ἀδελφῷ τῷ ὄντι μετ' ἐμοῦ· κἀκεῖνος πλησιάσας εἶδε καὶ αὐτὸς οὕτως. Καὶ εἴπομεν ἀμφότεροι, ὅτι
τινὰς ἐκ τῶν ἀρχόντων τῶν μεγιστάνων ἀπέστειλεν αὐτό.
Καὶ πάλιν κρούσαντες, ἠγέρθη καὶ ἐλάλησε· καὶ εἰσήλθα-
μεν καὶ βαλόντες μετάνοιαν, ἐκαθίσαμεν καὶ ὁμιλήσαντες
ἀριστήσαμεν.

And after they had prostrated themselves, he dismissed them in peace. And on the way back they described what they had seen with their own eyes, amazed at how close the blessed one was to God.

Chapter 29

The hieromonk Makarios from the holy Lavra, whose surname was Chamnos, said that he decided to go visit the blessed one in wintertime, and "After I had made some food," he said, "and taking another monk along with me, we walked there. And when we knocked on the door, he didn't answer. For, on account of the cold, he had taken a plaited wrap which he had made out of rushes, and covered himself up and gone to sleep. So when I saw that he was not answering, I thought that he had curled up and was sleeping because of the cold. And I went in and saw the blessed one asleep covered with a golden blanket. And the hut was lit up, as it seemed to me, by the blanket. And when I saw this I was amazed, and I went out and told the brother who was with me; and when he came close, he too saw this. And we said to each other that one of the grand officials must have sent it. And when we knocked again, he woke up and spoke. And we went in and, after prostrating ourselves, sat down, and after we had talked, we had our meal.

2 "Καὶ μετὰ τοῦ ἀρίστου ἠρώτησα τὸν ὅσιον, 'Τίς σε ἀπέστειλε, πάτερ, τοιοῦτον ὑφάπλωμα;' Καὶ ὁ γέρων ἀπεκρίθη, 'Οὐκ οἶδα τί λέγεις.' Κἀγὼ εἶπα, "Ὑφάπλωμα εἴδαμεν χρυσοῦν καὶ ὑπέρλαμπρον, ὑπνοῦντά σε ὄντα, καὶ σκέποντά σε ὅλον· καὶ ἐκ τῆς λαμπρότητος αὐτοῦ ἔλαμπεν ὅλον σου τὸ κελλίον ἀπ' αὐτῆς.' Καὶ ὁ γέρων μειδιάσας πρός με λέγει, 'Συνεχόμενος ἀπὸ τῆς ψυχρότητος ἐσκεπάστην τὴν πλοκοτὴν τῶν καλάμων, καὶ συνέσφιξε τὰ ῥάκιά μου καὶ ἐθερμάνθη· καὶ ἀφύπνωσα, ὅτι τῇ νυκτὶ ταύτῃ ἀπὸ τῆς ψυχρότητος οὐκ ἐκοιμήθην.' Καὶ λαβόντες εὐχὴν ἀπὸ τοῦ ἁγίου, ὡς ἠκούσαμεν ταῦτα, ἐξήλθομεν θαυμάζοντες καὶ δοξάσαντες τὸν Θεὸν τὸν ποιοῦντα θαυμαστὰ μυστήρια, πῶς τοὺς αὐτὸν δουλεύοντας σκέπει καὶ διαφυλάττει ἀπὸ ψυχρότητος καὶ παντὸς κακοῦ."

30

Δαμιανός τις μοναχὸς ἀμπελικὸς ἐκ συνεργίας τοῦ Πονηροῦ εἶχεν ἀπιστίαν εἰς τὸν ἅγιον, καὶ τοσοῦτον ὡς οὐδὲ ὀρθόδοξον Χριστιανὸν αὐτὸν ἐνόμιζεν εἶναι. Θέλων οὖν ὁ πάντας ἀνθρώπους θέλων σωθῆναι καὶ εἰς ἐπίγνωσιν ἀληθείας ἐλθεῖν [1 Timothy 2:4], ἵνα καὶ ὁ ἀδελφὸς διορθωθῇ καὶ τὸν ἅγιον δοξάσῃ, τί ποιεῖ; Λαβὼν ὁ Δαμιανὸς τῇ Κυριακῇ κατὰ τὸ σύνηθες τὴν διακονίαν τῆς ἑβδομάδος, ἐκ τοῦ μοναστηρίου ἐξῆλθεν εἰς τὸν ἀμπελῶνα, ὃν ἐγεώργει·

"And after the meal I asked the blessed one, 'Who sent ₂ you such a blanket, father?' And the elder replied, 'I don't know what you're talking about.' And I said, 'We saw a brilliant golden blanket completely covering you while you were sleeping, and your whole cell was lit up by its brilliance.' And the elder smiled at me and said, 'I was suffering from the cold, so I covered myself with the wrap made from rushes, and it held together my rags and warmed me up; and I fell asleep because I hadn't been able to sleep last night because of the cold.' And, after we had received a blessing from the holy one, once we had heard this, we left, amazed and glorifying God who works strange wonders, <having witnessed> how He shelters and protects His servants from extreme cold and every evil."

Chapter 30

Damianos, a monk who was a vinedresser, had no faith in the holy one due to the efforts of the Evil One, and to such an extent, indeed, that he did not even think Maximos was an orthodox Christian. So, because *He who wishes that all men should be saved and come to recognize the truth* also wished that this brother might be set straight and might glorify the holy one, what did He do? Damianos, who, as usual, was carrying out his weekly work on Sunday, left the monastery for the vineyard which he was cultivating. And after he had

καὶ διακονηθείς, τῇ αὐτῇ ἑσπέρᾳ ἀφύπνωσε. Καὶ τῷ ὄρθρῳ ἀναστὰς πρὸς τὸ ποιῆσαι τὸν κανόνα αὐτοῦ, ἐπείνασε τοσοῦτον πολλὰ ὥστε μὴ δύνασθαι ποιῆσαί τι· καὶ καθίσας ἐθαύμαζε, τί ἐστι τοῦτο. Τότε ἀνάψας πῦρ καὶ λαβὼν κρόμμυα καὶ συγκόψας αὐτὰ καὶ βαλὼν εἰς χύτραν μετὰ ἐλαίου καὶ ὕδατος εἰς τὸ πῦρ, καὶ λαβὼν οὓς εἶχεν ἄρτους ξηροὺς ἔβαλεν εἰς πινάκιον μέγα· καὶ βαλὼν ἐπάνω τὸ ἔψημα καὶ καλύψας αὐτὸ ἐπρόσμενεν, ἕως ὅτου διαφαύσῃ ἡ ἡμέρα. Ἀναγκαστεὶς οὖν ἀπὸ τῆς πολλῆς πείνης οὐδὲν ἐκαρτέρησεν, ἀλλ᾽ ἤρξατο ἐσθίειν· καὶ φαγὼν μίαν μετὰ πολλῆς βίας κατέπιεν, ὅσον μόνον ὁποῦ ἐγεύσατο, σχεδὸν εἰπεῖν, καὶ πλέον οὐκ ἠδυνήθη· καὶ καθίσας ἐθαύμαζεν ἐν ἑαυτῷ, τί ἐστι τοῦτο. Τότε καλύψας τὸ πινάκιον εἶπε, "Σήμερον μέλλω σκάπτειν εἰς τὸν ἀμπελῶνα, ὥστε με ποιῆσαι ὄρεξιν τοῦ φαγεῖν."

2   Ὡς δὲ ἔφαυσεν ἡ ἡμέρα, ἔκρουσέ τις ἔξωθεν τοῦ κελλίου καὶ λέγει πρὸς αὐτόν, "Ἐλθὲ ἔσω, εἴ τι ἂν καὶ εἴης." Καὶ εἰσελθών, θεωρεῖ ὅτι ὁ ὅσιος ἦν· καὶ λέγει πρὸς αὐτόν, "Πολλὰ ἐτάχυνας, πάτερ." Καὶ ὁ γέρων λέγει, "Φέρε τὸ ἔψημα, ἵνα φάγω, ὅτι ὀγδόη ἡμέρα ἔχω ἄσιτος, ἐπεὶ οὐδὲ εἰς ἐπαρέβαλε πρός με, ἵνα φέρῃ τι." Εἶχε γὰρ συνήθειαν ὅτι ποτὲ εἰς τὴν καλύβην οὐκ ἐκράτει τί ποτε, οὔτε ἄρτον, οὔτε ἄλλο τι βρώσιμον, μόνον ὕδωρ ὀλίγον. Τότε κατανυγεὶς ὁ Δαμιανὸς καὶ βαλὼν μετάνοιαν εἶπε πρὸς τὸν ὅσιον, "Ἀληθῶς, πάτερ ἅγιε, ὁ Θεὸς ἐμαγείρεψε διὰ σοῦ." Καὶ βαλὼν τράπεζαν καὶ τὸ ἔψημα καὶ ἄρτους καὶ οἶνον καὶ εἴ τι ἄλλο βρώσιμον εἶχεν εἰς τὸ κελλίον αὐτοῦ, καὶ καθίσας μετὰ τοῦ ὁσίου ἔφαγε καὶ ηὐφράνθη καὶ ἠγαλλιάσθη καὶ

done his work, he slept there that evening. And when he got up in the morning to say his office, he was so hungry that he couldn't do anything. And he sat there, wondering what was going on. Then, after he had lit a fire, he took some onions, cut them up and put them on the fire in a cooking pot with oil and water; he also took what dry bread he had and put it in a big dish. And he put the stew on top, covered it up, and was waiting for daybreak. But then, driven by his great hunger, he couldn't wait any longer, but began to eat. He took one bite and violently gulped it down, but then it was as though he could eat no more than just the taste he had had. And he sat there wondering to himself what was going on. Then he covered up the dish and said, "Today I'm going to dig in the vineyard to give myself an appetite to eat."

But at daybreak someone knocked outside his cell and he said to him, "Come in, whoever you are!" And when the person came in, Damianos saw that it was the holy one; and he said to him, "You're up and about very early, father." And the elder said, "Bring the stew, so that I can eat, because I've been without food for eight days, as not a single person has come to see me to bring anything." For it was his practice never to keep anything in his cell, neither bread nor any other food, only a little water. Then Damianos was filled with contrition and prostrated himself and said to the blessed one, "Truly, holy father, God cooked for you." Then he set the table with the stew and bread and wine and whatever other food he had in his cell, and he sat down with the

σώματι καὶ πνεύματι. Καὶ μετὰ τοῦ ἀρίστου πάλιν ἔβαλε μετάνοιαν καὶ ἐξωμολογήσατο, πῶς ἐλοιδόρει τὸν γέροντα καὶ ἐμέμφετο. Καὶ λαβὼν συγχώρησιν παρ᾽ αὐτοῦ, ἀπῆλθεν ὁ ὅσιος ἐν τῇ καλύβῃ αὐτοῦ. Καὶ ἔκτοτε ἔλαβε πληροφορίαν πίστεως εἰς τὸν ὅσιον καὶ ἐδόξαζε τὸν Θεὸν καὶ τὸν αὐτοῦ θεράποντα. Τοῦτό μοι διηγήσατο ὁ αὐτὸς Δαμιανὸς ἔνδον τῆς ἁγίας Λαύρας.

31

Ἦν δὲ καὶ ἄλλα πολλὰ θαύματα καὶ προοράματα ᾀδόμενα καὶ λεγόμενα καὶ γενόμενα παρὰ τοῦ ὁσίου πατρὸς ἡμῶν, ἅπερ ἀκήκοα κἀγώ, καὶ καθώς μοι ἐδήλωσαν καὶ ἕτεροι ἀψευδεῖς πατέρες, ὅ τε Γρηγόριος ἀπὸ τῆς Πέτρας Σίμωνος τοῦ μυροβλύτου καὶ Ματθαῖος μοναχὸς καὶ ἄλλος Ματθαῖος ἱερομόναχος καὶ ἕτεροι, ἅτινα ἔμελλον γράφειν καταλεπτῶς, διὰ δὲ τὴν ἰδιωτείαν μου καὶ τὴν ἄγονόν μου ψυχὴν καὶ τὴν τοῦ νοὸς ἔλλειψιν καὶ τὴν ἀδυναμίαν μου, καὶ διὰ τὸ μῆκος τοῦ λόγου κατέπαυσα ἕως ὧδε. Αὐτὸς γοῦν ὁ μαθητὴς καὶ μιμητὴς τοῦ Χριστοῦ τοιαύτην ὁδὸν ἐβάδισε στενὴν καὶ τεθλιμμένην [see Matthew 7:14], ὅπως τὸ κατ᾽ εἰκόνα τηρήσῃ ἀλώβητον, καὶ οὕτως ἔφθασεν εἰς τὸ καθ᾽ ὁμοίωσιν [Genesis 1:26]. Ἐγὼ δὲ ὁ πανάθλιος, ὁ πάσης ἀνομίας ἐργάτης τί ποιήσω; Τί πράξω; Τίς γένωμαι; Πῶς φύγω τὰς κολάσεις; Πῶς τύχω σωτηρίας;

blessed one and ate and was content and glad in body and spirit. And after the meal he prostrated himself again and confessed how he had abused the elder and found fault with him. And when Damianos had received forgiveness from him, the blessed one went off to his hut. And from then on he had complete faith in the blessed one and glorified God and His servant. Damianos told me this himself in the holy Lavra.

Chapter 31

And there were many other celebrated miracles and prophecies performed and foretold by our blessed father, which I myself have heard and which likewise also other trustworthy fathers, such as Gregory from the Rock of Simon who exudes perfumed oil, and the monk Matthew, and another hieromonk Matthew, and others have disclosed to me, which I was going to write down in detail, but, due to my uncouthness and the sterility of my soul and the deficiency of my mind and my lack of ability, and also on account of the length of the work already, I have stopped here. This disciple and imitator of Christ, Maximos, trod such a *narrow and difficult* path so that he might preserve *the image* of God unblemished, and he thus attained *the likeness* of God. But what shall I, this totally wretched and completely iniquitous laborer, do? What shall I contrive? What is to become of me? How may I escape eternal punishment? How

Τίς δώσῃ τῇ κεφαλῇ μου ὕδωρ καὶ τοῖς ὀφθαλμοῖς μου πηγὴν δακρύων [Jeremiah 9:1], ὅπως θρηνήσω καὶ ἀποκλαύσω τῶν ἀπείρων μου πράξεων τὰ δεινὰ ἀνομήματα καὶ παραπτώματα; Ὅμως διὰ τῶν ἁγίων εὐχῶν τοῦ ὁσίου πατρὸς δώῃ ὑμῖν ὁ Θεὸς σωτηρίαν τοῖς ἀκούουσι τῷ παρόντι ἰδιωτικῷ συγγράμματι, κἀμοὶ τῷ ἁμαρτωλῷ καὶ ἀναξίῳ ἐλεήσῃ καὶ σώσῃ εἰς τὴν βασιλείαν αὐτοῦ ὡς ἀγαθὸς καὶ φιλάνθρωπος.

may I obtain salvation? *Who will provide my head with water and my eyes with a fountain of tears,* so that I may lament and bewail the dreadful faults and transgressions of my boundless deeds? May God, however, through the holy prayers of the blessed father, give salvation to you who hear this present amateurish composition, and may He, who is good and compassionate, also have mercy on me, a sinful and unworthy man, and bring me safe into His kingdom.

LIFE OF MAXIMOS THE HUTBURNER BY THEOPHANES

Βίος καὶ πολιτεία καὶ ἄσκησις καὶ φαιδροὶ ἀγῶνες καὶ θαύματα τοῦ ὁσίου καὶ θεοφόρου πατρὸς ἡμῶν Μαξίμου τοῦ τὴν καλύβην πυρπολοῦντος ἐν τῷ Ἁγίῳ Ὄρει τῷ Ἄθωνι

Ποίημα καὶ πόνημα Θεοφάνους τοῦ Περιθεωρίου καὶ προηγουμένου τοῦ Βατοπεδίου

I

Οἱ τὴν ἤπειρον κατ᾽ ἐπιστήμην καὶ θάλατταν διερχόμενοι ἄνθρωποι, οἱ μὲν τὰς νάπας καὶ τοὺς ζυγούς, ὄρη καὶ πεδιάδας, οἰκουμένην τε καὶ ἀοίκητον, καὶ τὰς ὁδοὺς αὐτῶν καὶ τὰς θέσεις καὶ τὰς διαφορὰς πάσας διαμετροῦσιν, ὅσον ἡ γνῶσις ἀπὸ πείρας λάβοιεν, ἵν᾽ ἐξηγήσαιντο· οἱ δὲ πελάγη διάφορα διαδραμόντες καὶ πορθμοὺς καὶ λιμένας, ἀκτὰς καὶ αἰγιαλοὺς καθιστορήσαντες ἀκριβῶς καὶ τῶν κύκλῳ ἀνέμων τὰς κινήσεις ἐν γνώσει καταλαβόντες, διηγοῦνται τοῖς πᾶσιν ἐγγράφως τε καὶ ἀγράφως εἰς ὠφέλειαν τῶν ἀκουόντων ἅμα καὶ μνήμην ἀγαθὴν τοῦ μηνύοντος. Ταὐτὸ δὴ καὶ ὁ ἀρετὴν ἐξηγούμενος τἀνδρὸς ἀγαθοῦ, πρῶτον μὲν εὐφροσύνην ἐντίθησι ταῖς ἀκοαῖς τῶν πιστῶν, εἶτα δὲ καὶ σκιρτᾶν ἐμποιεῖ τὰς καρδίας αὐτῶν, ὥς φησι

The life, conduct, ascetic discipline, splendid struggles, and miracles of our holy and divinely inspired father Maximos, who used to burn his hut on the Holy Mountain of Athos

The work and labor of Theophanes, <metropolitan> of Peritheorion and former superior of Vatopedi

Chapter 1

Among men who travel the land and sea in search of knowledge, some explore valleys and hilly ridges, mountains and plains, inhabited and uninhabited regions of the world, and all their roads, locations, and everything that distinguishes them, so that they may describe in detail what they have learned from their experience; others voyaging through the various seas, making accurate observations of straits and harbors, promontories and shores, and gaining knowledge of the swirling winds, set this out in every detail in writing and orally, both for the benefit of their listeners as well as for the sake of the informant's own good reputation. The same is true of one who describes the virtue of the good man: first he instills joy in the ears of the faithful, then he

Σολομών· "Ἐγκωμιαζομένου δικαίου εὐφρανθήσονται λαοί"
[see Proverbs 29:2].

2   Ἀλλ᾽ ὁ εἰδὼς ἐκεῖνος τὰ τοῦ δικαίου, ὡς ἐκεῖνοι κατ᾽
ἐπιστήμην θαλαττάν τε καὶ ἤπειρον, οὗτος καὶ εἰκότως ἂν
δίκαιον τὰ τοῦ δικαίου ἐγκώμια πλέξασθαι, καὶ μάλιστα ὁ
τὸν λόγον ἔχων ἐκ τοῦ Λόγου τὸ λέγειν, τοιούτους δὲ καὶ
ὀφείλει λογογραφεῖν καὶ ἐγκωμιάζειν δικαίους. Ἀλλ᾽ ὁ
λόγος πᾶσι μὲν τοῖς λογικοῖς πρῶτον μὲν ὡς ἐνδιάθετος
κατὰ νοῦν βρεφουργεῖται καὶ τὴν διάνοιαν, εἶτα γίνεται
καὶ εὐδιάχυτος διὰ χειλέων καὶ πνεύματος, εἶθ᾽ οὕτως
ἔναρθρος καὶ πρόσφατος, εἰς ἓν τοῖς τοῦ λόγου μέρεσιν
† ὡς ἀνὴρ † ἑδραζόμενος τὸ ῥῆμα τῆς διαλέξεως. Καὶ εἰ
μὲν κατ᾽ ἐπιστήμην μαθημάτων ὁ νοῦς τὸν λόγον κινήσει
μόνον, θαυμάζεται μὲν τοῖς λογίοις καὶ μόνοις, ἀλλ᾽ οὐκ
ἐπανατέλλει καὶ οὕτως ἐπὶ πᾶσιν τὴν χάριν καὶ τὴν εὐφροσύνην τοῦ Πνεύματος· εἰ δ᾽ ἐκ τοῦ Πνεύματος ὁ νοῦς τὸν
λόγον κινήσειεν, οὐ μόνον ἐν τῇ ἀκοῇ τῶν λογίων θαυμάζεται, ἀλλὰ καὶ τοῖς μὴ εἰδόσι τὸν λόγον, καὶ πάντων εὐ-
κρινεῖ καὶ εὐφραίνει καρδίας πλουσίως ἐν χάριτι.

3   Ὧν ἐπ᾽ ἀμφοτέροις αὐτὸς πάνυ ὡς ἀδαὴς χωλανῶ καὶ
ὡς ἀμύητος· ὅθεν τὴν ἀβελτηρίαν ὁρῶν τοῦ νοὸς καὶ τοῦ
ἐμοῦ λόγου τὸ ἀκαλλές (ξένος γάρ εἰμι ἐκ τῶν ὧν μέμνημαι δύο, τῆς τε μαθήσεως καὶ τῆς χάριτος), λέγειν οὐ
βούλομαι· καὶ ναρκῶ μὲν τῇ χειρί, πεπέδημαι δὲ τῇ γλώττῃ
λαλεῖν καὶ γράφειν τὰ ὑπὲρ δύναμιν. Ὅμως θαρρήσας τῇ
εὐχῇ τοῦ δικαίου, κατὰ τὸ δυνατὸν ἡμῖν οὕτως αὐτὸν
καταλέξομεν ἐγκωμίοις καὶ στέψομεν, ὃν ἡ ἁγία Τριὰς

makes their hearts to leap, as Solomon says: "*When the righteous man is praised, the people will rejoice.*"

But someone who knows all about the righteous man, just 2 like those who traverse sea and land in search of knowledge, would rightly think he should compose encomia of the righteous man, and that he has an obligation to write about and praise such righteous men, especially if he is someone who has received skill in using words from the Word of God. But words are first engendered in all rational beings as something immanent in the mind and thought, and then they are spontaneously disseminated through the lips and breath; then, being thus articulated and freshly uttered, like man being created, they are assigned to one of the parts of speech and take on the phrasing of discourse. If the mind sets words in motion only through a skill it has learned, it is admired only by erudite men, but it does not manifest at all in this way the grace and joy of the Spirit; but if the mind sets words in motion through the Spirit, not only are they admired by the erudite men who hear them, but also by those who are not learned, and they explain things clearly and make the hearts of all rejoice abundantly in grace.

I myself limp along, almost completely ignorant and un- 3 initiated in both of these qualities; and so, seeing the stupidity of my mind and the gracelessness of my words (for I am a stranger to the two qualities that I have mentioned, both learning and grace), I have no wish to speak. My hand is numb and my tongue is tied, so that I cannot speak and write that which is beyond my abilities. Nonetheless, taking courage from the intercessory prayer of the righteous Maximos, I will thus describe him as best I can with encomia, and will crown him whom the Holy Trinity crowned with both

ἐστεφάνωσεν φῶς ἅγιον ἄνωθεν καὶ χάριν ἣν ἐκέκτητο
ἀνεκλάλητον κατά τε διάκρισιν, διόρασιν καὶ προόρασιν.

4 Ὡς γὰρ προφήτης ὑπέρτατος πάντα τοῖς πᾶσιν ἐπροΰ-
λεγε καὶ τὰ μακρὰν ὡς ἔγγιστα ἐσαφήνιζεν ἐν τῷ Πνεύματι·
Πνεῦμα γὰρ ἅγιον ἐπὶ τὸν δίκαιον κατεσκήνωσεν καὶ τὸ
ὀπτικὸν τῆς ψυχῆς αὐτοῦ ἀπεκάθηρεν καὶ τὸν φωτισμὸν
τῆς χάριτος αὐτοῦ αὐτῷ πλουσίως ἐξέχεεν. Διὰ τοῦτο καὶ
οὐχὶ ὑπὸ τὸν μόδιον, ἀλλ᾽ ἐπὶ τὴν λυχνίαν τὴν ὑψηλὴν ἐτέθη
τοῦ Πνεύματος, *καὶ ἔλαμψεν τὸ φῶς αὐτοῦ τοῖς πᾶσιν* [see
Matthew 5:15], ὥς φησι τὸ ἀληθινὸν φῶς, ὁ Χριστός. Καὶ
ἦν ἀεὶ φῶς ὁ δίκαιος οὗτος ἡμῖν ἐν τῷ Ὄρει τῷ κεκλημένῳ
Ἁγίῳ διαλάμπων καὶ καταλάμπων καὶ εὐφραίνων καὶ ψυ-
χαγωγῶν, ὡς ὁ φαιδρότατος ἥλιος ἀνατέλλων φαιδρύνει
τοὺς ἐν Ὄρει καθεύδοντας καὶ τὰ ὕψη ἐκτρέχοντας, ὥς
φησι τοῦτο καὶ Σολομών· *"Φῶς δικαίοις διὰ παντός"*
[Proverbs 13:9] καὶ *"Ἐν τῷ φωτί σου ὀψόμεθα φῶς"* [Psalm
35(36):9].

5 Οὐκ ἐν ῥητορικῇ γλώττῃ καὶ πιθανότητι, οὐ σοφιστι-
κοῖς νοήσεσιν καὶ συλλογισμοῖς καὶ ἀριθμητικοῖς καὶ πυ-
θαγορικοῖς μυθεύμασι καὶ μαντεύμασι τοὺς πάντας εἷλκεν
ἐκ μακρόθεν οὕτω πρὸς ἑαυτὸν τοῦ κατατρέχειν κόπῳ
πολλῷ *τοῦ ἀκούειν καὶ λέγειν καινότερα* [Acts 17:21], ὡς
κατὰ τὸν Ἄρειον πάγον ποτέ· ἀλλ᾽ ἐν ἁπλοῖς καὶ ἀπεριέρ-
γοις ἤθεσί τε καὶ λόγοις, καὶ ἁγίοις ἄνθεσιν ἀρετῆς, ἧς
κεκόσμητο, ἀειθαλέσιν ἐν Πνεύματι, καὶ ἐξαισίοις καρποῖς
χαρισμάτων ἐν θεωρίαις ἁγίαις, οἷς ἐχορηγεῖτο πλουσίως
καὶ ἐχορήγει αὖθις τοῖς πᾶσι πλουσίως. Τούτου γε χάριν
κεκμηκότες ἅπαντες, εἴτε ἡμεῖς οἱ κατοικοῦντες ἐν Ὄρει,

holy light from on high and the ineffable spiritual gift which he received of discernment, clairvoyance and foresight.

For, as a superlative prophet, he foretold in the Spirit everything to everyone and revealed distant things as if they were close at hand; for the Holy Spirit took up residence in the righteous man, refined the visual acuity of his soul, and shed the illumination of Its grace abundantly on him. Therefore *he was not placed beneath a bushel, but on the* high *lampstand* of the Spirit, and his light *shone upon all men,* as the true Light, Christ, says. And this righteous man was always a light for us on the Mountain that is called Holy, shining, gleaming, making us rejoice, and guiding our souls, just as the most brilliant sun, as it rises, illumines those who sleep on the Mountain and traverse its heights; as Solomon says: *"The righteous always have light,"* and *"We will see light in your light."* 4

For it was not through an eloquent tongue and persuasiveness, not through sophistic conceits, syllogisms, mathematics, Pythagorean tales and oracles, that he thus drew everyone from far and wide to come to him with much effort, so as *to hear and tell new things,* as once happened on the Areopagus; rather it was through his simple and artless conduct and speech, through the holy flowers of virtue, always blooming in the Spirit, with which he was adorned, and through the extraordinary fruits of spiritual gifts in the holy visions, the fruits which he was granted in abundance and in turn granted abundantly to all. This is why everyone, whether those of us who live on the Mountain, or countless 5

εἴτε ἐξ ἀνατολῶν καὶ δύσεων καὶ τῆς παραλίου Ἑλλάδος
καὶ νησαέων Κυκλάδων καὶ αὐτῶν τῶν βαρβάρων Τρι-
βάλλων ἄπειρα πλήθη ἀεὶ πρὸς τὸν δίκαιον ἐκατέτρεχον,
καθώσπερ καὶ τῶν μελιττῶν τὰ γένη τοῦτο ποιοῦσιν, ὅταν
ἔν τισι τόποις τὴν γλυκύτητα τοῦ μέλιτος αἰσθανθῶσιν, ἐν
ὄρεσι καὶ σπηλαίοις καὶ ταῖς ὀπαῖς τῆς γῆς [Hebrews 11:38].

6   Ἀλλ' ἀρκτέον ἡμῖν ἄνωθεν τὰ τοῦ δικαίου, μᾶλλον δὲ
τὰ τοῦ ὁσίου πατρός, διηγήσασθαι ἀπὸ μέρους, ὅσα ἡ
χάρις τὸ μνημονευτικὸν ἡμῶν χαρίσει τῇ εὐχῇ ἐκείνου καὶ
ὁδηγήσειεν· οὐ γὰρ δυνησόμεθα τὰ πάντα ἐκείνου θεῖα
πλεονεκτήματα καταλαβεῖν καὶ εἰπεῖν, ὡς οὐδὲ τοῦ ἡλίου
τὸ φέγγος τις ὅλον καταλαβεῖν δυνήσοιτο ἂν καὶ εἰπεῖν·
ἀλλ' ὡς ὁ τοῦ ἡλίου τὸ φῶς κατιδὼν τοσοῦτον καὶ δύναται
μόνον εἰπεῖν, οὕτω καὶ ἡμεῖς ὅσον καὶ μόνον ἐθεασάμεθα
φῶς τοῦ δικαίου τούτου καὶ ὁσίου πατρὸς ἡμῶν Μαξίμου,
τοῦτο καὶ φιλαλήθως ὑμῖν διηγησόμεθα. Πρὸς δὲ τὸ πᾶν
οὐχ ὁρμῶ, ἐπειδὴ ἄβυσσός ἐστιν ἡ τἀνδρὸς ἀρετὴ καὶ
πέλαγος ἄπειρον, ἀνεξάντλητον.

2

Οὗτος ὁ ὅσιος πατὴρ ἡμῶν Μάξιμος ὡς ἥλιος φαιδρὸς
ἐξ ἑῴας ἀνατείλας τὸ πρῶτον (ἐκεῖθεν γὰρ ὥρμητο, ἐκ
Λαμψάκου τῆς μητροπόλεως τὴν πατρίδα ἔχων τῷ γένει),
γεννήτορας μὲν ἔσχεν οὐκ ἀγενεῖς, ἀλλ' ἐπισήμους καὶ

hordes of people from East and West, from coastal Greece and the Cycladic Islands, even from among the barbarous Triballoi themselves, always kept exerting such effort to hasten to the righteous one, just as bees do when they perceive the sweetness of honey in certain places, *in mountains and dens and the caves of the earth.*

But I must begin from the beginning to narrate in detail   6 the deeds of the righteous one, or rather the deeds of the holy father, to the extent that grace will favor and guide my memory through his intercessory prayer. For I will not be able to include and describe all of his divine accomplishments, just as one would not be able to fully include and describe the light of the sun. But just as someone who has seen the light of the sun can only say so much about it, so also I can only say as much about the light of this righteous and holy father of ours, Maximos, as I have seen, but this I will narrate truthfully to you. I do not, however, aim to recount everything, since the man's virtue is a deep abyss and an infinite and inexhaustible sea.

Chapter 2

This holy father of ours, Maximos, first arose like a shining sun from the east (for he came from there, having his family homeland in the metropolis of Lampsakos). He did not have ignoble parents, but ones who were distinguished

ἀγαθοὺς κατά τε ἀρετὴν καὶ εὐσέβειαν· καὶ τοῦτο δῆλον ἡμῖν ἐκ τοῦ τοιούτου βλαστοῦ, οὗ ἐκεῖνοι ἐβλάστησαν κατ᾿ ἀξίαν τῆς πρὸς Θεὸν ἐκείνων πιστῆς καὶ ὀρθῆς προσευχῆς. Καὶ γὰρ καθώσπερ ἡ Ἄννα τὸν Σαμουήλ, οὕτω καὶ ἡ μήτηρ τοῦ ὁσίου σὺν τῷ συνεύνῳ τῇ προσευχῇ μετὰ δακρύων ἐσχόλαζον, τέκνον ἄρρεν ζητοῦντες τὸν Κύριον μᾶλλον ἢ θῆλυ ὡς ἐπεπόθησαν· καὶ οἶμαι τοῦτο, ἐν ταῖς καρδίαις ἐκείνων τοῦ τοιούτου μέλλοντος γενέσθαι ὑψηλοτάτου ἐν ἀρεταῖς τὴν τοιαύτην προσευχὴν καὶ ἔφεσιν ἐνέθηκεν [ἐν ταῖς καρδίαις] ἡ χάρις τοῦ Πνεύματος. Καὶ πρὸ τοῦ γεννηθῆναι ἔσχον τὴν ἀγάπην αὐτοῦ· καὶ τοσούτως τοῖς γονεῦσιν μετὰ τὸ τεχθῆναι γέγονεν ποθητός, ὅτι καὶ τῷ Θεῷ φέρον<τες> ἀνέθηκαν· καὶ μετὰ τὸ βαπτίσαι καὶ ἱερὰ μαθεῖν γράμματα μετὰ πόθου δεδώκασιν, ἔτι μειράκιον ὄν. Κἀκ τούτου καὶ τὸν νέον Σαμουὴλ ὁ λεγόμενος Μανουὴλ ἐνδεικνύμενος ἦν ὅλως, *προκόπτων ἡλικίᾳ καὶ χάριτι* [see Luke 2:52]. Καὶ ἦν *μακάριος* καὶ ποθητὸς οὗτος τοῖς πᾶσιν, ὅτι *οὐκ ἐπορεύετο ἐν βουλαῖς τῶν ἀφρόνων* [see Psalm 1:1] ὡς νέος, ἀλλ᾿ ὡς τέλειος ὢν τῷ φρονήματι ἀκμὴν παῖς ὑπάρχων ταῖς διδαχαῖς ἐσχόλαζε τῶν γερόντων.

2 Ἔτυχεν γὰρ ἐκεῖσε πλησίον ἀνδράσιν οὖσιν ὁσίοις ἐν ἀγωνίσμασιν ἡσυχαστηρίοις, καὶ ἀεὶ ποδηγούμενος Πνεύματι ἐκείνοις καὶ συνωμίλει καὶ ὑπηρέτειν, ὅσον ὁ καιρὸς ἐκάλει πρὸς ὥραν, διὰ τὴν ὑποταγὴν ἀκμὴν τῶν γονέων. Οὕτως καὶ τοῖς γονεῦσιν ὑπήκοος ἦν κατὰ πάντα, καὶ τῷ ναῷ προσήδρευεν τῆς Παναγίου, καὶ αὐτὴν ἀεὶ ποτνιώμενος ἔψαλλεν μετὰ ἡδυφωνίας καὶ πόθου θείου καὶ ἔρωτος. Ἀλλ᾿ ὁ πόθος ἐνίκα ἐξελθεῖν ἐκ τοῦ κόσμου καὶ πρὸς

and good as regards both their virtue and piety. This is clear to us from the nature of their offspring, whom they produced in a manner merited by their faithful and correct prayer to God. For just as Anna did with Samuel, so the holy one's mother and her husband devoted themselves to tearful prayer, begging the Lord for a male rather than a female child, as they fervently desired. And this is my belief, that the grace of the Spirit instilled in their hearts this kind of prayer and longing for the sort of child who was going to be outstanding in virtues. Even before he was born they loved him; and he was so cherished by his parents after his birth, that they brought him to God as an offering. And after his baptism, while he was still a young boy, they eagerly handed him over to learn holy Scripture. As a result the child, who was called Manuel, showed that he really was a new Samuel, *increasing in stature and favor.* And he was deemed *blessed* and beloved by all, because *he did not walk in the counsel of the* foolish, like a young man, but, although still a child, like a man of mature mind he used to devote himself to the teachings of the elders.

For there happened to be holy men nearby, engaged in ascetic struggles in their hermitages, and Maximos, who was always guided by the Spirit, used to converse with them and serve them, to the extent that opportunity permitted, because he was still subject to his parents. For he was indeed obedient to his parents in all things, and used to visit the church of the all-holy Virgin and, constantly calling upon her in supplication, would chant the psalms with a sweet voice and divine desire and love. But his desire was forcing him to depart from the world and journey toward the 2

ἡσυχίαν ὁδεῦσαι διὰ τοῦ σχήματος. Διὰ τοῦτο καὶ τὰ ἱμάτια αὐτοῦ ἀπεκδύετο καὶ τοῖς ἐνδεέσιν ἐσκέπαζεν, αὐτὸς
δὲ τῷ κρύει πηγνύμενος ἔτρεμεν. Ταὐτὸ καὶ ἄρτους τοῖς
πεινῶσιν ἐχορήγειν κρύφα πλουσίως· καὶ ὡς ἔξηχος ὑπεκρίνετο τοῖς γονεῦσιν εἶναι καὶ πᾶσιν· ἀλλ᾽ οὐκ ἔλαθεν
αὐτοῖς ἡ ἀρετὴ τούτου τἀνδρός. Καὶ οἱ μὲν γονεῖς αὐτοῦ
ἔσπευδον τάχα εἰς ἑτοιμασίαν τοῦ γάμου, ὡς ἔθος τοῦτο
τοῖς ἐν κόσμῳ ποιεῖν, ἵν᾽ αὐτὸν παγιδεύσουσι καὶ συνδήσου-
σιν ἐν τῷ κόσμῳ καὶ τὸν ποθούμενον ἔχουσιν ἐπὶ χεῖρας
καὶ καθορῶσιν ἀεί· ἀλλ᾽ οὐκ ἔτυχον τοῦ σκοποῦ τούτου
καὶ τὴν πρᾶξιν ποιῆσαι, ἐπειδὴ ἄνωθεν ἡ πρόνοια ταύτην
τὴν βουλὴν παρηκόντισεν.

3

Καὶ οὔπω τὸν ἴουλον φθάσας, ἑπτακαίδεκα ἐτῶν ὢν
οὗτος δρασμὸν ποιεῖ θεῖον, καὶ ἀπὸ Λαμψάκου διαπεράσας
εἰς τὸ ὄρος τὸ καλούμενον Γάνου, ἐκεῖ τὸ σχῆμα τῆς μοναδικῆς πολιτείας ἐνδύεται, καὶ ὑπὸ γέροντα τέτακτο
δόκιμον, τὴν μοναδικὴν ἐν ὑποταγῇ μαθεῖν πολιτείαν· ἀλλ᾽
οὗτος καὶ πρὸ τούτου πεπαιδευμένος ἦν τῆς μοναδικῆς
ἀρετῆς τὰ μαθήματα· καὶ δόκιμος ἐν τούτῳ τοῖς γέρουσιν
ἀναφανεὶς ἐπί τε νηστείαν, ἀγρυπνίαν, προσευχήν, χα-
μευνίαν, κακουχίαν καὶ πάντων ὑπεροψίαν ματαίων καὶ
αὐτοῦ τοῦ ἰδίου σώματος, ἠγαπᾶτο μὲν παρὰ πάντων,

contemplative life by taking the monastic habit. For this reason he used to remove his clothes and cover the needy with them, while he himself shivered, frozen with the cold. In the same way he used to distribute bread to the hungry secretly and in abundance. He pretended to his parents and everyone else to be deranged; but the man's virtue did not escape their attention. And so his parents hastened to make arrangements for his marriage, as is customary for those in the world to do, so that they might ensnare him and bind him to the world and keep their beloved child at hand and always in their sight; but they did not succeed in taking this action, since heavenly providence thwarted their plan.

Chapter 3

At the age of seventeen, when the down upon his cheek had not yet begun to grow, he resorted to divinely sanctioned flight, and crossed from Lampsakos to the mountain called Ganos, where he donned the habit of monastic life and was assigned to an experienced elder to learn the monastic life in obedience. But Maximos had been previously trained in the lessons of monastic virtue; and so, since he appeared to the elders to be experienced in fasting, keeping vigil, prayer, sleeping on the ground, mortification, and disregard of all vanities and of his own body, he was beloved by

ἐσκώπτετο δὲ ὑπὸ τοῦ ἰδίου γέροντος διὰ τὸ τραχὺ τῆς ὁδοῦ καὶ ἀνένδοτον. Μικρὸν δὲ χρόνον ἐκεῖσε ποιήσας, ὁ μὲν ὅσιος τούτου γέρων τε καὶ διδάσκαλος ἀπῆρεν ἀπὸ γῆς πρὸς τὰς αἰωνίους μονάς· καὶ θάπτεται χερσὶ τοῦ νέου Μαξίμου ὁ Μάρκος ὁ ἅγιος· τοῦτο γὰρ ἦν τὸ ὄνομα τοῦ ὁσίου ἐκείνου τοῦ διαλάμψαντος ἐν ὅλῃ Μακεδονίᾳ, ὡς ἀστὴρ φαεινότατος.

4

Κὰκ τούτου δὲ οὗτος ὁ κλεινὸς Μάξιμος ἀπάρας ἐκ Γάνου τὴν Μακεδονίαν διέρχεται καὶ τὰ πλησιόχωρα ὄρη κατερευνᾷ, εἴ που καὶ τύχοιεν θησαυροῦ, οὗ ἐκέκτητο, τοιούτου γέροντος κατιδεῖν· καὶ ταύτην τὴν ἔφεσιν ἐκπληροῖ, ὡς ἐσπούδαζεν, ὁ Θεός. Γενόμενος γὰρ πρὸς τὸ Παπίκιον ὄρος εὗρεν ἐκεῖσε ἄνδρας ἁγίους ἴσα τοῖς μεγάλοις πατράσιν ἐκείνοις, Ἀντώνιον λέγω καὶ τὸν Εὐθύμιον, Ἀρσένιον καὶ Παχώμιον, ἀοίκους, ἀπροΐτους, πελαζομένους ἐν ὄρεσιν ὑψηλοῖς καὶ σπηλαίοις ἡσύχοις καὶ ἀβάτοις τόποις, ἀπαρακλήτους, ἔχοντας μεθ᾿ ἑαυτῶν οὐδέν, εἰ μὴ μόνον τὰ ῥάκη ἃ περιβέβληντο οἱ γενναῖοι. Καὶ τούτους ὁμιλήσας κατὰ πολύ, ὡς καθαρώτατος σπόγγος τὰς ἀρετὰς ἐκείνων εἰς ἅπαν ἀνακραθείς, ἢ μᾶλλον ὡς κηρὸς τὸν χαρακτῆρα ἐκείνων τῆς ὑπὲρ ἄνθρωπον ἀρετῆς ὡς ἐκμαγεῖον εἰς ἑαυτὸν ὅλως ἀναλαβών, καὶ γενόμενος ὑπερόπτης ἔτι

them all, but mocked by his own elder *on account of the rough-ness* and rigidity *of the road*. After Maximos had spent a short time there, his blessed elder and teacher departed from earth to the heavenly abodes; and the holy Mark was buried by the young Maximos with his own hands; for Mark was the name of that holy man who shone throughout Macedonia like a most brilliant star.

Chapter 4

Then this illustrious Maximos departed from Ganos and, traveling through Macedonia, searched the nearby mountains to see if he might find anywhere a treasure, in the form of an elder, such as he had formerly possessed; and God fulfilled this desire, as Maximos eagerly wished. For when he came to Mount Papikion, he found holy men there equal to those great fathers of old, I mean Antony and Euthymios, Arsenios and Pachomios, living without a home, in seclusion, spending their time in lofty mountains, tranquil caves, and inaccessible places, without comforts, and having no possessions except for the rags which these noble souls wore. After having long conversations with them, and completely soaking up their virtues like the purest sponge, or rather taking upon himself the impression of their super-human virtue like wax from a mold, and becoming even

πλεῖον τῶν πάντων, ἀπάρας ἐκ Παπικίου πρὸς τὴν μεγαλόπολιν τὴν Κωνσταντίνου ἀπῄει.

2   Καὶ τὰ κάλλη τῶν νεῶν καθιστορήσας καὶ τὰ ἐν ἐκείνοις τεθησαυρισμένα ἅγια προσκυνήσας, πρὸς τὴν κυρίαν ἡμῶν τὴν πάναγνον Θεοτόκον τὴν Ὁδηγήτριαν τρέχει, τὰ μέγιστα θαύματα κατιδεῖν· ἃ καὶ ἰδὼν καὶ προσκυνήσας ἐξεπλάγη τῷ θαύματι. Καὶ ὅλως σύννους γενόμενος ἐκεῖσε, τὴν Πάναγνον εἰς οὐρανοὺς κατενόει, ὁποίαν δόξαν κέκτηται ἐπὶ θρόνου θεότητος, καὶ θρόνον αὐτὴν τῆς Τριάδος ὁ νοῦς τοῦ γέροντος ἀπλανῶς ἐπεσφράγιζεν. Ἐν τούτῳ καὶ νυκτερεύων ἐφαίνετο ἐν ταῖς ἡμέραις τοῦ θαύματος ὅλως ἐκπληττόμενος τῆς Θεοτόκου τὰ θαύματα, ἀνυπόδετος, ἀσκεπής, μόνον τρίχινον ἓν διεζωσμένος ἱμάτιον καὶ αὐτὸ διερρηγμένον τὰ πλεῖστα. Ἀπὸ δὲ τῆς ἐκστατικῆς αὐτοῦ θεωρίας τοῖς πᾶσιν ἐδόκειν ὡς ἔξηχος, αὐτὸς καὶ τοῦτο ὑποκρινόμενος τάχα μωρολογίαν προσέπλαττεν, ὡς ὁ διὰ Χριστὸν Ἀνδρέας ἐκεῖνος ὁ μέγιστος· ὅθεν καὶ πάντες ὡς ἐκεῖνον ὑπετόπαζον εἶναι καὶ Μάξιμον μωρίαν ὑποκρινόμενον διὰ Κύριον· καὶ διὰ θαύματος μᾶλλον εἶχον αὐτὸν καὶ ἑώρων ἢ σαλὸν καὶ μωρὸν λογιζόμενοι. Τούτου δὲ ἡ τοιαύτη πολιτεία ἀκουστὴ γέγονεν τοῖς κρατοῦσιν τότε ἐν θαύματι.

more disdainful of all material things, he departed from Papikion and went to the great city of Constantine.

After viewing the beauties of the churches and venerat- 2 ing the holy relics stored in them, Maximos hastened to the church of our Lady the all-holy Mother of God the Hodegetria to witness the greatest miracles; and after seeing them and worshipping there, he was overwhelmed by the miracle-working image. And becoming completely absorbed in meditation there, Maximos perceived the all-pure Virgin in heaven, and what kind of glory she possessed before the *throne of divinity;* and the elder's mind unerringly confirmed her as being the throne of the Trinity. He spent his nights there and, on the days of <the procession of> the miracle-working image, appeared to be completely overwhelmed by the miracles of the Mother of God, going barefoot and bare-headed, and wearing only one garment made of haircloth which itself was mostly in rags. After his ecstatic vision he seemed to everyone to be deranged, and he himself proba-bly feigned this and exaggerated his folly, like Andrew, that greatest fool for Christ. As a result everyone suspected that Maximos was like him, and feigned folly for the sake of the Lord. And they held and looked at him in wonder rather than considering him truly a fool and deranged. And this be-havior of his was a source of wonder to the current rulers when they heard about it.

5

Ἀνδρόνικος ἦν ἐκεῖνος ὁ μέγας ἐν βασιλεῦσιν ὁ Παλαιολόγος, ὁ καὶ μετονομαστεὶς Ἀντώνιος· καὶ πατριάρχης, ὁ ἐν ἁγίοις Ἀθανάσιος ὁ οἰκουμενικὸς καὶ θαυμάσιος. Ὅθεν καὶ προσκαλεσάμενος εἰς τὰ βασίλεια τοῦτον, ὁ βασιλεὺς ἤρξατο ὁμιλεῖν τὸν ὅσιον μέσον πολλῶν. Αὐτὸς δ᾽ ὡς ἔθος εἶχεν, ἐκ τοῦ Θεολόγου πρὸς τὸν λόγον τοῦ ἄνακτος λόγους φέρων ἀνταπεκρίνετο· καὶ τοῖς ῥήτορσιν ἔπληττεν, πῶς ἀπὸ στήθους τὰ τοῦ Θεολόγου ἀναφωνεῖ καὶ πᾶσαν θείαν Γραφήν. Ἐπεὶ δὲ γραμματικὴν οὐ μεμάθηκεν οὗτος ὁ ὅσιος, ἐν τοῖς ῥήμασιν ἀδαὴς ἐνοεῖτο· διὰ τοῦτο καὶ παρὰ τοῦ μεγάλου λογοθέτου ἐκείνου ἀκούσας τοῦ κανικλείου τό· "Ἡ μὲν φωνὴ φωνὴ Ἰακώβ, αἱ δὲ χεῖρες χεῖρες Ἡσαύ" [Genesis 27:22], ἀπελθὼν ᾤχετο, ματαιόφρονας καλέσας ἐκείνους καὶ ἄφρονας· καὶ πλεῖον εἰς τὰ βασίλεια οὐκ ἐγένετο.

2 Πρὸς δὲ τὸν πατριάρχην τὸν ἅγιον συνήθης γενόμενος ἀεὶ εἰσελήλυθεν, καὶ αὐτοῦ τοῖς γλυκυτάτοις λόγοις κατετρύφαν καὶ ἐπευφραίνετο, νέον Χρυσόστομον λέγων εἶναι αὐτόν. Πολλὰ δ᾽ ὁ πατριάρχης κατηγωνίσατο εἰσάξαι αὐτὸν ἐν τοῖς κοινοβίοις, οἷς ἀνήγειρεν καὶ ἐκτήσατο ἐν τῇ Κωνσταντινουπόλει μονύδρια· ἀλλ᾽ οὐ κατένευσεν οὗτος ὁ ὅσιος, τὴν καταμονὴν ἔχων ἐν ταῖς πύλαις τῆς παναχράντου κυρίας καὶ Θεοτόκου Βλαχέρνης, ὡς πένης ἄοικος προσεδρεύων ἐν πείνῃ καὶ δίψῃ, ἐν ἀγρυπνίᾳ καὶ στάσει καὶ προσευχῇ, ἐν κλαυθμῷ καὶ δακρύων πλήθους

Chapter 5

These were Andronikos Palaiologos, great among emperors, who later changed his name to Antony, and the ecumenical patriarch, the sainted and wondrous Athanasios. And so, after summoning him to the palace, the emperor began to converse with the holy one, in the midst of many people. But Maximos, as was his custom, responded to the ruler's words with the words of the Theologian; and the orators were astonished at how he declaimed by heart the words of the Theologian and all the holy Scriptures. For since the holy one had not studied grammar, he was considered ignorant of learned discourse. For this reason, when he heard the great *logothetes,* the keeper of the inkwell, say this: "*The voice is Jacob's voice, but the hands are the hands of Esau,*" he left, calling them weak-minded and silly men, and he did not go to the palace any more.

Maximos did, however, become friendly with the holy patriarch and used to visit him frequently, and took delight and pleasure in his most sweet discourse, saying that he was a new Chrysostom. The patriarch tried very hard to have him enter the cenobitic monasteries which he had constructed and possessed in Constantinople; but the holy one refused, and stayed in the doorway of the church of the all-pure Lady and Mother of God of Blachernai. He remained there every night like a poor homeless man, in hunger and thirst, in vigil, standing, and prayer, in weeping, shedding a

ῥοῇ καὶ στεναγμοῖς ἀνενδότοις ταῖς ὅλαις νυξί. Ταῖς δὲ ἡμέραις ἐλογίζετο τοῖς ἄφροσιν ἄφρων, ὑποκρινόμενος τοῦτο κατὰ σοφίαν τοῦ Πνεύματος, ἵνα μὴ τὸν καρπὸν αὐτοῦ ἐκτινάξῃ ἡ κάκιστος ἀνθρωπαρεσκία, ἡ ὑπερήφα-νος.

6

Κἀκ τούτου πάλιν ἀπάρας ἐκ Πόλεως πρὸς τὴν Θεσ-σαλονίκην ἐγένετο, ἵν᾽ ὅπως κατίδῃ καὶ προσκυνήσῃ τὸν μυροβλύτην καὶ θαυματουργὸν τὸν ἐν μάρτυσι μέγαν Δημήτριον. Καὶ ταύτην τὴν ἔφεσιν ἐκπληρώσας δρομαίως εἰσέδυν ἐν Ὄρει Ἁγίῳ· καὶ ἅμα τὰς ἱερὰς θείας μονὰς ὅλας μετὰ πόθου δραμὼν καὶ ἰδὼν καὶ προσκυνήσας καὶ εὐξάμε-νος τῷ Θεῷ ἐν αὐταῖς, πρὸς τὴν Λαύραν γέγονεν τοῦ ἁγίου Ἀθανασίου· κἀκεῖ προσευξάμενος τῷ Θεῷ τὸν βίον τοῦ ἁγίου ἀνέγνω καὶ τὰ παλαίσματα, ὁμοίως καὶ Πέτρου τοῦ ἁγίου ἐκείνου τοῦ Ἀθωνίτου καὶ μάκαρος· καὶ τοῦ μὲν τὸ ἥσυχον ἐπαινῶν καὶ θαυμάζων, τοῦ δὲ τὸ κοινωνικὸν καὶ σπουδαῖον ἐν ταῖς ἐντολαῖς τοῦ Χριστοῦ καὶ Θεοῦ ἡμῶν, κατανῶν ἀμφοτέρους, ἐγλίχετο ἐν αὐτῷ τῷ τόπῳ τοῦ Ἄθωνος καὶ αὐτὸς ἀμφοτέρων τοὺς βίους ἀναλαβεῖν καὶ ἄρξασθαι διὰ πράξεως, ὡς ἐκεῖνοι [οὕτως] ἐποίησαν.

2   Ἀλλ᾽ ὡς ἔθος τοῦτο τοῖς σπουδάζουσιν, ἐρωτᾶν πρῶτον προσήκει, εἶθ᾽ οὕτως τῆς ὁποιασοῦν ὁδοῦ ἄρξασθαι· τοῖς

multitude of tears, and endless lamentation. And by day he was considered a fool by foolish people, feigning this in the wisdom of the Spirit, so that a most wicked and arrogant love of popularity might not *shake off* his *fruit*.

Chapter 6

Then Maximos left the City again and went to Thessalonike in order to observe and venerate the exuder of perfumed oil and worker of miracles, Demetrios, great among martyrs. After fulfilling this desire, he headed quickly for the Holy Mountain of Athos; and after eagerly visiting all the holy and divine monasteries and seeing them, and venerating and offering prayers to God in them, he came to the Lavra of the holy Athanasios. After praying to God there, he read the Life of the saint and about his struggles, and likewise that of the holy and blessed Peter the Athonite. Approving and admiring the latter's love of spiritual tranquility, and the former's zeal for the cenobitic life in accordance with the commandments of Christ our God, and gaining an understanding of them both, he yearned to adopt the lifestyle of both men here on Athos itself, and to begin to act as they had done.

But as it is customary for those who are eager to do this 2 first to make appropriate inquiries, and only then begin a

τότε ἁγίοις πατράσιν ἐπερωτᾷ ὁ θεόφρων Μάξιμος, τί ἄρα
καὶ ποιήσειεν πρότερον· καὶ δὴ τὰ τῆς ὑποταγῆς αὐτὸν
ὁδηγοῦν καὶ τῆς μακαρίας ὑπακοῆς ὑποδεικνύουσιν τὰ
παλαίσματα, "Φαιδροὶ μαργαρῖται," λέγοντες, "εἶναι οἱ
διαλάμποντες μέσον ἡμῶν ἐν τῇ σεβασμίᾳ Λαύρᾳ ταύτῃ·
καὶ ταύτης τῆς ὁδοῦ καὶ σὺ ἀπάρξου τὸ πρότερον, ἵνα
θεμέλιον θήσῃς καὶ καταβάλῃς πρῶτον ἐπὶ τὴν πέτραν
Χριστοῦ τὴν θείαν ταπείνωσιν· διὰ γὰρ τῆς ὑποταγῆς καὶ
ὑπακοῆς ἡ ταπείνωσις κτίζεται καὶ συνίσταται, καὶ ἡ ἀρετὴ
οὕτω πρὸς ὕψος ἐπαίρεται τοῖς θεόφροσιν. Ἀπάρξου τοίνυν
τὰ τῆς ὁδοῦ καὶ αὐτὸς ἐπὶ τὴν μονὴν ἔνδοθεν πρότερον,
ἵνα διὰ πολλῶν ποδηγούμενος εὐμαρῶς ὁδεύσῃς πρὸς τὴν
ταπείνωσιν (ἥτις ἐστὶν ἀρχὴ καὶ ῥίζα πασῶν ἀρετῶν) καὶ
ἀνάπαυσιν, εἶθ᾽ οὕτως καὶ τὰ τῆς ἐρήμου ἀναδράμῃς καὶ
κατίδῃς καθίσματα καὶ πρὸς ἡσυχίαν ὁδεύσῃς, ὡς βούλεσαι."

7

Ταῦτα καὶ τὰ τοιαῦτα ἀκούσας, ὁ ὅσιος οὗτος ἀνὴρ
φέρων ἑαυτὸν δίδωσι τῷ τῆς σεβασμίας Λαύρας πατρὶ εἰς
ὑποταγήν, καὶ πᾶσι τοῖς ἀδελφοῖς ἐκεῖσε ἐγκατέμειξεν
ἑαυτὸν εἰς ὑπακοὴν τοῦ Χριστοῦ. Ἔνθεν τοι καὶ δοκιμάζε-
ται πρότερον ἐν τοῖς ἐσχάτοις, οὕτω ὡς ἔθος, διακονήμα-
σιν· εἶθ᾽ οὕτως ἀνάγεται καὶ κατατάττεται ἐν τῷ χορῷ τῆς

course of action, so the divinely inspired Maximos made inquiries of the holy fathers who were there at that time as to what he should do first; and they guided him on the path of submission and showed him the struggles of blessed obedience, saying, "Those who shine in our midst in this venerable Lavra are gleaming pearls; you should start out initially on this path, so that you may first establish a solid footing and lay down divine humility on the rock of Christ as a foundation; for humility is built up and established through submission and obedience, and thus virtue is raised to a higher level by those who are godly minded. So start out initially on this path within the monastery, so that, being gently guided by many people, you may journey toward both humility (which is the beginning and root of all virtues) and repose, and then you may return to and explore the hermitages in the wilderness and journey toward spiritual tranquility, as is your wish."

Chapter 7

After hearing these and similar words, this holy man went and gave himself up in submission to the father of the venerable Lavra, and joined all the brethren there in obedience to Christ. Thus, as is customary, he was first tested in the most menial duties; and then he was promoted and

ἐκκλησίας, τοῦ ὑμνεῖν ἐν ἱεροῖς μελῳδήμασιν καὶ ᾠδαῖς λογικοῖς τὸν ἐνυπόστατον Λόγον καὶ Υἱὸν τοῦ Θεοῦ, ἅμα Πατρὶ καὶ τῷ Πνεύματι, καὶ τὴν Θεομήτορα, τὴν παναγίαν ἡμῶν καὶ κυρίαν τὴν Δέσποιναν. Ἔτυχε γὰρ μεμαθηκὼς καὶ ἱεροῖς μελῳδήμασι νεαλὴς ὤν· διὰ τοῦτο καὶ τὴν λογικὴν λατρείαν προσετάγην ποιεῖν τότε ἐν τῇ ἐκκλησίᾳ τῆς Λαύρας. Καὶ οὕτως ὢν τὸν μὲν στίχον εἶχεν ἐν στόματι καὶ ἐν τῇ γλώττῃ τὸ ᾆσμα, τὸν δὲ νοῦν ὅλον εἶχεν ἐν ὑψίστοις [see Luke 2:14], ἐν τῷ ἀοράτῳ καὶ ἀθανάτῳ Θεῷ ἐκθαμβούμενος. Διὰ τοῦτο εἶχεν ἀεὶ τοὺς ὀφθαλμοὺς ἐν τοῖς δάκρυσιν, ὡς ἐκπλήκτους ἀνεῳγμένους ἐν θαύματι.

2   Ταὐτὸ καὶ ἐν τοῖς ἱεροῖς ἀναγνώσμασιν ὅλος ἔκθαμβος ἦν ἐπὶ τὸν νοῦν τῆς Γραφῆς καὶ ἐξεπλήττετο πρὸς τὴν φιλανθρωπίαν Χριστοῦ, τὴν δωρησαμένην ἡμῖν τοιαῦτα κατανοεῖν ἐν τῷ σώματι διὰ Πνεύματος. Εἶχεν δὲ τὴν καρδίαν οὗτος ὁ ἅγιος ὅλην αὐτοῦ ἐξάπτουσαν διὰ πυρὸς θείου ἀΰλου ἄνθρακος [Isaiah 5:24], ὡς ὁ προφήτης ποτέ, καὶ τὰ σπλάγχνα ἐφλέγετο ὑπὸ τῆς ἐνοικούσης ἐν αὐτῷ θείας χάριτος. Διὰ τοῦτο καὶ τὴν εὐχὴν εἶχεν ἀσχόλαστον ἀεὶ κινουμένην καὶ λέγουσαν τῷ στόματι τῆς καρδίας ἅμα σὺν τῷ νοΐ, τὴν ἐξαίρετον· ὅ ἐστι σπάνιον καὶ δυσεύρετον, ταύτην οὕτως κατέχειν ἀνεμποδίστως μέσῳ πολλῶν. Ἀλλ᾽ οὗτος οὕτως πλουσίως εὐμοίρειν τῆς προσευχῆς ἐκ παιδόθεν, ὡς ἄλλος εἴ τις ἔχων ἐν ἐρήμοις τόποις καὶ ἡσυχίοις αὐτήν· ἐκεῖ γὰρ ὅπου ἐπιδημήσῃ τὸ Πνεῦμα τὸ ἅγιον, τοιαῦτα ὑπερφυῆ νοεῖ καὶ λέγει ὁ λαμπρυνθεὶς ἐκ τοῦ Πνεύματος, ὥς φησι τοῦτο ὁ υἱὸς τῆς βροντῆς [see Mark 3:17], ὁ

assigned to the church choir, to hymn with holy melodies and spiritual odes the substantial Word and Son of God, together with the Father and the Spirit, and the Mother of God, our all-holy Lady and Mistress. For he had studied holy chant in his youth; and for this reason was then assigned to perform this kind of spiritual veneration in the church of the Lavra. And thus, while he had the verses on his lips and the melody on his tongue, he had his entire mind *in the highest,* astounded by the invisible and immortal God. For this reason he always had tears in his eyes, as they were wide open, astonished in wonder.

In the same way during the holy readings he was always astounded at the meaning of Scripture and amazed by Christ's love of mankind, which has been given to us so that we may understand such things through the Spirit while still in our bodies. The entire heart of the holy one was burning with the immaterial *coal* of divine *fire,* as the prophet once said, and his insides were inflamed by the divine grace dwelling in him. Therefore, without pause, the prayer of the heart was always moving and being uttered by his lips at the same time as in his mind, something that is extraordinary; but what is really rare and hard to find is that he could continue this prayer unimpeded in the midst of many people. But this man, from childhood, was as richly endowed with the gift of prayer as someone else might be only in deserted and tranquil places. For wherever the Holy Spirit takes up residence, the one illuminated by the Spirit thinks and says such extraordinary things, as the *son of thunder* says,

2

ἠγαπημένος Χριστῷ Ἰωάννης ὁ θεολόγος, ὅτι "*οὐδεὶς λέγει Κύριον Ἰησοῦν, εἰ μὴ ἐν Πνεύματι ἁγίῳ*" [1 Corinthians 12:3].

3   Καὶ ταῦθ᾽ οὕτως ἔχων ὁ ὅσιος πάλιν ἐν κακουχίᾳ διῆγεν, ὡς πρότερον ἐν Βλαχέρναις, καὶ οὔτε κέλλαν ἔνδοθεν τῆς Λαύρας ὑπεκτήσατό τε, οὔτε τὰ τῆς κέλλης ὑλώδη ἐπαγωνίσματα καὶ χρειώδη, ἀλλ᾽ ὡς ἄσαρκος ὑπῆρχεν οὕτω ἐν τῇ μονῇ. Τὰ πρὸς τροφὴν ἐκ τῆς τραπέζης <τῆς> μονῆς ἐλάμβανεν ἐγκρατῶς εἰς τὸ ζῆν. Ἐπὶ τοῖς σκάμνοις δὲ τῆς ἐκκλησίας τὴν πᾶσαν εἶχεν καταμονὴν ἐν τῷ νάρθηκι, μᾶλλον δὲ ἐν τῇ παννύχῳ στάσει καὶ ἀγρυπνίᾳ ἣν ἐπαγωνιζόμενος ἀεί, ὡς ἔθος αὐτῷ ἄνωθεν.

8

Ἀλλ᾽ ὡς τὸν Μωϋσῆν τὸ Σίναιον ὄρος καὶ τὸν Ἠλίαν ὁ Κάρμηλος καὶ τὸν Ἰεζεκιὴλ ἐκάλει τὸ ὄρος Χωρὴβ καὶ τὸν Ἰωάννην ἡ ἔρημος, οὕτωῒ καὶ τὸν ὅσιον Μάξιμον ἀνακαλεῖται ὁ Ἄθων, τὸ ἄνθος τῶν ὀρέων, ἵν᾽ ἀνθήσῃ ὁ δίκαιος ἐν αὐτῷ καὶ καρπὸν φέρῃ πλουσίως τὸν ὥριμον τοῦ Πνεύματος *ἐν τριάκοντα καὶ ἐν ἑξήκοντα καὶ ἐν ἑκατόν* [Mark 4:20]. Ὡς γὰρ *ἄμπελος Κυρίου Σαβαώθ* [see Isaiah 5:7] ὑπάρχει οὗτος ὁ ἐκλεκτὸς Ἄθων, Κυρίῳ καὶ τῇ Θεομήτορι πανάγνῳ καὶ Δεσποίνῃ τῇ κυρίᾳ ἡμῶν ἄνωθεν ἀνατεθειμένος εἰς κατοικίαν τῶν θελόντων σωθῆναι καὶ ὁμιλῆσαι Θεῷ διὰ καθαρότητος· καθὼς τοῦτο σαφῶς

John the Theologian the beloved of Christ, that "*no one can say that Jesus is Lord except by the Holy Spirit.*"

In this way the holy one again lived a life of mortifica- 3 tion, as formerly at Blachernai, and he did not even possess a cell within the Lavra, and thus not the material snares and necessities of a cell either, but lived in the monastery like someone without flesh. He took the food he needed to live on in moderation from the monastery table. And he would always retire to the benches of the church in the narthex, or rather he stood there all night long and was always striving to keep vigil, as was his custom from the beginning.

Chapter 8

But just as Mount Sinai called to Moses, and Carmel to Elijah, and Mount Horeb to Ezekiel, and the wilderness to John, so Athos, the flower of mountains, called out to the holy Maximos, so that the righteous man might blossom upon it and bear abundantly the ripe fruit of the Spirit *thirty and sixty and one hundredfold.* For this chosen Athos is like *a vineyard of the Lord Sabaoth,* having been dedicated from the beginning by the Lord and the all-pure Mother of God, our Lady and Mistress, as an abode for those who wish to be saved and converse with God in purity. This is exactly what

παρὰ τῇ Θεοτόκῳ ἐχρηματίσθη ὁ ἁγιώτατος Πέτρος
ἐκεῖνος, ὁ καλούμενος Ἀθωνίτης διὰ τὴν ἐν αὐτῷ καταμονὴν καὶ τὴν ὑπὲρ ἄνθρωπον ἄσκησιν, καὶ ὁ ἐν ἀσκηταῖς
πατράσιν ἁγιώτατος καὶ μέγιστος πατὴρ ἡμῶν Ἀθανάσιος, ὁ τῆς ἀθανασίας ὄντως ἐπώνυμος, παρὰ τῆς Θεοτόκου
καὶ οὕτω χρηματισθεὶς καὶ ὅτι *εὐκληματίσει αὕτη ἡ ἄμπελος ἕως θαλάσσης τὰς παραφυάδας αὐτῆς* [see Psalm
79(80):11] καὶ *ἐξανθήσει ὡς κρίνον* [see Isaiah 35:1] καὶ *ἀνα-
τείλη ὡς ῥόδον καὶ καρπὸν δώσει ὥριμόν τε καὶ εὔσταχυν*
τῷ δημιουργῷ τῶν ἁπάντων Χριστῷ τῷ Θεῷ ἡμῶν. Καὶ
ὡς ἄν εἴποι τις, διὰ τοῦτ᾽ ἔφη Δαβίδ· *"Τὸ ὄρος, ὃ εὐδόκησεν
ὁ Θεὸς κατοικεῖν ἐν αὐτῷ, ὄρος πῖον, ὄρος τετυρωμένον, ὄρος
θεῖον"* [Psalm 67(68):16, 15].

2   Διὰ τοῦτο καὶ "Ἅγιον" μόνον τοῦτο προσηγορεύκασιν
οἱ πατέρες ἡμῶν ὑπὲρ πάντα τὰ ὄρη τῆς κτίσεως τὸ τοῦ
Ἄθωνος, ὃ ἐσαεὶ βρύει τῶν μοναχῶν τὰς ἀγέλας, ὡς πόλις
ἄλλη ζῶντος Θεοῦ παντοκράτορος. Καὶ ὡσπερεὶ *τὸ ἅρμα
τοῦ Θεοῦ μυριοπλάσιον γέγονεν ἐν τῷ Σιναίῳ ὄρει* [Psalm
67(68):17] ποτέ, μάλιστα δὲ καθώσπερ στρατιαὶ ἐν οὐρανοῖς κατὰ τάξιν, αἱ τάξεις τῶν ἀγγέλων καὶ ἀσωμάτων
θείων δυνάμεων τῷ Θεῷ παρίστανται καὶ λειτουργοῦσιν
ἐν ὕμνοις ἀκαταπαύστοις ἀεὶ ὡς κτίστην καὶ δημιουργὸν
αὐτὸν τοῦ παντός, οὕτωῗ κατίδοις καὶ τὸ Ἅγιον Ὄρος τὸ
ἐν τῷ Ἄθωνι· κύκλωθεν μὲν τὰ πρόποδα τούτου βρύει τοῖς
ἡσυχάζουσιν καὶ ἀσκοῦσιν ἐν Πνεύματι· καθώσπερ Ἠλίας
καὶ Ἰωάννης ποτέ, πάντες ἀγωνισταί, πάντες θεόπται
καὶ θεοφόροι ὑπάρχοντες, πάντες παννύχιον στάσιν καὶ
ἀγρυπνίαν ποιούμενοι, οἱ μὲν συστάδην διὰ ψαλτῆρος καὶ

that most holy Peter was clearly told by the Mother of God, Peter who is called the Athonite on account of his residence and super-human asceticism here. And the holiest of ascetic fathers, our greatest father Athanasios, who truly bore the name of immortality, was also told this by the Mother of God, and that this vine will *send forth its shoots as far as the sea* and will *flower like a lily,* and grow like a rose and produce ripe and abundant fruit for Christ our God, the creator of all things. One might even say that for this reason David said, *"This is the mountain which God has delighted to dwell in, a rich mountain, a swelling mountain, a* divine *mountain."*

For this reason our fathers gave the name "Holy" only to Athos out of all the mountains of creation, Athos which forever teems with flocks of monks, like another city of the almighty living God. And as *the chariot of God* once appeared *on Mount Sinai ten thousand fold,* and, in particular, as the ranks of the angels and the incorporeal divine powers, those armies marshaled in the heavens, stand next to God and continually celebrate Him with unceasing hymns as the founder and creator of all, so you might also visualize the Holy Mountain on Athos. For its lower slopes teem all round with those who engage in spiritual tranquility and practice asceticism in the Spirit. Just like Elijah and John of old, all are warriors, all are people who see God and are divinely inspired, all engage in standing all night and keeping vigil. Some by actively devoting themselves to the reading of the

2

ἀναγνώσεως πρακτικῶς, οἱ δὲ κατὰ μόνας ἐν προσευχῇ
νοερᾷ καὶ ἡσυχίᾳ καρδιακῇ, οἱ δὲ ἐν θεωρίαις καὶ μόναις
τοῦ Πνεύματος σχολάζοντες, μετάρσιοι οὕτω ἐν τῷ Πνεύματι κατὰ νοῦν γίνονται καὶ θείων ἀποκαλύπτονται μυστηρίων, ὥς φησι· "Σχολάσατε καὶ γνῶτε, ὅτι ἐγώ εἰμι Θεός"
[Psalm 45(46):10].

3   Ἄτεροι δὲ τοῖς τοιούτοις γέρουσιν καὶ ἁγίοις ὑπο-
τασσόμενοι τῷ πόθῳ Χριστοῦ τετρωμένοι εἶν ἐσαεὶ καὶ τὰς
ἐντολὰς αὐτοῦ ἀθλίπτως ποιοῦσιν κατὰ τὴν δύναμιν ἕκαστος, μηδὲν τὰ ὡραῖα τοῦ κόσμου ποθοῦντες ἰδεῖν, ἀλλὰ
τὰ κάλλη τοῦ νοητοῦ παραδείσου σπουδάζοντες εὐμοιρῆσαι
καὶ κατιδεῖν, ὥς φησι τοῦτο σοφός, ὅτι τοῖς ἐρημικοῖς
ἄπαυστος ὁ θεῖος πόθος ἐγγίνεται, κόσμου οὖσι τοῦ μα-
ταίου ἐκτός. Διὰ τοῦτο καὶ ἐν ὑπομονῇ πολλῇ τὸν σκληρὸν
τόπον τοῦτον καὶ δύσβατον ἐκ τοῦ κόσμου παντὸς συναχθέντες οὗτοι οἱ μάκαρες κατοικοῦσιν ἐπὶ τῷ Ἄθωνι
κύκλωθεν ὡς ἐν λειμῶνι ἀειθαλεῖ ὄντες καὶ ἐπευφραίνονται ἐν τῷ Πνεύματι. Καὶ οὐ μόνον τὰ κύκλωθεν τούτου
τοῦ ὑψηλοτάτου Ἄθωνος οὕτω ἀειλαμποῖς φωστῆρσιν
κεκόσμητο, ἀλλὰ καὶ πάντα τὰ ἐν τῷ Ἁγίῳ Ὄρει τούτῳ
φαιδρότατα καὶ ἱερὰ μοναστήρια ἀνδρῶν ἁγίων καὶ ἱερῶν
πλήθει ἀπείρῳ τοιούτους ἐν ἀρεταῖς θείαις ὄντας πλουσιοπαρόχως κεκόσμητο Χριστοῦ χάριτι καὶ ἀντιλήψει τῆς
Θεομήτορος. Καὶ ἦν τὸ Ἅγιον Ὄρος, ὡς ἔφημεν, ἄλλος
οὐρανὸς ἐπίγειος, τάγμασι καὶ πλήθει τῶν μοναζόντων
ἀντὶ ταγμάτων τῶν ἐπουρανίων πλουτῶν, κατὰ τάξιν τῶν
ἄνω ὑμνούντων ἀεννάως τῆς δόξης τὸν Κύριον καὶ τῇ
παναγνῳ Θεομήτορι εὐφημίζοντες. Ἀλλὰ τί πάθω; Καὶ

psalter while standing together, others by themselves in mental prayer and with spiritual tranquility in their hearts, and yet others only in visions of the Spirit thus become elevated in their minds through the Spirit and uncover the sacred mysteries, as it is said, *"Be still and know that I am God."*

Others, who are subject to elders and holy men of this sort, are always smitten with desire for Christ, and each one carries out His commandments to the best of his ability and without restraint, not desiring to see the beauties of the world, but striving to share happily in and observe the beauties of the intelligible paradise, for, as a wise man says, divine desire becomes unceasing for those in the wilderness, since they are beyond the vanity of the world. For this reason and with much endurance, these blessed men have gathered together in this harsh and inaccessible place from all over the world, and live all around Athos, as if in a meadow that is always in flower, and they rejoice in the Spirit. Not only are the areas all around this most lofty Athos thus adorned with eternally shining luminaries, but also all the most splendid and holy monasteries on this Holy Mountain are abundantly adorned through the grace of Christ and the succor of the Mother of God with innumerable multitudes of holy and hallowed men, such men as are richly endowed with divine virtues. And, as we said, the Holy Mountain was another heaven on earth, rich with ranks and multitudes of monks instead of ranks of celestial beings, monks who praise the all-pure Mother of God in the same way that those on high hymn with eternal praise the Lord of glory. But what am I to

γὰρ νικᾷ με ὁ πόθος τοῦ ἁγίου Μαξίμου καταλιπεῖν τὴν
διήγησιν ταύτην τῶν φαιδρῶν μαργαρίτων τῶν κατοι-
κούντων ἐν Ὄρει Ἁγίῳ καὶ αὐτοῦ πάλιν ἄρξασθαι τὰ ὑπὲρ
ἄνθρωπον θεῖα παλαίσματα.

9

Οὗτος ὁ ἅγιος, πειθόμενος τοῖς ἁγίοις ἐκείνοις πατράσιν, ἐμποδίζετο μὲν τὴν πρὸς ἐρημίαν ὁδεῦσαι ὁδὸν παρ'
αὐτοῖς, ἐσπουδάζετο δὲ παρὰ τῇ θείᾳ ῥοπῇ. Καὶ διὰ τοῦτο
ἡ Θεοτόκος καθ' ὕπνους φησί, ἐν ἀγκάλαις ἔχουσα τὸν
Κύριον· "Δεῦρο δή, ἀκολούθει μοι, πιστότατε Μάξιμε, τὰ
πρὸς ἀνάβασιν τούτου τοῦ Ἄθωνος, ἵν' ὅπως κατὰ τὸ σὸν
ἐφετὸν λάβῃς καὶ τὰ πυξία [Exodus 24:12] τῆς χάριτος."
Καὶ δὶς καὶ τρὶς τοῦτο παθών (καθ' ὕπαρ μᾶλλον ἢ κατ'
ὄναρ τοῦτο αὐτῷ ἐγεγόνει, ἐπεὶ ἄϋπνος ἦν τῷ παντί), τί
γίνεται;

2   Καταλιπὼν τὴν μεγάλην καὶ θαυμαστὴν Λαύραν, τὴν
ἄνοδον πρῶτον ταχοῖς δρόμοις ἐπιζητεῖ τὴν τοῦ Ἄθωνος,
ὅπου καὶ τὰ πυξία τῆς χάριτος παρὰ τῆς Θεοτόκου εὐηγ-
γελίσατο· καὶ νῆστις οὕτω καταλαμβάνει ἐν τῇ ἑβδόμῃ·
πρώτη γὰρ ἦν ἡ ἡμέρα ἐκείνη τῆς Ἀναλήψεως, ἡ λεγομένη
Κυριακὴ τῶν ἁγίων Πατέρων. Κἀκεῖ γενόμενος ἐν τῇ κορυφῇ καὶ προσκυνήσας καὶ εὐξάμενος τῷ Θεῷ πάννυχον,
ὡς ἔθος αὐτῷ ἦν, τὴν πᾶσαν νύκταν διετέλεσεν ἄγρυπνος

do? For my desire for the holy Maximos is forcing me to abandon this account of the shining pearls who dwell on the Holy Mountain and to take up again the account of his divine and superhuman struggles.

Chapter 9

The holy one, obeying those holy fathers, was prevented by them on the one hand from following the path to the wilderness, but on the other was troubled by divine influence. To this end the Mother of God appeared in his sleep, holding the Lord in her arms, and said, "Come here, most faithful Maximos, follow me in the ascent of this Athos, so that in accordance with your objective you too may receive *the tablets* of grace." After experiencing this a second and third time (and this happened to him in a waking vision rather than in a dream, since he was completely awake), what happened?

Leaving the great and wondrous Lavra, he first set off at full speed on the ascent of Athos, where the tablets of grace were promised by the Mother of God. And thus he reached it, without eating anything, on the seventh <Sunday after Easter>; for that day was the first <Sunday> after the Ascension, the so-called Sunday of the Holy Fathers. After arriving at the summit there and prostrating himself and praying to God, as was his custom every night, he spent the whole

μετὰ καὶ μοναζόντων τινῶν. Ἀλλ᾽ ἐπειδὴ οἱ μοναχοὶ τῷ πρωῒ ἀπεδήμησαν ἅπαντες καὶ ἀπελείφθην οὐδείς, αὐτὸς ἐκεῖσε προσεκαρτέρησεν μόνος ἐν νυχθημέροις τρισὶν πάλιν ἀνέσθιος καὶ μονόχιτος, προσεδρεύων Θεῷ· καὶ τὴν Θεομήτορα ἐν τῇ γλώττῃ, νοῒ καὶ καρδίᾳ διὰ προσευχῆς εἶχεν νοερᾶς ἀεννάως ἐν Πνεύματι.

3 Ἀλλὰ τίς διηγήσεται τὰ τοῦ Ἐχθροῦ ἐκεῖσε μηχανουργεύματα; Ἔδοξεν γὰρ βροντὰς ποιῆσαι καὶ ἀστραπὰς καὶ συσσεῖσαι τὸ ὄρος τὸ μέγα τοῦ Ἄθωνος, καὶ σπάσματα πετρῶν καὶ βουνῶν γεγωνέναι οὕτω ψευδῶς. Καὶ ταῦτα μὲν τῇ νυκτί· τῇ δὲ ἡμέρᾳ φωνὰς ἀγρίας πολλῶν ἐφάνταζεν εἶναι ὄχλων πλησίον αὐτοῦ καὶ ταραχάς, καὶ πολλοὺς ἐδείκνυεν κύκλωθεν ἀειδεῖς τὴν κορυφὴν τοῦ Ἄθωνος ἀναβαίνοντας καὶ πρὸς αὐτὸν καθορμῶντας τὸν ἅγιον μετὰ σφενδονῶν καὶ κοντῶν καὶ λογχῶν. Οὐ γὰρ ἔφερον οἱ κατάρατοι τὴν τοῦ ἁγίου ἐκεῖσε καταμονὴν καθορᾶν· ὅθεν καὶ τοιαύτοις προσέβαλλον τοῖς παλαίσμασιν, ἵνα τάχα ἐκ τῆς κορυφῆς αὐτὸν καταγάγωσιν. Καὶ ταῦτα μὲν οἱ κατάρατοι δαίμονες, οἳ τοῖς ἁγίοις τοιαῦτα προσάπτουσιν πανουργεύματα.

4 Ὁ δὲ ἅγιος, ὡς ἔχων τὴν χάριν τοῦ ἁγίου Πνεύματος ἔνδοθεν, τὰ ἔξωθεν γενόμενα τοιαῦτα ἀθύρματα οὐκ ἐφρόντισεν, μόνον δὲ ἦν μόνος τῇ προσευχῇ ἀεννάως προσεδρεύων Θεῷ καὶ τῇ Θεομήτορι, τῇ ἀναδόχῳ αὐτοῦ καὶ προστάτιδι. Καὶ δῆτα καθ᾽ ὕπαρ ἡ Θεοτόκος φαίνεται τῷ ἁγίῳ ὡς δέσποινα κυκλουμένη ὑπὸ ἀρχόντων νέων πολλῶν, φέρουσα ἐν χερσὶν αὖθις καὶ τὸν Υἱὸν τὸν δημιουργὸν πάσης τῆς κτίσεως. Καὶ τοῦτο κατανοήσας ὁ ἅγιος

night in vigil together with some monks. But when all the monks departed in the morning and no one was left behind, he remained there alone for three entire days and nights without food and wearing only a single garment, in the service of God. And he constantly had the name of the Mother of God on his tongue, in his mind and heart through mental prayer in the Spirit.

But who will describe the machinations of the Enemy in 3 that place? For he seemed to make thunder and lightning and to shake the great mountain of Athos, and thus to make the rending of rocks and hills resound deceptively. This is what happened during the night; but during the day the Enemy made it seem as though there were wild voices and the tumult of great crowds in his vicinity, and he showed many ugly people ascending the summit of Athos on all sides and attacking the holy one with slings and spears and javelins. For the accursed ones could not bear to see the holy one staying there, and thus launched such tricky attacks upon him, so that they might perhaps force him to descend from the summit. These were the deeds of the accursed demons, who inflict such villainous tricks on holy men.

The holy one, however, inasmuch as he had the grace of 4 the Holy Spirit dwelling within him, paid no attention to such external distractions, and continued his constant and solitary prayer in service to God and the Mother of God, his guardian and protector. And indeed the Mother of God appeared to the holy one in a waking vision, as a lady surrounded by many young officials, again also holding in her arms her Son, the demiurge of all creation. When the holy

ἐκ τοῦ ἀστέκτου καὶ ἀδύτου θείου φωτὸς τοῦ ἐν τῇ Θεοτόκῳ ὄντος καὶ διαλάμποντος κύκλωθεν ἐκεῖνα τὰ πέρατα,
ὅτι οὐκ ἦν πλάνη, ἀλλὰ ἀλήθεια, τὸ "Χαῖρε κεχαριτωμένη,
ὁ Κύριος μετὰ σοῦ" [Luke 1:28], καὶ τὸ "Ἄξιόν ἐστιν ὡς ἀληθῶς" μετ᾽ εὐφροσύνης καὶ χαρᾶς ἀνεκφράστου τῇ Θεοτόκῳ πρῶτον ἀνύμνησεν.

5   Εἶθ᾽ οὕτως καὶ πεσὼν προσεκύνησεν τῷ Κυρίῳ ἅμα τῇ
Θεομήτορι, καὶ τὴν εὐλογίαν παρὰ Κυρίου ἐδέξατο καὶ
τὸν λόγον παρὰ τῆς Δεσποίνης οὑτωΐ προεκροάσατο·
"Δέξου τὴν χάριν κατὰ δαιμόνων, ὁ σεπτὸς ἀθλοφόρος,
καὶ κατοίκησον ἐπὶ τὰ πρόποδα τῆς κορυφῆς τοῦ Ἄθωνος·
τοῦτο γὰρ βουλητὸν τῷ Υἱῷ μου γέγονει, ἵνα σύ, ὡς ἔφην,
ἀναδράμῃς πρὸς ὕψος ἀρετῆς τῆς ἐρήμου καὶ γένῃς
ὁδηγὸς καὶ διδάσκαλος ἐν ἐρήμῳ τοῖς πᾶσιν, τὸν νέον
Ἰσραὴλ ὁδηγῶν εἰς τὰ εὐσεβῆ θεῖα τοῦ Υἱοῦ μου ἐντάλματα,
ὅπως καὶ διασώσῃς αὐτούς, ὥς ποτε Μωυσῆς καὶ Ἡλίας
τὸν παλαιὸν ἐκεῖνον Ἰσραὴλ τὸν φυγάδα." Ἐν τούτῳ καὶ
ἄρτος οὐράνιος ἐδόθη αὐτῷ εἰς τροφὴν καὶ ἀνάψυξιν
φύσεως. Καὶ ἅμα τοῦ ἄρτου λαβὼν καὶ τοῖς ὀδοῦσι βαλών,
φῶς θεῖον περιεκύκλωσεν αὐτὸν ἄνωθεν καὶ ὕμνος γέγονεν ἀγγελικός· καὶ οὕτω ἡ Θεοτόκος ἀπῆρεν ἐξ ὀφθαλμῶν
τοῦ ἁγίου πρὸς τὰ οὐράνια, τὸν ὕμνον ἐπάδοντες οἱ
ἀσώματοι ἐπὶ τὴν ἀνάβασιν τῆς Δεσποίνης ἐκείνην τὴν
θαυμαστήν. Ἔλεγεν γὰρ ὁ ἅγιος, ὅτι μετὰ τὴν τοιαύτης
ἀνάβασιν τὴν ἔνδοξον καὶ φαιδρὰν τοσαύτη ἦν ἔλλαμψις
καὶ εὐωδία ἐν τῇ κορυφῇ τότε τοῦ Ἄθωνος, ὡς ἔκθαμβον
γεγονέναι ἐν τούτῳ τὸν ἅγιον καὶ κατοικεῖν οὕτω

one realized, from the unbearable and never-setting divine light which was in the Mother of God and which illuminated that area all around, that this was not an illusion but reality, he began with joy and ineffable happiness to sing to the Mother of God the hymns that begin, "*Hail, one who is filled with grace, the Lord is with you,*" and "*Truly it is worthy.*"

Then he fell to his knees and venerated the Lord and the 5 Mother of God, and received a blessing from the Lord and heard the following prophetic words from our Lady: "Receive the grace of power over demons, O revered contender, and dwell on the slopes of the summit of Athos. For this is the will of my Son, that, you, as I said, should ascend to the heights of virtue out of the wilderness and become a guide and teacher for all in the wilderness, guiding the new Israel toward the divine and pious commandments of my Son, so that you may save them, as Moses and Elijah once saved the people of ancient Israel in exile." And at the same time heavenly bread was granted to him for his physical nourishment and recovery. As soon as he took the bread and bit into it, divine light surrounded him from above and an angelic hymn began. Thus the Mother of God disappeared from the holy one's sight toward heaven, while the incorporeal angels sang their hymn at our Lady's wondrous ascent. For the holy one said that after her glorious and brilliant ascension there was then such illumination and fragrance on the summit of Athos that he was astonished at this and wished to dwell

βουληθῆναι ἐν αὐτῷ μᾶλλον ἀεὶ ἢ κατελθεῖν καὶ ὑστε-
ρηθῆναι τῆς εὐοδμίας ἐκείνης καὶ τῆς ἐλλάμψεως.

6   Ὅθεν καὶ τρεῖς ἡμέρας ποιήσας ἐν αὐτῷ τῷ τόπῳ τῆς
εὐωδίας, κατέρχεται οὕτω κατὰ τὴν κέλευσιν τῆς Δεσποίνης ἡμῶν Θεοτόκου μέχρι τὸν ναὸν αὐτῆς τὸν λεγόμενον
Παναγίαν. Κἀκεῖ οὖν ἡμέρας τινὰς διατρίψας, πάλιν ἐπὶ
τὴν κορυφὴν ἀνῆλθεν τοῦ Ἄθωνος καὶ τὸν τόπον ἐκεῖνον
ἠσπάζετο, ἐν ᾧ ἡ Θεοτόκος ἐδόκει σταθῆναι μετὰ τῆς
δόξης· καὶ μετὰ δακρύων ἐζήτει πάλιν τὸ ὁραθέν, ἀλλ᾽ οὐκ
ἔτυχεν· φῶς γὰρ μόνον καὶ εὐωδία θεία ἀκόρεστος ταῖς
αἰσθήσεσιν τοῦ ἁγίου ἐνέπιπτεν ἀοράτως, ὡς πρότερον,
καὶ τοῦτον εὐφροσύνην ἐπλήρουν καὶ χαρᾶς ἀνεκφράστου.
Καὶ τοῦτο δὶς καὶ τρὶς ἐκ τῆς Παναγίας ἀνελθὼν καὶ
λαχών, ἔκτοτε κατελθὼν <καὶ> εἰς τὸ Καρμήλιον γεγονὼς
κἀκεῖσε εὑρών τινα μονάζοντα γέροντα, προσεῖπεν τὸ
ὁραθέν.

10

Ὅ δ᾽ ὁ γέρων ταῦτα ἀκούσας ἔδοξεν πλάνην εἶναι τὸ
ὁραθέν· διὰ τοῦτο καὶ προσῆψεν αὐτῷ τῆς πλάνης τὸ ὄνομα, τὸν φωστῆρα πλανημένον ἀποκαλῶν ὁ ἀνόητος. Ἀπὸ
τούτου καὶ παντὶ τὸν αὐτὸν λόγον προσῆπτον αὐτῷ καὶ
κατεδίωκον μὴ προσεγγίσαι τινί, ἀποσειόμενοι αὐτὸν ὡς
πλανημένον καὶ βδελυττόμενοι. Ἀλλ᾽ ὁ ἀπλανὴς οὗτος

there forever rather than to descend and be deprived of that fragrance and illumination.

Thus, after spending three days in this place of fragrance, 6 he descended at the bidding of our Lady the Mother of God as far as her church, the one called Panagia. After spending some days there, he went up again to the summit of Athos and kissed the spot where the Mother of God had appeared to stand in glory. He tearfully sought to see the vision once again, but he did not succeed; for only light and unceasing divine fragrance fell invisibly upon the holy one's senses, as before, and filled him with joy and inexpressible happiness. After going up two or three times from the Panagia and being granted this experience, he then went down from there and, going to Karmelion, found a solitary elder there and told him about his vision.

Chapter 10

When the elder heard this, he thought the vision was a delusion; and for this reason dubbed Maximos "the vagrant," the foolish man calling the radiant one deranged. As a result everyone began to apply the same term to him and they chased him away to stop him from approaching anyone, rejecting him as someone who was deranged and reviling him. But this unerring luminary embraced even this,

φωστήρ, καὶ τοῦτο ἐγκολπωσάμενος, τὸ καλεῖσθαι πεπλα-
νημένος ἢ μάλιστα ἅγιος, εὐφραίνετο ἐν τούτῳ καὶ πλεῖστα
ἔχαιρεν· καὶ ὑπεκρίνετο οὕτως ὡς πλανημένος ἀείποτε,
ὅταν ὡμίλει τισίν, καὶ ἐμώραινεν, ἵνα τὴν ὑπερήφανον
ἀνθρωπαρέσκειαν καὶ οἴησιν ἐξ αὐτοῦ ἀφανίσῃ καὶ ἀνθήσῃ
τὴν ταπεινοφροσύνην τὴν φυλάττουσαν τὴν χάριν τοῦ
Πνεύματος.

2   Τούτου γε χάριν καὶ οὐκ ἐν ἑνὶ κατῴκησεν τόπῳ τοῦ
Ἄθωνος, ὡς οἱ πλείονες ἐν ἡσυχίοις κελλίοις τοῦτο ποιοῦσιν, ἀλλ᾽ ὡς πλανώμενος ἀπὸ τόπον εἰς τόπον πλησίον
μετέβαινεν· καὶ κέλλας τάχα ἐπήγετο, καὶ αὖθις ταύτας
κατέκαπτεν διὰ πυρός· τὸ ξένον τοῦτο τοῖς μονάζουσιν,
μᾶλλον δὲ τοῖς ἀνθρώποις ἐγχείρημα. Μὴ δίκελλαν, μὴ
σκαλίδαν, μὴ πήραν, μὴ σκάμνον, μὴ τράπεζαν, ἢ χύτραν,
ἢ ἄλευρον, ἢ ἔλαιον, ἢ οἶνον, ἢ ἄλλο τι τῶν ἀναγκαίων
ὑλῶν, ἢ ἄρτον ὑπεκτήσατο πώποτε ὁ μακάριος, ἀλλ᾽ ἐν
ἀΰλοις τόποις ὡς ἄϋλος ὤν, οὕτως μόνον ἐν ὑποκρίσει
μικρὸν κελλίον, ὅσον ἐχώρει καὶ μόνον τὸ πολύαθλον
αὐτοῦ σωμάτιον, καὶ ταύτην ἐκ χόρτου συστησάμενος,
συντόμως κατέκαπτεν ἐν πυρί. Διὰ τοῦτο καὶ ἀπλανὴς ὢν
πλανημένος ἐλέγετο, καὶ σὺν αὐτῷ καὶ Καψοκαλύβης
λέγεσθαι προσετέθην αὐτῷ παρὰ τοῖς γεώφροσιν, μὴ
ὁρῶντες τὴν ἐν αὐτῷ θείαν χάριν τοῦ Πνεύματος τὴν φωταυγῆ, τὴν σκέπουσαν ὡς σκηνὴν αὐτῷ θείαν οὐράνιον
καὶ γλυκαίνουσαν, καὶ τὴν δροσίζουσαν αὐτὸν ἐλπίδαν καὶ
προσευχὴν τὴν ἀέναον πάντοτε.

that is, being called deranged rather than holy, and rejoiced at this and was extremely joyful. And so he always pretended to be deranged whenever he talked with people, and he played the fool so as to eradicate from himself the pride and self-conceit which tries to court popularity and so as to bring into flower the humility which preserves the grace of the Spirit.

For this reason he did not settle in one place on Athos, as 2 most monks do in tranquil cells, but kept moving from one place to another nearby like a vagrant. He would quickly build huts, and then burn them down again with fire. This behavior was strange for the monks, and even for people in general. The blessed one never possessed a digging fork or hoe, nor a purse, nor a bench, a table, a pot, flour, oil, or wine, nor any other material necessity, nor bread, but living like an immaterial being in places untouched by materiality, he thus possessed only the semblance of a small hut, large enough only to contain his much-suffering body. And after building this out of grasses, he would soon burn it down. For this reason, although he was not in error, he was considered deranged, and at the same time he was given the sobriquet Hutburner by earthly-minded people, who did not see in him the illuminating divine grace of the Spirit which sheltered him like a divine, celestial tent and spread sweetness, and the eternal hope and prayer which always refreshed him like dew.

II

Ἀλλὰ τίς διηγήσηται τὰ θεῖα παλαίσματα, μᾶλλον δὲ ἀγωνίσματα τοῦ τοιούτου ἁγίου ἀνδρός, ἐν οἷς ἀνδρικῶς κατεπάλαιεν, πείνῃ καὶ δίψῃ καὶ τῇ γυμνότητι [see Deuteronomy 28:48; 2 Corinthians 11:27], παγετοῖς καὶ τῷ καύσωνι, ἐν χειμῶνι καὶ θέρει, αἴθριος, μονόχιτος, ἀνυπόδετος; Παρὰ δὲ μηδέτινος ἐπισκεπτόμενος τὰ πρὸς χρείαν, εἰ μήτι ἂν αὐτὸς ἐπαρέβαλεν πώποτε πρός τινι· καὶ τότε παράκλησιν ἐποίει τῷ σώματι, ἄρτῳ καὶ οἴνῳ καὶ ἅλατι καὶ πλέον οὐδέν.

2   Οὗτός ἐστιν, ὃν ἔφη Χριστός· "Ἐμβλέψατε εἰς τὰ πετεινὰ τοῦ οὐρανοῦ, ὅτι οὐ σπείρουσιν οὐδὲ θερίζουσιν οὐδὲ συνάγουσιν εἰς ἀποθήκας, καὶ ὁ Πατὴρ ὑμῶν ὁ οὐράνιος τρέφει αὐτά" [Matthew 6:26]. Ὡς γὰρ πετεινὸν οὐράνιον οὗτος ὁ ἅγιος, μᾶλλον δ᾽ ὡς ἄγγελος τὴν ἔρημον ταύτην κατῴκησεν, καὶ τὸ περισσότερον, ὅτι καὶ τὰς καλιὰς αὐτοῦ ἐκατέφλεγεν. Οὗτός ἐστιν, ὃν ἔφησεν Παῦλος· "Περιῆλθεν ἐν μηλωταῖς, ἐν αἰγείοις δέρμασιν, ὑστερούμενος, θλιβόμενος, κακοχούμενος, κολαφιζόμενος, ὑβριζόμενος· οὗ οὐκ ἦν ἄξιος ὁ κόσμος" [Hebrews 11:37–38]. Ὄντως οὗτος τὴν σάρκα ἐσταύρωσεν σὺν τοῖς παθήμασι καὶ ταῖς ἐπιθυμίαις [Galatians 5:24], καὶ τὸν σταυρὸν ἦρεν, ὡς ἔδει, ἐπ᾽ ὤμων καὶ τῷ Χριστῷ πιστῶς ἠκολούθησεν [see Matthew 16:24; Mark 8:34] ἀόκνως. Τίς οὐ θαυμάσειεν τὴν τοιαύτην αὐτοῦ οὐράνιον διαγωγήν; Τίς οὐκ ἐκπλαγῇ ἀκούων τὰ ὑπὲρ ἄνθρωπον ὑπερφυῆ αὐτοῦ θεῖα ἐπαγωνίσματα, τὴν αὐτοῦ

Chapter 11

But who could describe the divine struggles, or rather the contests of such a holy man, in which he contended manfully, in hunger *and thirst and nakedness,* in freezing cold and burning heat, in winter and summer, living in the open air, with only a single garment, and no shoes? No one ever visited him to bring provisions, unless he himself ever went to visit someone; and then he would offer some solace to his body, nothing more than bread and wine and salt.

This is the man of whom Christ said, "*Look at the birds of* 2 *the air; they neither sow nor reap nor gather into barns, and yet your heavenly Father feeds them.*" For this holy one dwelt in this wilderness like a bird of the air, or rather like an angel; and even more so, because he used to burn down his huts. This is the man of whom Paul said, "*he went about in skins of sheep and goats, destitute, afflicted, ill-treated,* being beaten and abused, *of whom the world was not worthy.*" Truly this man *crucified the flesh with its passions and desires* and *carried the cross,* as he should have, on his shoulders, and without hesitation *followed* Christ faithfully. Who would not marvel at his heavenly behavior? Who would not be astonished to hear about his superhuman and extraordinary divine struggles, his great

μεγάλην ὑπομονήν, τὴν νηστείαν τὴν ὑπεράμετρον, τὴν δίψαν, τὴν ἀγρυπνίαν, τὴν προσευχὴν καὶ τὸ δάκρυον, τὴν στάσιν καὶ τὴν μετάνοιαν, τὴν τύψιν τῆς κεφαλῆς ἐπὶ τὸ πετρῶδες ἔδαφος, τὸ ἥσυχον καὶ πρᾷον καὶ ταπεινὸν τῆς ἀπλανῆς ἐκείνης φωταυγοῦς θείας χάριτος, ἧς κατετρύφα ἀεί;

3   Καὶ ἀπὸ θεωρίαν εἰς θεωρίαν οὕτω μετάρσιος καθ' ἑκάστην ἐγένετο ἐν τῷ Πνεύματι, καὶ ἁρπαγὴν νοὸς ὑφίστατο πρὸς τὰ ἄδυτα, καὶ θείων μυστηρίων κατηξίωτο, ὡς Παῦλός ποτε καὶ Ἀντώνιος, οἱ μεγάλοι φωστῆρες τῆς οἰκουμένης καὶ τῆς ἐρήμου οἰκήτορες· μᾶλλον δ' ὡς ὁ Πέτρος ὁ Ἀθωνίτης καὶ ὁ μέγιστος Ἀθανάσιος, οἱ τοῦ Ἁγίου Ὄρους καὶ τῆς Δύσεως ἁπάσης ὡς ἀειλαμπεῖς ἥλιοι ἀνατέλλοντες· οὕτω καὶ οὗτος κατὰ μικρὸν ἀναβὰς εἰς τὰ ὕψη ἐκείνων κατ' ἀρετήν, πρᾶξιν λέγω καὶ θεωρίαν, ἐξανέτειλεν μέσον ἡμῶν ἐν ἐρήμῳ, καὶ τὴν κτίσιν ἐφαίδρυνεν καὶ ἡμᾶς πάντας ἐψυχαγώγησεν, ὡς φαιδρότατος ἥλιος.

12

Οὗτος δὲ ὁ ἅγιος γέγονε συνήθης μεγάλοις τισὶ γέρουσιν, τοῖς ἐν χαράδραις τὴν κατοίκησιν ἔχουσι, λέγω δὴ τὸν ἐν τοῖς Βουλευτηρίοις Γερόντιον καὶ τὸν ἐν τοῖς μέρεσιν τοῦ ἁγίου Μάμαντος Κορνήλιον καὶ Αὐξέντιον καὶ

endurance, his extreme fasting, his thirst, his lack of sleep, his prayers and tears, his standing vigils and prostrations, the way he beat his head against the rocky ground, the tranquility and mildness and humility of the unerring illuminating divine grace which he always enjoyed?

And with vision after vision he thus became uplifted every day in the Spirit, and experienced *rapture of mind* unto the innermost secrets, and was deemed worthy of the divine mysteries, just like Paul of old and Antony, the great illuminators of the inhabited world and dwellers in the desert, or rather like Peter the Athonite and the great Athanasios, who rose like eternally shining suns over the Holy Mountain and all the West. Thus Maximos, gradually ascending to their heights of virtue, I mean of practice and contemplation, arose in our midst in the wilderness, and illuminated creation and guided all our souls like a most brilliant sun.

Chapter 12

The holy one became acquainted with some great elders, who had their dwellings in ravines, I mean Gerontios in the monastery of Bouleuteria and Kornelios in the region of Saint Mamas, and Auxentios and Isaiah and the wondrous

Ἠσαΐαν καὶ ἐπὶ τὸν ἅγιον Χριστοφόρον τὸν θαυμάσιον Μακάριον τὸν ἱερόν, ἀλλὰ δὴ καὶ τὸν ἐν τῇ Στραβῇ Λαγκάδᾳ λογιώτατον τὸν καὶ ἄρτον οὐράνιον ὑπ᾿ ἀγγέλου τραφέντα Γρηγόριον, καὶ τὸν ἐν Δωροθέοις καθήμενον καὶ ἐν ταῖς Λεύκαις, λέγω δὴ καὶ τοὺς ἐπὶ τὸν λεγόμενον Μελανέαν ἁγίους γέροντας ὄντας καὶ ἡσυχάζοντας, τὸν Ἁγιομαμίτην ἐκεῖνον καὶ τὸν Γερόντιον, Θεόδουλον, Ἰάκωβον τὸν ἐπικεκλημένον Μαρούλην, Τραπεζούντιον ἕτερον Ἰάκωβον, τὸν ἱερὸν Κλήμην ἐκεῖνον καὶ Γαλακτίωνα τοὺς ἡσυχάζοντας, Μάρκον ἐκεῖνον τὸν Ἁπλοῦν καὶ θαυμάσιον, καὶ ἄλλους πλείονας γέροντας, ὧν τὰ ὀνόματα διὰ τὸ μῆκος τοῦ λόγου παραιτητέον· καὶ ὅτι τούτων ἁπάντων *ἐγράφησαν ἐν τοῖς οὐρανοῖς* [see Luke 10:20], διὰ τοῦτο οὐκ ἀναγκαῖον ἡμῖν ἐνθάδε γραφῆναι.

2   Οὗτοι πάντες, τὸν ἅγιον Μάξιμον διὰ θαύματος ἔχοντες, πῶς τὰς κέλλας αὐτοῦ ἐκτρίβει διὰ πυρός, αὐτὸς δὲ ἀφερέοικος καὶ ἀπρονόητος οὕτως διῆγεν ἐπὶ παντί, ἀλλὰ δὴ καὶ διὰ τῆς αὐτοῦ ὁμιλίας καταλαβόντες καὶ τὴν ἐνοικοῦσαν ἐν αὐτῷ θείαν χάριν, οὐκέτι πεπλανημένον ἔκτοτε αὐτὸν ἔλεγον, ἀλλὰ Καψοκαλύβην καὶ τίμιον Μάξιμον καὶ φωστῆρα ὑπέρλαμπρον.

13

Ἐλθὼν δὲ καὶ ὁ ἡσυχαστικώτατος ἐκεῖνος ἐξ Ἱερουσαλὴμ ὁ κύριος Γρηγόριος ὁ Σιναΐτης (ὁ καὶ θαυματουργὸς

holy Makarios on the island of Saint Christopher, as well as the most learned Gregory of Strabe Langada, who was nourished with heavenly bread by an angel, and the one residing in the monastery of Dorotheos and at Leukai; I am also referring to the holy elders who lived in spiritual tranquility on what is called the Melanea, Gerontios of Saint Mamas, Theodoulos, Iakobos surnamed Maroules, another Iakobos from Trebizond, the holy Clement and Galaktion who lived in spiritual tranquility, the wondrous Mark the Simple, and many other elders, whose names must be omitted because of the length of my narrative. And because all *their names are written in heaven,* for that reason we need not record them here.

All these men, marveling at how holy Maximos used to destroy his huts by fire and always lived without shelter and without taking thought for the future, but also perceiving from conversation with him the divine grace that dwelt within him, from that time on no longer called him deranged, but the Hutburner and the honorable Maximos and an exceedingly brilliant luminary. 2

Chapter 13

When that greatest contemplative, Kyr Gregory the Sinaite (the wonderworker who became a saint and later

καὶ ἅγιος γενόμενος ὕστερον ἐν τοῖς τῆς Μακεδονίας μέρεσιν καὶ πολλοὺς φωτίσας κἀκεῖ ἐν λόγοις καὶ ἔργοις πρὸς ἡσυχίαν καὶ μοναδικὴν πολιτείαν), καθίσας καὶ οὗτος ἐπὶ τοῖς μέρεσιν τούτου τοῦ Ἄθωνος γέγονεν τοῖς πᾶσιν ποθητὸς καὶ ἐπέραστος, τοῖς ἐν ὅλῳ τῷ Ὄρει πατράσιν οἰκοῦσιν καὶ ἀδελφοῖς, περισσοτέρως δὲ τοῖς ἡσυχάζουσι γέρουσιν. Ὑπῆρχεν γὰρ οὗτος θαυμαστὸς διδάσκαλος ἐν τῇ νοερᾷ ἡσυχίᾳ καὶ καρδιακῇ προσευχῇ καὶ τὰς φορὰς τῶν πνευμάτων ἐνόει μάλα σαφῶς, τὸ δυσεύρετον ἐν τοῖς γέρουσί τε καὶ σπάνιον.

2　　Διὰ τοῦτο καὶ πρὸς αὐτὸν ἀναδραμόντες οἱ ἡσυχάζοντες κατεμάνθανον τὰ τῆς καρδιακῆς εὐχῆς, τὰ μυστήρια τὰ ἀπλανῆ τὰ τῆς χάριτος, καὶ ὁποῖα τὰ τῆς πλάνης σημεῖα. Καὶ ἴδοις ἂν κατέρρεον ἅπαντες ἐπὶ τοῦτον, ὡς ἐπὶ τὸν Ἰησοῦν οἱ πεντακισχίλιοι τότε διὰ τὸ θαῦμα τῆς ἐσθιάσεως. Ἀλλ᾽ ὡς ἐκεῖνον οἱ μαθηταὶ καὶ μόνοι τότε κατηκολούθησαν, οὕτω καὶ τὸν κλεινὸν Γρηγόριον ἐκλεκτοί τινες ἑπόμενοι τοῖς αὐτοῦ ἴχνεσιν ἠκολούθησαν, καὶ φωστῆρες ἀνεδείχθησαν φαεινότατοι.

14

Τούτων δὲ οὕτω ὄντων καὶ ὁμιλούντων Γρηγορίῳ τῷ διδασκάλῳ, τῷ φωτὶ τῶν φωστήρων, γέγονεν καὶ λόγος περὶ τοῦ ὁσίου τούτου καὶ θεοφόρου πατρὸς ἡμῶν τοῦ

through his words and deeds enlightened many in the region of Macedonia so as to lead them toward the solitary life of spiritual tranquility), arrived from Jerusalem, he also settled in the region of Athos and became beloved and cherished by all: by the fathers and brethren dwelling all over the Mountain, but especially among the elders who lived in spiritual tranquility. For this man was a wondrous teacher of mental contemplation and prayer in the heart and understood very clearly the impulses of people's souls, something hard to find and rare among elders.

For this reason those who lived in spiritual tranquility hastened to him and learned the prayer of the heart and the unerring mysteries of grace, and the signs of error. And you could see how everyone flowed toward him, just as of old the five thousand flowed to Jesus on account of the miracle of the feeding of the multitudes. But just as His disciples alone followed Jesus then, so certain chosen ones followed the celebrated Gregory and walked in his footsteps, and were revealed as most shining luminaries. 2

Chapter 14

While these men were thus associating and conversing with Gregory the teacher, the light of luminaries, there was talk of this holy and divinely inspired father of ours, the

Καψοκαλύβη, λέγοντες καὶ ἐξηγούμενοι τὴν τούτου πᾶσαν ὑπὲρ ἄνθρωπον θείαν διαγωγὴν καὶ τὴν ὑποκρινομένην μωρίαν καὶ πλάνην τὴν ἀπλανῆ. Καὶ ταῦτα παρὰ πάντων ἀκούσας ὁ Σιναΐτης μέγας Γρηγόριος, διὰ θαύματος εἶχεν τὸν ὅσιον καὶ ἰδεῖν ἐπεθύμει καὶ ὁμιλῆσαι συχνῶς ὡς μέγαν τῆς ἐρήμου καὶ τοῦ ὄρους τούτου οἰκήτορα καὶ φωστῆρα ὑπέρλαμπρον.

2   Ὅθεν καί τινας ἐκπέμψας ἐκ τῶν αὐτοῦ φοιτητῶν σὺν Μάρκῳ τῷ προμνημονευθέντι Ἁπλῷ, ἔφη· "Σκύλθητι πρὸς ἡμᾶς, τιμιώτατε πάτερ καὶ ἀδελφὲ Μάξιμε, ἵν' ἴδωμεν τὴν σὴν ἀγάπην καὶ ἁγιότητα καὶ δοξάσωμεν τὸν ἐν ὑψίστοις Θεόν." Καὶ τοῦτον ἰχνεύσαντες ἐν ταῖς λόχμαις δυσὶν ἡμέραις, οὐχ εὕρισκον, ἐπειδὴ τὴν καλύβην προέκαυσεν καὶ διῆγεν οὕτως ἐν λόχμαις καὶ τοῖς σπηλαίοις καὶ ἐν χαράδραις. Χειμέριος γὰρ ἦν ὁ καιρός, καὶ πολλὰ κεκμηκότες ὑπὸ τοῦ κρύους, στραφέντες εἰς τὸν Ἁγιομαμίτην κατέφυγον ἀναψύχοντες.

3   Ἔτι δὲ ὄντων ἐκείνων ἐκεῖσε, καταλαμβάνει καὶ ὁ ζητούμενος οὗτος ἐκεῖ Μάξιμος, ὡς μαργαρίτης ἀναφανεὶς αὐτοῖς ὁ θαυμάσιος· καὶ εἴτε ἡ πρόνοια τοῦτον καὶ ἡ εὐχὴ τοῦ γέροντος κινήσας ἤφερεν, εἴτε αὐτὸς προορατικῷ ὄμματι κατιδὼν οὕτω γέγονεν πρὸς αὐτούς, οὐκ ἔχω τοῦτο εἰπεῖν· τοῦτο μόνον, ὅτι προσαγορεύει τοῖς ὀνόμασι πάντας καὶ τοῦ γέροντος τὴν βουλὴν προμηνύει· ἐβούλετο γὰρ ὁ γέρων ἀπᾶραι ἀπ' Ὄρους πρὸς τῆς Μακεδονίας τὰ ἄκρα, εἰς τὰ Παρόρια. Διὰ τοῦτο καὶ τὸν ῥηθέντα Μάρκον κατέσκωπτε, "Μὴ τολμήσῃς," λέγων αὐτῷ, "ἀκολουθῆσαι τῷ γέροντι ἀπαγομένῳ εἰς τὰ Παρόρια." Καὶ ταῦτα μὲν ὁ

Hutburner, as they spoke of and described his totally divine and superhuman behavior and his feigned foolishness and unerring wandering. When the great Gregory the Sinaite heard this from everyone, he marveled at the holy one and desired to see him and spend much time in conversation with him as a great inhabitant of the wilderness and of this mountain and an exceptionally bright luminary.

He thus sent some of his disciples, together with the 2 aforementioned Mark the Simple, and said: "Hurry to us, most venerable father and brother Maximos, so that we may see your love and holiness and may glorify God in the highest." But although they searched for Maximos in the thickets for two days, they did not find him, because he had previously burned his hut and was living in the thickets and caves and ravines. And so, exhausted by the cold, for it was wintry weather, they turned back and sought refuge at the Saint Mamas monastery to recover.

While they were still there, however, this Maximos whom 3 they were seeking arrived, the wondrous man appearing among them like a pearl. Whether providence and the prayer of the elder Gregory moved him and brought him there, or whether he himself saw them with a clairvoyant eye and came to them, I cannot say; but I know only this, that he addressed everyone by name and predicted the elder's wishes; for the elder wanted to depart from the Mountain to the borders of Macedonia, to Paroria. For this reason Maximos mocked the aforesaid Mark, saying to him, "I don't think you'll dare follow the elder when he goes away to Paroria." This was what the marvelous Maximos said; but

θεσπέσιος Μάξιμος· οἱ δὲ ἀδελφοὶ τὸν λόγον προσαγο-
ρεύουσιν αὐτῷ τοῦ γέροντος καὶ μηνύουσιν. Ὁ δὲ οὐκ
ἀνεβάλετο, ἀλλ᾽ εὐθὺς σὺν αὐτοῖς εἴχετο τῆς ὁδοῦ καὶ
ψάλλων ὑπέψαλλεν τό· "Ἦρα τοὺς ὀφθαλμούς μου εἰς τὰ
ὄρη, ὅθεν ἥξει ἡ βοήθειά μου παρὰ Κυρίου τοῦ ποιήσαντος
τὸν οὐρανὸν καὶ τὴν γῆν" [see Psalm 120(121):1–2]. Καὶ ἄλλα
τινὰ ἄναρθρα ψιθυρίζων ὑπέψαλλεν, μὴ δυναμένων τῶν
συνοδευόντων καταλαβεῖν τὴν ᾠδήν.

4   Φθασάντων δὲ ἀμφοτέρων εἰς τὴν κέλλαν τοῦ γέροντος, λέγει τούτοις ὁ Μάξιμος· "Ὁ γέρων ἤδη κοπιάσας
πλεῖστα ἐκ τῆς εὐχῆς ἀναπαύεται, καὶ μείνατε μικρὸν
ἡσυχάζοντες. Αὐτὸς δὲ μικρὸν ἀναπαύσομαι μέχρις ἂν ἴδω
τὸν γέροντα." Καὶ τοῦτο εἰπών, αὐτοὶ μὲν εἰς τὸ κελλίον
ἡσύχασαν· ὁ δὲ ἅγιος πάλιν εἰσέδυ ἐν λόχμῃ, καὶ ταῖς
εὐχαῖς ἠγωνίζετο μετὰ δακρύων καὶ ἔψαλλεν· "Κατευ-
θυνθήτω, Κύριε, τὰ διαβήματά μου ἐνώπιόν σου, καὶ μὴ
κατακυριευσάτω μου πᾶσα ἀνομία. Λύτρωσαί με ἀπὸ συκο-
φαντίας ἀνθρώπων" [Psalm 118(119):133–34], καὶ τὰ ἑξῆς.
Τὴν δὲ ᾠδὴν ταύτην ἀποπληρώσας μετὰ δακρύων ὁ ἅγιος,
ἀνακαλεῖται τοῦτον ὁ Σιναΐτης ὁ θεῖος Γρηγόριος, καὶ
παραυτίκα πρὸς τῇ κελεύσει προσγίνεται, καὶ ἀλλήλοις
ἀσπάζονται θείῳ φιλήματι. Καὶ πάντας ἐκβαλὼν ὁ Γρηγόριος κατέχει μόνον τὸν θεοφόρον τοῦτον Μάξιμον,
καταλαβεῖν ἀκριβῶς τὰ περὶ αὐτοῦ παρ᾽ αὐτοῦ σαφῶς
βουλόμενος.

the brethren greeted him and informed him of the words of the elder Gregory. And Maximos did not delay, but immediately set out on the journey with them, and he chanted in song the psalm, "*I lifted up mine eyes to the mountains, whence my help shall come from the Lord who made the heaven and the earth.*" And he recited certain other indistinct words under his breath, so that his travel companions could not catch the song.

When they all arrived at the elder's cell, Maximos said to them, "The elder is very tired at present from his prayers and is resting, so wait a while in contemplation. I myself will rest a bit before seeing the elder." And after he said this, the others sat in contemplation in the cell, while the holy one went again into a thicket, and contended with tearful prayers, and chanted, "*O Lord, let my steps be ordered* before *you, and let not any iniquity have dominion over me. Deliver me from the false accusation of men,*" and the rest of the psalm. After the holy one completed his song with tears, the divine Gregory the Sinaite called to him, and he immediately answered his call, and they greeted each other with a divine kiss. Then Gregory dismissed everyone and kept with him only this divinely inspired Maximos, wanting to learn clearly and exactly all about him. 4

15

Καὶ δὴ ἐρωτηθεὶς παρ' αὐτοῦ ἀνυποκρίτως οὕτως
φησίν· "Συγχώρησον, πάτερ, πλανημένος εἰμί." Καὶ ὁ
γέρων· "Ἄφες ἄρτι [Matthew 3:15]. Λέγε διὰ τὸν Κύριον
τὴν σὴν ἀρετήν, ἵνα φωτίσῃς ἡμᾶς· εἰ δ' οὖν, ἵν' οἰκοδο-
μηθῶμεν ἀλλήλοις πρὸς ἀρετὴν Χριστοῦ χάριτι· οὐ γὰρ
τοιοῦτοί ἐσμεν, ὥς τινες ἐν λόγῳ παγιδεύουσιν [Matthew
22:15] τὸν πλησίον, ἀλλὰ φιλοῦντες τὸν πλησίον ὡς ἑαυτούς
[see Matthew 22:39]. Καὶ λέγε διὰ τὸν Κύριον."

2   Τότε ὁ ἅγιος τὰ ἐκ νεότητος πάντα εἰπὼν αὐτῷ, τὸν
ζῆλον τὸν ἔνθεον, τὸν δρασμόν, τὴν ὑποταγήν, τὴν ὑποκρινομένην μωρίαν καὶ σαλότηταν, τὰ ἆθλα, τὰ σκάμματα,
τὴν ὀπτασίαν τῆς Θεοτόκου ἐκείνην τὴν φοβεράν, τὸ φῶς
τὸ περικυκλῶσαν αὐτὸν καὶ περικυκλοῦν, τῶν δαιμόνων
τοὺς πειρασμοὺς καὶ τὰ ἔνεδρα, περικόψας ὁ γέρων αὐτόν·
"Λέγε μοι, ἀξιῶ, κρατεῖς τὴν νοερὰν προσευχήν, τιμιώτατε;" Καὶ μειδιάσας φησίν· "Ἐκ νεότητος ταύτης λαχὼν
οὐκ ἀποκρύψω τὸ θαῦμα. Ἐγώ, τίμιε πάτερ, πίστιν καὶ
ἀγάπην ἔχων ὅ τι πολλὴν εἰς τὴν πάναγνον κυρίαν τὴν
Θεοτόκον, μετὰ δακρύων ἐζήτουν τὴν χάριν τῆς προσευχῆς λαβεῖν παρ' αὐτῆς. Καὶ δῆτα γενόμενος ἐν μιᾷ, ὡς
ἔθος εἶχον, ἐν τῷ ναῷ τῆς Πανάγνου, μετὰ δακρύων ὑπὲρ
τούτου πάλιν τῇ Θεοτόκῳ ἱκέτευον· καὶ ἀσπασάμενος
μετὰ πόθου τὴν ἄχραντον εἰκόνα αὐτῆς, εὐθὺς ἐγένετό
μοι θέρμη ἐν τῷ στήθει καὶ τῇ καρδίᾳ ὅ τι πολλή, οὐ
καταφλέγουσα, ἀλλὰ δροσίζουσα καὶ γλυκαίνουσα καὶ

Chapter 15

And, in fact, when he was questioned by Gregory, Maximos answered thus without any pretense: "I'm sorry, father, I am deranged." And the elder said, "*Let it be so for the present.* Speak of your virtue through the Lord, so that you may enlighten us, or at least so that we may edify each other in pursuit of virtue through the grace of Christ. For we are not the sort of men who *trap* their neighbor *in his own words, but* are those who *love their neighbor as themselves.* Speak through the Lord."

Then the holy one told him all about his life from his youth onward, his divinely inspired zeal, his flight, his submission, his feigned folly and foolishness, his struggles, his contests, that fearsome vision of the Mother of God, the light which surrounded him and continued to surround him, the temptations and snares of demons; but the elder interrupted him, saying, "Tell me, I beg of you, most honorable one, have you mastered mental prayer?" And Maximos replied with a smile, "Because I have possessed this gift since my youth, I will not conceal the miracle. Honorable father, since I had very great faith in and love for the all-pure Lady, the Mother of God, I tearfully sought to receive from her the grace of this prayer. And one day, when I was in the church of the all-pure one, as was my custom, I again entreated the Mother of God with tears for this gift; and, immediately after I lovingly kissed her immaculate image, a great warmth arose in my chest and heart, not a burning heat, but refreshing like dew and instilling sweetness and

κατάνυξιν ἐμποιοῦσά με πολλήν. Ἔκτοτε, πάτερ, ἤρξατό μου ἡ καρδία λέγειν τὴν προσευχὴν ἔνδοθεν· ὁμοίως καὶ τὸ λογιστικὸν ἄμφω σὺν τῷ νοΐ τὴν μνήμην ἔχει τοῦ Ἰησοῦ καὶ τῆς Θεοτόκου μου, καὶ οὐδέποτέ μου ἀπέστην, συγχώρησον."

3   Καὶ ὁ Σιναΐτης· "Καὶ λεγομένης τῆς εὐχῆς, ἅγιε, ἐγένετό σοι ἀλλοίωσις ἢ ἔκστασις ἢ ἄλλο τι τῆς προσευχῆς ἄνθος καὶ καρπὸς *Πνεύματος*;" [Galatians 5:22]. Καὶ ὁ ἅγιος· "Διὰ τοῦτο, πάτερ, τὴν ἔρημον ἔτρεχον καὶ τὴν ἡσυχίαν ἐπόθουν ἀεί, ἵνα τὸν καρπὸν τῆς προσευχῆς εὕρω πλουσίως, ὅς ἐστιν ἔρως θεῖος καὶ ἁρπαγὴ νοὸς πρὸς τὸν Κύριον." "Καὶ ἔχεις ταῦτα, παρακαλῶ;" φησὶν ὁ Γρηγόριος. Καὶ μειδιάσας μικρόν· "Δός μοι φαγεῖν, καὶ μὴ ἐρεύνα τὴν πλάνην." Καὶ ὁ Γρηγόριος· "Εἴθ᾽ ἐπλανήθην κἀγὼ ὡς σύ, ἅγιε. Ἀλλὰ δέομαί σου, ἐν τῇ ἁρπαγῇ τότε σου τοῦ νοός, τί καθορᾷ τοῖς νοεροῖς ὀφθαλμοῖς τότε ὁ νοῦς; καὶ ἡ ἄρα τότε δύναται σὺν τῇ καρδίᾳ ἀνάγειν τὴν προσευχήν;"

4   Καὶ ὁ ἅγιος· "Οὐμενοῦν. Ὅταν ἐπιδημήσῃ, πάτερ, τὸ Πνεῦμα τὸ ἅγιον ἐν τῷ ἀνθρώπῳ τῆς προσευχῆς, σχολάζει τότε ἡ προσευχή, διότι *καταποθεῖται ὁ νοῦς ὑπὸ τῆς παρουσίας τοῦ ἁγίου Πνεύματος*, καὶ οὐ δύναται τὰς δυνάμεις αὐτοῦ ἐφαπλοῦν, ἀλλ᾽ ὅλως ὑποτάσσεται, ὅπου ἂν τὸ Πνεῦμα βουληθῇ ἆραι αὐτόν, ἢ εἰς ἀέραν ἄϋλον ἀμηχάνου θείου φωτός, ἢ εἰς ἄλλην ἔκθαμβον θεωρίαν οὕτω ἀσαφήν, ἢ εἰς θείαν ὁμιλίαν τὴν ὑπερβάλλουσαν· καὶ καθὼς βούλεται, οὕτω καὶ χορηγεῖ κατ᾽ ἀξίαν ὁ Παράκλητος ἐπὶ τοῖς δούλοις αὐτοῦ τὴν παράκλησιν. Τοῦτο δὲ μέμνημαι, πάτερ ἅγιε, τῶν προφητῶν ἐκείνας τὰς θεωρίας, μάλιστα δὲ τῶν

much contrition in me. From that time on, father, my heart began to recite the prayer internally; similarly the rational part of me, together with my mind, remembers Jesus and my Mother of God, and it has never left me; forgive me."

The Sinaite responded, "Holy one, while you were recit- 3 ing the prayer, did you ever experience any change or ecstasy or any other flower of prayer and *fruit of the Spirit?*" And the holy one responded, "That is why I have always hastened into the wilderness, father, and longed for spiritual tranquility; in order to find in abundance the fruit of prayer, which is divine love and *rapture of the mind* unto the Lord." "Please tell me, do you possess this?" said Gregory. And smiling a little, Maximos said, "Give me something to eat and do not seek out my error." And Gregory said, "If only I were deranged like you, holy one. But I beg of you, when you experience rapture of the mind, what then does your mind see with its mind's eye? And is it then able to elevate the prayer to a higher plane together with the heart?"

And the holy one said, "By no means. When, father, the 4 Holy Spirit takes up residence in the man of prayer, at that time the prayer ceases, because *the mind is consumed* by the presence of the Holy Spirit, and it cannot deploy its faculties, but is completely subservient; the Spirit may raise him wherever it wishes, either into the immaterial air of ineffable divine light, or into another wondrous vision that is equally incomprehensible, or into overwhelming divine intercourse. And the Comforter, just as He wills, provides appropriate comfort for His servants. This reminds me, holy father, of those visions of the prophets, and especially of the

ἀποστόλων ἐπὶ τὴν τοῦ Πνεύματος χάριν τὴν φωταυγῆ, πῶς ἐλογίζετο παρὰ τοῖς ἄλλοις πλάνη καὶ μέθη καὶ εἰς οὐδέν, καὶ ταῦτα λεγόντων· *Εἶδον τὸν Κύριον ἐπὶ θρόνου ὑψηλοῦ καὶ ἐπηρμένου*' [Isaiah 6:1], καθὼς καὶ Παῦλος σὺν τῷ πρωτομάρτυρι Στεφάνῳ, 'Εἶδον,' φάσκοντες, 'τὸν Ἰησοῦν *καθήμενον ἐπὶ θρόνον θεότητος ἐν ὑψίστοις ἐν δεξιᾷ τοῦ Πατρός*' [see Acts 7:55–56; Colossians 3:1]. Καὶ θαυμάζω πῶς καὶ νῦν ἀπιστοῦνται τὰ ὁραθέντα τισί, ὅπου ἡ χάρις τοῦ Πνεύματος ἐξήνθησεν ἐν τοῖς πιστοῖς, ὥς φησιν τοῦτο καὶ Ἰωὴλ ὅτι *Ἐκχεῶ ἀπὸ τοῦ πνεύματός μου ἐπὶ πᾶσαν σάρκα*' [Joel 2:28]. Καὶ νῦν τὸ παράκλητον Πνεῦμα δέδωκεν ἡμῖν ὁ Χριστός· διὰ τοῦτο λαμβάνει τὸ Πνεῦμα τὸν νοῦν, οὐχ ἵνα πάλιν τὰ κατὰ συνήθειαν αὐτῷ νοούμενα διδάξῃ, οἷον τὰ ὄντα, ἀλλ' ἐκεῖνα διδάσκῃ αὐτὸν τὰ ὑπὲρ ὄντα καὶ ὑπερκόσμια, οἷον τὰ περὶ τῆς θεότητος ὄντα καὶ τὸ ὄν, αὐτὸν τὸν Θεόν, ἃ *ὀφθαλμὸς σωματικὸς οὐ τεθέαται οὐδὲ καρδία γεώφρονος ἀνεβίβασεν* [see 1 Corinthians 2:9] πώποτε.

5   "Λάβε δέ μοι τοιαύτην διάνοιαν· ὥσπερ ὁ κηρὸς κηρός ἐστιν μόνος χωρὶς πυρός, ἐπὰν δὲ ὁμιλήσῃ τὸ πῦρ, συναιρεῖται καὶ διαλύεται καὶ συμφλογίζεται ἅμα τῷ πυρὶ καὶ οὐ δύναται ἀντισχεῖν, ἀλλ' ἐξάπτει σὺν τῷ πυρὶ φῶς ὅλον, ἕως οὗ ὑπάρχει τῇ φύσει καὶ φῶς ὅλον γίνεται, εἰ καὶ κηρός· οὕτω μοι νόει τὴν τοῦ νοὸς δύναμιν εἶναι ὡσεὶ κηρόν· καὶ ἕως οὗ ἵσταται κατὰ φύσιν, νοεῖ μόνον τὰ κατὰ τὴν αὐτοῦ φύσιν καὶ δύναμιν, ὅταν δὲ τὸ πῦρ τῆς θεότητος, αὐτὸ τὸ Πνεῦμα τὸ ἅγιον πλησιάσῃ αὐτόν, τότε συναιρεῖται τῇ δυνάμει τοῦ Πνεύματος καὶ συμφλογίζεται τῷ πυρὶ τῆς

apostles, regarding the illuminating grace of the Spirit; how the others considered it delusion and intoxication and nothing else when the prophets said these words: '*I saw the Lord sitting on a high and exalted throne,*' just as Paul and Stephen the First Martyr said, 'I have seen Jesus *sitting* on the throne of divinity on high *at the right hand of the Father.*' And I marvel at how, even now, there is disbelief of the things that have been seen by some people, when the grace of the Spirit has blossomed among the faithful, as Joel also says, '*I will pour out of my spirit upon all flesh.*' And now Christ has given us the Spirit as comforter. For this reason the Spirit takes the mind, not in order to teach it again its customary thoughts, such as things to do with reality, but to teach those things that are above reality and transcendent, such as things to do with divinity and that which is God himself, *which no* corporeal *eye has seen* nor has the *heart* of any earthly-minded person ever *conceived*.

"Consider this thought with me; just as wax is wax only in the absence of fire, but as soon as it comes into contact with fire, it is reduced and dissolved and is set ablaze along with the fire and cannot resist it, but in doing so turns together with the fire into a flame that is pure light, as long as the wax physically continues to exist and becomes pure light, even if it is wax. In the same way then think, along with me, of the power of the mind as being like wax; and as long as it stays true to its nature, it understands things only in accordance with its nature and power, but when the fire of divinity, the Holy Spirit itself, comes close to it, then it is reduced by the power of the Spirit and is set ablaze with the fire of

θεότητος καὶ διαλύεται ταῖς νοήσεσι, καὶ καταποθεῖται ὑπὸ τοῦ θείου φωτὸς καὶ ὅλως φῶς γίνεται θεῖον ὑπέρλαμπρον."

6 Ἐν τούτῳ ὑπολαβὼν ὁ θεῖος Γρηγόριος ἔφησε τῷ ἁγίῳ· "Καψοκαλύβη μου, ἀλλ᾽ ἔστιν καὶ ἕτερον τοιοῦτον τῆς πλάνης λεγόμενον." Καὶ ὁ ἅγιος· "Ἄλλα τὰ τῆς πλάνης σημεῖα, καὶ ἄλλα εἰσὶν τὰ τῆς χάριτος καὶ τῆς ἀληθείας τοῦ Πνεύματος. Ἐκεῖνα γὰρ τῆς πλάνης εἰσίν· ὅταν πλησιάσῃ τὸ πονηρόν, συγχέει τὸν νοῦν καὶ ἀγριωπὸν αὐτὸν καθιστᾷ, ποιεῖ τὴν καρδίαν σκληράν, ἀλλὰ καὶ δειλίαν ἐντίθησι καὶ ἀπόνοιαν καὶ σκότος ἐν ταῖς φρεσὶ καὶ ἀγριαίνει τοῖς ὀφθαλμοῖς, τὸν δ᾽ ἐγκέφαλον συνταράττει καὶ φρίκην ποιεῖ τὸ σωμάτιον· φαντάζει δὲ τοῖς ὀφθαλμοῖς καὶ φῶς πυρῶδες τῆς πλάνης καὶ οὐχ ὑπέρλαμπρον· ἐξιστᾷ δὲ τὸν νοῦν καὶ δαιμονιώδην ποιεῖ ἔκτοτε· καὶ φθέγγεται διὰ γλώττης οὗτος ῥήματα ἀπρεπῆ καὶ βλάσφημα, θυμοῦται, ὀργίζεται ὡς τὰ πολλά. Οὐκ ἔστιν ταπείνωσις ἐν αὐτῷ οὐδὲ προσευχή, οὐδὲ δάκρυον ἀληθινόν, ἀλλὰ καυχᾶται ἀεὶ ἐν τοῖς αὐτοῦ κατορθώμασιν καὶ δοξάζεται, καὶ πάντα πάντοτε τοῖς πονηροῖς πάθεσιν κοινωνεῖ ἀδεῶς. Καὶ ἕως οὗ ποιήσῃ αὐτὸν ἔξηχον καὶ παραδώσῃ αὐτὸν εἰς ἀπώλειαν, οὐκέτι μεθίσταται ἀπ᾽ αὐτοῦ. Ἧς πλάνης, ἅγιε, ῥύσοιτο ἡμᾶς Κύριος ἐκ τοῦ Πονηροῦ.

7 "Σημεῖα δὲ πάλιν τῆς χάριτος τοιαῦτά εἰσιν· ὅταν πλησιάσῃ τὸ ἅγιον, τὸν νοῦν συνάγει καὶ ποιεῖ αὐτὸν σύννουν καὶ ταπεινὸν καὶ μέτριον· τὴν μνήμην τοῦ θανάτου καὶ τῆς κρίσεως καὶ τῶν πταισμάτων, ἀλλὰ δὴ καὶ τῆς κολάσεως τοῦ πυρὸς ἐντίθησι τῇ ψυχῇ· καὶ ποιεῖ τὴν

divinity, and is dissolved by its thoughts, and is consumed by the divine light, and becomes purely divine and exceptionally bright light."

Interrupting at this point, the divine Gregory said to the holy one, "But, my Hutburner, there is also another such light called that of delusion." The holy one replied, "The signs of delusion are one thing, and the signs of grace and the truth of the Spirit are another. For these are the signs of delusion: when the wicked light approaches, it confuses the mind and bewilders it, it hardens the heart, but also instills cowardice and madness and darkness into the wits and makes the eyes wild, it agitates the brain and makes the body tremble. It presents to the eyes a fiery light of delusion that is not exceptionally bright. It confounds the mind and makes it demonic from that point on; and this person utters uncouth and blasphemous words with his tongue, he grows angry, he becomes extremely irate. There is no humility in him, nor prayer, nor true tears, but he always boasts of his accomplishments and glorifies himself, and always does everything fearlessly in common with the wicked passions. And the wicked light does not leave him until it drives him crazy and delivers him to perdition. Holy one, may the Lord save us from this delusion of the Evil One.

"Again the signs of grace are as follows: when the holy light approaches, it focuses the mind and makes it thoughtful and humble and modest; and it instills in the soul the recollection of death and of the last judgment and of sins, and indeed also of the punishment of hellfire; and it makes

καρδίαν εὐκατάνυκτον, πενθοῦσαν καὶ κλαίουσαν· τοὺς ὀφθαλμοὺς πραεῖς καὶ δακρυρρόους ποιεῖ. Καὶ ὅσον πλησιάζει, ἡμεροῖ καὶ παρακαλεῖ τὴν ψυχὴν διὰ τῶν τιμίων παθῶν τοῦ Χριστοῦ καὶ τὴν ἄπειρον φιλανθρωπίαν αὐτοῦ. Ἐντίθησι τῷ νοῒ θεωρίας ὑψηλοτάτας, τὰς ἀπλανεῖς· πρώτην τὴν ἀκατάληπτον δύναμιν τὴν ποιητικήν, τὴν τὸ πᾶν συστησαμένην ἐκ μὴ ὄντος ὑπ᾽ οὐδενός, τὴν συνεκτικὴν καὶ τὴν προνοοῦσαν οὕτω τὸ πᾶν, τῆς τρισυποστάτου θεότητος τὸ ἀκατανόητον καὶ ἀπερίγραπτον, τὸ ἀκατάληπτον καὶ ἀνεξιχνίαστον πέλαγος, τὸ ὑπὲρ πάντα τὰ ὄντα Ὄν· καὶ οὕτω φωτίζει αὐτὸν φωτισμὸν γνώσεως θεϊκῆς. Καὶ ἐκ τοῦ ἀδύτου θείου φωτὸς ἁρπαγεὶς ὁ νοῦς ἐν τῷ Πνεύματι φωτίζεται ἐν τῷ φωτὶ τούτῳ τῷ θείῳ καὶ ὑπερλάμπρῳ. Καὶ γαληνόμορφον ἐκτελεῖ τὴν καρδίαν· καὶ χαρίζει τὸν τοιαῦτα λαχόντα κατὰ νοῦν καὶ λόγον καὶ πνεῦμα ἄρρητον εὐφροσύνην καὶ ἀγαλλίασιν." Καὶ ὅλως ἦν οὗτος ἀεὶ μετάρσιος τῷ Πνεύματι, τὸν καρπὸν ἔχων τοῦ Πνεύματος, ὥς φησι Παῦλος ὁ μέγιστος ὅτι "Ὁ καρπὸς τοῦ Πνεύματός ἐστιν χαρά, εἰρήνη, μακροθυμία, χρηστότης, ἀγαθωσύνη, ἀγάπη, συμπάθεια καὶ ταπείνωσις" [see Galatians 5:22].

the heart contrite, sorrowful and tearful, and makes the eyes meek and full of tears. As it approaches, it calms and comforts the soul through the venerable sufferings of Christ and His infinite love of mankind. It instills in the mind the most lofty, unerring visions: first the incomprehensible creative power, that which makes everything from nothingness by no one, that which holds together and takes care of everything, the inconceivability and indescribability of the divinity in three hypostases, the incomprehensible and unsearchable sea, the Being which is above all things that are; and thus the holy light illuminates the mind with the illumination of divine knowledge. And the mind, when seized with the rapture of the divine light that never sets, is illuminated in the Spirit in this divine and exceptionally bright light. And *it makes the heart calm,* and grants ineffable joy and happiness to the one who attains such things in mind and reason and spirit." And this holy one was always completely elevated in the Spirit, possessing *the fruit of the Spirit,* since the great Paul says that, "*The fruit of the Spirit is joy, peace, patience, kindness, goodness, love,* compassion and humility."

16

Ταῦτα ἀκούσας ὁ τῆς ἡσυχίας διδάσκαλος καὶ τῆς προσευχῆς, ὁ Σιναΐτης θεῖος Γρηγόριος ἔκθαμβος γέγονεν καὶ ὅλως ἐξέστην ταῖς τοῦ ἁγίου ταύταις προσρήσεσιν, καὶ διὰ θαύματος εἶχεν μεγάλου τὸν ἅγιον. Ἔκτοτε τοίνυν καὶ ἄγγελον ἐπίγειον ἐκάλει αὐτὸν καὶ οὐκ ἄνθρωπον· ὅθεν καὶ ἀξιοῖ τὰ πλεῖστα αὐτόν, λέγων· "Παῦσαι ἀπὸ τοῦ νῦν, παρακαλῶ, τοῦ μὴ κατακαίειν τὴν κέλλαν, ἀλλ' ὥς φησιν ὁ σοφὸς Ἰσαὰκ ὁ Σύρος τῷ γένει, *σύναξον ἑαυτὸν ἐν ἑνὶ τόπῳ* καὶ κάθισον, *ἵνα καὶ καρπὸν πλείονα φέρῃς* [John 15:2]· καὶ πολλοὺς ὠφελήσεις ὡς δοκιμώτατος. Καὶ γὰρ καὶ τὸ γῆρας ἰδοὺ κατατρέχει, καὶ ὁ σπόρος *πληθύνεσθαι* [see 2 Corinthians 9:10] βούλει, ὁ δὲ θάνατος ἄωρος. Διὰ τοῦτο μετάδος τὸ τάλαντον καὶ τὸν θεῖον σπόρον διὰ καθίσματος τὸν λαὸν τοῦ Θεοῦ, πρὶν ἢ τὸ τέλος προφθάσῃ, ἵν' ἕξῃς ἐν οὐρανοῖς τὸν μισθὸν πλείονα, ἁγιώτατε.

2   "Καὶ γὰρ τοῖς ἀποστόλοις ἁγιάσας ὁ Κύριος οὐκ εἰς τὰ ὄρη αὐτοὺς ἐξαπέστειλεν τοῦ διάγειν ἀεί, ἀλλὰ μᾶλλον πρὸς τοὺς ἀνθρώπους, ἵνα διὰ τῆς κοινωνίας τῆς ἁγιότητος καὶ οἱ ἐναγεῖς ἅγιοι γίνωνται καὶ σωθῶσιν δι' ἁγιότητος. Διὰ τοῦτο ἔφη αὐτοῖς· *Λαμψάτω τὸ φῶς ὑμῶν ἔμπροσθεν τῶν ἀνθρώπων'* [Matthew 5:16], καὶ οὐκ ἔμπροσθεν τῶν πετρῶν. *Λαμψάτω* τοίνυν καὶ τὸ σὸν *φῶς ἔμπροσθεν τῶν ἀνθρώπων, ὅπως ἴδωσι τὰ σὰ καλὰ ἔργα καὶ δοξάσουσι τὸν Πατέρα ἡμῶν τὸν ἐν τοῖς οὐρανοῖς* [Matthew 5:16], καὶ ἄφες τοῦ μωραίνειν καὶ σαλίαν ἀπὸ τοῦ νῦν

Chapter 16

When the teacher of spiritual tranquility and prayer, the divine Gregory the Sinaite, heard these words, he was astonished and completely changed his opinion at the holy one's discourse, and marveled greatly at the holy one. Therefore from that time on Gregory called him an earthly angel and not a human; and he thus implored Maximos, saying, "Please, stop burning your cell from now on, and instead, as the wise Isaac the Syrian says to his <spiritual> kin, '*Stay in one place* and remain there, *so that you may bear more fruit.*' Being so experienced you will benefit many people. For behold, old age rapidly approaches, and *the seed* wants *to be multiplied,* but *death is untimely.* So share the talent and the divine seed with the people of God by remaining in one place, before the end arrives, so that you may have a greater reward in heaven, most holy one.

"For the Lord, after blessing the apostles, did not send them to the mountains to live, but rather to mankind, so that by sharing in their holiness those who are accursed might become holy and be saved through holiness. And for this reason he said to them, '*Let your light shine before men,*' and not before rocks. Therefore *let your light shine before men* too, *so that they may see your good works and glorify our Father who is in heaven.* And leave off playing the fool and feigning

2

ὑποκρίνεσθαι· ὅτι σκάνδαλον γίνεται τοῖς μὴ εἰδόσι τὰ σά. Τοίνυν ὅρα τὴν συμβουλὴν καὶ θείαν ὑπακοήν, καὶ ποίησον ἅ σοι ἐντέλλομαι, ὡς φίλος σοι ἄριστος καὶ ἀδελφός. Γέγραπται γάρ· Ἀδελφὸς ὑπὸ ἀδελφοῦ βοηθούμενος ὡς πόλις ὀχυρά'" [Proverbs 18:19].

3   Ταῦτα μαθόντες καὶ οἱ τῶν καθισμάτων ἕτεροι μέγιστοι γέροντες, οὓς καὶ προμεμνήμεθα, καὶ συναινέσαντες τοῖς λόγοις τοῦ Σιναΐτου καταπειθῆ τὸν ἅγιον τοῦ καθίσαι οὕτω πεποίηκαν. Καὶ ἰδοὺ πλησίον τοῦ Ἡσαΐου ὡσεὶ μίλια τρία, ποιεῖ θριγκίον μιᾶς ὀργυίας τὸ πλάτος καὶ μῆκος, οὐκ ἐκ ξύλων τετραγώνων ἢ καρφίων, περονίων ἢ πετρῶν καὶ σανιδίων· ἀλλ᾽ ὡς ἔθος αὐτῷ ἦν, ἄλση λαβὼν καὶ μικρὸν χόρτον, ἔδοξεν κέλλαν ποιεῖν· ἐν ᾗ καὶ ἔκτοτε καθίσας καὶ μὴ κατακαύσας αὐτήν, τὸν τῆς ζωῆς αὐτοῦ χρόνον ἐν ἐκείνῃ διεβίβασεν ἅπαντα, μὴ κτησάμενός τι τὸ οἱονοῦν ἐκ τῶν τῆς χρείας, ὡς οἱ πολλοί· ἀλλ᾽ ἄϋλον εἶχεν τὴν κέλλαν παντί, τοσοῦτον ὅτι οὐδὲ ῥαφίδαν οὐδὲ σκαλίδαν οὐδὲ δύο χιτῶνας, οὐκ ἄρτον, οὐ πήραν, οὐδ᾽ ὀβολὸν [see Matthew 10:10; Mark 6:8; Luke 9:3] ὑπεκτήσατο πώποτε, τὴν ὑπὲρ ἄνθρωπον ἄσκησιν πάλιν τηρῶν ἐν αὐτῇ τῇ κέλλῃ ὡς ἄσαρκος. Ὅθεν καὶ ὀρύσσει μνῆμα ἴδιον πλησίον αὐτῆς καὶ καθ᾽ ἑκάστην ἐθρήνει ὁ Καψοκαλύβης τὸν Μάξιμον, ὀρθρίζων ἐκεῖ καὶ ᾠδάρια πενθικὰ νεκρώσιμα οἴκοθεν ἔλεγεν πρὸς τό· "Ἐν οὐρανῷ τοῖς ἄστροις κατακοσμήσας ὡς Θεός."

madness from now on; for this is a stumbling block for those who are not familiar with you. So take heed of my advice and divine obedience, and do as I tell you, as your best friend and brother. For it is written, '*A brother helped by a brother is as a strong city.*'"

When the other great elders of the hermitages, whom 3 we have previously mentioned, learned about these developments, they agreed with the words of the Sinaite and persuaded the holy one to settle down. And lo and behold, near Kyr Isaiah, about three miles distant, he made a fenced enclosure six feet long and wide, not out of rectangular pieces of wood or nails, rivets or stones and boards, but as was his custom, taking brushwood and some grass, he built a cell. And from then on he settled there and did not burn it down, but spent all the rest of his life in it, not possessing any necessities at all, as most people do; but he kept his cell completely untouched by materiality, so that he never possessed a needle, or a digging fork, *or two tunics, or bread, or a purse, or an obol,* maintaining a superhuman asceticism in the cell as if he were without flesh. Therefore he even dug his own grave nearby, and every day the Hutburner lamented for Maximos; as he said his morning prayers there, he used to repeat by heart the mournful funeral hymns according to the *heirmos* for, "*Like God adorning the heaven with stars.*"

17

Ἀλλ' ὁ μὲν Σιναΐτης ἐκεῖνος ὁ καὶ θεῖος Γρηγόριος κατὰ τὴν τοῦ ἁγίου Μαξίμου πρόρρησιν ἀπεδήμησεν ἐκεῖσε εἰς τὰ Παρόρια. Ἐξερχομένου δὲ καὶ τοῦ προρρηθέντος Μάρκου καὶ γενομένων ἐν τῇ Κομητίσσῃ, φωνὴν ἀκούει ὁ Μάρκος τοῦ ἁγίου στραφῆναι εἰς τὰ ὀπίσω. Καὶ ἅμα σὺν τῇ φωνῇ στραφεὶς τῷ βλέμματι ὄπιθεν, ὁρᾷ ξένα παράδο-ξα, ἅ μοι καὶ διηγήσατο. Ὁρᾷ κύκλωθεν ὅλῳ τῷ ὄρει ὑπὸ κοκκίνων πύργων ὡς κάστρον κτισμένον ἐν ὕψει ἐπαιρόμε-νον· πρὸς δὲ τὴν λεγομένην Μεγάλην Βίγλαν παλάτια χρύσεα πάντερπνα, βασίλισσαν φέροντα τὴν Θεοτόκον σὺν ἀσωμάτοις ἀπείροις καὶ ἀρχαγγέλοις, καὶ τὰ πλήθη κύκλωθεν τῶν μοναζόντων τῇ Θεοτόκῳ ὑμνούντων καὶ προσκυνούντων. Καὶ τοῦτο ἰδὼν καὶ μνησθεὶς τὴν πρόρρη-σιν Μαξίμου τοῦ ἁγίου, βαλὼν μετάνοιαν τῷ καθηγητῇ αὐτοῦ Γρηγορίῳ τῷ Σιναΐτῃ, στραφεὶς εἰς τὴν Λαύραν κατῴκησεν ἡσυχάζων, καὶ ἐγένετο ἀνὴρ διακριτικώτατος.

18

Ὁ δὲ Σιναΐτης κύριος Γρηγόριος γενόμενος ἐκεῖσε εἰς τὰ Παρόρια, ὡς ἥλιος φαιδρὸς τοῖς ἐσκοτισμένοις ἐκεῖσε ἀνέτειλεν, καὶ χορτάζει ἄρτον ζωῆς τοῖς πεινῶσι πᾶσι τὸν

Chapter 17

But that divine Gregory the Sinaite, in accordance with the prediction of the holy Maximos, departed for Paroria. The aforementioned Mark also set out but, when they were at Kometissa, Mark heard the holy one's voice, instructing him to look back. As he turned at the sound of the voice to look behind him, he saw something strange and marvelous, which he also related to me. For he saw the entire mountain surrounded by red towers, like a fortress built and raised upon a height; and toward the so-called Great Watchtower there were delightful golden palaces, bearing upon them as queen the Mother of God together with countless incorporeal beings and archangels, and all around were multitudes of monks singing hymns to the Mother of God and venerating her. When Mark saw this, he remembered holy Maximos's prophecy, prostrated himself before his master Gregory the Sinaite and, returning to the Lavra, remained there living a life of spiritual tranquility; and he became a man of greatest discernment.

Chapter 18

When Kyr Gregory the Sinaite arrived there at Paroria, he shone upon the benighted people there like a brilliant sun, and he nourished with the bread of life all those who

σωτήριον ἐκεῖ. Οὐκ ἔχω πῶς διηγήσασθαι κἀκείνου τοῦ ἀνδρὸς τὰ σεπτὰ ἀριστεύματα· γίνεται πηγὴ ἀνεξάντλητος τῷ λόγῳ, τῇ πράξει καὶ θεωρίᾳ. Μανθάνει τοῦτο ἡ μεγαλόπολις καὶ ὅλη ἡ Θράκη καὶ ἡ Μακεδονία, ἀλλὰ καὶ ἡ πᾶσα τῶν Βουλγάρων κατοίκησις καὶ τὰ πέρα Ἴστρου καὶ τῆς Σερβίας· καὶ τρέχουσιν ἄπειρα πλήθη τῶν ἐκλεκτῶν πρὸς αὐτόν, ζητοῦν χορτασθῆναι ἐκ τῆς πηγῆς τῶν διδαγμάτων αὐτοῦ τῶν ἀειζώων, καὶ δὴ καὶ χορτάζονται· καὶ ποιεῖ τὰ πρώην ἄοικα ὄρη καὶ τὰ Παρόρια ἔνοικα, ὥστε πλεονάζειν ταῖς ἀγέλαις τῶν μοναχῶν, οὓς ἰδίαις χερσὶν ἐπεσφράγιζεν. Καὶ τοὺς βασιλεῖς τῆς γῆς, Ἀνδρόνικον λέγω καὶ τὸν Ἀλέξανδρον, Στέπανον καὶ Ἀλέξανδρον, ἐπιθυμητὰς αὐτοῦ πεποίηκεν δι᾽ ἐπιστολῶν διδακτικῶν θαυμασίων.

2   Ἔνθεν τοι καὶ πληθύνεται τὸ σχῆμα τῶν μοναζόντων ἐν τοῖς τόποις ἐκείνων καὶ πόλεσι τῇ ἀρετῇ καὶ τῇ διδαχῇ τοῦ ὁσίου πατρὸς Γρηγορίου τοῦ Σιναΐτου. Ἀνήγειρεν δὲ καὶ μονύδρια ἐν ἐκείνοις τοῖς Παρορίοις· καὶ ἴδοις ἂν ὡς Ὄρος ἄλλον Ἅγιον εὐρίζοντα τὸ σωτήριον ἀγαλλίαμα [see Psalm 47(48):1–2]. Καὶ γέγονε τῶν Βουλγάρων ἡ οἴκησις πόλις τῶν μοναχῶν ἐν τῇ ζωῇ ἐκείνου τοῦ διδασκάλου καὶ μάκαρος. Ἐκ δὲ τῶν μαθητῶν ἐκείνου πολλοὶ ἐξανέτειλαν ὡς φαιδροὶ ἀστέρες μετὰ τὴν ἐκείνου κοίμησιν καὶ τὴν πρὸς Θεὸν ἄνοδον καὶ τὰ πέρατα κατεκόσμησαν. Καὶ ταῦτα μὲν τοῦ μακαρίτου Γρηγορίου ἐκείνου τοῦ Σιναΐτου ἀπὸ μέρους διὰ τὸ μῆκος τοῦ λόγου ἐμνημονεύσαμεν.

hungered for salvation there. It is impossible for me to relate that man's venerable achievements; he was an inexhaustible spring, in word, deed, and contemplation. The great city of Constantinople and all of Thrace and Macedonia learned about him, as well as the entire area inhabited by the Bulgarians and the lands beyond the Danube and Serbia; and a countless host of chosen people hastened to him, seeking to be filled from the spring of his teachings of eternal life, and indeed they received their fill. And he caused the previously uninhabited mountains and Paroria to become inhabited, so that they were filled with flocks of monks, upon whom he set his seal with his own hands. And through wondrous edifying letters he made the rulers of the earth, I mean Andronikos and Alexander, Stefan and Alexander, eager to meet him.

So the monastic ranks in those regions and cities were 2 multiplied through the virtue and teaching of the blessed father Gregory the Sinaite. He also built monasteries in Paroria; and one could see him *establishing* salvific *exultation like* another *Holy Mountain*. And so the land of the Bulgarians became a city of monks during the lifetime of that blessed teacher. Many of his disciples also sprang up like shining stars after his death and ascent to God and adorned the frontiers. I have only partially recorded the facts about the late Gregory the Sinaite because of the length of my narrative.

19

Ἀλλ᾽ ἔλθωμεν πάλιν ἐπὶ τὰ τοῦ ἁγίου Καψοκαλύβη ἀνδραγαθήματα, ὅσα καὶ οὗτος ἐν Ὄρει πάλιν ὡς γίγας ἠνδραγαθήσατο. Καθίσας οὗτος ἐν τῷ κελλίῳ, ὡς ἔφημεν, οἱ μὲν δαίμονες συναχθέντες πόλεμον μετὰ τοῦ ἁγίου καθ᾽ ἑκάστην ἐποιοῦντο, καὶ ἔσπευδον ἐκ τοῦ τόπου ἐκείνου ἐξῶσαι τὸν ἅγιον. Ἀλλ᾽ εἰς μάτην ἐλιθοβόλιζον οἱ κατάρατοι· ἀντεβάλλοντο γὰρ ταῖς βολαῖς τῆς νοερᾶς αὐτοῦ προσευχῆς καὶ ὡς καπνὸς διελύοντο. Ἐν τούτῳ καὶ δύναμις θεία ἀκαταμάχητος αὐτὸν ἔκτοτε περιεκάλυπτεν, ὡς ἐν εἴδει πυρός, καθὼς ὡράθη τισὶν ἀξίοις, καταφλέγουσα τοὺς ὑπεναντίους. Καὶ φῶς ἰαματικὸν ἄνωθεν κατηύγαζεν ἐν τοῖς λόγοις αὐτοῦ· καὶ λόγῳ μόνῳ πολλοὺς δαιμονιώδεις ἰάσατο, ὡς ἔγνωμεν ἀληθέστατα, καὶ ἀπέλυ<εν> ἐν εἰρήνῃ ἐν τοῖς τόποις αὐτῶν, παραγγέλλων αὐτοῖς ἀπέχεσθαι μήνης, πορνείας καὶ ἀδικίας, μέθης καὶ ἐπιορκίας, καὶ διὰ νηστείας κρεῶν καὶ ἐλεημοσύνης τὸ κατὰ δύναμιν καὶ καθάρσεως ἀξίους ποιεῖν ἑαυτοὺς ἐν ἐπισήμοις ἑορταῖς τῶν ἁγιασμάτων καὶ ἀχράντων θείων μυστηρίων Χριστοῦ, ἵν᾽ ὅπως ὑγιαίνωσι πάντοτε.

Chapter 19

But let us return again to the brave accomplishments of the holy Hutburner, which, like a giant, he accomplished on the Mountain. When he had settled in his cell, as we have said, the demons assembled and waged war against the holy one every day, and strove to drive him from that place. But the accursed ones threw stones at him in vain; for they were repelled with the missiles of his mental prayer and were dissolved like smoke. In that place an invincible divine power protected him from then on, like fire in its appearance, as it was perceived by certain trustworthy men, burning his enemies with flames. A healing light also shone brightly from above in his words; and, as we have learned most truthfully, he healed many demoniacs with words alone and sent them away in peace to their homes. He counseled them to avoid anger, fornication and injustice, drunkenness and perjury, and through abstinence from meat and through almsgiving in accordance with their means and purification to make themselves worthy to receive on feast days the sacraments and immaculate divine mysteries of Christ, so that they might always be healthy.

20

Καί τινα Μερκούριον μοναχόν, ἐν μιᾷ προύτρέψας αὐτὸν διὰ λόγου, καὶ αὐτὸς ἐν τῷ ὀνόματι Ἰησοῦ Χριστοῦ ἔμπροσθεν τοῦ ὁσίου δαιμονιώδην ἰάσατο, τὸ καινότατον. Καὶ ἄλλον ὑπουργὸν γέροντος ὑπὸ δαίμονος δεινῶς πάσχοντα ἐν ὁδῷ ἀπαντήσας, ἐνετείλατο αὐτῷ λέγων· "Ὕπαγε, ὑποτάγηθι τῷ πνευματικῷ σου πατρὶ ὁλοκλήρως καὶ νήστευσον τυροῦ καὶ οἴνου καὶ μιασμοῦ· καὶ ὑγιανεῖς ἐν τῷ ὀνόματι τοῦ Χριστοῦ·" καθὼς καὶ ἰάθην ἀπὸ τῆς ἡμέρας ἐκείνης.

2 Πάλιν μιᾷ τῶν ἡμερῶν μοναχοὶ ἐκ τῆς Λαύρας παραγενόμενοι πρὸς αὐτὸν ὠφελείας χάριν, παρεγένετο σὺν αὐτοῖς καὶ ἕτερος κοσμικός. Καὶ ὡς εἶδεν αὐτὸν ὁ ὅσιος, ἀπεδίωξεν μακρόθεν αὐτόν, Ἀκινδυνᾶτον λέγων εἶναι καὶ ἄπιστον, μὴ γινωσκόμενον παρ᾽ ἄλλων τινῶν μέχρι τῆς ὥρας ἐκείνης. Πολλὰ γὰρ κατὰ τοῦ Ἀκινδύνου ἐφέρετο οὗτος ὁ ἅγιος, καὶ Κακοκίνδυνον αὐτὸν ἐπωνόμαζε καὶ δαιμονιώδη καὶ κοινωνὸν πάσης αἱρέσεως καὶ ὑπουργὸν Ἀντιχρίστου· διὰ τοῦτο τοὺς τοιούτους μακρὰ ἀπεβάλλετο καὶ ἀναθεμάτιζεν παρρησίᾳ. Πάλιν δέ τινες μονάζοντες παραγενόμενοι πρὸς αὐτόν, ὡς εἶδεν αὐτούς, μεγάλῃ τῇ φωνῇ ἀνεβόησεν· "Διώξατε τὸν Μασσαλιανὸν ὄπιθεν, καὶ οὕτως ἔλθετε πρός με." Καὶ τὸ ὄνομα προσηγόρευσεν· ὅπερ ἀκούσαντες ἔντρομοι καὶ ἔμφοβοι γεγόνασιν οἱ συνοδεύοντες καὶ τὸν ἀσεβῆ κατεδίωξαν τῆς ὁμιλίας αὐτῶν.

3 Ἄλλον δέ τινα μοναχόν, βουλόμενον μετὰ πλοίου

Chapter 20

One day Maximos encouraged a certain monk Merkourios with his words, and in the holy one's presence Merkourios healed a demoniac in the name of Jesus Christ, something truly novel. And once, on his way, Maximos met another servant of an elder who was suffering terribly from a demon; he instructed him, saying, "Go, subject yourself completely to your spiritual father and abstain from cheese and wine and pollution; and you will be healed in the name of Christ." And he was healed from that day on.

Again, when some monks came to him one day from the Lavra for their spiritual benefit, a layman accompanied them. When the holy one saw the layman, he sent him away when he was still far off, calling him Akindynatos and an unbeliever, although he was not recognized as such by others until that moment. For the holy one held many things against Akindynos, and called him Kakokindynos, and a demoniac, and an adherent of every heresy, and a servant of the Antichrist; for this reason he sent such people far away and outspokenly anathematized them. Again when some monks approached him, as soon as he saw them, he shouted with a loud voice: "Send back the Messalian, and then come to me." And he spoke the man's name. When they heard it, his companions were terrified and fearful and chased the impious man away from their company.

He also mocked another monk, who wanted to sail on

Θεσσαλονικαίου πρὸς τὴν Κωνσταντινούπολιν πλεῦσαι διά τινα χρείαν, κατέσκωψεν, τοῦ πλοίου τὸν κίνδυνον προειπών. Παρελθουσῶν γὰρ τριῶν ἡμερῶν καὶ τὸ πλοῖον αὔτανδρον γέγονε, μέσον θαλάττης πλέοντα καὶ καταχθέντα εἰς ἄβυσσον. Πάλιν ἄλλον πλοῖον ἀπὸ νήσου ἐλθὸν ἐν τῷ λιμένι τῆς Λαύρας, οἱ τοῦ πλοίου πρὸς τὸν ἅγιον παρεγένοντο ἔχοντες μεθ' ἑαυτῶν καί τινα δαιμόνιον ἔχοντα τῆς ἀπληστίας· ἤσθιεν γὰρ ὡσεὶ πέντε ἀνδρῶν τροφὴν καθ' ἑκάστην καὶ οὐκ ἐχορτάζετο. Καὶ τοῦτον ἐπὶ τοὺς πόδας τοῦ ἁγίου κλίναντες ἱκέτευον σὺν αὐτῷ τυχεῖν παρ' αὐτοῦ τῆς ἰάσεως· καὶ δῆτα λαβὼν ἀπαξαμᾶν τῷ πάσχοντι δέδωκεν, λέξας αὐτῷ· "Τοσοῦτον ἔσθιε καὶ χορτάζου ἐν τῷ ὀνόματι τοῦ Κυρίου ἡμῶν Ἰησοῦ Χριστοῦ, καὶ εἰρήνευε." Ἔκτοτε οὖν ὁ τοιοῦτος τὸν τῆς ἀχορτασίας δαίμονα ἠλευθέρωτο καὶ πλεῖον τοῦ ἀπαξαμάτου τὸ μῆκος οὐκ ἤσθιεν. Διὰ τοῦτο καταλιπὼν πάντα, γυναῖκα καὶ τέκνα καὶ βίον καὶ πλοῖον καὶ συνοδίαν, γέγονεν δοκιμώτατος μοναχός, πλησίον τοῦ ἁγίου καθίσας καὶ παρ' αὐτοῦ πρὸς Θεὸν ποδηγούμενος καὶ *προκόπτων ἐν χάριτι* [see Luke 2:52].

4   Καὶ Βαρλαάμ τις μοναχὸς ὑποτασσόμενος γέροντι, ἐλθὼν εἰς τὸν ἅγιον κατεσκώπτετο παρ' αὐτοῦ διὰ τὸ *σκληροτράχηλον* [see Acts 7:51] αὐτοῦ καὶ παρήκοον, λέγων αὐτῷ· "Τούτου γε χάριν μέλλεις τελειωθῆναι ὑπὸ κρημνοῦ·" ὃ καὶ γέγονεν. Καὶ ἄλλον Ἀθανάσιον τὸν Κροκᾶν, τὸ τέλος αὐτῷ προεῖπεν, ὅτι "Παρὰ τῶν Ἰσμαηλιτῶν μέλλεις τελειωθῆναι." Καὶ γέγονεν οὕτως. Εἶχεν γὰρ τὴν χάριν πλουσίαν ἐκ Πνεύματος θείου τοῦ προορᾶν,

some business to Constantinople on a Thessalonican ship, predicting that danger would befall the ship. Three days later the ship sank with all hands aboard, as it was sailing on the open sea, and was dragged down into the abyss. Again, when another ship came from an island into the harbor of the Lavra, the sailors came to the holy one, bringing with them a man suffering from a demon of insatiability, for every day he ate as much food as five men and was not satisfied. They made him bend down at the feet of the holy one and, together with him, begged that he might receive healing from him. Then indeed, Maximos took a rusk and gave it to the afflicted man, saying to him: "Eat this much and be satisfied in the name of our Lord Jesus Christ, and be in peace." From then on the man was delivered from the demon of insatiability and did not eat more than one piece of rusk. For this reason he abandoned everything, wife, children and livelihood, ship and companions, and became a most esteemed monk, settling near the holy one and being guided by him toward God and *advancing in grace.*

A monk named Barlaam, who was in submission to an elder, came to the holy one, who mocked him because he was *stiff-necked* and disobedient, saying to him: "For this reason you are going to die by falling off a cliff," which indeed happened. He also foretold the death of another man, Athanasios Krokas, saying, "You are going to be killed by the Ishmaelites." And it happened in that way. For the noble one had the gift of foresight in abundance from the Holy Spirit, 4

ὡς προέφημεν, ὁ γεννάδας, καὶ τὰ πόρρω ὡς ἐγγὺς καθ-
ηρμήνευσε καὶ τὰ ἄδηλα καὶ μέλλοντα ἑκάστῳ προύλεγεν
δι' αἰνίγματος σοφωτάτου καὶ κατεμήνυεν. Ἔνθεν τοι καὶ
τὴν συνέλευσιν τὴν πρὸς τὸν ἅγιον γενομένην τῶν βασιλέων τοῖς πᾶσι προὐμήνυσεν λέγων· "Οἱ βασιλεῖς τῶν
Ῥωμαίων παραγενέσθαι μέλλουσιν πρὸς ἡμᾶς προφητείας
χάριν ἢ μᾶλλον ψυχικῆς ὠφελείας."

21

Καιροῦ δὲ παρῳχηκότος ὀλίγου, καὶ οἱ βασιλεῖς τῶν
Ῥωμαίων πρὸς αὐτὸν παρεγένοντο, Καντακουζηνὸς
ἐκεῖνος καὶ Ἰωάννης οἱ τότε βασιλεύοντες. Καὶ τὰ μέλλοντα συμβαίνειν αὐτοῖς ὡς προφήτης κατήγγειλεν· τὴν
ἀποστασίαν, τὰ σκάνδαλα, τοὺς φόνους, τοὺς ἐμφυλίους
πολέμους, τὰ ἔνεδρα, τῶν ἐθνῶν τὴν δυναστείαν, τὴν ἐπι-
δρομὴν καὶ τὴν κάκωσιν, καὶ πάλιν τὴν ἐπανάκλησιν τῶν
πιστῶν καὶ τὴν ἀγαλλίασιν τὴν μέλλουσαν ἐν καιρῷ
γενέσθαι τῷ ὁρισθέντι διὰ σημείων, ὥς φησι Κύριος.

2   Καὶ ταῦτα εἰπών, πρὸς διδασκαλίαν ἐτράπην λέγων
αὐτοῖς· "Ὀφείλετε ὑμεῖς, εἰ καὶ βασιλεῖς εἶτε τῆς γῆς, ἵν'
ἀείποτε ὁρᾶτε πρὸς τὸν βασιλέα τὸν ἐπουράνιον, καὶ τὸν
νόμον αὐτοῦ κατέχειν ὡς σκῆπτρον οὐράνιον, καὶ ποιεῖν
πρῶτον ὑμεῖς αὐτοῦ τὰ θεῖα ἐντάλματα, καὶ μιμεῖσθαι
αὐτοῦ κατὰ τὸ δυνατὸν ἐπὶ πάντα, ὡς γέγραπται·
'Παιδεύθητε πάντες οἱ κρίνοντες τὴν γῆν, δουλεύσατε τῷ

as I have already mentioned, and described things that were far away as though they were close, and through most clever riddles foretold and announced secrets and things that were going to happen to each person. In this way, then, he even predicted to everyone the emperors' joint visit to him, saying, "The emperors of the Romans are going to come to me for a prophecy, or rather for their spiritual benefit."

Chapter 21

After a short time had passed, the emperors of the Romans did indeed come to him, Kantakouzenos and John who were reigning then. And he announced, like a prophet, what was going to happen to them in the future: the rebellion, the scandals, the murders, the civil wars, the ambushes, the rise to power of the pagan nations, the invasion and the oppression, and the restoration of the faithful again, and the joy which is going to occur at a time designated by signs, as the Lord says.

After saying all this, he turned to instruction, saying to   2 them: "Even if you are rulers of the earth, you are still always obliged to look to the heavenly king, and uphold His law like a heavenly scepter, to carry out His divine commandments first, and imitate Him in all things to the best of your ability, as it is written in Scripture: *'Be instructed, all ye that judge the earth. Serve the Lord with fear, and rejoice in Him*

Κυρίῳ ἐν φόβῳ, καὶ ἀγαλλιᾶσθε αὐτῷ ἐν τρόμῳ· δράξασθε παιδείας, μήποτε ὀργισθῇ Κύριος, καὶ ἀπολεῖσθε ἐξ ὁδοῦ δικαίας, ὅταν ἐκκαυθῇ ἐν τάχει ὁ θυμὸς αὐτοῦ [Psalm 2:10–12]· εἶθ' οὕτως διδάσκειν ὑμᾶς καὶ τὸ ὑπήκοον ἅπαν ὑμῶν πίστιν, δικαιοσύνην, ἀλήθειαν, ἀγάπην, εἰρήνην καὶ ἁγιότηταν· τὸ κάλλος δὲ καὶ τὸ κράτος τῆς καθολικῆς ἐκκλησίας κρατεῖν καὶ τηρεῖν τὴν τιμὴν διὰ τὸν Χριστὸν κατὰ τὸ τεταγμένον καὶ ὀφειλόμενον ἄνωθεν αὐτῇ. Συμπαθεῖτε τοὺς πταίοντας, μακροθυμεῖτε πρὸς πάντας [1 Thessalonians 5:14], ἐλεεῖτε τοὺς πένητας, τοὺς ἀσθενεῖς ἐπισκέπτεσθε, τοὺς μοναχοὺς ἀγαπᾶτε καὶ ἀναδέχεσθε ὡς στρατιώτας καὶ φίλους τοῦ παμβασιλέως Χριστοῦ, καὶ ἐπαρκεῖτε τὰ πρὸς χρείαν κατὰ τὴν αἴτησιν αὐτῶν. Ὁρᾶτε, μὴ θροεῖσθε [Matthew 24:6] πρὸς τὰ ἐπερχόμενα λυπηρά, ἀλλ' ὑπομένετε, ἵνα τὸν στέφανον τῆς βασιλείας καὶ ἐν οὐρανοῖς ἕξετε παρὰ Χριστοῦ τοῦ Θεοῦ ἡμῶν."

3   Καὶ προπέμπων αὐτοῖς, πρὸς τὸν Καντακουζηνὸν οὕτως ἔφη· "Ἔδε, ἡγούμενος εἰς μοναστήριν·" πρὸς δὲ τὸν Παλαιολόγον· "Κράτει, ἀκράτητε, καὶ μὴ πλανῶ· τὸ γὰρ σὸν κράτος μακρὸν καὶ ἀχαμόν, καὶ χειμῶνα πολὺν φέρει ἐν σοί. Χαίρετε καὶ ὑπάγετε ἐν εἰρήνῃ." Μετὰ δέ τινα καιρὸν ἀπαξαμᾶν ἕνα καὶ κρόμμυον καὶ σκόροδον ἐξαπέστειλεν τὸν Καντακουζηνὸν ἐν τῇ Πόλει, προμηνύων ἐν τούτῳ τῆς μοναχικῆς πολιτείας τὰ σήμαντρα· ἐν ᾧ καὶ δι' ὀλίγου ἄκων ἀποκαρεὶς παρὰ τοῦ Ἰωάννου γέγονε μοναχός. Τὸν παξαμᾶν τότε λαβὼν καὶ φαγὼν καὶ μνησθεὶς τοῦ ἁγίου τὴν πρόρρησιν, διὰ θαύματος εἶχεν αὐτόν· ταὐτὸ καὶ Παλαιολόγος ὁ κράτιστος Ἰωάννης.

with trembling. Accept correction, lest at any time the Lord be angry, and ye should perish from the righteous way, whensoever His wrath shall be suddenly kindled.' In the same way you are obliged to teach all your subjects faith, righteousness, truth, love, peace and holiness; and to maintain the beauty and the power of the universal Church and preserve its honor for the sake of Christ in accordance with the command and obligation to do so from above. Be compassionate toward those who sin; *be patient with them all,* have mercy on the poor, visit the sick, show love to the monks and receive them as soldiers and friends of Christ, the emperor of all, and give them what they need when they ask for it. *See that you are not alarmed* at the coming troubles, but endure them, so that you may obtain the crown of empire from Christ our God in heaven as well."

And as he was escorting them on their departure, he said 3 this to Kantakouzenos: "See, you will be a superior at a monastery"; and to Palaiologos, "Keep on ruling, you who cannot be ruled, and do not waver; for your reign will be long but weak, and will bring many storms upon you. Farewell and depart in peace." Sometime later he sent a rusk, an onion and a head of garlic to Kantakouzenos in the City, indicating in this way the markers of monastic life; and not long after Kantakouzenos was tonsured against his will by John Palaiologos and became a monk. Then he took the rusk and ate it and remembered the holy one's prediction, and marveled at him; and the most excellent John Palaiologos had the same reaction.

22

Ὁ δὲ ἁγιώτατος πατριάρχης ὁ Κάλλιστος πρὸς τὴν Σερβίαν ἀπαίρων μετὰ τοῦ κλήρου αὐτοῦ διὰ τὴν τῆς ἐκκλησίας ἕνωσιν καὶ εἰρήνην, γενόμενος ἐν Ὄρει τοῦτον τὸν ἅγιον ἰδεῖν ἐπεζήτησεν. Καὶ δὴ γενόμενος ἐν τῷ κελλίῳ τοῦ γέροντος μετὰ τοῦ κλήρου αὐτοῦ, προϋπήντησεν τὸν πατριάρχην ὁ γέρων καὶ ηὐλόγητο παρ' αὐτοῦ. Καὶ χαριεντιζόμενος μετὰ τὸν ἀσπασμὸν οὕτως ἔφη· "Οὗτος ὁ γέρων τὴν γραῖάν του ἔχασεν. Ἔλα, ὠργισμένε, εἰς τὸ χωρίον, ἔλα, ἄτυχε, εἰς τὸ ὁσπῖτιν." Καὶ μετὰ τῆς ὁμιλίας προπέμπων αὐτόν, ἔψαλλεν τὸ "Μακάριοι οἱ ἄμωμοι ἐν ὁδῷ, οἱ πορευόμενοι ἐν νόμῳ Κυρίου" [Psalm 118(119):1], τὰ πρὸς ταφὴν αὐτοῖς προμηνύων· καθώσπερ τοῦτο τότε καὶ γέγονεν. Γενόμενος γὰρ ἐν τῇ Σερβίᾳ ὁ πατριάρχης μετὰ τοῦ κλήρου, ἔθνηξεν σὺν αὐτοῖς δι' ὀλίγου μετὰ τοῦ φάρμακος οὕτω παγιδευθείς, ὡς οἱ πλείονες ἔφησαν τοῦτο· καὶ τέθαπτο ἐν τῇ ἐκκλησίᾳ Σερρῶν. Καὶ ταῦτα μὲν περὶ τῶν βασιλέων καὶ τοῦ πατριάρχου ἡ πρόρρησις τοῦ ἁγίου εἰς πέρας πρόδηλος τοῖς πᾶσιν ἐγένετο.

23

Ὁ δὲ Μεθόδιος, ἀνὴρ ἀσκητὴς καὶ αὐτὸς ὤν, ἐλθὼν ἐν μιᾷ ἵνα ἴδη τὸν ὅσιον, φῶς θεῖον κατεῖδε περιαστράπτον

Chapter 22

When the most holy patriarch Kallistos was going to Serbia with his clergy for the unification and peace of the Church, upon his arrival at the Mountain he sought an audience with the holy one. And when he came with his clergy to the elder's cell, the elder went out to meet the patriarch and received his blessing. And joking with him after their embrace, Maximos said, "This old man has lost his old lady. Come, angry one, to the village, come, unfortunate one, to the house." With these words he sent him on his way, as he chanted the verse: *Blessed are the blameless in the way, who walk in the law of the Lord,* predicting his burial service to them, as indeed then occurred. For when the patriarch arrived in Serbia with his clergy, he died soon afterward along with them after falling victim to poison, as most people recounted; and he was buried in the church of Serres. Thus the holy one's prediction about the emperors and the patriarch came to pass, as was clear to all.

Chapter 23

When Methodios, who was himself an ascetic, came one day to see the blessed one, he saw divine light flashing

ἐπὶ τὸν ὅσιον κύκλωθεν· καὶ οὐκ ἐτόλμα πλησιάσαι, ἕως
οὗ, κελεύσας τοῦτον ὁ ὅσιος, ἐπλησίασεν. Καὶ ἄλλος
ἐλθὼν μοναχός, Ἀρσένιος ὀνόματι, πρὸς τὸν ἅγιον, πῦρ
ἐδόκει ὁρᾶν τὴν κέλλαν αὐτοῦ καταλαβοῦσαν καὶ μὴ
φλέγουσαν. Ὁμοίως καὶ τὰ πέριξ τῶν ἄλσεων φλόγα
ὡρᾶτο δροσίζουσα, τὸ καινότατον. Καὶ πάλιν ὁ αὐτὸς Ἀρσένιος ἐλθὼν καὶ μηνύσας αὐτὸν τὴν ἔφοδον τῶν Ἰσμαηλιτῶν, καὶ τὰς χεῖρας ὁ ἅγιος ἐκτείνας πρὸς οὐρανόν, πῦρ
πάλιν ἐδόκει ἐκ τοῦ στόματος αὐτοῦ ἐξερχόμενον καὶ
ἀνιπτάμενον καὶ κυκλοῦντα τὸν ἅγιον καὶ δροσίζοντα· ὃ
καὶ ἰδὼν σύντρομος καὶ ἔμφοβος γέγονεν ὁ Ἀρσένιος καὶ
τοῖς πᾶσιν ἐκήρυξεν τὸ θεώρημα διὰ θαύματος.

24

Καὶ τοῦτο ἐλέγετο παρὰ πᾶσιν, ὅτι ἄρτον οὐράνιον
ἐδέχετο, τὸ ἐξαίρετον. Μιᾷ γὰρ τῶν ἡμερῶν ἐν καιρῷ χει-
μερίῳ παραγενόμενος ὁ νοσοκόμος τῆς Λαύρας, Γρηγόριος τοὔνομα, μετὰ καὶ ἄλλου ἀδελφοῦ εἰς ἐπίσκεψιν τοῦ
ἁγίου, οὐχ εὗρον κύκλωθεν μαλαγήν τινα τοῦ κελλίου
αὐτοῦ διὰ τὸ πολὺν χιόνα πεσεῖν ἐκεῖσε· καὶ κοπὴν οὗτοι
καινὴν ποιησάμενοι, εἰσήλθοσαν εἰς τὸν ἅγιον ἔχοντες
μεθ᾽ ἑαυτῶν ἄρτον ξηρὸν καὶ οἶνον καὶ ἄλλα τινὰ τὰ πρὸς
παράκλησιν ἐπιτήδεια. Ὡς δὲ εἶδον ἐν τῇ κέλλῃ τοῦ ἁγίου
ἄρτον ζέοντα καθαρώτατον, εὐωδίαν ἀποπληροῦντα τῇ

all around the blessed one; and he dared not approach until the blessed one told him to do so, and then he drew near. And when another monk, Arsenios by name, visited the holy one, he seemed to see fire enveloping his cell but not burning it. Similarly, he saw flame covering the area around the thicket like dew, something most strange. Again, when the same Arsenios came to warn him of the attack of the Ishmaelites, and the holy one extended his hands to the heavens, once more fire seemed to be coming out of his mouth and flying up and encircling the holy one and covering him like dew. When Arsenios observed this, he was terrified and fearful and, in awe, told everyone about the sight.

Chapter 24

And everyone said that he was the recipient of heavenly bread, something extraordinary. For one day in wintertime, when the infirmarian of the Lavra, Gregory by name, came with another brother to visit the holy one, they did not find any tracks around his cell, because a lot of snow had fallen there; and after laboriously making a fresh path, they made their way in to the holy one, having with them dry bread and wine and some other refreshments. But as they saw very fine warm bread in the holy one's cell, filling it with a strange and

κέλλη καινὴν καὶ θαυμάσιον, κύκλωθεν περιεργασάμενοι, εἰ πυρὸς σημεῖον φανεῖεν, καὶ μὴ εὑρόντες, ἔκθαμβοι καὶ οὗτοι γεγόνασιν τὸν οὐράνιον ἄρτον θαυμάζοντες. Καὶ δὴ πεσόντες ἐπὶ τοὺς πόδας τοῦ ἁγίου, ἠτοῦντο λαβεῖν ἐκ τοῦ ἄρτου μερίδα· καὶ σπλαγχνισθεὶς κλάσας δέδωκεν αὐτοῖς τοῦ ἄρτου τὸ ἥμισυ, φήσας αὐτοῖς· "Λάβετε, φάγετε [Matthew 26:26]· καὶ τοῦτό τιναν μὴ ἐξείπητε, ἕως οἰκῶ ἐν τῷ σώματι." Ἀλλὰ καὶ ὕδωρ πότιμον καὶ γλυκύτατον εἰς πόσιν δέδωκεν τούτοις, ὡς ἐπὶ Θεῷ ἐμαρτύρησαν ὕστερον ἡμῖν τοῦτο μετὰ τὴν κοίμησιν τοῦ ἁγίου. Ἀλλὰ καὶ ὕδωρ θαλάττιον εἰς ἡμερότητα καὶ γλυκύτητα μετεβάλετο, καὶ πιὼν δέδωκεν καὶ ἄλλοις, ὡς ἐμαρτύρησαν.

25

Ὁ δὲ ἡγούμενος τοῦ Προδρόμου τοῦ Μικροαθωνίτου ἡτοιμάσατό ποτε τὰ πρὸς ἐσθίασιν, ἵν᾽ ἐλθὼν ὁμιλήσῃ τὸν ἅγιον. Καὶ πρὸ τοῦ ἐλθεῖν εἰς τὸν ἅγιον ἀπὸ τοῦ κελλίου αὐτοῦ, ἔφησεν οὕτως· "Καρτέρει με, Καψοκαλύβη, νὰ φά-γωμεν." Ὅταν δὲ προσήγγισεν τῇ κέλλῃ τοῦ ἁγίου, ὁ ἅγιος τῷ ἱερεῖ τοῦτο ἐφώνησεν· "Ἔλα, παπᾶ, καρτερῶ σε." Ὅπερ ἀκούσας ἐθαύμασεν, πῶς τοσοῦτον διάστημα οὐκ ἔλαθεν τοῦτο τὸν ἅγιον, ὅσον ἀστείως ἐλάλησεν ὁ ἡγούμε-νος.

wondrous fragrance, they looked all around to see if there was any sign of fire, and when they found none, they were astonished, marveling at the heavenly bread. Falling at the holy one's feet, they asked for a piece of the bread; and taking pity on them, he broke the bread and gave them half of it, saying to them, "*Take, eat;* and do not tell anyone about this, as long I'm still alive." He also gave them fresh and very sweet water to drink, as they testified to me later, after the holy one's death, swearing by God. He also changed sea water into fresh sweet water, and after drinking it gave it to others, as they attested.

Chapter 25

The superior of the monastery of the Prodromos on Little Athos was once preparing some food, so that he might go and visit the holy one. Before leaving his cell to go to the holy one, he said this: "Wait for me, Hutburner, so we can eat." When he approached the holy one's cell, the latter called out to the priest: "Come along, *papas,* I'm waiting for you." When he heard this, he was astonished that, even at such a distance, this had not escaped the holy one's notice, as the superior humorously reported.

26

Ἄλλος δὲ μοναχὸς ἐκ τῶν Καρεῶν γενόμενος πρὸς τὸν ἅγιον ἐζήτει θεραπευθῆναι τὴν χεῖρα, ἣν κακῶς ἔπασχεν ὑπὸ ρεύματος. Καὶ λέγει αὐτῷ· "Παῦσαι τοῦ λογισμοῦ τῆς Πόλεως, ὅτι οὐ δύνασαι θεραπευθῆναι ἐκεῖσε· καὶ γύρου γύρου καὶ μέσα καρτέρει· καὶ ὑπομένων ὑπόμενε [see Psalm 39(40):1], ὅτι ἐδόθη σκόλοψ τῇ σαρκί, κατὰ τὸν ἅγιον Παῦλον, ἵνα μὴ ὑπεραίρεσαι [see 2 Corinthians 12:7] καὶ σωθήσῃ. Ἔχεις καὶ ἀργύρια· καὶ διάνεμε ταῦτα τοῖς πένησι, καὶ μὴ κατόρυττε, ἵνα μὴ κολασθῇς ἐν τῷ τέλει."

2   Ἐλθὼν δὲ καὶ μοναχὸς Μάρκος ὀνόματι καὶ ἕτερος μετ᾽ αὐτοῦ εἰς τὸν ἅγιον, λέγει τῷ ἑνί· "Ὑπέρπυρα ἔχεις δώδεκα, καὶ ὕπαγε, δὸς αὐτὰ τοῖς πτωχοῖς" [Mark 10:21; see Matthew 19:21; Luke 18:22]. Καὶ ὁ Μάρκος φησίν· "Ἐγὼ τριάκοντα δουκᾶτα κέκτημαι μόνα." Καὶ προλαβὼν ὁ ἅγιος εἶπε· "Ψεύδεσαι, διότι ἑξήκοντα κέκτησαι." Καὶ ταῦτα ἀμφότεροι ὡμολόγησαν, ὡς προέγνω ὁ ἅγιος. Καὶ Δαμιανός τις μοναχὸς ἐλθὼν πρὸς τὸν ἅγιον ἔφη αὐτῷ· "Ἀββᾶ, ἔχομεν εἰς τὸ μοναστήριν μοναχὸν τὸν ὁδεῖνα καλλίονά σου." Καὶ ἀποκριθεὶς λέγει αὐτῷ· "Αὐτὸς ἑξήκοντα ἔχει ὑπέρπυρα· καὶ δι᾽ ὀλίγου μέλλει καὶ τελευτῆσαι." Ὁ καὶ γέγονεν· δι᾽ ὀλίγου γὰρ τελευτήσας, ηὑρέθησαν εἰς ἐκεῖνον καὶ τὰ ἑξήντα ὑπέρπυρα· καὶ τοῦτο πάντες ἐθαύμασαν.

3   Ἄλλος δέ τις Κασσιανὸς μακρόθεν ὡσεὶ μίλια δύο καθεύδων ἀπὸ τὸν ἅγιον, πίταν ποιήσας καὶ εἰπών, "Ἔλα,

Chapter 26

Another monk came from Karyes to the holy one and sought to have his hand healed, for it was badly affected by a flux. Maximos said to him, "Stop thinking about the city of Constantinople, since you can't be healed there. So stick around <here> and *wait patiently,* because *a thorn has been given to your flesh,* in the words of Saint Paul, *so that you will not be too elated,* and thus you will be saved. You also have money; distribute this to the poor, and do not bury it, so that you may not be punished at the end."

When the monk named Mark and another companion 2 came to the holy one, Maximos said to one of them: "You have twelve *hyperpyra,* so *go, give* them *to the poor."* Mark replied, "I possess only thirty ducats." But the holy one interrupted him, saying, "You are lying, because you have sixty ducats." And both men acknowledged this, as the holy one foresaw. A monk called Damianos came to the holy one and said to him: "*Abba,* we have at the monastery the monk so-and-so who is better than you." In response Maximos said to him, "He has sixty *hyperpyra;* and in a little while he is going to die." Which indeed happened; for when he died soon after, the sixty *hyperpyra* were found on him and everyone marveled at this.

Another monk, Kassianos, who used to sleep about two 3 miles away from the holy one, made *pita* bread and said,

Καυσοκαλύβη, νὰ φάγωμεν," δι' ὀλίγου ἐλθὼν ἔφη, "Ἐλάλησάς με καὶ ἦλθα. Θὲς τὴν πίταν νὰ φάγωμεν· ἔχεις καὶ
οἶνον, καὶ φέρε." Τοῦ δὲ Κασσιανοῦ λέγοντος, "Οὐκ ἔχω
οἶνον," λαβὼν τὴν χεῖραν αὐτοῦ ὁ ἅγιος λέγει αὐτῷ· "Ἀκολούθει μοι, ἵνα σοι δείξω τὸν οἶνον." Καὶ ἐξελθὼν ἐνεφάνι-
σεν τὸν κεκρυμμένον οἶνον. Καὶ πολλὰ θαυμάσας ὁ Κασσιανὸς τὴν πρόγνωσιν τοῦ ἁγίου τοῖς πᾶσιν ἐκήρυττε.

4   Ἄλλοτε δὲ ἐν καιρῷ τρυγητοῦ, καθαροῦ τοῦ ἀέρος
ὄντος καὶ τοῦ ἡλίου αὐγάζοντος, μοναχοὶ δύο παρεγένοντο εἰς τὸν ἅγιον. Καὶ μετὰ τὴν ὁμιλίαν αὐτῶν λαβὼν
ἀπαξαμᾶν δέδωκεν αὐτοῖς εἰπών, "Πορεύεσθε συντόμως
εἰς τὴν μονὴν Δωροθέου, ἵνα μὴ κινδυνεύσετε ἐκ τοῦ χειμῶνος." Καὶ θαυμάζοντες πῶς χειμῶνα λελάληκεν γενέσθαι εὐδίας οὔσης μεγάλης, ἐξελθόντες μέχρι πρὸ τοῦ
Δωροθέου γενέσθαι αὐτοὺς ὡσεὶ μίλια τέσσαρα, τροπὴ
γέγονεν φοβερὰ ἐν ἀνέμῳ εὔρῳ βιαίῳ καὶ πλῆθος ἀστρα-
πῶν καὶ βροντῶν καὶ χάλαζα ῥαγδαία μεθ' ὕδωρ πολύ,
ὥστε τὸν τρυγητὸν παῦσαι τὸ σύνολον· τὰς γὰρ ἀτρύγους
ἀμπέλους ὡς τρυγημένας ἀνέδειξεν καὶ τελείως ἠφάνισεν.
Ταῦτα ἰδόντες οἱ μοναχοί, τὸ "Κύριε ἐλέησον" ἀνεβόησαν
καὶ τοῖς παρατυχοῦσιν ἐν Δωροθέοις τὴν πρόρρησιν τοῦ
ἁγίου διὰ θαύματος ἀνεκήρυξαν· καὶ πάντες ἐξέστησαν ἐν
τῷ θαύματι τῆς προγνώσεως.

5   Ἐν ἄλλοτε πάλιν οὗτοι οἱ μοναχοὶ προσωμίλουν τὸν
ἅγιον, καὶ λέγει πρὸς αὐτούς· "Κερατᾶδες ἔρχονται πρὸς
ἡμᾶς καὶ λυποῦνται πολλά." Παρελθούσης δὲ μιᾶς ὥρας,
ἦλθασιν τρεῖς κοσμικοὶ βάλλοντες μετάνοιαν ἐπ' ἐδάφου
τὸν ἅγιον, καὶ μετὰ λύπης σφοδρᾶς ἠγκαλοῦσαν τὰ γύναια

"Come, Hutburner, so that we may eat." A short time later Maximos came and said, "You have spoken to me and I have come. Set out the *pita* so that we may eat; you also have wine, so bring it out as well." When Kassianos said, "I don't have any wine," the holy one took his hand and said to him, "Follow me, so that I may show you the wine." And going outside he showed him the concealed wine. And Kassianos reported the holy one's clairvoyance to everyone with much amazement.

On another occasion, at harvest time, when the sky was 4 clear and the sun was shining, two monks came to the holy one. After their conversation Maximos took a rusk and gave it to them, saying, "Go quickly to the monastery of Dorotheou, so that you are not endangered by the storm." They marveled at how he spoke of a storm, when the weather was very good. But after they had journeyed to within four miles of Dorotheou, there was a fearful change in the weather with such a violent east wind and much thunder and lightning and raging hail with a downpour of rain, that it brought the harvest to a complete halt. For it caused the unharvested vines to be stripped of grapes as if they had been harvested, and completely destroyed them. When the monks saw this, they cried out, "Lord have mercy," and reported with amazement to those present at Dorotheou the holy one's prediction; and everyone was astonished at the miracle of his prophecy.

On another occasion when these monks were conversing 5 with the holy one, he also said to them, "Cuckolds are coming to us and they are very upset." After one hour passed, three laymen came and prostrated themselves on the ground before the holy one and, with extreme grief, accused their

καὶ τὴν ὕβριν αὐτῶν ἀπεκλαίοντο. Καὶ μικρὸν ἀναψύξας τοῖς λόγοις ὁ ἅγιος ἀπέλυσεν αὐτοὺς ἐν εἰρήνῃ.

6 Ὁ δὲ ἀββᾶς Χαρίτων μικρὰν ἐσθίαν ποιήσας καὶ ἐλθὼν εἰς τὸν ἅγιον, μετὰ τὴν εὐχὴν ἤσθιον. Καὶ λέγει ὁ ἅγιος, "Φέρε καὶ τοὺς βότρυας," ἐπιλαθομένου τοῦ Χαρίτωνος ταύτας. Καὶ λέγει πρὸς τὸν ἅγιον, "Οὐκ ἔχομεν βότρυας." Καὶ ὁ ἅγιος, "Ἔχετε, καὶ φέρετε, ὅτι ἔρχονται καὶ ἄλλαι πλεῖσται, καὶ χορτασθήσεσθε." Τότε μνησθεὶς ὁ Χαρίτων τοὺς βότρυας δέδωκεν. Καὶ μετ᾽ ὀλίγα ἐλθὼν ἄλλος ἤφερεν κοφῖνιν βότρυας· καὶ ὁ Χαρίτων σὺν τοῖς ἄλλοις τὸ διπλοῦν τῆς προοράσεως τοῦ ἁγίου ἰδόντες ἐξέστησαν.

7 Ἐν ἄλλοτε πάλιν πολλοὶ μοναχοὶ παραγενόμενοι πρὸς αὐτὸν ὠφελείας χάριν, καὶ ἐσθιόντων, λαβὼν ποτήριον ἀστείως οὕτως ἔφη· "Ῥάπτης εἶμαι ἐκ τὸ Προσφόριν· καὶ βαστῶ χύτραν ἰχθύας καὶ βρεμένος ἕως τὴν μέσην." Καὶ ἐν ὀλίγῃ ὥρᾳ ἐλθὼν κοσμικὸς ἐκ τὸ Προσφόριν μὲ χύτραν ἰχθύας, τῷ μεγάλῳ μετάνοιαν ἔβαλεν, φήσας αὐτῷ· "Ῥάπτης εἶμαι ἐκ τὸ Προσφόριν, καὶ ἐβράχην ἕως τὴν μέσην ἐκ τοῦ πλοίου θαλασσώσας·" ἐν ᾧ καὶ πάντες οἱ παρατυχόντες μεγάλως ἐθαύμαζον εἰς τοῦ ἁγίου τὴν πρόγνωσιν.

8 Πάλιν ὁ ἐκκλησιάρχης τῆς Λαύρας παραγενόμενος ἐν μιᾷ πρὸς τὸν ἅγιον, καὶ ὁμιλοῦντες ἀμφότεροι μετὰ καὶ ἄλλων πολλῶν μοναχῶν, ἔφη ὁ ἅγιος· "Καὶ ὁ Κανάκης ποῦ; Ἰχθύας μέλλει φαγεῖν." Καὶ μετ᾽ ὀλίγον ἐλθὼν ὁ Κανάκης, λέγει ὁ ἅγιος· "Ῥάπτης εἶμαι ἐκ τὸ Λουπάδιν, καὶ βαστῶ ἰχθύας πλήρεις." Καὶ ἰδοὺ καὶ ὁ ράπτης διὰ μιᾶς στιγμῆς παρεγένετο βαστάζων ἰχθύας ὀπτάς, καὶ

wives and lamented their wanton behavior. After consoling them a little with his words, the holy one dismissed them in peace.

Abbas Chariton made a small meal and came to visit the 6 holy one, and they ate this after their prayers. The holy one said, "Bring out the grapes as well," since Chariton had forgotten about them. And he said to the holy one, "I don't have any grapes." The holy one responded, "You do have some, so bring them out, because many other grapes are about to arrive as well, and you can eat your fill." Then Chariton remembered the grapes, and gave them to him. A little while later another man came carrying a basket of grapes; and Chariton and the others were astonished at the holy one's double prophecy.

On another occasion a large group of monks came to him 7 for their spiritual benefit and, while they were eating, he took a cup and said humorously to them: "I'm a tailor from Prosphorin; and I'm holding a pot of fish and I'm soaked to the waist." In a short time a layman came from Prosphorin with a pot of fish, and prostrated himself before the holy one, saying to him: "I'm a tailor from Prosphorin; and I was drenched to the waist when I fell into the sea from my boat." And all who were present marveled greatly at the holy one's prophecy.

Again, the sacristan of the Lavra came one day to the holy 8 one, and as they were both conversing, together with many other monks, the holy one said, "And where is Kanakes? He's going to eat fish." When Kanakes came a little while later, the holy one said, "I'm a tailor from Loupadin, and I'm carrying many fish." And lo and behold, an instant later the tailor appeared, carrying grilled fish. Prostrating himself

βαλὼν μετάνοιαν πρὸς τὸν ἅγιον ἔφη, "Ῥάπτης εἶμαι ἐκ
τὸ Λουπάδιν." Καὶ τοῦτο ἰδόντες οἱ παρατυχόντες μετὰ
τοῦ ἐκκλησιάρχου μεγάλως ἐθαύμαζον πῶς καὶ τὸν Κανά-
κην ἀπὸ μακρόθεν προέγνω καὶ τοῦ ῥάπτῃ τὴν προσηγορίαν καὶ τὸ Λουπάδιν καὶ τοὺς ἰχθύας προεῖπεν.

27

Πάλιν δὲ ἐλθών τις γραμματεὺς νουνεχὴς λόγιος εἰς
τὸν ἅγιον, ἀπὸ τὴν μεγαλόπολιν ὤν, οὗτος ὡς εἶδεν
αὐτόν, τοὺς λογισμοὺς αὐτοῦ κακοὺς εἶναι καὶ πονηροὺς
ἔλεγεν, καὶ κατέσκωπτεν αὐτὸν καὶ ὠνείδιζεν λέγων· "Ποῦ
ἔγνως ἐσὺ τῶν ἁγίων τοὺς πόνους καὶ τὰ παλαίσματα
ὁπόσοι εἰσίν, καὶ πάλιν τὴν τοῦ Θεοῦ χάριν τὴν δοθεῖσαν
αὐτοῖς; Καὶ βλασφημεῖς πρὸς αὐτοὺς λέγων· Ὀλίγα οἱ
ἅγιοι ἐκοπίασαν, ἀμὴ οἱ γράφοντες τοὺς βίους αὐτῶν
πλεῖστα χαρίζοντες κενῶς προσέθηκαν.' Καὶ τὴν χάριν
τῶν θαυμάτων ψευδὴν εἶναι λογίζεσαι. Παῦσαι τοῦ τοιούτου νοήματος, ὅ ἐστιν ἐκ τοῦ Πονηροῦ, ἵνα μὴ τύχῃς
σκηπτοῦ ἐκ Θεοῦ τῆς ὀργῆς· οἱ γὰρ ἅγιοι ὁλοκλήρως τῷ
Θεῷ ἑαυτοὺς ἀναθέμενοι, πάντα τὰ νοούμενα καὶ
πραττόμενα ὑπ᾽ αὐτῶν διὰ Θεὸν καὶ Θεοῦ εὐαρέστησιν
ἐσπουδάζοντο ἐν ὅλῃ τῇ ζωῇ. Τίς οὖν, εἰπέ μοι, δύναται
διαγράψαι πᾶσαν τὴν βιοτήν τῶν ἁγίων, ὡς ἦν ἑκάστου
κατὰ διπλοῦν; Ἀλλὰ σημεῖά τινα σχεδιάζουσιν, ἐκ τῶν
ἀπείρων ὀλίγα, εἰς μαρτύριον τῶν ἁγίων.

before the holy one, he said: "I'm a tailor from Loupadin."
When those present with the sacristan saw this, they marveled greatly at how Maximos predicted the arrival of
Kanakes from far away and foretold the tailor's greeting as
well as Loupadin and the fish.

Chapter 27

On another occasion a smart and erudite scholar, who
was from the great city of Constantinople, came to the holy
one. When Maximos saw him, he said that his thoughts
were evil and wicked, and mocked and reproached him, saying, "How does someone like you know the nature of the labors and struggles of the saints, as well as the grace given
them by God? You blaspheme against them when you say:
'The saints toiled little, but those who write their lives,
by enhancing many things, have groundlessly embellished
them.' You also think that the grace of miracles is false. Stop
this sort of thinking, which comes from the Evil One, so
that you do not fall victim to a thunderbolt from the wrath
of God. For the saints dedicated themselves entirely to
God, and strove throughout their lives that everything they
thought and did should be for God and pleasing to God.
Who then, tell me, can possibly describe the entire life of
the saints, unless he is a duplicate of each one? But these
writers sketch out certain signs, a few out of an infinite
number, as evidence for the saints.

2 "Ταὐτὸ καὶ τὴν χάριν νόμισον εἶναι πλουσίαν ἐν τοῖς ἁγίοις διὰ τοῦ ἁγίου Πνεύματος, οὐχ ὅσην ὁρῶμεν, ἀλλὰ πλουσίαν καὶ ἀκατάληπτον καὶ ἀχώρητον, ὑπερβαίνουσαν πάντα νοῦν καὶ διάνοιαν τῶν ἀνθρώπων. Εἰ σοφὸς ἀληθὴς βούλεσαι εἶναι, τὴν τῶν Ἑλλήνων μωρολογίαν κατάπτυσον, καὶ σχόλασον κατὰ τὸν Δαβίδ, ἵνα νοήσῃς Θεόν [see Psalm 45(46):10], ἵν' ὅπως διὰ γνώσεως καὶ προσεδρίας πνευματικῆς οἰκειωθῇς τῷ Θεῷ κατὰ τὸ σὸν ἐφετὸν καὶ ἐφικτόν. Καὶ τότε γνώσει τὴν χάριν τοῦ Πνεύματος καὶ Θεοῦ θεῖα θαυμάσια ἀκατάληπτα, καὶ θαυμάσεις τότε. Καὶ σεαυτὸν καταγνῷς νοήσας τὸ σκότος, ὅσον ἐστὶν ἐν σοί· χωρὶς γὰρ τοῦ φωτὸς τὰς αὐγάς, τὸ σκότος οὐκ ἀπελέγχεται. Τοίνυν γενοῦ ἐν φωτὶ ἡσυχίας καὶ προσευχῆς, καὶ φεύξεταί σου τὸ σκότος πρῶτον μακρά· καὶ τότε ὄψει τῶν ἁγίων τὴν χάριν καὶ δύναμιν, καὶ ποθήσεις τυχεῖν καὶ αὐτός."

3 Ταῦτα ἀκούσας ὁ γραμματεὺς σύντρομος καὶ ἔμφοβος γέγονεν, ὅτι τοὺς κεκρυμμένους λογισμοὺς αὐτοῦ δήλους ἐκεῖσε πεποίηκεν καὶ ὠνείδισεν· ἐν τούτῳ καὶ πλεῖστα ὠφεληθεὶς διωρθώσατο τὸ βλάσφημον νόημα, καὶ ἄλλους ἔκτοτε οὗτος διωρθοῦτο τοὺς ἄφρονας ἐν τῇ σοφίᾳ τοῦ σοφοῦ διδασκάλου καὶ μάκαρος.

"Consider this too, that grace is abundant in the saints 2
through the Holy Spirit, not such as we observe it, but abundant and incomprehensible and uncontainable in a way that
surpasses every human mind and thought. If you wish to be
a truly wise man, spit upon the folly of the Hellenes, and
in the words of David, *Be still so that you may understand God,*
so that through knowledge and spiritual perseverance you
may become intimate with God in accordance with your desire and ability. Then you will know the grace of the Spirit
and the incomprehensible divine marvels of God, and then
you may marvel. And you will condemn yourself, after you
have understood the darkness which is within you; for without rays of light, darkness is not exposed. Therefore embrace the light of spiritual tranquility and prayer, and first
the darkness will flee far away from you; and then you will
see the grace and power of the saints, and you yourself will
desire to attain it."

When the scholar heard these words, he trembled and 3
was fearful because Maximos had revealed and reproached
his hidden thoughts. He was helped a great deal in this way,
corrected his blasphemous thinking, and from then on corrected other foolish people through the wisdom of the wise
and blessed teacher.

28

Καὶ αὐτὸς ἐπὶ Θεῷ μάρτυρι οὐκ ἀποκρύψω, ὃ ἑώρακα εἰς τὸν ἅγιον. Συνήθης γὰρ καὶ αὐτὸς τῆς ὁμιλίας τούτου γενόμενος, ἐν μιᾷ τῶν ἡμερῶν ἐκ τῆς μονῆς τοῦ Βατοπεδίου μετὰ καὶ ἄλλου ἐλθὼν οὐχ εὗρον τὸν ἅγιον εἰς τὸ κελλίον αὐτοῦ. Καὶ κύκλωθεν τῆς κέλλης κατασκοπήσας οὐχ εὗρον πάλιν αὐτόν, καὶ ἀσχάλλων τῷ πνεύματι ἐζήτουν ἰδεῖν τὸν ποθούμενον. Καὶ μικρὸν ὄπιθεν ἀνελθὼν ἑώρων πρὸς τὴν ὁδὸν τοῦ κυρίου Ἡσαΐου καὶ μετὰ προσοχῆς κατεσκόπευον ἰδεῖν τὸ ζητούμενον.

2 Καὶ ἰδοὺ εἶδον αὐτὸν εἰς τὴν γοῦρναν τοῦ ἀγελαρίου τὴν κατ<αβ>ιβάζουσαν ὕδωρ ἐκεῖσε, ὡσεὶ μίλια δύο τὸ διάστημα ὄν, ἐξ οὗ ἱστάμην καὶ ἔβλεπον· ἔστι δὲ τὸ μέσον τούτου δύσβατον καὶ πετρῶδες, οὐ κατ᾽ εὐθεῖαν τὸν δρόμον ἔχον, ἀλλὰ στραγγαλιὸν καὶ ἐπίβαθον. Καὶ τοῦτον ἑώρων, ὡς ἐπὶ Θεῷ μάρτυρι, ἀναχθέντα καὶ ὡς ὑπόπτερος ἀετὸς ἄνω ἐπὶ τοῦ ἄλσους καὶ τῶν μεγίστων λίθων πετόμενον καὶ πρός με ἐρχόμενον. Καὶ ὡς εἶδον αὐτὸν οὕτως, σύντρομος γέγονα ὅλως καὶ ἐξέστην τῷ θαύματι καὶ τὸ "Μέγας εἶ, Κύριε," ἀνεβόησα.

3 Καὶ μικρὸν ὄπιθεν ἑαυτὸν ἐκ τοῦ φόβου συστείλας, ὡς ἐν ῥιπῇ καὶ ὁ ἅγιος εἰς τὸν τόπον ὅπου ἱστάμην ἐγένετο, ψάλλων ἃ οὐ κατέλαβον ἐκ τοῦ θαύματος. Καὶ πεσὼν ἐπὶ τοὺς πόδας αὐτοῦ, ὁ ἅγιος συχνῶς κατηρώτα με, "Πόσην ὥραν ἔχεις ἐν τῷ τόπῳ ἐτούτῳ;" Εἶτα λαβών με ἐκ τῆς χειρὸς εἰς τὴν κέλλαν εἰσήγαγεν, καὶ πολλὰ διδάξας καὶ

Chapter 28

And, as God is my witness, I will not conceal what I my-self saw with regard to the holy one. I myself regularly used to spend time in conversation with him, and so one day, when I came from the Vatopedi monastery with another monk, I did not find the holy one in his cell. After looking all around his cell I still did not find him; and, being dis-tressed in spirit, I sought to see the object of my desire. I went up a short distance behind his cell in order to see in the direction of the path to Kyr Isaiah, and I looked very care-fully to catch sight of the man I sought.

And lo and behold, I saw him at the sheep trough which 2 brings water down there, at a distance of about two miles from where I was standing and looking; and the intervening space is rough and rocky, and the path is not straight but twisting and full of potholes. As God is my witness, I saw him raised up and flying like a winged eagle above the forest and the huge rocks and coming toward me. When I saw him like this, I trembled with fear and was astonished at the mir-acle and cried out, "*Thou art great, O Lord.*"

I recoiled a bit out of fear, and in a twinkling the holy one 3 appeared at the spot where I was standing, chanting some-thing which I did not understand in my wonder. As I fell at his feet, the holy one kept asking me: "How long have you been in this place?" Then he took me by the hand and led me to his cell; after much teaching and instruction, he said to

νουθετήσας ἔφησε πρός με· "Ὅρα μὴ ἐξείπῃς τινὶ ὅπερ
ἑώρακας, ἕως ὑπάρχω ἐν σώματι. Σὺ δὲ ἡγούμενος ἔχεις
γενέσθαι καὶ μητροπολίτης Μοραχριδῶν· καὶ πολλὰ
μέλλεις παθεῖν, καὶ ὑπόμεινον μιμούμενος τὸν ἐπὶ ξύλου
τανυθέντα Χριστόν· αὐτὸς γάρ σου γενήσεται βοηθὸς ἐν
τοῖς πειρασμοῖς καὶ στέφανος ἐν τῇ δόξῃ αὐτοῦ. Καὶ χαῖρε,
ὅταν πλέῃς ἐν πειρασμοῖς, ὅτι εἰς μαρτύριόν σου γενήσονται τῆς ἀθλήσεως." Ἅτινα καὶ ἀπετελέσθησαν, ὡς προεῖπεν ὁ ἅγιος.

29

Πάλιν δὲ ἕτεροι μοναχοὶ ἀπὸ τῆς μονῆς τοῦ Ἀλυπίου
ἐλθόντες, λέγει αὐτοῖς ὁ ἅγιος· "Σήμερον ἐν τῇ ὥρᾳ ταύτῃ
ψάλλουσιν ἅπαντες εἰς τὸ μοναστῆρί σας τὸ 'Μακάριοι οἱ
ἄμωμοι' [Psalm 118(119):1]· καὶ ψάλλετε καὶ ὑμεῖς." Καὶ στα-
θεὶς σὺν αὐτοῖς, τοὺς τρεῖς ψαλμοὺς ἀπεπλήρωσαν· καὶ οἱ
μοναχοὶ σημειώσαντες τὴν ὥραν καὶ στραφέντες εἰς τοῦ
Ἀλυπίου, εὗρον ὅτι ἐν αὐτῇ τῇ ὥρᾳ ἔψαλλον τὸ λείψανον
τοῦ κοιμηθέντος κυρίου Ἰωσὴφ τοῦ γραμματικοῦ καὶ λο-
γίου καὶ ἐναρέτου.

2   Καὶ τοῦτο οὐ σιωπήσω, ὃ εἶδον. Μοναχός τις Λαυ-
ριώτης, Ἰάκωβος τοὔνομα, ἐλθὼν ἐπαρεκάλει τὸν ἅγιον,
ἵνα ποιήσῃ γράμμαν αὐτῷ τῆς ζητήσεως διὰ τὴν αἰχμαλωσίαν τοῦ αὐταδέλφου αὐτοῦ. Καὶ μικρὸν προσσχὼν

me: "See that you do not tell anyone what you have seen as long as I'm still alive. You will become a superior and the metropolitan of Morachrida. You're going to suffer a lot, but persevere in imitation of Christ Who was stretched out on the cross, for He will be your helper in your tribulations and you will obtain a crown in His glory. And so rejoice, when you sail into tribulations, because they will be a testimony of your struggle." And everything came to pass as the holy one foretold.

Chapter 29

On another occasion some monks came from the monastery of Alypios, and the holy one said to them: "Today at this very hour all the monks at your monastery are chanting the psalm that begins, '*Blessed are the blameless,*' and you must chant it too." And as he stood with them, they chanted the three sections of the psalm in their entirety. The monks noted the time, and when they returned to Alypiou, they found that at that very hour they had been chanting psalms over the body of the deceased Kyr Joseph, the erudite and virtuous teacher of grammar.

Nor will I remain silent about the following incident 2 which I observed. A Lavriot monk, called Iakobos, came to ask the holy one to write a petition for him with regard to his brother's captivity. After listening to him for a bit,

αὐτῷ μετὰ αὐστηρότητος λέγει· "Ὕπαγε, ἔβγαλε τὰ ἑξήκοντά σου ὑπέρπυρα ἐκ τοῦ τείχους τοῦ πύργου, καὶ δὸς εἰς τὴν σὴν ἀγοράν· καὶ μὴ ἔσο πλεονέκτης καὶ ψεύστης, ἵνα μὴ πάλιν τὴν αἰχμαλωσίαν δουλεύσῃς." Καὶ τοῦτο ἀκούσαντες ὡμολόγησαν καὶ συγχώρησιν τοῦ τολμήματος ἔλαβον.

3   Πάλιν κοσμικός τις ἐλθὼν πρὸς τὸν ἅγιον μετὰ κλαυθμοῦ λέγει αὐτῷ· "Βοήθησόν με, ἅγιε τοῦ Θεοῦ, ὅτι ἱερεύς με ἠφόρισεν καὶ ἀπέθανεν· καὶ οὐκ ἔχω τί πράξειν ὁ ἄθλιος." Καὶ ταῦτα ἀκούσας ὁ ἅγιος, σπλαγχνισθεὶς λέγει πρὸς αὐτόν· "Πορεύου εἰς τὸν ἅγιον τὸν μητροπολίτην Βεροίας κύριον Διονύσιον, ὅστις καὶ τὸν ἱερέαν ἐκράτει, ἵνα συγχωρήσῃ σοι κατὰ νόμους." Ὁ καὶ γέγονεν, καὶ παρ' ἐκείνου τὴν συγχώρησιν ἔλαβεν.

4   Ἐκεῖσε καὶ ἕτερος μοναχὸς τῇ ὥρᾳ ταύτῃ εἰς τὸν ἅγιον ὤν, καὶ πρὸς αὐτὸν ὁ ἅγιος ἔφησεν· "Πορεύου καὶ σὺ πρὸς τὸν παπᾶν Ἰωάννην, ἵνα σε συγχωρήσῃ πρὸ τοῦ ἀποθανεῖν, ὅτι ἀφωρισμένον σε ἔχει, ἐξ ὅτου δέδωκας αὐτὸν μετὰ ὕβρεως παλαμαίαν." Καὶ τοῦτο θαυμάσας ὁ μοναχός, πῶς ἐξεῖπεν αὐτοῦ τὸ κεκρυμμένον μυστήριον, ἐπορεύθη καὶ αὐτὸς εἰς τὴν Βέροιαν, ἀσθενὴς ὤν, σὺν τῷ προλεχθέντι κοσμικῷ καὶ τὴν συγχώρησιν ἔλαβεν. Καὶ νεαλὴς πάλιν ἐλθὼν πρὸς αὐτὸν κοσμικός, λέγει ὁ ἅγιος πρὸς αὐτόν· "Ἰωάννη, μοναχὸς μέλλεις γενέσθαι καὶ ἱερεὺς καὶ ἡγούμενος·" ὅπερ καὶ γέγονεν.

Maximos said to him very severely, "Away with you, take your sixty *hyperpyra* out of the wall of the tower, and use them to pay your ransom; and do not be greedy and a liar, so that you are not taken captive a second time." When they heard this, they confessed and received forgiveness for their offense.

On another occasion a layman came to the holy one and said to him tearfully: "Help me, holy one of God, because a priest has excommunicated me and then died; and, wretch that I am, I don't know what to do." When the holy one heard this, he took pity on him and said to him, "Go to the holy metropolitan of Berrhoia, Kyr Dionysios, who had authority over the priest, so that he may pardon you in accordance with the legal regulations." This happened, and he received the pardon from him. 3

There was another monk there with the holy one at that time, and the holy one said to him: "You too should go to the priest John, so that he may pardon you before he dies, since he has excommunicated you for striking him insolently with your hands." The monk was amazed at how he spoke of his hidden secret, and so, even though he was ill, he set out for Berrhoia, together with the previously mentioned layman, and received pardon. On another occasion a youthful layman came to him, and the holy one said to him, "John, you are going to become a monk and a priest and a superior," which also happened. 4

30

Καὶ ὁ ἀρχιερεὺς Τραϊανουπόλεως ἐρχόμενος μετὰ τοῦ μαθητοῦ αὐτοῦ εἰς τὸν ἅγιον, ἐν μέσῳ τῆς ὁδοῦ λαβὼν τὸ μανδύον τοῦ μαθητοῦ ἀνεβάλετο, καὶ τὸ τῆς ἀρχιερωσύνης πάλιν τὸν μαθητήν, βουληθεὶς δοκιμάσαι τὸν ἅγιον. Καὶ δῆτα ἐλθὼν πρὸς αὐτόν, ὁ ἀρχιερεὺς πρῶτον ὡς μαθητὴς λέγει τὸν ἅγιον· "Ἔρχεται ὁ ἀρχιερεὺς νά σε ἴδῃ καὶ ποιῇ σε μετάνοιαν· ἐγὼ δέ εἰμι μαθητὴς ἐκείνου, καὶ εὐλόγησόν μοι." Ὁ δὲ ἅγιος λέγει πρὸς αὐτόν· "Σὺ εἶ ὁ ἀρχιερεύς, καὶ εὐλόγησόν με." Καὶ πάλιν ὁ ἀρχιερεύς· "Εἶπόν σοι, ὅτι ὁ ἀρχιερεὺς ἔξω ἵσταται, ὅστις καὶ τῆς ἀρχιερωσύνης τὰ σήμανδρα περιβέβληται· καὶ ἂν ὁρίσῃς, νὰ ἔλθῃ." Τότε λέγει ὁ ἅγιος πρὸς αὐτόν· "Σὺ εἶ ὁ ἀρχιερεύς, καὶ εὐλόγησόν με. Καὶ μηδέν με λέγῃς τὰς κλεψίας σου· ἐκεῖ γὰρ ἤμην ἐπάνωθεν τοῦ λάκκου, ὅταν ἐποιήσατε τὴν κλεψίαν." Καὶ τοῦτο εἰπών, βαλὼν μετάνοιαν ὁ ἀρχιερεὺς εὐλόγησεν τὸν ἅγιον καὶ ἠσπάσατο, καὶ διὰ θαύματος μεγάλου εἶχεν αὐτόν.

31

Ἔλεγεν δὲ ὁ ἅγιος καὶ τοῦτο <πρὸς> τὸν ὅσιον καὶ θεοφόρον Νίφωνα τὸν Ἀθωνίτην, ὅτι ἐπάνωθεν [δὲ] τῆς καλύβης αὐτοῦ ἦν σπήλαιον μικρόν· καὶ μιᾷ τῶν ἡμερῶν

Chapter 30

The archbishop of Traianoupolis, who was coming with his disciple to the holy one, took his disciple's cloak and put it on while they were on the way, and gave his archiepiscopal mantle to his disciple, as he wished to test the holy one. Indeed, when he came to Maximos, the archbishop, as if he were the disciple, first said to the holy one, "The archbishop is coming to see you and make obeisance to you; but I am his disciple so, please, bless me." But the holy one retorted, "You're the archbishop, and should bless me!" The archbishop said again, "I told you, the archbishop is standing outside; he's even wearing the insignia of the archbishopric, so please ask him to come in." Then the holy one said to him, "You're the archbishop, and should bless me. And don't tell me any more of your lies; for I was there above the cistern when you plotted this deception." When Maximos said this, the archbishop did obeisance and blessed the holy one and embraced him, and considered him a great marvel.

Chapter 31

The holy one also said this to the blessed and divinely inspired Niphon the Athonite: that there was a small cave above Maximos's hut; and one day he went into the cave and

εἰσῆλθεν εἰς τὸ σπήλαιον καὶ ἀφύπνωσε. Καὶ ἀναστὰς ἐκάθισεν· καὶ θεωρεῖ γύναιον ἐστολισμένον ἔμπροσθεν τοῦ σπηλαίου. Γνοὺς οὖν τὴν ἐπίνοιαν τοῦ πανπονήρου δαίμονος, καὶ ποιήσας ἐκ τρίτου σταυροῦ τὸ σημεῖον, ἄφαντος ἐγένετο. Καὶ ὀλίγων ἡμερῶν παρελθόντων, ἔλεγεν ὁ μέγας ὅτι "Μοναχός τις ἦλθεν ἡμέρᾳ δευτέρᾳ καὶ ἐκάθι<σεν> ἔμπροσθεν τοῦ σπηλαίου, ὃν οὐκ εἶδά ποτε. Ἦν δὲ κατάξηρος ἀπὸ τῆς πολλῆς ἐγκρατείας. Καὶ τῇ Τρίτῃ πρωῒ ἦλθε πρός με καὶ ὡμιλήσαμεν· καὶ μὴ ἔχων ἄρτον τοῦ φαγεῖν ἀμφότεροι ἢ ἄλλο τι τοῦ συνεσθιαθῆναι, ἐξῆλθεν καὶ ἐκάθητο ἄνωθεν ἕως τῇ Πέμπτῃ πρωῒ. Καὶ πάλιν ἦλθεν καὶ ὡμιλήσαμεν, καὶ πάλιν ἀνέβη καὶ ἐκάθητο ἕως τῷ Σαββάτῳ πρωῒ. Τότε ἐξῆλθον καὶ ἐγὼ διὰ σωματικὴν παράκλησιν καὶ ἔκτοτε οὐκ εἶδον αὐτόν."

2 Ἐτῶν οὖν διάστημα τεσσαρεσκαίδεκα ἐν τῷ προειρημένῳ σπηλαίῳ πλησίον τῆς Παναγίας διανύσας, ἐξῆλθεν ἀπ᾽ ἐκεῖ καὶ ἦλθεν πλησίον, ὅσον ἀκούονται τὰ πνευματικὰ ὄργανα τῆς ἱερᾶς Λαύρας· πήξας μικρὸν καλύβιον ἐκάθητο, ἐν ᾧ καὶ ἐτελειώθη.

3 Εἰσὶ δὲ ἄλλα πολλά, προοράσεις καὶ ἀληθεῖς θαυματουργίαι ᾀδόμεναί τε καὶ λεγόμεναι καὶ γενόμεναι παρὰ τοῦ ὁσίου πατρός, ἅπερ ἀκήκοα κἀγώ, καὶ καθώς μοι ἐδήλωσαν καὶ ἄλλοι πατέρες, ὅ τε Γρηγόριος ἀπὸ τῆς Πέτρας Σίμωνος τοῦ μυροβλύτου καὶ Ματθαῖος μοναχὸς καὶ ἄλλος Ματθαῖος ἱερομόναχος καὶ ἕτεροι. Ἀλλὰ τίς διηγήσηται τῆς προοράσεως αὐτοῦ τὰ χαρίσματα, ἅτινα ὡς ψάμμος θαλάττιος ἐπληθύνθησαν ἐφ᾽ ὅλην τὴν ὑφήλιον τῶν πιστῶν; Εἰ γὰρ βουληθείημεν πάντα συγγράψαι, ὅπερ

fell asleep. When he awoke he remained there; and he saw a finely dressed woman in front of the cave. After he realized that this was a device of the most evil demon, he made the sign of the cross three times, and she disappeared. And a few days later, as the great man said, "A monk, whom I had never seen before, came on Monday and sat in front of the cave. He was all withered up from his great asceticism. On Tuesday morning he came to me and we talked together; and since neither of us had any bread to eat nor any other food, he went outside and stayed above the cave until Thursday morning. Then he came again and we talked, and again he went up and stayed there until Saturday morning. Then I went out to relieve myself, and from that time I did not see him."

After spending a period of fourteen years in the previously mentioned cave near the Panagia, he left it and came nearer, to where the spiritual instruments of the holy Lavra could be heard. He built a small hut there and remained in it until his death. 2

There are also many other things, prophecies and true miracles performed by the holy father which are to be praised and celebrated, things which I myself have heard about and which other fathers have described to me, such as Gregory from the Rock of Simon who exudes perfumed oil, and the monk Matthew and another hieromonk Matthew, and others as well. But who will be able to narrate his gifts of prophecy, which multiplied like the sand of the sea over the entire world of the faithful? For even if I wished to write them all 3

ἀδύνατον, ἐπιλείψει ἡμῖν διηγούμενον ὁ χρόνος. Ἀλλὰ κοτύλην μίαν ἐκ τοῦ πελάγους τῶν θαυμάτων αὐτοῦ προλαβόντες διὰ τὸ μῆκος τοῦ λόγου, εἰς μαρτύριον συνεγράψαμεν τοῦ ἁγίου, ἵνα ἴδωμεν οἱ πιστοὶ πῶς καὶ νῦν δοξάζει ὁ Κύριος τοὺς δοξάζοντας αὐτὸν [see 1 Kings 2:30] ἐν αὐτοῖς ὁλοκλήρως.

32

Ὅθεν καὶ ἐκ μέρους τὴν διδασκαλίαν αὐτοῦ σημειώσωμεν, ἐν ᾗ πάντας διδάσκων ἐφώτιζεν ἐν τῷ Πνεύματι, καὶ οὕτω πρὸς τὴν κηδείαν αὐτοῦ καταδράμωμεν καὶ τὸν λόγον αὐτοῦ τελειώσωμεν. Τοίνυν συντείνατέ μοι τὸν νοῦν, ἀκοὴν καὶ διάνοιαν, ὅσα πρὸς φωτισμὸν οὐράνιον καὶ οὗτος τοῖς πᾶσιν ὡδήγει καὶ πρὸς γνῶσιν ἀπλανῆ τὴν τοῦ Πνεύματος ἀνεβίβαζεν.

2 Παρήνει γὰρ λέγων ὅτι "Πᾶς ἄνθρωπος ὀφείλει τηρεῖν τὸ κατ' εἰκόνα ἑαυτοῦ ἀλώβητον ἐκ τῶν σκανδάλων τοῦ Πολεμήτορος, ἅτινά εἰσιν· ἀλαζονεία καὶ ἔπαρσις, ὑπερηφάνεια καὶ οἴησις, πλάνη καὶ πονηρία, ἀπανθρωπία καὶ ἀθεΐα, ἀσέλγεια καὶ ἀσέβεια, μῖσος καὶ ἀφοβία, ψεῦδος καὶ βλασφημία, καὶ πάντων τῶν κακῶν δεσμός, ἡ ἀντικείμενος δύναμις, ἥτις ἀρχὴν λαβοῦσα ἐκ τῆς πτώσεως τοῦ πρώτου Ἀδὰμ εἰσέρχεσθαι πειρᾶται εἰς τὴν φύσιν ἡμῶν τοῦ μιαίνειν αὐτήν, καὶ πάντας πολεμεῖ καθ' ἑκάστην, ἵν' ἀχρειώσῃ εἰς πάντας τὸ κατ' εἰκόνα Θεοῦ τὸ ἐξαίρετον.

down, which is impossible, there would not be enough time for me to narrate them. But after selecting only one cupful from the sea of his miracles, on account of the length of my tale, I have written them down as a testimony to the holy one, so that in them we faithful may see how, even now, the Lord completely *glorifies those who glorify Him.*

Chapter 32

Let me, then, also note down in part his teaching, by means of which he instructed everyone and enlightened them in the Spirit, and thus let me move on rapidly to his funeral and complete his story. So concentrate your mind, ears and intellect along with me, on how this man guided everyone toward heavenly enlightenment and elevated them to unerring knowledge of the Spirit.

For he used to advise them, saying, "Every man ought 2 to preserve his own image, undefiled by the snares of the Enemy, which are boastfulness and arrogance, pride and self-conceit, error and wickedness, inhumanity and godlessness, lasciviousness and impiety, hatred and temerity, falsehood and blasphemy, and the bonds of all evils, the opposing power which, taking its beginnings from the fall of the first Adam, tries to insinuate itself into our nature so as to defile it, and makes war against everyone on a daily basis, so that it may corrupt in everyone the distinguishing feature of being in God's image.

3 "Δι' οὗ καὶ ὁ Χριστὸς ἐλθὼν καὶ ἀναπλάσας αὐτὸ διὰ θείου βαπτίσματος νόμον δέδωκεν τὸν σωτήριον τοῦ ἀπέχεσθαι ἐκ πάντων ἡμᾶς τῶν πονηρῶν ἔργων τοῦ Διαβόλου, καὶ ποιεῖν ὅσα ἐντέλλεται ἡμῖν τὰ σωτήρια, ἅτινά εἰσιν· ἀγάπη, πίστις καὶ πόθος πρὸς τὸν Θεόν, καὶ ἁγιασμὸς ὁ τοῦ σώματος, ἀγάπη πρὸς τὸν πλησίον ἀνυπόκριτος, ταπείνωσις καὶ ἀλήθεια, εἰρήνη, μακροθυμία καὶ ἀγαθότης, συμπάθεια καὶ τὸ ἔλεος, ὑπεροψία πάντων ματαίων καὶ πονηρῶν καὶ ἄρνησις παθῶν ψυχοφθόρων, ἀλήθειαν καὶ δικαιοσύνην ἀσκεῖν καὶ φόβον ἔχειν Θεοῦ, καὶ ὑπομένειν τὰ ἐπερχόμενα θλιβερὰ διὰ τὴν βασιλείαν τῶν οὐρανῶν. Ὀφείλει πᾶσι τοίνυν ἡμῖν τοῖς πιστοῖς τοῦ μιμνῆσθαι τὰς ὑποσχέσεις ἀεί, ἃς ἐποιήσαμεν ἐν τῷ ἁγίῳ βαπτίσματι, καὶ ἐν τίνι βεβαπτίσμεθα καὶ πιστεύομεν· καὶ βιοτεύειν ὡς υἱοὶ Θεοῦ παντοκράτορος ἀκολουθοῦντες Χριστῷ, τὸν δὲ Πονηρὸν καταπτύειν καὶ πᾶσι τοῖς ἔργοις αὐτοῦ καὶ πάσῃ τῇ πομπῇ αὐτοῦ, ἵνα ἐλθὼν ὁ Κύριος *ἐνοικήσῃ ἐν ἡμῖν καὶ ἐμπεριπατήσῃ* [see 2 Corinthians 6:16] καὶ σὺν τῷ κατ' εἰκόνα καὶ θεοὺς κατὰ μέθεξιν ἀπεργάσεται.

4 "Ὁρᾶτε πρὸς τὸν βασιλέα τῶν οὐρανῶν, ὁρᾶτε πρὸς τὰ ἀποκείμενα ἡμῖν αἰώνια ἀγαθὰ ἐν τοῖς οὐρανοῖς· σπουδάσατε λαβεῖν τὴν βασιλείαν τῶν οὐρανῶν, ὡς οἱ ἅγιοι ἅπαντες, ἵνα σὺν ἐκείνοις αἰωνίως ἀγάλλεσθε. Τίς ὑμῖν ὠφέλεια ἐπὶ τῶν ματαίων καὶ πονηρῶν, ἅτινα καὶ πρὸ τοῦ τέλους ἀφανίζονται καὶ ὑμᾶς ἀφανίζουσι καὶ κολάζουσιν; Ὁρᾶτε πρὸς τοὺς τάφους τῶν ἀνθρώπων, οἱ ἄνθρωποι· νοήσατε τοῦ κόσμου τὸ μάταιον, τοῦ πλούτου καὶ τῆς δόξης τὸ

"For this reason Christ, Who came and restored that image through divine baptism, has given us the salvific law that we should avoid all the wicked deeds of the Devil, and perform those salvific acts which He enjoins upon us, namely: love, faith and desire for God, and sanctification of the body, unfeigned love for one's neighbor, humility and truth, peace, patience and goodness, compassion and mercy, disdain for all vain and wicked things and rejection of soul-destroying passions; and to practice truth and righteousness and have fear of God, and endure the afflictions that beset us for the sake of the kingdom of heaven. For all we faithful people ought to remember always the vows which we made at holy baptism, and in Whom we have been baptized and believe; and to live like sons of God the almighty, following Christ, and to spit upon the Evil One and all his works and all his pomp, so that when the Lord comes *He may live within us and move* with a person who is in His image and make us gods by participation. 3

"Look to the king of heaven, look to the eternal blessings that are stored up for us in heaven. Make haste to attain the kingdom of heaven, like all the saints, so that you may rejoice eternally with them. For what benefit is there for you in vain and wicked things, which vanish even before your death and cause you to vanish and torment you? O men, look at the graves of men; understand the vanity of the world, the uncertainty and transience of wealth and 4

ἄστατον καὶ ἀκλήρωτον. Ποῦ δόξα ἢ εὐγένεια ἢ πλοῦτος ἐν τοῖς τάφοις, εἰ μὴ μόνον ὀστέα γυμνὰ καὶ ταῦτα κεχωσμένα ἐν κόνει ὀζώδει;

5   "Μέμνησθε, παρακαλῶ, τὰς αἰωνίους κολάσεις, ἐν αἷς κοιτάζονται οἱ ἁμαρτωλοὶ καὶ κολάζονται ἔκαστος κατὰ τὴν ἁμαρτίαν αὐτοῦ, ὡς προγέγραπται. Μέμνησθε τὸν ἐρχόμενον Κριτὴν καὶ Θεὸν ἡμῶν, τὸν μέλλοντα κρῖναι πάντας βροτούς, ὅστις καὶ ἀποδώσει ἑκάστῳ κατὰ τὴν πρᾶξιν αὐτοῦ [Matthew 16:27]. Θρηνήσατε πρὸ τοῦ θρήνου ἐκείνου τῆς ἀποφάσεως, κλαύσατε πρὸ τοῦ κλαυθμῶνος τοῦ ἀπαρακλήτου ἐκείνου. Σπουδάσατε, ἕως καιρὸν ἔχετε, μήπως προφθάσῃ τὸ τέλος ἐν ἀνομίαις ὑμᾶς καὶ πορευθῶμεν εἰς γέενναν τοῦ αἰωνίου πυρός [Matthew 5:22]. Σπεύσατε ἐν μετανοίᾳ λαβεῖν, οἱ ἁμαρτωλοί, τὴν συγχώρησιν πρὸ τοῦ τέλους ὑμῶν, ἵνα ἐλέους τύχητε Θεοῦ καὶ φιλανθρωπίας, ὡς εὔχομαι, καὶ βασιλείας τῶν οὐρανῶν· ἀμήν, γένοιτο πρεσβείαις τῆς Θεομήτορος."

33

Καὶ ταῦτα μὲν τοῖς κοσμικοῖς διδάσκων ἐφθέγγετο, τοῖς δὲ μονάζουσιν τὰ τῆς ὑπομονῆς καὶ ἀσκήσεως καὶ ὑπακοῆς καὶ ἡσυχίας παλαίσματα καὶ χαρίσματα τὰ οὐράνια, λέγων· "Σπουδάζετε, τρέχετε πρὸς οὐράνια, οἱ στρατιῶται Χριστοῦ. Βάλετε τὰ βέλη τῆς πίστεως κατ᾽

glory. Where is glory or nobility or wealth in the grave if there are only bare bones and even those are covered with foul-smelling dirt?

"Be mindful, I beg you, of the eternal punishments in 5 which sinners must rest, each of them punished in accordance with his sin, as has been previously written. Be mindful of our Judge and God Who will come, Who is going to judge all mortals, Who *will repay every man for what he has done.* Lament before the lamentation of that judgment, weep before that inconsolable weeping. Make haste while you still have time, lest death anticipate you in your lawlessness and we proceed into *the gehenna of* eternal *fire.* O sinners, make haste before your death to receive forgiveness through repentance, so that you may obtain the mercy and compassion of God, and the kingdom of heaven, as I pray. Amen, may this come to pass through the intercessions of the Mother of God."

Chapter 33

He used to utter these words of instruction to the laymen, but to the monks he spoke of the heavenly struggles and gifts of perseverance, asceticism, obedience, and spiritual tranquility, saying, "Make haste, run toward what is heavenly, O soldiers of Christ. Hurl the missiles of faith

Ἐχθροῦ, ὅπως αὐτὸν ἐκνικήσητε, ἅτινά εἰσιν· νηστεῖαι, ἀγρυπνίαι, προσευχαί, δάκρυα, μετάνοια καὶ ταπείνωσις, ἐξαγόρευσις τῶν λογισμῶν καὶ καρτερία ἐν πειρασμοῖς, ὑπακοὴ καὶ ὑποταγὴ καὶ ὑπομονὴ ἐπὶ πάντα. Ὡς ἄλλον ἅλας οὐράνιον, *χαίρετε, οἱ μονάζοντες, οἱ παρθενίαν ἀσκοῦντες, ὅτι ὁ μισθὸς ὑμῶν πολὺς ἐν τῷ οὐρανῷ ὑπάρχει*." Διὰ τοῦτο καὶ *ἐπαγαλλόμενος ἔχαιρεν* [see Matthew 5:12–13], ὅταν ὡμίλειν τοῖς μοναχοῖς, καὶ *ἐσκίρταν* [see Luke 6:23] τῷ Πνεύματι.

2   Ταὐτὸ καὶ τοῖς ἡσυχάζουσιν τὰ τῆς καρδιακῆς προσευχῆς καὶ θεωρίας τῆς νοερᾶς τὰ σημεῖα καὶ τὰς ἀπλανεῖς ἐν αὐτῶν ἐνεργείας σοφῶς καθηρμήνευεν καὶ ἐφώτιζεν λέγων· "Ὅταν ἐν ἡσυχίᾳ ἀρεμβάστῳ καὶ εἰρηνικῇ καταστάσει ὁ νοῦς τῶν πάντων ἀπορραγῇ πραγμάτων καὶ νοημάτων καὶ μόνος γένηται ἐν τῇ μνήμῃ Χριστοῦ καὶ σὺν τῇ καρδίᾳ τὴν προσευχὴν ἀεννάως ἱερουργῇ ἐν αὐτῇ, τότε μετὰ ταπεινώσεως ὀφείλει ὡς σκῆπτρον κατέχειν τὴν προσευχήν, ἵνα μὴ κλαπῇ ἐξ οἰήσεως. Ὅταν δ᾽ ἐπιμόνως τὴν εὐχὴν ὁ νοῦς ἐν τῇ καρδίᾳ σὺν τῇ μνήμῃ κατέχῃ τοῦ Ἰησοῦ, εἰ μὲν ἀπλανῶς, πρῶτον μὲν φωτίζεται τῷ νοΐ καὶ κατανύσσεται τῇ καρδίᾳ, εἶθ᾽ οὕτως καὶ πρὸς θεῖα ὑπερφυῆ νοήματα καταυγάζεται ἐξ ἀΰλου θείου φωτὸς ἐν τῷ πνεύματι καὶ πρὸς θεωρίας ἀνάγεται λαμπροτέρας, τὸν Χριστὸν ἔχων ἔνδον ἐν τῇ καρδίᾳ ἐνθρόνιον, ἵν᾽ εἴπω μεμορφωμένον, τὴν ταπείνωσιν, τὴν ἀγάπην καὶ τὴν εἰρήνην σὺν δάκρυσι σημειούμενον ἔξωθεν. Εἰ δὲ ἐξ οἰήσεως κατέχει τάχα τὴν προσευχήν, πρῶτον μὲν σκοτίζεται τῷ νοΐ, εἶθ᾽ οὕτως σκληρύνεται καὶ καρδίαν ὁ ἄθλιος καὶ

against the Enemy, so that you may vanquish him; those missiles which are: fasts, vigils, prayers, tears, repentance and humility, confession of wicked thoughts and endurance in tribulation, obedience, submission, and perseverance in all things. Like another heavenly *salt, rejoice,* O monks, you who practice celibacy, because *your reward* is *great in heaven.*" Therefore he used to *rejoice* and *be glad* when he spoke to the monks, and *leaped for joy* in the Spirit.

In the same way he used to explain wisely and enlighten those who lived in spiritual tranquility about the signs of the prayer of the heart and mental contemplation and their unerring energies, saying: "When, as a result of unwavering spiritual tranquility and peaceful composure, the mind is torn away from all mundane matters and thoughts, and is given solely to recollection of Christ and, along with the heart, constantly devotes itself to prayer, then the mind should hold onto that prayer with humility like a staff, so that it may not be stolen away by self-conceit. When the mind clings steadily to the prayer of the heart together with the recollection of Jesus, if it does so unerringly, first of all the person is enlightened in the mind and stricken with contrition in the heart, then he is illuminated in the spirit by immaterial divine light toward divine supernatural thoughts, and is led upward toward more brilliant visions, having Christ internally enthroned in his heart, so that, dare I say, the fact that he is conformed with Him internally is signified externally by his humility, love and peace with tears. But if, on the other hand, he should cling to this prayer out of self-conceit, first of all his mind will be darkened, then the wretched man will be hardened in his heart and become

γίνεται πνεῦμα πλάνης ὑπόπτωτος, καὶ θυμοῦται, ὀργίζεται, δοξομανεῖ βλοσυρῷ τῷ ὄμματι καὶ ἀδακρυτί· σκοτεινὰ
νοήματα καὶ πονηρά, καὶ ἐργασίαι οὐκ ἁρμόζουσαι."

3   Ταῦτα διδάσκων ἐφώνει τοῖς ἡσυχάζουσιν· "Ὁρᾶτε,
προσέχετε ἑαυτούς, μήπως ἀντὶ προβάτου λύκον προσ-
άξετε. Ὁ δοκῶν ἑστάναι βλεπέτω μὴ πέσῃ" [1 Corinthians
10:12]. Καὶ ταῦτα λέγων, ἐν μιᾷ τῶν ἡμερῶν ἐλθὼν Νικόδημος μοναχός, λέγει αὐτῷ· "Ἀδελφὲ Νικόδημε, συντόμως
ἔχω τελειωθῆναι." Καὶ τὴν ἡμέραν δήλην ἐποίησεν τῆς
κοιμήσεως· καὶ τοὺς μέλλοντας τυχεῖν εἰς τὴν κηδείαν αὐτοῦ, τὰς ἐπωνυμίας προεῖπεν.

34

Καὶ οὕτως ἐκοιμήθην ὁ ἅγιος Μάξιμος ὁ Καυσοκαλύβης τῇ τρισκαιδεκάτῃ τοῦ Ἰανουαρίου μηνός, ἐτῶν
γενόμενος πέντε καὶ ἐνενήκοντα· καὶ ἐτάφη ἐν τῷ μνημείῳ
τῷ λαξευθέν<τι> ὑπ' αὐτοῦ πλησίον τοῦ κελλίου αὐτοῦ,
κηδεύσαντες αὐτὸν καὶ μόνοι οὓς προεῖπεν ὁ ἅγιος. Οὐ
γὰρ ἐβούλετο μετὰ παρρησίας καὶ πλήθους λαοῦ γενέσθαι
τὴν κοίμησιν αὐτοῦ· διὰ τοῦτο κατὰ τὴν κέλευσιν αὐτοῦ
καὶ οὕτως ἐγένετο· νόμον δοὺς τοῖς κηδεύσασιν τὸ ἅγιον
αὐτοῦ λείψανον, ἵνα μὴ γένηταί ποτε τούτου μετάθεσις ἐν
ἄλλῳ τόπῳ διὰ τὴν δόξαν, μηδ' ἐκ τοῦ ἁγίου λειψάνου
μερίδαν τις ἄρῃ ποτέ, ἀλλὰ μένειν σῶον οὕτως ἐν ἀδοξίᾳ,
ἐν ᾧ τόπῳ ἡσύχασεν.

subject to a spirit of error, and grow angry, become enraged, and thirst for fame with a grim look in his eyes and no tears. His thoughts are dark and wicked, and his deeds inappropriate."

After these words of instruction, he told those who lived ₃ in spiritual tranquility: "See that you pay attention to yourselves, lest you introduce a wolf instead of a sheep. *Let anyone who thinks that he is standing take heed lest he fall.*" After he said these words, one day the monk Nikodemos came, and Maximos said to him: "Brother Nikodemos, I am going to die soon." And he indicated the day of his death, and foretold the names of those who were going to attend his funeral.

Chapter 34

Thus the holy Maximos the Hutburner died on the thirteenth day of the month of January, at the age of ninety-five; and he was buried in the grave which he had excavated near his cell, and only those whose names the holy man had foretold attended his burial. For he did not wish his burial to be conducted lavishly and with a multitude of people. For this reason the following also happened in accordance with his bidding: with regard to his holy corpse, he gave binding instructions to those who buried him, that it should never be translated to another location for the sake of glory, nor should anyone ever take a piece of his holy corpse, but that it should remain intact in obscurity, in the place where he had lived as a contemplative solitary.

2   Ὡς δὲ δήλη ἡ μετάστασις τοῦ ἁγίου τοῖς πᾶσιν ἐγένετο, ἡ μὲν Μεγίστη Λαύρα ὡς ἄλλην ὀρφανίαν τοῦτ᾽ ἐλογίσαντο, ὥσπερ ἐν τῇ μεταστάσει τοῦ ἁγίου Ἀθανασίου, καὶ μετὰ πένθους καὶ δακρύων πολλῶν συναχθέντες ἔνδον τῆς Λαύρας, τὰς ᾠδὰς ἀνεπλήρωσαν τῆς αὐτοῦ κοιμήσεως μετὰ λαμπάδων καὶ θυμιαμάτων πολλῶν. Βουληθέντες δὲ μετακομίσαι καὶ τὸ ἅγιον αὐτοῦ λείψανον ἐν τῇ θαυμαστῇ Λαύρᾳ καὶ κηδεῦσαι ἐντίμως ὡς πρέπει ἁγίοις, οὐκ ἐτόλμησαν τοῦτο ποιῆσαι διὰ τὸν νόμον ὃν ἔθετο, τοῦ ἀμετάθετον μεῖναι τὸ ἅγιον αὐτοῦ λείψανον ἐν τῷ κελλίῳ αὐτοῦ, ὡς ἔφην ὁ ἅγιος. Καὶ οὕτως μὲν οἱ ἐν τῇ Λαύρᾳ.

3   Οἱ δ᾽ ἔξωθεν ἅπαντες, οἱ καθήμενοι ἐν τῷ Ἄθωνι κύκλωθεν ἡσυχάζοντες καὶ ἀσκοῦντες, μοναστοὶ καὶ μιγάδες, νέοι καὶ γέροντες, κατασυστάδην γενόμενοι πρῶτον μὲν τὴν ὀρφανίαν καὶ οὗτοι μεγάλως ἐπένθησαν· ὡς γὰρ πατέρα καὶ φωστῆρα ὑπέρλαμπρον εἶχον ἐν μέσῳ αὐτῶν καὶ διδάσκαλον τἀληθῆ ἡσυχίας καὶ μοναδικῆς πολιτείας. Εἶθ᾽ οὕτως καὶ τὰ τῆς ταφῆς καὶ μνήμης μνημόσυνα τοῦ ἁγίου ἐποίησαν καὶ ποιοῦσιν κατ᾽ ἔτος· καὶ πρὸς τὸν τάφον αὐτοῦ παραγίνονται, πόθον ἀποπληροῦντες ὃν εἶχον ἅπαντες οὗτοι εἰς τὸν ἅγιον Μάξιμον.

4   Τὰ δὲ κύκλωθεν τοῦ Ἁγίου Ὄρους βασιλικὰ σεβάσμια μοναστήρια, τούτου μαθόντες τὴν κοίμησιν, οὐκ ἔχ᾽ ὅπως διηγήσασθαι τὴν λύπην ἣν ἔσχον οἱ μονάζοντες ἐν αὐτοῖς μοναχοὶ καὶ σεβάσμιοι γέροντες, μετὰ δακρύων καὶ οὗτοι ἀποκλαιόμενοι τοῦ ἁγίου τὴν στέρησιν, λέγοντες· "Οἴμοι, τί πεπόνθαμεν, ζημιωθέντες τῆς ὁμιλίας τοῦ ἁγίου πατρός, τοῦ διδασκάλου, τοῦ φωστῆρος, τοῦ ἀπλανοῦς ὁδηγοῦ,

When the holy one's passing became known to everyone, 2 the Great Lavra regarded this as though it had been orphaned again, just as at the passing of the holy Athanasios, and after assembling with sorrow and many tears within the Lavra, they performed the hymns for his laying to rest with candles and much incense. Although they wished to transfer his holy corpse into the wondrous Lavra and give it the honorable burial fitting for holy men, they did not dare to do this because of the binding instructions he had laid down that his holy body should remain untranslated in his cell, as the holy one said. This is what those at the Lavra did.

As for everyone elsewhere, those who resided all over 3 Athos in spiritual tranquility and ascetic practice, solitaries and cenobitics, young monks and elders, they assembled and first greatly lamented their orphanhood; for they viewed him as a father and exceedingly bright luminary in their midst, and as a true teacher of spiritual tranquility and monastic conduct. Then they carried out the funeral and commemoration of the holy man's memory, and they continue to do so every year; and they come to his grave, fulfilling the yearning which they all had for the holy Maximos.

As for the venerable imperial monasteries all over the 4 Holy Mountain, I cannot describe the sorrow felt by the monks and venerable elders who lived in them when they learned of his death; and they too tearfully bewailed the loss of the holy man, saying, "O woe, what have we suffered, being deprived of the company of the holy father, the teacher, the luminary, the unerring guide, the seer and prophet and

τοῦ προγνώστου καὶ προφήτου καὶ βοηθοῦ πάντων ἡμῶν
ἐν ταῖς θλίψεσι; Τίς ἄλλος ἡμῖν τοιοῦτος γένηται ὁδηγὸς
ἀγαθὸς καὶ παρήγορος ὡς οὗτος ὁ ἅγιος;" Ἐν τούτῳ καὶ
οὗτοι τὰ μνημόσυνα ἀπετέλεσαν καὶ ἀποπληροῦσιν ἀεί-
ποτε· καὶ τὰ τοῦ ἁγίου ἀνδραγαθήματα καὶ θεῖα χαρίσματα
εἰσαείποτε διηγούμενοι τοῖς πᾶσιν ἀνακηρύττουσιν. Καὶ
οὕτω μὲν ἐν Ὄρει Ἁγίῳ τὸν ἅγιον δοξάζουσι καὶ ἀνυμνοῦ-
σιν ὡς ἅγιον.

5   Ἄνω δὲ ἐν οὐρανοῖς ἡ Τριάς, Πατήρ, Υἱὸς καὶ ἅγιον
Πνεῦμα, τὸ καθαρώτατον καὶ ἡγιασμένον αὐτοῦ πνεῦμα
ὑποδεξαμένη ἐν σκηναῖς ἁγίων κατέταξεν καὶ ἐδόξασεν ὡς
θεράποντα μέγιστον *τῆς τρισηλίου αὐτῆς μιᾶς καὶ ἀδι-
αιρέτου θεότητος*. Καὶ φωτίζεται ἐξ αὐτῶν τῶν τριῶν φῶς
ἄστεκτον, ἀδιαίρετον, ἀνεκλάλητον, ἐν ᾧ φωτίζονται πάντων τῶν ἀσωμάτων θείων δυνάμεων αἱ τάξεις καὶ τῶν
ἁγίων πᾶσα πανήγυρις. Καὶ γὰρ διὰ φωτὸς βιοτεύσας
ἁγίου (ὥς φησι, "Φῶς δικαίοις διὰ παντός" [Proverbs 13:9]),
ἀπ᾽ ἐντεῦθεν πρὸς φῶς ἀνέσπερον τῆς θεότητος διὰ φωτὸς
ἁγίου ἐκεῖσε ἐγένετο καὶ παρίσταται τῷ Χριστῷ, ὃν ἐπόθη-
σεν ἐκ νεότητος, καὶ πρεσβεύει ὑπὲρ ἡμῶν καὶ ἀγάλλεται
σὺν ἁγίοις καὶ ἀσωμάτοις θείαις δυνάμεσι.

6   Θαυμαστὸν δὲ οὐδέν, εἰ καὶ οὐ γεγόνασιν θαύματα ἐν
τῇ κοιμήσει αὐτοῦ. Ἐπειδὴ τὸ ἄδοξον καὶ πενιχρὸν καὶ
ἄκομπον ἐν ὅλῃ τῇ ζωῇ αὐτοῦ ἠγάπαν ὁ ἅγιος, διὰ τοῦτο
καὶ ἐν τῇ κέλλῃ αὐτοῦ εἰς τόπον ἥσυχον κατετέθη καὶ οὐχὶ
εἰς τὴν Μεγάλην Λαύραν τὴν θαυμαστήν. Εἰ γὰρ καὶ τοῦτο
ἐπόθειν, ἵνα καὶ μετὰ τὴν κοίμησιν αὐτοῦ ἀποτελῇ οὕτω
θαυμάσια καθὼς ἐν τῇ ζωῇ αὐτοῦ, πλουσιοπαρόχως ἂν

helper of us all in our tribulations? Who else can be such a good and consoling guide for us as this holy man?" In addition they too have performed and celebrated his commemoration in perpetuity; and narrating in perpetuity the holy man's feats and divine gifts, they proclaim them to all. And in this way they glorify the holy man on the Holy Mountain and hymn him as a saint.

Above, in heaven, the Trinity, Father, Son and Holy Spirit, 5 after receiving his most pure and hallowed spirit into the tabernacles of the saints, ordained and glorified him as a very great servant of *the one* and indivisible *godhead of three suns*. And by those three he was illuminated as an unbearable, indivisible, ineffable light, by which the ranks of all the incorporeal divine powers and all the assembly of saints are illuminated. For after spending his life in holy light (as is said, "*The righteous always have light*"), he then came through holy light toward the unsetting light of divinity and now stands before Christ, Whom he had desired since his youth, and intercedes on our behalf and rejoices with the saints and incorporeal divine powers.

It is not surprising that miracles did not occur at the time 6 of his death. Since the holy one loved obscurity and poverty and modesty throughout his entire life, he was laid to rest, for this reason, in his cell in a tranquil spot and not at the wondrous Great Lavra. For if it had been his desire to perform miracles after his death as he did during his life, he

ἀπετέλει, ὡς ἔχων τὴν χάριν πλουσίαν ἀείποτε. Ἀλλ' ὡς φησιν ὁ Σωτήρ· "Μὴ χαίρετε, ὅτι τὰ δαιμόνια ὑμῶν ὑποτάσσεται, ἀλλὰ χαίρετε, ὅτι τὰ ὀνόματα ὑμῶν ἐγράφη ἐν τοῖς οὐρανοῖς" [Luke 10:20]. Ἀλλ' οὐδὲ χρεία θαυμάτων ἐν ἐρήμῳ διὰ τὸ ἥσυχον· εἰ γὰρ ἐγένοντο θαύματα καὶ ἐν Ὄρει, ὁ κόσμος ἂν εἰσήρχετο καὶ τὸ ἥσυχον τοῦ Ὄρους ἐσκανδαλίζετο, καὶ ἐγεγόνει ἂν ἀντ' ὠφελείας βλάβη τοῖς ἡσυχάζουσιν· ἵνα δὲ μὴ σκανδαλίσῃ ἐν τούτῳ τοὺς πλείονας, οἶμαι, ἀκμὴν τῶν θαυμάτων κατέπαυσεν τὴν ἐνέργειαν.

35

Ὅμως ἐν τῷ τάφῳ αὐτοῦ μοναχός τις προσελθών, ὀνόματι Διονύσιος ὁ Κοντοστέφανος, τὴν κεφαλὴν αὐτοῦ κακῶς πάσχων ἐν ἡμέραις πολλαῖς, ὡς τῷ τάφῳ τοῦ ἁγίου μετὰ πίστεως καὶ πλῆθος δακρύων προσήγγισεν, καὶ μικρὸν ἀφυπνώσας, ἔξυπνος ἅμα καὶ ὑγιὴς γέγονεν, καὶ τὸν ἅγιον τὰ μέγιστα ηὐχαρίστησεν· καὶ ἐκ τοῦ χοὸς τοῦ τάφου τοῦ ἁγίου ἔμπροσθεν μικρὰν κόνιν λαβών, ὡς μύρον ἀνεφάνη θαυμάσιον, εὐωδίαν ἀποπληρῶν τὰς αἰσθήσεις ἀκόρεστον τῶν εἰδότων τὴν κόνιν καὶ μαρτυρούντων τῷ θαύματι.

2   Καὶ αὐτὸς ἐγὼ ἐκ τῆς ἱερᾶς μονῆς ὢν τοῦ Βατοπεδίου, ὁ καὶ ἰδὼν τὸν ἅγιον ἀνιπτάμενον τῆς γῆς ὕπερθεν, πολλὰ ἀσθενήσας καὶ πρὸς θάνατον καταντήσας καὶ τὰ λοίσθια

would have performed them in abundance, since he always had abundant grace. But as the Savior says, "*Do not rejoice in this, that the spirits are subject to you; but rejoice that your names are written in heaven.*" Anyway, there is no need for miracles in the wilderness on account of its tranquility; for if miracles kept occurring on the Mountain too, the world would run to it and the tranquility of the Mountain would be disturbed, and this would result in harm instead of benefit to those who live in spiritual tranquility; and I think it was so as not to disturb the majority in this way, that he now stopped working his miracles.

Chapter 35

Nonetheless, a monk named Dionysios Kontostephanos, who had suffered from a severe headache for many days, came to his grave; after he approached the holy one's grave with faith and many tears, he fell asleep for a while, and, as soon as he awoke, was cured; and he thanked the holy man very much. And when he took a little bit of dust from the dirt in front of the holy man's grave, it resembled a wondrous, perfumed oil, filling with unceasing fragrance the senses of those who experienced the dust and attested to the miracle.

I myself, who am from the holy monastery of Vatopedi, 2 the one who saw the holy man flying above the earth, I tearfully called upon the holy man when I was very ill and on

πνέοντα, μετὰ δακρύων τὸν ἅγιον ἐπεκαλεσάμην· καὶ ὡς δι' ὀνείρου φανεὶς ἀνεκτήσατό μοι, καὶ ἔζησα, καὶ τὸν Θεὸν οὕτως καὶ τὸν ἅγιον ηὐχαρίστησα καὶ ἐδόξαζον τὸ θαῦμα τῆς ἀναστάσεως.

3   Καὶ ἄλλος ἱερομόναχος, Νίφων ὀνόματι, ἅγιος ἡσυχάζων μετὰ καὶ ἄλλου ἀσκητοῦ, βουλόμενοι ἀποπειράσαι τοῦ ἁγίου τὸν τάφον, θείῳ ζήλῳ ὑπερβάντες τοῦ ἁγίου τὸν ὅρον, τολμηρῶς προσῆλθον τοῦ ἁγίου τὸν τάφον· καὶ σκαλίδας λαβόντες μόχθῳ πολλῷ ἀπὸ τῆς δεξιᾶς μερίδος τοῦ τάφου κατώρυξαν, καὶ ἐκ τοῦ ἁγίου λειψάνου μικρὰν μερίδα προσέλαβον· καὶ τοσαύτη, ἔλεγον, εὐωδία ἐκ τοῦ ἁγίου τὸν τάφον πλείστη ἐξῆλθεν, ὅσην οὐκ ἠδύναντο φέρειν ὑπερεύοσμον. Τὸ δὲ ἅγιον λείψανον ἦν ὥσπερ βρύον τὰ μύρα. Ἐν τούτῳ καὶ τὴν ἁγίαν μερίδα, ἣν ἀνελάβοντο, ἀπομάξαντες μετὰ σπόγγου ἐν ὕδατι μετέλαβον, καὶ τὰς αἰσθήσεις αὐτῶν καὶ τὰ πρόσωπα πιστῶς κατερράντισαν. Εἶτα συνέστειλαν πάλιν τὴν μερίδα ἐν τῷ ἁγίῳ λειψάνῳ ὡς πρότερον, ἵν' ὅπως ὑπάρχῃ σῶον, ὡς ἐδίδαξεν αὐτοῖς τοῦτο ὁ ἅγιος· καὶ χοῦν λαβόντες τὸν τάφον πάλιν κατησφαλίσαντο, ὡς τὸ πρότερον, εὐχαριστήσαντες καὶ δοξάσαντες τὸν Θεὸν τὸν οὕτω δοξάζοντα τοὺς ἁγίους αὐτοῦ. Καὶ πολλὰ εὐφραινόμενοι καθ' ἑκάστην πρὸς τὸν τάφον ἐγένοντο τοῦ ἁγίου καὶ τῆς εὐωδίας ἀπέλαυον. Ταὐτὸ καὶ πάντες οἱ πλησίον καθήμενοι.

4   Ὅθεν καὶ ἡμεῖς οἱ τὰ θαύματα καὶ τὸν βίον τοῦ ὁσίου τούτου καὶ θεοφόρου πατρὸς ἡμῶν Μαξίμου τοῦ Καυσοκαλύβη ἀκούοντες, πιστῶς προσδεξώμεθα· καὶ εὐχαριστήσωμεν καὶ δοξάσωμεν τὸν ἐν Τριάδι Θεόν, τὸν

the brink of death and breathing my last; and appearing as if in a dream he brought about my recovery and I survived, and therefore gave thanks to God and the holy man, and glorified the miracle of my recovery.

Another hieromonk, Niphon by name, a holy man who lived a life of spiritual tranquility, along with another ascetic, wished to make trial of the holy man's grave; in their divine zeal they transgressed the rule laid down by the holy one, and boldly attacked the holy one's grave. Taking shovels, they excavated the right side of the grave with much effort, and took a small piece of the holy corpse; and such a great fragrance was emitted from the holy one's grave, they said, that they were unable to endure the overpoweringly sweet smell. The holy corpse was bursting with perfumed oils, as it were. Meanwhile, they wiped off with a sponge the holy fragment which they had retrieved, transferred the perfumed exudations into water and, with faith, sprinkled their sensory organs and their faces. Then they put the piece back in the holy body as it was before, so that it could remain whole, as the holy one had instructed them; and taking dirt, they restored the grave to its former condition again, giving thanks and glorifying God Who thus glorifies His saints. And they used to visit the holy one's grave every day with great joy, and would savor the fragrance. The same was true of all those who lived nearby.

So let us, who hear about the miracles and the life of this our holy and divinely inspired father, Maximos the Hutburner, accept them with faith; and let us give thanks and

δοξάζοντα οὕτω τοὺς ἁγίους αὐτοῦ, ᾧ πρέπει πᾶσα δόξα, τιμὴ καὶ προσκύνησις τῷ Πατρὶ καὶ τῷ Υἱῷ καὶ τῷ ἁγίῳ Πνεύματι, νῦν καὶ ἀεὶ καὶ εἰς τοὺς αἰῶνας τῶν αἰώνων, ἀμήν.

glorify God in the Trinity, Who thus glorifies His saints, to Whom is due all glory, honor and reverence, to the Father and the Son and the Holy Spirit, now and forever and unto the ages of ages, Amen.

LIFE OF NIPHON
OF ATHOS

Βίος καὶ πολιτεία τοῦ ὁσίου καὶ θεοφόρου πατρὸς ἡμῶν Νίφωνος τοῦ ἐν τῷ Ἄθῳ Ὄρει ἀσκήσαντος

I

Οὗτος ὁ ὅσιος πατὴρ ἡμῶν ὑπῆρχεν ἀπὸ τὸ δεσποτᾶτον τὸ διακείμενον μέσον Ἀχαΐας καὶ Ἰλλυρικοῦ, ἐκ κώμης καλουμένης Λουκόβης, παντοίοις κομώσης καρποῖς· ἐν ᾗ κατῴκει τῶν τοῦ Χριστοῦ μυστηρίων ἱερεύς, εὐλαβείᾳ τεθραμμένος καὶ ὅλος τοῦ Πνεύματος τοῦ ἁγίου, ὃν δηλώσει ὁ ἐξ αὐτοῦ γεννηθεὶς οἷος ἦν τὴν ἀρετὴν διαβόητος, εἴπερ ἐκ τοῦ καρποῦ τὸ δένδρον γινώσκεται [Matthew 12:33]. Ἐκ τούτου ὁ ὅσιος πατὴρ γεννηθείς, εὐθὺς ἐκ πρώτης τριχὸς τῆς ἀρετῆς ἦν ἐραστὴς ὁ ἀκρότατος. Τῷ γὰρ δεκάτῳ ἔτει τῆς ἡλικίας αὐτοῦ ὁ πρὸς πατρὸς αὐτῷ θεῖος, ἐκκλησιάρχης ὢν τῆς ἐκεῖσε τοῦ παμμάκαρος ἁγίου Νικολάου μονῆς (ἣν ὁ ἀοίδιμος ἐκεῖνος βασιλεὺς ὁ Μονομάχος ἐν τῷ Μεσοποτάμῳ οὕτω καλουμένῳ ἀνήγειρε), προσλαβόμενος πρῶτα μὲν αὐτὸν τὰ ἱερὰ ἐξεπαίδευσε γράμματα, ἔπειτα κατὰ μοναχοὺς ἀποκείρει· καὶ ἀναγνώστην τοῦ ἱεροῦ ἀποστόλου σφραγίσας, μετὰ μικρὸν ὡς εἶδε τῇ ἡλικίᾳ συναύξουσαν καὶ τὴν ἀρετήν, καὶ ἱερέα καθίστησι τοῦ Χριστοῦ μυστηρίων.

The life and conduct of our holy and divinely inspired father, Niphon, who lived the ascetic life on Mount Athos

Chapter 1

This holy father of ours, Niphon, came from the despotate that lies between Achaia and Illyrikon, from a village called Loukove, renowned for producing all sorts of fruit. In this village lived a priest of Christ's mysteries, who was nourished with piety and full of the Holy Spirit, a claim that, if ever *a tree is known by its fruit,* will be proved by his son, who was so famous for his virtue. The holy father, being born to such a man, was a consummate lover of virtue, right from the time he grew his first hair. When he was ten years old, his paternal uncle took charge of him. This man, who was sacristan at the monastery of the all-blessed Saint Nicholas there (which the renowned emperor Monomachos had founded at the place called Mesopotamon), first taught Niphon the holy Scriptures and then tonsured him as a monk. He confirmed him as a lector of the holy apostolic epistles, and, a short time after, when he saw that Niphon's virtue had increased with his age, also ordained him as a priest of Christ's mysteries.

2   Ὁ δὲ φύσεως ὀξύτητι καὶ τὴν παρ' ἑαυτοῦ σπουδὴν συνεισενεγκών, πλείστων ἐν ὀλίγοις ἔτεσι ἐπιΐστωρ ἐγένετο. Ἀλλ' ἔπληττε θεῖος ἔρως αὐτὸν καὶ ἡσυχίας σπινθὴρ ὀλίγος καταβληθεὶς εἰς μέγα ἀνεδίδου πυρσόν. Καὶ δὴ πλησίον ἐκεῖσε γέροντα καταλαμβάνει τινὰ πρὸ χρόνων ἀπὸ τοῦ Σιναΐου ἀφιγμένον ὄρους, ἐν ὄρει καθήμενον οὕτω καλούμενον Γηρομέριον, καὶ μόνῳ Θεῷ προσανέχοντα· παρ' οὗ κανόνας ἡσυχίας καὶ τύπους ἀκριβεῖς μονώσεως πειραθεὶς οὐκέτι κατέχειν οἷός τε ἦν ἑαυτόν, τῇ τῆς ἡσυχίας ἡδονῇ καταβακχευθείς. Πρὸς γὰρ τοῖς ἄλλοις οἷς κατὰ Θεὸν προέκοπτε καὶ ἐπὶ μεῖζον ἐξῄρετο, καὶ τοῦτο ἦν κατωρθωκὼς τῇ τοῦ Χριστοῦ χάριτι· εἰς γὰρ ἕνα πόδα ἱστάμενος ὅλον ἀπεστομάτιζε τὸ ψαλτήριον.

2

Ἀκηκοὼς δὲ τὸν Ἄθω πολλοὺς ἔχοντα τότε διαφανεῖς ἁγίους καὶ τοῦ Θεοῦ μιμητάς, καὶ πατρίδα καὶ γένος καὶ τὴν ἄλλην πᾶσαν οὐσίαν χαίρειν εἰπών, ὅλῳ ποδὶ πρὸς τὸν Ἄθω χωρεῖ. Καὶ σκοπήσας ὅπου πλεῖστοι καὶ κάλλιστοι τῶν ἁγίων τυγχάνουσιν, ὁδηγεῖται θεόθεν· καὶ πρὸς τὰ μέρη τῆς Λαύρας γενόμενος, εὑρίσκει τινὰ μοναχὸν καὶ ὀνόματι καὶ σχήματι καὶ ταῖς κατὰ Θεὸν ἀναβάσεσιν ὄντως Θεόγνωστον, ἔνθα πρὶν Πέτρος ὁ Ἀθωνίτης ἀρετῆς τὸ θεμέλιον κατεβάλετο· ᾧ τὰ μὲν καθ' ἑαυτὸν ἀνατίθησι

Niphon, who combined natural astuteness with innate   2
zeal, became well versed in most matters in a few years. But
he was smitten with divine love and, when a tiny spark of
spiritual tranquility was struck, this burst into a great blaze.
He went to an elder near there who had come from Mount
Sinai some years before, but who had now settled down on
the mountain known as Geromerion, where he had devoted
himself to God alone. When Niphon had been trained by
this elder in the experience of the rules of spiritual tranquility and the precise forms of the solitary life, he could no
longer restrain himself, for he had become obsessed with
the pleasure of spiritual tranquility. In addition to the other
matters in which he made progress toward God and grew
better, he even managed by Christ's grace to accomplish this
feat: recite the whole psalter while standing on one foot.

Chapter 2

Niphon heard that there were many illustrious holy men
and imitators of God on Athos at that time, and so he bid
farewell to his homeland, his family, and all his possessions,
and traveled the whole way to Athos on foot. After he had
found out where most of the outstanding holy men were living, he was led there by God. When he reached the region
of the Lavra, at the spot where Peter the Athonite had in the
past laid the foundations of his virtue, he came across a
monk who, by name, disposition, and spiritual development
truly was Theognostos. Niphon told him about himself and

καὶ τὸν ἴδιον ἀνακαλύπτει σκοπόν, ἡσυχίας χάριν παραγενέσθαι εἰπών· τὸ δὲ τῆς ἱερωσύνης οὐκ ἐξεῖπεν ἀξίωμα οὐδὲ τῶν παρ' ἑαυτῷ πλεονεκτημάτων τὸ πλῆθος. Ὁ δὲ ἀσμένως τε δέχεται καὶ δίδωσι τὰ παρ' ἑαυτοῦ καὶ λαμβάνει τὰ παρ' ἐκείνου. Μετὰ δὲ τρίτον ἐνιαυτὸν ἐγνώστη τῷ γέροντι τὰ κατὰ τὸν μέγαν, ὡς εἴη μὲν ἱερεύς, ἔστι δὲ καὶ χάρισι πλείσταις κεκοσμημένος· καὶ τοῦ λοιποῦ μηκέτι καθ' ὑποταγὴν αὐτῷ συνεῖναι τὸν μέγαν ἠξίου, ἀλλ' ἀδελφικῶς ἄμφω καθῆσθαι τὸ χρυσοῦν τῆς ἀρετῆς ζεῦγος ἐλαύνοντας. Ὁ δέ, "Πῶς ἄν τις," ἔφη, "καθ' ἑαυτὸν ἡσυχάσειεν, μὴ πρότερον ὑποταγῇ τὰ μέλη κολάσας καὶ τὰς αἰσθήσεις χειραγωγῶν πρὸς τὴν ἡσυχίαν τε καὶ τὴν μόνωσιν;" Ὡς δ' οὐδὲν εὕρισκε καταπειθῆ τὸν Θεόγνωστον, ἐκεῖθεν ἀναχωρεῖ, μέγιστον κέρδος ἐπιφερόμενος ὅπερ ἐκεῖσε κατώρθωσε δάκρυον. Καὶ πρὸς τὸ κάθισμα τοῦ ἐν ἁγίοις πατρὸς ἡμῶν Βασιλείου τοῦ μεγάλου παραγεγονὼς τεσσαρεσκαιδέκατον ἔτος ἐκεῖσε διήνυσεν, ἅπαξ τῆς ἑβδομάδος γευόμενος ἄρτου ξηροῦ.

3

Κατ' ἐκεῖνο τοίνυν καιροῦ λοιμική τις νόσος ἐνέσκηψε τῇ ἱερᾷ Λαύρᾳ καὶ τῇ τοῦ θανάτου ὀξείᾳ ῥομφαίᾳ τοὺς πάντας σχεδὸν συνδιέφθειρεν, ὥστε καὶ τοὺς ἱερεῖς συναπολέσθαι καὶ ὀλίγους καταλειφθῆναί τινας. Μεταπεμψάμενος οὖν αὐτὸν ὁ τότε τῆς ἱερᾶς καὶ διαφανοῦς

revealed his personal goal to him, saying that he had come to achieve the grace of spiritual tranquility; but he did not mention his priestly rank nor his host of accomplishments. Theognostos gladly welcomed Niphon, and gave him what he had to offer while receiving the same from Niphon. After three years had passed, however, the elder found out that the great Niphon was both a priest and had been adorned with very many spiritual gifts. From then on Theognostos no longer thought it appropriate for the great one to live in obedience to him, but instead wanted them both to live as monastic brothers together, *driving the golden chariot* of virtue. But Niphon replied, "How can anyone achieve spiritual tranquility on his own without having first disciplined the parts of his body by obedience and having trained his senses for spiritual tranquility and solitude?" He was unable to persuade Theognostos, however, and so he left that place, taking with him the greatest profit he achieved there, the gift of tears. He went to the hermitage of our father among the saints, Basil the Great, and spent fourteen years there, eating dry bread once a week.

Chapter 3

At that time a pestilential epidemic fell upon the holy Lavra and destroyed almost everyone with the sharp sword of death, so that even the priests perished and only a few of them were left alive. The superior of the holy and illustrious

προϊστάμενος Λαύρας, εἰσελθεῖν εἰς τὸ μοναστήριον ἠξίου καὶ τῷ ἱερατείῳ καταλεγῆναι. Ὁ δὲ ἰδιωτείαν καὶ ἀγροικίαν προβαλλόμενος τὴν ἐπαινετήν, ἑτέραν ἐνεχειρίσθη διακονίαν, τοῖς ἐκτὸς καθίσμασι πᾶσιν ἐπιφοιτᾶν καὶ τὴν συνήθη ἀκολουθίαν διέρχεσθαι καὶ τὴν ἱερὰν μυσταγωγίαν ἐκτελεῖν· ὅπερ μόλις μέν, κατεδέξατο δ' οὖν, ὀφείλων καὶ πρὸς τὸν ἀρχηγὸν τῆς μονῆς τὴν ὀφειλομένην ὑποταγήν· καὶ διετέλεσεν οὕτω τὴν τοιαύτην λειτουργίαν διακονῶν χρόνοις ἐπὶ τρισίν. Εἶτα ὁ τῆς ἡσυχίας αὖθις πόθος διάπυρος ἐπιστὰς ἐτυράννει τε καὶ ἀνέφλεγε καὶ οὐκ εἴα τὸν ἅγιον ἠρεμεῖν. Διὰ τοῦτο καὶ πάντα θέμενος οὐδέν, εἰς τὰ Βουλευτήρια παραγίνεται.

4

Κἀκεῖσε χρόνοις συχνοῖς διετέλεσεν ἄστεγος καὶ μόναις βοτάναις τρεφόμενος, ὥστε καὶ πολλοὺς εἰς φθόνον κινηθέντας πλάνην τοῦ ἁγίου καταψηφίσασθαι. Οἳ καὶ πρὸς τὸν τῆς Λαύρας προϊστάμενον ἀπελθόντες ἀναστῆσαι κείμενον ἐν τῷ τῆς πλάνης σκότῳ τὸν μέγαν ἠξίουν. Ὁ δ' αὖθις τοῦτον μεταπεμψάμενος, "Ἵνα τί," φησίν, "ἄσαρκον καὶ ἀναίμονα βίον ἀνύεις, παρ' οὗ καὶ οἴησις ἀναφύεται καὶ πλάνη, καὶ οὐ τὴν ἀπλανῆ καὶ μέσην βαδίζεις, ἥτις ἐστὶν εὐχερής τε καὶ ἀδιάπτωτος; Εἰς γὰρ τὰς ἐρήμους οἱ πατέρες διὰ τοῦτο βοτάναις ἐτρέφοντο, διὰ τὴν ἀπορίαν τῶν

Lavra at that time thus summoned Niphon and asked him to enter the monastery and be enrolled as a cleric. Niphon, however, used his laudable rusticity and uncouthness as an excuse, and was entrusted with a different duty, that of visiting all the outlying hermitages, reciting the regular liturgy, and celebrating the holy sacrament. Even this duty he agreed to reluctantly, and only because he owed obligatory obedience to the superior of the monastery. He thus spent three years performing this ministry. But then the burning desire for spiritual tranquility came over the holy Niphon again and overpowered him and inflamed him and would not leave him in peace. For this reason, and because he considered that nothing else mattered, he went to Bouleuteria.

Chapter 4

Niphon spent many years there, living in the open air and eating only plants. As a result many became envious and condemned the saint for going astray. These men even went to the superior of the Lavra and asked him to raise up the great Niphon who lay in the darkness of error. The superior summoned him again and said, "Why are you leading a life that is not one of flesh and blood, one that, moreover, gives rise to conceit and error, rather than treading the sure, middle path which is without risk and free of snares? The reason the fathers ate plants in the desert was because they lacked

ἄρτων. Ἐνταῦθα δὲ καὶ ἄρτος καὶ ἕτερα πρὸς διατροφὴν ἐπιτήδεια· κἀκείνοις ἀρκούμενον δεῖ τὴν οἴησιν ἀποπέμπεσθαι." Ὁ δὲ τὴν ἰδίαν μᾶλλον ταπείνωσιν ἐνδεικνύμενος πείθεται ταῖς ἐκείνου ὑποθήκαις· καὶ πρὸς τὸν σεβάσμιον ναὸν τοῦ Σωτῆρος παραγίνεται· ἔνθα τὴν ἱερὰν καθαιρεθεῖσαν τράπεζαν εὑρών, τὸν Ἱερισσοῦ ἠξίου ἐπίσκοπον ὡς ἂν αὐτὸς ἐκεῖσε παραγενόμενος αὖθις αὐτὴν ἀποκαταστήσῃ. Ὁ δὲ τοῦτον ἐπιτρέπει τοῦτο ποιῆσαι καὶ ἀρκεῖν ἀντ᾽ ἐκείνου φάναι. Καὶ δὴ καὶ πεποίηκε.

2 Καὶ τὴν ἱερὰν ἐκεῖσε διετέλει μυσταγωγίαν. Ὡς δὲ συχνὸν ἐκεῖσε πατέρων πλῆθος συνῆκτο, ὑπὸ καθηγητῇ τῷ μεγάλῳ τελεῖν ἐθελόντων καὶ ῥυθμίζεσθαι παρ᾽ ἐκείνου καὶ διαπλάττεσθαι πρὸς τὰς τρίβους τῆς ἀρετῆς, ἀναχωρεῖ μὲν ἐκεῖθεν εὐθύς, πρὸς δὲ τὸν πυρπολοῦντα τὴν καλύβην Μάξιμον παραγίνεται· καὶ πολλοὺς ἐκεῖσε διαβιβάσας ἡλίους, οὕτω δεσμοῖς ἀγάπης συνεδέθη τῷ γέροντι ὡς ὁμοψύχους εἶναι καὶ ἀλλήλους ἐν ἀλλήλοις ὁρᾶσθαι· οὕτω τὸ χρυσοῦν τῆς ἀρετῆς ζεῦγος ἐλαύνοντες ἦσαν ἀμφότεροι, ὅτε καὶ τῆς ἑαυτοῦ κέλλης ὁ μακάριος Μάξιμος ὑπεκστὰς δέδωκε ταύτην τῷ γέροντι, ἑτέραν ἑαυτῷ ἀνῳκοδόμησε.

5

Ἐκεῖθεν δὲ ὁ μακάριος Νίφων ἀναχωρήσας πρός τι σπήλαιον ἄντικρυ τοῦ ἐπ᾽ ὀνόματι ἁγίου Χριστοφόρου,

bread, but here there is both bread and other food to eat, so to avoid conceit you should be content with these." Niphon then gave a further demonstration of his characteristic humility and was persuaded by the superior's advice. He went to the venerable church of the Savior, and, as he discovered that the holy altar there was in ruins, he asked the bishop of Hierissos to come there and restore it again; but the bishop permitted Niphon himself to do this and said that he could substitute for him. And this is indeed what he did.

He also celebrated the holy sacrament there. But because 2 a large crowd of fathers gathered there, wanting to serve under the great teacher and be trained by him and molded in the ways of virtue, he immediately left there and went to Maximos the Hutburner. He spent many days there, bound to the elder with such bonds of love that they were kindred spirits and saw themselves in each other. They both *drove the golden chariot* of virtue together to such an extent that, when the blessed Maximos left his cell he gave it to the elder Niphon and constructed another for himself.

Chapter 5

From there the blessed Niphon moved away to a cave facing the islet named after Saint Christopher; he entered it on

εἰσέδυ γνώμῃ τοῦ μακαρίου Μαξίμου. Καὶ μετὰ μικρὸν
ἐκεῖσε πλησίον ἕτερον κελλίον οἰκοδομεῖ. Ἔνθα τις Μάρκος ἐξ Ἰλλυρίων προσελθὼν καὶ πολλὰ δεηθεὶς τῆς ἁγίας
ψυχῆς ἐκείνης ὡς ἂν ἡσυχίας ὅρους ὑπ᾽ ἐκείνῳ διδαχθῇ
καὶ ὑποταγῆς, δέχεται μέν, ἐπιτρέπει δὲ ἑτοιμάσαι κελλίον
εὐρυχωρότερον, "ὡς ἄν," φησί, "καὶ ὁ σὸς μεθ᾽ ἡμῶν συν-
διάγῃ αὐτάδελφος." Ἔτυχε δὲ ὢν ἐκεῖνος εἰς Ἰλλυρίους,
γυναικὶ συνοικῶν καὶ παῖδας γνησίους τρέφων. Διὰ τοῦτο
καὶ ὁ Μάρκος, ὥσπερ πρὸς τὸν τοῦ γέροντος λόγον κατα-
πλαγείς, "Πῶς ἂν ὁ ἐμός," ἔφη, "πάτερ, αὐτάδελφος, ὑπὸ
γυναικὸς ὢν καὶ παίδων καὶ πραγμάτων ἐπιμελούμενος;"
Ὁ δέ (ὦ ψυχῆς εἰς βάθος ταπεινώσεως ἐμπεσούσης),
"Παραφρονῶν, ἀδελφέ, τοῦτο εἴρηκα," λέγει· "σοὶ δὲ οἰκο-
δομηθήτω τὸ κελλίον ὡς βούλει." Ἠβούλετο γὰρ οἰκο-
δομήσειν αὐτόν, ὅτε τὴν τῆς προρρήσεως ἔκβασιν τελε-
σθεῖσαν θεάσεται.

2   Ἑορτῆς δὲ τότε τοῦ ὁσίου πατρὸς ἡμῶν Ἀθανασίου τοῦ
Ἀθωνίτου ἐν τῇ κατ᾽ αὐτὸν ἱερᾷ τελουμένης Λαύρᾳ, πέμ-
πεται μὲν ὁ Μάρκος παρὰ τοῦ γέροντος διά τινα χρείαν
εἰς τὴν εἰρημένην μονήν. Παρακελεύεται δὲ μεθ᾽ ἑαυτοῦ
λαβόντα ἐπανελθεῖν τὸν ἴδιον ἀδελφόν, "ὡς ἄν," φησί,
"καὶ αὐτὸν θεασώμεθα." Ὁ δὲ καὶ πάλιν τὴν αὐτὴν ἀπόκρι-
σιν ἐδεδώκει. Ἀπελθὼν δὲ εἰς τὴν Λαύραν βλέπει ἐκτὸς
τοῦ πυλῶνος τὸν ἀδελφόν· καὶ τῷ τῆς θέας ἀπροσδοκήτῳ
καταπλαγεὶς καὶ τῇ προρρήσει τοῦ γέροντος περιεκέχυτο
μὲν καὶ κατεσπάζετο τὸν αὐτάδελφον καὶ ἀπὸ τῆς χαρᾶς
οὐκ εἶχεν ὅ τι καὶ γένοιτο· ἐτιτρώσκετο δὲ τὴν ψυχήν, ὡς
ἀπιστίαν νοσῶν καὶ πρὸς τὴν τοῦ γέροντος ἀμφιβάλλων

the advice of the blessed Maximos. After a short time he built another cell nearby. Then a man called Mark arrived from Illyria. After Mark had implored that holy soul Niphon many times to teach him the rules of spiritual tranquility and obedience, the latter accepted him, but he told him to prepare a more spacious cell, "so that your brother can live with us," said Niphon. That man was in Illyria, however, living with his wife and raising his children. For this reason Mark was completely bewildered by the elder's words. "Father," he said, "how can you mean my brother when he has a wife and children and is taking care of his business?" But then Niphon (oh, soul that plumbed the depths of humility), replied, "I must have been crazy to have said this, brother; so it's up to you whether you build the cell." For Niphon wanted to edify Mark, when he saw the complete fulfillment of his prophecy.

At the time when the feast of our holy father Athanasios the Athonite was being celebrated in his holy Lavra, Mark was sent by the elder Niphon on some errand to the aforesaid monastery. He told Mark to bring his brother back with him, "so that I can see him too," he said. Mark gave the same answer as before, but when he got to the Lavra he saw his brother outside the gateway. He was astonished at the unexpected sight and was overwhelmed by the elder's prediction. He embraced his brother and was beside himself with joy, but at the same time he was wounded in his soul for suffering from doubt and being skeptical about the elder's

προφητείαν. Λαβὼν οὖν τὸν ἀδελφὸν ἀπήει πρὸς τὸν γέροντα, συγχώρησιν αἰτῶν τοῦ προτέρου δισταγμοῦ. Καὶ μετὰ μικρὸν πάρεσις λαμβάνει ὁλομελής, ὡς μηδὲν τῶν μελῶν εὐχερῶς κινεῖν δύνασθαι, ἀπιστίας, οἶμαι, τῆς προτέρας διδάσκοντα. Ἱκέτης οὖν ἐλεεινὸς γίνεται καὶ συμπάθειαν μὲν ἐξαιτεῖται παρὰ τοῦ ὁσίου· ἀποπέμπεται δὲ οἰκονομικῶς ὡς ἂν μάθῃ ταῦτα καὶ παρακοῆς καὶ δυσπιστίας ἔργα τυγχάνοντα. "Ταῦτα γὰρ Ἀναργύρων," ἔφη, "τῶν ἁγίων εἰσὶ τῶν ψυχικῶν ἰατρῶν καὶ σωματικῶν· ἐγὼ δὲ ἀνήρ εἰμι ἁμαρτωλός [Luke 5:8], ὃν ὁ Θεὸς οὐκ ἀκούει." Ὡς δὲ καὶ τὸν αὐτάδελφον αὐτοῦ συναχθόμενον εἶδε καὶ δυσωποῦντα ὑπὲρ ἐκείνου, ἔλαιον ἐκ τῆς φωταγωγοῦ λαβὼν καὶ χρίσας ἅμα τὸ σῶμα, ὑγιῆ παραχρῆμα ἀποκατέστησεν, "Ἴδε, ὑγιὴς γέγονας," λέγων· "μηκέτι ἁμάρτανε, ἵνα μὴ χεῖρόν τί σοι γένηται" [John 5:14].

6

Ἀλλὰ καὶ πάλιν ὁ Μάρκος παρακοῆς τιτρώσκεται δήγματι καὶ πάλιν εἰς βάθος ἐμπίπτει κακῶν καὶ πάλιν τῆς συμπαθεστάτης ἐκείνης πεῖραν λαμβάνει ψυχῆς· ἀγρεύειν γὰρ ἰχθύας δι' ἐφέσεως ἔχων ὅτι πολλῆς, πολλὰ μὲν ἐδυσώπει τὸν γέροντα συγχωρῆσαί οἱ πρὸς θάλασσαν ἀπελθεῖν καὶ ἰχθύας ἀγρεῦσαι, "πρὸς παράκλησιν ἡμετέραν," φησίν. Ὁ δ' οὐκ ἐνεδίδου, "Λογισμοὺς ἀγρεύειν

prophecy. So he took his brother and went to the elder to seek forgiveness for his former doubt. Shortly afterward Mark became paralyzed all over, so that he was unable to move any of his limbs easily. This was, I think, to teach him a lesson for his earlier lack of faith. So Mark became a pitiful suppliant, begging for compassion from the holy Niphon. Niphon, however, deliberately sent him away so that he might learn the results of disobedience and lack of belief. "This is a matter for the holy Anargyroi," he said, "who are physicians of both our souls and bodies, whereas *I am a sinful man* to whom God doesn't listen." But when he saw Mark's brother grieving as well and pleading on his behalf, Niphon took oil from the lamp and, after he had anointed Mark's body, he restored him to health on the spot. "*See, you are well!*" Niphon quoted, "*Sin no more that nothing worse befall you.*"

Chapter 6

Mark was, however, wounded again by the sting of disobedience and again fell into the depths of evil and was again tested by that most compassionate soul, Niphon. Because he very much liked to go fishing, he often asked the elder for permission to go to the sea and catch fish, "as a treat for us," he said. But Niphon would not give it, saying, "You need to learn to fish out wicked thoughts, and always

διδάσκεσθαι," λέγων, "χρεών, καὶ τούτους ἀεὶ στηλιτεύειν, ἵνα μὴ ὑπ᾽ ἐκείνων βρωθῇς· θαλάσσης δὲ καὶ ἰχθύων ἀπέχεσθαι, ἵνα μὴ εἰς θάλασσαν ἐμπέσῃς κακῶν." Ὁ δὲ μήτε τῆς τοῦ πατρὸς νουθεσίας ἐπιστραφεὶς καὶ ὅλος τοῦ ἰδίου θελήματος γεγονὼς κάτεισιν εἰς τὴν θάλασσαν ὡς δῆθεν πλῦναι τὰ ῥάκια αὐτοῦ. Καὶ παρὰ γνώμην τοῦ γέροντος ζωγρεῖ μὲν ἰχθύας ἀγκίστρῳ καὶ τῷ δελέατι· ἔμελλε δὲ αὐτὸς ἰχθύος ἄγρα μεγάλου γενέσθαι, εἰ μὴ προφθάσασα ἡ τοῦ γέροντος εὐχὴ τοῦτον ἐρρύσατο· κύων γὰρ θαλάσσιος ἐκδραμὼν ἔμελλε τὸν Μάρκον καταπιεῖν, εἰ μὴ τὰς εὐχὰς τοῦ γέροντος ἐπικαλεσάμενος καὶ μικρὸν πρὸς τὴν ξηρὰν παρακλίνας αἰσθητοῦ καὶ νοητοῦ θηρὸς ἀπηλλάττετο.

2   Καὶ σύντρομος ἀπῄει εὐθὺς πρὸς τὸν γέροντα, καὶ οὓς εἷλεν ἰχθύας ἐπιφερόμενος. Ὁ δὲ ἡγιασμένος ἐκεῖνος προφθάσας, "Μὴ ἀπίστει," ἔφη, "παρήκοε Μάρκε· ὁ εἰς ὄφιν τὸ πρὶν μεταβαλὼν ἑαυτὸν καὶ παρακοὴν ὑποβαλὼν τοῖς προπάτορσιν, ἐκεῖνός σοι σήμερον θαλάσσιος κύων γενόμενος, δι᾽ ἣν σοι παρακοὴν ὑπέθετο πρότερον εἰς ἀπωλείας κατενεγκεῖν ἠβούλετο βάραθρον, εἰ μὴ Χριστὸς ὁ εἰς καθαίρεσιν ἐκείνου παραγενόμενος, χεῖρά σοι ὤρεξε καὶ τοῦ κινδύνου ἐρρύσατο εἰς μετάνοιαν συμπαθῶς ἐκκαλούμενος. Ἄγραν δὲ παρακοῆς οὐκ ἄν ποτε γεύσωμαι." Ὁ δὲ ῥίπτει μὲν οὓς ἐπεφέρετο ἰχθύας μακράν· ῥίπτει δ᾽ ἑαυτὸν τοῖς τοῦ ἁγίου ποσὶ καὶ συγχώρησιν ἐξαιτεῖται καὶ λαμβάνει εὐθύς. Καὶ τοῦ λοιποῦ διετήρησεν ἑαυτὸν ἐν ὑπακοῇ. Καὶ μετὰ μικρὸν ἀπῆλθε πρὸς Κύριον, τῆς ἐλπίδος

to censure them, so that you are not consumed by them. And you should keep away from the sea and from fish so that you don't fall into a sea of evils!" Mark, however, did not pay attention to the father's warning and, entirely following his own inclination, went down to the sea, under the pretense of washing his habit. Contrary to the elder's advice he caught some fish with bait on a hook, but he himself would have become the prey of a great big fish if the elder's prayer had not anticipated this and protected him. For a shark swam up and would have swallowed Mark if he had not invoked the elder's prayers and, having dodged aside onto dry land, escaped from what was both a physical and spiritual beast.

Trembling, Mark went straight back to the elder, carrying the fish he had caught. The blessed Niphon had anticipated this and said, "Have no doubt, disobedient Mark, that the Devil, who once transformed himself into a serpent and suggested disobedience to our forefathers, became a shark for you today because he wanted to carry you down into the pit of destruction through the disobedience he suggested to you earlier. <And he would have done so> if Christ had not come to destroy him, and stretched out a hand to you and protected you from danger, summoning you compassionately to repentance. But I'll never eat something that's been caught as a result of disobedience." So Mark flung the fish which he had brought a long way away, but flung himself at the saint's feet and begged forgiveness and received it at once. And from then on he kept himself in obedience. After a short time he departed to the Lord, receiving thence the

ἐντεῦθεν τοὺς ἀρραβῶνας λαβών. Κατέλιπε δὲ εἰς ὑπηρεσίαν τῷ γέροντι τὸν ἑαυτοῦ ἀδελφόν.

7

Γαβριὴλ οὗτος τὸ ὄνομα· οὗ τὸν πατέρα Δοσίθεον ἡ τοῦ
σχήματος αὐτοῦ ἀξία προσηγόρευσε. Χρείας κατεπειγούσης ἀξιοῖ συγχωρηθῆναι παρὰ τοῦ γέροντος τὸν Γαβριὴλ καὶ ἀπελθεῖν εἰς τὴν τοῦ Βατοπαιδίου μονήν. Ὁ δὲ
νεύει μὲν πρὸς τὴν αἴτησιν· ἀποστέλλει δ᾽ αὐτὸν ὡρισμένην
ἐνστήσας ἡμέραν, καθ᾽ ἣν θέλοντος τοῦ Θεοῦ ἐπαναστρα-
φήσεται. Τῆς οὖν ὡρισμένης παρελθούσης καὶ Ἀχαιμε-
νιδῶν τὰ ἐκεῖσε μέρη ληϊζομένων, ἐδόκει τῷ τοῦ Γαβριὴλ
πατρὶ ὡς ἀνδράποδον ὁ υἱὸς ἐρχόμενος ἐγεγόνει· καὶ πανταχόθεν εἰς ἀπορίαν ὑπὸ τῆς ἀφορήτου λύπης ἐνέπιπτεν.
Ἡ δὲ θαυμαστὴ καὶ συμπαθὴς ἐκείνη ψυχή, "Μὴ κλαῖε,
γέρον," διεμηνύσατο· "ἐλεύθερον γάρ φημι εἶναι τὸν ἀδελφόν, ἐπεὶ ἀπέσταλται παρ᾽ ἐμοῦ." Καὶ μήπω τοῦ ἡλίου ἀπο-
λελοιπότος τὴν γῆν, ἀκίνδυνος ἐπανῆλθεν ὁ ἀδελφός,
πεῖραν μηδὲ τοῦ τυχόντος δεινοῦ ἐσχηκώς.

guarantee of his hopes. But he left behind his brother in service to the elder.

Chapter 7

The name of Mark's brother was Gabriel, and his father, after he received the monastic habit, was Dositheos. Because of some pressing need Dositheos asked the elder Niphon to allow Gabriel to go to the monastery of Vatopedi. He agreed to the request and sent Gabriel off after setting a day on which, God willing, he was to return. When the appointed day passed, however, and some Achaimenids were plundering in the area, Gabriel's father thought that his son had been captured while on his way back. He fell into all kinds of despair because of his unbearable grief. "Don't weep, elder," that wondrous and compassionate soul, Niphon, advised him, "for I tell you, the brother is free because he was sent out by me!" And the sun had not yet set when the brother returned safely without having encountered any problem whatsoever.

8

Οὗ δὲ ὁ λόγος ἄνωθεν ἐμνήσθην μακαριωτάτου Μαξίμου, τοῦ τὰς καλύβας πυρπολοῦντος, ἐγγὺς ὄντος περὶ τὸ τέλος (μετὰ γὰρ ἓξ μῆνας κεκοίμηται), ὁ θεῖος οὗτος ἀνὴρ ἀναστὰς ἔφη πρὸς τοὺς περὶ αὐτόν· "Ἀπελευσώμεθα πρὸς τὸν Μάξιμον καὶ θεασώμεθα αὐτόν, ὅτι οὐκέτι αὐτὸν ἐνταῦθα κατὰ τὸν παρόντα θεασόμεθα βίον." Ἀπελθόντες οὖν καὶ ἀσπασάμενοι ἐκεῖνον, "Χαίρετε," ἔφη, "τοῦτο ὕστατον πρόσφθεγμα· οὐκέτι γὰρ ἀλλήλους κατὰ τὸν παρόντα ὀψόμεθα βίον." Καὶ γέγονε κατὰ τὴν τῶν ἀμφοτέρων πρόγνωσίν τε καὶ προφητείαν.

9

Ἐτῶν οὖν παρελθόντων πολλῶν καὶ πάλιν ἐνέσκηψε λοιμός. Καὶ τοῦ εἰρημένου Γαβριὴλ τὴν ἐπιχωριάζουσαν τότε νοσήσαντος νόσον, ὁ πατὴρ αὐτοῦ τὸν υἱὸν ὁρῶν οὕτω πρὸς θάνατον βλέποντα ἔκλαιε ὡς εἰκὸς καὶ ὠδύρετο· ὃν ὁ γέρων ἀνέχων καὶ ἀναλαμβανόμενος· "Μὴ σύ γε, ἀδελφέ, θρηνῇς οὕτως ἐπὶ τῷ ἀδελφῷ· τεθνήξεται γὰρ οὐδαμῶς τὸ παρόν, ἐπεὶ κατὰ τὴν τοῦ Θεοῦ ἐντολήν μοι ὑπηρέτησεν· ἐγὼ δὲ ὅσον οὔπω τεθνήξομαι." Καὶ στραφεὶς κατὰ ἀνατολὰς εὐχὴν ὑπὲρ ἐκεῖνον μακρὰν

Chapter 8

When the most blessed Maximos the Hutburner, whom I mentioned above, was nearing his end (he died six months later), the godly Niphon arose and said to his companions, "Let's go see Maximos, because we're not going see him here again in this present life." So they went to visit him and embraced him. "Welcome," said Maximos, "this is our last conversation, for we won't see each other again in this present life." And it turned out as both of them had predicted and prophesied.

Chapter 9

Many years later another outbreak of plague occurred, and the above mentioned Gabriel caught the disease that was then attacking the region. When his father Dositheos saw that his son was close to death, he wept and mourned as was to be expected. The elder Niphon, however, supported him and raised him up saying, "Brother, don't weep like this for brother Gabriel. He's not going to die at the present time, since he has served me according to God's commandment; but I myself will soon breathe my last." Niphon turned toward the east and whispered a long prayer for

ὑπεψιθύρισε. Καὶ ὁ κείμενος ἀναστὰς ἐδόξαζε τὸν Θεόν. Στραφεὶς δὲ ὁ γέρων λέγει πρὸς τοὺς ἐκεῖσε· "Ὁ μὲν ἀδελφὸς ἰδοὺ σὺν Θεῷ τῆς ὑγείας ἀπήλαυσεν· ἐγὼ δὲ κατὰ τὴν ἐρχομένην νηστείαν τεθνήξομαι."

10

Ἐκεῖνος μὲν οὖν οὕτως ἔλεγε, τὴν τῶν ἁγίων ἀποστόλων σημαίνων νηστείαν· οἱ δὲ τὴν τοῦ σωτηρίου πάθους ὑπέλαβον· καὶ διεληλυθυίας ἐκείνης, "Ἀλλ᾽ ἰδού," φασί, "πάτερ, ἡ νηστεία παρῆλθεν." Ὁ δέ, "Οὐκ ἔστι παρὰ ταύτην," ἔφη, "νηστεία ἑτέρα τις;" Τῆς οὖν τῶν ἁγίων ἀποστόλων ἐν-στάσης, ἀναστὰς καὶ προσευξάμενος καὶ τῶν φρικτῶν τοῦ Χριστοῦ κοινωνήσας μυστηρίων, λέγει πρὸς τοὺς συνήθεις· "Ἰδού, τῆς ἐμῆς ἐν Χριστῷ ἀναλύσεως ὁ καιρὸς [2 Timothy 4:6] ἤγγικεν." Τῶν δὲ πρὸς τὸ ῥῆμα διαταραχθέντων, "Ὁ μὲν ἡμέτερος," αὖθις ἔφη, "πεπλήρωται καιρὸς καὶ ἀπέρχο-μαι πρὸς τὸν ἐμοὶ ποθεινότατον Ἰησοῦν. Ὑμῖν δὲ λυπεῖσθαι οὐκ ἔδει· ἕξετε γὰρ ἡμᾶς ὑπὲρ ὑμῶν Χριστῷ ἐντυγχά-νοντας, μόνον εἰ τῶν ἐντολῶν ἐκείνου τῶν σεπτῶν μὴ ὀλι-γωρήσετε." Καὶ ἀναστὰς τὸ πρωῒ (ἦν γὰρ ἡ κυρία τῶν ἡμερῶν), "Ἀριστήσατε," πρὸς ἐκείνους φησί, "καὶ τὸ ἡμέ-τερον ὑπανοίξατε μνῆμα, ὡς ἂν πρὸς ἐκείνην ἐξ ἧς ἐλήφθην [Genesis 3:19] ἀφίξωμαι." Οὕτως οὖν κατὰ τὸ κελευσθὲν ἤδη ποιήσαντες, πρὸς ἐκεῖνον ἀτενὲς ἑώρων, εἴ τι ἂν

Gabriel. And Gabriel, who had been lying down, got up and glorified God. The elder then turned around and said to those present, "Look, with God's help the brother has recovered his good health. But I'm going to die during the coming fast."

Chapter 10

In saying this, Niphon meant the fast of the Holy Apostles, but they understood him to mean the fast of the Savior's passion which had already ended. "But, look, father," they said, "the fast is already over." "Isn't there another fast beside that one?" he replied. When the fast of the Holy Apostles began, Niphon arose, prayed, and partook of Christ's awesome mysteries. Then he said to his companions, "Behold, *the time* has come *for my departure* in Christ." When they were dismayed at his words, he said again, "My time has been fulfilled and I am departing to my most dearly beloved Jesus. But you needn't be sad, for you'll have me as your intercessor with Christ, as long as you don't neglect His holy commandments." When he got up the next morning (for it was Sunday), he said to them, "Have your morning meal and then open up my tomb so that I may return to the dust *from which I came.*" When they had carried out Niphon's instructions, they paid careful attention to him in case he

κελεύσειε τοῦ λοιποῦ. Ὁ δὲ ἀναστὰς καὶ ὄμματα καὶ χεῖρας εἰς οὐρανὸν ἀναβλέψας, παρέτεινε τὴν εὐχὴν ὡς οὐδέποτε ἄλλοτε. Καὶ στραφεὶς καὶ πάντας εὐλογήσας καὶ "Συγχωρήσατέ μοι τῷ ἁμαρτωλῷ" ἐπειπὼν καὶ πᾶσι συγχώρησιν ἐπευξάμενος, σχηματίζει μὲν ἑαυτὸν σταυροειδῶς, τὸ δὲ πνεῦμα εἰς χεῖρας παρατίθησι [see Psalm 30(31):5; Luke 23:46] τοῦ Θεοῦ, ἀστράψας ὑπὲρ τὸν ἥλιον καὶ πᾶσι σύμβολα διδοὺς ἀκριβῆ τῆς ἐκείνου πρὸς Θεὸν παρρησίας.

2   Ἐκοιμήθη μὲν οὖν ὁ ὅσιος οὗτος πατὴρ κατὰ τὴν ιδʹ τοῦ Ἰουνίου μηνός. Ἔζησε δὲ τὰ πάντα αὐτοῦ ἔτη ϟϛʹ, θαύματα πλεῖστα παρ' ὅλον αὐτοῦ τὸν βίον καὶ ἀξιάκουστα ἐκτελῶν· ἀφ' ὧν ὀλίγα τοῖς φιλοχρίστοις ἐκ τῶν πολλῶν παραθήσομαι.

II

Γέρων τις, πνευματικὸς ἀνὴρ καὶ ὅλος τῆς ἀρετῆς, Θεόδουλος τοὔνομα, ὠφελείας χάριν ἀνελθεῖν ἠβούλετο πρὸς τὸν γέροντα· ἦν γὰρ ἐξ ἱκανοῦ μὴ θεασάμενος αὐτόν. Ἀναστὰς οὖν εἴχετο τῆς ὁδοῦ· καὶ διερχόμενος τόπον κρημνώδη καὶ δύσβατον, ὠλίσθησε μὲν ὡς δῆθεν ἀποπεσεῖν· προσέκρουσε δὲ λίθῳ μεγάλῳ τὸν ἑαυτοῦ πόδα, ὡς καὶ τὴν ἑαυτοῦ ζωὴν ἀπολέγεσθαι ἤδη· τοσοῦτον γὰρ ἐξέρευσεν αἷμα ἐκ τῆς πληγῆς ὡς ὀλιγοψυχῆσαι τὸν γέροντα καὶ μηδὲ φωνὴν ἀφιέναι δύνασθαι. Ἰδὼν οὖν

should give them further orders. But he stood up, raised his eyes and hands to heaven and prayed for a longer time than ever before. Then he turned round, blessed everyone and said, "Forgive me, for I am a sinner." When he had prayed for forgiveness for everyone, he positioned himself in the form of the cross and *committed his spirit into the hands* of God, shining more brightly than the sun and giving everyone a clear sign of his intimacy with God.

The holy father died on the 14th of June. He lived for a full ninety-six years and during his life accomplished very many miracles which are worth hearing. I am now going to set down a few of these, from among the many, for those who love Christ. 2

Chapter 11

An elder called Theodoulos, a spiritual man who was full of virtue, wanted to visit the elder Niphon for spiritual benefit, for he had not seen him for some time. So he got up and took the path there, but while he was traversing a very steep and rugged stretch, he slipped and nearly fell off the path. He struck his foot on a large rock so badly that he almost lost his life there and then. So much blood flowed from the wound that the elder felt faint and was unable to

ἑαυτὸν ἐς τοσοῦτον βάθος ἀκοντισθέντα κακῶν, φωνὴν ἐκ βάθους καρδίας μόλις ἀνενεγκών, "Κύριε Ἰησοῦ Χριστέ, Υἱὲ τοῦ Θεοῦ," ἀνεβόησεν, "εἰ ὅλως ἅγιος ὁ ἱερὸς Νίφων ἐστί, καθὰ λογίζονται περὶ ἐκείνου πολλοί, στήτω μὲν ἡ ῥύσις τοῦ αἵματος, αἱ δὲ ὀδύναι παυσάσθωσαν· καὶ ἔργον τῶν ἐκείνου εὐχῶν ἡ ἡμετέρα γενέσθω ἀνάκτησις, ὡς ἂν μὴ θηρίοις ἐν ἐρημίᾳ ἀνθρώπων πολλῇ βορὰ γένωμαι." Εἶπε, καὶ παραυτίκα (τῶν θαυμασίων σου, Χριστὲ βασιλεῦ!) ἡ μὲν ῥύσις ἔστη τοῦ αἵματος, ὀρθὸς δ᾽ ὁ πρὶν τραυματίας καὶ ὑγιὴς ἔστη, δοξάζων μὲν τὸν Θεόν, ἀκριβῶς δὲ πληροφορηθεὶς ὅτι ἅγιος ὄντως ὁ γέρων ἐστί. Πρὸς ὃν ἀπελθὼν καὶ εὐλογίας τυχὼν ἐπανῆλθε καὶ χαίρων καὶ θαυμάζων καὶ εὐλογῶν τὸν Θεόν.

12

Ἀδελφός τις ἐκ τῆς ἱερᾶς καὶ θείας Λαύρας ἔλαιον μνήμης μικρᾶς χάριν ἀπέστειλε πρὸς τὸν γέροντα διά τινος τῶν ἐκείνου ὁμιλητῶν. Καὶ τῆς ὁδοῦ τραχείας οὔσης καὶ ἀποτόμου, προσκόψας λίθῳ ὁ ἀδελφὸς ἀνετράπη καὶ πέπτωκε· καὶ πάντων ἃ ἐπεφέρετο συντριβέντων, τὸ ἐλαιοδόχον ἀγκεῖον διατηρηθὲν ἀβλαβὲς ἀποκεκόμισται παρὰ τοῦ ἀδελφοῦ πρὸς τὸν γέροντα. Ὁ δὲ σεμνὸν ὑπομειδιάσας, "Ἴδε," φησί, "πόσον ἡ πίστις ἐνήργησε τοῦ πέμψαντος ἡμῖν τὸ ἔλαιον ἀδελφοῦ, ὥστε καὶ σὲ τοῦ κινδύνου

call out. Realizing the depth of his predicament, however, he just managed to raise a cry from the bottom of his heart. "Lord Jesus Christ, Son of God," he called out, "if the holy Niphon really is a saint, as many think he is, let the flow of blood be staunched and the pain cease, and let me recover through his prayers, so that I do not become food for wild animals in a place deserted by men." As soon as he had spoken (oh, your miracles, Christ the King!), the bleeding stopped and the injured man now stood up restored to health again, glorifying God and fully convinced that the elder Niphon truly was a saint. Theodoulos went on to see Niphon, received his blessing, and then returned, rejoicing and marveling and praising God.

Chapter 12

A brother from the holy and divine Lavra once sent some oil as a small memento to the elder Niphon by means of one of his disciples. The path was rough and precipitous and the brother tripped on a stone, stumbled and fell. Although everything else he was carrying was broken, the oil flask remained undamaged and was brought by the brother to the elder. Smiling gravely, Niphon said, "See what the faith of the brother who sent me the oil has managed to do! It has

λυτρωθῆναι καὶ τὸ ἔλαιον σῶον διασωθῆναι, τῶν ἄλλων διαφθαρέντων ἁπάντων." Καὶ θαυμάσας ἐπὶ τούτῳ ὁ ἀδελφὸς πῶς καὶ πρὸ τοῦ ἀναγγεῖλαι τοῦτον πρὸς τὸν γέροντα τὰ συμβάντα ἐν τῷ κρημνῷ εἶπε ταῦτα, καὶ ἀπῄει θαυμάζων καὶ δοξάζων τὸν Θεόν.

13

Μοναχός τις κεφαλαλγίαν νοσῶν καὶ χρόνοις πλείστοις ἐξεταζόμενος ὑπ᾽ αὐτῆς καὶ ἰατροῖς προσαναλώσας πολλά, ὡς οὐδὲ τυχούσης παραμυθίας ἀπήλαυσεν, ἄνεισι μετὰ πίστεως πρὸς τὸν γέροντα καὶ τοῖς ἐκείνου προσπίπτει ποσὶ καὶ τὴν ὑγείαν ἐξαιτεῖται θερμοτέροις τοῖς δάκρυσι· "Γενήσεται γάρ," ἔφη, "ῥᾳδίως ὅπερ αἰτήσεις Θεόν, ἁγιώτατε πάτερ, ὑπὲρ οὗ τὴν ἔρημον ταύτην κατῴκησας." Ὁ δὲ τῆς ταπεινώσεως χρησάμενος ῥήμασι, "Παρὰ ἁμαρτωλῷ," φησίν, "ἀνδρὶ τίς ἡ περὶ τούτων ὠφέλειά σοι γενήσεται;" Ὡς δὲ ἐνέκειτο καὶ αὖθις γονυκλιτῶν ὁ νοσῶν, εἰς συμπάθειαν ὁ ἅγιος κινηθεὶς εὐχὴν ὑπεψιθύρισεν ἐπὶ τῇ ἀλγούσῃ κεφαλῇ. Καὶ ὁ νοσῶν εὐθὺς ὑγιὴς ἐγένετο, εὐλογῶν καὶ δοξάζων τὸν Θεόν· καὶ ὡς ὅρκοις ἡμᾶς ἐπληροφόρησεν ὕστερον, "Ἀναγινώσκοντος," ἔφη, "τοῦ γέροντος τὴν εὐχήν, ἦχος ἐκ τῆς ἐμῆς κεφαλῆς ἐξήρχετο ὡς ἀνέμου βιαίου."

preserved you from danger and kept the oil safe when everything else has been destroyed." The brother was astonished at how, even before he had told the elder, Niphon reported what had happened on the cliff. And he went away marveling and glorifying God.

Chapter 13

A monk suffered from a headache and was tormented by it for many years. He had spent a lot on doctors but, as he could not get rid of it and find any relief, he went with faith to the elder Niphon, fell at his feet, and begged for a cure with scalding tears. "Most holy father," he said, "whatever you ask of God, for whose sake you live in this wilderness, it will readily come about." Niphon replied with humility, "What help will you get for this from a sinful man?" But when the sick man begged him again on bended knee, the saint was moved to compassion and whispered a prayer over his aching head. The sick man was immediately cured, blessing and glorifying God. As he later assured us with oaths, "While the elder was reciting the prayer, a sound erupted from my head like a violent wind."

14

Ἕτερός τις μοναχός, ἰδιορρυθμίᾳ ἑαυτὸν κατακλείσας καὶ μηδενὶ τῶν αὐτόθι πατέρων τὰ καθ' ἑαυτὸν ἀνατιθέμενος, ἔλαθε σκότους ἄγγελον ἀντὶ φωτὸς εἰσδεξάμενος· παρ' οὗ πολλὰ τῶν ἀτοπωτάτων ὡς οὐκ ὤφειλε μυηθείς, ἑαυτὸν ὑπὲρ ἄλλους ᾤετο εἶναι καὶ πλείστοις χαρίσμασι τῶν πάντων κρατεῖν· τοιούτου γὰρ διδασκάλου τοιαῦτα καὶ τὰ μαθήματα. Παραβαλὼν οὖν πρὸς τὸν ἅγιον καὶ παρ' ἐκείνου ἐρωτηθεὶς δι' ἣν αἰτίαν ἀφῖκται, "Ἐλήλυθα," φησί, "θεάσασθαί σε ὡς γέροντα." Ὁ δέ, "Πῶς πρὸς ἡμᾶς ὁ τοσοῦτος τοὺς ταπεινοὺς ἐλήλυθας καὶ αὐτὸς τυγχάνων ὑπὲρ ἡμᾶς;" "Ἀλλὰ Θεοῦ," ἔφη, "τὸ χάρισμα· Θεὸς ὁ ταύτην μοι δωρησάμενος εὐεργεσίαν." Ὁ δέ, "Θεοῦ," ἔφη, "τὸ ταπεινοῦσθαι, Θεοῦ τὸ λογίζεσθαι ἑαυτὸν πάντων ἔσχατον, Θεοῦ τὸ μεγάλοις πλεονεκτοῦντα χαρίσμασιν ἑαυτὸν εὐτελέστερον πάντων ἡγεῖσθαι. Ταῦτα δὲ πλάνης, ἀδελφέ, καὶ τοῦ ταύτης σπορέως τοῦ Σατανᾶ." Ὁ δὲ ὥσπερ πρὸς ἑαυτὸν γεγονώς, "Εἰ ἐκ τοῦ Σατανᾶ, πάτερ, ταῦτα," φησίν, "εὐχῇ μοι τὴν πλάνην κατάστειλον καὶ τῶν τοιούτων με λύτρωσαι φαντασιῶν." Ὁ δὲ εἰς οὐρανὸν ἀναβλέψας, "Κύριε Ἰησοῦ Χριστέ," ἔφη, "ὁ τὸ πεπλανημένον πρόβατον καὶ ἀπολωλὸς ζητήσας καὶ εὑρὼν καὶ τοῖς λοιποῖς συγκαταριθμήσας καὶ ἀπλανέσι, καὶ τὸν αὐτὸ διασπαράξαι λύκον ζητοῦντα καθελών, καὶ τρίβους ἡμῖν σωτηρίας ἀπλανέσιν ὑποθέμενος, αὐτὸς καὶ τὸν ἁπλουστέρῳ τούτῳ φρονήματι ταῖς τοῦ πλάνου μεθοδείαις πρὸς πλάνην

Chapter 14

Another monk, who had shut himself away to pursue an individualistic way of life and who did not communicate with any of the other fathers there, had unwittingly admitted an angel of darkness instead of one of light; this had given him all sorts of absurd ideas that he should not have had. He thus considered himself to be better than other people and to possess far more spiritual gifts than anyone else, for such are the lessons given by such a teacher. He came to the saint, who asked him why he had come. "I've come to see you, as you are an elder," he said. Niphon replied, "Why has someone who is so superior to me come to someone as humble as I am?" "But it's a gift from God," said the monk, "God has given me this advantage." "Being humble is from God," said Niphon. "Considering oneself to be last of all is from God. Believing that being greedy for great spiritual gifts makes one inferior to everyone is from God. But your ideas come from error, brother, and from Satan, the sower of error." As if coming to his senses, the monk said, "If these ideas are from Satan, father, correct this error by praying for me and deliver me from such delusions." Niphon looked up to heaven and said, "Lord Jesus Christ, who sought the sheep that had wandered and was lost and, having found it, brought it back into the fold with the others which had not wandered, and destroyed the wolf that was seeking to tear it in pieces; Lord Jesus Christ, who has established pathways to salvation for us so that we may not wander; Lord Jesus Christ, free from his delusions this man, who

κατασπασθέντα τῶν ἐκείνου φαντασιῶν ἐλευθέρωσον, ὅπως σε γινώσκῃ μόνον Θεὸν ἀληθινόν [John 17:3], τὸν δι᾽ ἡμᾶς καὶ σταυρὸν καὶ ταφὴν ὑπομείναντα, καὶ σοῦ δοξάζῃ τὸ ὄνομα τὸ εὐλογημένον εἰς τοὺς αἰῶνας, ἀμήν." Εἶπε καὶ παρευθύς, ὥς τι νέφος τῶν ὀφθαλμῶν διασκεδασθέν, γνῶσιν ἀκριβῆ τῷ πεπλανημένῳ παρέσχεν, ὅποι κακῶν ἐμπεπτωκὼς ὁ ἄθλιος ἦν· καὶ τοῦ λοιποῦ σωφρόνως διαβιοὺς τῶν σκοτεινῶν ἀπηλλάγη φαντασιῶν.

15

Ὡρολόγος τις ἐκ τῆς ἱερᾶς Λαύρας διά τι πταίσιμον ἐκδιωχθεὶς τοῦ πυλῶνος ἀπῆλθε πρὸς τὸν ὅσιον καὶ ἀπήγγειλεν αὐτῷ τὸ γεγονός, ὅτι "Ἐπειδὴ ἀδίκως ἐδιώχθην, οὐ χρήζω πλέον στραφῆναι ἐκεῖ· καὶ ἀξιῶ τὴν σὴν ἁγιωσύνην δεχθῆναί με, καὶ ποιήσας κελλίον καθεστῆναι πλησίον σοῦ, ὁδηγούμενος ὑπὸ τὴν σὴν χεῖρα." Ὁ δὲ ἅγιος λέγει πρὸς αὐτόν, "Ἄπελθε εἰς τὸ μοναστήριον, ὅτι οὐ δυνήσει ὑπομεῖναι ἐνταῦθα καὶ ἀδόκιμος γενήσῃ καὶ μοναστηρίου καὶ τῆς ἐρήμου. Ἀλλ᾽ ἐπανελθεῖν σε βούλομαι εἰς τὸ μοναστήριον, διότι μέλλεις γενέσθαι ἐκκλησιάρχης καὶ ἡγούμενος, εἰ μετὰ ταπεινώσεως ὑπομείνῃς εἰς τὴν σεβασμίαν Λαύραν." Καὶ μειδιάσας εἶπεν αὐτῷ, "Ὅταν ἡγούμενος γένῃς, τότε ἐνθυμοῦ ἵνα παραγγείλῃς τοῖς ἀδελφοῖς τοῦ διακονεῖν ἡμᾶς." Καὶ καθὼς εἶπεν, οὕτως ἐγένετο καὶ ἐκκλησιάρχης καὶ ἡγούμενος.

has been dragged down into error with this foolish idea by the wiles of the deceitful one, so that he may *know you, the only true God* who was crucified and who submitted to burial for our sake, and may glorify your blessed name, forever, Amen." Niphon said this and immediately, as though a cloud had lifted from his eyes, the monk understood clearly that he had been in error and what a wretch he was for having fallen into such evils. From then on he lived circumspectly, set free from his dark delusions.

Chapter 15

A timekeeper from the holy Lavra, who had been expelled for some fault, came to the holy one and told him what had happened: "I don't want to go back there anymore, because I've been expelled unjustly. I beg your holiness to accept me, and let me build a cell and set myself up near you so that I may be guided by your hand." But the saint replied to him, "Go back to the monastery because you won't be able to stand it here and then you'll be discredited in both the monastery and the wilderness. But I want you to go back to the monastery again because you're going to become sacristan and superior, if you remain with humility in the venerable Lavra." He also said to him, with a smile, "When you become superior, make sure you encourage the brothers to take care of me!" And, just as he said, the monk became both sacristan and superior.

16

Μοναχοὶ τρεῖς παρέβαλον χάριν εὐλογίας πρὸς τὸν ἅγιον, καὶ ὁ μὲν εἷς ὑπῆρχε νέος ἀγένειος. Καὶ πλησίον τοῦ τόπου γενόμενοι εἴασαν τὸν νέον πόρρω τῆς κέλλης, αἰδούμενοι τὸν ἅγιον. Ἐλθόντες δὲ οἱ δύο καὶ ἀσπασάμενοι τὸν ἅγιον κατὰ τὸ σύνηθες ἐκαθέστησαν. Λέγει πρὸς αὐτοὺς ὁ ἅγιος, "Διὰ τί οὐκ ἐάσατε τὸν νέον εἰσελθεῖν πρός με; Αὐτὸς γάρ, εἰ καὶ νέος εἶν, ἀλλὰ κατοικητήριον τοῦ ἁγίου Πνεύματος μέλλει γενέσθαι." Καὶ ἐθαύμασαν τοῦ ἁγίου τὴν πρόρρησιν, καὶ ἐξελθόντες ἐκάλεσαν αὐτόν· καὶ εὐλογηθεὶς παρὰ τοῦ ὁσίου, ἐκάθισαν ἀμφότεροι. Καὶ οἱ τρεῖς καὶ ὁμιλήσαντες μετὰ τοῦ ὁσίου καὶ ὠφεληθέντες ἀπῆλθον δοξάζοντες τὸν Θεὸν καὶ τὸν αὐτοῦ θεράποντα. Ὁ δὲ νέος ἐχρημάτισε δόκιμος μοναχὸς κατὰ τὴν τοῦ ἁγίου πρόρρησιν.

17

Ἕτερος ἀδελφὸς παρέβαλε τῷ ὁσίῳ· ἦν γὰρ πένης, καὶ ἐκόμιζε κοπτὸν κεχρὶν πρὸς τὸ ἀριστῆσαι μετὰ τοῦ ὁσίου. Καὶ αἰδεσθεὶς ὁ ἀδελφὸς διὰ τὸ εἶναι κεχρίν, κατέλιπεν τοῦτο μήκοθεν τῆς κέλλης· καὶ εὐλογηθεὶς παρὰ τοῦ μεγάλου ἐκάθισεν. Καὶ μιλήσας μετ᾽ αὐτὸν ἕως ἔφθασεν ὁ

Chapter 16

Three monks, one of whom was a beardless youth, came to the saint for a blessing. When they were near the place, they left the boy at a distance from the cell out of respect for the saint. The two came and embraced the saint in the usual way. The saint said to them, "Why didn't you let the youth come to me? Even if he is a youth, he's going to become a dwelling place for the Holy Spirit." They were amazed at the saint's foresight and went out and called the youth; when he had been blessed by the holy one, they all sat down together. The three conversed with the holy one and, after receiving helpful advice, went away praising God and his servant. And the youth came to be known as an excellent monk in accordance with the saint's prediction.

Chapter 17

Another brother came to the holy one. He was a poor man and had brought some crushed millet to eat at the morning meal with the holy one. But the brother was ashamed that it was only millet and left it some distance from the cell. After he had been blessed by the great man, he sat down and talked with him until the time came for the

καιρὸς τοῦ ἀρίστου, λέγει ὁ ὅσιος πρὸς τὸν ἀδελφόν·
"Καιρὸς εἶν τοῦ ἀρίστου· ἐτράφημεν ψυχικῶς, ἀνάγκη εἶν
τοῦ τραφῆναι καὶ σωματικῶς. Κόμισον οὖν ἐνταῦθα τὸ
κεχρὶν ὃ κατέλιπες ἔξω, ἵνα ἀριστήσωμεν." Ἀριστήσας οὖν
ὁ ἀδελφὸς μετὰ τοῦ ὁσίου καὶ ὠφεληθεὶς ἀπῆλθε χαίρων
καὶ ἀγαλλόμενος δοξάζων τὸν Θεόν.

18

Μετὰ τὸ ἀναιρεθῆναι τὸν δεσπότην Οὔγκλεσιν ὑπὸ
τῶν Ἰσμαηλιτῶν, θρασυνθέντες οἱ τοιαῦτοι Ἰσμαηλῖται
συνῆξαν στόλον μέγαν πλοίων καὶ ἦλθον κατὰ τοῦ Ἁγίου
Ὄρους καὶ κατὰ πάντων τῶν Χριστιανῶν μετὰ τῶν ὅπλων
τῶν Σερβῶν, βαστάζοντες καὶ τειχομαχικὰ ἐργαλεῖα διὰ
τὰ κάστρη τοῦ Ἁγίου Ὄρους. Ὡς γοῦν ἦλθον, ἰδόντες
αὐτοὺς ἅπαντες ἐτρόμαξαν, τοσοῦτον ὅτι καὶ ὁ μέγας πρι-
μικήριος οὐκ ἐτόλμησε καταπροσωπῆσαι αὐτούς. Καὶ ἀπὸ
τοῦ φόβου μὴ ἔχοντες ἄλλο τι δρᾶσαι, ἔπεσον εἰς ἱκεσίαν
πρὸς τὸν οἰκτίρμονα Θεὸν καὶ εἰς τὴν πάναγνον αὐτοῦ
μητέρα, τὴν τοῦ Ἁγίου Ὄρους καὶ πάντων τῶν Χριστιανῶν
μεσίτριαν καὶ τροφὸν καὶ βοήθειαν· καὶ οὐκ ἀπέτυχον.

2   Ἀπέστειλεν οὖν καὶ ὁ τότε προϊστάμενος τῆς ἱερᾶς
Λαύρας πρὸς τὸν ὅσιον, διαγγέλλων αὐτῷ τὴν βίαν καὶ
τὴν ἀνάγκην ἥτις ἦλθεν ἐκ τῶν ἀπροσδοκήτων, ἐκλιπαρῶν
αὐτὸν τοῦ ποιῆσαι εὐχὴν πρὸς τὸν Κύριον, "ὅπως

meal. The holy one said to the brother, "It's time for the morning meal. We've nourished ourselves spiritually, but we also need to nourish ourselves physically. So bring the millet here that you left outside, so that we can have our meal." So the brother had his meal with the holy one and, after receiving helpful advice, went away rejoicing and happily glorifying God.

Chapter 18

After the despot Uglješa was killed by the Ishmaelites, some such Ishmaelites were emboldened and, after assembling a large fleet of ships, also attacked the Holy Mountain and all the Christians; they came with Serbian forces, bringing siege engines against the fortified monasteries of the Holy Mountain. When they came, everyone was so terrified at the sight of them that even the *megas primikerios* did not dare confront them. Unable to do anything else because of their fear, they cast themselves down in supplication to God, who is merciful, and to His all-pure Mother, who is the intercessor and nurturer and helper of the Holy Mountain and of all Christians. And they did not fail.

The superior of the holy Lavra at the time thus sent to 2 the holy one, telling him of the violent assault that had come from this unexpected source and begging him to say a prayer

ρυσθῶμεν ἐκ τοῦ παρόντος κινδύνου." Καὶ ἀπεκρίθη ὁ μέγας, "Ὁ Κύριος ρύσεται ἡμᾶς ἐκ τῶν ἀοράτων Ἰσμαηλιτῶν· περὶ δὲ τῶν ὁρωμένων, ἐλπίζω εἰς τὸν Κύριον καὶ Θεόν μου Ἰησοῦν Χριστόν· καὶ διὰ πρεσβειῶν τῆς παναγίας μητρὸς αὐτοῦ καὶ τοῦ πανοσίου καὶ θεοφόρου πατρὸς ἡμῶν Ἀθανασίου, οὐδὲν ἡμᾶς βλάψωσιν, ἀλλὰ μᾶλλον καταλυθήσονται καὶ εἰς ἀφανισμὸν γενήσονται." Ὃ καὶ γέγονε· εὐθὺς καὶ ἀπροσδοκήτως ἦλθον τρία μεγάλα καὶ θαυμαστὰ πλοῖα τῶν Βενετίκων ὡπλισμένα εἰς τὴν Λαύραν· καὶ μαθόντες περὶ τῶν Ἰσμαηλιτῶν τὴν ἔφοδον, συνήχθησαν μετὰ τοῦ πριμικηρίου καὶ συνέβαλον πόλεμον καὶ κατὰ κράτος κατέλυσαν αὐτοὺς κατὰ τὴν πρόρρησιν τοῦ ἁγίου· καὶ λαβόντες αὐτῶν πάντα τὰ πλοῖα μετὰ τῶν ὅπλων καὶ πάντων ὧν ἐκέκτηντο, ἠφάνισαν αὐτοὺς παντελῶς. Εὐεργέτησαν δὲ καὶ τὴν σεβασμίαν Λαύραν πλοῖον ἓν καὶ ἕτερα ἐκ τῶν σκευῶν αὐτῶν ἀναγκαῖα, εὐχαριστοῦντες τὸν Κύριον ἡμῶν Ἰησοῦν Χριστὸν καὶ τὴν πάναγνον αὐτοῦ μητέρα καὶ Θεοτόκον καὶ τὸν ὅσιον καὶ θεοφόρον πατέρα ἡμῶν Ἀθανάσιον.

19

Διά τινα χρείαν ἦλθεν εἰς τὸν ὅσιον ὁ τοῦ Γαβριὴλ πατὴρ ὁ προρρηθεὶς Δοσίθεος λέγων, "Συγχώρησόν μοι, πάτερ, ἵνα ἀποστείλω τὸν Γαβριὴλ εἰς τὴν μονὴν τῶν

to the Lord, "that we may be delivered from our present danger." The great one replied, "The Lord will surely deliver us from the invisible Turks. As for the visible ones, I have hope in my Lord and God, Jesus Christ, and through the intercession of his all-holy Mother and of our most saintly and divinely inspired father Athanasios, that they will not harm us, but will rather be destroyed and exterminated." And that is what happened. For immediately and unexpectedly three wonderful big ships, manned by the Venetians, arrived at the Lavra. When they learned about the attack by the Turks, they joined forces with the *primikerios,* engaged in battle, and destroyed them with all their might in accordance with the saint's prediction. They captured all the Turkish ships, along with their weapons and all their plunder, and completely exterminated them. They also donated one ship to the venerable Lavra and other provisions from their supplies, in thanks to our Lord Jesus Christ and his all-pure Mother the Theotokos, and our holy and divinely inspired father Athanasios.

Chapter 19

Gabriel's father Dositheos, who has already been mentioned, came to the holy one on some business. "Father," he said, "please let me send Gabriel to the monastery of Iviron."

Ἰβήρων." Ἀποκριθεὶς δὲ ὁ μέγας λέγει, "Γίνωσκε ὅτι, ἐὰν ἀπέλθῃ, κινδυνεῦσαι ἔχει ὑπὸ τῶν Ἰσμαηλιτῶν." Ὁ δὲ Δοσίθεος ἐπέκειτο λέγων, "Ἀφοβία ἐστί, πάτερ, ὅτι ἐὰν παραγένηται ταύτῃ τῇ νυκτὶ ἕως τοῦ Μολφινοῦ, καὶ αὔριον ἀπελθεῖν εἰς τῶν Ἰβήρων, ἐλπίζω, οὐ μὴ συναντήσῃ κακόν." Ὁ δὲ ἅγιός φησι πρὸς αὐτόν· "Εἰ κινδυνεύσει ὁ υἱός σου, ἀναίτιος ὑπάρχω ἐγώ· καὶ ποίησον ὡς βούλει." Ἀκούσας δὲ ὁ Δοσίθεος ἐσιώπησεν, οὐδὲν πλέον εἰπών. Καὶ τῇ αὐτῇ ἑσπέρᾳ ἐλθών τις ἀνήγγειλε τῷ ὁσίῳ ὅτι ἐφάνη πλοῖον καὶ ἠχμαλώτευσε τρεῖς ἀνθρώπους ἀπεδόθεν τοῦ Μολφινοῦ, καθὼς ὁ μέγας ἦν προειπὼν ὅτι "Ἀπεδόθεν τοῦ Μολφινοῦ ἔχει κινδυνεῦσαι."

20

Μοναχός τις ἐλθὼν ἀνήγγειλε τῷ ἁγίῳ ὅτι "Ἠχμαλώτευσαν οἱ Ἰσμαηλῖται τὸν πνευματικὸν κῦρ Ἰωαννίκιον μετὰ καὶ ἑτέρων μοναχῶν καὶ τοῦ πλοίου, ἀπερχομένων ἐκ τῆς Λαύρας εἰς τὴν σκήτην. Καὶ νῦν συνάσουν ἀργύρια ἵνα αὐτοὺς ἐξαγοράσωσι· καὶ δέδωκα κἀγὼ δι᾽ αὐτοὺς ἕνα χρυσόν." Καὶ ἀπεκρίθη ὁ γέρων· "Εἰ τῶν πτωχῶν εἶχες δώσῃ, κρεῖσσον ὑπῆρχεν, ὅτι καὶ ὁ πνευματικὸς καὶ οἱ μετ᾽ αὐτοῦ καλῶς ἔχουσι, καὶ οὐδὲν συνήντησεν αὐτοὺς κακόν· μάλιστα ἐν ἀνέσει μεγάλῃ διάγουσι καὶ παράκλησιν μεγάλην ἔχουσιν σήμερον. Εἴθε εἴχαμεν καὶ ἡμεῖς ἐκ τοιαύτης

But in reply the great one said, "You should be aware that he'll be in danger from the Ishmaelites, if he goes." Dositheos pressed him, saying, "There's nothing to be afraid of, father, because, if he gets as far as the Amalfitans tonight, my hope is that he'll reach Iviron safely tomorrow without coming to any harm." But the saint replied to him, "If you put your son in danger, I won't be to blame. But do as you wish!" When Dositheos heard this he kept quiet and said no more. But that same evening someone came and told the holy one that a ship had appeared and taken three men prisoner this side of the Amalfitans, just as the great one had foretold, "He could be in danger this side of the Amalfitans."

Chapter 20

A monk came and told the saint, "The Ishmaelites have captured the spiritual father Kyr Ioannikios along with some other monks and their boat, as they were going from the Lavra to the hermitage. Now they're collecting money to pay the ransom; I've given one gold coin for them myself." The elder replied, "You would have been better off giving it to the poor, because the spiritual father and those who are with him are well and have met with no harm. In fact they're living in great comfort and are having a great treat today. I

παρακλήσεως." Ἐσημειώσατο γοῦν ὁ μοναχὸς τὴν ἡμέραν·
καὶ ἐλθόντος τοῦ πνευματικοῦ, ἠρώτησεν αὐτόν. Καὶ εἶπεν ὅτι "Τὴν ἡμέραν ἐκείνην ἔτυχεν ἡμᾶς ἄγρα ἰχθύων
μεγάλων, καὶ οὐ μετρίως ἐπαρεκλήθημεν, ἐσθίοντες καὶ
πίνοντες *εἰς δόξαν Θεοῦ* [1 Corinthians 10:31], καθώς φησιν
ὁ ἀπόστολος." Ταῦτα ἀκούσας ὁ ἀδελφὸς καὶ θαυμάσας
τοῦ ἁγίου τὸ χάρισμα, ἐδόξασε μεγάλως τὸν δοξάζοντα
τοὺς ἑαυτοῦ θεράποντας· ὅτι καὶ τὰ πόρρω ὡς ἐγγὺς βλέ-
πουσιν ἀληθῶς οἱ δουλεύοντες αὐτῷ γνησίως, χάριτι καὶ
φιλανθρωπίᾳ τοῦ Κυρίου καὶ Θεοῦ καὶ Σωτῆρος ἡμῶν
Ἰησοῦ Χριστοῦ, ᾧ πρέπει κράτος, δόξα, τιμὴ καὶ προσκύνησις σὺν τῷ ἀνάρχῳ αὐτοῦ Πατρὶ καὶ τῷ παναγίῳ καὶ ζωο-
ποιῷ αὐτοῦ Πνεύματι, νῦν καὶ ἀεὶ καὶ εἰς τοὺς αἰῶνας.

wish we too had such a treat!" The monk made note of the day and, when the spiritual father came back, he asked him about this. And he said, "That day we had a haul of big fish, and we had a real treat, and ate and drank *to the glory of God,* as the apostle says." When the brother heard this, he was amazed at the saint's spiritual gift and gave glory to Him who glorifies His servants, and because those who truly serve Him see things that are far off as though they were present, by the grace and benevolence of our Lord, God, and Savior Jesus Christ, to whom belongs power, glory, honor and worship together with His eternal Father and His all-holy and life-giving Spirit, now and always and forever.

LIFE OF PHILOTHEOS OF ATHOS

Βίος καὶ πολιτεία τοῦ ὁσίου καὶ θεοφόρου πατρὸς ἡμῶν Φιλοθέου τοῦ ἀσκήσαντος ἐν τῷ Ἄθω Ὄρει

Εὐλόγησον, πάτερ.

I

Μάτην οἱ πολλοὶ τὸν χρόνον αἴτιον ἀξιοῦσιν εἶναι τοῦ περὶ τὰ καλὰ ζήλου καὶ τῶν ἄκρων τῆς ἀρετῆς βαθμῶν καὶ τῆς ἄχρι τέλους πρὸς αὐτὴν ἀναβάσεως· τοὺς μὲν πάλαι γεγενημένους σφοδροὺς ἐπιθυμητὰς αὐτῆς καὶ ζηλωτὰς ὑπάρξαι λέγοντες, τοὺς δέ γε νῦν ἢ μικρῷ πρόσθεν γενομένους ἀμβλείας καὶ μαλακὰς καὶ ψυχροτέρας ἔχειν τὰς πρὸς ἐκείνην ὁρμάς, καὶ μηδὲ μέχρι τοῦ μέσου ταύτης ἀναβῆναι σπουδὴν τιθεμένους οὐδὲν ἀσφαλὲς οὐδ᾽ ἐχέγγυον ὑπὲρ τούτου λέγοντες. Ὥσπερ γὰρ κἂν τοῖς παλαιοτέροις τῶν χρόνων πολλοί τινες ἦσαν, οἳ μὴ μόνον ῥαθύμως τῆς ἀρετῆς ἥπτοντο, ἀλλὰ καὶ εἰς ἅπαν ὀλιγωροῦντες αὐτῆς πρὸς κακίαν ἐχώρουν, οὕτω δὴ κἂν τοῖς μετὰ ταῦτα καὶ μέχρι τοῦ νῦν οὐκ ὀλίγοι θερμῷ τῷ πρὸς αὐτὴν διατετήκασιν ἔρωτι καὶ τὴν ἐκεῖσε φέρουσαν συντόνως ὁδοιποροῦντες· παρὰ τοῦτο δὴ καὶ τῶν ἄκρων αὐτῆς βαθμίδων οὐκ εἰς μακρὸν τὸν χρόνον ἐπιλαμβάνονται.

Life and conduct of our blessed and divinely inspired father
Philotheos who lived an ascetic life on Mount Athos
    Bless us, father.

Chapter 1

*M*ost people foolishly consider the age in which a man is born
to be the determining factor in his zeal for the good, his most impor-
tant steps toward virtue, and the completion of his ascent toward
this goal. For on the one hand they say that those who were born in
the past strove hard for virtue and were zealous for it, while on the
other hand they consider those who live now or shortly before this
time to have a feeble, soft, and less ardent desire to attain virtue,
making no effort to ascend even to its middle point, nor offering any
certain or reliable evidence to that end. However, just as in the past
there were many who not only sought after virtue in a lax manner,
but were indeed entirely negligent of it and proceeded toward evil,
thus even among those who have lived ever since and up to the pres-
ent day many also have maintained a fervent desire for virtue and
earnestly travel the road leading to it. Because of this they reach the
pinnacle of virtue in a short time.

2

*T*οιοῦτός ἐστι καὶ ὁ σήμερον ἡμῖν εἰς ἑορτὴν προκείμενος, ὁ θεσπέσιός φημι καὶ τῷ Θεῷ φίλος Φιλόθεος, ὃς τῷ χρόνῳ πολλοστὸς ὢν ἐν τοῖς πρὸς ἀρετὴν εὐδοκιμηκόσιν οὐδενὸς ἐκείνων εὑρίσκεται δεύτερος· μᾶλλον μὲν οὖν ὅσον ὑστερεῖ τοῖς χρόνοις, τοσοῦτον ἐν πόνοις πρωτεύων δείκνυται. Δηλώσει δὲ περὶ τούτων ὁ λόγος τοῖς τὴν ἀκοὴν ἐλευθέραν παρέχειν αὐτῷ βουλομένοις.

2 Φύει μὲν τοῦτο δὴ τὸ θεῖον φυτὸν ἐκ τῆς Χρυσοπόλεως τῆς Μακεδονίας, οἱ δὲ γονεῖς αὐτοῦ ὑπῆρχον ἐκ πόλεως Ἐλατείας οὐ μακρὰν οὖσαν Ἀσιανῶν ἐπαρχίας· διὰ δὲ τὸν φόβον τῶν Ἀγαρηνῶν μετανάσται γίνονται ἐκ τῆς ἐνεγκαμένης ἐν τῇ προειρημένῃ πόλει. Ἱκανὸν δὲ χρόνον διατριψάντων ἐν τῇ αὐτῇ χώρᾳ καὶ ὁ πατὴρ αὐτοῦ τῶν τῇδε μετέστη. Ἔμεινε δὲ ὁ θεῖος παῖς μετὰ τῆς μητρὸς σὺν ἑτέρῳ ἀδελφῷ αὐτοῦ, ὀνειδιζόμενοι καὶ κακουχούμενοι ὑπὸ τοῖς ἀγχιστοῖς αὐτῶν ὡς ξένοι καὶ πάροικοι [Ephesians 2:19] καὶ ὀρφανοί, καὶ ὀρφανίαν τὴν χαλεπωτάτην, οὔτε συγγενῆ τινα ἢ πατρὸς ἢ μητρὸς ἢ μόνον τὸν Θεὸν καὶ τὴν κατὰ σάρκα μητέρα αὐτῶν.

3 Ἐν δὲ τῷ καιρῷ ἐκείνῳ ἐξῆλθε πρόσταγμα παρὰ τοῦ κρατοῦντος εἰς συλλογὴν παιδίων, ὡς ἔθος ἐστὶ τοῖς Ἀγαρηνοῖς, μᾶλλον δὲ βουλῇ τοῦ πατρὸς αὐτῶν τοῦ Διαβόλου [John 8:44], τοῦ μισοκάλου καὶ φθονεροῦ δράκοντος, τοῦ ἀπ᾽ ἀρχῆς Πολεμίου τοῦ γένους τῶν Χριστιανῶν. Οἴμοι, πόσοι ἐκ τοῦ ἡμετέρου γένους ἐγένοντο τέκνα τοῦ

Chapter 2

Such a person is the man whose feast we celebrate today, I mean the marvelous Philotheos, the friend of God, *who may be much more recent in time but was never second to any of those men who excelled in virtue. Rather he made up for his lateness in time by proving himself first in effort. My narrative will reveal these things to those who are willing to listen.*

This divine plant sprang up from Macedonian Chrysopolis, 2
while his parents were from the city of Elateia, which was not far from the province of Asia. Because of their fear of the Agarenes they emigrated from their homeland to the aforementioned city. After they had lived in that land for some time, his father died. The holy child remained, together with his mother and another brother, but they were ridiculed and abused by their neighbors as *strangers and outsiders* and orphans, being orphans of the worst kind with no paternal or maternal relatives, but only God and their birth mother.

At that time a command was issued by the ruler for a levy 3
of male children, as is customary among the Agarenes, or rather by the will *of their father the Devil,* that despiser of good, that envious serpent, the Enemy of Christians from the beginning of time. Alas, how many among our own people were made into children of the Antichrist! Woe is me!

Ἀντιχρίστου! Φεῦ μοι! Ἐγένοντο καὶ οὗτοι οἱ καλοὶ παῖδες μετὰ τῶν ἄλλων παίδων, οὓς προεκόμιζον τῷ ἀμηρᾷ. Ἐκ πάντων μέν, οὓς εἶχον τέκνα ἢ δύο ἢ τρία ἢ καὶ δέκα, ἕνα καὶ μόνον ἐκράτουν καὶ αὐτὸ μετὰ βίας· οἱ δὲ οὗτοι διὰ τὸ μὴ ἔχειν τινὰ ἐκ τοῦ γένους αὐτῶν, ἵνα εἴπῃ ἢ ἀντιτείνῃ τι, ἐπῆραν ὁμοῦ καὶ τοὺς δύο ἀδελφούς.

4   Ἡ δὲ μήτηρ αὐτῶν ἐκ πάντων ἀπορουμένη, οὔτε συγγενῆ τινα εἶχεν οὔτε ἄλλην τινὰ παραμυθίαν ὡς σύνηθες τοῖς ἀνθρώποις, ἔκλαιε καὶ ὠδύρετο τὴν στέρησιν τῶν φιλτάτων, τί μὲν λέγουσα, τί δὲ πράττουσα, καὶ οὐκ εἶχεν τὸν βοηθοῦντα. Ἐν ἀμηχανίᾳ δὲ συσχεθεῖσα ἔκειτο ἄφωνος. Μόλις ποτὲ ἐλθοῦσα εἰς ἑαυτὴν ἐκ τῆς ἄγαν ἀθυμίας (καὶ πάνυ μὲν οὖν ἀθυμεῖν αὐτήν, διότι εἰς ἀλλοτρίαν καὶ ἀλλοδαπὴ χώραν ὑπῆρχε καὶ οὔτε γονεῖς οὔτε ἀνὴρ ἤ τις τῶν κατὰ συνήθων ἦν αὐτῇ ἢ μόνον εἰς τὸ ἔλεος τοῦ φιλανθρώπου Θεοῦ καὶ εἰς τὴν ὑπέραγνον καὶ δέσποιναν ἡμῶν Θεοτόκον, τὴν μεσίτριαν τῶν γνησίως ἐπικαλουμένων αὐτήν), ὅπως γένηται ἵλεως εἰς τοὺς φιλτάτους καὶ ἐξέλῃ αὐτοὺς ἐξ ἀθέων καὶ μιαρῶν χειρῶν.

5   Τί οὖν ἡ πανάμωμος καὶ εὔσπλαχνος μήτηρ τοῦ Κυρίου ἡμῶν Ἰησοῦ Χριστοῦ; Κάμπτεται τοῖς σπλάχνοις· οὐ βούλεται παριδεῖν τὴν ὄντως γνησίως ἱκετευομένην αὐτήν, ἀλλὰ θαυμασίως πως καὶ οἰκονομικῶς αὐτῇ ἐξάγει αὐτοὺς ἐκ τοῦ δεσμωτηρίου, ὦ τοῦ θαύματος! Ἐν μιᾷ τῶν νυκτῶν ἀωρὶ φαίνεται πρὸς τοὺς παῖδας ὡς οἷα μήτηρ καὶ φησὶ πρὸς αὐτούς, "Ὦ τέκνα, ἔπεσθε ἐμοί!" Οἱ δὲ ἐκ πολλῆς περιχαρίας ἠκολούθουν αὐτῇ· μηδὲν δύνανται φθέγξαι τι, ἀλλ' ὡς ἐν ἐκστάσει κεκώλυνται.

These fine boys were taken along with the other boys who were brought to the emir. All those who had children, either two, or three or even ten, could scarcely keep one. But because the two brothers did not have kinsmen to object or resist somehow, the Agarenes took both brothers at the same time.

Their mother, who was completely destitute and had nei- 4 ther a relative nor any other kind of comfort as people usually have, wept and bewailed the loss of her beloved children, but no matter what she said or did there was no one to help. Overcome by helplessness she lay there unable to speak. When she recovered a little from her great distress (and she was greatly distressed indeed, for since she was in a strange and foreign land, and had neither parents nor husband nor friends, her only recourse was to the mercy of the benevolent God and our Lady the most pure Theotokos, who intercedes for those who sincerely entreat her), <she prayed> that the Theotokos might be merciful to her beloved children and deliver them from godless and polluted hands.

So, what did the faultless and compassionate Mother of 5 our Lord Jesus Christ do? She was swayed to mercy, and was unwilling to disregard the woman who was sincerely beseeching her, but rather, in a wondrous and providential manner, she freed the children from prison. Oh, what a miracle! One evening, in the dead of night, she appeared to the children as if she were their mother and said to them, "Children, follow me!" They followed her with great rejoicing, unable to utter a word, but speechless as if in a trance.

6 Περὶ δὲ ὄρθρου βαθέως καταλαμβάνουσι τὴν Νεάπολιν, ἐν ᾧ ἔστι μοναστήριον ἔχον τὴν ἐπωνυμίαν αὐτῆς. Ἐνταῦθα τοὺς παῖδας προσέταξε διαμένειν καὶ ὑποτάσσεσθαι τῷ ἡγουμένῳ καὶ τοῖς ἀδελφοῖς πᾶσι "ἕως καὶ πάλιν ἐλθεῖν τοῦ ἰδεῖν ὑμᾶς" [see Romans 1:11], καὶ ἀπέστη ἀπ' αὐτῶν, ὡς οἶδεν αὐτή. Τοῦ ὄρθρου δὲ πληρωθέντος φαίνονται καὶ οὗτοι οἱ θεῖοι παῖδες εἰς τὸν προεστῶτα καί φησι πρὸς αὐτούς, τίνες εἶεν καὶ πόθεν. Οἱ δὲ ἀπαγγέλουσιν αὐτῷ πάντα τὰ καθ' ἑαυτῶν. Καὶ γνοὺς ὅτι θεία δύναμις ἔσωσεν αὐτούς, ἐδόξασεν τὸν Θεόν, μηδενὶ ἀποκαλύψας τὸ δρᾶμα. Καὶ παραλαβὼν αὐτοὺς ἔδωκέν τινι τῶν νεωκόρων ἐκπαιδεύεσθαι τοῖς ἱεροῖς γράμμασι καὶ ὑπηρετεῖν εἰς τὸν θεῖον ναόν. Οἱ δὲ νέοι ἀόκνως καὶ σπουδαίως ἐποίουν τὴν προστασίαν ἣν κεκλήρωντο ὥστε θαυμάζειν πάντας. Τί δὲ λέγειν περὶ πασῶν τῶν ἀρετῶν, ὧν κεκόσμηνται οἱ παῖδες; Ἐν τοῖς ἁπάντων στόμασιν ἦν καὶ ἔχαιρον καὶ ἠγάλλοντο ἐπ' αὐτοῖς.

3

Ἰλιγγιῶ καὶ συγχέεταί μοι ὁ νοῦς, πῶς ἐξείπω τὰ περὶ τῆς κατὰ σάρκαν χρηματισάσης αὐτῶν μητρός. Τί εἴπω καὶ τί λαλήσω; Τὴν στέρησιν τοῦ συνεύνου, τὴν χηρείαν λέγω, ἣν καλεῖ ὁ μέγας Χρυσόστομος σιδηρᾶν κάμινον, ἢ τῶν παίδων τὴν στέρησιν, ὧν καὶ ζῶσιν εἰς ἀλλοφύλων

By early dawn they reached Neapolis where there is a 6
monastery bearing her name. There she commanded the
boys to take up residence and be obedient to the superior
and all the brothers "until I return again to *see you*," and then
she left them, in her own mysterious manner. When the
matins service was over, these holy children appeared before the superior and he asked them who they were and
where they came from. They told him all about themselves.
And the superior, knowing that a divine power had saved
them, gave glory to God, but disclosed the events to no one.
He took them in and handed them over to one of the church
custodians to be trained in holy letters and to serve in the
holy church. The young boys performed untiringly and earnestly the duties which they were assigned, to the amazement of all. What can one say regarding all the virtues with
which the boys were adorned? They were on everyone's lips,
and all rejoiced and were gladdened by them.

Chapter 3

I become dizzy and my mind reels, as to how I might tell
what happened to their earthly mother. What should I say
and what can I tell? Shall I speak more of her lack of a husband, I mean her widowhood, which the great Chrysostom
calls the *iron furnace,* or of the loss of her children, who lived

αὐλάς; Πλέον τοῦτο ἢ κἀκεῖνο; Τί οὖν ποιεῖ ἡ ἀδαμάντινος ἐκείνη ψυχή; Βουλὴν βουλεύεται ἀγαθήν (καὶ τοῦτο τῆς θείας προνοίας ἐνεργησάσης), ἵνα καταλιπεῖν πάντα καὶ συνεῖναι Θεῷ· ὃ καὶ πεποίηκε.

2 Δοῦσα δὲ πάντα τὰ προσόντα ὅσον τε κινητὰ καὶ ἀκίνητα εἰς τοὺς δεομένους, ἀφίκετο εἴς τινα μοναστήριον, ἐν ᾧ οἱ παῖδες αὐτῆς ἔμενον. Ἦν δὲ τὸ μοναστήριον κεχωρισμένον εἰς δύο τμήματα, τὸ ἓν τῶν μοναχῶν καὶ τὸ ἕτερον μοναχαῖς, καὶ ἐποιμαίνοντό τε παρὰ ἑνὸς πατρός. Ἐν τούτοις καταλήγει ἡ καλὴ Εὐδοκία, ἀποκαρεῖσα παρὰ τοῦ προεστῶτος, καὶ κατηχήσαντος αὐτῇ τὰ εἰκότα, ἐπρόσταξεν ἐμμένειν μετὰ τὰς παρθένους πάσας ἐντὸς τοῦ προαστείου.

3 Ἄξιόν ἐστι μὴ παραδραμεῖν τὴν ξένην ἀναγνώρισιν τῶν τέκνων αὐτῆς, τοῖς βουλομένοις παρέχειν ἀκοὴν ἐλευθέραν. Ἦν δὲ ἑορτὴ τῶν ἐπισήμων. Συνέρρεον πᾶσαι αἱ μοναχαὶ εἰς τὴν θείαν ἱερουργίαν, ἐλθοῦσα δὲ καὶ αὐτὴ μετ᾽ αὐτῶν. Καὶ τελεσθείσης τῆς θείας λειτουργίας οἱ πάντες ἀνεχώρουν. Μόνον οἱ παῖδες αὐτῆς ἔμεινον ἐν τῷ ναῷ, ἐν ᾧ καὶ νεωκόροι ἐτύγχανον. Ἐκάλει γὰρ ἕτερος τοῦ ἑτέρου τὴν κλῆσιν, καθὼς ὠνομάσθησαν παρὰ τοῦ θείου βαπτίσματος· τοῦτο γὰρ οἰκονομίᾳ Θεοῦ. Ἡ δὲ μήτηρ αὐτῶν ἔξω ἑστηκυῖα καὶ ἀκούουσα αὐτοὺς καὶ ῥινηλατεῖν αὐτοὺς ἤθελε. Καὶ ἰδοῦσα ἀκριβῶς ὅτι τὰ ἔκγονα αὐτῆς εἰσίν, κάμπτεται τοῖς σπλάγχνοις καὶ γίνεται ὡς τοῖς πολλοῖς χαρμολύπη. Ἐκ δὲ τῆς ἀφάτου περιχαρίας ἐδόκει ὄναρ ὁρᾶν, μόλις δὲ ἐδυνήθη ἀφικέσθαι πρὸς αὐτούς.

in the courts of foreigners? Shall I tell more of one or the other? What then did *that adamantine soul* do? She devised an excellent plan (and this was through the action of divine providence), that she should abandon everything and unite herself with God. And this what she did.

After giving away all her belongings, both movable and immovable, to the poor, she went to a monastery, the one in which her children resided. For the monastery was divided in two sections, one for monks and one for nuns, and they were both shepherded by one father. Here the good Eudokia ended her journey and was tonsured by the superior; after he had given her appropriate instruction, he bade her reside with all the nuns in the monastic complex. 2

For those who are willing to pay close attention it is worthwhile not to pass over the wondrous way in which she recognized her children. It was an important holiday. All the nuns gathered together for the holy liturgy, and she too came along with them. After the divine liturgy was completed, everyone departed. Only her children remained in the church, where they served as custodians. Each called the other by name, using the names they had been given at holy baptism, for this was God's providence. Their mother, who was standing outside and heard them, decided to observe them more closely. After she saw clearly that they were her offspring, she was overwhelmed with emotion and was overcome with joyful sadness. Because of her ineffable joy she thought she was dreaming, and was barely able to approach them. 3

4   Τότε οἱ θεῖοι καὶ ἱεροὶ ὅρπηκες, ἰδόντες τὴν βλαστήσασαν αὐτούς, ἀναγνωριοῦσιν αὐτὴν καὶ δραμόντες πίπτουσιν εἰς τοὺς πόδας αὐτῆς, ἣν καὶ περιπλακέντες καταφιλοῦσιν αὐτήν. Ἡ δὲ λέγει πρὸς αὐτούς, "Ὦ τέκνα, πόθεν ἦλθεν τοιοῦτον ἔλεος; Καὶ τίς ὁ ἐλευθερώσας ὑμᾶς καὶ ἀφίξατε ὧδε;" Οἱ δὲ ἀνταποκρινόμενοι λέγουσιν αὐτῇ, "Τάχα ἡ μήτηρ ἡμῶν δοκιμαστικῶς πως εἴρηκεν ἡμῖν; Οὐ σύ ἐστιν ἡ ἐκσπάσασα ἡμᾶς ἐκ τῶν χειρῶν τῶν Ἰσμαηλιτῶν καὶ ὥρισας ἡμᾶς προσμένειν ἐν τῷ μοναστηρίῳ, ἕως οὗ πάλιν ἐπανακάμψῃς πρὸς ἡμᾶς;" Ἡ δὲ ἐκπλαγεῖσα ἐπὶ τὰ λαληθέντα καὶ μηδὲν πλέον εἰποῦσά τι, μόνον αἶνον καὶ εὐχαριστίαν ἀνέπεμπεν τὴν ὑπέραγνον καὶ εὔσπλαχνον μητέρα τοῦ Κυρίου ἡμῶν Ἰησοῦ Χριστοῦ, "ὅπως ἐρρύσατο ὑμᾶς ἐκ τῆς πανωλεθρίας καταδίκης."

5   Ἐδηλώθη δὲ καὶ ἐν τῷ μοναστηρίῳ τὸ τεράστιον καὶ ἔχαιρον ἅπαντες καὶ εὐφραίνοντο ἐπ' αὐτοῖς. Ἡ δὲ μήτηρ αὐτῶν προσμείνασα ἐν τῷ παρθενῶνι, οἱ δὲ παῖδες ἐν τῷ μοναστηρίῳ ἐν ᾧ ἐκλήθησαν, προκόπτοντες χάριτι Θεοῦ εἰς πᾶν εἴ τι καλὸν καὶ εὐάρεστον αὐτοῦ. Πᾶσα δὲ ἡ ἀδελφότης σὺν τῷ καθηγουμένῳ ἔχαιρον καὶ εὐφραίνοντο ἐπ' αὐτοῖς. Μόνον δὲ ὁ ἀρχέκακος καὶ ἀπ' ἀρχῆς Πολέμιος τοῦ ἀνθρωπείου γένους ἤσχαλλεν, ἐδυσφόρει, ἐλεεινῶς ὠδύρετο· καὶ μὴ φέρων τὴν ἧτταν ἐκ τοιούτων μειρακίων, τί τεχνουργεῖται ὁ παμπόνηρος κατὰ τοῦ γενναίου Φιλοθέου; Εὑρὼν ἓν ὄργανον καὶ κατοικεῖ πᾶν τὸ πλήρωμα τοῦ ἀντικειμένου εἰς αὐτό· μονάστρια γὰρ ἦν.

6   Ὥσπερ γὰρ καὶ ἐν τῷ προπάτορι ἡμῶν, οὕτω καὶ νῦν καὶ πάλαι, ὡς ἁπαλωτέρας καὶ πειθανωτέρας τῆς γυναικός,

Then her divine and holy offspring saw the woman who   4
had given birth to them. They recognized her and ran to her,
fell at her feet, and embracing her, covered her with kisses.
She said to them, "My children, where did such mercy come
from? And who set you free so you were able to come here?"
They replied to her, "Is our mother saying this to test us
somehow? Weren't you the one who removed us from the
hands of the Ishmaelite Turks and ordered us to wait in the
monastery until you came back to us again?" Their mother
was astonished at their words, and said no more, only giving
praise and thanksgiving to the most pure and compassionate mother of our Lord Jesus Christ, "as she delivered you
from a sentence of death."

The miracle was announced in the monastery as well, and   5
all were glad and rejoiced for them. Their mother remained
in the nunnery, and the boys in the male side of the monastery to which they had been summoned by the Virgin, advancing by the grace of God in everything that was good and
pleasing to Him. The entire brotherhood together with the
superior were glad and rejoiced for them. Only the originator of evil, the Enemy of the human race from the very beginning, was vexed and distressed, and lamented piteously.
Unable to bear his defeat by such young lads, what did the
most wicked one devise against the noble Philotheos? He
found an instrument for his wickedness and made it the ve-
hicle for the fulfillment of his animosity; and it was a nun!

For just as he did against our forefather, now as in the   6
past, the accursed one strove to tempt us through woman,

δι' αὐτῆς σπουδάζει ὁ κατάρατος ἐγεῖραι ἡμᾶς. Ὁ δὲ γεννναῖος τὴν ψυχὴν καὶ θεῖος Φιλόθεος ἀντέκρουσεν αὐτῇ μετὰ πάσης πραότητος καὶ ἐπιεικείας, λέγων καὶ ὑπομιμνήσκων τὴν γέενναν τοῦ πυρός [Matthew 5:22], τὸν σκώληκα [see Mark 9:48], τὸν βρυγμὸν τῶν ὀδόντων [see Matthew 8:12] καὶ τὰ ἑξῆς. Ἡ δὲ μᾶλλον σφοδρότερον αὐτὸν ἠνώχλει, τί δὲ λέγουσα, τί δὲ πράττουσα, ὅπως ἑλκύσῃ αὐτὸν εἰς αἰσχρὰν μίξιν. Ὁ δὲ γενναῖος καὶ ἀδαμάντινος τὴν ψυχήν, μὴ ἔχων τί ποιῆσαι, εἰς συμμαχίαν καλεῖ τὸν Κύριον ἡμῶν Ἰησοῦν Χριστόν, ὃν καὶ εὑρών· καὶ ὁδηγεῖ αὐτόν.

7   Καὶ ἀπαγγέλλει τὸ συμβὰν τῷ καθηγουμένῳ τῆς μονῆς. Ὁ δὲ σοφὸς ἐκεῖνος ἀνήρ, καλέσας τὸν τρίπλοκον ὄφιν ἐκεῖνον καὶ ὡς εἰκὸς ἐπιτιμήσας, ἐξήλασεν αὐτὴν ἐκ τῆς μονῆς. Καὶ οὐκ ἔλαθεν ἅπαντας, ὥσπερ οὐ δύναται πόλις κρυβῆναι ἐπάνω ὄρους κειμένη [Matthew 5:14]. Κἀκ τούτου τὸν ἅγιον ἀνευφήμουν, λαμπρὸν νικητὴν ἐκάλουν αὐτόν. Καὶ ἐδόξαζον τὸν Θεὸν ἅπαντες, λέγοντες, "Εἴδομεν γὰρ ἐν ταῖς ἡμέραις ἡμῶν νέον Ἰωσήφ." Ὡς ἐκεῖνος τὴν Αἰγυπτίαν ἐξέφυγεν, οὕτως καὶ αὐτὸς τὴν ὁμόσκηνη καὶ ὁμόθρησκη. Καὶ οὐκ ἦν φόβος ἐν τ' αὐτῷ, ὥσπερ τῷ Ἰωσήφ, ἐκ τοῦ Κυρίου αὐτοῦ· πλέον δὲ θαυμάσειέ τις τὸ παρὸν ἢ τὸ παλαιόν.

since she is more malleable and more easily persuaded. But the divine and spiritually courageous Philotheos rebuffed her very gently and mildly, telling and reminding her of the *gehenna of fire, the worm, the gnashing of teeth* and the rest. Still she persisted even more forcefully, saying and doing everything to lure him into a shameful union. He who was brave and *adamantine in his soul,* not knowing what to do, called upon our Lord Jesus Christ for support; and indeed he found Him and He gave him guidance.

Philotheos revealed the situation to the superior of the monastery. That wise man summoned that thrice-twined serpent and, as was right, expelled her from the monastery after reprimanding her. Nor did this escape anyone's notice, just *as a city that lies atop a mountain is unable to conceal itself.* Because of this they acclaimed the holy man, calling him a radiant victor. And all gave glory to God, saying, "We have seen in our days a new Joseph." Just as he escaped from the Egyptian woman, so did this man from the woman with whom he shared a residence and a religion. And just as in the case of Joseph, the Lord made him fearless. Once again one should marvel more at the present event than at the ancient one.

4

Ὁ δὲ λαμπρὸς Φιλόθεος καὶ ἀφιλόκομπος τὴν ψυχήν, μὴ φέρων τὴν δόξαν τῶν ἀνθρώπων καὶ θέλων ἐκφυγεῖν ταύτην, προφασίζεται τοιοῦτο δρᾶμα, μήπως πάλιν ἐπεστῇ πειρασμὸς ὡς τὸ πρότερον· καὶ αἰτεῖ συγχώρησιν παρὰ τοῦ προεστῶτος τοῦ ἐξελθεῖν τῆς μονῆς. Ὁ δὲ ἠντιβόλει αὐτὸν λέγων, "Μὴ χωρισθῇς ἀφ᾽ ἡμῶν." Καὶ πάντα λίθον κινήσας, οὐκ ἐκάμπτετο τοῖς λόγοις αὐτοῦ. Ἰδὼν δὲ τὸ ἀμετάτρεπτον τοῦ νέου καὶ ὅτι εἰς κωφὸν ᾄδειν, καὶ ἄκων ἀπέλυσεν αὐτόν. Καὶ εὐθὺς βαλὼν μετάνοιαν καὶ εὐλογίαν λαβὼν παρὰ τοῦ πνευματικοῦ πατρὸς αὐτοῦ καὶ ἀσπασάμενος τοὺς ἀδελφοὺς πάντας, ἐξῄει τῆς μονῆς. Ἡ δὲ μήτηρ αὐτοῦ ἀπεβίω πρὸ ἱκανοῦ χρόνου.

2   Καὶ εὑρὼν ὁ θεῖος Φιλόθεος εὔλογον αἰτίαν ὥρμησεν εὐθὺς τῆς ὁδοῦ τοῦ ἐν τῷ Ἄθῳ ὡς ἔλαφος διψῶσα ἐπὶ τὰς διεξόδους τῶν ὑδάτων [see Psalm 41(42):1–2]. Καὶ λαχὼν εἰς κοινόβιον, ὅ ἐστι τοῦ Διονυσίου, οἰκεῖ ἐν αὐτῷ. Καὶ ποιεῖ μετάνοιαν τῷ καθηγουμένῳ, ὡς ἔθος ἐστί, καὶ καταλέγει ἑαυτὸν τοῖς ἀδελφοῖς καὶ ὑπηρετεῖν ὡς καὶ οἱ λοιποί. Οὕτως ἀόκνως καὶ δραστηρίως ἐποίει τὴν ὑπηρεσίαν τοῦ ναοῦ καὶ ἐν πάσαις ταῖς διακονίαις ὥστε θαυμάζειν πάντας. Καὶ ἔχαιρον ἐπ᾽ αὐτὸν καὶ ἐδόξαζον τὸν Θεὸν τὸν χορηγήσαντα τοιοῦτον μέγιστον ἀγαθὸν εἰς αὐτούς.

3   Ἱκανὸν δὲ χρόνον ἐνδιατρίψας ἐν τῷ κοινοβίῳ, οὐκ ἠρέμα ἀλλὰ καὶ ἀκάθεκτος ἦν καὶ διψῶν μόνος μεμονωμένος λαλῆσαι Θεῷ. Προφασισάμενος δὲ ὅτι ἠσθενηκὼς

Chapter 4

But the radiant Philotheos, who was humble in his soul, was unable to endure the glorification of mankind and wanted to escape it, so he devised the following course of action, lest temptation should come upon him again as before. He requested the superior's permission to depart from the monastery. The latter implored him, saying, "Do not leave us." But even though the superior *left no stone unturned,* the holy man was not swayed by his words. Seeing the steadfastness of the youth and that he *was singing to the deaf,* the superior reluctantly released him. After prostrating himself and receiving the blessing of his spiritual father and embracing all the brothers, Philotheos left the monastery. His mother had died some time before.

Having found a reasonable excuse, the divine Philotheos 2 hastened immediately along the road to Athos *like a thirsty deer toward streams of water.* He came to a cenobitic monastery, that of Dionysiou, and took up residence there. He prostrated himself before the superior, as is customary, and enrolled himself among the brethren in order to serve as did the others. He performed his services in the church and in all other duties so untiringly and vigorously that all were amazed. And they rejoiced in him and glorified God who had provided them with such a great blessing.

After living in the cenobitic monastery for some time, 3 however, he did not find repose but was restless and thirsting to converse with God in complete isolation. He pretended

<ἦν> καὶ ἐκωφώθη, λύπη δὲ ἔσχε τὸν προεστῶτα καὶ τοῖς ἀδελφοῖς πᾶσι περὶ τοῦ Φιλοθέου, νομίζων ὅτι ἀληθῆ λέγει. Ἔκτοτε οὖν λαβὼν ἀφορμὴν εὔλογον, αἰτεῖ παρὰ τοῦ καθηγουμένου συγχώρησιν τοῦ οἰκῆσαι ἔξω τῆς μονῆς, ἣν καὶ λαβὼν ἐξῄει τοῦ μοναστηρίου· καὶ ὁδεύσας ὡσεὶ στάδια ἓξ μήκοθεν τῆς μονῆς καὶ πήξας σκηνὴν [see Exodus 33:7] εἰς τραχὺν καὶ εἰς δύσβατον τόπον, κἀκεῖ τὰς εὐχὰς τῷ Κυρίῳ ἐκπληρῶν καὶ ἦν, διαιτώμενος ἄρτον καὶ ἅλας ἡμέραν παρ' ἡμέραν, προσθεὶς δὲ Σάββατον καὶ Κυριακὴν μόνον σιτίζεσθαι.

5

Ὁ γοῦν ἀρχέκακος καὶ ἀπ' ἀρχῆς Πολέμιος, μὴ φέρων τὴν προκοπὴν τοῦ ἁγίου, πειρᾶται ὑποσκελίσαι αὐτόν· καὶ σχηματίσας ἑαυτὸν ὁ κατάρατος ὡς δῆθεν ἐκ ναυαγίου ἐλθὼν καὶ πλανώμενος ἐν τῷ κρυμῷ βοῶν καὶ λέγων, "Ἐλέησόν με, δοῦλε τοῦ Θεοῦ, ὅτι κακῶς ἀπόλλομαι ἐν τῇ νυκτὶ ταύτῃ." Ὁ δὲ ἅγιος, μὴ γνοὺς τὴν πανουργίαν τοῦ Διαβόλου, ἐξῆλθε τοῦ οἰκτειρίσαι αὐτόν. Ὁ δὲ κατάρατος συμποδίζει καὶ ὠθεῖ κατὰ τοῦ κρυμοῦ τὸν ἅγιον. Ἀλλὰ καὶ πάλιν κεναῖς ἔμεινε ταῖς ἐλπίσιν ὁ παλαμναῖος · ὁ δὲ ἅγιος, διαφυλαχθεὶς τῇ τοῦ Θεοῦ χάριτι, οὐδὲν κακὸν πεπονθώς, παρά τινος μοναχοῦ διασωθεὶς ἐκ τοῦ κρυμοῦ.

2 Καὶ ἔμεινεν ἱκανὸν χρόνον· ὡς οὐκέτι κωφεύων

that he was ill and suffering from deafness. The superior and all the brothers were saddened regarding Philotheos, believing that he spoke the truth. Then using this reasonable pretext, he requested the superior's permission to reside outside the monastery. Upon receiving it, he departed. After making a journey of six stades beyond the monastery, *he established his residence* in a harsh and inaccessible place; and there he performed his prayers to the Lord and lived on bread and salt every other day, adding other food only on Saturday and Sunday.

Chapter 5

Then the originator of evil, our Enemy from the very beginning, was unable to bear the holy man's spiritual progress, and attempted to trip him up. The accursed one disguised himself as if he had escaped from a shipwreck, and wandered among the cliffs, shouting and saying, "Have mercy on me, servant of God, for I am in terrible danger tonight." The holy man, failing to realize the Devil's villainy, came out to help him. Then the accursed one tripped him and pushed the holy man toward the precipice. But again the miscreant remained empty-handed, and the holy man, who was preserved through God's grace, suffered no harm and was saved from the cliff by a monk.

He remained there for some time; no longer able to feign   2

(ἀνεγνώσθη δὲ παρά τινος μοναχοῦ ὅτι ὑποκρινόμενος ἦν), ἐξῆλθε τῆς κέλλης καί, ἀπελθὼν εἰς ἕτερον τόπον πλησίον ἄλλου μοναστηρίου, οἰκεῖ ἐν αὐτῷ καὶ ποιήσας μαθητὰς τρεῖς εἰς τύπον τῆς ἁγίας Τριάδος. Καὶ πάλιν ὁ Πειράζων ὁπλίζεται κατὰ τοῦ ἁγίου καὶ καλεῖ εἰς συμμαχίαν πλοῖον Ἀγαρηνῶν, ὧν καὶ προσώρμησαν τῇ κέλλῃ τοῦ ἁγίου. Ἰδόντες δὲ οἱ μαθηταὶ αὐτοῦ φυγὰς ᾤχοντο. Ὁ δὲ ἅγιος τῷ τιμίῳ τοῦ σταυροῦ σφραγισάμενος καὶ ἐκτείνας τὰς χεῖρας εἰς τὸν οὐρανὸν καὶ τὴν εὐχὴν ἐπειπών, "Κύριε Ἰησοῦ Χριστέ, ὁ Θεὸς ἡμῶν, ὁ σώσας τοὺς Ἰσραηλίτας ἐκ χειρὸς Φαραώ, οὕτω καὶ νῦν, Δέσποτα, σῶσον ἡμᾶς ἐν τῇ ὥρᾳ ταύτῃ." Καὶ παραχρῆμα ἐγείρεται κλύδων ἐν τῇ θαλάσσῃ καὶ οὐκ εἶδαν οἱ κατάρατοι πόθεν ἀπέδρασαν. Καὶ ἔμεινεν ὁ ἅγιος ἀβλαβὴς σὺν τῇ συνοδίᾳ αὐτοῦ τῇ τοῦ Θεοῦ χάριτι.

3 Χρόνῳ δὲ πολλῷ προστετηκὼς ἑαυτόν, προσθεὶς νηστείαν τῇ νηστείᾳ, ἀγρυπνίᾳ τὴν ἀγρυπνίαν καὶ πληθύνων πληθύνων τὰς εὐχὰς τῷ Κυρίῳ, ἠξίωται προορατικοῦ χαρίσματος. Καί ποτε ἐλθὼν εἰς τὴν σύναξιν (ἑορτῆς γὰρ οὔσης τῶν ἐπισήμων, ἐν ᾗ ἱερούργουν ἅπαντες οἱ ἱερεῖς τοῦ μοναστηρίου ἐν ᾧ ἐστι τοῦ Βατοπεδίου), καὶ πήξας ἑαυτὸν ἐν κόγχῃ τοῦ ναοῦ ἐπροσηύχετο. Καὶ γινομένης τῆς Μεγάλης Εἰσόδου παρὰ τῶν ἱερέων, ὁρᾷ ὁ θειότατος γέρων κόρακα προπορευόμενον ἔμπροσθεν τῶν μανουαλίων· καὶ ἐθαύμασε τὸ τί ἂν εἴη τὸ ὁραθέν, καὶ ἐρευνήσας τὸ δρᾶμα, εὗρεν ἑνὶ τῶν ἱερέων εἰς πτῶμα πεσών· καὶ κατηχήσας αὐτὸν ἐκώλυσε τοῦ ἱερουργεῖν. Καὶ οὐκέτι πλέον ὁ σκολιὸς ἐφάνη κόραξ. Καὶ πάντας ἐπιτιμήσας ἢ

deafness (as it was revealed by a monk that he was only pretending to be deaf), he left his cell and went to a different place near another monastery, where he took up residence and trained three disciples on the model of the Holy Trinity. And again the Tempter armed himself against the holy man and summoned to his aid a ship of the Agarenes who had cast anchor near the holy man's cell. When his disciples saw this, they rushed away in flight. But the holy man made the sign of the holy cross and, extending his hands to the heavens, said a prayer: "Lord Jesus Christ, our God, who saved the Israelites from the hands of Pharaoh, in the same way now, Lord, save us at this hour." Immediately the sea billowed with waves and the accursed ones were unable to escape. The holy man remained unharmed along with his companions through God's grace.

After many years of emaciating himself, adding fast to 3 fast, vigil to vigil and multiplying multitudes of prayers to the Lord, he was deemed worthy of the gift of foresight. Once when he came to services (for it was one of the important feasts in which all the priests of the monastery of Vatopedi were performing the liturgy), after ensconcing himself in an apse of the church, he devoted himself to prayer. While the priests were performing the ceremony of the Great Entrance, the most holy elder Philotheos saw a crow flying in front of the candelabra and wondered what the vision might mean. When he looked into the situation, he discovered that one of the priests had fallen into sin. After questioning him, he forbade him to perform the liturgy. Subsequently the evil crow appeared no more. And after

καὶ διδάξας ἱκανῶς, ἐπορεύθη εἰς τὴν κέλλαν αὐτοῦ μετὰ τῶν αὐτοῦ μαθητῶν.

4 Καὶ ἐν βαθὺ γῆρας ἐλάσας, πρὸς Κύριον ἐξεδήμησεν, ἐτῶν ὑπάρχων τέσσαρσι πρὸς τοῖς ὀγδοήκοντα. Ἐκοιμήθη δὲ εἰκοστῇ πρώτῃ τοῦ Ὀκτωβρίου μηνός. Τοὺς δὲ μαθητὰς αὐτοῦ τὴν συνήθη εὐλογίαν ἀφείς, καὶ ἐντολὴν δίδωσιν αὐτοῖς τοῦ μὴ θάψαι τὸ σῶμα αὐτοῦ, ἀλλ᾽ ἐᾶσαι αὐτὸ ἄταφον τοῦ βρωθῆναι ὑπὸ θηρίων, τὸν μέγαν γὰρ Εὐφραὶμ μιμησάμενος. Οἱ δὲ μαθηταὶ τὰ κελευσθέντα ὑπὸ τοῦ διδασκάλου ἐποίουν προθύμως καὶ ἔσυραν τὸ ἅγιον αὐτοῦ λείψανον ἕως σταδίων ἐννέα καὶ ἔασαν αὐτὸ ἐν τῇ ὕλῃ, μηδενὸς γιγνώσκοντος.

6

Περὶ δὲ τῶν θαυμάτων, ὧν ἐποίει ὁ ἅγιος καὶ μετὰ θάνατον, οὐ δύναται γραφῇ παραδοῦναι. Ἡμεῖς δὲ τῇ συντομίᾳ χρώμενοι ἓν καὶ μόνον ἐπιμνησθῶμεν ἐξαίρετον καὶ θαυμασιώτατον, τὰ πολλὰ ἐάσαντες. Ὑμεῖς, ὦ φιλόθεοι καὶ φιλήκοοι, τὸν νοῦν προσεκτικώτερον στήσατε ἐπὶ τῇ διηγήσει τοῦ θαύματος. Ἐν ἐκείνῳ τῷ καιρῷ μοναχός τις ἐπορεύθη ἐν τῷ αἰγιαλῷ τοῦ ἁλιεύειν, ἵνα ἀγρεύσῃ τι, καὶ ἔμεινεν ὅλην τὴν νύκτα διανυκτερεύων. Καὶ πρωῒ ἔτι σκοτίας οὔσης, ἐρχόμενος ἐν τῇ μονῇ, ὁρᾷ φῶς ἐν τῇ ὕλῃ. Καὶ προσδοκῶν ὅτι πυρκαϊά ἐστι, ὥρμησεν εὐθὺς εἰς τὸ πῦρ, ὅτι ψῦχος ἦν, εἰς τὸ θερμανθῆναι.

either censuring or rather instructing them all for some time, he returned to his cell along with his disciples.

At a very old age, he departed to the Lord, being eighty-four years old. He died on the twenty-first of October. Bestowing upon his disciples the customary blessing, he charged them not to bury his body, but to leave it exposed to be consumed by the beasts, imitating the great Ephraim. The disciples complied willingly with their teacher's instructions, and dragged his holy remains nine stades and left it in the woods unbeknownst to all. 4

Chapter 6

Regarding the miracles that the holy man performed even after death, it is not possible to commit them to writing. Cutting the story short, we will only call to mind a single remarkable and most wondrous example, and leave the majority aside. O my God-loving attentive audience, pay close attention to my description of the miracle. At that time a monk went to the seashore to catch fish, and he remained there awake all night. In the morning while it was still dark, as he was going toward the monastery, he saw a light in the woods. Supposing that it was a fire, he rushed immediately toward the flames to warm himself, for it was cold.

2   Καὶ πλησιάσας τὸ φῶς, ὁρᾷ τὴν κεφαλὴν τοῦ ὁσίου ὡς ἀστέρα φαεινὸν ἐπάνω τῶν ὀστέων αὐτοῦ. Καὶ ἰδὼν τὸ θαῦμα ἐξέστη καὶ ὥρμησεν εἰς τὸ φυγεῖν. Καὶ πάλιν ἐλθὼν εἰς ἑαυτόν (καὶ τοῦτο τῆς θείας χάριτος, τὸ μὴ κρύπτεσθαι τοιοῦτος θησαυρός), ἐθάρρυνε τὸν μοναχὸν τοῦ λαβεῖν τοῦ ὁσίου τὴν κάραν, ὃ καὶ πεποίηκεν. Καὶ γνοὺς αὐτὴν ὅτι τοῦ ὁσίου πατρὸς καὶ πνευματικοῦ Φιλοθέου ἐστίν, ἔλαβεν αὐτὴν μετὰ πολλοῦ τοῦ δέους. Ὤιχετο ἐν τῇ κέλλᾳ αὐτοῦ μετὰ φόβου καὶ χαρᾶς πολλῆς καὶ ἔθηκεν αὐτὴν ἐν ἐπισήμῳ τόπῳ, ἣν καὶ μυρίσας καὶ θυμιάσας, ὡς εἰκὸς ἦν. Καὶ βουλόμενος ποιῆσαι τὸ δρᾶμα ἀφανές, καὶ τῇ ἐπιούσῃ νυκτὶ πάλιν θυμιάσας καὶ ἀσπασάμενος αὐτὴν ἐπὶ τῆς στρωμνῆς ἐχώρει. Εἰσελθὼν δὲ εἰς αὐτὸν φόβος καὶ δειλία, ὥστε οὐδὲ ὑπνώττει, καθεκτὸς ἦν. Ἔμεινε δὲ ὅλῃ τῇ νυκτὶ ἐκείνῃ ἄυπνος τὸ καθόλου, ἕως οὗ κρούσαντος τοῦ ξύλου εἰς τὴν ὀρθρινὴν ὑμνῳδίαν.

3   Καλεῖται καὶ αὐτὸς ἐν τῷ νεῷ ἐκτελέσων τὰς εὐχὰς τῷ Κυρίῳ. Καὶ ἔστησαν ἀνάγνωσιν ὡς ἔθος ἐστί. Ἐκαθέζοντο πάντες ἐν τοῖς αὐτῶν τόποις, ὁ δὲ μοναχὸς ὁ τὸ ἕρμαιον ἔχων ὕπνωσεν ἐν τῷ στασιδίῳ αὐτοῦ, ἀγρυπνημένου γὰρ ὄντος· καὶ ὁρᾷ τὸν ἅγιον ἐν ὁράματι ἐκφοβοῦντα καὶ ἐπιτιμῶντα αὐτῷ μετὰ σοβαροῦ τοῦ φρονήματος καὶ λέγοντα, "Ἀπόδος τὴν κεφαλήν μου ἐν τάχει εἰς τοὺς μαθητὰς τοὺς ἐμούς, ἵνα μὴ χεῖρόν τί σοι γένηται." Ὁ δὲ ἄκων καὶ μὴ βουλόμενος ἀπέδοτο αὐτὴν εἰς αὐτούς. Καὶ ἰδόντες αὐτὴν ἐχάρησαν σφόδρα καὶ ἐδόξαζον τὸν Θεὸν τὸν δοξάσαντα τὸν διδάσκαλον καὶ πατέρα αὐτῶν. Καὶ εἶχον αὐτὴν ἕρμαιον καὶ φυλακτήριον ὡς ἔτι ζῶντος

Approaching the light, he saw the holy man's head shin- 2
ing like a star above his bones. At the sight of the miracle he
was amazed and hastened to get away. But coming again to
his senses (this was through divine grace, so that such a treasure might not be hidden), the monk was emboldened to
take the holy man's head, and this is what he did. Knowing
that it was the head of the holy spiritual father Philotheos,
he took it with much awe. He went to his cell with fear and
great joy, put it in a prominent place, applied perfumed oil
to it and censed it, as was appropriate. However, he wanted
to keep the matter secret. The next evening he again censed
it and kissed it and then went to bed. But such fear and
fright overwhelmed him that he could not sleep at all, and
remained awake. He spent that entire night completely
sleepless, until the striking of the wooden sounding board
for matins.

He too was summoned to the church to perform prayers 3
to the Lord. They set up the reading, as is customary. They
all sat in their places and the monk who possessed the godsend fell asleep at his stand, since he had been sleepless. In a
vision he saw the holy man threatening and censuring him
with a severe demeanor and saying, "Give my head back to
my disciples immediately, so that nothing worse may happen to you." Reluctantly and against his will he returned it
to them. When they saw Philotheos's head, they rejoiced
greatly and glorified God who had glorified their teacher
and father. They kept it as a godsend and an amulet, as if he

αὐτοῦ εἰς ἀνατροπὴν παντὸς ἐπηρεασμοῦ ψυχικοῦ τε καὶ σωματικοῦ· ὧν γένοιτο καὶ ἡμᾶς ἐπιτυχεῖν τῆς τοιαύτης ἀντιλήψεως, χάριτι καὶ φιλανθρωπίᾳ τοῦ Κυρίου ἡμῶν Ἰησοῦ Χριστοῦ, μεθ᾽ οὗ τῷ Πατρὶ ἅμα τῷ ἁγίῳ Πνεύματι δόξα, κράτος, τιμὴ καὶ προσκύνησις, νῦν καὶ ἀεὶ καί εἰς τοὺς αἰῶνας τῶν αἰώνων, ἀμήν.

were still alive, to overcome every temptation either spiritual or physical. May we too attain such succor, through the grace and compassion of our Lord Jesus Christ to whom, along with the Father and the Holy Spirit, belong glory, power, and veneration, now and always and to the ages of ages, Amen.

Abbreviations

BHG = F. Halkin, ed., *Bibliotheca Hagiographica Graeca* (Brussels, 1957)

BMFD = J. T. and A. C. Hero, eds., *Byzantine Monastic Foundation Documents*. 5 vols. (Washington, D.C., 2000)

BZ = *Byzantinische Zeitschrift*

CPG = E. Leutsch and F. G. Schneidewin, eds., *Corpus Paroemiographorum Graecorum*. 2 vols. (Göttingen, 1851; repr. Hildesheim, 1965)

DOP = *Dumbarton Oaks Papers*

Follieri, *Initia* = E. Follieri, ed., *Initia Hymnorum Ecclesiae Graecae*. 5 vols. (Rome, 1960–1966)

Grumel, *Chronologie* = V. Grumel, *La Chronologie* (Paris, 1958)

Janin, *Constantinople byz.* = R. Janin, *Constantinople byzantine* (Paris, 1964)

Janin, *EglisesCP* = R. Janin, *La géographie ecclésiastique de l'empire byzantin, I: Le siège de Constantinople et le patriarcat oecuménique, 3: Les églises et les monastères*² (Paris, 1969)

Janin, *Grands centres* = R. Janin, *Les églises et les monastères des grands centres byzantins* (Paris, 1975)

LbG = E. Trapp, ed., *Lexikon zur byzantinischen Gräzität* (Vienna, 1994–)

LSJ = H. G. Liddell, R. Scott, et al., eds., *A Greek-English Lexicon* (Oxford, 1968)

Meyer, *Haupturkunden* = P. Meyer, *Die Haupturkunden für die Geschichte der Athosklöster* (Leipzig, 1894)

MM = F. Miklosich, J. Müller, eds., *Acta et diplomata graeca medii aevi sacra et profana.* 6 vols. (Vienna, 1860–1890)

ODB = A. P. Kazhdan et al., eds., *Oxford Dictionary of Byzantium.* 3 vols. (New York, 1991)

PG = J.-P. Migne, ed., *Patrologiae cursus completus, series Graeca.* 161 vols. (Paris, 1857–1866)

PGL = G. W. H. Lampe, ed., *A Patristic Greek Lexicon* (Oxford, 1961–1968)

PLP = E. Trapp, ed., *Prosopographisches Lexikon der Palaiologenzeit.* 12 vols. (Vienna, 1976–1996)

PmbZ = R.-J. Lilie et al., eds., *Prosopographie der mittelbyzantinischen Zeit.* Series 1, 6 vols.; Series 2, 8 vols. (Berlin, 1998–2013)

Sturz, *Etymologicum* = F. Sturz, ed., *Etymologicum Graecae linguae Gudianum* (Leipzig, 1818; repr. Hildesheim, 1973)

SynaxCP = H. Delehaye, ed., *Synaxarium ecclesiae Constantinopolitanae: Propylaeum ad Acta sanctorum Novembris* (Brussels, 1902)

TLG = *Thesaurus Linguae Graecae* (http://www.tlg.uci.edu/)

Note on the Texts

LIFE OF EUTHYMIOS THE YOUNGER

The *Life of Euthymios the Younger* has already been edited by the French Assumptionist scholar Louis Petit in the *Revue de l'Orient chrétien*.[1] That edition, however, although based on three of the four manuscripts that preserve the entire text, is marred by numerous misreadings and, occasionally, by rather unnecessary or infelicitous emendations.[2] This is the result not only of the editor's hasty work, but also of his decision to tacitly give preference to the text provided by the most recent manuscript, the *Athonensis Panteleemonos* 207 (= P) of the nineteenth century[3] (a paper codex of both late date and inferior quality), at the expense of the other two.[4] Petit was not able to consult the fourth manuscript, the parchment *Mosquensis Bibl. Synod.* 174 (Vladimir 387) (= M in the present edition), which is possibly the earliest one (tenth/eleventh century), a manuscript that originally belonged to the Great Lavra.[5] He did, however, use another early manuscript, that is, the parchment *Athonensis Megistes Lavras* Δ.78 (= L) of the eleventh century.[6] The third manuscript used by Petit was the paper *Athonensis Vatopediou* 631 of the year 1422 (= V).[7] In his introduction to the edition, Petit claims that he used L as the basic manuscript[8] and that he was also able to check the entire text in P. Unfortunately,

as he remarks, while consulting V, the difficult circumstances of their expedition to Athos did not permit them to collate the variants beyond fol. 150[v].[9] Sporadic indications in the critical apparatus of this edition show also that Eduard Kurtz contributed some emendations to the text and sent Petit a few readings from M after inspection *in situ*.

As becomes readily evident from their common mistakes, L and M copy the same lost archetype. This can be easily explained by the fact that both were originally copied in the monastery of the Great Lavra, although only one, L, remains there to this day. M is marred by numerous mistakes of iotacism, confusion between omicron and omega or other similarly sounding vowels, duplication of single consonants, and simplification of double ones. In many instances the same mistakes are extant in L, but a second hand has corrected most of them above the line. V diverges slightly from L and M and, on occasion, is more reliable than all the other witnesses. It possibly copied a manuscript that was textually very close to the lost archetype of L and M. In a number of cases I have given preference to its readings against those of all other manuscripts. Finally, P seems to have copied in a rather careless fashion either L or M or their archetype. Some of its mistakes are repeated in Petit's edition.

For the present edition I have used all four manuscripts that are extant, but efforts have been made to restrict the notes to the most significant variants and errors, including those of Petit's edition. For this reason, omissions of double letters or the opposite, iotacisms and other similar errors, and mistaken readings and variants transmitted by only one manuscript are omitted, unless they offer a defensible read-

ing. As indicated in the Notes to the Texts, a few passages remain problematic.

Life of Athanasios of Athos, Version B

The Greek text is based on the excellent edition of Jacques Noret,[10] which has required almost no emendation at all; we have included in the endnotes two suggestions made by Jan Olof Rosenqvist in his *Byzantinische Zeitschrift* review of 1983. As in the texts of all the *Lives* except that of Euthymios, we have mostly limited ourselves to the addition of paragraph numbers within each chapter, a few changes in punctuation, especially with regard to quotation marks, and some capitalization of proper names. We have also indicated a few additional scriptural and patristic references missed by Noret. We thank the publisher for granting us copyright permission to reproduce the Noret text, without its critical apparatus.

Lives of Maximos the Hutburner by Niphon and by Theophanes

The texts of the two versions of the *Life of Maximos* included in this volume were originally published in 1936 by François Halkin.[11] His edition was based on a transcription by the Lavriot monk Eulogios Kourilas, supplemented by photographs of the manuscripts. Both vitae were edited from single manuscripts preserved in Athonite monasteries: that by Niphon from Lavra Θ 58 of the sixteenth or seventeenth century, and that by Theophanes from Panteleimon 552 of the sixteenth century. For the most part we have faithfully reproduced the text established by Halkin, who deliberately

retained some phrases of unorthodox Greek that Kourilas would have preferred to normalize; we agree with Halkin's argument that they reflect the spoken Greek of the fourteenth century and are thus not without interest to the scholar. In only a few places have we suggested different readings.

LIFE OF NIPHON

Halkin also published the edition of this vita, four years after those of Maximos.[12] This work was edited from three Athonite manuscripts of the sixteenth to eighteenth centuries. The first, Lavra Θ 58 of the sixteenth or seventeenth century is the same manuscript as that containing Niphon's *Life of Maximos*. Halkin argues this was likely the source of the second witness, the seventeenth-century Dionysiou 132, although the scribe of the latter has engaged in some reworking of the style; the third manuscript, Kausokalyvia 12, is a relatively late eighteenth-century luxury edition of Athonite saints' *Lives,* in which the *Life of Niphon* has undergone substantial manipulation.

In this volume the Greek text is reproduced virtually unchanged from the 1940 edition of Halkin; we have made only some tacit changes in the punctuation and capitalization.

LIFE OF PHILOTHEOS

We have used a very slightly modified version of the edition of Basilike Papoulia,[13] which is based on a single seventeenth-century manuscript (codex 132) at the Dionysiou monastery on Athos, copied by the monk Daniel of the same monas-

tery. The previously published Greek text contains a few errors, which we have endeavored to correct, and presents some difficulties that could not be resolved by inspection of a digital reproduction of the original codex.

NOTES

1 Petit, "St. Euthyme le Jeune."

2 Here is an example of Petit's work. On page 184 of his edition, in the very first line of the critical apparatus, for the reading προθύμως adopted in the main text, Petit inserted the remark: "4. προθύμους LVP: on attendrait προθύμως . . ."; however, all three (in fact, all four) manuscripts preserve the reading προθύμως.

3 Description in S. P. Lambros, *Catalogue of the Greek Manuscripts on Mount Athos* (Cambridge, 1900), 2:329, no. 5714.

4 An example of Petit's misplaced preference for the nineteenth-century manuscript is this: on the same page 184, line 28, Petit has adopted the reading πολυπλασίονα ἀποποιεῖσθαι, which makes no sense within the particular context. In the critical apparatus is inserted the indication: "28. ποιεῖσθαι V." The manuscripts preserve the reading, πολυπλασίονα ποιεῖσθαι LMV and πολυπλάσιον ἀποποιεῖσθαι P. Evidently Petit simply improved on what is extant in P instead of consulting the other two manuscripts (L and V) at his disposal.

5 Description in Vladimir (Archimandrite), *Sistematičeskoe opisanie rykopisej Moskovskoj Sinodalnoj (Patriaršei) biblioteki* (Moscow, 1894), 1:582. We are grateful to Dr. Emilia Shulgina and her colleagues at the State Historical Museum in Moscow for providing a digital file of this manuscript. We also acknowledge the generous assistance in this matter of Dr. Nadezhda Kavrus-Hoffmann, who suggests that this manuscript may date as early as the late tenth century (personal communication).

6 Description in Spyridon Laureotes-S. Eustratiades, Κατάλογος τῶν Κωδίκων τῆς Μεγίστης Λαύρας (τῆς ἐν τῷ Ἁγίῳ Ὄρει) (Paris, 1925), 69–70. In this catalog the manuscript bears the number 454.

7 Description in S. Eustratiades-Arkadios Vatopedinos, Κατάλογος τῶν ἐν τῇ Ἱερᾷ Μονῇ Βατοπεδίου ἀποκειμένων κωδίκων (Paris, 1924), 124–25.

We are grateful to the brethren of the Monastery of Vatopedi for their kind offer of digital reproductions of folios 131^v–134 of this manuscript.

 8 Petit, "St. Euthyme le Jeune," 162.

 9 Ibid., 163.

10 Noret, *Vitae duae.*

11 Halkin, "Deux vies."

12 Halkin, "Niphon."

13 Papoulia, "Philotheos."

Notes to the Texts

The notes are referenced by chapter and paragraph number. The following abbreviations and symbols are used in the text and textual notes:

add. = added in/by
post corr. = after correction
fol(s). = folio page(s)
in marg. = in margin
om. = omitted in/by
ms = manuscript
<. . .> = editorial insertion
[. . .] = editorial seclusion
† = corrupt reading

LIFE OF EUTHYMIOS THE YOUNGER

Sigla

L = *Athonensis Μεγίστης Λαύρας* Δ.78 (454) (11th cent., fols. 142–163ᵛ)
M = *Mosquensis Bibl. Synodal.* 387 (10th–11th cent., fols. 143–179)
P = *Athonensis Παντελεήμονος* 207 (19th cent., fols. 1–32) [Lambros 5714]
V = *Athonensis Βατοπεδίου* 546 (1422, fols. 131–169ᵛ)
Petit = L. Petit, ed., "Vie et office de St. Euthyme le Jeune," in *Revue de l'Orient chrétien* 8 (1903): 155–205, 503–36.

Title   Βίος . . . Εὐλόγησον πάτερ: μηνὶ τῷ αὐτῷ ιε΄: λόγος κδ΄ *in marg.* L; ΜΗΝΙ ΌΚΤΩΒΡΊῼ ΙΕ΄ φύλλα λζ΄ *in marg.* M; τῷ αὐτῷ μηνὶ, ιε΄ λόγος στ΄ φύλλα λθ΄ βίος καὶ πολιτεία τοῦ ὁσίου πατρὸς ἡμῶν εὐθυμίου τοῦ νέου, τοῦ ἐν θεσσαλονίκῃ· συγγραφεὶς παρὰ βασιλείου ἀρχιεπισκόπου θεσσαλονίκης, εὐλό-

γησον πάτερ V; Ὀκτωβρίου ιδ´ βίος τοῦ ὁσίου πατρὸς ἡμῶν Εὐθυμίου, τοῦ ἐν Θεσσαλονίκῃ τοῦ ὑπὲρ τῶν ἁγίων εἰκόνων ἀγωνισαμένου. Εὐλόγησον πάτερ. P

1.2   εὐπρεπέστατα οἷς: εὐπρεπέστατα οἷς Petit, τοῖς LMVP

2.1   ἐποφειλῶς: ἐπωφελῶς *post corr.* P, Petit

2.3   διαπορθμεῦσαι δυνήσεται: διαπορθμεῦσαι δυνήσηται LMP, Petit

      τοῦτο τῶν ὅσοι: τῶν Petit *(corr. by Kurtz),* τοῖς LMVP

      θήσει τὰ νικητήρια: θέσει τὰ νικητήρια LVP

3.2   ῥᾳθυμίᾳ: ῥᾳθύμως P, Petit

3.4   στρατείᾳ τε καταλεγομένους: τε *om.* V, Petit

      ἀπονεύοντας: *Here we have accepted P's reading of* ἀπονεύοντας, *instead of* ὑπονεύοντας *of LVM and Petit. Alexakis prefers* ὑπονεύοντας.

      ὅτι καὶ μᾶλλον: καὶ *om.* LVP, Petit

      προτροπῇ ἀλλήλους: προτροπῇ ἀλλήλους V, Petit, ἀλλήλοις LMP

      ὃς δύναιτ᾽: ὃς *post corr.* LMV, ὡς P, Petit

3.6   ὁ φάνας μὲν τότε: ὅτε LMVP *(corr. by Kurtz)*

4.1   καταλήγουσαν: *Here we prefer* καταλήγουσαν *of LMP; Petit emends to* καταλήγουσα; *Alexakis prefers* κατάγουσα *of V.*

      ὅτε τῷ βίῳ: ὅταν τῷ βίῳ LMP, Petit

5.1   ὁ μὲν πατὴρ: ὁ μέγας πατὴρ V

      προσηγόρευτο: προσηγορεύετο P, Petit

      γενέσεως: γεννήσεως P, Petit

      θεοπρόπου: θεοπρόπου *(corr. by Talbot),* θεοτρόπου Petit, θεοπρόπτου LMVP

6.1   ἐλπιζομένην: ἐλπιζομένης LMP

      εἰσοισαμένης: εἰσοικισαμένης MP

      βουλευθεῖσιν: βουληθεῖσιν P, Petit

      καθ᾽ ἣν ἔθιμον: καθ᾽ ἣν ἔθιστο LP

7.2   μοναχῷ γενομένῳ: μοναχῷ γεναμένωι LM

7.3   δόκιμον: δοκίμιον LMP

8.1   τῷ καθηγητῇ βουλομένου τοῦ ὀνόματος: τοῦ καθηγητοῦ βουλομένου (-ῳ P) τῷ ὀνόματι Petit

ὅτε διὰ γυναικὸς: ὅταν διὰ γυναικὸς LMP, Petit

9.1 τῷ τῶν Πισσαδινῶν . . . κοινοβίῳ: τῷ *om.* LV, Petit

10.1 ἀγνώς τις: ἀγνωστὴς LMVP *(corr. by Petit)*

10.2 τῆς διηγήσεως γενομένου: τῆς διηγήσεως γεναμένου LM, γι- νομένου P, γενομένῳ Petit

παραδραμόντος: παραδραμόντι Petit

<τὸ> τουτωνὶ: τοτωνὶ P, τὸ <του>τωνὶ Petit

τῇ παρὰ μικρὸν παρανεύσει Petit: τῇ κάρᾳ μικρὸν παρανεύσει LMVP

τῷ . . . ἀπομάχεσθαι: τὸ Petit

11.2 ἑαυτὸν λογιζόμενος: αὐτὸν LM

τὸν προγενόμενον: προσγενόμενον V, Petit

ἢ καὶ ἐπιγινόμενον: *om.* V, Petit

θείων λόγων: θείων λογίων V, Petit

12.2 Ἐπὶ δέκα δὲ: δὲ *om.* LVP, Petit

ἀνονήτως ἀπομάχεσθαι: ἀνοήτως ἀπομάχεσθαι LMP

13.2 ἐπεμηχανήσατό: ἐνεμηχανήσατο L, ἐμηχανήσατο VP, Petit

ἀποσκευασάσης: ἀποτελεσάσης V, Petit

14.1 τοῦ ἱεροῦ ποιμένος αὐτοῦ: τοῦ ἱεροῦ ποιμένος αὐτῷ LMP, Petit

14.2 τοῦ ἁγίου . . . προσχήματος: *om.* V, προσχήματος P, Petit

εὐχῆς αὐτῷ γενομένης: εὐχῆς αὐτῷ γεναμένης LM

τῆς πρὸς τὸν Ἄθω πορείας: τὴν . . . πορείαν LM

τοῖς αὐτοῦ συνασκηταῖς: αὐτοῦ *om.* LM

15.2 περὶ ἑαυτοῦ: περὶ αὐτοῦ LMP

καθορκώσας: κατορκώσας LM, κατορθώσας P

ὡς καὶ αὐτὸς: καὶ *om.* V, Petit

15.3 Εἰ δ᾽ οὖν: εἰ δ᾽ οὔ Petit

16.1 διεντέταλτο: διετέταλτο LMP

16.2 ἀϊδίῳ: ἀϊδίως P, Petit

17.2 πρὸ: πρὸς MP, Petit

τῆς ἀσκητικῆς αὐτοῦ παλαίστρας: τὴν ἀσκητικὴν αὐτοῦ πα- λαίστραν Petit

ἑαυτοὺς ἐπιλογισώμεθα: αὐτοὺς ἐπιλογισώμεθα LM

18.1 προσειθίζοντο: προσηθίζοντο LMVP

τοῦ τέλους βίου: τέλους *om.* LMP

18.2   προθύμως: προθύμους Petit

19.2   αὐτοῖς ὁ καιρὸς: ὁ καιρὸς αὐτοῖς V, Petit

        πολυπλασίονα ποιεῖσθαι: πολυπλάσιον ἀποποιεῖσθαι P, πολυ-
πλασίονα ἀποποιεῖσθαι Petit

20.2   ἑαυτὸν περιφράττοντος: αὐτὸν περιφράττοντος LMP

21.1   τεθνάναι: τεθναίειν LMVP, τεθνάναι *(corr. by Kurtz)*

21.2   ἐπὶ ἑτέραν συμβολὴν: πάλιν *post* ἑτέραν *add.* M

22.2   προσνεκρωθὲν: προνεκρωθὲν MV

        πόρρω καθίστασθαι: πόρρω καθέζεσθαι V

        ἐγλίχετο: ἔγλιχε LMP, Petit

22.3   ἀπηγορευκὼς: ἀπαγορευκὼς LMVP

23.1   ἐκγόνους: ἔκγονας LMVP, Petit *(corr. by Alexakis)*

23.2   Πρώτως: πρῶτος LMP, Πρῶτον Petit

        προσεξακουόμενος: προεξακουόμενος Petit

23.3   πολὺς ἦν: ἦν *om.* Petit

24.1   ἔστιν οὓς: ἔστιν ὧν LV, οὖν MP *(corr. by Kurtz)*

        Ἄθῳ: Ἄθωνι M

24.2   ἀνδράσιν ἁγίοις: ἀνδράσιν ἱεραγίοις V

24.3   ὁμόγνωμον: ὁμογνώμων Petit

25.1   ἡ ἑτέρα δὲ: ἡ δὲ ἑτέρα P, Petit

25.2   ἡμῖν τὸ τοῦ πλοὸς: *om.* V

        †δέος μέχρις ἐνθυμούμενον†: *we have obelized the phrase* δέος . . .
ἐνθυμούμενον (ἐνθυμουμένων V)

        τῷ θείῳ δυσμενεῖν ἐπιχειροῦντες βουλήματι: *om.* V

25.3   Ὡς δὲ ταῦτα εἰπόντος: *om.* V

        ἐπευφήμησαν: *post* ἐπευφήμησαν V *add.* καὶ

25.4   ἀπέδοσθε: ἀπέδοσθαι LMV, ἀποδέδοσθε P

25.5   ἐπικατελάβετο: ἐπεκατελάβετο LMVP

26.1   χωρία ἄσυλα ἑαυτοῖς: χωρία ἄσυλα ἑαυτοὺς LMP, ἑαυτῶν Petit

        ὁ καθ᾽ εἷς: ὁ καθεὶς LMP, καθεῖς Petit

26.2   πρεσβύτης ἤδη γενόμενος: πρεσβύτης ἤδη γενάμενος LM

        ὁ Θεὸς ἡμῶν: ὁ Θεὸς ἡμᾶς LMP *(corr. by Petit)*, *om.* V

        τὰ μὲν γραφῇ: τὰ μὲν γραφῆς LVP

        τὰ δὲ: καὶ *add.* P, Petit *post* τὰ δὲ

27.3   οὐ καλὸν γὰρ ἔτι: οὐ καλὸν γάρ ἐστι P, Petit

28.1   ὁ θεοπειθὴς ἐκεῖνος: ἐκεῖνος ὁ θεοπειθὴς P, Petit
         προσηγορεύοντο: προσηγόρευτο V, προσηγορεύετο P
         τελοῦν: τελῶν LM, τελῶν VP, Petit

28.2   ἐπικατελάβετο: ἐπεκατελάβετο LMVP

28.3   ἐπικατελάβετο: ἐπεκατελάβετο LMVP

29.1   ἐπικατελάβοντο: ἐπεκατελάβοντο LMVP
         σηκὸν: οἶκον P, Petit

29.2   κατεαγῆναι παρεσκεύασαν: καταραγῆναι παρεσκεύασαν V
         ἀβλαβοῦς: om. Petit
         τῷ γενομένῳ σημείῳ: τῷ γεναμένῳ σημείῳ LMP

29.4   γέλωτος ἀξίας: γέλωτος ἀξίους LMVP
         ἀπέφηνεν: ἀνέφηνεν Petit

29.5   ὁ Θεὸς: ᾧ Θεὸς Petit
         περαιώσειν: περαίωσιν P, Petit

29.6   ‚ϛτοθ΄: ἑξακισχιλιοστὸν τριακοσιοστὸν ἑβδομηκοστὸν ἔνατον
         V, 6379 P
         τῆς . . . ‚ωοθ΄: om. V, Petit, 879 P

30.1   ὡς ἂν ἡμῖν: ὡς ἂν ὑμῖν Petit
         πέλωσι: πέλουσι LMP, Petit
         διεπεραίνοντο: διεπεραίννον LM, διαπεραίνουσιν P, διεπέραι-
         νεν Petit. *Before this word Petit postulates a lacuna, which should be
         placed after it. Possibly a phrase like* αἱ δὲ ἡμέραι ἐν ἐργασίᾳ *was
         missing in the manuscript(s) copied by LMVP.*
         προελήφθη: προελείφθη LMP, ἐλήφθη V

30.2   τὴν οὐρανίαν κατάσχεσιν: τὴν οὐράνιον κατάσχεσιν P, Petit

30.3   τῷ αὐτοῦ ἀξίῳ θεράποντι: τῷ ἀξίῳ αὐτοῦ θεράποντι P, Petit
         ἄλογος: ἄλλως V

30.5   *σου οἱ οἶκοι:* οἱ οἶκοι σου LMP, Petit

31.1   ἠρυθροδανωμένα: ἐρυθροδανομένα LM, ἐρυθροδανωμένα V,
         ἐρυθρῷ δανωμένα P
         σπουδῆς ἢ περιουσίας: σπουδῆς ἢ om. Petit

32.1   ποιήσοιτο: ποιήσοι τὸ M, ποιήσει τὸ P, Petit

33.1   *καταπίῃ:* καταπίει LMVP
         διαμαρτήσομεν: διαμαρτήσωμεν MP, Petit

33.2   ὁ μὴ συμπεριφερόμενος: Petit om. ὁ

ἀλλὰ καὶ: καὶ *om.* LMP, Petit

33.3 ἡ ἀγάπη ἀνυπόκριτος: ἐν ἀγάπῃ ἀνυποκρίτῳ Petit

33.4 ὑπὲρ ἀλλήλων προσεύχησθε: ὑπὲρ ἀλλήλων προσεύχεσθε LM, Petit

33.5 ἀρετῶν ἰδέαν: ἀρετῶν εἰδέαν LM, Petit

34.1 ἀποκείρας: ἀποκρίνας V

34.2 τὰ ἡμέτερα μόνα: τὰ ἡμέτερα μόνον Petit

35.1 ἐν τῷ Δημητρίου νεῴ: ἐν τῷ Δημητρίου ναῷ P, Petit
μεθ᾽ ἑαυτοῦ προσλαβόμενος: μεθ᾽ ἑαυτοῦ προσλαμβανόμενος LMV

35.2 ἐπιγίνεσθαί: ἐπιγενέσθαι P, Petit

36.1 Ἰωάννῃ τῷ Τζάγαστῃ: Τσάγαστῃ *post corr.* P, Petit
σημειωσάμενοι: σημειωσάμενον LMP, σημειωσαμένων V

36.3 ἐν τῷ Ἄθωνι: τῷ *om.* Petit

37.1 τεσσαρεσκαίδεκα ἐνιαυτῶν: τεσσαρεσκαίδεκα ἐνιαυτοὺς P, Petit
τοῖς συγγενεῦσι: τοῖς συγγενέσι VP, Petit

37.2 ἱδρύσαι ἐν αὐτοῖς: ἱδρύσαι ἐν αὐταῖς V, Petit

37.3 τὴν ἐρημίαν: τὴν ἠρεμίαν Petit
τῇ ιεʹ τοῦ αὐτοῦ Ὀκτωβρίου μηνός: πεντεκαιδεκάτῃ V, 14 P
ᾧ ζῶν: ὁ ζῶν L, Petit, ὁ ζῶν P

LIFE OF ATHANASIOS OF ATHOS, VERSION B

6.1 Δύο δὲ τῶν δούλων αὐτοῖς: *Rosenqvist suggests emending* αὐτοῖς *to* αὐτῶν, *but there is no support for this in the manuscript tradition.*

7.2 ἐφαίνετο καὶ ἠγνόηκεν: *We have tentatively suggested the emendation of* ἠγνόηκεν *from* ἐγίνωσκεν *of the Noret ed.*

30.2 "ἀρκεῖν ἡμῖν," ". . . εἰς τὴν βασιλεύουσαν.": *We have added here quotation marks that are missing in the Noret ed.*

31.3 καὶ [ὅτι] φησίν: ὅτι *of the Noret ed. has been secluded.*

35.3 πρὶν ἢ δὲ ταύτην: πρινὴ *of the Noret ed. has been emended to* πρὶν ἤ.

61.2 κατατολμήσαντα: κατατολμήσαντος *of the Noret ed. has been emended to* κατατολμήσαντα, *following the suggestion of Jan Olof Rosenqvist.*

LIFE OF MAXIMOS THE HUTBURNER BY NIPHON

Unless noted below, all editorial additions, seclusions, and obelizations are those of Halkin.

1.1 πρόξενον σωτηρίας ὑπάρχει: *Kourilas suggests the emendation* πρόξενοι σωτηρίας ὑπάρχουσιν.

1.3 ἀλλὰ κατ᾽ἐπίγνωσιν: *Emended, following Kourilas's suggestion, from* ἀλλ᾽ οὐ κατ᾽ἐπίγνωσιν *of the Halkin ed.*

2.1 ἔπειθον μένειν: *Emended following Halkin's alternative reading for* ἔπασχον μένειν.

7.1 καὶ πάλιν τούτου . . . συνέβαλεν: *At the suggestion of Alexander Alexakis, we have moved the first sentence of chap. 8.1 in the Halkin ed. to the end of chap. 7.1.*

10.3 πεῖσον αὐτόν: *Emended following Halkin's suggested alternative for* ποίησον αὐτόν.

15.1 ἦλθόν τινες μοναχοὶ: *Emended from Halkin's* ἔλαχόν τινες μοναχοὶ. *The parallel passage in the* Life *by Theophanes, 26.4, has* παρεγένοντο.

27.1 τὰ πώματα: *Emended from Halkin's* τὰ πόματα.

29.1 ἀπέστειλεν αὐτό: *Emended from* ἀπέστειλεν αὐτόν *of the Halkin ed.*

LIFE OF MAXIMOS THE HUTBURNER BY THEOPHANES

Unless noted below, all editorial additions, seclusions, and obelizations are those of Halkin.

1.5 νησαέων Κυκλάδων: *This rare form of the genitive plural of* νῆσος *is unattested in the* TLG.

2.1 μᾶλλον ἢ θῆλυ: *We have here reversed the word order in Halkin's text,* ἢ μᾶλλον, *to* μᾶλλον ἤ.

ἐν ταῖς καρδίαις ἐκείνων: *After* ἐκείνων *we have secluded the superfluous article* ἥ.

[ἐν ταῖς καρδίαις]: *Halkin secluded the phrase* ἐν ταῖς καρδίαις, *which is repeated from two lines above.*

5.2 δακρύων πλήθους ῥοῇ: πλῆθος *of the Halkin ed. has been emended to* πλήθους.

6.2 ἀνάπαυσιν: ἀνάπαυσις *of the Halkin ed. has been emended to* ἀνάπαυσιν.

7.1 ἐκπλήκτους ἀνεῳγμένους: *We have here accepted Halkin's emendation of* ἐκπλήτους *to* ἐκπλήκτους.

7.3 ἐκ τῆς τραπέζης <τῆς> μονῆς: *We have emended* μόνης *of the Halkin ed. to* <τῆς> μονῆς.

8.3 πλήθει ἀπείρῳ: *We have followed here the reading of Kourilas instead of the* πλήθη ἄπειρα *of Halkin.*

9.3 γεγωνέναι οὕτω ψευδῶς: *We have emended* γεγονέναι *of Halkin to* γεγωνέναι.

13.1 ἐν τῇ νοερᾷ ἡσυχίᾳ καὶ καρδιακῇ προσευχῇ: *We have moved* καρδιακῇ *from before* ἡσυχίᾳ *to before* προσευχῇ.

15.4 τὰς δυνάμεις αὐτοῦ ἐφαπλοῦν: *We have emended the* ἐφαπλοῖν *of the Halkin ed. to* ἐφαπλοῦν.

15.5 συναιρεῖται καὶ διαλύεται: *We have emended* συναίρεται *of the Halkin ed. to* συναιρεῖται.

τότε συναιρεῖται τῇ δυνάμει: *We have emended* συναίρεται *to* συναιρεῖται, *as just above in the same paragraph.*

19.1 παραγγέλλων αὐτοῖς ἀπέχεσθαι μήνης: *Halkin suggests emendation of* μήνης *to* μήνιδος.

20.1 προὐτρέψας: *Sic.*

26.7 ἐκ τὸ Προσφόριν: *We have corrected* Πορσφόριν *of the Halkin ed. to* Προσφόριν.

27.1 πᾶσαν τὴν βιοτήν τῶν ἁγίων: *Following the suggestion of Halkin, we have moved* τῶν ἁγίων *from after* τῇ ζωῇ *in the previous sentence to after* βιοτήν.

29.1 καὶ οἱ μοναχοὶ: *Before* καὶ *we have secluded* οἱ *as suggested by Halkin.*

29.2 Ὕπαγε, ἔβγαλε: *We have emended the* ἔυγαλε *of the ms to* ἔβγαλε.

31.1 <πρὸς> τὸν ὅσιον: *We have inserted* πρός *before* τὸν ὅσιον.

ἕως τῇ Πέμπτῃ πρωΐ: *We have added a* μ *to the* πέπτῃ *of the ms.*

33.2 γίνεται πνεῦμα πλάνης ὑπόπτωτος: *We have accepted Halkin's suggestion to change* ὑπόπτερος *to* ὑπόπτωτος.

35.2   τὰ λοίσθια πνέοντα: *We have emended* ὀλίσθια *to* λοίσθια *as suggested by Kourilas.*

LIFE OF PHILOTHEOS

Before the title the scribe inserted the notation Μηνὶ Ὀκτωβρίῳ κα΄ λόγος γ΄, *i.e., October 21, Oration 3.*

3.3   πᾶσαι αἱ μοναχαὶ: *McGrath emended from* πάντες οἱ μοναχαῖς *of the ms and Papoulia ed.; Greenfield prefers to emend to* πάντες οἱ μοναχοί.

3.4   ἀνέπεμπεν: *Emended from* ἀνέπεμπον *of the ms and Papoulia ed.*

4.3   ἠσθενηκὼς <ἦν>: ἦν *added by Papoulia.*

5.1   οἰκτειρίσαι: *Emended from* οἰκτηρίσαι *of the ms and Papoulia ed.*

5.2   καὶ ἔμεινεν . . . ἐξῆλθε τῆς κέλλης: *The punctuation of the first part of the paragraph has been slightly changed in the effort to make sense of this passage.*

5.3   πληθύνων πληθύνων: *sic* in Papoulia ed.

        ἐν ᾗ ἱερούργουν: *Emended from* ἐν ᾧ ἱερούργουν *of the ms and Papoulia ed.*

        ἐν κόγχῃ: *Emended from* ἐνὶ κόγχῃ *of the ms and Papoulia ed.*

6.3   ἐκτελέσων τὰς εὐχὰς: *Before this phrase Papoulia secluded* τοῦ.

Notes to the Translations

1.1   *Those who had . . . lost their initial standing:* That is, the descendants of Adam and Eve, who before their expulsion from Paradise were immortal and had no physical cares.

To combine living well: That is, living correctly.

2.1   *Commemoration day of our father:* The feast day of Saint Euthymios the Younger is October 14.

Deservedly: The adverb ἐποφειλῶς (deservedly) seems to be a hapax in Greek, unattested in the *TLG*.

3.1   *Land of the Galatians:* Galatia was a region of central Anatolia, with its capital at Ankyra.

3.2   *Opso:* This town near Ankyra is otherwise unattested.

3.3   *A group . . . same village:* This suggests that Euthymios's parents became local community leaders or at least exemplars.

3.4   *For it seemed . . . involved <in military service>:* Translation of this sentence has proved challenging. Alexander Alexakis prefers the reading of ὑπονεύοντας το ἀπονεύοντας and takes ταύτης as referring to "virtue" rather than "service." He suggests the following translation: "although they . . . enrolled in the army and were seemingly obliged to surrender a little of their virtue to its violence, they neither considered nor even slightly consented to be caught straying from it (i.e., the virtue)."

3.5   *The others:* Probably an allusion to the "group" of chap. 3.3.

Both a silent and vocal encouragement: Gregory of Nazianzos, *Or. 43, In laudem Basilii Magni* (PG 36:580C).

3.6   *Epiphaneios . . . named after the divine epiphany:* Epiphaneios (*PmbZ* 1, no. 1527), who died in 831, is not attested elsewhere.

Anna, who bore the name of grace: Anna (*PmbZ* 1, no. 458) is known only from the *Life of Euthymios*. Hannah means "grace" in Hebrew. The interpretation of the name Anna as *charis* (grace) is found in Philo, *De somniis* 1.254.2–3 and elsewhere.

4.1   *Heresy of the iconoclasts:* An allusion to the second period of iconoclasm, which began in 815 under the emperor Leo V (r. 813–820).

Leo the beastly named: Leo V was murdered on Christmas Day 820 in the palace church of Saint Stephen.

Michael, the former exkoubitor: Michael II (r. 820–829) was Domestic of the *exkoubitoi* before his accession to the throne.

Terminated in the seventh year of his reign: Our translation of this passage, based on a minor emendation of the punctuation of the Greek text and a rejection of Petit's reading of one word, represents a departure from the traditional interpretation of it. The Greek participle καταλήγουσα, emended by Petit from the καταλήγουσαν of the manuscripts LMP and apparently inspired by the reading κατάγουσα of manuscript V, when coupled with the previously accepted punctuation, had to be taken as referring to the heresy of iconoclasm. But this posed difficulties of sense and implied a mistake on the part of the author, Basil, who was evidently suggesting that iconoclasm "ceased" during Michael II's reign in 827. In fact, it ended seventeen years later, in 843 under Michael III and Theodora, something Basil clearly did know, given his statement to this effect in chap. 8.1. Alexakis prefers the reading of V, κατάγουσα, and retaining the punctuation of the manuscripts: thus iconoclasm "was still current" when Michael was in the seventh year of his reign. We feel, however, that our approach is simpler, accords with the broader manuscript tradition, and makes more sense of the passage and the vita. Traditionally Niketas/Euthymios's birth has been assigned to 823/4, accepting at face value the *anno mundi* (AM) date given in this chapter. Our present reading, however, when coupled with a new understanding of the dating provided in chap. 6.1 (see below) and a rejection of the AM dating here as a later, and mistaken, interpolation, may confirm a revised date for Niketas/Euthymios's birth as 820, the seventh year of Leo V's reign—the year in which he was as-

sassinated and Michael II came to power. Given the nature of the DOML series, this issue cannot be discussed here in the detail it deserves, but it will form the subject of a future publication by Richard Greenfield.

6332: The year 6332 is equivalent to 823/4 CE, since the Byzantines dated the creation of the world in 5508. This AM date does not correlate with the seventh year of Leo's reign cited just above (820), or the seventh year of Michael's reign on the traditional reading (827). It is possible that it is a later, and inaccurate, insertion.

5.1   *In his seventh year:* Richard Greenfield has suggested the possibility that an iota has dropped out of the Greek numeral ιζ΄ (17) in an earlier version of the text, so that the text should read "seventeenth" instead of "seventh" (ζ΄). This would remove the problem of a seven-year-old boy being enrolled for military service, which has puzzled historians. See note below.

Maria . . . Epiphaneia: Epiphaneios's daughters Maria (*PmbZ* 1, no. 4740) and Epiphaneia (*PmbZ* 1, no. 1526) are known only from the *Life of Euthymios*.

Enrolled in the military registers: This passage has puzzled scholars, who do not understand how a boy of seven could be enrolled for military service, and how he could simultaneously look after his widowed mother's household. John Haldon (*Recruitment and Conscription in the Byzantine Army c. 550–950: A Study on the Origins of the Stratiotika Ktemata* [Vienna, 1979], 47) suggests that he enrolled at age seven but was not expected to actually serve until he reached the age of eighteen, while Martha Gregoriou-Ioannidou has proposed that the hagiographer conflated events and that Euthymios did not actually enroll until he was eighteen ("Ζητήματα στρατολογίας στὸ Βυζάντιο· ἡ περίπτωση τοῦ ὁσίου Εὐθυμίου τοῦ Νέου," *Byzantiaka* 10 [1990]: 151–58).

Birth name of Niketas: The name Niketas is derived from the Greek noun νίκη, "victory."

5.2   *Euphrosyne:* Euphrosyne (*PmbZ* 1, no. 1710), whose name means "good cheer" or "joy" in Greek, is not attested elsewhere.

6.1   *Anastaso:* Anastaso (*PmbZ* 1, no. 343) is known only from the *Life*

of Euthymios. Her name derives from the Greek word for resurrection, *anastasis.*

Feast day of the . . . cross: The feast of the Elevation (Exaltation) of the Cross, on which see *ODB* 1:551, under "Cross, Cult of the."

The martyr Niketas: Niketas the Goth was martyred on a September 15 during the reign of the Visigothic king Athanaric (r. 364–376).

Feast day . . . of . . . Niketas . . . Sunday: There is a chronological inconsistency here with the AM date of 6350 (= 841 CE) given at the end of this chapter, since September 15, 841, fell on a Thursday, not a Sunday. Traditional scholarship, as represented by Petit ("St. Euthyme le Jeune"), Papachryssanthou ("Vie de saint Euthyme"), and the *PmbZ* (2, no. 21912), has thus concluded that Basil was here in error; Petit (ibid., 529, n. 5), for example, suggests that placing Niketas/Euthymios's departure on a Sunday was simply authorial embellishment. Instead, scholars have placed their faith in the AM date of 841 for Niketas/Euthymios's abandonment of his family and, given the assertion just below that this was his eighteenth year, have consequently set his birth date as 823/4. This does indeed agree with the AM date given in chap. 4.1, but, as noted there, we believe that that AM date may be both a later interpolation and an inaccuracy. If so, the present AM date would also be suspect and likely determined by a simple mathematical calculation. It seems more plausible to imagine that the coincidence of his name day with a Sunday, when coupled with this dramatic turn in his life, would have remained more vivid in the holy man's mind when recounting his story than an AM or incarnation date would have. Indeed, if the AM dating of 841 is rejected, a number of alternative years may be suggested (using Grumel's perpetual calendar, *Chronologie,* 316–17), in which September 15 fell on a Sunday. Of these, however, the only plausible one is 838. Accepting this would place Niketas/Euthymios's birth year as 820, which agrees nicely with the reading we have adopted for the text in Chap 4.1. This revision has some consequences for other dating traditionally ascribed to his life; see notes below.

Son of Kis . . . lost asses: When Saul went to look for his father's asses, he encountered Samuel, who anointed him as king of Israel; see 1 Kings 9–10.

850th year: Either the date of 850 is incorrect or the era of 5500 (instead of 5508) is being used; see Papachryssanthou ("Vie de saint Euthyme," 234–35).

7.1   *Walking through the air:* According to the *TLG* this is the earliest attested usage of the word ἀεροβάμων.

Olympos: Mount Olympos in Bithynia, a holy mountain famed for its monasteries.

Ioannikios: Ioannikios lived on Mount Olympos for much of his monastic career, from the late eighth century up to his death in 846. For an English translation of his vita by Peter, see Denis Sullivan, "Life of St. Ioannikios," in *Byzantine Defenders of Images,* ed. Alice-Mary Talbot (Washington, D.C., 1998), 243–351.

7.2   *Leopard . . . versatility:* See pseudo-Eustathios of Thessalonike, *Comm. on Hexaemeron,* PG 18:741.34–37: a leopard emits a sweet smell from its mouth to attract its prey and they follow it because they are delighted by the "versatility" or "spottedness" of its body.

8.1   *Man . . . called John:* John (*PmbZ* 1, no. 3218) was the superior of a monastery on Bithynian Mount Olympos.

Theodora and Michael: After the death of the iconoclast emperor Theophilos in 842, his iconophile widow, Theodora, served as regent for her young son, Michael III (842–867); icon veneration was restored in March 843. Euthymios's tonsuring is thus dated to 842/3. Traditional dating of his departure from his family to 841 suggests that this took place quite soon after his arrival on Olympos. However, the revised date of September 15, 838, suggested above in the note to chap. 6.1, requires four or five years to have passed. This is not inconsistent with the information provided in chap. 7.1 that he visited a number of places on his way to Olympos and encountered many holy men there before he met with Ioannikios, or with the fact that the present chapter does not specify how long he spent with the latter.

Relative representation: Official doctrine on the veneration of images distinguished between the "relative" *(schetike)* or "honorific" *(timetike)* veneration of images and the genuine worship *(latreia)* of the sacred person depicted.

9.1 *First and second stage:* The Greek adjective πρωτοδεύτερος is extremely rare, appearing only four times in the *TLG,* in all cases but ours in a medical context. *LbG* does not cite this passage, and translates "the first and the second, one after the other." The meaning of the term in this context is not completely clear.

Pissadinoi: On the monastery of Pissadinoi, see Janin, *Grands centres,* 173–74. It is mentioned in only one other source besides the *Life of Euthymios* and is only attested in the ninth century, in an uncertain location in the region of Mount Olympos.

9.2 *Superior ... Nicholas:* Nicholas (*PmbZ* 1, no. 5603) was superior of the Pissadinoi monastery from 843 to 858.

10.2 *Determination:* The Greek noun παράνευσις is an apparent hapax, for which we suggest the meaning "determination" or "inclination."

11.2 *Despondency:* The vice of accidie (ἀκηδία) to which monks were considered prone, often translated as "torpor," "listlessness," or "boredom" but also including what we would recognize as depression or despondency.

12.1 *Carmel of Elijah:* The prophet Elijah was associated with Mount Carmel, where to this day he is venerated in a cave called the "Grotto of Elijah."

12.2 *Methodios:* Patriarch of Constantinople from 843 to 847.
Ignatios: Ignatios's first patriarchate was from 847 to 858.
Stepped down from ... the ... throne and Church: Ignatios, who had been appointed patriarch by the empress Theodora, during the minority of her son Michael III, without ratification by a synod, found himself caught in a power struggle between Stoudite monks and moderates led by Gregory Asbestas. Subsequently, when Caesar Bardas, Theodora's brother, dethroned her from the regency and banished her from the palace, Ignatios had to resign the patriarchate.

His own monastery: The monastery of Satyros, on the Asian shore of the Bosporos; see Janin, *Grands centres,* 42–43.

12.3 *The new patriarch:* This is Photios, whose first patriarchate was from 858 to 867. His controversial appointment was opposed especially by monastic leaders and led to the so-called Photian Schism with the papacy, which supported Ignatios.

The blessed Photios: Photios's name contains the root (φωτ-) of the word for light.

His father's loss of his property and exile: This was the *spatharios* Sergios the Confessor, an iconodule saint of the second period of iconoclasm, who suffered confiscation of his property and exile during the reign of the iconoclast emperor Theophilos (r. 829–842); see *SynaxCP* 682–84; *PmbZ* 1, no. 6665.

13.2 *Reunited the Church:* The ecclesiastical dispute between the parties of Ignatios and Photios lasted until Photios was forced to step down from the patriarchal throne in 867, at which point Ignatios was restored.

14.2 *Theodore:* The monk Theodore (*PmbZ* 1, no. 7724) is known only from the *Life of Euthymios.* Given the statement in chap. 14.1 that Euthymios was prompted in this decision by the departure of Nicholas, which itself was linked to the resignation of the patriarch Ignatios, Theodore must have vested him with the great habit in 858 or 859.

Theosteriktos: The monk Theosteriktos (*PmbZ* 1, no. 8395), known only from the *Life of Euthymios,* accompanied Euthymios to Athos in 858 or 859.

Fifteen years . . . on Olympos: If his departure from Olympos is dated to 858 or 859, then Euthymios/Niketas should have arrived there in 843 or 844. This is apparently inconsistent (on both traditional and revised chronology) with the dating derived from his abandonment of his family in 841 or 838 (see above, chap. 6.1) if, as is usually assumed, he went straight to Olympos. It is possible, however, that he spent a number of years making his way to the mountain (see chap. 7.1: "Moving then from place to place and passing from city to city. . ."), but perhaps it is more likely that Basil (and thus Euthymios him-

self, if he is his source for this information) is counting from his tonsure, which is dated (chap. 8.1) to 842/3.

15.1   *Nikomedeia:* An important bishopric of Bithynia and port city on the Sea of Marmara.

    Were afraid to take monastic vows: Evidently they did not want to commit to monastic life, if there was a chance that Euthymios might return to their household.

15.2   *As a token of blessing:* For this meaning of ἐν παραθέσει, see *PGL*, under παράθεσις, 7.

    Let those . . . no possessions: The various English translations of this passage from Corinthians differ substantially; note also that parts of verses 30 and 31 have been omitted by the hagiographer.

17.2   *Joseph:* The monk Joseph (*PmbZ* 1, no. 3457; *PmbZ* 2, no. 23511) is known only from the *Life of Euthymios.*

    We will feed . . . like cattle: Solitaries who ate only wild plants that they foraged were called *boskoi,* or "grazers," and are first attested in the Judean Desert; see John Wortley, "'Grazers' (βοσκοί) in the Judean Desert," in *The Sabaite Heritage in the Orthodox Church from the Fifth Century to the Present,* ed. Joseph Patrich (Leuven, 2001), 37–48; a further extreme of this ascetic practice was to crawl along the ground on all fours munching wild greens.

18.1   *We will undergo the good change:* See Gregory of Nazianzos, *Or.* 40 (PG 36:416.31).

18.2   *Of Armenian descent:* An example of anti-Armenian prejudice in Byzantium.

    The spiritual man: See, for example, 1 Corinthians, chaps. 2–3, esp. 2:13, 15 and 3:1, but also 15:42–50.

19.1   *Barefoot people . . . whom mythic tales admire:* In Homer (*Iliad,* 16:235) these people have unwashed rather than bare feet.

19.3   *Partner:* The Greek σύννομος literally means "fellow grazer" and may allude to Joseph's stint as a "grazer," who ate only wild grasses and plants.

20.2   *Someone important:* See Galatians 6:2, ἀπὸ δὲ τῶν δοκούντων τι, "from those who were reputed to be something."

The great Antony: Antony the Great (ca. 251–356), an early desert father in Egypt and model for all hermit saints, was famed for his stalwart resistance to the demons who tormented him in his solitude.

22.1   *The angelic habit:* See chap. 14.2 above. "Angelic habit" is another term for the "great habit" *(mega schema),* which was the highest level of monastic profession. A *megaloschemos* monk wore a cowl *(koukoulion)* and scapular *(analabos).*

22.2   *Makrosina:* Petit ("St. Euthyme le Jeune," 531) assumes that this spot must be near Hierissos.

22.3   *Church of . . . Sozon:* This church, dedicated to an early Christian martyr, is known only from this text; see Janin, *Grands centres,* 411.

23.2   *The new Thesbite:* That is, Elijah (the "Tishbite" in English translation).

23.3   *The great Symeon:* There were two stylite saints named Symeon: the Elder (ca. 389–459), whose column was at Qal'at Sem'an in Syria, and the Younger (521–592), whose column was situated on the Wondrous Mountain near Antioch. Stylite monks were relatively uncommon in the Middle Byzantine period, but the ascetic practice of living on top of a column continued until at least the eleventh century, as can be seen from the *Life* of Lazaros of Mount Galesion.

24.1   *Theodore:* Theodore's exact dates as archbishop are unknown (*PmbZ* 1, no. 7727; *PmbZ* 2, no. 27618) but definitely included the years 868 to 879, since he was a signatory to the acts of the councils of 869 and 879/80.

24.2   *John Kolobos:* Some years later, between 866 and 883, John Kolobos founded a cenobitic monastery near Hierissos, just outside the precincts of Mount Athos (*PmbZ* 1, no. 3318; *PmbZ* 2, no. 22783). It bore his name and was dedicated to Saint John the Baptist. John Kolobos had the same name as a famed fourth-century monk of the Egyptian desert, John the Little or the Dwarf.

Symeon: This monk (*PmbZ* 2, no. 27451) is known only from the *Life of Euthymios.*

Neoi: An island about eighteen miles southwest of Lemnos in the northern Aegean Sea, also known as Hagios Eustratios; it is about fifty-three miles southeast of the tip of the Athonite peninsula. See Johannes Koder, *Aigaion Pelagos (Die nördliche Ägäis)* (Vienna, 1998), 240–41, and chaps. 57.1 and 71.1 of the *Life of Athanasios,* below.

Euthymios . . . harbor: In order to make better sense in English of this paragraph, which is a single rambling sentence in the Greek text, we have broken it up into three sentences and moved some of the clauses around.

24.3 *Saracens . . . Arabs:* In the ninth century, following their capture of the island of Crete circa 826, Muslim pirates raided the coasts of the Greek mainland and islands with relative impunity. On these "Saracens," see further the note on "Cretans" in the *Life of Athanasios,* chap. 13.2, below.

25.2 *We will be prevented:* We have obelized the unintelligible phrase δέος μέχρις ἐνθυμούμενον that comes before ἐπισχεθησόμεθα, "we will be prevented," in the Greek text. Richard Greenfield suggests that possibly δέος could be emended to δέον and ἐνθυμούμενον to ἐνθυμῶμεν and the phrase translated "for that long we need to bear in mind."

26.1 *To avoid dangerous places:* A quotation from *Theodori Studitae epistulae,* ed. George Fatouros (Berlin, 1992), 2:334.

26.2 *Siderokausia:* A village in the Chalkidike peninsula, northwest of Hierissos.

Hellas: The theme or district of Hellas, here probably referring to the mainland of central Greece.

Brastamon: A village in the Chalkidike peninsula, west of Hierissos and north of Sermylia (Ormylia).

Joseph, whom we have often mentioned: See chaps. 17–19 and 22, above.

Already elderly: PmbZ 2, no. 23511, interprets πρεσβύτης here as "priest," but it is used throughout the *Life* to denote Euthymios and most likely is simply a term of respect for an elderly person.

27.1   *Onouphrios:* The monk Onouphrios (*PmbZ* 2, no. 26189) is known only from this text.

27.3   *Peristerai:* Located fifteen miles southeast of Thessalonike, on the slopes of Mount Chortiates.

        Sanctuary of Andrew: The church, dated to 871, still survives in the village of Peristera.

28.1   *Ignatios . . . Ephraim:* The monks Ephraim (*PmbZ* 2, no. 21687) and Ignatios (*PmbZ* 2, no. 22719) were disciples of Euthymios, known only from this passage in the *Life of Euthymios.*

28.3   *Apse of the holy sanctuary:* Nikolaos K. Moutsopoulos (Περιστερά, ο ορεινός οικισμός του Χορτιάτη και ο Ναός του Αγίου Ανδρέα [Thessalonike, 1986], 15–16, 33–72) argues, on the basis of preliminary soundings in the church, that he discovered the remains of an early Christian church. His views are rejected, however, by Robert Ousterhout, who finds no evidence of an earlier building on the site (personal communication of March 11, 2015).

29.1   *Precincts for the holy Forerunner . . . and Euthymios the Great:* These may refer to separate chapels dedicated to John the Baptist and Euthymios the Great.

29.2   *Building's wooden scaffolding:* This is our interpretation of the phrase τὰ ξύλα τῆς οἰκοδομῆς, following the Dumbarton Oaks Hagiography Database and Robert Ousterhout, *Master Builders of Byzantium* (Princeton, N.J., 1999), 185. For another description of scaffolding in a church, see the *Life of Athanasios,* below, chap. 66.1–2.

29.3   *The demons shook . . . the structure:* Perhaps an allusion to the earthquake that struck Constantinople in 869; see Grumel, *Chronologie,* 479. This would have occurred just before the completion of the church in 870/1; see note below to chap. 29.6.

29.5   *In his spirit:* Or perhaps "in the Holy Spirit."

29.6   *Basil and Constantine the augoustoi:* As Petit ("St. Euthyme le Jeune," 532, n. 29) and Papachryssanthou ("Vie de saint Euthyme," 235–36, in some detail) have pointed out, there are a number of problems with the combination of datings provided here: both AM 6379 and the fourth year of the reign of Basil I

and Constantine are September 1, 870 to August 31, 871, but indiction five is September 1, 871 to August 31, 872, and none of these dates matches the 879 provided as the year of the Incarnation. Clearly there is some confusion, but a date *range* for the completion of the monastery of Peristerai between 870 and 872 does emerge, with 871 being that accepted by existing scholarship, including *PmbZ* (2, no. 21912, p. 320).

30.2　*Beseleel:* The chief architect of the tabernacle, according to Exodus 31:2.

　　　Egypt . . . confusion of this world: See Cyril of Alexandria, *De adoratione et cultu in spiritu et veritate* (PG 68:200.18).

　　　The gloomy sin: Gregory of Nazianzos, *Or.* 45 (PG 36:644.12).

30.4　*Men from all over the earth:* This Homeric-sounding phrase may be drawn from R. Janssen, ed., *Das Johannes-Evangelium nach der Paraphrase des Nonnus Panopolitanus* (Leipzig, 1903), 7.151.

33.1　*On both accounts:* That is, love of the Lord and fear of hell.

33.5　*John of the Ladder:* A Sinaite monk and superior of the seventh century. He wrote a classic monastic treatise, entitled *The Heavenly Ladder,* which presents the virtues and vices typical of monastic life.

　　　Apostles. . . by the Holy Spirit: An allusion to Pentecost.

34.1　*He tonsured me in . . . Sermylia:* Here the hagiographer Basil (*PmbZ* 2, no. 20858), who first introduces himself in chap. 26.2, describes his investiture with the monastic habit, circa 875. He reveals his name in the following chapter. Sermylia is present-day Ormylia, in Chalkidike on the Gulf of Cassandra.

　　　Antony of Kraneai: The article on Antony in *PmbZ* 2 (no. 20486) voices doubts about Petit's identification of this monk as a Paulician author ("St. Euthyme le Jeune," 532, n. 31), contemporary with Euthymios, and suggests that he may be a much earlier figure. Petit's identification of Kraneai with Kranaia or Kranea, a site near Hierissos, is also questioned in the same entry.

　　　The Apocrypha of the Gospel: Or perhaps *The Hidden Meanings of the Gospels.*

36.1　*John . . . Tsagastes:* John (*PmbZ* 2, no. 22835) was a monk at the

monastery of Peristerai; he is evidently from the family mentioned in an act of the Lavra monastery, dated 897; see Lemerle, *Actes de Lavra,* Act no. 1.

Antony: This monk (*PmbZ* 2, no. 20487) is attested only in this passage.

Koroneia: A lake about seven and a half miles east of Thessalonike.

36.2   *Hilarion:* This monk (*PmbZ* 2, no. 22604) is not attested elsewhere.

37.1   *Shepherding . . . forty-two years:* If one accepts the traditional chronology for Euthymios's life, this information suggests that the reunion with his family took place around 884 (so *PmbZ* 2, no. 21912, p. 320) if he left them in 841/2. It also appears to set the foundation of Peristerai (or at least the start of work there) fourteen years earlier, in circa 870, thus agreeing (though barely) with the dating provided above in chap. 29.6 for the completion of the work in 871; further, it sets the foundation of the women's convent to 884. The revised chronology suggested above (see chaps. 4.1, 6.1) would, however, place the family reunion and the foundation of the convent in 880 (forty-two years after 838); it is possible, but too complex to discuss in detail here, to fit this dating with the other information about Peristerai, if the "shepherding of the community," which would now begin in 866, refers to the proto-community at Brastamon or dates the start of Euthymios's work at Peristerai as many as five years before the completion of the church.

Joseph: Joseph, son of Jacob, was reunited with his family after many years in Egypt; see Genesis, chaps. 45 and 46.

37.2   *Methodios . . . of Thessalonike:* Methodios, who was archbishop of Thessalonike in the 880s, died in 889 (*PmbZ* 2, no. 25072). His predecessor Gregory was still alive in 883, thus providing a *terminus ante quem* for Methodios's accession to the episcopal throne.

Installation of saints' relics . . . and dedicated: What is somewhat odd here (a point discussed and potentially explained by Papachryssanthou, "Vie de saint Euthyme," 238, n. 17) is that the translation of relics and the "dedication to God" of Peristerai

(along with the convent) apparently have to be dated at the earliest to 883 (see previous note), at least eleven or twelve years after the (male) monastery's completion in 871/2.

Grandson Methodios . . . and Euphemia: Methodios (*PmbZ* 2, no. 25073) and Euphemia (*PmbZ* 2, no. 21786) were two of the children of his sole daughter, Anastaso.

37.3   *Euthymios the Great:* Euthymios the Great (d. 473) was a founder of cenobitic monasticism in fifth-century Palestine.

Hiera: The identification of this island is uncertain. Petit ("St. Euthyme le Jeune," 534) suggests, without firm evidence, that the island was Gioura (Yioura), one of the northern Sporades.

George: The monk George (*PmbZ* 2, no. 22105), a disciple of Euthymios, is known only from this passage.

October of the second indiction: This corresponds to 898.

38.1   *The monk Paul and the priest Blasios:* Paul (*PmbZ* 2, no. 26317) and Blasios (*PmbZ* 2, no. 21178) are known only from this passage in the *Life of Euthymios.*

It had remained in the cave: The account of his death in the previous chapter omits the detail that he died in a cave.

38.2   *Is transferred from . . . Hiera:* The use of the present tense in chap. 38.2 suggests that this vita may have been composed by Basil on the occasion of the transfer of Euthymios's relics from Hiera.

Illuminated by the candles: The noun κηροφάνεια appears in the *TLG* only for this passage.

Lying in this holy coffin: Chap. 38 does not make clear whether the final burial place of Euthymios was Thessalonike, where he had spent time as a stylite, or his monastery at Peristerai, as hypothesized by Papachryssanthou ("Vie de saint Euthyme," 242–44). The second location seems more plausible, but no marked tomb is preserved in the church today, although Moutsopoulos (Περιστερά, 55–58) has hypothesized that the skeleton he found in grave T₁ may be that of Euthymios.

39.2   *Of my position:* That is, as a bishop.

The interceder of the Old and New Testaments: See Gregory of Nazianzos, *Or.* 21.3 (PG 35:1085B); *Or.* 39 (PG 36:353.6).

39.3   *Peter . . . Andrew:* The stress here on the apostles Peter and Andrew is noteworthy. Since Andrew was patron saint of the Peristerai monastery, it is logical that Basil would single him out; it
is also a possible indication that Basil was writing the *Life of
Euthymios* on commission from the monastery, as suggested by
Papachryssanthou ("Vie de saint Euthyme," 228). Papachryssanthou also suggested (ibid., 234 and n. 63) that the allusion to
Peter in the following sentence means that Basil's bishopric
was part of Illyrikon and subject to the papacy, while the *PmbZ*
entry on Basil (2, no. 20858) argues that the allusion is merely
to Peter as founder of the universal Church.

Life of Athanasios of Athos, Version B

1.3   *To do one's best . . . sensible of men:* Gregory of Nazianzos, *Or.* 43, *In
laudem Basilii Magni,* chap. 69 (PG 36:589C).

       We will begin . . . at the point where: Gregory of Nazianzos, *Or.* 39,
In sancta lumina, chap. 8 (PG 36:341D–344A).

       His first birth: His monastic tonsure was considered his second
birth.

2.1   *Byzantion:* That is, Constantinople.

       Trebizond: A major city on the southern coast of the Black Sea.

       Kolchis: Kolchis was a region of Asia Minor at the eastern end of
the Black Sea; its name was sometimes used, by metonymy, for
its principal city, Trebizond.

2.2   *Naming him Abraamios:* Abraamios was his baptismal name, Athanasios his monastic name.

3.1   *Abandon all childish things:* Surely an allusion to 1 Corinthians
13:11, although the vocabulary differs.

3.2   *Received . . . realized . . . set forth:* The three Greek verbs for "received," "realized," and "set forth" are all based on the same
root verb λαμβάνω, a subtlety impossible to convey in English.

4.1   *Queen of Cities:* That is, Constantinople.

4.2   *Who provides . . . in difficulty:* John Chrysostom, *In Genesim* (PG
54:425.2)

       Romanos . . . the Elder . . . the Younger: Romanos the Elder refers to

Romanos I Lekapenos, who seized power during the minority of Constantine VII Porphyrogennetos and ruled from 920 to 944. Romanos the Younger is Romanos II (r. 959–963).

Kommerkiarios: A fiscal official who supervised trade and merchants.

4.3   *Man named Athanasios:* This teacher is known only from the two vitae of Athanasios; see *PmbZ* 2, no. 20673.

5.1   *Zephinazer:* This was Theodore Zephinazer (also spelled Zephinezer), on whom see *PmbZ* 2, no. 27682.

6.1   *Eat pure food:* The verb ἀγνοφαγέω is a hapax, although a cognate form, ἀγνοφαγία, appears in chap. 32 of the Lips *typikon,* ed. Hippolyte Delehaye, *Deux typica byzantins de l'époque des Paléologues* (Brussels, 1921), 124.20. For the translation, see *LbG,* under ἀγνοφαγία.

Follis: A large bronze coin worth forty *nummi,* and equal to one twenty-fourth of the silver *miliaresion.*

7.2   *Had forgotten how much love he had for him:* The translation of this final clause poses difficulties. We have suggested the emendation of ἐγίνωσκεν to ἠγνόηκεν in order to make sense of it. Alternatively, one could follow the reading of vita A, Noret, *Vitae duae,* chap. 16.11–12, καίτοι πολὺ τὸ περὶ αὐτὸν εἰδότα φίλτρον αὐτοῦ, and translate "even though he knew that Abraamios had much love for him."

Emperor: This is most likely Constantine VII Porphyrogennetos (r. 945–959).

8.1   *Aegean Sea:* Zephinazer was *strategos* of the Aegean Sea in the 940s.

Abydos: A port on the eastern shore of the Hellespont, near modern Çanakkale.

Lemnos: An island in the northeastern Aegean, off the coast of Turkey, and forty miles distant from Athos.

8.2   *Maleinos . . . Kyminas:* Michael Maleinos (ca. 894–961) was superior of the *lavra* on Mount Kyminas in Bithynia and became a saint; on him, see *PmbZ* 2, no. 25124. The precise location of Kyminas is uncertain, but it was evidently near the Gallos (Göksu) River east of Nicaea (Janin, *Grands centres,* 115–18).

8.3   *Governor of the Anatolikon:* The technical Greek term used here

(strategos) refers to the military governor of a Byzantine theme (a territorial unit). The Anatolikon, stretching from the Aegean to Lykaonia and Isauria in west central Asia Minor, was one of the original Anatolian themes, founded in the seventh century.

Nikephoros: The future Nikephoros II Phokas, emperor from 963 to 969 (*PmbZ* 2, no. 25535).

9.1   *Trial period:* That is, the standard period of the novitiate.

Athanasios instead of Abraamios: In the Middle Byzantine period it was common practice (although by no means mandatory) that a monk took a new monastic name beginning with the same letter as his baptismal name.

9.2   *Sacristan:* The sacristan *(ekklesiarches)* was a monastic official responsible for preparing the church for services, ensuring that these were carried out properly and seeing that discipline was observed.

10.1   *Lavra:* A *lavra* was a type of monastery that permitted some of its monks to live as solitaries. They lived in cells at some distance from the *lavra,* returning on weekends for the liturgy and a meal in the refectory and to pick up food supplies for the coming week.

Three periods of Lent: The three periods of lenten fasting alluded to here were the Great Lent preceding Easter, and two lesser lents, preceding the Nativity of Christ and the feast of Saints Peter and Paul at the end of June; see, for example, the rules in the eleventh-century typikon of Pakourianos, *BMFD* 2:535, (23) Pakourianos, chap. 10. For a similar phrase, see chap. 42.1 below.

11.1   *Patrikios Leo:* Leo Phokas, a famous Byzantine general, on whom see *PmbZ* 2, no. 24423. *Patrikios* was a high-ranking dignity. The Domestic of the Schools originally commanded a unit of the standing professional army called the *scholae,* hence the term. In the tenth century there were two Domestics of the Schools, one in the East and one in the West.

12.3   *Praxapostolos:* A liturgical book used at the Eucharist, containing the Acts of Paul and the Epistles of Paul and other apostles.

13.2   *Cretans:* These "Cretans" were Andalusian *muwallad,* Muslim

converts of an Iberian background led by Abu Hafs 'Umar ibn Shuaib al-Iqritishi. They were expelled from al-Andalus by Emir al-Hakam (r. 796–822) and had originally settled in Alexandria, where they took control of the city, before being moved on by 'Abdallah ibn Tahir. They captured Crete from the Byzantines in the mid-820s and held it until 961. Cretan pirates used the island as a base for raids throughout the Aegean, including Athos.

14.1   *Magistros Leo:* On Leo see note on chap. 11.1 above. *Magistros* was a high-ranking dignity like *patrikios.*

      Zygos: One of the earliest monasteries in the vicinity of Mount Athos, its ruins can still be seen near present-day Ouranoupolis, about forty yards outside the boundary wall of the Holy Mountain.

15.1   *Abbas:* A general title of respect for Greek monks; it could also mean "superior" or "abbot," but that is clearly not the case here. For a more detailed discussion of the term, see note to chap. 14.1 in Niphon's *Life of Maximos* below.

16.1   *Command of all the East:* That is, he became Domestic of the Schools for the East.

16.3   *Protos:* A *protos,* literally, "first monk," was head of a group of scattered monasteries and hermitages, often on a holy mountain such as Mount Athos. According to vita A (Noret, *Vitae duae,* chap. 44.26–27), this *protos* was Stephen, who served from 958 to 959; see *PmbZ* 2, no. 27292; Papachryssanthou, *Prôtaton,* 129.

      Synaxis: An assemblage of the monks of Mount Athos in the church of the Virgin at the Protaton of the *lavra* at Karyes, which served as capital of the confederation of monasteries. Papachryssanthou dates this particular *synaxis* to Christmas 958 (*Prôtaton,* 72–73).

17.1   *Three times a year:* At Easter, the Dormition of the Virgin (August 15), and Christmas.

17.2   *The Theologian:* Gregory of Nazianzos, bishop of Constantinople (380–381), one of the primary Orthodox church fathers. The assigned text was probably Gregory's Oration 38 on Christmas (PG 36:312–34).

18.1   *Paul of Xeropotamou:* Paul (*PmbZ* 2, no. 26352) is traditionally be-
        lieved to have been the founder of the Xeropotamou monas-
        tery, one of the oldest establishments on Mount Athos. It had
        been established shortly before Athanasios's arrival on the
        Holy Mountain. His role in the original foundation is uncer-
        tain, but he was definitely its superior by 980.

19.1   *Solitary cell:* A *kellion,* the abode of a solitary, often connected
        with a *lavra.*

19.2   *Loukitzes:* Loukitzes (*PmbZ* 2, no. 24792) is known only from the
        two vitae of Athanasios of Athos.
        And as payment . . . nothing else: If we have interpreted this sen-
        tence correctly, the subject shifts in the final clause from
        Loukitzes to Athanasios.

20.1   *Nomadic Scythians:* This is a reference to Leo's victory over the
        Magyars who had crossed the Danube. His surprise attack is
        probably to be dated to 960.

21.1   *Melana:* Located at the southern tip of the Athonite peninsula.
        Workshop of virtue: See, for example, Gregory of Nazianzos, *Or.*
        43, *In laudem Basilii Magni,* chap. 12 (PG 36:509B).

21.2   *Our Enemy . . . never sleeps:* That is, the Devil; note the wordplay
        between "black" *(melanos)* and the promontory of Melana; see
        below, chap. 35.3.
        Despondency: The Greek term is ἀκηδία, or "accidie," a state of
        torpor, listlessness, or even depression, a condition known to
        afflict monks, especially solitaries.

21.4   *Luminous:* Athanasios's transfiguration with light at the third
        hour is reminiscent of the descent of holy fire upon the apos-
        tles at Pentecost; see Acts 2:3, 15.

22.1   *Crete:* In 960 Nikephoros Phokas led a naval expedition to
        Arab-controlled Crete, recovering the island for the Byzan-
        tines by March 961 (see below, chap. 23.2).

22.3   *Agarenes:* The Byzantines called the Arabs Agarenes, in the be-
        lief that they were descended from Hagar, the maidservant of
        Abraham.
        Cells designed for spiritual tranquility: The Greek term is ἡσυχα-
        στικὰ κελλία, probably denoting simple stone huts.
        Cenobitic community: It is puzzling that Nikephoros uses the

term *koinobion* here, since he is clearly describing a *lavra,* not a cenobitic monastery, as he states just below.

23.1 *Methodios:* On this intimate of Nikephoros Phokas, see *PmbZ* 2, no. 25077.

23.2 *The year 6469 . . . 4th indiction:* The AM 6469 is equivalent to 961 CE. The indiction is a year within a repeated fifteen-year cycle, which the Byzantines used in their chronological system in addition to the year calculated from the Creation (5508 BCE). The indiction year ran from September to August.

Chapel . . . of the all-glorious Prodromos: This chapel of Saint John the Baptist is located inside the Lavra, near its southern wall.

24.1 *Worker of evil:* A common term for the Devil in the Church Fathers; see, for example, John Chrysostom, *In Joannem, Hom.* 36, chap. 2 (PG 59:206.5).

Trisagion prayer: This is a reference to the "thrice-holy hymn," sung at the beginning of the Eucharist, "Holy [is] God, holy [and] mighty, holy [and] immortal!" See *ODB* 3:2121, under "Trisagion."

25.1 *Oratories:* In fact, these two side chapels, the Forty Martyrs to the north, and Saint Nicholas to the south, were not added during the lifetime of Athanasios, but in the eleventh century; see Mylonas, "Le plan initial du catholicon de la Grande-Lavra," 95–96. This passage thus provides a rough *terminus post quem* for the composition of vita B.

Great habit: The great habit *(megaloschema)*, which included a cowl and scapular, symbolized the highest level of monastic profession.

Isaiah: This monk (*PmbZ* 2, no. 22586) is known only from the two vitae of Athanasios.

25.2 *Seventy stades:* A stade was equivalent to about six hundred feet, and so seven stades would equal forty-two thousand feet, or about eight miles.

25.3 *Stream of water:* The Greek here, πέτων, is an apparent hapax, meaning a stream of water according to *LbG:* that is, a millrace, the current of water that drives a mill wheel.

25.4   *Metochion:* A smaller satellite outpost of a monastery, which could be in a rural setting or in a nearby town.

26.1   *Ordinances and rules:* Here the hagiographer summarizes some of the prescriptions from Athanasios's rule for the Lavra dating to 963 or shortly thereafter, which incorporates many of the provisions of the earlier *typikon* for the Stoudios monastery in Constantinople; for details on this, see the annotated English translation in *BMFD* 1:205–31.

Choir: The term χορός could refer either to a group of singers or to the place in the church where they stood; see Mylonas, "Le plan initial du catholicon de la Grande-Lavra," 98.

Epistemonarches: A disciplinary official who oversaw the singing of hymns; in some monasteries, as here, he was a more general watchdog against unnecessary conversation and idleness.

He was not to permit . . . as he entered: See (11) *Ath. Rule,* chap. 17, *BMFD* 1:224–25.

26.3   *Doorkeepers:* On the doorkeepers *(thyroroi),* see (11) *Ath. Rule,* chap. 17, *BMFD* 1:225.

"*Glory in the Highest*": The doxology at the end of the matins service.

26.5   *Sacristan:* On the duties of the sacristan *(ekklesiarches),* see note on chap. 9.2 above.

28.1   *Matthew:* A monk of the Lavra *(PmbZ* 2, no. 25018), known only from vita B of Athanasios.

28.2   *Woman escorted by two eunuchs:* Evidently the Virgin accompanied by two angels.

Miliaresion: A silver coin worth one-twelfth of a gold *nomisma.*

Folles: On the bronze coin called a *follis,* see note above on chap. 6.1. Twelve *folles* = half of a *miliaresion.*

29.1   *Monastic rule:* For more detailed rules about the refectory, see chaps. 21–31 of (11) *Ath. Rule, BMFD* 1:225–28. The account in vita B, however, provides information on some additional regulations not in the rule.

Monitors: For more on the monitors *(epiteretai),* see Athanasios's rule for the Lavra ([11] *Ath. Rule,* chap. 21, *BMFD* 1:225), where

the monitor is to ensure that the monks take their seats in an orderly manner.

29.2   *Reader:* The reader *(anagnostes)*, to be distinguished from the clerical order of lector, also *anagnostes,* read aloud to the monks while they ate in the refectory.

29.4   *Outsider:* A monk tonsured in a different monastery. The quoted phrases in this chapter are a modified version of (13) *Ath. Typikon,* chap. 29, *BMFD* 1:258. For the Greek text, see Meyer, *Haupturkunden,* 112.

29.5   *Kephas:* Simon Peter; see John 1:42.

        Apollos: An Alexandrian Jew who preached about Christ at Ephesus and Corinth; see Acts 18:24–28, 19:1.

29.6   *In all these matters . . . humble self:* This is a slightly modified version of the translation of chap. 3 of Athanasios's Testament found in *BMFD* 1:274. Before καθηγουμένῳ vita B omitted the words ἐμῷ διαδόχῳ καὶ, which appear in the Testament, drafted sometime after 993, and in chap. 214 of vita A. For the Greek text, see Meyer, *Haupturkunden,* 124.

30.1   *Nikephoros had been proclaimed emperor:* This occurred in July 963.

30.2   *Abydos:* A port on the Asian shore of the Hellespont; see also chap. 8.1 above.

        Euthymios: A Lavriot monk, known only from the two vitae of Athanasios; see *PmbZ* 2, no. 21944.

        Theodotos: This monk is known only from the two vitae of Athanasios; see *PmbZ* 2, no. 27979.

30.3   *Antony:* As we learn from later passages (chaps. 32.2, 78.2), the monk Antony was a physician and was to become Athanasios's closest disciple. Later on, he was superior of the Lavra and then of the Panagiou monastery in Constantinople; see *PmbZ* 2, no. 20498.

        Gerontikon: A book containing the deeds and sayings of the early ascetics, especially the Desert Fathers.

        Isidore: Isidore of Pelousion (ca. 360/70–after 433), an Egyptian monk who wrote over two thousand letters on theological subjects.

        Sketis: An Egyptian monastic settlement in the Wadi Natrun, west of the Nile Delta.

'*Actually . . . except the face of the patriarch*': See *Apophthegmata patrum,* PG 65:221B.

31.1   *Monastery of the Priests:* Probably to be identified with the Hagia Mone northeast of Paphos, supposedly founded in the sixth century.

32.1   *Other side:* Anatolia is meant here, since in chap. 33 Theodotos encounters Athanasios in Attaleia. Thus Athanasios and Antony probably embarked on the north coast of Cyprus, perhaps at Morphou, and disembarked at Anemourion (Anamur) or Alanya. From there they proceeded on foot northwest toward Attaleia.

         Incursion of the . . . Agarenes: Probably a reference to raids made in Anatolia by Arab emirs based in Aleppo and Tarsos.

32.2   *Poor and meager provisions:* The phrase τῆς ἀπόρου καὶ στενοτά-της ζωῆς is difficult to translate; the French translation has "ces pauvres et misérables vivres," perhaps following the slightly different phrase in vita A, Noret, *Vitae duae,* chap. 97.20, τῆς ἀπόρου καὶ στενοτάτης διαίτης.

33.2   *Attaleia:* A port city (modern Antalya) on the southern coast of Anatolia.

         Proceed on foot: He was probably headed for Alanya or Anemourion.

         Lampe: A town in northwestern Anatolia near Adramyttion (Edremit). The monastery of Dioungiou is otherwise unknown and is not listed in Janin, *Grands centres.*

33.3   *Sourdough starter:* At the Lavra the monks used a vinegary sourdough starter instead of yeast to leaven their bread dough. For more details, see below at chaps. 40.4 and 48.

         Paul of Larissa: A monk of the Lavra in the 960s; he is mentioned only in the two vitae of Athanasios. See *PmbZ* 2, no. 26355.

34.2   *Nathan did to David:* See 2 Kings 12:1–13.

34.3   *Great Monastery:* This somewhat puzzling phrase, ἡ Μέγα παρ' αὐτοῖς ἔστι τε καὶ ὀνομάζεται Μοναστήριον, is identical in vitae A and B. We have omitted the words παρ' αὐτοῖς in the translation because the referent is unclear. There is no "Great Monastery" in Thessalonike proper, but Lemerle has argued convincingly that the author is referring to the region of Thes-

salonike, and identifies it as the monastery of Saint Andrew in Peristerai, fifteen miles southeast of Thessalonike; see Lemerle, *Actes de Lavra,* 1:38, 86–87. Nikephoros Phokas gave the monastery to the Lavra in 964/5, but it remained independent until the death of its superior, Stephen, when it became a *metochion* of the Lavra; see [Sisters of Ormylia], Ὁ ἅγιος Ἀθανάσιος ὁ Ἀθωνίτης (Ormylia, 2003), 483. See also the description of the foundation of the monastery in the *Life of Euthymios,* above in this volume, chaps. 28–33.

Stipend of three pounds: One pound = 72 *nomismata* (gold coins), thus three pounds would be 216 *nomismata.*

35.1   *Steward of blessings:* See K. Mras, ed., *Die Praeparatio Evangelica* (= *Eusebius Werke,* vol. 8.1) (Berlin, 1956), 1.1.4.3.

35.3   *Military commander:* Literally, *chiliarches,* commander of one thousand soldiers.

    Pitch-black commander . . . Melana: There is a pun in the Greek on "pitch-black" *(pammelanos)* and the promontory of Melana, meaning "black." For Melana, see note on chap. 21.1 above, and for a similar wordplay, 21.2.

35.5   *Gerontikon:* See note above on chap. 30.3. Claudia Rapp suggests that this may allude to a tradition of pious copying of manuscripts during Lent; see Rapp, "Holy Texts, Holy Men and Holy Scribes," in *The Early Christian Book,* ed. William Klingshirn and Linda Safran (Washington, D.C., 2007), 209.

36.1   *Emperor Nikephoros:* Nikephoros was murdered in his bedchamber in 969 as the result of a conspiracy between his wife Theophano and John Tzimiskes.

    John: John I Tzimiskes became emperor (r. 969–976) after engineering the murder of Nikephoros II.

37.1   *Thomas:* The elder Thomas is known only from the two vitae of Athanasios; see *PmbZ* 2, no. 28315.

    Black dwarves: Literally, "Ethiopian dwarves."

    Egyptian dwarves . . . Melana: On this, see also chaps. 21 and 35.3 above. There may be a wordplay here, between the black dwarves (literally, Ethiopian or Egyptian) and Melana, meaning the "black place." We thank Claudia Rapp for this suggestion.

38.1   *And the voice . . . hands of Esau:* This same quotation is used in the

Life of Maximos by Theophanes, 5.1, as a derogatory reference to Maximos at the imperial palace.

Abel . . . Cain: See Genesis 4:8–16.

40.1   *Apathetic:* The Greek word πάρετος can mean "paralyzed," but we think here it refers to a mental paralysis or languor, for which see the listing in *PGL*.

Indolent: The Greek word φίλαργος is an apparent hapax.

40.3   *Brethren in Christ:* This phrase, which also appears in chaps. 41.1 and 49.1, may refer to hermits on Athos who were not subject to Athanasios's authority but who occasionally sought alms, food, or medical care at the Lavra. A passage in chap. 49.2 suggests that these monks were mendicants who subsisted by begging for alms.

40.4   *Assisting with the leavened dough:* The hard work is kneading the sourdough starter into the flour paste to make the leavened dough.

41.1   *Infirmarian:* The Greek term is *nosokomos.*

42.1   *Three lenten periods:* See chap. 10.1 and note above.

Blessed bread: The blessed bread *(antidoron)* distributed to the congregation at the close of the liturgy is to be distinguished from the bread consecrated during the Eucharist.

43.1   *Common guardian and protector:* See Gregory of Nazianzos, *Or.* 43, *In laudem Basilii Magni,* chap.42 (PG 36:552C).

43.2   *Iberia:* That is, Georgia.

Patriarch Nicholas: Nicholas II Chrysoberges was patriarch of Constantinople from 979/80 to 991/92 (*PmbZ* 2, no. 26019).

Charonites: Apparently a surname for a monk or cleric; see *PmbZ* 2, no. 21234. He is known only from the two vitae of Athanasios.

Andrew of Chrysopolis: Andrew, probably the superior of a monastery in Chrysopolis (across the Bosporos from Constantinople), is known only from the two vitae of Athanasios; see *PmbZ* 2, no. 20384.

Akakios: Akakios (*PmbZ* 2, no. 20202) is known only from the two vitae of Athanasios.

43.3   *Nikephoros:* This hermit from Calabria (*PmbZ* 2, no. 25610) is mentioned as a traveling companion of Saint Phantinos in chap. 36 of the vita of Phantinos, ed. Enrica Follieri, *La vita di*

San Fantino il Giovane (Brussels, 1993). For further details on Nikephoros, sometimes called *ho gymnos,* "the naked," see op. cit., 125–28.

Phantinos: Phantinos the Younger (*PmbZ* 2, no. 26576) was a tenth-century monk from Calabria who became the spiritual director of Saint Neilos of Rossano and later moved to Thessalonike.

43.4   *Transferred into one of the tombs:* As was common in Byzantine monasteries, some years after the initial burial of a holy man, his remains might be ceremonially translated to a different location. During this ceremony a miraculous exudation of *myron* (perfumed oil) was observed on Nikephoros's bones. Despite the allusion to his sanctification, there is no evidence that Nikephoros was ever recognized as a saint; he is not listed in *BHG.*

Fruit . . . root: This is an allusion to Matthew 7:16–20, 12:33, and Luke 6:43–44.

44.1   *Nicholas the cook:* Nicholas (*PmbZ* 2, no. 26106) is known only from vita B of Athanasios.

Theodoritos: This monk (*PmbZ* 2, no. 27614) should perhaps be identified as the Theodoritos who was one of Athanasios's successors as superior of the Lavra, from 1010 to 1016 (*PmbZ* 2, no. 27612).

Word of advice about perseverance: This is reminiscent of the *logoi,* or sayings, of the Desert Fathers, which were collected in the *Apophthegmata Patrum.*

Eupraxia: A fifth-century ascetic saint who lived in the Thebaid, a region of southern Egypt that was a center of monasticism; for her vitae, see *BHG* 631–631m. It is noteworthy that Athonite monks would read the vitae of holy women, despite the prohibition of members of the female sex on the Holy Mountain.

44.3   *Cellmates:* It was common practice at some monasteries for a cell to be shared by two, or even three, monks; for examples, see index listings in *BMFD* 5:1873, under "cells, monastic *(kellia)*: occupied by two monks" and "occupied by three monks." It is not clear why he stood on the bed instead of the floor.

I stood outside: The monks were normally seated during the readings.

44.4   *Martyr Nikephoros:* Nikephoros Phokas, who was murdered in his sleep in 969, was celebrated as a martyr on Athos in an *akolouthia* (liturgical office), probably composed by Theodore the Deacon; see Louis Petit, "Un office inédit en l'honneur de Nicéphore Phocas," *BZ* 13 (1904): 398–420.

I had grown weak: This translation of κατωφερής, suggested by Erich Trapp, makes sense in this context. The word has the literal meaning, however, of "descending downward" (see LSJ), which would seem to refer to his imminent rupture.

Internal organs . . . my knees: He evidently suffered from some sort of hernia or prolapse.

45.1   *Most beneficial passages:* Claudia Rapp has suggested that the reference is perhaps to a *Gerontikon,* or collected sayings of the Desert Fathers.

45.3   *Completely receptive:* Literally, "impregnated with mordant," that is, saturated with a caustic corrosive used to prepare wool for dyeing.

47.1   *Amalfitan elders:* Probably monks from the monastery of the Amalfitans founded on Mount Athos at the end of the tenth century, on which see Agostino Pertusi, "Monasteri e monaci italiani all' Athos nell' alto Medioevo," in *Le Millénaire du Mont-Athos, 963–1963* (Chevetogne, 1963), 1:217–51.

Garum: A type of fermented fish sauce condiment popular in Roman and Byzantine cuisine.

48.2   *Bema:* The Greek word ἀναβάθρα refers to a raised platform, in this case probably the *bema* (sanctuary) of the church. The corresponding term in vita A, Noret, *Vitae duae,* is ὀκρίβας, rendered as "Tribüne" (tribune) or "Podest" (pulpit) by *LbG.*

48.3   *Sourdough mix:* A more literal translation would be "vinegary leaven," but we assume the reference is to the sourdough starter that was used instead of yeast to leaven the bread dough.

48.4   *Contraption, easily turned by oxen:* The need for Athanasios to invent an ox-driven bread dough mixer gives some idea of the

huge amount of bread that had to be baked to feed the monks and visitors to the Lavra.

49.1   *Mylopotamos:* The name of a Lavriot *metochion* located some ten miles northwest of the Lavra on the northeastern coast of Mount Athos. It was famed for its olive trees and vineyards.

Training facility: The Greek term is φροντιστήριον, which can mean either "monastery" or "school." Here it seems to mean a training facility for novices of the Lavra, who were deliberately kept separate from the monks during the period of their novitiate; this is manifestly the case in chap. 57.1, which states that the island of Neoi ("youths") was so called διὰ τὸ φροντιστήριον γεγονέναι ἐν αὐτῇ καὶ προγυμνάζεσθαι ἐκεῖσε τοὺς νεωτέρους τῶν μοναχῶν. The comparable passage in vita A (Noret, *Vitae duae,* chap. 208) states that the island was an imperial gift to the Lavra, εἰς φροντιστήριον δὲ καὶ γυμναστήριον νέων μοναχῶν ἐπωνύμως μετασκευασθεῖσα.

Belas: An anchorage on the northeastern coast of the Athonite peninsula.

Brethren in Christ: See chap. 41.1 above for a similar reference to "brethren in Christ," perhaps hermits, and, as made clear below, mendicant monks.

50.1   *The great Athanasios:* Archbishop of Alexandria (328–373); his feast day is celebrated on January 18 and May 2.

The storeroom keeper . . . Athanasios: For Athanasios, the *apothekarios* (storeroom keeper), also mentioned in chap. 62.1, see *PmbZ* 2, no. 20682. He is known only from the two vitae of Athanasios of Athos.

50.3   *Impulsive eating from the tree:* See Genesis 2:17, 3:7, for the story of how Eve, tempted by the serpent, took an apple from the tree of knowledge of good and evil and shared it with Adam.

50.4   *Monks be placed in confinement:* Chap. 19 of Athanasios's rule for the Lavra refers to these places of confinement for disobedient monks; see (11) *Ath. Rule,* chap. 19, *BMFD* 1:225.

I will bear the . . . punishment: That is, Athanasios will take the blame for having wrongly punished the monks, if such should be the Lord's ruling at the Last Judgment, but he will not relent now.

51.3   *On account of his transgression:* That is, that of Adam.

52.2   *Monk John:* John (*PmbZ* 2, no. 23212) was *docheiarios* of the Lavra,
        a title that could refer to either the treasurer or the cellarer of
        the Lavra. Since below, in chaps. 61.4 and 75, the term *kellarites*
        is used for the cellarer (as in the *typikon* for the Lavra, (13) *Ath.
        Typikon,* chap. 32, *BMFD* 1:259), we have decided to translate
        docheiarios here as "treasurer." John is known only from the two
        vitae of Athanasios.

52.3   *Theodore the hunter:* The hunter Theodore (*PmbZ* 2, no. 27792) is
        known only from the two vitae of Athanasios. He seems to
        have been affiliated with the Lavra, and one wonders for whom
        he was hunting game, since the monks could not eat meat. Per-
        haps lay workmen or the monastery cats?

        Kerasea: Also called Kerasia, a small monastic settlement at the
        tip of the Athonite peninsula, southwest of the Great Lavra.

        Chalasmata: A site of uncertain location near the tip of the
        Athonite peninsula.

        A monk: This monk, unnamed in vita B, is called Theophylaktos
        in vita A (ed. Noret, *Vitae duae,* chap. 52), where he is described
        as a former monk at the Lavra; see *PmbZ* 2, no. 28234.

53.2   *Peter, a Cypriot:* On Peter, see *PmbZ* 2, no. 26520; he is known
        only from the two vitae of Athanasios.

        Sank momentarily: See Matthew 14:30–31.

54.1   *Matthew:* The Lavriot monk and coppersmith Matthew (*PmbZ*
        2, no. 25019) is known only from the two vitae of Athanasios.

54.2   *Something precious:* Claudia Rapp suggests emending τι τῶν τι-
        μίων to τίνα τῶν τιμίων, and translating "as an important per-
        son and a family relation."

54.3   *Ambrosios:* This Lavriot monk (*PmbZ* 2, no. 20272) is known only
        from the two vitae of Athanasios.

55.3   *One of his customary retorts:* For example, just above, in chap. 54.5.

56.1   *Monk Theodore:* This monk at the Lavriot *metochion* of Mylopota-
        mos (*PmbZ* 2, no. 27790) is known only from the two vitae of
        Athanasios.

        Timothy, the physician: For Timothy, see *PmbZ* 2, no. 28353.

56.2   *Does not get better in a short time:* The version in vita A (ed. Noret,

Vitae duae, chap. 205), renders this phrase, "always walks crookedly and proceeds to the worse."

56.3   *Mylopotamos:* See note on chap. 49.1 above.

57.1   *Neoi:* Island about eighteen miles south of Lemnos in the northern Aegean Sea, also known as Hagios Eustratios; it is about fifty-three miles southeast of the tip of the Athonite peninsula. As the text here suggests, it may have taken the name of Neoi ("youths," "young people") because it was the location of a preparatory school for novices, although it already had this name in the ninth century, when it was a deserted island (see *Life of Euthymios,* above, chap. 24.2). On the island, see Johannes Koder, *Aigaion Pelagos,* 240–41.

Emperors of blessed memory: A reference to the emperors Basil II (r. 976–1025) and Constantine VIII (r. 976–1028). This provides a *terminus post quem* of 1025 for the date of composition of the vita. Actually, the emperor Basil gave it with a chrysobull to John the Iberian, who gave the island in turn to the Lavra in 984; see Lemerle, *Actes de Lavra,* 136 and Act 6.15–16, and Denise Papachryssanthou, Ὁ Ἀθωνικὸς μοναχισμός. Ἀρχὲς καὶ ὀργάνωση (Athens, 1992), 231.

Goats which yielded the finest wool: This may be a reference to Angora goats, which produce a fine wool called mohair.

57.3   *Rose-colored pastors:* A species of European starling, which congregates in large flocks, often in the vicinity of herds of sheep. They are known to have a preference for a diet of locusts.

58.2   *Protos . . . John Phakenos:* On the *protos* of Athos, see note above on chap. 16.3. John Phakenos (*PmbZ* 2, no. 23134) held this position from 991 until 996.

58.3   *Campaign against the barbarians:* This apparently refers to Basil II's renewed offensive in the Balkans between 991 and 994; see article by Catherine Holmes at www.roman-emperors.org/basilii.htm, consulted September 23, 2011.

58.5   *Turks:* According to Gyula Moravcsik, *Byzantinoturcica* (Berlin, 1958), 1:555, the reference is probably to Hungarians or Vardariots (on whom, see Moravcsik, 1:86–87).

60.1   *Monk Gerasimos:* On Gerasimos, who worked in both the vine-
        yard and the bakery of the Lavra and went on a mission to the
        Holy Land, see *PmbZ* 2, no. 22281. He is known only from vita
        B of Athanasios.

60.2   *Salvific tomb . . . in Jerusalem:* This passage provides a valuable
        reference to pilgrimage to the Holy Sepulcher by Athonite
        monks in the second half of the tenth century. It also demon-
        strates some sort of relationship between the Lavra and the
        patriarchate of Jerusalem or a monastery in the holy city.

60.3   *Church of the Holy Apostles:* Most probably the cemetery chapel,
        located to the west of the Lavra. It is sometimes called the cha-
        pel of Saints Peter and Paul.

61.4   *Kerasea:* See note above on chap. 51.3.

        Paul . . . the cellarer: On Paul the cellarer (*kellarites*), see chap. 75
        below, and *PmbZ* 2, no. 26370. He is known only from vita B of
        Athanasios.

62.1   *Mylopotamos:* Mylopotamos had a *metochion* where new monks
        received training; see chap. 49.1 above and relevant notes.
        Athanasios the storeroom keeper was already mentioned
        above, in chap. 50.

        There is nothing wrong with you: Athanasios used the same expres-
        sion in chap. 42.3 above.

63.1   *Mark, from Lampsakos:* The Lavriot monk Mark (*PmbZ* 2, no.
        24999) is known only from vita B of Athanasios. Lampsakos is
        a city on the eastern shore of the Hellespont.

64.1   *Let us compare Athanasios:* Here the author begins the *synkrisis,* or
        comparison of his hero with great figures of the past, a tradi-
        tional feature of Byzantine hagiography, borrowed from an-
        cient rhetoric.

64.2   *Arsenios:* Arsenios the Great (354–445), after many years in impe-
        rial service in the palace in Constantinople, fled to Egypt,
        where he lived in various locations as a hermit.

64.3   *Sabas:* Sabas the Great (439–532), founder of the *lavra* of Saint
        Sabas in the Judean Desert, southeast of Jerusalem.

        Monastic complexes: The Greek term is φροντιστήριον, which oc-
        curs four times in this vita. In chap. 25.1 we translate it as "mo-

nastic complex," as here; in chaps. 49.1 and 57.1 it has the meaning of a training facility or preparatory school.

Pachomios: Pachomios (ca. 290–346), one of the founders of cenobitic monasticism in Egypt.

Antony: Antony the Great (ca. 251–356), one of the founders of eremitic monasticism in Egypt.

65.1   *As I have said above:* See above, chap. 43.1–3.

Enlarge the church: Mylonas ("Le plan initial du catholicon de la Grande-Lavra," 96–97) argues that this "enlargement" or "widening" refers to the addition of the semicircular choirs to the north and south sides of the church to form the triconch plan.

65.2   *Theodore the Stoudite:* Theodore (759–826), superior of the Stoudios monastery in Constantinople, was a famed monastic reformer whose rule for Stoudios had great influence on subsequent monastic foundations, including the Great Lavra. The "catechetical instruction" he delivered was no doubt one of his *Great Catecheseis* or *Small Catecheseis,* which were favored reading materials in monastic communities.

It is better . . . slip of the tongue: John of the Ladder, *Scala paradisi,* chap. 11 (PG 88:852.33).

65.3   *Cowl of . . . Maleinos:* See chap. 12.3 above.

66.1   *Scaffolding:* This word is not in the Greek but seems warranted by the allusion to "wooden beams" at the end of 66.2. For another example of scaffolding in a church, see the *Life of Euthymios,* above, at chap. 29.2.

Daniel, the mason: Daniel, the *oikodomos,* or mason, is known only from the two vitae of Athanasios; see *PmbZ* 2, no. 21403.

66.2   *Hands and feet and fingernails:* Evidently a proverbial expression, but we cannot find a reference in either the *CPG* or the *TLG.*

Synthronon: The *synthronon* was a semicircular tier of benches in the apse of a church reserved for the clergy.

66.3   *A death unworthy of the saints:* Indeed, an accidental death is most unusual for Byzantine holy men.

67.1   *Assembly of elders:* The *gerousia* was the assembly of Athonite elders that met at Karyes three times a year; it was composed of superiors of the Athonite monasteries and heads of *kellia;* see Papachryssanthou, *Prôtaton,* 116–17.

His face ... was like snow: Perhaps an allusion to Revelations 1:14.

68.1 *The calligrapher John:* A well-attested scribe *(kalligraphos)* at the Lavra, from whose hand eight manuscripts are known; see *PmbZ* 2, no. 23154.

68.2 *Drank up ... my marrow:* See Gregory of Nazianzos, *Or.* 2, *Apologetica,* chap. 71 (PG 35:480A).

68.3 *The father ... reality and name:* See Gregory of Nazianzos, *Or.* 7, *In laudem Caesarii fratris,* chap. 1 (PG 35:756A).

69.1 *The monk Antony:* This Antony, whom Athanasios designated as his successor as superior of the Lavra, is apparently to be identified with Athanasios's bosom companion on his flight to Cyprus and Asia Minor in 963–964 (see chap. 30.3); he is also the teacher of the author of vita A (see Lemerle, *Actes de Lavra,* 1:48 and passim). The dates when he held office cannot be determined, but he probably died before 1010. Antony's mission to Constantinople is alluded to in chap. 66.4.

Mount Ganos: A holy mountain in Thrace, on the western shore of the Sea of Marmara, near Rhaidestos.

Croup: Dog-quinsy (κυνάγχη), or croup, is an inflammation of the larynx common in small children. A typical feature of the disease is that the sick child makes a barking sound like a dog.

Symeon: This monk *(PmbZ* 2, no. 27529) is called "the Corinthian" in vita A of Athanasios (Noret, *Vitae duae,* chap. 247).

70.1 *Oreon:* A small town in Euboea.

Arrived here at the Lavra: This passage provides an important clue to the fact that vita B was composed at the Lavra.

71.1 *Eustratios:* Eustratios, who was indeed superior of the Lavra for only a short time, between 1016 and 1018, died before March 1030. See Lemerle, *Actes de Lavra,* 1:49; *PmbZ* 2, no. 21898.

Neoi: In vita A (Noret, *Vitae duae,* chap. 208.32–33), he is called the "superior of the island," a reference to the *metochion* on the island of the Neoi, on which see chap. 57.1 and note above, and chap. 24.2 of the *Life of Euthymios* above.

71.2 *Up to the city:* The entry for Eustratios in *PmbZ* (2, no. 21898) assumes that this means Constantinople; this interpretation is supported by the author's use of the verb ἀναπλεῖν, "to sail up (north)." It should be noted, however, that in vita B Constanti-

nople is usually referred to as "Byzantion," the "Queen of Cities," the "imperial city," or the "great city."

71.3   *Superior:* The Greek term here is προεστώς, usually a synonym for ἡγούμενος. The entry on Eustratios in *PmbZ* (2, no. 21898) suggests, however, that it might mean "acting superior" in this case.

72.1   *Smyrna:* A major port city (modern Izmir) on the west coast of Anatolia.

In the middle of the day: As opposed to morning or evening, when private devotions of this sort would have been more usual.

73.1   *Elephant leprosy:* In Greek, the term elephant leprosy or elephant disease *(elephantiasis)* is used to denote true leprosy as opposed to other skin diseases; it was so called because the skin becomes dark, thickened, and cracked like the skin of an elephant. See Timothy S. Miller and John W. Nesbitt, *Walking Corpses: Leprosy in Byzantium and the Medieval West* (Ithaca, N.Y., 2014), 10–12, 14, 29–30, 57, 60–61, 120–21.

74.1   *A man called Athanasios:* This Athanasios *(PmbZ* 2, no. 20695) is known only from vita B of Athanasios.

75.1   *Paul the cellarer:* See chap. 61.4 above.

Theoktistos: His dates as superior at the Lavra are unknown, but Lemerle places him before Theodoritos, who became superior in 1010; see Lemerle, *Actes de Lavra,* 1:55; *PmbZ* 2, no. 28059. He is mentioned only in vita B of Athanasios.

75.2   *Realized . . . condemned:* There is a nice wordplay in the Greek between the verbs for "realized" (ἐπέγνω) and "condemned" (κατέγνω), but one impossible to render in English.

76.1   *Symeon and George:* Symeon was mentioned in a similar context in chap. 69.1 above. The monk George *(PmbZ* 2, no. 22263) is known only from vitae A and B of Athanasios.

Peukia: Seaport of unknown location, possibly on the Asiatic side of the Bosporos near Chalcedon (Janin, *Constantinople byz., 503*).

76.3   *Another miracle . . . described:* See Gregory of Nazianzos, *Or.* 43, *In laudem Basilii Magni,* chap. 54 (PG 36:564B).

77.1   *Erisos:* Also called Hierissos, a small town located in Chalkidike at the neck of the Athonite peninsula.

Metochion: See above note on chap. 25.4; the *metochion* of the Lavra at Hierissos is mentioned in Lemerle, *Actes de Lavra* in Act 40.1 of 1080.

Ioannikios: The monastic steward *(oikonomos)* Ioannikios *(PmbZ* 2, no. 23464) is known only from vitae A and B of Athanasios.

Strymon: This could refer either to the river or to the theme established in the ninth century.

The barbarous people: No doubt a reference to the Slavs who began to settle in the region in the late seventh century.

Gold . . . save one from death: This is an allusion to a false etymology, connecting χρυσός, "gold," with ῥύσις, "deliverance from captivity, ransom"; see Sturz, *Etymologicum,* under χρυσέω.

77.4   *Octopus . . . rocky chamber:* See Homer, *Odyssey,* 5:432; Gregory of Nazianzos, *Or. 43, In laudem Basilii Magni,* chap. 19 (PG 36:521AB).

78.2   *Kosmas:* Kosmas, sacristan *(ekklesiarches)* of the Lavra *(PmbZ* 2, no. 24172) is mentioned in both vitae A and B of Athanasios.

Panagiou: A monastery in Constantinople closely associated with the Great Lavra on Mount Athos. The monk Athanasios of Panagiou wrote vita A of Athanasios of Athos.

The monk Antony: Antony, who served for a while as superior of the Lavra after Athanasios's death, is also mentioned in chaps. 30.3, 31.3, 32.1–4, 55.4, 66.4, and 69.1 of vita B.

78.3   *The icon maker . . . Pantoleon:* Pantoleon *(PmbZ* 2, no. 26258) was also a painter of illuminated manuscripts, known from his many signed miniatures in the Vatican's *Menologion of Basil II.*

79.2   *You watch over us . . . guide us:* See Gregory of Nazianzos, *Or. 24, In laudem S. Cypriani,* chap. 19 (PG 35:1193B); *Or. 43, In laudem Basilii Magni,* chap. 82 (PG 36:604D).

LIFE OF MAXIMOS THE HUTBURNER BY NIPHON

1.1   *Hieromonk:* A hieromonk (ἱερομόναχος) was an ordained monk. For Niphon's ordination, which occurred before the canonical age, see *Life of Niphon,* 1.1.

1.2   *Unerring guides for those who went astray:* The translation attempts to capture the range of meaning inherent in the Greek root

πλαν-, which has connotations of both "wandering" and "error." See also the note to chap. 2.2, below.

1.3   *Condemnation . . . God:* A direct quotation, with minor adaptations from Mode 4 of the Matins sung at the Pre-sanctified Liturgy on Holy Tuesday; see *Τριόδιον Κατανυκτικόν* (Rome, 1879), 633.

2.1   *Lampsakos:* Lampsakos (modern Lapseki) was a port city on the eastern shore of the Hellespont.

After he had spent a long time there: Niphon was evidently unaware of, or thought it unnecessary to record, a number of details of Maximos's early life that are included in the *Life of Maximos* by Theophanes, chaps. 2–5; see below.

The venerable Lavra: The monastery founded by Saint Athanasios of Athos in 963; see the *Life of Athanasios* above in this volume.

Timekeeper: The monastic timekeeper *(horologos),* an official responsible for summoning the brothers to church; see *BMFD* 2:749. Another timekeeper from the Lavra is mentioned in the *Life of Niphon,* 15.1.

After this he went up to Constantinople: In the *Life of Maximos* by Theophanes, chaps. 4–5, Maximos's visit to Constantinople is made prior to his arrival on Athos.

Relics: On these and other relics at Constantinople, see Holger Klein, "Sacred Relics and Imperial Ceremonies at the Great Palace of Constantinople," *BYZAS* 5 (2006): 79–99. Most of the more famous of these relics had, however, been removed during the sack of Constantinople in 1204 or during the years of the Latin occupation, around a century before Maximos's stay in Constantinople, which probably took place in the middle of the first decade of the fourteenth century.

Onouphrios: Onouphrios was an Egyptian hermit who lived circa 400.

Peter the Athonite: The semilegendary ninth-century Peter the Athonite was one of the earliest documented monks to reside on Mount Athos, where he spent fifty-three years as a hermit. His *Life* by Nicholas was published by Kirsopp Lake, *The*

Early Days of Monasticism on Mount Athos (Oxford, 1909), 18–39. There is an Italian translation of his *Life* (*BHG* 1505) by Antonio Rigo, *Alle origini dell'Athos: La Vita di Pietro l'Athonita* (Magnano, 1999). On him, see also Denise Papachryssanthou, "La vie ancienne de Saint Pierre l'Athonite. Date, composition et valeur historique," *Analecta Bollandiana* 92 (1974): 19–61.

2.2 *Panagia:* A small chapel situated at almost five thousand feet on the precipitous and barren southern slope below the peak of Mount Athos. It lies about three miles west-southwest of the Lavra.

   Deranged: It is impossible to capture in simple English translation all that is implicit in the Greek verb πλανάω and its cognates, which are used widely in relation to Maximos, both in this *Life* and that by Theophanes. The term thus contains a sense not only of "derangement" and "madness," as well as "vagrancy," which relate to its root meaning of (physical) "wandering," but also of "spiritual and theological error."

3.1 *Hermitages:* In the Athonite context *skete* (σκήτη) indicates a small monastic community. The term is derived from the celebrated fourth-century Egyptian monastic settlement of Sketis (Wadi Natrun).

3.2 *There was a small cave:* This and the following paragraph are included, with acknowledgment of the source, almost verbatim in the *Life of Maximos* by Theophanes, 31.1–2.

3.3 *Spiritual instruments:* A reference either to bells or to the *semandron,* the wooden board that was struck to summon monks to church services.

4.1 *The emperors Kantakouzenos and John Palaiologos:* John VI Kantakouzenos and John V Palaiologos. Outside the *Lives* of Maximos there is no other allusion to this imperial visit to Athos, which must have occurred between 1347 and 1352; the *PLP* (16810) dates it to around 1350. It is possible that chap. 26.1 also refers to this visit. A more elaborate version is provided by Theophanes in his *Life of Maximos* at 20.4–21.3.

5.1 *Glorify God ... glorify Him:* See 1 Kings 2:30.

Merkourios: Merkourios (*PLP* 17918), an Athonite monk. A less detailed version of this episode is provided by Theophanes in his *Life of Maximos* at 20.1.

5.2 *Bother the elder:* The Greek verb πειράζω also has the sense of "making trial of," "testing," or "tempting."

Healed from that time: Theophanes, *Life of Maximos,* 20.1, also gives a slightly different version of this episode.

Virtue . . . envelops it: A more or less direct quotation from the *Vita Lucae Junioris Steiriotae,* 27:1–3, ed. and trans. Carolyn and Robert Connor, *The Life and Miracles of St Luke* (Brookline, Mass., 1994), 40–41.

Shake off his fruit: See John Chrysostom, *Interpretatio in Danielem prophetam* (PG 56:215.43).

6.1 *Some monks once approached Maximos:* Compare the somewhat different account of this and the following incident in Theophanes, *Life of Maximos,* 20.2.

Akindynatos: A follower of Gregory Akindynos, an anti-Palamite theologian (d. 1348). He was condemned at the Council of Constantinople in 1341 and excommunicated at the Council of 1347, dying in exile soon afterward.

7.1 *Ecumenical patriarch . . . Kallistos:* Kallistos I was patriarch of Constantinople 1350–1353 and 1355–1363. An Athonite monk in his youth, he was a hesychast and disciple of Gregory of Sinai. He presided over the Council of Constantinople in 1351, which supported Palamite doctrine. He died in 1363 in Serres during a mission to the Serbs seeking the reunification of the bishopric of Serres with Constantinople. This episode is described by Theophanes at greater length in his *Life of Maximos,* 22.1.

So . . . immense: At the suggestion of Alexander Alexakis, we have moved the first sentence of chap. 8.1 to the end of 7.1.

8.1 *Methodios:* A monk known only from the *Lives* of Maximos (*PLP* 17607). The episode involving Methodios, and the subsequent incidents recorded in this chapter, are summarized by Theophanes, *Life of Maximos,* 23.1.

8.2   *Arsenios:* Arsenios (*PLP* 1413) is perhaps identical with the Arsenios (*PLP* 1417) mentioned in chap. 23.1 below.

8.3   *Ishmaelites:* A term for the Turks.

9.1   *I need to bring this up:* Theophanes provides a somewhat embroidered version of this story, *Life of Maximos,* 24.1.

        Gregory the infirmarian: This monk (*PLP* 4582) is also mentioned by Theophanes, *Life of Maximos,* 24.1.

        We were astounded: The unexpected switch here to first person plural is puzzling. Perhaps Niphon, in recalling too vividly the story told him by Gregory and the other monk, has made an editorial slip, but it also seems possible that this is self-referential and for a moment, by mistake, he reveals his own identity as the other monk.

        Summit . . . Christ the Savior: There was a chapel of the Transfiguration at the summit.

10.1   *Teacher . . . Athos:* Probably a reference to Dionysios, who founded the monastery of Saint John the Baptist (Prodromos), more commonly called Dionysiou, between 1356 and 1366. This is situated on the west coast of the peninsula at the foot of Little Athos (Antiathos), a mountain peak around two and a half miles northwest of the main summit of Athos; see *BMFD* 1:266, n. 16. In the *Life of Maximos* by Theophanes (25.1) he is called "superior" of the monastery.

        Papas: A Greek word for priest.

        I'm waiting for you: Theophanes's version of this episode, *Life of Maximos,* 25.1, is slightly reworked, although the direct speech remains almost identical.

10.2   *Another man again:* Theophanes's version of this story appears in his *Life of Maximos,* 26.1.

        Karyes: A village on Mount Athos that housed the central administration of the monastic community on the Holy Mountain.

        Hyperpyra: Hyperpyron was the name for the type of gold coin struck in Byzantium between the late eleventh and mid-fourteenth centuries; in 1367 it was replaced by a heavy silver coin called initially *hyperpyron argyron* (silver *hyperpyron*) and

later *stavraton*. We thank Cécile Morrisson for clarification of this point. The mention of this coin may thus provide a *terminus post quem* for Maximos's death, on which see further in the Introduction.

10.3   *Serres:* A town in Macedonia, about forty miles northeast of Thessalonike.

10.4   *Mark:* Mark (*PLP* 17065) is known only from the *Lives* of Maximos. For this episode see Theophanes, *Life of Maximos,* 20.2.

Messalian heretic: Messalians were members of an ascetic sect that originated in Mesopotamia in the fourth century and spread to Syria, Egypt, and Asia Minor. They emphasized prayer as a tool to expel demons from one's soul. In the fourteenth century the term referred to Bogomils, who were condemned at two synods of Constantinople in 1316 and 1325; see MM 1:296. The heresy spread on Mount Athos and was associated with the controversy over the teachings of Gregory Palamas; see Janet and Bernard Hamilton, *Christian Dualist Heresies in the Byzantine World c. 650-c.1450* (Manchester, 1998), 52–54, 278–82.

Another time again: Theophanes gives a rather garbled account of this episode in his *Life of Maximos,* 26.1, immediately after that of the man from Karyes (above, 10.2).

Hyperpyra: In Theophanes's version of this episode (26.2), Mark is said to have sixty ducats. By the time of Maximos, *hyperpyron* was a money of account, which explains why Mark actually had Venetian ducats in his possession. We again thank Cécile Morrisson for her assistance with this note.

11.1   *Damianos:* Damianos (*PLP* 5076) is known only from the *Lives* of Maximos. Theophanes gives an abbreviated and slightly altered account of this episode, *Life of Maximos,* 26.2.

11.2   *Theodoulos:* Theodoulos (*PLP* 7277) is known only from this text.

Bag: In *LbG* the rare term περσικάριον is rendered as "Quersack" or "Bettelsack," both being types of shoulder bag. Note, however, that the feminine noun περσικάρια is defined in Emmanouel Kriaras, *Λεξικό της μεσαιωνικής ελληνικής δημώδους γραμματείας, 1100–1669* (Thessalonike, 1968–), 16:182, as a type of watercress.

Like this for three days: Probably Maximos means to say that he has been without food for three days.

11.3   *Kallinikos:* Kallinikos (*PLP* 10413) is known only from this text. It is conceivable he could be identified with the *abbas* of the same name mentioned below in 16.1.

11.4   *Kassianos:* Kassianos (*PLP* 11348) is known only from the *Lives* of Maximos. Theophanes provides an abridged version of this episode, *Life of Maximos,* 26.2.

12.1   *Barlaam:* Barlaam (*PLP* 2278) is known only from this passage in the *Lives.*

Ioannikios from Exypolytos: Ioannikios (*PLP* 8843) is known only from this text. Halkin notes that the small cell of Exypolytos was attached to the Athonite monastery of Karakalou in 1324. Theophanes provides a similar, but not identical, account of this and the following episode, *Life of Maximos,* 20.4.

Athanasios Krokas: Athanasios Krokas (*PLP* 13813) is known only from this passage in the *Lives.*

Nikodemos: Nikodemos (*PLP* 20363) is again known only from the *Lives* of Maximos.

Present at his funeral: Theophanes includes this episode somewhat later in his version of the *Life of Maximos,* 33.3. It is curious that Niphon does not describe Maximos's death.

13.1   *Niphon:* This Niphon (*PLP* 20642), who is known only from the *Lives* of Maximos, is to be distinguished from the author of the current *Life of Maximos* (*PLP* 20687). Halkin suggests that he must also be distinguished from Niphon (*PLP* 20644), hieromonk from the Lavra and former *kanonarches* of Dionysiou, mentioned shortly below in chap. 15.1. Given, however, that Theophanes in his version of the present story, *Life of Maximos,* 35.3, also describes this Niphon as a hieromonk, it is at least possible they could be same man. Overall, Theophanes's account of this episode contains some new details but lacks others found here.

Gerasimos: It is conceivable that this Gerasimos (*PLP* 3764), who is not named in Theophanes's parallel account, could be the *abbas* Gerasimos of the Lavra, Niphon's source for the episodes

recorded in chaps. 19 and 20, although he is distinguished by the *PLP* (3695/91611) from that man. See further below, chap. 19.1.

Maximos had cleaned it out: Theophanes twice mentions that Maximos had dug his own grave: *Life of Maximos,* 16.3 and 34.1.

13.2   *Dionysios . . . Kontostephanos:* Dionysios (*PLP* 13119) is known only from the *Lives* of Maximos. Theophanes includes this episode before the preceding one, *Life of Maximos,* 35.1.

14.1   *Abbas Daniel:* Daniel (*PLP* 5099) is also known only from this vita. The term *abbas* (ἀββᾶς), derived from the Aramaic term for "father" and used on a number of occasions in the New Testament (e.g., Mark 14:36), can indicate both a respected monk or priest and, more specifically, a monastic superior, hence "abbot." Although the *PLP* here interprets it in the latter sense, there is no necessary reason for doing so. The *PLP* is not consistent in its interpretation of the term in this *Life* (Kallinikos, Gerasimos, and Ignatios of chaps. 16, 19, and 22 are interpreted as superiors, but Chariton of chap. 15.3 is described as a monk), and there is no independent witness to any of these men being a superior (see below, note on Gerasimos in 19.1). It seems more likely that Niphon uses the term as one of general respect for a monastic elder; it is thus left as *abbas* in the translation. See also chap. 15.1 of the *Life of Athanasios,* above.

Lights: Or "stars." Halkin suggests this passage may reflect Daniel 12:3, but the use of φωστῆρες in Philippians is perhaps more likely to be the source: ". . . that you may be blameless and innocent, children of God without blemish in the midst of a crooked and perverse generation, among whom you shine as lights in the world."

15.1   *Hieromonk Niphon:* On this Niphon (*PLP* 20644), see above, chap. 13.1 and note. A briefer version of this episode and the next are included by Theophanes in his *Life of Maximos,* 26.4–5.

Precentor: The *kanonarches,* or precentor, was the choir leader and an important official in the monastery administration.

Dorotheou: A monastery that no longer exists on Mount Athos.

Took a rusk: A rusk (παξαμᾶς, ἀπαξαμᾶς) is a hard and crisp twice-baked bread.

15.3 *Chariton:* Chariton (*PLP* 30655) is known only from the *Lives* of Maximos. In Theophanes's version of this episode, *Life of Maximos, 26.6*, the meal is made by Chariton.

Double insight: Niphon's account is rather elliptical here. Theophanes's version makes it clear that Chariton had grapes but had forgotten about them. Niphon's double insight thus refers to the fact that he knows about these, as well as predicting that someone is coming with more.

15.4 *Theodoulos:* Theodoulos (*PLP* 7278) is known only from this vita. Theophanes has a somewhat different introduction to his briefer account of this story, *Life of Maximos, 26.6.*

Berrhoia: As Halkin notes, "Deux vies," 54, n. 1, there was a monastery on Athos τοῦ Βερριώτου, which was attached to Vatopedi in 1312. It is unclear if this monk came from that monastery or actually from Berrhoia in Macedonia, since Maximos seems to have had other visitors from that city; see Theophanes, *Life of Maximos, 29.3–4.*

Prosphorin: A place near Hierissos on the isthmus between the peninsula and the mainland. It was a *metochion* dependent on the monastery of Vatopedi. See Halkin, "Deux vies," 54, n. 2.

16.1 *Kallinikos:* The *PLP* 10381 suggests Kallinikos was a monastic superior, but this is not necessarily so; see above, note on *abbas* in 14.1. It is thus conceivable he could be identified with the monk of the same name mentioned above in chap. 11.3.

Meletios: Meletios (*PLP* 17741) is known only from this episode.

17.1 *A ship once came into the harbor:* Theophanes has a slightly different version of this episode, *Life of Maximos, 20.3.*

18.1 *Superior . . . Athos:* See Theophanes, *Life of Maximos, 25.1,* and note on chap. 10.1, above.

Panagia: See above, note on chap. 2.2.

Enclosure: The Greek term παράδεισος means both "garden" and "paradise" but is also used of a monastery courtyard or enclosure. Given the barren location of the peak and the obviously miraculous appearance of the apples there, the term must be used in the latter sense, but the original reader would certainly

pick up the narrator's intended allusion to the apples of the tree of life in the Garden of Eden and the temptation of Eve by the serpent of Genesis (chaps. 2–3).

19.1 *Gerasimos:* Identified by the *PLP* (3695/91611) as the Gerasimos who was superior of the Lavra from 1305 to 1314 and from 1318 to 1322. Given, however, that the present Gerasimos is also said to have recounted the story concerning Maximos's message to John VI Kantakouzenos in the following chapter, the identification seems impossible: Kantakouzenos did not become emperor until 1347, abdicating in 1354, while the superior Gerasimos died before 1333. On Niphon's use of the term *abbas* as not necessarily implying a monastic superior, see above note on *abbas* at 14.1. It is thus conceivable that this Gerasimos could be the same man as the monk Gerasimos (*PLP* 3764), who was one of the monks who excavated Maximos's tomb (chap. 13).

Went . . . with some other monks: Theophanes includes a somewhat abbreviated version of this story in his *Life of Maximos,* 26.7. He does not mention the source.

Kanakes: Also mentioned in Theophanes, *Life of Maximos,* 26.8, Kanakes is tentatively identified by *PLP* 10874 as a monk from the Lavra, although this passage provides no evidence for such an assertion. Kanakes is a family name rather than a monastic name.

Loupadion: There is a relatively important town and fortress called Lopadion in northwestern Asia Minor, but this probably refers to a place in Thrace, known under the same name from a document of 1287; see Halkin, "Deux vies," 57, n. 2.

20.1 *Go to the emperor:* Theophanes attaches this episode to his account of the visit to Athos of the emperors John VI Kantakouzenos and John V Palaiologos, *Life of Maximos,* 21.3.

Empress: John VI Kantakouzenos's empress was Irene Asanina, a great-granddaughter of Michael VIII Palaiologos.

Sign of the monastic life: Kantakouzenos was forced by John V Palaiologos to resign as emperor, and he retired to a monastery under the name Ioasaph in 1354.

21.1 *Feast day of the Holy Apostles, on Friday:* The feast day of the Holy Apostles is celebrated on June 29. I am grateful to Alex-

ander Alexakis for confirmation of the translation of this date, which may provide some indication of dating for the composition of the *Life*. Subsequent to the earliest possible date for Maximos's death in 1367, June 29 fell on a Friday in the years 1369, 1375, 1380, 1386, 1397, 1403, and 1408. If we assume Niphon, who died in 1411, to be tired and sick because of advancing old age, then perhaps 1403 or 1408 would be most likely.

Fourth hour of the day: Late morning, according to the Byzantine system of measuring time.

22.1   *A . . . scholar once came . . . to the holy Lavra:* Theophanes has a significantly elaborated version of this episode, *Life of Maximos,* 27.1–3.

Martyrdom: That is, their *passiones*. This chapter provides a particularly clear example from Byzantium of skepticism concerning the saints and their miracles; on such attitudes, although the present passage is not considered, see Anthony Kaldellis, "The Hagiography of Doubt and Skepticism," in *The Ashgate Research Companion to Byzantine Hagiography,* ed. Stephanos Efthymiades (Farnham, 2014), 2:453–77.

Abbas Ignatios: PLP 8004 suggests Ignatios was a monastic superior, but this is not necessarily so; see above note on *abbas* in chap. 14.1.

23.1   *Arsenios:* Arsenios (*PLP* 1417) is possibly to be identified with the Arsenios (*PLP* 1413) of chap. 8.2–3 above and the *Life of Maximos* by Theophanes, 23.1. Theophanes includes a version of this episode at the start of chap. 20.3.

Iakobos: Iakobos (*PLP* 7916) is known only from the *Lives* of Maximos. Theophanes recounts the second episode of this chapter, which he says he witnessed himself, at chap. 29.2.

Came with his brother: Since Iakobos's brother is actually present, Niphon's account of this problematic episode is somewhat clearer than that of Theophanes, below chap. 29.2, although the latter claims to have been an eyewitness. It is, however, unclear why, if he was a captive, Iakobos's brother should have been at liberty to visit Maximos. There is evidently some confusion in the telling of this story in both accounts.

May use: The Greek verb διακονιστῶ is a hapax. See *LbG,* under διακονίζω.

24.1 *Joseph:* The monk Joseph of the Alypios monastery *(PLP* 9055) is also mentioned in some Athonite acts. He signed an act of Esphigmenou dated 1353–1356? (see Jacques Lefort, *Actes d'Esphigménou* [Paris, 1973], 150–52) and an act of Chilandar in 1366 *(Actes de Chilandar,* ed. Louis Petit [= *Vizantiiskii Vremennik,* suppl. to vol. 17, St. Petersburg, 1911; repr. Amsterdam, 1975], 322).

Monastery of Alypios: This monastery, which no longer exists, was located below the monastery of Koutloumousiou. It is attested several times in the fourteenth century. Theophanes's version of this episode is at *Life of Maximos,* 29.1.

Blessed are the blameless: The first verse of Psalm 118 (119), whose recitation was a standard part of the Byzantine monastic funeral rite.

Joseph the scholar: Joseph *(PLP* 8988) is known only from the *Lives* of Maximos.

25.1 *Matthew:* The *PLP* 17384 suggests that Matthew was a monk from the monastery of Saint Romanos in Constantinople, but no such monastery is attested in Janin, *EglisesCP,* only the church of that dedication, on which see the following note. The initial episode of this chapter is not included by Theophanes.

Hagioromanitai: This term is a hapax that seems to refer to people from the district of Saint Romanos. This district, near the important gate of Saint Romanos (Top Kapısı) in the center of the land walls of Constantinople, was named after a nearby church (Janin, *EglisesCP,* 448–49).

Modinos: Modinos *(PLP* 19218) is known only from the *Lives* of Maximos.

John: John *(PLP* 8419) is known only from the *Lives* of Maximos. This episode is included by Theophanes at the end of chap. 29.4 in his *Life of Maximos.*

26.1 *Menas:* Menas *(PLP* 18022) is known only from this vita.

Alypios: For the monastery of Alypios, see above, note on chap. 24.1.

Hieromonk Gregory: Gregory (*PLP* 4497) is known only from this vita.

Gregory Palamas: Gregory Palamas (ca. 1296–1357) was archbishop of Thessalonike and one of the foremost theologians of the late Byzantine period, renowned for his elaboration of the mystical doctrine of hesychasm. He was officially declared a saint of the Orthodox Church in 1368. A collection of his miracles was incorporated into his biography written by Philotheos Kokkinos, but the present chapter presents clear evidence that these were being circulated as a separate text. See Alice-Mary Talbot, introduction to *Miracle Tales from Byzantium,* trans. Alice-Mary Talbot and Scott F. Johnson (Cambridge, Mass., 2012), xviii–xix, and, for the miracles themselves, 300–405.

27.1 *Traianoupolis:* A town in Thrace about nine miles northeast of Alexandroupolis. A somewhat abbreviated version of this episode is included by Theophanes, *Life of Maximos,* 30.

28.1 *Vatopedi:* Vatopedi was one of the first monasteries to be founded on Mount Athos, being established in the late tenth century, not long after the Great Lavra of Athanasios. It is located on the northeastern coast of the peninsula and has always been one of the principal monasteries on the Holy Mountain. Theophanes, who was one of the two witnesses to this episode, gives a much fuller and more developed version in his *Life of Maximos,* chap. 28.

With their own eyes: The implication here seems to be that they told Niphon, thus explaining how he came to know of the episode. It does, however, contradict the charge laid on the monks by Maximos in Theophanes's own version, not to tell anyone while he was still alive.

29.1 *Makarios:* Makarios Chamnos (*PLP* 30559) is known only from this vita.

30.1 *Damianos:* Damianos (*PLP* 5078) is known only from this vita. Although the Damianos of chap. 11.1 above and Theophanes, *Life of Maximos,* 26.2, also has a low opinion of Maximos, the content of the stories in Niphon's *Life of Maximos* seems to indicate that they are different people.

Vineyard: The vineyard evidently belonged to the Lavra.

31.1   *Gregory from the Rock of Simon:* Gregory of Simonopetra (*PLP* 4575) is a monk known only from the *Lives* of Maximos. According to tradition, the Simonopetra monastery was founded in the thirteenth century by Simon the Athonite, also known as *myroblytes,* the one who exudes *myron* (perfumed oil), but it is not firmly attested until circa 1368, when the Serbian ruler Jovan Uglješa provided substantial funds for its construction. It is located on the southwestern coast of the peninsula.

    Matthew . . . hieromonk Matthew: Matthew (*PLP* 17379) and the hieromonk Matthew (*PLP* 17318) are known only from the *Lives* of Maximos. Theophanes includes the first part of this chapter in his *Life of Maximos,* 31.3.

LIFE OF MAXIMOS THE HUTBURNER BY THEOPHANES

Title   *Theophanes, metropolitan of Peritheorion and former superior of Vatopedi:* For the hagiographer Theophanes, see *PLP* 7616, and chap. 28.3 of this vita, where Maximos predicts that he will be metropolitan of Morachrida. Peritheorion was a town in the Rhodope mountains, where the Vatopedi monastery had a dependency *(metochion).* Vatopedi was one of the first monasteries to be founded on Mount Athos, being established in the late tenth century, not long after the Great Lavra of Athanasios. It is located on the northeastern coast of the peninsula and has always been one of the principal monasteries on the Holy Mountain. At the beginning of his career, in the early fourteenth century, the pioneering hesychast theologian Gregory Palamas made a brief stay at Vatopedi.

1.2   *Words from the Word of God:* Here and below Theophanes is playing on the multiple meanings of the word *logos* in Greek, ranging from "word," "discourse," "reason," or "account" to "the Word," that is, the second person of the Trinity.

    Like man: These words have been obelized in the Greek text, and the translation is uncertain.

1.4   *Mountain that is called Holy:* That is, Mount Athos.

1.5   *New things . . . Areopagus:* An allusion to Paul's visit to Athens, and the "new teaching" that he preached there.

       Triballoi: The Serbs.

2.1   *Lampsakos:* Lampsakos (modern Lapseki) was a port city on the eastern shore of the Hellespont. Theophanes agrees with Niphon's account (2.1) on this point, but subsequently includes much supplementary detail concerning Maximos's early life.

       Anna . . . Samuel: See 1 Kings 1:10–11, 20.

       Manuel: The baptismal name of Maximos.

2.2   *Pretended . . . deranged:* This is the first allusion in the vita to Maximos's behavior as a "holy fool" or "fool for Christ's sake."

3.1   *Ganos:* Mount Ganos was a holy mountain in Thrace, on the western coast of the Sea of Marmara, which housed a number of monastic communities.

       On account of . . . the road: See Theodore of Stoudios, *Magna catechesis* 71, ed. Giuseppe Cozza-Luzzi, *Nova Patrum bibliotheca* 9/2 (Rome, 1888), 200.44.

       Mark: PLP 17067, which dates this encounter to circa 1297.

       Young Maximos: The term νέος may have a double meaning here, "young" and "new," that is, referring to Maximos as a "new" or "second" Maximos the Confessor.

4.1   *Mount Papikion:* Another holy mountain in Thrace, near modern Komotini.

       Antony . . . Pachomios: References to Antony the Great and Arsenios the Great, the Egyptian desert fathers, and Euthymios the Great and Pachomios, the founders of cenobitic monasticism in Palestine and Egypt, respectively.

       In seclusion: The Greek adjective ἀπρόϊτος literally means "without going out" and is often used in hagiography to describe recluses or hermit saints who secluded themselves in caves or huts.

       Great city of Constantine: In Niphon's version (2.1), which contains none of the detail found here, Maximos's visit to Constantinople takes place after an initial stay on Athos.

4.2   *Miracle-working image:* We have here translated θαύματι (literally, "miracle") as "miracle-working image," following Lampe,

s.v. 8. Theophanes is most probably referring to the weekly procession of the icon of the Virgin Hodegetria, which performed healing miracles; see George Majeska, *Russian Travelers to Constantinople in the Fourteenth and Fifteenth Centuries* (Washington, D.C., 1984), 362–66. The monastery of the Hodegon was located next to the shore at the eastern edge of Constantinople. The Hodegetria icon depicts the Virgin holding the Christ child in her left arm.

Throne of divinity: See pseudo-Epiphanios of Salamis, *Hom. 5 in laudes sanctae Mariae Deiparae* (PG 43:501.12), where Mary is described as the "throne of divinity," and earlier in the same homily (PG 43:492.2) where she is said to illuminate the throne of divinity.

Andrew . . . fool for Christ: On Saint Andrew, a fictional holy fool who supposedly lived in the fifth century and who also experienced a vision of the Virgin in Constantinople, see Lennart Rydén, *The Life of St. Andrew the Fool,* 2 vols. (Uppsala, 1995), esp. 1:254–55.

Source of wonder: Both here and just above the Greek word for "wonder" is *thauma,* the same word used for "miracle" and "miracle-working image" in this paragraph.

5.1   *Andronikos Palaiologos:* Andronikos II Palaiologos (r. 1282–1328) took the monastic habit as the monk Antony after being driven from the throne in 1328.

Athanasios: Athanasios I was twice patriarch of Constantinople (1289–1293 and 1303–1309) and was declared a saint in the mid-fourteenth century.

Words of the Theologian: Although the term "the Theologian" often refers to Gregory of Nazianzos, here we think the author has in mind Saint John the Theologian and evangelist, author of the fourth gospel. Once again in this paragraph, Theophanes is making extensive play on the word *logos,* which is also included both in this epithet and in the title *logothetes* below.

Grammar: Literally, *grammatike,* the second stage of the Byzantine educational curriculum, focusing on the study of classical Greek poetry.

Great logothetes, keeper of the inkwell: The identity of this individual is unclear. Halkin ("Deux vies," 71, n. 4) assumes that the reference is to Theodore Metochites, *great logothetes* from 1321 to 1328. Metochites never held the position of keeper of the inkwell, however. Theophanes might also be referring to Constantine Akropolites, *great logothetes* from 1305/6 to 1321. This would fit better with the dates of the second patriarchate of Athanasios I (1303–1309).

The voice . . . hands of Esau: This same biblical quotation is found in the *Life of Athanasios,* 38.1, above.

5.2   *New Chrysostom:* John Chrysostom, bishop of Constantinople (398–404), who was famed for his rhetorical skills.

Cenobitic monasteries . . . in Constantinople: An allusion to Athanasios's double monastery in the Xerolophos region of Constantinople.

Church . . . of Blachernai: One of the principal shrines to the Virgin in Constantinople, located in the northwestern corner of the city. Note that above (4.2) Maximos is described as spending his nights at the church of the Hodegetria; this might refer to a different phase of his stay in Constantinople, or perhaps Theophanes has become confused in his recollection, which is here colored by the association of Blachernai with visions of the Virgin, as in the *Life of Andrew the Fool* (above note on 4.2), or that of Irene of Chrysobalanton, for which see Jan Olof Rosenqvist, *The Life of St Irene Abbess of Chrysobalanton* (Uppsala, 1986), 56–61.

6.1   *Exuder of perfumed oil:* The shrine of Saint Demetrios, the patron saint of Thessalonike, was famous for its perfumed oil, or *myron,* which performed healing miracles.

Lavra of . . . Athanasios: The monastery founded by Saint Athanasios of Athos in 963; see his vita above.

Peter the Athonite: One of the earliest documented monks to reside on Mount Athos. For bibliography of his vita, see Niphon's *Life of Maximos,* above, chap. 2.1 and note.

7.1   *This holy man . . . venerable Lavra:* The phase of Maximos's career described in chap. 7 is covered in one sentence in Niphon's version of the *Life of Maximos* (2.1) and is placed before his visit to

Constantinople. Niphon, however, includes the information that Maximos was timekeeper at the Lavra.

Spiritual odes: In Greek the word λογικός, here translated as "spiritual," carries also a sense of "verbal" and "rational," which ties it to "the Word of God" and revisits the plays on "word/ *logos*" above in chaps. 1.2 and 5.1.

7.2 *Prayer of the heart:* A form of deeply contemplative prayer also referred to as "mental prayer" that culminates in the "Jesus prayer" of hesychasm and later Orthodoxy. See also chaps. 8.2, 9.1, 13.1 (with note), 15.2, 19.1, and 33.2.

No one can say . . . Holy Spirit: This citation is not from Saint John, but from Paul, 1 Corinthians 12:3.

8.1 *Athanasios . . . name of immortality:* The Greek word for immortality is *athanasia.*

8.2 *Be still:* This is the same verb σχολάζω that we have translated just above as "devoting themselves to."

8.3 *As a wise man says:* We have not been able to identify the source of this quotation.

9.1 *Troubled:* For this meaning of the verb σπουδάζω, see LSJ, s.v., II.2b, and Job 22:10, 23:16.

Tablets of grace: Maximos is here and below compared to Moses receiving the tablets on Mount Sinai (Exodus 19:16).

9.2 *Sunday of the Holy Fathers:* The first Sunday after the Feast of the Ascension, thus the seventh Sunday after Easter, and the feast day of the 318 fathers of the Council of Nicaea (325 CE). The Ascension was a movable feast, celebrated on the Thursday that comes forty days after Easter.

9.4 *Hail . . . the Lord is with you:* A hymn based on Luke 1:28; see Follieri, *Initia,* 5.1:57.

Truly it is worthy: First words of the hymn "Ἄξιόν ἐστιν," a hymn to the Virgin sung during the liturgy and at other services as well.

9.5 *As I said:* This seems to refer to the summons by the Mother of God in chap. 9.1 above.

The new Israel: A frequent phrase in medieval Greek texts to denote the Byzantines as a second "chosen people."

9.6 *Panagia:* A small chapel situated below the peak of Mount Athos. See further, Niphon's *Life of Maximos,* chap. 2.2.

Karmelion: A hill at the tip of the Athonite peninsula.

10.1 *Dubbed... the "vagrant":* The Greek means literally "gave him the name of wandering." As noted in chap. 2.2 of Niphon's version of the *Life of Maximos,* the Greek word πλάνη and its cognates have multiple connotations; in this chapter the root word lies behind the repeated theme of vagrancy, derangement, and error.

10.2 *Kept moving . . . like a vagrant:* This chapter represents a development of material contained in chap. 2.2 of Niphon's version.

Deranged: As above in 10.1, the hagiographer is playing on the multiple meanings of the Greek root πλαν-: ἀπλανής means literally "not wandering," "not in error," while πλανημένος here can mean "wandering," "in error," and hence "deranged."

Hutburner: The Greek term used here, Kapsokalyves, is a variant on the more common form of his sobriquet, Kausokalyves.

11.2 *Bird of the air:* See Matthew 6:26; Mark 4:32; Luke 8:5, etc.

Heavenly behavior: This seems to refer back to the description of Maximos earlier in this paragraph as a "bird of the air"; the same term οὐράνιος, "pertaining to the sky/heavens/air," is used both times.

11.3 *Rapture of mind:* See *Syméon le Nouveau Théologien. Traités théologiques et éthiques,* ed. Jean Darrovzès (Paris, 1966), 1:296.

Paul of old: Given the association with Antony and the desert, this must refer to Paul of Thebes, the first hermit in the Egyptian desert. Note, however, that the apostle Paul was also "caught up" in rapture: 2 Corinthians 12:2. Theophanes seems to slip from one parallel to another.

12.1 *Gerontios:* PLP 3883. According to the Ἀκολουθία τῶν ἐν τῇ σκήτῃ Ἀγίας Ἄννης ὁσίων (Athens, 1929), 46–47, Gerontios, the superior of Bouleuteria, was honored as a saint; see Halkin, "Deux vies," 81, n. 3.

Bouleuteria: The monastery of Bouleuteria, no longer extant, was located near the west coast of Athos, at the foot of the hermitage of Saint Anna. See Halkin, "Deux vies," 81, n. 3.

Kornelios: Kornelios (*PLP* 13223) was a monk of the Saint Mamas monastery on Mount Athos, no longer extant. It was probably

near the hermitage of Kausokalyvia; see Halkin, "Deux vies," 81, n. 4.

Auxentios . . . Isaiah . . . Makarios: Auxentios (*PLP* 1683) and Isaiah (*PLP* 6735) are known only from this vita; Makarios (*PLP* 16214) was perhaps a hieromonk.

Saint Christopher: An island opposite the hermitage of Kausokalyvia.

Gregory of Strabe Langada: PLP 4565. Strabe Langada means "crooked ravine."

Dorotheos: An Athonite monastery that is no longer extant.

Leukai: A site near Krya Nera of the Lavra; see Halkin, "Deux vies," 82, n. 1. The vita of Maximos by Kochylas (ed. Patapios Kausokalyvites, "Ἱερομονάχου Ἰωαννικίου Κόχιλα, Βίος ὁσίου Μαξίμου τοῦ Καυσοκαλύβη [14ᵒˢ αἰ.]," *Γρηγόριος ὁ Παλαμᾶς* 819 [2007], 513–77, at 539.46) reads "Dorotheos at Leukai."

Melanea: More usually Melana, a promontory at the extreme tip of the Athonite peninsula, where Athanasios the Athonite lived in solitude for a year before founding his *lavra;* see chaps. 21–22 of his vita, above.

Gerontios of Saint Mamas: PLP 3886.

Theodoulos: PLP 7284.

Iakobos . . . Maroules: PLP 17151; a physician who became a monk at the Lavra on Mount Athos between circa 1320 and 1341. He was the nephew of Germanos Maroules and provided Philotheos Kokkinos, the hagiographer and patriarch of Constantinople, with information for his vita of Germanos.

Iakobos from Trebizond: PLP 7909.

Clement and Galaktion: PLP 11827 and 3483.

Mark the Simple: PLP 17086, a Palamite disciple of Gregory Sinaites, and monk on Mount Athos.

13.1   *Gregory the Sinaite:* Gregory of Sinai (*PLP* 4601) was a famed hesychast monk and writer; the dates of his birth (ca. 1255 or 1265?) and death (after 1337) are uncertain, as is the chronology of other events in his life. After spending his early monastic

career on Cyprus, Mount Sinai, Jerusalem, and Crete, he lived on Mount Athos but left circa 1330 for Paroria, where he founded a monastery on Mount Katakekryomene. Maximos's encounter with Gregory is omitted from Niphon's version of the *Life*.

Prayer in the heart: Gregory of Sinai reportedly introduced to Athos the technique of mental prayer known as the "Jesus prayer" or "prayer of the heart." See also above, note on chap. 7.2.

13.2 *Feeding of the multitudes:* See Mark 6:44.

14.2 *Mark the Simple:* See note above on chap. 12.1.

    Saint Mamas monastery: See note above on chap. 12.1.

14.3 *Paroria:* A region of the Strandzha mountains in southern Bulgaria, about nineteen miles south southwest of Sozopolis.

15.1 *Let it be . . . for the present:* These were the words spoken by Jesus to John the Baptist when he was hesitant to baptize him. The phrase could also be translated "Leave that now," in the sense of "stop/leave off playing the fool"—that is, as it is used in chap. 16.2 below at the end of their conversation.

15.2 *Mental prayer:* See notes above on chaps. 7.2 and 13.1.

15.3 *Rapture of the mind:* See note above on chap. 11.3.

    My error: Once again there is wordplay with πλάνη, meaning "error, delusion, derangement."

15.4 *The mind is consumed:* See *Makarios/Symeon Reden und Briefe,* ed. Heinz Berthold, vol. 2 (Berlin, 1973), *Hom.* 49, chap. 2.4.7.

    The Comforter: This is the Paraclete, or Holy Spirit.

    Delusion and intoxication: See Acts 2:13.

15.6 *Delusion:* Yet another instance of the use of πλάνη with multiple meanings.

15.7 *It makes the heart calm:* See John of Damascus, *Carm.* 12 (PG 96:833A).

16.1 *To his <spiritual> kin:* This is our suggested translation of the Greek term τῷ γένει, whose meaning is unclear.

    Stay in one place: This phrase is found in the title of Isaac the Syrian's *Logos asketikos* 26, in Τοῦ ὁσίου πατρὸς ἡμῶν Ἰσαὰκ τοῦ

Σύρου τὰ εὑρεθέντα ἀσκητικά, ed. Ioakeim Spetsieres (Athens, 1895; repr. Thessalonike, 1997), 109.

Death is untimely: This phrase, used by classical authors, was also adopted by Christian writers, such as John Chrysostom in, for example, *Adversus oppugnatores vitae monasticae (lib. 1–3),* PG 47:372.3; *Syméon le Nouveau Théologien, Catéchèses,* ed. and trans. Basile Krivochéine and Joseph Paramelle, vol. 2 (Paris, 1964), *Cat.* 19.135, p. 324.

Share the talent: This is a reference to the parable of the talents in Matthew 25:14–30.

16.3   *Kyr Isaiah:* The monastic settlement of Kyr Isaiah is about one hour walking distance south of the Lavra; it has cells and a chapel of the Holy Trinity.

Six feet: The Greek measurement was one *orgyia,* the length of the outstretched arms, or a fathom.

Dug his own grave: See below, chap. 34.1, and Niphon's version of the *Life of Maximos,* 13.1.

"*Like God . . . with stars*": The quotation is the *incipit* of a model stanza *(heirmos)* of a hymn for Saturday; see Follieri, *Initia* 3:126–27. Theophanes has slightly changed the wording of the verse, which should be ὁ οὐρανὸν τοῖς ἄστροις κατακοσμήσας.

17.1   *Kometissa:* As Halkin notes ("Deux vies," 89, n. 4), the present-day Koumitsa, a *metochion* of the monastery of Chilandar, is at the entrance to the Holy Mountain.

Related to me: This is the first time the author Theophanes refers to himself.

Great Watchtower: As Halkin notes ("Deux vies," 90, n. 1), the Megale Vigla is the chain of hills that marks the boundary of Mount Athos.

Palaces, bearing . . . the Mother of God: The image seems to be of the Virgin standing on the palace roof.

18.1   *Andronikos and Alexander, Stefan:* Andronikos III, emperor of Byzantium (r. 1328–1341); Ivan Alexander, tsar of Bulgaria (r. 1331–1365); Stefan IV Dušan, tsar of Serbia (r. 1321–1355).

*Alexande*r: Halkin ("Deux vies," 90, n. 3) proposes that this sec-

ond Alexander might be Alexander I, hospodar of Wallachia (r. 1338–1364), brother-in-law of Alexander of Bulgaria. Kourilas suggested that one of the two references to Alexander should be deleted.

20.1   *Merkourios:* An Athonite monk (*PLP* 17918). The vita by Niphon (5.1) clarifies that Merkourios was commanded by Maximos to heal the possessed man.

      Servant . . . suffering . . . from a demon: Niphon has a slightly fuller version of this episode, *Life of Maximos,* 5.2.

20.2   *A layman accompanied them:* Theophanes follows Niphon's version of this episode (*Life of Maximos,* 6.1) quite closely at the start but then adds commentary. In the second half of the paragraph, where Niphon continues with a second Akindynatos story, Theophanes substitutes a truncated rendering of Niphon's account of the Messalian (10.4).

      Akindynatos: A follower of Gregory Akindynos, on whom see further Niphon's *Life of Maximos,* 6.1 and note.

      Kakokindynos: The Greek epithet, meaning "evil danger," is a pun on the name Akindynos, "without danger."

      Messalian: Messalians were members of an ascetic sect that originated in Mesopotamia in the fourth century, although here the term refers to Bogomils. See further, Niphon's *Life of Maximos,* 10.4 note.

20.3   *Mocked another monk:* In Niphon's version of this story, *Life of Maximos,* 23.1, the monk is named as Arsenios from the Lavra. The story of the man with the insatiable demon that follows here is told in greater detail by Niphon in chap. 17.1.

20.4   *Monk named Barlaam: PLP* 2278. He is known only from this episode in the *Lives.* Niphon's version, which includes a few more details, is at chap. 12.1.

      Athanasios Krokas: PLP 13813. He is known only from this passage in the *Lives.* Niphon's version (12.1) is almost identical but is followed by Maximos's prediction of his own death to Nikodemos, which Theophanes includes in chap. 33.3 below.

21.1   *Kantakouzenos and John:* John VI Kantakouzenos (r. 1347–1354) and John V Palaiologos (r. 1341–1391). Apart from the *Lives,*

there is no other allusion to this imperial visit to Athos. If it really took place, it must have occurred between 1347 and 1352. Theophanes here provides an elaborated version of Niphon's brief account, which comes toward the start of his *Life of Maximos,* 4.1.

As the Lord says: See Luke 21:25–28.

21.3　　*He sent a rusk . . . to Kantakouzenos:* This episode is recounted separately by Niphon, *Life of Maximos,* 20.1.

22.1　　*Kallistos I:* Patriarch of Constantinople from 1350 to 1353 and from 1355 to 1363. See further, the *Life of Maximos* by Niphon, 7.1 and note. Theophanes's version of the episode is much fuller than Niphon's.

This old man . . . to the house: We are unable to identify the source of this cryptic quotation, which we assume to be from a contemporary vernacular source. We can suggest only that the "old man" is Kallistos and the "old lady" is the Church.

Chanted the verse: This is the first verse of Psalm 118 (119), chanted as part of a monk's funeral service; hence Maximos was alluding to the patriarch's impending death.

23.1　　*Methodios:* A monk known only from the *Lives* of Maximos; *PLP* 17607.

Divine light flashing: The episodes recounted by Theophanes from 23.1 to 26.1 follow exactly the order of Niphon's version of the *Life of Maximos,* 8.1 to 10.2.

Arsenios: PLP 1413, perhaps identical with *PLP* 1417, a monk from the Lavra, mentioned in Niphon's *Life of Maximos,* 23.1.

24.1　　*Gregory: PLP* 4582, known only from the *Lives* of Maximos.

25.1　　*The superior of . . . the Prodromos:* Probably Dionysios, the founder of the monastery of Saint John the Baptist (Prodromos), which is more commonly called Dionysiou. The monastery lies at the foot of Little Athos, a peak to the northwest of the summit of Athos. See further Niphon's *Life of Maximos,* 10.1 and note.

Papas: A Greek word for priest.

26.1　　*Karyes:* A village on Mount Athos that housed the central administration of the monastic community of the Holy Mountain.

Stick around <here>: We have supplied this clarification following the parallel passage in the vita of Maximos by Kochylas
(Patapios Kausokalyvites, "Ἱερομονάχου Ἰωαννικίου Κόχιλα,"
chap. 49, p. 556).

A flux: The Greek word ρεῦμα means the discharge of a humor
from the body, but in this case it may well refer to rheumatism,
since Niphon simply describes his ailment as "a pain in the
hand" (*Life of Maximos,* 10.2).

You also have money ... do not bury it: A reference to the parable of
the talents; see Matthew 25:18, 24–30.

26.2   *Monk named Mark:* PLP 17065; known only from the *Lives* of
Maximos. In Niphon's slightly longer account, *Life of Maximos,*
10.4, this Mark is also associated with the Messalian episode
recounted by Theophanes above at 20.2.

Twelve hyperpyra: On the Byzantine gold coins called *hyperpyra,*
see the note to chap. 10.2 of Niphon's *Life of Maximos.*

Sixty ducats: According to Cécile Morrisson (personal communication of September 2011), sixty Venetian ducats were indeed
equivalent to twelve *hyperpyra.*

Damianos: PLP 5076; known only from the *Lives* of Maximos.
Niphon recounts this episode in his version of the *Life of Maximos,* 11.1.

26.3   *Kassianos:* PLP 11348, where the name is spelled with only one
sigma; known only from the *Lives* of Maximos. Theophanes
here omits two other tales concerning Maximos's clairvoyance
with regard to food that appear at this point in Niphon's account (*Life of Maximos,* 11.2–3); the story of Kassianos appears
there at 11.3.

26.4   *Two monks came to the holy one:* This and the following three episodes (26.4–7) follow the same order as Niphon's version of the
Life of Maximos, 15.1–4.

Dorotheou: A monastery that no longer exists on Mount Athos.

26.6   *Abbas Chariton:* PLP 30655; a monk known only from the *Lives*
of Maximos. On the term *abbas,* which is used on a number of
occasions in Niphon's version, apparently as a mark of respect,
see his chap. 14.1 and note. It does not necessarily imply the

role of monastic superior; see *PGL,* under ἀββᾶς. Theophanes employs the term only here and in chap. 26.2.

Made a small meal: In Niphon's version of the *Life of Maximos* (15.3), the food has been made by another monk called Niphon, who is the source for the story.

26.7 *Large group of monks:* In Niphon's version, *Life of Maximos,* 15.4, only two monks are present.

Prosphorin: A place near Hierissos on the isthmus between the peninsula and the mainland. See further, Niphon's version, 15.4 and note.

26.8 *Kanakes: PLP* 10874; known only from the *Lives* of Maximos, it is unclear whether he was a monk or a layman. Niphon's version of this story is at chap. 19.1.

Loupadin: This probably refers to a place in Thrace. See further, Niphon's version of the *Life of Maximos,* 19.1 and note; there, however, it is spelled Loupadion.

27.1 *A smart and erudite scholar . . . came to the holy one:* In his account of this episode, Theophanes supplies Maximos's lengthy speech, which is only referred to indirectly in Niphon's version, *Life of Maximos,* 22.1. On the evidence it provides for Byzantine skepticism regarding the saints, see the note there.

28.1 *What I myself saw:* Theophanes, as an eyewitness, provides a much fuller version of this strange episode than does Niphon, *Life of Maximos,* 28.1

Kyr Isaiah: See above, chap. 16.3 and note.

28.2 *Thou art great, O Lord:* This is the beginning of a prayer in the office for Epiphany, toward the end of the section blessing the water; see Μηναῖον τοῦ Ἰανουαρίου (Athens, 1896), 82.

28.3 *Superior . . . metropolitan of Morachrida:* As we know from the title of the vita, Theophanes became superior of Vatopedi. Morachrida was an unknown bishopric; see Halkin, "Deux vies," 100, n. 1, for further discussion.

You're going to suffer . . . crown in his glory: This passage seems to be inspired by 1 Peter 4:12–5:4.

29.1 *Monastery of Alypios:* On this monastery, which no longer exists, see further Niphon's version of the *Life of Maximos,* 24.1 and note.

Blessed are the blameless: The first verse of Psalm 118 (119), whose recitation was a standard part of the Byzantine monastic funeral rite; see note above on chap. 22.1.

Kyr Joseph: PLP 8988; known only from the *Lives* of Maximos. Further on him, see Niphon's version of the *Life,* 24.1 and note.

29.2   *Lavriot monk, called Iakobos:* PLP 7916, known only from the *Lives* of Maximos. Niphon's version of this episode, 23.1, does not mention the presence of Theophanes.

His brother's captivity: Although Theophanes claims to be an eyewitness here, this passage is clearer in Niphon's version, chap. 23.2 above, which states that Iakobos approached Maximos together with his brother; this explains the reference to a second captivity and the plural verbs of the last sentence, but not what the brother was doing on Athos if he were indeed a captive. There is evidently some confusion in the telling of this story in both accounts.

29.3   *Kyr Dionysios:* PLP 5481; an anti-Palamite, Dionysios of Berrhoia (in Macedonia) is mentioned in acts of 1330 and 1351. He died before 1364.

He received the pardon from him: This episode is not in Niphon's version of the *Life of Maximos.*

29.4   *Priest John:* PLP 8681; a priest of Berrhoia, mentioned only in this vita.

Striking . . . with your hands: The Greek word for "striking with the hands" is παλαμαία, a hapax unattested in the *TLG* but included in *LbG.*

Received pardon: This episode is also absent from Niphon's version of the *Life of Maximos.* That which immediately follows, however, appears there in the second half of chap. 25.1.

John . . . monk . . . priest . . . superior: PLP 8419, known only from the *Lives* of Maximos.

30.1   *Traianoupolis:* A town in Thrace about nine miles northeast of Alexandroupolis; it was the seat of an archbishop.

Gave his archiepiscopal mantle to his disciple: Niphon provides a slightly more detailed version of this story, *Life of Maximos,* 27.1.

31.1   *The holy one said this to . . . Niphon:* The first and only acknowledgment by Theophanes of his main source, Niphon (*PLP* 20687),

the Athonite monk and author of the previous *Life of Maximos* in this volume. He is himself the subject of the *Life* that follows. For Niphon's account of the material in chap. 31.1–2, see his version of the *Life of Maximos,* 3.2–3.

31.2   *Spiritual instruments:* A reference either to bells or to the *semandron,* the wooden board that was struck to summon monks to church services.

31.3   *Gregory from the Rock of Simon:* Gregory of Simonopetra (*PLP* 4575) is a monk known only from the *Lives* of Maximos. According to tradition, the Simonopetra Monastery was founded in the thirteenth century by Simon the Athonite, also known as *myroblytes,* "the one who exudes perfumed oil." See further Niphon's version of the *Life of Maximos,* 31.1 and note.

Monk Matthew and another hieromonk Matthew: PLP 17379 and 17318; these two monks named Matthew are known only from the *Lives* of Maximos.

There are also . . . others as well: The first part of this paragraph, including the statement "things which I myself have heard about," is taken almost word for word by Theophanes from Niphon's final chap. 31.1.

32.1   *His teaching:* Theophanes's account of Maximos's teaching in chaps. 32–33 is absent from Niphon's version of the *Life of Maximos.*

32.5   *Eternal punishments . . . in accordance with his sin:* We cannot find this phrase in the *TLG,* but Maximos may have in mind the κόλασις αἰώνιος of Matthew 25:46.

Inconsolable weeping: See Matthew 8:12: "The sons of the kingdom will be thrown into the outer darkness; there men will weep and gnash their teeth."

33.2   *Monk Nikodemos:* PLP 20363; known only from the *Lives* of Maximos. Niphon includes this prediction at the end of chap. 12.1 of his version of the *Life of Maximos* but has nothing parallel to the account of Maximos's death provided by Theophanes in the following chapter.

34.1   *Died . . . at the age of ninety-five:* The year of his death is uncertain, between 1367 and 1380. The *PLP* suggests 1375.

34.2   *Passing of the holy Athanasios:* For the death of Athanasios, the

tenth-century founder of the Great Lavra, see above, Introduction, xii, and vita B of Athanasios of Athos, chap. 66.

34.4   *Company:* The Greek word ὁμιλία also conveys a further sense of conversation and instruction.

34.5   *Godhead of three suns:* See Niketas Patrikios, *Vita of St. Andrew of Crete,* ed. Athanasios Papadopoulos-Kerameus, in Ἀνάλεκτα ἱεροσολυμιτικῆς σταχυολογίας (Jerusalem, 1888; repr. Brussels, 1963), 5:170.7.

35.1   *Dionysios Kontostephanos: PLP* 13119; known only from the *Lives* of Maximos. Niphon includes this story in his version of the *Life of Maximos,* 13.2.

35.2   *The holy man flying above the earth:* See chap. 28.2 above.

35.3   *Another hieromonk, Niphon by name:* On this Niphon (*PLP* 20642), see further the hagiographer Niphon's version of this episode, *Life of Maximos,* 13.1 and note.

        Another ascetic: According to Niphon's version he was called Gerasimos (*PLP* 3764); see chap. 13.1 and note.

LIFE OF NIPHON

1.1   *Despotate:* The despotate of Epiros. During the period between 1315 and the late 1330s, when Niphon lived there, the region was subject to extensive political instability with control disputed between various Greco-Latin and Italian powers, Serbia, and Constantinople.

        Loukove: Modern Lukovë, situated on the Albanian coast some twelve miles north of the island of Corfu.

        His son: Celibacy was not required of the lower clergy in the Byzantine church, and most regular priests appear to have been married.

        Monomachos: The emperor Constantine IX Monomachos (r. 1042–1055).

        Mesopotamon: An important monastery situated to the south of modern Delvinë, which lies some ten miles inland, east-southeast of Lukovë.

        Lector: The lector *(anagnostes)* was at this time a minor cleric who read the Epistles during the liturgy.

A short time after . . . ordained him as a priest: The minimum age for ordination as a reader was eighteen, for a priest, thirty. It seems likely, however, that Niphon was only about twenty when he was ordained priest. See Halkin, "Niphon," 8.

1.2   *Geromerion:* Geromerion lies about twenty-three miles southeast of Delvinë. The monastery there had been founded not long before, around 1330, by Neilos Erichiotes; see Donald Nicol, *The Despotate of Epiros, 1267–1479* (Oxford, 1957), 243. It still stands today, some three miles north of Philiates in Epiros, just inside the Greek border with Albania.

2.1   *The Lavra:* The Great Lavra, founded by Athanasios of Athos in 962/3 near the southeastern tip of the peninsula. On this, see above in the Introduction and the *Life of Athanasios.*

Peter the Athonite: The hermit Peter, who died circa 885, was an important early figure in the development of Athos. For bibliography on his vita, see note on chap. 2.1 of Niphon's *Life of Maximos,* above.

Theognostos: The monk Theognostos (*PLP* 7075) is known only from the *Life of Niphon.* His name literally means "known to God."

Driving the golden chariot: See *Jean Chrysostome. Sur le sacerdoce,* ed. Anne-Marie Malingrey (Paris, 1980), Hom. 1.213, p. 408; vita A of Athanasios of Athos in Noret, *Vitae duae,* chap. 40.13.

Hermitage of . . . Basil the Great: The hermitage of Saint Basil is situated on the northern coast of Athos near the Serbian monastery of Chilandar, some distance from the region of the Lavra.

3.1   *Pestilential epidemic:* The Black Death struck the Balkans in 1348–49. If the chronology of the vita is correct, this must refer to a subsequent outbreak in the mid-1350s or to some other epidemic.

Sharp sword of death: See Revelations 6:8.

Rusticity: The same term (ἀγροικία) is used of Athanasios of Athos's supposed lack of literary ability in the *Life of Athanasios,* above, chap. 17.2.

Bouleuteria: A community located high on the southwestern tip of Athos and controlled by the Lavra after 1030.

4.1   *Free of snares:* Or "unerring."

        Church of the Savior: Perhaps the church of the Transfiguration, which lies half a mile below the hermitage of Kavsokalyvia at the southern tip of Athos.

        He asked . . . what he did: The meaning of this passage remains rather unclear.

        Bishop of Hierissos: Athos fell under the jurisdiction of the bishop of Hierissos.

4.2   *Maximos the Hutburner:* On Maximos, see the *Lives* by Niphon and Theophanes, above in this volume.

        Drove the golden chariot: For this citation from John Chrysostom, see note to chap. 2.1 above.

        When the blessed Maximos left his cell: Compare Niphon's *Life of Maximos,* chap. 3.3, where he states that he inherited Maximos's final hut only on the holy man's death; there thus appears to be a discrepancy with the present account here and in chaps. 5.1 and 8.1.

5.1   *Islet named after Saint Christopher:* Close to the southeastern coast of the peninsula some four and a half miles southeast of the Lavra.

        Mark: The monk Mark (*PLP* 17066) is known only from the *Life of Niphon.*

        To edify Mark: There is a wordplay in the Greek here that is hard to capture in English; the verb οἰκοδομέω, used both here and in the previous sentence, can mean not only to "build" or "construct" but also to "edify." Taken a different way, the sentence could thus also mean "he wanted him [Mark] to build it [the cell]." Our thanks to Alexander Alexakis for help with this passage.

5.2   *Feast of our holy father Athanasios:* The feast day of Athanasios of Athos is July 5.

        Holy Anargyroi: This is a reference to the physician saints, Kosmas and Damian, venerated and sought out for their free *(anargyros)* medical assistance.

6.1   *Flung the fish . . . away:* Compare the action of Athanasios in the *Life of Athanasios,* above, chap. 46.2.

        Receiving . . . hopes: See 2 Corinthians 1:22, 5:5; Ephesians 1:14.

7.1   *Gabriel . . . Dositheos:* The monks Gabriel (*PLP* 3420) and Dositheos (*PLP* 5646) are known only from the *Life of Niphon.* It is not entirely clear from the Greek, either here or below in chaps. 9.1 and 19.1, whether Dositheos was Mark's (and thus Gabriel's) birth father or his spiritual father; the *PLP* assumes the former.

       Vatopedi: A major monastery located on the northeastern coast of the peninsula; see further the note to chap. 28.1 in Niphon's *Life of Maximos,* above.

       Achaimenids were plundering: Achaimenid, like Ishmaelite, was a common term for the Ottoman Turks. Chap. 18, below, reports an Ottoman attack on Athos, in 1372 or 1373. See further on this and other Turkish attacks on Mount Athos in the fourteenth century, in Angeliki Laiou-Thomadakis, "Saints and Society in the Late Byzantine Empire," in *Charanis Studies: Essays in Honor of Peter Charanis,* ed. Angeliki Laiou-Thomadakis (New Brunswick, N.J., 1980), 92–95.

10.1   *Fast of the Holy Apostles:* The fast of the Holy Apostles lasted from the second Monday after Pentecost until the feast of Saints Peter and Paul (June 29).

       Fast of the Savior's passion: That is, Great Lent.

10.2   *Died on the 14th of June:* In 1411, see Introduction. According to Grumel's perpetual calendar, *Chronologie byzantine,* 316, this was a Wednesday.

11.1   *Theodoulos:* Theodoulos (*PLP* 7292) is known only from this vita.

14.1   *An individualistic way of life:* The term ἰδιορρυθμία refers to a style of monasticism in which individuals living alone or in a loose community set their own pattern of life rather than following those of the standard eremitic or communal cenobitic regime. *Idiorrhythmia* was generally regarded with much suspicion, as here, but by this time had apparently become quite well established on Athos. See the criticism of Niphon himself, above, chap. 4.1.

       Angel of darkness . . . light: See 2 Corinthians 11:14.

       Wandered: The Greek verb πλανάω contains the sense of "erring" as well as "wandering." See also above, the notes to chaps.

1.2 and 2.2 in Niphon's *Life of Maximos,* and to chap. 10.2 in Theophanes's *Life of Maximos.*

Was lost: See Luke 15:4–6; Matthew 18:12–13.

Wolf . . . pieces: See John 10:12.

Dark delusions: The Greek adjective σκοτεινός contains the sense of "being blind" as well as "evil," in addition to that of "darkness."

15.1   *Timekeeper:* The monastic timekeeper *(horologos)* was an official responsible for summoning the brothers to church; see *BMFD* 2:749. In chap. 2.1 of his *Life of Maximos,* Niphon mentions that Maximos fulfilled this role at the Lavra for a while.

16.1   *Beardless youth:* Normally beardless youths were prohibited on the Holy Mountain.

Let the youth come to me: See Matthew 19:14.

18.1   *Uglješa:* Jovan Uglješa was lord of Serres and western Thrace in the 1350s and 1360s after the death of the great Serbian ruler Stefan Dušan in 1355. Jovan's brother, Vukašin Mrnjavčević, was coruler with Stefan's son Stefan Uroš V and controlled the area of Prilep and Ochrida. Both brothers were killed while fighting against the Ottoman Turks in the important battle of Černomen, on the Marica River near Edirne, in September 1371.

Ishmaelites: The author uses the traditional archaic descriptor "Ishmaelites" for the Turks in this chapter.

The megas primikerios: The reference is undoubtedly to John the *primikerios,* who, with his brother Alexios (the *stratopedarches*), founded the Pantokrator monastery on Athos circa 1357. The rank of *primikerios,* which had once belonged to the master of ceremonies at court, was by this time a more general, but highly honorific, title. The brothers had established themselves as military strongmen in eastern Macedonia in the chaotic political situation in the region in the mid-fourteenth century. The location of the Pantokrator, on a low headland by the sea, midway down the eastern coast of the peninsula, made it particularly vulnerable to attacks of the type mentioned in this episode and helps to explain its founder's role here.

19.1   *Dositheos . . . mentioned:* See chaps. 7.1 and 9.1 above.

Monastery of Iviron: Iviron, a tenth-century foundation, lies on the east coast of the peninsula some two miles southeast of Karyes. It was about nine miles north of Niphon's cave, but considerably further on foot, since the peak of Athos lay in the way.

The Amalfitans: The monastery of the Amalfitans was a Latin monastery founded in the late tenth century; although it had once been one of the leading monasteries on Athos, it became a dependency of the Lavra in the late thirteenth century. It was situated about three miles north of the Lavra and four miles south of Iviron.

20.1 *Hermitage:* Halkin speculates that the reference to an otherwise unidentified hermitage (*skete*) here may be an error for the island of Skyros, an alternative manuscript reading. The Lavra owned a *metochion* there.

Gave glory . . . servants: See 1 Kings 2:30.

LIFE OF PHILOTHEOS

1.1–2.2 *Many people . . . sprang up:* The passage in italics extending from the beginning of 1.1 to the beginning of 2.2 is taken word for word from the prologue of the *Life of St. Paul of Latros* with the substitution of Philotheos's name and the wordplay "friend of God" in place of Paul's name. The identical wording of the texts suggests that the tenth-century vita of Paul of Latros was the model for the introduction to the vita of Philotheos of Athos, if one assumes that there was no intervening text in the line of transmission. For the *Life* of Paul of Latros, see *Vita S. Pauli Junioris,* ed. Hippolyte Delehaye in *Der Latmos,* ed. Theodor Wiegand (Berlin, 1913), 105–35, at 105.

2.1 *Feast we celebrate:* The feast day of Philotheos of Athos is October 21.

2.2 *Chrysopolis:* Macedonian Chrysopolis was located at the mouth of the Strymon River; see *ODB* 1:454.

Elateia: The location of Elateia has not been identified. The text specifies that it was a city in the province of Asia. Basilike Pa-

poulia, "Philotheos," 260–61, considers this an anachronistic reference to the Roman province of Asia, but it is possible that the author was referring to the ecclesiastical province of Asia that encompassed a stretch of the Aegean coastline from Assos to Priene.

Agarenes: Agarenes (on whom, see note to chap. 22.3 of the *Life of Athanasios* above) was a Byzantine term for Turks as well as Arabs.

Strangers: The term πάροικοι *(paroikoi)* in this context is synonymous with the biblical "stranger," "recent settler."

2.3   *A command . . . by the ruler:* Although the Greek is very differently phrased, this clause is reminiscent of Luke 2:1. The author uses the very generic term κρατοῦντος for "ruler," probably the Ottoman governor.

Levy of male children: This rare early description of the *devşirme,* or "child-levy," dating to the very end of the fourteenth century, indicates that the practice of recruiting children was already customary among the Turks at this time; see V. L. Ménage, "Some Notes on the Devshirme," *Bulletin of the School of Oriental and African Studies* 29 (1966): 64–78. The hagiographer's account seems to exaggerate the number of children recruited from a single household.

The Agarenes took both brothers: The recruitment of all the male children in Philotheos's family contradicts normal practice and may be explained by the family's refugee status and consequent social vulnerability.

2.6   *Neapolis:* Most likely the modern city of Kavala. The exact location of the monastery and convent is uncertain. Papoulia, "Philotheos," has a discussion of the double monastery at p. 262 and of Neapolis at pp. 261–2.

"To see you": The author appears to be referencing Romans 1:11 by inserting the direct quotation "ἰδεῖν ὑμᾶς," a passage discussed extensively in the writings of the Church Fathers.

Church custodians: The Greek term *neokoros* designates a member of a minor order of the clergy, concerned with menial work in the church.

Be trained in holy letters: The standard expression for learning how to read, since the psalms served as the basic primer.

3.1   *Iron furnace:* See Malingrey, *Jean Chrysostome,* 1.2.60.

Courts of foreigners: The Greek, ἀλλοφύλων αὐλάς, can be interpreted a number of different ways. It is possible that the author writes with a distinct knowledge of the fate of Christian children gathered through the *devşirme* and their service in the Ottoman court.

That adamantine soul: See, for example, John Chrysostom, *In epistulam primam ad Thessalonicenses Commentarius,* PG 62:421.28–29.

3.2   *Monastery was divided into two sections:* For a further discussion of double monasteries, see Alice-Mary Talbot, "A Comparison of the Monastic Experience of Byzantine Men and Women," *The Greek Orthodox Theological Review* 30 (1985): 5–7.

The good Eudokia: Here is the first mention of Eudokia by name.

Monastic complex: Normally a *proasteion* was a parcel of land or an estate at a distance from a city or village; see Franz Dölger, *Beiträge zur Geschichte der byzantinischen Finanzverwaltung, besonders des 10. und 11. Jahrhunderts* (Leipzig, 1927; repr. Hildesheim, 1960), 115.39–43. For more extensive discussion of the function of monastic *proasteia,* see Michael Angold, *Church and Society in Byzantium under the Comneni, 1081–1261* (Cambridge, 1995), 326–29. In this passage, however, the term must refer to the monastic complex itself, rather than an outlying estate.

3.3   McGrath has suggested the emendation πᾶσαι αἱ μοναχαί, "all the nuns," arguing that it refers to the entire complement of nuns coming in a group to the liturgy. Greenfield prefers to emend to πάντες οἱ μοναχοί and translate "all the monastics."

Joy and sadness: The Greek term χαρμολύπη, sometimes translated as "bitter joy," is a postclassical word, almost never found in Byzantine hagiography, but it is attested in the popular monastic treatise of John of the Ladder.

3.4   *Delivered you from . . . death:* This statement seems to be an ex-

cerpt from Eudokia's words to her sons, evoking the phrasing of 2 Corinthians 1:10.

3.6   *Adamantine in his soul:* See the note on 3.1.

3.7   *Thrice-twined serpent:* The adjective "thrice-twined" evokes the Devil; see, for example, the twelfth-century vita of Cyril Phileotes written by Nicholas Kataskepenos, which mentions "the thrice-twined [τρίπλοκον σχοινίον] snare of Satan": vainglory, avarice, and lasciviousness; see Etienne Sargologos, *La Vie de Saint Cyrille le Philéote moine byzantin (†1110)* (Brussels, 1964), 35.5.

Joseph . . . Egyptian woman: For the story of Joseph and Potiphar's wife, see Genesis 39:7–19.

Shared a residence: The author is referring to the double monastery housing both monks and nuns in separate sections (see note above on 3.2).

Marvel more at the present event: The author is connecting the text to the theme of the *Life*'s introduction.

4.1   *Left no stone unturned:* A proverbial expression; see *CPG* 1:146, 293; 2:201.

Singing to the deaf: A proverbial expression; see *Aristaeneti epistularum libri ii,* ed. Otto Mazal (Stuttgart, 1971), 1:28; *CPG* 1:370, note to Gregory of Cyprus, no. 32.

4.2   *Dionysiou:* The monastery of Dionysiou is located on the west coast of the Athos peninsula, near its southern tip.

4.3   *Six stades:* A distance of a little over half a mile.

Lived on bread and salt: For saints' fasting practices, see Béatrice Chevallier Caseau, "Childhood in Byzantine Saints' Lives," in *Becoming Byzantine: Children and Childhood in Byzantium,* ed. Arietta Papaconstantinou and Alice-Mary Talbot (Washington, D.C., 2009), 147–49.

5.2   *He remained . . . he left his cell:* The proper punctuation of the Greek text and the translation of this passage are not certain.

5.3   *Vatopedi:* A major monastery located on the northeastern coast of the peninsula; see further the note to chap. 28.1 in Niphon's *Life of Maximos,* above.

Great Entrance: A ritual procession that opens the second half of the liturgy, during which the Eucharist is celebrated.

5.4   *The great Ephraim:* Ephraim (Ephrem) the Syrian (d. 373) was a deacon in Nisibis, theologian, hymnographer, and saint. Over the centuries he was transformed by Syriac tradition "into a virtual paradigm of the Byzantine ascetical ideal"; see Joseph P. Amar, "Byzantine Ascetic Monachism and Greek Bias in the Vita Tradition of Ephrem the Syrian," *Orientalia Christiana Periodica* 58 (1992): 123–56, at 123. The traditions about his death and burial are contradictory. The various versions of the Syriac vita of Ephrem, in contrast to the story here, report that his body received a proper burial; see Joseph P. Amar, trans., *The Syriac Vita Tradition of Ephrem the Syrian* (Louvain, 2011), chap. 42. A metrical homily in Syriac, "On Hermits and Desert Dwellers," probably erroneously ascribed to him, contains several verses (e.g., 277–97, 317–25, 341–53) extolling hermits for not being buried in graves but allowing their bodies to decay in whatever corner of the forest or desert they happened to die; see Joseph P. Amar, "Hermits and Desert Dwellers," in *Ascetic Behavior in Greco-Roman Antiquity. A Sourcebook,* ed. Vincent Wimbush (Minneapolis, 1990), 66–89. We thank Susan Ashbrook Harvey for her assistance with this note.

Nine stades: A distance of a little less than a mile.

6.2   *Wooden sounding board:* The *semandron,* a wooden board that was struck to summon monks to church services and to the refectory.

Bibliography

EDITIONS AND TRANSLATIONS

Life of Euthymios the Younger

Petit, Louis, ed. "Vie et office de St. Euthyme le Jeune." *Revue de l'Orient chrétien* 8 (1903): 155–205, 503–36.

Life of Athanasios of Athos, Version B

Dumont, Pierre, trans. "Vie de saint Athanase l'Athonite." *Irénikon* 8 (1931): 457–99, 667–89; 9 (1932): 71–95, 240–64.

Noret, Jacques, ed. *Vitae duae antiquae Sancti Athanasii Athonitae,* 127–213. Turnhout, 1982.

Lives of Maximos the Hutburner by Niphon and Theophanes

Halkin, François, ed. "Deux vies de s. Maxime le Kausokalybite, ermite au Mont Athos (XIVe s.)." *Analecta Bollandiana* 54 (1936): 38–112.

Life of Niphon

Halkin, François, ed. "La vie de Saint Niphon ermite au Mont Athos (XIVe s.)." *Analecta Bollandiana* 58 (1940): 42–65.

Life of Philotheos

Papoulia, Basilike. "Die Vita des Heiligen Philotheos vom Athos." *Südost Forschungen* 23 (1963): 259–80.

Secondary Literature

Life of Saint Euthymios the Younger

Papachryssanthou, Denise. *Actes du Prôtaton*. Paris, 1975.

——. "La vie de saint Euthyme le Jeune et la métropole de Thessalonique." *Revue des études byzantines* 32 (1974): 225–45.

Life of Athanasios of Athos, Version B

Krausmüller, Dirk. "The Lost First Life of Athanasius the Athonite and Its Author Anthony, Abbot of the Constantinopolitan Monastery of Ta Panagiou." In *Founders and Refounders of Byzantine Monasteries*, edited by M. Mullett, 63–86. Belfast, 2007.

Lemerle, Paul, et al., eds. *Actes de Lavra*. 4 vols. Paris, 1970–1982.

Mylonas, Paul. "Le plan initial du catholicon de la Grande-Lavra au Mont Athos et la genèse du type du catholicon athonite." *Cahiers archéologiques* 32 (1984): 89–112.

Lives of Maximos the Hutburner by Niphon and Theophanes

Kapetanaki, Sophia. "Transmission of Byzantine Hagiographical Texts in the Palaeologan Period: The Case of the *Life of Maximos Kausokalyves*." *Acta Academiae Scientiarum Hungaricae* 48 (2008): 179–85.

Ware, Kallistos. "St. Maximos of Kapsokalyvia and Fourteenth-Century Athonite Hesychasm." In *ΚΑΘΗΓΗΤΡΙΑ: Essays Presented to Joan Hussey for Her 80th Birthday,* edited by J. Chrysostomides, 423–30. Camberley, Surrey, 1998.

Index

References are to vita, chapter, and paragraph number. The vitae are abbreviated as VEuth *(Life of Euthymios the Younger)*, VAth *(Life of Athanasios of Athos)*, VMaxN *(Life of Maximos the Hutburner by Niphon)*, VMaxTh *(Life of Maximos the Hutburner by Theophanes)*, VNiph *(Life of Niphon of Athos)*, and VPh *(Life of Philotheos of Athos)*.

References in parentheses indicate that the individual or item is implicit in that paragraph but not specifically named. References to notes are indicated by an "n" (for example, VMaxN 6.1n points to note 6.1 for the *Life of Maximos by Niphon* in the Notes to the Translations).